Poems

Available from the Simms Initiatives and the University of South Carolina Press

The Army Correspondence of Colonel John Laurens, ed.
As Good as a Comedy
Beauchampe
Border Beagles
Carl Werner, an Imaginative Story, 2 vols.
The Cassique of Accabee
The Cassique of Kiawah
Castle Dismal
Charlemont
Charleston and Her Satirists, 2 vols.
The Charleston Book, ed.
Confession
Count Julian
The Damsel of Darien, 2 vols.
Donna Florida
Eutaw
Father Abbot
The Forayers
The Geography of South Carolina
The Golden Christmas
Guy Rivers
Helen Halsey
The History of South Carolina
Joscelyn
Katherine Walton
The Letters of William Gilmore Simms, Vol. 1
The Letters of William Gilmore Simms, Vol. 2
The Letters of William Gilmore Simms, Vol. 3
The Letters of William Gilmore Simms, Vol. 4
The Letters of William Gilmore Simms, Vol. 5
The Letters of William Gilmore Simms, Vol. 6 (exp. ed.)
The Life of Captain John Smith
The Life of Chevalier Bayard
The Life of Francis Marion
The Lily and the Totem
Marie de Berniere
Martin Faber and Other Tales, 2 vols.
Mellichampe
Michael Bonham
The Partisan
Pelayo, 2 vols.
Poems, Descriptive, Dramatic, Legendary, and Contemplative, 2 vols.
The Remains of Maynard Davis Richardson
Richard Hurdis, 2 vols.
Sack and Destruction of the City of Columbia
The Scout
Selections from the Letters and Speeches of the Hon. James H. Hammond, ed.
Simms's Poems Areytos
Slavery in America
South Carolina in the Revolutionary War
Southward Ho!
Stories and Tales
A Supplement to the Plays of William Shakespeare
Vasconselos
Views and Reviews in American Literature, History and Fiction, 2 vols.
Voltmeier
War Poetry of the South
The Wigwam and the Cabin
Woodcraft
The Yemassee

Poems

Descriptive, Dramatic, Legendary, and Contemplative

William Gilmore Simms

Critical Introduction by Matthew C. Brennan

With a Biographical Overview by David Moltke-Hansen

The University of South Carolina Press

Cloth original published by Redfield, 1853
Paperback published by the University of South Carolina Press
Columbia, South Carolina 29208

www.sc.edu/uscpress

Manufactured in the United States of America

22 21 20 19 18 17 16 15 14 13
10 9 8 7 6 5 4 3 2 1

ISBN 978-1-61117-055-9 (pbk)

Published in cooperation with the Simms Initiatives, a project of the University of South Carolina Libraries with the generous support of the Watson-Brown Foundation, and with additional funding by the John Govan Simms Endowment.

William Gilmore Simms: A Biographical Overview

David Moltke-Hansen

Introduction

Harper's Weekly put it succinctly in its July 2, 1870, issue: "In the death of Mr. Simms, on the 11th of June, at Charleston, the country has lost one more of its time-honored band of authors, and the South the most consistent and devoted of her literary sons" (qtd. In Butterworth and Kibler 125–26). Indeed no mid-nineteenth-century writer and editor did more than William Gilmore Simms to frame white southern self-identity and nationalism, shape southern historical consciousness, or foster the South's participation and recognition in the broader American literary culture. No southern writer enjoyed more contemporary esteem and attention, at least after Edgar Allan Poe moved north. Among American romancers (or writers of prose epics), only New Yorker James Fenimore Cooper was as successful by the 1840s. In those same years, Simms was the South's most influential editor of cultural journals. He also was the region's most prolific cultural journalist and poet, publishing an average of one book review and one poem per week for forty-five years.

Before his death Simms saw his national reputation fall along with the Confederacy he had vigorously supported and with the slave regime that many in the North had come to despise. Nevertheless reprints of most of the twenty titles in the selected edition of his works, first published between 1853 and 1860, appeared up until World War I. Thereafter only *The Yemassee*, an early romance about an Indian war in South Carolina, continued in print. The tide began to turn in the 1950s, when five volumes of Simms's letters appeared and a growing number of his works were issued in new editions. Publication in 1992 of the first literary biography, by John C. Guilds, and establishment of the William Gilmore Simms Society and the *Simms Review* the next year at once reflected and fostered this revived interest. Yet not until the 2011 launch of the digital Simms edition of the South Caroliniana Library of the University of South Carolina did scholars of southern, American, and nineteenth-century culture have the prospect of ready access to all of Simms's separately published works. With the University of South Carolina Press's cooperation, readers also will have access to sixty works in paperback editions by the end of 2014. Simms himself never saw nearly so many of his works in print at one time.

Clearly the decline in the critical standing of, and historical attention to, Simms and his oeuvre in the century after his death has reversed in the years since. The last three decades of the twentieth century saw more published on Simms than the previous hundred years (Butterworth and Kibler 126–200; MLA International). The last decade of the twentieth and first decade of the twenty-first centuries saw more dissertations and theses on him (forty-one) than had appeared in all the years before. This is not to say that Simms is yet given the attention directed to some of his contemporaries. For the first decade of the twenty-first century, the Modern Language Association International Bibliography lists roughly four times as many scholarly publications on James Fenimore Cooper, more than ten times as many on Nathaniel Hawthorne, and sixteen times as many on Edgar Allan Poe. Not surprisingly, therefore, Simms is not yet included in most anthologies of American literature, although he is a subject or a source in an expanding and ever more diverse body of scholarship.

To prepare to read Simms, it is important to see his writings in multiple contexts. He rarely wrote about himself outside of his more personal poems and his letters (some fifteen hundred of the many thousands of which survive). Yet he systematically drew on his background, personal experience, and relationships in his work. He also shaped that work through a progressively developed poetics and philosophy of life, history, and art. He did so in the context of his very broad reading of both contemporary and earlier Western literature and in the midst of multiple professional engagements and responsibilities. The richness and variety of these writings and involvements make Simms a key figure for future understanding of the literary culture, issues, and networks in mid-nineteenth-century America.

Background

Simms's family history reflected the dynamics that fueled the spread southward and westward of the populations, plantation economy, and society of the South Atlantic states. Simms's ancestry also reflected the Scots-Irish and English roots of what became identified as southern culture by the 1830s, a generation after the end of most immigration to the region. Two of Simms's grandparents, William and Elisabeth Sims, were Scots-Irish and migrated to South Carolina from Ulster. One, John Singleton, was an American-born son of putatively English immigrants, who had come to South Carolina from Virginia. The fourth, Jane Miller, was daughter of two Scots-Irish and Irish descended people—John Miller, of North and then South Carolina, and Jane Ross. Ross's family also migrated to South Carolina from western Virginia, where members lived cheek by jowl with other Scots-Irish families, who migrated to the Carolinas (White, *Ross*). Simms's father and Uncle James migrated in 1808 from Charleston to Tennessee, then to Mississippi. This was after the bankruptcy of the elder William's business and the deaths of his wife and their other two sons. Following the last of these losses, the elder Simms's hair turned white in a week. To his anguished eyes, Charleston appeared "a place of tombs" (qtd. in Guilds 6, 12).

For the son, however, Charleston was home—so much so that he refused to leave his maternal grandmother and move to Mississippi when his uncle came to get him in 1816. Then the fifth largest and by far the wealthiest city, as well as one of the greatest ports, in America, Charleston was at the peak of its influence (Moltke-Hansen, "Expansion" 25–31; Rogers). Cotton culture on the sea islands to the south, begun in 1790, and rice culture in impounded lowcountry tidal marshes meant that the port was filled not only with sailors of many lands and languages, but also with enslaved people of many African and Creole cultures and speech ways (slaves continued to be imported legally in large numbers until 1808). This street life made vivid the transnational nature of plantation agriculture and the fact that the developing region's dramatically expanding borders "were not just geographic; they also were human, historical, and intellectual" (Moltke-Hansen, "Southern" 19).

Even more important for the future author, the expanding region's borders and nature were taking imaginative shape. The West of the senior William Gilmore Simms and the first Creek War in which he fought, the Revolutionary War of the young Simms's maternal grandfather, the backcountry of many related Scots-Irish settlers, all these became grist for a lonely, energetic boy, who spent as much time with books as he could (Simms, *Letters* 1:161). The possibilities of such settings, incidents, and characters were not confined to history alone. Simms reported that he "used to glow and shiver in turn over 'The Pilgrim's Progress,'" while "Moses' adventures in 'The Vicar of Wakefield' threw [him] into paroxysms of laughter" (Hayne 261–62). Sir Walter Scott's Border and medieval romances and James Fenimore Cooper's Leatherstocking tales also deeply colored his imagination (Simms, *Views* 1:248, and Moltke-Hansen, "Southern" 6–15). As affecting were the ghost stories and Revolutionary War tales of his grandmother and the verses sent, and tales told, by his father.

These diverse tales became reasons to explore—in books, but also on the ground. As a boy, Simms ranged through the city and along the banks of the Ashley River, which fed into Charleston Harbor. He did so in search of scenes of colonial and Revolutionary battles and incidents (*Letters* 1:lxii). He first heard his uncle's and father's many Irish and frontier stories when they visited in Charleston in 1816 and 1818, respectively. He heard more on his trips to Mississippi during the winter of 1824 through the spring of 1825 and again in 1826. The first trip took him through Georgia and Alabama, where he saw elements of the Creek and Cherokee nations. At the time, Simms later reported, he was a boy "cumbered with fragmentary materials of thought, . . . choked by the tangled vines of erroneous speculation, and haunted by passions, which, like so many wolves, lurked, in ready waiting, for their unsuspecting prey" (*Social* 6). When he first got to Mississippi, traveling partly by stage, partly by riverboat, and partly by horse, Simms learned that his father had just come back from "a trip of three hundred miles into the heart of the Indian country" (Trent 15). Later father and son "rode together on horseback to various settlements on the frontier of Alabama and Mississippi" (Guilds 10–11, 17–18). Simms recalled as well "having traveled 150 miles beyond the Mississippi" (Shillingsburg, "Literary Grist" 120). The next year he returned to the Southwest by ship. "During this [second] trip he carried a 'note book.'" There he jotted episodes, encounters, stories heard, characters seen, and descriptions of the landscapes unfolding around him. He also wrote "at least sixteen poems" (Kibler, "First"; Shillingsburg, "Literary Grist" 123).

Simms took a third western trip five years later, writing letters back to the newspaper that by then he was editing (*Letters* 1:10–38). Together these three trips provided materials for his writings over more than forty years. "The first . . . produced mainly short fiction; the second inspired much poetry; . . . the first and third . . . yielded three novels written in the 1830s" (Shillingsburg, "Literary Grist" 119). This was, in part, because of the trips' timing. Sixteen years after the first trip, Simms told students at the University of Alabama that in the interval their world had changed from a howling wilderness into a place of growing civilization (Simms, *Social* 5–6). Had he not gone when he did, he would have been too late to see the frontier. Later travels took him many other places and also provided much grist for his writing. Never again, however, did he experience the frontier firsthand. Furthermore, on these later trips Simms was a practiced professional writer, no longer that boy haunted by passions.

Personal Life

After the ten-year-old boy's momentous refusal to leave Charleston, his grandmother sent Simms for two years to the grammar school taught on the campus and by the faculty of the nearly moribund College of Charleston. By then he already was "versifying the events of the war [of 1812]," just concluded, publishing "doggerel" in the local papers, and learning to read in several languages (*Letters* 1:285). His trip west a decade later helped him decide to pursue both literature and a career in law, but back in Charleston—this despite his father's urging that he stay in Mississippi. Upon his return home, he began to read law and also launched a literary weekly, the *Album*, which ran for a year. He became engaged as well to Anna Malcolm Giles, daughter of a grocer and former state coroner.

A year later the young couple married. This was six months before Simms was admitted to the South Carolina bar, on his twenty-first birthday, not long before he was appointed as a city magistrate. Although living up the Ashley River in the more healthful, less expensive village of Summerville, Simms kept a law office in the city. Shortly after using his maternal inheritance to buy the *City Gazette* at the end of 1829 and moving down to Charleston Neck, just north of the city limits where he had lived as a boy, Simms lost both his father and his maternal grandmother. He also found himself attacked because of his Unionist stance in the Nullification crisis resulting from South Carolina's rejection of a federal tariff. Then, in early 1832, Simms's wife died. Soon after, he took his four-year-old daughter back to Summerville to live and determined to sell his newspaper and leave the state for a literary life in the North.

Fueling his ambition was the correspondence Simms had begun several years earlier with an accountant whom he had published in his *City Gazette* but not yet met—Scots immigrant James Lawson. At the time Lawson, seven years Simms's senior, edited a New York City newspaper and, in addition to writing plays and poetry, was a friend (and, later, informal literary agent) to a wide circle (McHaney, "An Early"). Simms's trip north in the summer of 1832 saw the two begin a lifelong friendship, cemented as they squired ladies about and interacted with Lawson's literary circle. In subsequent years Simms multiplied the number of his friendships, in both the North and the South, making them in some measure a replacement for the family that he had lost. Lawson remained the closest of his northern friends, while James Henry Hammond, a future governor and U.S. senator, became his closest friend in South Carolina.

Late in 1833, after his Summerville house burned, Simms wrote Lawson to say that he was enamored of "a certain fair one" (*Letters* 1:73). Seventeen-year-old Chevillette Eliza Roach was the daughter of "a literary-minded aristocrat of English descent" with two plantations on the banks of the Edisto River in Barnwell District (later County) (Guilds 70). The courtship was protracted, as Simms felt it necessary first to clear debts that friends had bought up on his behalf. He also was determined "to marry no woman" before he was "perfectly independent of her resources, and her friends" (*Letters* 1:78). Therefore he did not propose until the spring of 1836. The nuptials took place seven months later, and as a result, Simms came to call the four thousand acres of Woodlands Plantation, with its seventy slaves, home. It was twenty years, however, before he took over management of the plantation and, then, only in the wake of his father-in-law's final sickness and death. Five years after that, he lost his wife, the mother of fourteen of his fifteen children. Nine of the children Chevillette bore him had already died, devastating Simms repeatedly. Five were still living (three sons and two daughters), as was Simms's daughter by his first marriage, who helped raise the youngest of her siblings. Those remaining children—even Gilly, who fought in the Confederate army—all outlived their father. Gilly and a brother-in-law ran Woodlands after the war, when Simms, though dying of cancer, was earning what he could by writing again for publications in the North and editing one or another South Carolina newspaper.

Career

The trip north in 1832 did not result in Simms moving there. Except during the Civil War, however, he returned almost every year. This was because the contacts he made, and the exposure to literary culture that he enjoyed, helped him define his future as an author. Earlier he had written fiction and criticism as well as journalism, filling the pages of several short-lived cultural journals and his newspaper, but between the ages of nine and twenty-six Simms had focused his literary efforts primarily on poetry. Beginning with his first book of verse in 1825, he had published five small volumes in Charleston. A couple had received positive notice in New York, and in the fall of 1832, J. & J. Harper issued the sixth anonymously from there, *Atalantis: A Story of the Sea.* Coming back the following summer, Simms had in hand for the Harpers a gothic novella, *Martin Faber,* and after his return south, he also would send the manuscript of his first two-volume border romance, *Guy Rivers: A Tale of Georgia.*

The reception of these and the romances and short stories that followed quickly made Simms one of the nation's most successful fictionists. He continued to issue poetry as well—roughly a collection every three years over the thirty-seven years that he worked as a professional author. But this output was dwarfed by the fiction—on average a title every year (counting several serialized works but not counting the many revised editions). Then there were the two dozen separately published orations, histories, and biographies as well as edited collections of documents and dramas and a geography of South Carolina. Add to these the revised editions and the further printings and issues of his own works and it appears that Simms saw a title coming off the presses at the rate of one every three months or so. Making that figure all the more astounding is the fact that, during more than a dozen of those years (the early-to-mid 1840s, the late 1840s-to-early 1850s, and the mid-to-late 1860s), he also was editing a cultural journal or newspaper. Furthermore he contributed reams of reviews and poems, hundreds of op-ed pieces and columns, and dozens of short stories and public addresses, which were never collected and published in volume form.

His career mapped an arc. It ascended meteorically in the 1830s and peaked in the early-to-mid 1840s, before beginning to descend. One reason was the popularity of the historical fiction that Simms began to write. When he left behind the law, his first newspaper, and the Nullification controversy, as well as his sadness, historical fiction was all the rage. Sir Walter Scott had fueled the craze, beginning with the publication of his first Border romance in 1814. He died in September 1832. Seventeen years Simms's senior, James Fenimore Cooper, the closest America had to a Scott at the time, was at the peak of his reputation and success, having started publishing his romances in 1820. Thus the way had been prepared for a writer of Simms's historical imagination and preoccupations. Within five years of his first trip north, moreover, Lawson's (and now his) circle became loosely affiliated with a nationalistic and Democratic group, self-styled Young America, this after Young Italy and similar ethnic, nationalist, European, cultural and political movements (Moltke-Hansen, "Southern"). Edgar Allan Poe and other members gave Simms's first fictions positive, if not uncritical, attention.

By the end of the 1830s, paradoxically, Simms, like Cooper, found his success attracting unauthorized editions of his works because Britain and America did not have an international copyright agreement. Further, in the wake of the panic of 1837, Americans bought fewer books. Simms's response was to diversify his portfolio. He turned to biography and history, including his hugely successful *Life of Francis Marion* (1844). He also returned to the editor's chair, overseeing one and then another cultural journal. These were unlike the ones he had edited in the 1820s: they included contributions by numerous authors, not just those from Charleston, but from the region and also the North. The ambition motivating the journals was to connect and promote Charleston intellectually. Consequently the journals more closely resembled metropolitan quarterly reviews in their offerings.

The mid-1840s saw Simms involved in politics, even serving a term in the South Carolina legislature. By the middle of the Mexican-American War in 1847, he had concluded that the South needed to become an independent nation. Thereafter, although he maintained ties with many in the Young America circle, he no longer promoted his writings as fostering Americanism in literature (*Views*). Instead he increasingly emphasized the ways in which his three romance series—the colonial, the Revolutionary, and the border—were making tangible and meaningful the origins and development of the future southern nation and the sad but inevitable consequences for Native Americans (Watson, *From Nationalism*; compare Nakamura).

Sectional politics colored more and more of Simms's perceptions, speeches, and private communications. The rising tide of abolitionism had him aghast. It also fed his growing sense that his position in American letters was slipping. He returned to editing, and his poetry, which was more often explicitly about the South, became increasingly patriotic in tone. Although his first biographer, William Peterfield Trent, insisted that Simms's declining standing reflected the change in literary fashion from historical romances to realistic novels, Simms in fact wrote more and more as a social realist in the 1850s (Wimsatt, "Realism").

The Civil War consumed Simms. As he wrote Lawson, "Literature, especially poetry, is effectually overwhelmed by the drums, & the cavalry, and the shouting" (*Letters* 4:369–70). He did manage to editorialize often and to rework and finish things long on his desk, including poems, a novel, and a dramatic treatment of Benedict Arnold, the northern traitor in the Revolutionary War. Then, in the wake of the Confederacy's loss and the failure of his vision for the South, he found himself recording the loss in a new newspaper, dealing with the trauma in his poetry, and becoming more existential and psychological in his fictional treatments. Simms's old New York friends tried to help. He did edit and see through publication a volume of Confederate war poetry. Yet it is a measure of his reduced stature that the several new romances he published appeared only in serial form. In part this may have been because he was in a sense competing with himself. Publishers were beginning to reprint volumes out of the selected edition of his writings. Many of Simms's works were available in book form, just not new works.

Associations

As the *Letters* testify, Simms had complex, overlapping networks of friends and colleagues. As a boy and young man, he received the friendship, patronage, and commendation of a variety of well-placed people in Charleston, including Charles Rivers Carroll. It was Carroll with whom he read law, to whom he dedicated his first romance, and after whom he named a son. Both men were Unionists during the Nullification controversy. So were Hugh Swinton Legare (later U.S. attorney general) and the considerably older William Drayton, as well as lawyer and editor Richard Yeadon and Greenville, South Carolina, newspaper editor Benjamin Franklin Perry. Also considerably older was James Wright Simmons, who had joined with Simms to launch the *Southern Literary Gazette* in 1828, when Simms was twenty-two. Through him Simms had direct contact with such British literary figures as Leigh Hunt and Byron (Kibler, *Poetry* 15).

The next group of influential friends and collaborators that Simms acquired were members of the Lawson circle and included such figures as Edwin

Forrest, the Shakespearean actor, and Evert Duyckinck, who published several of Simms's volumes in Wiley and Putnam's series Library of American Books, which he edited. Among the many others were poets and editors William Cullen Bryant and Fitz-Greene Halleck. Simms also made nonliterary friends in New York and Philadelphia, such as John Jacob Bockee and William Hawkins Ferris, the cashier at the U.S. Treasury office in New York who, after the war, helped Simms, Henry Timrod (poet laureate of the Confederacy), and others.

As a Barnwell planter, Simms met a widening circle of South Carolina's leaders and literati. For instance his acquaintance with James Henry Hammond began in the late 1830s and deepened into a friendship in the early 1840s. It was in the early 1840s, too, when he again was editing cultural journals, that Simms became friends with many southern writers. He regarded several of them, including Virginians George Frederick Holmes, Edmund Ruffin, and Nathaniel Beverley Tucker as members, together with Hammond and himself, in a "sacred circle." Uniting the circle were members' devotion to the South and a shared sense of the marginal status and critical importance of the life of the mind in a largely rural and unintellectual region (Faust, *Sacred*). Others of Simms's wide connections in the region did not interact as much with each other, but Simms long corresponded with Maryland novelist and lawyer John Pendleton Kennedy, Irish-born Georgia poet Richard Henry Wilde, Alabama lawyer and writer Alexander Beaufort Meek, and Louisiana historian and assistant attorney general Charles Gayarré, among others. By the 1850s, when Simms once more returned to editing a cultural journal, many of the writers whom he recruited were members of a younger generation. Poets Paul Hamilton Hayne and Henry Timrod were two. Often they and a half dozen others of Simms's and their generations met in John Russell's Charleston Book Shop and adjourned to dinner at Simms's Smith Street home, "dubbed 'The Wigwam'" (*Letters* 1:cxxxvi). Shortly before his death fifteen or so years later, Simms wrote Hayne, "I am rapidly passing from the stage, where you young men are to succeed me" (*Letters* 5:287).

Thought

The welter of Simms's works disguises unities and dynamics of the thought underlying them. From early on Simms was convinced that art ennobles or transforms, as well as gives voice to individuals and societies; therefore it must be cultivated assiduously. Without the potential for high artistic attainment, he insisted, societies are not ready for the independence and regard of free peoples. This is where Simms the historian joined Simms the poet. Societies develop, he argued (using the stadialism of the Scottish historical school), from imitation through self-assertion to achievement and also from savagery through strife to settled agricultural communities and, ultimately, to a hierarchical civilization supporting a rich artistic life. It was the job of the artist to help envision the goal, inspire the pursuit, and inform the process. That process was at once progressive and dialectical. Order, without dynamism, stifled development, as did the obverse—the dominance by ungoverned impulses or uncontrolled license. This was true in the individual, but also in societies as a whole. War was necessary for civilization, but its success was measured in the securities of the home, the center of cultural production and reproduction.

Whether in the public or in the domestic arena, "the true governor, as [Thomas] Carlyle call[ed] him—the king man—" guided rather than impeded the forces of change and progress (Simms, "Guizot's" 122). There were few such men with the capacity to lead. The same was true of nations. Neither all people nor all peoples were equal in either capacity or attainment. That was why Native Americans were overrun and Africans had been enslaved by European peoples in the New World. Indeed, Simms argued, "slavery in all ages has been found the greatest and most admirable agent of Civilization," giving education and examples to less evolved peoples (*Letters* 3:174). The degree to which a people had evolved mattered. That was why, he held, Americans had won independence from the most powerful empire in the world. They had done so through their Revolution, led by an elite that felt correctly its time had come (Simms, "Ellet's" 328). By mid-1847 that also was Simms's judgment for the South: the region had evolved enough to become independent (*Letters* 2:332). The hope inspired and then failed him and the people he sought to lead.

While not all men could rise to the highest rank, they all had the same responsibility at home. There the father was patriarch, protector, and head, while the mother was nurturer, moral instructor, and heart. There, too, children's characters and minds were formed by age twelve ("Ellet's"). Children's upbringing was critical to citizenship, and it was through her sons and the support of her husband, father, and brothers that a woman shaped the public sphere. The culture and character instilled in the child expressed and informed not just the household, but the larger society—the people.

"The history of peoples and their embodiments in institutions, states, and artistic productions—these were the great subjects" in Simms's view (Moltke-Hansen, "Southern" 120). Yet "poets were the only class of philosophers who had recognized" this until his own day, when at last "we now read human histories. We now ask after the affections as well as the ceremonies of society" ("Ellet's" 319–20). Peoples or races—that is, ethnic groups—were not unchanging any more than were their politics and their cultures. They either advanced or were overrun by history. Further, new peoples emerged, and old identities were submerged. The Spanish conquistadors were the creation of centuries of conflict with the Moors: their motivation was the glory of conquest, not the routine of trade or the plow. On the other hand, the English settlements in North America reflected the impulse to transform the wilderness into verdant farms and build society (*Views* 64, 178–85; *Social* 8). The same impulse drove Americans westward in Simms's own day and gave Americans their Manifest Destiny.

To explore these facts of the South's settlement and its place in international conflicts, Simms wrote all together, between 1833 and 1863, two romances set in eighth-century Spain, two set during the Spanish exploration and conquest of the Americas and two during the later English colonization of South Carolina, seven set during the American Revolution, and—depending on how one counts—perhaps eight set on the borders of the nineteenth-century South. After the war he published one more Revolutionary romance and two more that, like it, were set beyond the boundaries of civilization. He also left two unfinished romances, also set beyond society's normal reach. These late works, however, no longer had as their framing justification the cultivation of the South's future and civilization.

White southerners had their independence foreclosed by the war. In his last works, therefore, Simms found himself exploring the psychological, philosophical, and historical impulses that led to the Confederacy's demise and what, in the aftermath, it meant to be a good man and to build for the future, however impoverished. On the first score, he argued that the impulse to idealism behind abolitionism ignored historical realities, becoming inhuman in its consequences. On the latter score, he affirmed responsibility for one's dependents and the virtues of stoicism, as well as a continued commitment to the beauty and truth of art and the impulses to the cultivated life and fields. Therefore, in the face of the burning of his Woodlands home and library in February 1865—during Sherman's march and in the midst of desperate circumstances—he insisted that home, or the ideals and past characterizing its potential, still was at the center of true civilization, but only if elevated by art (*Sense* 8, 17). It was wrong to measure civilization by the getting, spending, and mad dashing, or material progress and utilitarianism, characteristic of both a capitalistic North and also many southerners. These traits he often had attacked even before the war, insisting that "the work of the Imagination, which is the Genius of a race, is only begun when its material progress is supposed to be complete" (*Poetry* 12).

Writings

Simms expressed many of his ideas most personally in letters and most cogently in essays, speeches, and occasional introductions to his books. But he illustrated them most fully in his fiction and poetry. By the time he arrived in New

York in 1832, he had formed many of the core ideals and beliefs that would shape his work. His application of them, however, modified his understanding over time. Growing as a writer and growing in knowledge and experience, he also grew as a thinker.

In his hierarchy of values, poetry came first. It was a prophetic calling as well as evocative of the deeply felt (or, sometimes, the fleeting) and thus testimony to the perdurance and transcendence of the beautiful and the human spirit. Yet, as Simms often ruefully reflected, prose spoke to many more people. That was a principal reason why he turned to writing prose epics or romances. He gave his most concerted consideration of poetry's value and roles in three lectures in Charleston in 1854. Over the prior three years he had given portions of them in Augusta, Georgia, Washington, D.C., and Richmond and Petersburg, Virginia. Entitled *Poetry and the Practical*, they did not see print until 1996, as Simms never found the time to expand them as he wanted. On the other hand, his last address on the same themes, *The Sense of the Beautiful*, was issued soon after he delivered it, also in Charleston.

Many of his important reviews have not yet been gathered, but Simms collected some in 1845–46, and *Views and Reviews in American Literature, History and Fiction* came out in 1846 and 1847 in two "series." Beginning with a consideration of "Americanism" in literature, the first series explored the themes and periods of American history for treatment by the novelist. Simms argued there, and in forewords to several of his romances, that fiction rendered the past more truthfully, interestingly, and tellingly than histories and biographies could because fiction—like poetry—required imagination to look beyond what is not known or expressed. The second series examined additional American writers and what distinguished them, for instance, in their humor.

Despite their early success, Simms's romances, novellas, and stories provoked mixed reviews. Poe eventually concluded that Simms had become "the best novelist which this country has, on the whole, produced" but also insisted that "he should never have written 'The Partisan,' nor 'The Yemassee.'" This was in a review of *Confession*. That novel, like the gothic *Martin Faber*, demonstrated, Poe contended, that Simms's "genius [did] not lie in the outward so much as in the inner world." Yet he nevertheless wrote of Simms's short-story collection *The Wigwam and the Cabin* that "in invention, in vigor, in movement, in the power of exciting interest, and in the artistical management of his themes, he has surpassed, we think, any of his countrymen." Other critics, especially in the genteel and Whiggish Knickerbocker circle, joined Poe in condemning what they considered to be the excessively graphic and vulgar qualities of many characters and scenes, and Simms's prolixity and sententiousness, in his romances (Butterworth and Kibler 64, 50).

The violent realism and earthiness of the romances did not result in realistic novels. Although Simms received early praise for his characterizations (particularly of women), he used the romance formula, with its stereotypic heroes and heroines, predictable themes, and conventional polarities. People were on quests or had lost their way or were fighting long odds or were carrying forward the banner of (and modeling) civilization or were mired in the slough of despond or were resisting all the claims of civilized society and behavior or were pursuing love interests. Deceitfulness, selfishness, and greed opposed honor, high-mindedness, and honesty against the backdrop of the South's development from the earliest days of Spanish exploration to the westward movement in Simms's own youth.

It was only gradually that Simms married the psychological acuity of some of his portraits of the interior struggles of his gothic characters and fiction to the historical romance. Helping him think through how to do so were the biographies he wrote in the mid-1840s, but also the incidents on which he focused particular fictions, such as the murder in *Beauchampe; or, The Kentucky Tragedy* (1842). However incomplete the blending of realism and romanticism or of stereotypical and socially individuated renderings through the 1840s, by the 1850s Simms fundamentally had made the transition to social realism in such works as *Woodcraft* and *The Cassique of Kiawah.* Indeed some scholars have considered *Woodcraft* the first realistic novel in America (Bakker; Wimsatt, "Realism").

In some sense disguising the transition is the fact that Simms also increasingly wrote as a humorist and, in so doing, often rendered his late narratives fabulistically, when not writing social comedy or stories of manners. This dimension of Simms's work was largely hidden, however, until the 1974 publication of *Stories and Tales,* volume 5 in the Centennial Simms edition. There, for the first time, readers had access in print to "Bald-Head Bill Bauldy." There, too, for the first time one could read together that story, "Legend of the Hunter's Camp," and "How Sharp Snaffles Got His Capital and Wife," which was published posthumously in *Harper's Magazine* in October 1870. These and other stories and tales made it clear that Simms was a fecund contributor to southern and American humor.

Humor let Simms take up issues that he could not otherwise address in print and still expect to be well received. He did so both during and after the war. The war also pushed Simms past the emerging fashion of social realism. Having destroyed the familiar, the preoccupation of much realistic fiction, the war made the liminal central (Shillingsburg, "Cub"). While his romances and tales had often explored life on the edge or in extreme circumstances, whether in war or on the frontier or on the verge of madness or in fanciful realms, it had done so against a backdrop of, and with the goal of affirming, social norms and development. In the war's wake that goal seemed absurd. Mythologized memories of a healthy past might nurture a sense of the beautiful but could not help one deal with the present. Thus Simms's conclusion, in a March 1869 letter to Paul Hamilton Hayne: "Let us bury the Past lest it buries us!" (*Letters* 5:214). Fifteen months later he lay dead in the 13 Society Street, Charleston, home of his oldest daughter, with the shell holes in the walls of the bedroom he had shared with several children.

Posthumous Reputation

The twenty years after Simms's death saw him often respectfully treated, first in obituaries, later in memoirs and columns, and also in literary dictionaries and encyclopedias. Yet Charles Richardson's 1887 *American Literature: 1607–1885* proved a harbinger of a shift: Simms, Richardson observed, was "more respected than read," having "won considerable note because he was so sectional" and then having "lost it because he was not sectional enough," although he showed "silly contempt for his Northern betters" (qtd. in Butterworth and Kibler 130). Five years later Trent's biography of Simms appeared. It was the first full-length, scholarly treatment. Its central thesis was that Simms's environment frustrated his abilities: the South was inimical to art and the life of the mind, and Charleston high society's hauteur marginalized Simms despite his talent and character. Trent's second thesis was that Simms's commitment to the romance and his romanticism meant that his works had become largely unreadable in an age of literary realism. Although Vernon Parrington and later scholars recognized Simms's impulses to realism, the two theses long shaped Simms criticism and, indeed, also helped frame study of antebellum southern literature and intellectual life (Parrington 119–30).

A Virginian born in 1862, Trent was a progressive who wanted a New South radically different from the old. He saw his pioneering study of Simms as an opportunity to criticize what the Civil War had made untenable. From his perspective the Old South was not the expanding and rapidly developing environment, with a deep history, that Simms portrayed, but a place where slavery stultified and stunted the growth and progress displayed by the North. Southern—especially South Carolinian—writers occasionally challenged Trent's agenda and conclusions, but those critiques had little impact. Not until after publication of the Simms letters in the 1950s did scholars begin to consider the author in the historical and contemporary contexts that he had rendered in his poetry and fiction. And not until after the centennial of his death did a growing number of scholars, having concluded that southern intellectual history was not an oxymoron, begin to study in detail the culture in which Simms participated and to which he contributed so voluminously and variously.

Some of these scholars also have had agendas: they have wanted to see Simms included in the American literary canon, for instance, or they have wanted to defend the heritage that in their view Trent, and so many others, inappropriately belittled or ignorantly dismissed. More fruitfully, other scholars have begun to reframe the understanding of nineteenth-century American intellectual life by stripping away preconceptions that characterized earlier evaluations of Simms and his contemporaries. They are closely examining the historical record and transatlantic and other contemporary contexts and developments in the process. Although the pursuit of canonical status in a post-canonical age seems quixotic at this point, the explosion of the canon is leading to more varied fare being offered and may, therefore, mean that Simms, once his work is widely available, will be more often anthologized as well as studied. Defensiveness about Simms and the antebellum South may warm the hearts of like-minded people, just as critics of the Old South have been encouraged by shared presuppositions and disdain. Yet dueling cultural ideologies do not advance comity and may only reinforce mutual incomprehensions. Continued, deep research in original sources and the theoretical reframing that Atlantic history, the history of the book, and other perspectives offer—these approaches promise most for further study of Simms, his works, and his world.

Works Cited

For amplified readings by and on Simms and on his world, go to http://simms.library.sc.edu/bibliography.php.

Bakker, Jan. "Simms on the Literary Frontier; or, So Long Miss Ravenel and Hello Captain Porgy: *Woodcraft* Is the First 'Realistic' Novel in America." In *William Gilmore Simms and the American Frontier,* edited by John Caldwell Guilds and Caroline Collins, 64–78. Athens: University of Georgia Press, 1997.

Butterworth, Keen, and James E. Kibler Jr. *William Gilmore Simms: A Definitive Guide.* Boston: G. K. Hall, 1980.

Faust, Drew Gilpin. *A Sacred Circle: The Dilemma of the Intellectual in the Old South, 1840–1860.* Baltimore: Johns Hopkins University Press, 1977.

Guilds, John C. *Simms: A Literary Life.* Fayetteville: University of Arkansas Press, 1992.

Hayne, Paul Hamilton. "Ante-Bellum Charleston." *Southern Bivouac* 1 (October 1885): 257–68.

Kibler, James E. "The First Simms Letters: 'Letters from the West' (1826)." *Southern Literary Journal* 19 (Spring 1987): 81–91.

———. *The Poetry of William Gilmore Simms: An Introduction and Bibliography.* Columbia: Southern Studies Program, University of South Carolina, 1979.

McHaney, Thomas L. "An Early 19th-Century Literary Agent: James Lawson of New York." *Publications of the Bibliographical Society of America* 64 (Spring 1970): 177–92.

Moltke-Hansen, David. "The Expansion of Intellectual Life: A Prospectus." In *Intellectual Life in Antebellum Charleston,* edited by Michael O'Brien and David Moltke-Hansen, 3–44. Knoxville: University of Tennessee Press, 1986.

———. "Southern Literary Horizons in Young America: Imaginative Development of a Regional Geography." *Studies in the Literary Imagination* 42, no. 1 (2009): 1–31.

Nakamura, Masahiro. *Visions of Order in William Gilmore Simms: Southern Conservatism and the Other American Romance.* Columbia: University of South Carolina Press, 2009.

Parrington, Vernon L. *The Romantic Revolution in America, 1800–1860.* Vol. 2 of *Main Currents in American Thought.* New York: Harcourt, Brace and Company, 1927.

Rogers, George C., Jr. *Charleston in the Age of the Pinckneys.* Columbia: University South Carolina Press, 1980.

Shillingsburg, Miriam J. "The Cub of the Panther: A New Frontier." In *William Gilmore Simms and the American Frontier,* edited by John Caldwell Guilds and Caroline Collins, 221–36. Athens: University of Georgia Press, 1997.

———. "Literary Grist: Simms's Trips to Mississippi." *Southern Quarterly* 41, no. 2 (2003): 119–34.

Simms, William Gilmore. *Atalantis: A Story of the Sea: In Three Parts.* New York: J. & J. Harper, 1832.

———. *Beauchampe; or, The Kentucky Tragedy.* 2 vols. Philadelphia: Lea and Blanchard, 1842.

———. *The Cassique of Kiawah: A Colonial Romance.* New York: Redfield, 1859.

———. *Confession; or, The Blind Heart. A Domestic Story.* 2 vols. Philadelphia: Lea and Blanchard, 1841.

———. "Ellet's 'Women of the Revolution.'" *Southern Quarterly Review,* n.s. 1 (July 1850): 314–54.

———. "Guizot's Democracy in France." *Southern Quarterly Review* 15, no.29 (1849): 114–65.

———. *Guy Rivers: A Tale of Georgia.* 2 vols. New York: Harper & Brothers, 1834.

———. *The Letters of William Gilmore Simms.* Edited by Mary C. Simms Oliphant, Alfred Taylor Odell, and T. C. Duncan. 6 vols. Columbia: University of South Carolina Press, 1952–82.

———. *The Life of Francis Marion.* New York: Henry G. Langley, 1844.

———. *Martin Faber, the Story of a Criminal; and Other Tales.* 2 vols. New York: Harper & Brothers, 1837.

———. *Poetry and the Practical.* Edited by James E. Kibler. Fayetteville: University of Arkansas Press, 1996.

———. *The Sense of the Beautiful: An Address . . . before the Charleston County Agricultural and Horticultural Association, May 3, 1870.* Charleston: Charleston County Agricultural and Horticultural Association, 1870.

———. *The Social Principle: The Source of National Permanence. An Oration, Delivered before the Erosophic Society of the University of Alabama . . . December 13, 1842.* Tuscaloosa: Erosophic Society, University of Alabama, 1843.

———. *Stories and Tales.* Vol. 5 of *The Writings of William Gilmore Simms.* Centennial edition; introductions, explanatory notes, and texts established by John Caldwell Guilds. Columbia: University of South Carolina Press, 1974.

———. *Views and Reviews in American Literature, History and Fiction.* 2 vols. New York: Wiley and Putnam, 1845 (1846).

———. *The Wigwam and the Cabin.* 2 vols. New York: Wiley and Putnam, 1845–46.

———. *Woodcraft, or Hawks about the Dovecote: A Story of the South, at the Close of the Revolution.* New York: Redfield, 1854.

Trent, William Peterfield. *William Gilmore Simms.* Boston: Houghton, Mifflin, 1892.

Wakelyn, Jon L. *The Politics of a Literary Man: William Gilmore Simms.* Westport, Conn.: Greenwood Press, 1973.

Watson, Charles S. *From Nationalism to Secessionism: The Changing Fiction of William Gilmore Simms.* Westport, Conn.: Greenwood Press, 1993.

White, William B., Jr. *The Ross-Chesnut-Sutton Family of South Carolina.* Franklin, N.C.: Privately printed, 2002.

Wimsatt, Mary Ann. "Realism and Romance in Simms's Midcentury Fiction." *Southern Literary Journal* 12, no. 2 (1980): 29–48.

Critical Introduction

POEMS: DESCRIPTIVE, DRAMATIC, LEGENDARY, AND CONTEMPLATIVE

Matthew C. Brennan

William Gilmore Simms was a prolific poet, who wrote nearly 2,000 poems. Though in his own time and in ours he is best known as the author of such romances as *The Yemassee* and *Woodcraft*, he always considered poetry his first calling: He proclaimed in 1860, "Poetry, I hold to be my proper province" (*Letters* 6: 213). He even thought that in time his verse would outrank his novels (*Letters* 3: 190). Consequently, to ensure that his verse would be "on record for future judgment," in 1853 he collected many of his poems into a two-volume work, *Poems: Descriptive, Dramatic, Legendary and Contemplative* (*Letters* 3: 262). The work forms the most substantial and important collection of poetry in his canon. As the subtitle indicates, the volumes not only cover Simms's entire career from *Lyrical and Other Poems* (1827) through his verse drama *Norman Maurice* (1852), but also subsume a diverse range of styles, subjects, and themes; moreover, Simms revised many of the poems, hoping to strengthen them and make them last. In the 1860s he had hoped to assemble an expanded edition, but as with so many of his ambitions during the war years, this plan was scuttled. Consequently, Simms's reputation as a poet has hinged largely on the appraisal by both his contemporaries and later scholars of this selection of poems.

The Work

Poems: Descriptive, Dramatic, Legendary, and Contemplative appeared as the second release of the Redfield edition of his selected works, following on the heels of the novel *Vasconselos*. Though dated 1853 like the novel, *Poems* may have been published as late as January 1854 (*Letters* 6: 143); however, in letters of November 24 and December 17 Simms presumes that editors already possess the book (*Letters* 3: 261, 268). Volume 1 comprises 348 pages and four parts: (1) *Norman Maurice, a Tragedy*; (2) *Atalantis, a Tale of the Sea*, which he had initially published in 1832 with Harper and later revised for a second edition with Carey and Hart of Philadelphia in 1848; (3) "Tales and Traditions of the South," which includes "The Cassique of Accabee: A Legend of Ashley River," "The

Last Fields of the Biloxi," "The Hunter of Calawassee," and "Vasco Nunez"; and (4) *The City of the Silent*, which he had published in 1850. Volume 2, 360 pages long, uses these headings for its four parts: "Southern Passages and Pictures"; "Historical and Dramatic Sketches"; "Scripture Legends"; and "Francesca da Rimini," a reworking of Dante. Simms selected many of the poems from his 16 previous volumes of verse, but some verses had never before been collected and some never published under his name.

The more than seven hundred pages of verse vividly display Simms's range of subject matter and forms. The first work of the first volume is a blank-verse tragedy depicting contemporary politics; Simms wrote *Norman Maurice* with actor Edwin Forrest in mind but clearly based the satiric character of Colonel Ben Ferguson on Missouri Senator Thomas Hart Benton, who unlike Simms opposed the expansion of slavery west of Missouri. The other long works in volume 1 veer in radically different directions. *Atalantis* is dramatic, but its subject is fanciful, going far beyond "the merely human sentiment," as Simms states in his head note (*Poems* 1:121). Indeed, the cast of characters includes a human—a Spanish knight—but it is mostly populated by Sea-Demons, Nereids, and Fairies. *The City of the Silent*, on the other hand, is a solemn occasional poem composed in closed heroic couplets for the public ceremony dedicating Magnolia Cemetery in Charleston. Other poems treat death and mourning personally, such as "At a Child's Grave," one of Simms's lyrics to draw on his autobiography as a father whose lost children outnumber those who have survived. And his numerous poems about children—such as "Blessings on Children"—no doubt draw on his experience of fatherhood.

Many poems fit squarely in the Romantic tradition and evoke various aspects of nature. In fact, the opening pages of volume 2 present the reader with "Flight to Nature," "The Brooklet," "Sabbath in the Forest"—a sequence of six sonnets using nature as a source of escape and nurture—"First Day of Spring," and "Sonnet—By the Swanannoa," one of Simms's most often anthologized poems and one that illustrates his realism in employing the specific place names of his southern environment. Indeed, many poems in the second volume are distinctly southern, from poems on the Edisto and Congaree rivers in South Carolina to "The Edge of the Swamp" (probably about the terrain of his own plantation, Woodlands) to a poem on western emigration. Simms rendered southern climate in "The Streamlet," "The Shade-Trees," "The Traveller's Rest," "Night Storm," "Summer in the South," "The Approach of Summer," and a host of other poems. Sometimes, like Wordsworth, Simms probed the enduring effects of his childhood experiences in nature ("Nature's Favorite," "Forest Reverie by Starlight," and "Autumn Twilight"). And also like Wordsworth, in "Inutile Pursuit" and "Mental Solitude," he tackled the theme of being idle in nature and receptive to its spiritual powers versus getting and spending in the utilitarian marketplace.

If the various poems on nature show Simms writing out of his own ecological niche, he also chose subjects from literary tradition. For instance, "Sonnet—The Old Masters" delineates the greats from the past, Dante, John Milton, and "Michael Angelo." "Heads of the Poets" similarly pays tribute to Simms's artistic forefathers, who besides Milton this time include Geoffrey Chaucer, William Shakespeare, Edmund Spenser, Robert Burns, Walter Scott, William Wordsworth, and Lord Byron. The Bible also informs Simms's literary tradition and furnishes the content for "Saul at Endor," "Saul's Last Battle," and "The Rebellion of Absalom," three of the final four works in *Poems*. The poetic faculty itself more abstractly gives Simms his theme in "Imagination" and "The Bard."

Just as diverse as Simms's subjects are his poetic forms. Lyrics abound in the collection, including ballads and songs but especially sonnets. Simms was a master of this form and his rhyme schemes betray greater experimentation than the sonnets of any other nineteenth-century poet. As one would expect from a romantic poet, Simms frequently wrote blank-verse meditations, usually set in nature, as in "Moral Change" and "Autumn Twilight"; these are the types of poems Simms labeled "Contemplative." But if he showed the influence of romantic lyricism in the style of many works, he never turned from the past, as the topic of "Heads of the Poets" suggests. Hence, for "The City of the Silent," he revived the closed heroic couplet, the metrical form of his first book in verse, *Monody, on the Death of Gen. Charles Cotesworth Pinckney* (1825), which showed he had mastered Samuel Johnson and Alexander Pope. Significantly, too, Simms employs narrative, not just in dramatic works like *Norman Maurice* and *Atalantis*, but also in the poems that recount legends, such as "The Cassique of Accabee" and "The Hunter of Calawassee."

The Text

Simms first envisioned a collected edition of his poetry shortly after his 45th birthday. He told his friend James Henry Hammond, "When I can get $500 to spare, I will publish a complete collection of my verse, that the record may be ample, and all my material gatherable at a glance" (*Letters* 3: 127-28). Moreover, by then much of his poetry was unavailable. Both his first five books of poems and his most recent five were all published in Charleston; or as Simms clarified in his aborted preface to *Poems*, most of them "were printed rather for private distribution—than for sale—printed, in fact, without being *published*." Consequently, he said, these volumes "are not now to be had" (qtd. in Kibler, "Preface" 293). Surprisingly, he considered his poetic "career as pretty well over" and wanted "to revise" his work "and make" himself "as worthy as possible in the eyes of future criticism" (*Letters* 3: 155).

To this end, Simms entered into an agreement with Charleston publisher John Russell, who had brought out *Areytos: Or, Songs of the South* in 1846. Russell had a prospectus printed in the *New York Literary World* on 16 August 1851, soliciting subscriptions to the planned two-volume collection. However, so few subscribers answered the call that Simms sought alternate arrangements. J. S. Redfield, whose New York firm would publish most of Simms's works until the Civil War, stepped in and published the edition. Besides an edition bearing Redfield's imprint, Redfield produced an imprint for Russell to satisfy the original subscribers. According to James Everett Kibler, "The two imprints represent two states of the same impression, the Russell copies likely being run off first, for in Volume I, page 220, last line, the first words are lightly inked in the nine Russell copies examined; whereas all nine of the Redfield copies show the impression of type but are not inked" (*Intro* 96). The only key difference between the two issues is their bindings: Redfield's is dark green cloth while Russell's is dark brown cloth. The titles of both are stamped in gold on the spine, and "the cover has a multi-ruled blind-stamped box within a larger frame" (*Intro* 90-91).

In his unpublished preface to *Poems* Simms emphasized that he made many revisions in putting together his "best" verse: "In preparing this collection I have endeavoured to repair the defects of heedlessness & haste in the previous volumes" and "have sought to repair" as well the "faults of taste & temperament" since now he has higher standards for "nicety of finish" (qtd. in Kibler, "Preface" 293). Indeed, Simms had begun revising his early work in 1839 and was publishing improved versions "by the batch, in Magazines," such as the *Southern Literary Messenger*, "under the appropriate head of 'Early Lays'" (*Letters* 5: 356). Paul Hamilton Hayne was simply wrong when he wrote that Simms found revision repugnant and making corrections "distasteful" ("Poets" 159). In fact, while Simms viewed lyric poems as "*improvisations*" he insisted that they required later refinement "by exquisite art" (*Letters* 4: 432).

Many works selected for *Poems* from the books of his early twenties are significantly improved. One prime example, "Summer Night-Wind," was first published in the *Southern Literary Gazette* in 1828 and then collected in *The Vision of Cortes* the next year; but it was rewritten several times more, including for *Southern Passages and Pictures* (1839). Another example is "Night-Watching." It appeared twice in 1829, first in the *Southern Literary Gazette* and then in a longer form in *Vision of Cortes* Finally, it was revised for *Poems*. But other poems, as Simms mentions in the preface, are "fugitives" never before collected but now "reclaimed" for *Poems* (qtd. in Kibler, "Preface" 293). The chief sample of this type is "The Streamlet," written first in 1829 for the *Southern Literary Gazette* but revamped in 1835 for *American Monthly* and then revised once more for *Poems*. This final version deepens some effects, such as the vivid imagery of the natural scenery, but its added length perhaps introduces some redundancy as well. Considering the revised version in *Poems*, which consists of 22 stanzas, we observe the remnants of the earliest version in stanzas 4, 9, 12-17, and 19-21. The only modern reprinting of *Poems* is the edition of 1972, which forms part of the Arno Press series edited by Harold Bloom, The Romantic Tradition in American Literature. It was reprinted from a copy of the Redfield imprint in the Princeton University Library. Moreover, among its 193 poems Kibler's *Selected Poems of William Gilmore Simms* (1990; 2010) includes many works from the 1853 collection.

Although *Poems* was never reprinted in Simms's lifetime, he had entertained ambitions of publishing an expanded edition. In October 1867 Simms told Evert Augustus Duyckinck that he hoped to publish his "complete poetical & dramatic writings in 3 volumes" (*Letters* 5: 90-91); two months later, he planned to add two plays "to make 2 vols. of Dramas" and, by inserting his recent poems, "to make 2 vols. of Poems" (*Letters* 5: 100). However, his negotiations with Redfield's successor, William J. Widdleton, proved fruitless. To settle with Widdleton over unpaid royalties accrued during the Civil War, Simms had instructed James Lawson to take as compensation the plates of the two-volume edition of *Poems* (*Letters* 5: 99). The editors of *The Letters* note that "We do not know whether Simms got from Widdleton the plates for his *Poems* (1853); however, no collected edition of his 'poetical & dramatic writings' was published after" December 1867 (*Letters* 5: 91n).

The Context

Just before Simms started arranging for his collected poems, his reputation as a poet was mixed. The highest praise came in 1851 from James Warley Miles in the *Southern Literary Messenger*. Miles cited Simms's "originality of expression," "richness of imagination," and "command of language," coupled with "musical rhythm"—qualities found "in greater or less degree" in "all of" Simms's verse. Miles concluded, however, that Simms was capable of accomplishing much more than he already had (289, 291). The year before Duyckinck issued a harsher evaluation of Simms's poetry up to *The Cassique of Accabee* (1849). He asserted, "No man can deny that Mr. Simms is a poet; and yet no man in the country has sent before the world so much verse of doubtful character" (80-81). Between Miles and Duyckinck fell William Cullen Bryant, who thought Simms showed improvement in his poetry but had yet to fulfill his potential ("Simms"). These estimates surely reinforced Simms's desire to collect what he considered his best work so that his achievement could be fully and fairly judged. Indeed, just weeks before *Poems* was published he told Duyckinck that in his own mind his poems "exhibit the highest phase of the Imaginative faculty which this country has yet exhibited" (*Letters* 3: 261-62).

Compared to *Poems* Simms's earliest books were very well reviewed, a fact somewhat remarkable since, with the exception of *Atalantis* (1832), they were all published—or printed—locally in Charleston. The first two books attracted attention from two major voices in early American letters: Bryant in the *U. S. Review and Literary Gazette* and Timothy Flint in the *Western Monthly*. Moreover, the *New York Literary Gazette and American Athenaeum* also covered the books. Simms's third book, *The Vision of Cortes*, drew two reviews from Bryant in the *New York Evening Post*, as well as from two other northern sources, *The Yankee* and *The New-York Mirror*. The latter also reviewed *Atalantis*, one of the long works Simms later selected for volume one of *Poems*, as did *The Knickerbocker* and *New-England Magazine*. Even more impressive, Thomas Campbell, author of *The Pleasures of Hope* (1799), reviewed it in the *London Metropolitan Magazine* and, while "disappointed" that the poem "is so thoroughly English," Campbell described it as "well-written" and "polished throughout" (12b).

In contrast, although *Poems* was published in New York by Redfield, only three northern publications noticed it: *Norton's Literary Gazette*, *Harper's*, and *Graham's*, which singled out only the play *Norman Maurice*, though also generally lauding the less known poems for their "sweetness and melody" as well as their "power of description" ("Review of Redfield" 546). If, in the midst of growing sectional tensions and changing literary tastes, *Poems* seems ignored compared to Simms's earliest volumes of verse, it nevertheless enjoyed three strongly positive responses in southern journals from George Frederick Holmes, Miles, and Hayne. Writing at length in the *Richmond Semi-Weekly Enquirer*, Holmes alertly underscored Simms's originality as an American poet: "Mr. Simms is truly an American poet—much more so than his more belauded northern brethren. English subjects are not re-galvanized by his pen." Instead, Holmes insisted, Simms "selects his themes for himself, from the diversified scenes and incidents of American nature and life." Hayne actually reviewed *Poems* twice, when it first appeared in the *Charleston Weekly News* and later and more fully in *Russell's*. In the newspaper piece Hayne stated that in its "power of passionate utterance" Simms's poetry is rarely "excelled." In the longer essay from 1857, "The Poets, and Poetry of the South," Hayne's criticism is more measured, faulting Simms for his diffuse style but finding his poetry ultimately worthy of lasting beyond his lifetime.

Simms's verse has lasted well past his own time, but till the 1970s it hung by a thread above the dustbin of history. William Peterfield Trent, whose biography *William Gilmore Simms* appeared in 1892, shaped the reception of Simms's verse until the recent scholarly renaissance fostered by James Kibler. Trent bluntly dismissed Simms as a poet: His verse was a "failure" and has been deservedly "forgotten"; "Only by courtesy," Trent stated, can one call Simms's verse "poetry." Consequently, Trent considered the edition of *Poems* "needless" (327, 44, 143, 206). More surprising, and perhaps more damaging, are similar dismissals by critics who otherwise worked hard to revive Simms's reputation in the postwar era. T. C. Duncan Eaves served as one of the editors of the monumental *Letters*, but even he believed that "few of Simms's poems have any right of survival" (898). Donald Davidson, who wrote the introduction to the *Letters*, was hardly more sympathetic; in a sweeping statement he complained, "most of Simms' poetry" seems "too obviously worked up" from literary sources rather than from "deeper" origins (*Letters* 1: li). As a result, it is unsurprising that in the Twayne study of Simms, J. V. Ridgely announced that, since Simms's verse has "no significance," there is no need for him "to disinter" it (42). Not all critics were so harsh. Edd Winfield Parks suggested that culling Simms's complete works would produce "only a small volume of excellent poems" but one that would place Simms among "the better American poets" (xciii), and Allen Tate made a brief case for the neglected poetry when he affirmed that "by any test it deserved as much reading as" Simms's fiction (qtd. in Parks 343). Though much more favorable, these last two critical judgments are merely generalizations and apply to no specific works, not even *Poems*.

The fortunes of Simms's poetic reputation began to turn only after the centennial of his death. In 1979 James Kibler tracked Simms's canon and published an exhaustive bibliography of his books and poems, many of them unearthed and identified for the first time. This invaluable resource made modern scholarship on Simms's poetry finally possible. In addition, Kibler's introductory essay to the bibliography forms the first in-depth criticism of this verse since Paul Hamilton Hayne's. In contrast to Trent, Kibler remarked that Simms's two-volume edition of collected poetry "contains some fine poems" (*Intro* 3). A significant discovery uncovered by the bibliography is that Simms wrote many of his romantic poems "during the great period of romanticism" and thus preceded Nathaniel Hawthorne, Ralph Waldo Emerson, and Henry David Thoreau in incorporating elements of the British romantics' verse into American literature (*Intro* 5). Kibler spent the next decade, the 1980s, assembling Simms's *Selected Poems* (1990), which made a cross-section of Simms's poetic canon, including many samples from the collected edition, easily available to contemporary readers. The first scholar to use Kibler's edition was John Caldwell Guilds. His biography mentions numerous poems and discusses not only many works within *Poems* but also the circumstances surrounding its publication. Ultimately, Guilds found that "the excellence Simms attained as a poet is overshadowed by his achievement as a novelist," but he argued that Simms ranks "somewhere between Bryant and Whittier" among nineteenth-century poets (346). Similarly, in his introduction to *Selected Poems* Kibler maintained that Simms in many ways is comparable to Henry Wadsworth Longfellow, Emerson, and Bryant (xxii). Sacvan Bercovitch's *The Cambridge History of Nineteenth-Century American Poetry* (1999) refrained from such a lofty judgment, but its chronology of important books of verse includes *Poems* among the four worthy collections published in 1853 (502). Thus, the time seems ripe for Simms's poetry to receive its due.

Building on the sturdy foundations of Guilds's biography and Kibler's bibliography and editing, a few recent scholars have begun analyzing works in Simms's *Poems* with a seriousness typically brought to more canonical poets like Emerson or Walt Whitman. In 2003, in an article analyzing Simms's "The Streamlet," David W. Newton argued not only that Simms's 1853 collection "anticipates Emerson's attempt to situate Romanticism within a uniquely American context," but also that the best poems in the collection suggest Simms "is Emerson's intellectual equal, and, at times, a superior poet" (24). Another essay supplying an extended discussion of a particular work in *Poems* is Jason W. Johnson's "'Dazzling Outlawries of the Imagination.'" It argues that Simms's innovations in the experimental sonnet "The Lonely Islet" help demonstrate both his "Americanism" and his artistry. Further analysis of many poems from the 1853 collection appears in my own *The Poet's Holy Craft* (2010). I argue for Simms's status as a pioneer of early American romanticism, partly by showing his lifelong debt to Wordsworth and Samuel Taylor Coleridge, including the practice of writing contemplative poems similar to the British romantics' conversation poems; I also demonstrate how Simms's distinctly American and southern ecology parallels Wordsworth's Lake District environmentalism. And like Johnson I provide evidence of Simms's poetic craftsmanship, which often entails artful revision.

A recent issue of *The Simms Review*, edited by Nicholas Meriwether and based on papers from a conference organized by James Kibler, focuses on "Simms the Poet" (Summer/Winter 2009). Many poems never discussed before serve as subject matter for various articles, which is important, but only one article, Corey Mingura's on "The Western Emigrants" and the sonnet "The Age of Gold," centers on examples from *Poems*. The reprinting of the 1853 volume will ensure that scholars keep their eyes on the most important edition compiled by Simms himself. In fact, since most scholars know Simms only through *Selected Poems*, many overlooked works should now receive scrutiny. In a recent review-article Johnson sketched some aspects of Simms's poetry awaiting critical attention: "Simms and the Victorians"; "Simms and the Europeans"; "Simms and the ballad tradition"; "Simms and race/gender/ class, particularly in the narrative poetry"; and "Simms and Christianity and/or mysticism" (124). Many poems in the 1853 collection could advance this scholarship. Other long-needed studies would pair Simms and his contemporaries, for if we are to place Simms in his proper context as a canonical poet, we need criticism that compares him with figures such as Bryant, Emerson, Thoreau, Longfellow, John Greenleaf Whittier, Oliver Wendell Holmes, and Edgar Allan Poe. We need to test Simms's conviction that the poetry in *Poems* embodies "the highest phase of the Imaginative faculty which this country has yet exhibited." Simms knew his poetry would have to wait for posterity to receive a just measure of its value. Slowly, but emphatically, his judgment and ours are coming together.

Works Cited

Bercovitch, Sacvan, ed. *The Cambridge History of Nineteenth-Century American Poetry, 1800-1910*. Cambridge: Cambridge UP, 1999.

Bloom, Harold, ed. *Poems: Descriptive, Dramatic, Legendary and Contemplative*. 2 vols. 1853. The Romantic Tradition in American Literature. New York: Arno P, 1972.

Brennan, Matthew C. *The Poet's Holy Craft: William Gilmore Simms and Romantic Verse Tradition*. Columbia: U of South Carolina P, 2010.

Butterworth, Keen, and James E. Kibler, Jr. *William Gilmore Simms: A Reference Guide*. Boston: Hall, 1980.

Bryant, William Cullen. "Simms." *Homes of American Authors; Comprising Anecdotal, Personal and Descriptive Sketches, by Various Authors*. New York: Putnam, 1853.257-62.

Campbell, Thomas. "Notices of New Works." *London Metropolitan Magazine* Jan. 1834: 12b.

Davidson, Donald. Introduction. Oliphant, Odell, and Eaves 1: xxxi-lviii.

Duyckinck, Evert Augustus. Review of *The Cassique of Accabee* and *Father Abbott*. *New York Literary World* 26 Jan. 1850: 80-81.

Eaves, T. C. Duncan. "An Early American Admirer of Keats." *PMLA* 67 (1952): 895-98.

Guilds, John Caldwell. *Simms: A Literary Life*. Fayetteville: U of Arkansas P, 1992.

Hayne, Paul Hamilton. "The Poets, and Poetry of the South." *Russell's Magazine* (Nov. 1857): 152-60.

——. Review of *Poems*. *Charleston Weekly News* 7 Jan. 1854: 3.

Holmes, George Frederick. Review of *Poems*. *Richmond Semi-Weekly Enquirer* 4 Apr. 1854.

Johnson, Jason W. "'Dazzling Outlawries of the Imagination': William Gilmore Simms and the 'Americanism' of the Sonnets." *Simms Review* 14.2 (2006): 5-13.

——. Review. *Simms Review* 18.1/2 (2010): 117-25.

Kibler, James Everett. *The Poetry of William Gilmore Simms: An Introduction and Bibliography*. Columbia, SC: Southern Studies, 1979.

——. "The Unpublished Preface to W. G. Simms's Collected Poems." *Studies in Bibliography* 49 (1996): 291-93.

——, ed. Introduction. *Selected Poems of William Gilmore Simms*. 1990. Columbia: U of South Carolina P, 2010. xvii-xxvii.

Miles, James Warley. "Southern Passages and Pictures." *Southern Literary Messenger* May 1851: 289-96.

Mingura, Corey Don. "'Cash is Conqueror': The Critique of Capitalism in Simms's 'The Western Emigrants' and 'Sonnet—The Age of Gold.'" *Simms Review* 17.1/2 (2009):87-96.

Newton, David W. "Voices from the Enchanted Circle: Simms and the Poetics of the American Renaissance." *Southern Quarterly* 41.2 (2003): 23-36.

Parks, Edd Winfield. *Southern Poets*. New York: American Book, 1936.

"Review of the Redfield Edition." *Graham's* May 1854: 546.

Ridgely, J. V. *William Gilmore Simms*. New York: Twayne, 1962.

Simms, William Gilmore. *The Letters of William Gilmore Simms*. Ed. Mary C. Simms Oliphant, Alfred Taylor Odell, and T. C. Duncan Eaves. 6 vols. Columbia: U of South Carolina P, 1952-82.

Trent, William P. *William Gilmore Simms*. Boston: Houghton Mifflin, 1892.

Very faithfully, &c
W. Gilmore Simms

POEMS

DESCRIPTIVE DRAMATIC, LEGENDARY

AND

CONTEMPLATIVE

BY

WILLIAM GILMORE SIMMS, ESQ

IN TWO VOLUMES

VOL. I.

I. NORMAN MAURICE, A TRAGEDY
II. ATALANTIS, A TALE OF THE SEA
III. TALES AND TRADITIONS OF THE SOUTH
IV. THE CITY OF THE SILENT

REDFIELD
110 & 112 NASSAU-STREET, NEW YORK
1853

NORMAN MAURICE;

OR,

THE MAN OF THE PEOPLE.

DRAMATIS PERSONÆ.

NORMAN MAURICE.
ROBERT WARREN, *his kinsman and enemy.*
RICHARD OSBORNE, *an attorney and creature of Warren.*
HARRY MATTHEWS, *a friend of Warren.*
COL. BLASINGHAME, *a fire-eater.*
BEN FERGUSON, *a leading politician.*
COL. MERCER, } *Politicians of opposite party.*
COL. BROOKS, }
MAJOR SAVAGE, *a friend of Blasinghame.*
CAPT. CATESBY, U. S. A., *friend of Maurice.*
Citizens, Lawyers, &c.
MRS. JERVAS, *a widow.*
CLARICE DELANCY, *her niece, afterwards wife to Maurice.*
WIDOW PRESSLEY, *a client of Maurice*
KATE PRESSLEY, *her grand-daughter.*
BIDDY, *a servant girl.*

SCENE—First, in Philadelphia; afterwards, in Missouri.

NORMAN MAURICE.

ACT I.—SCENE 1.

A parlor in the house of Mrs. Jervas, in Walnut-street, Philadelphia. Mrs. Jervas and Robert Warren discovered—the latter entering hastily and with discomposure.

MRS. JERVAS, [*eagerly.*] Well?
WARREN. It is *not* well! 'Tis ill! She has refused me!
MRS. J. Has she then dared?
WARREN. Ay, has she! Something farther—
She does not scruple to avow her passion
For my most worthy cousin, Norman Maurice.
MRS. J. She shall repent it—she shall *dis*avow it,
Or she shall know!—I'll teach her!—
WARREN. She's a pupil
With will enough of her own to vex a master!
MRS. J. I have a will too, which shall master her!
Is she not mine?—my sister's child?—a beggar,
That breathes but by my charity! I'll teach her,
And she shall learn the lesson set for her,
Or I will turn her naked into the streets,
As pennyless as she came. But, wait and see,—
You shall behold—
WARREN. Nay, wait till I am gone,

Then use your best severity. She needs it—
Has no sufficient notion of her duty,
And—

MRS. J. No, indeed!

WARREN. But you must make her wiser.

MRS. J. I will!
I've treated her too tenderly!

WARREN. But show her
Some little glimpse of the danger in her path,—
Shame and starvation—

MRS. J. She deserves them both.

WARREN. And keep my worthy cousin from her presence.

MRS. J. He darks these doors no more! The girl, already,
Has orders to deny him.

WARREN. You've done wisely.
A little time,—but keep them separate,—
And we shall conquer her;—ay, conquer *him* too,
For I've a little snare within whose meshes
His feet are sure to fall.

MRS. J. What snare?

WARREN. No matter!
Be ignorant of the mischief till it's over,
And we enjoy its fruits! Meanwhile, be busy,—
Pursue the plan you purpose, and to-morrow,
We shall know farther. I shall use the moments,
'Twixt this and then, in labors which must profit,
Or fortune grows perverse. See you to *her*,
While I take care of *him*.

MRS. J. Oh, never fear me—
I'll summon her the moment you are gone,
And she shall know—

WARREN. That you may summon her—
For we must lose no time—I take my leave.

[*Ex. Warren.*

Mrs. J. The pert and insolent baggage! But I'll teach her!
I'll let her know from whose benevolent hand
She eats the bread of charity—whose mercy
It is, that clothes her nakedness with warmth.
[*Rings. Enter Biddy.*
Go, Biddy!—send my niece to me. [*Ex. Biddy.*] A beggar,
That fain would be a chooser!—So, Miss!

Enter Clarice.

Clarice. Dear Aunt!
Mrs. J. Ay, you would *dare* me in another fashion,
But you have met your match; and now I tell you,
Clarice Delancy, 'tis in vain you struggle—
Clarice. What *have* I done?
Mrs. J. Oh! you are ignorant,
And innocent seeming as the babe unborn,
If tongue and face could speak for secret conscience,
That harbors what it should not. So, you dare
Avow a passion for that beggarly Maurice,
Whom I've forbid the house!
Clarice. Forbidden Maurice!
Mrs. J. Ay, indeed! forbid!
Clarice. In what has he offended?
Mrs. J. His poverty offends me—his presumption.
Clarice. Presumption!
Mrs. J. He has the audacity to think of you
In marriage—he would heir my property;—
The miserable beggar! who, but lately—
Clarice. And, if the humble Clarice might presume,
There were no fitter husband! From the Fates
I do entreat no happier destiny
Than but to share, o'er all that wealth may proffer,
The beggary that he brings!
Mrs. J. But you shall never!

I am your guardian, in the place of mother,
And I will turn you naked from these doors
If you but dare—

CLARICE. Ah! that *were* guardianship,
Becoming the dear sister of a mother,
Who, when she left her hapless child to earth,
Ne'er dream'd of such remembrance, in the future,
Of what beseem'd the past. I've anger'd you,
But cannot chide myself, because my nature
Does not revolt at homage of a being
In whom no virtue starves. Suppose him poor!
Wealth makes no certain happiness to hope,
Nor poverty its loss. In Norman Maurice
I see a nobleness that still atones for
The lowly fortunes that offend your pride.
None richer lives in rarest qualities,—
More precious to the soul that feeds on worth,
Than all your city glitter. Do you think
To win me from a feast of such delights,
To the poor fare on common things that make
The wealth of Robert Warren? Madam—my aunt,—
I thank you for the bounty you have shown me!
It had been precious o'er most earthly things,
But that it hath its price, at perilous cost
To things more precious still. Your charity,
That found a shelter for this humble person,
Were all too costly, if it claims in turn
This poor heart's sacrifice. I *cannot* make it!
I will *not* wed this Warren,—for I *know* him—
And, if it be that I shall ever wed,
Will wed with Norman Maurice—as a man,
Whom most it glads me that I also know.

MRS. J. Never shall you wed with *him* while I have power
To keep you from such folly. You're an infant,

That knows not what is needful for your safety,
Or precious for your heart. Be ruled by me,
Or forth you pack. I cut you off forever,
From fortune as from favor.

CLARICE. Welcome death,
Sooner than bonds like these!

MRS. J. Ungrateful girl!
And this is the return for all my bounty?
But you shall not achieve your own destruction,
If I can help it. This Maurice never darkens
My dwelling with his shadow. He hath made you
Perverse and disobedient—but he shall not
Thrive by your ruin. See that you prepare
To marry Robert Warren.

CLARICE. With the grave first!—
Its cold and silence, and its crawling things,
Loathsome, that make us shudder but to think on,
Sooner than he!—a base, unworthy creature,
Who steals between his kinsman and the friend,
That gave him highest trust and held him faithful,
To rob him of the treasure he most values.
The reptile that keeps empire in the grave
Sooner than he, shall glide into this bosom,
And make it all his own.

MRS. J. Silence, I say!—
Before I madden with your insolence,
And lose the memory of that sainted sister
That left you in my trust.

CLARICE. My poor, dear mother!
She never dream'd of this, in that dark hour
That lost me to her own!

MRS. J. I'm in her place,
To sway your foolish fancies with a prudence
You will not know yourself. Once more I tell you,

You wed with Warren—Robert Warren, only!
This Maurice— [*noise without*] Ha! That noise?—
MAURICE. [*in the hall without.*] I *must*, my girl!
CLARICE. 'Tis Maurice now.
MRS. J. The insolent! will he dare!
BIDDY. [*in the hall without.*] Mrs. Jervas says, sir—
MAURICE. [*without.*] Ay! ay! she *says!*—
But when a lady means civilities,
'Tis still my custom to do justice to her,
By seeking them in person. There, my girl,
You've done your duty as you should. Now, please you,
I will do mine. [*Entering the room.*] Madam—
MRS. J. Was ever insolence—
BIDDY. [*entering.*] Mr. Maurice *would*, ma'am.
MRS. J. This conduct, sir—
MAURICE. Would be without its plea at common seasons,—
And he whose purpose was a morning visit,
The simply social object of the idler,
Who finds in his own time and company
The very worst offence, could offer nothing,
To plead for his intrusion on that presence,
Which, so politely, shuts the door against him.
MRS. J. Well, sir?
MAURICE. But I am none of these.
MRS. J. What plea, sir?—
MAURICE. Some natures have their privilege—some passions
Demand a hearing. There are rights of feeling,
That art can never stifle—griefs, affections,
That never hear the civil "Not at home!"
When home itself is perill'd by submission.
He's but a haggard that obeys the check,
When all that's precious to his stake of life
Is fasten'd on the string. Necessity
Makes bold to ope the door which fashion's portress

Would bolt and bar against him. 'Tis *my* fate,
That prompts me to a rudeness, which my nurture
Would else have shrunk from. But that I have rights
Which move me to defiance of all custom,
I had not vex'd your presence.

MRS. J. Rights, sir—rights?

MAURICE. Ay, madam, the most precious to the mortal!
Rights of the heart, which make the heart immortal
In those affections which still show to earth,
The only glimpses we have left of Eden.
Behold in her, [*pointing to Clarice,*] my best apology—
One, whom to gaze on silences complaint,
And justifies the audacity that proves
Its manhood in its error. Clarice, my love,
Is there from any corner of your heart
An echo to the will that says to Maurice,
Your presence here is hateful? [*Takes her hand.*]

CLARICE. Can you ask?

MAURICE. Enough!—

MRS. J. Too much, I say. Let go her hand,
And leave this dwelling, sir! I'm mistress here;
And shall take measures for security
Against this lawless insolence.

MAURICE. Awhile! awhile!
You *are* the mistress here;—I *will* obey you;—
Will leave your presence, madam, never more
To trouble you with mine. You now deny me
The privilege, that never act of mine
Hath properly made forfeit. You behold me
The suitor to your niece. You hear her language,—
How different from your own—that, with its bounty
Makes rich my heart with all the gifts in hers!
Sternly, you wrest authority from judgment,
To exercise a will that puts to scorn

Her hopes no less than mine! I would have pleaded
Your calm return to judgment;—would entreat you
To thoughts of better favor, that might sanction,
With the sweet blessing of maternal love,
The mutual passion living in our hearts;
But that I know how profitless the pleading,
Which, in the ear of prejudice, would soften
The incorrigible wax that deafens pride.
I plead not for indulgence—will *not* argue
The cruelty that finds in charity
Commission for that matchless tyranny
That claims the right to break the orphan's heart
Because it finds her bread.

CLARICE, [*aside to Norman.*] Spare her, Norman.

MAURICE, [*aside to Clarice.*] Oh! will I not! Yet wherefore need I spare,
When, if the Holy Law be not a mock,
The justice which must break this heart of stone,
Will send her howling through eternity.
'Twere mercy, which in season speaks the truth,
That, in the foretaste of sure penalties,
May terrify the offender from his path,
And send him to his knees.

CLARICE, [*aside to Maurice.*] For my sake, Norman.

MAURICE, [*to Mrs. J.*] Yet, madam, in this freest use of power,
Which drives me hence, be merciful awhile,
And, if this heart, so dearly link'd with mine,
Through love and faith unperishing, must turn
Its fountains from that precious overflow
That kept my flowers in bloom—yet, ere the word,
That leaves me sterile ever thence, be said,
Suffer us, apart awhile, to speak of parting!
Words of such import still ask fewest ears,
And words of grief and hopelessness like ours,

Must needs have utterance in such lowly tones,
As best declare the condition of the heart,
That's muffled for despair. But a few moments
We'll walk apart together.

Mrs. J. It is useless!
What needs—

Maurice. What need of sorrow ever! Could earth speak,
Prescribing laws to that Divinity,
That still smites rock to water, we should hear,
The universal voice of that one plea,
That claims for man immunity from troubles
Which make proud eyes o'erflow. Who should persuade
His fellow to opinion of the uses
That follow from his tears? What school, or teacher,
Would seek to show that chemistry had art,
To fix and harden the dilating drops
To brilliants as they fall,—such as no crown
In Europe might affect? One finds no succor,
Sovereign to break the chain about his wrist,
From all the fountains that o'ersluice the heart;
Yet will he weep, though useless. He who stands,
Waiting upon the scaffold for the signal,
That flings him down the abyss, still hoards each minute
That niggard fate allows. That single minute
Still shrines a hope;—if not a hope, a feeling,
That finds a something precious even in pain,
And will not lose the anxiety that racks him,
Lest he make forfeit of a something better
Which yet he cannot name. And, at the last,
I, whom you doom to loss of more than life,
May well implore the respite of a moment,
If but to suffer me to count once more,
The treasure that I lose. A moment, madam?

Mrs. J. [*walks up the stage.*] A single moment, then.

MAURICE. Oh! you are gracious!
A single moment is a boundless blessing
To him you rob of time! Clarice, my love.
CLARICE. My Norman!
MAURICE. Oh! is it thus, my Clarice—is it thus?
CLARICE. We have been children, Norman, in our dreams!
We are the sport of fate!
MAURICE. And shall be ever,
If that there be no courage in our hearts
To shape the fates to favor by our will.
CLARICE. What mean you, Norman?
MAURICE. What should Norman mean,
But, if he can, to grapple with his fortune,
And, like a sturdy wrestler in the ring,
Throw heart and hope into the perilous struggle?
What should I mean but happiness for thee,—
Thou willing, as myself? Who strives with fate,
Must still, like him, the mighty Macedonian,
Seize the coy priestess by the wrist, and lead her
Where yet she would not go! Suppose me faithful
To the sweet passion I have tender'd you,
And what remains in this necessity,
But that, made resolute by grim denial,
I challenge from your love sufficient courage,
To take the risks of mine!
CLARICE. Within your eye
A meaning more significant than your words,
Would teach me still to tremble. That I love you,
You doubt not, Norman! That my heart hath courage
To match the love it feels for you—
MAURICE. It hath—it hath!
If that the love be there, as I believe it,
That love will bring, to nourish needful strength,
A virtue that makes love a thing of soul,

And arms its will with wings. Oh! read you not,
My meaning—

MRS. J. [*approaching.*] Your moment is a long one, sir.

MAURICE. Ah, madam!
Who chides the executioner when he suffers
The victim his last words—though still he lingers
Ere he would reach the last? But a few moments,
And I have spoken all that my full heart
Might not contain with safety.

MRS. J. [*retiring up the stage.*] Be it so, sir.

MAURICE. You hear, my Clarice. We've another moment:
But one, it seems, unless your resolution
Takes its complexion from the fate that threatens
And shows an equal will. If then, in truth,
You love me—

CLARICE. Oh! look not thus!

MAURICE. I doubt not;—
And yet, dear Clarice, if indeed you love me,
The single moment that this woman gives us,
Becomes a life;—to me, of happiness,—
To thee, as full of happiness as thou
Might hope to gain from me. She would deny us,—
Would wed thee to that subtle Robert Warren—

CLARICE. I'll perish first!

MAURICE. No need of perishing
When I can bring thee to security.
I knew thy straits—the tyranny which thou suffer'st
Because of thy dependence; and my struggle,
Since this conviction reached me—day and night—
Was, that I might from this condition snatch thee,
And, in thy happier fortunes, find mine own!
I have prepared for this.

CLARICE. What would'st thou, Norman?

MRS. J. [*approaching.*] Your moments fly.

MAURICE. I soon shall follow them.

MRS. J. [*retiring again.*] The sooner, sir, the better.

MAURICE. She would spare me,
The argument which shows thee what is needful.

CLARICE. Speak! I have courage equal to my love!

MAURICE. I try thee though I doubt not! If thou lov'st m
Thou'lt yield, without a question, to my purpose,
And give me all thy trust.

CLARICE. Will I not, Norman?

MAURICE. Then, with the night, I make thee mine, Clarice!
Steal forth at evening. There shall be a carriage,
And my good hostess, whom thou know'st, in waiting.
Our future home is ready.

CLARICE. Let me think, Norman.

MAURICE. That's as your excellent aunt, who now approaches,
May please:—but, surely, when to my fond pleading
You sweetly vow'd yourself as mine alone,
The proper thought that sanctions my entreaty
Was all complete and perfect.

CLARICE. But Norman, how—
How should I, in your poverty, encumber
Your cares with a new burden?

MAURICE. There is no poverty,
Which the true courage, and the bold endeavor,
The honest purpose, the enduring heart,
Crowned with a love that blesses while it burdens,
May not defy in such a land as ours!
We'll have but few wants having one another!—
And for these wants, some dawning smiles of fortune
Already have prepared me. Trust me, Clarice,
I will not take thee to a worse condition,
In one whose charities shall never peril
The affections they should foster.

MRS. J. [*approaching.*] Sir,—again!

MAURICE. Yes, yes—most excellent madam—yes—again!
There's but a single syllable between us,
Your niece hath left unspoken.—My Clarice!

CLARICE. I'm thine!

MAURICE. *'Tis spoken!*
And now I live again!

MRS. J. Well, sir—art done at last?

MAURICE. Done! Ay, madam—done!
You've held me narrowly to a strict account—
And yet, I thank you. You've been merciful
After a fashion which invokes no justice,
And yet may find it, madam. Yet—I thank you!
The word *is* said that's needful to our parting;
And that I do not in despair depart,
Is due to these last moments. Fare you well!
Be you as safe, henceforth, from all intrusion,
As you shall be from mine. Clarice—farewell!

CLARICE. Norman.

MAURICE. [*embracing her.*] But one embrace!

MRS. J. Away, sir.

MAURICE. In earnest of those pleasant bonds hereafter,
That none shall dare gainsay. Clarice—Remember!
[*Exit Maurice.*

CLARICE. Go, Norman, and believe me.

MRS. J. Get you in! [*Exeunt.*

SCENE II.

A Lawyer's office in Philadelphia. Richard Osborne at a desk writing.

Enter Robert Warren.

WARREN, [*eagerly.*] Hast drawn the paper, Osborne?

OSBORNE. It is here.

WARREN. The copy this?—

OSBORNE. And this the original.

WARREN, [*examining papers.*] 'Tis very like! You've done it famously:
One knows not which is which; and Norman Maurice,
Himself, would struggle vainly to discover
The difference 'twixt the words himself hath written,
And these your skill hath copied to a hair.
We shall deceive him.

OSBORNE. Why would you deceive him?

WARREN. Eh! Why? It is my instinct! Are you answer'd?
I hate him! Would you have a better answer?

OSBORNE. Why hate him when his kindness still have served you?
This very obligation which hath bound him,
And given us cruel power o'er his fortunes,—
His purse—perhaps his honor—

WARREN. Why, perhaps?
Is it doubtful, think you, that this fatal writing,
Made public,—will disgrace him?

OSBORNE. An error only,—
The thoughtless sport of boyhood—wholly guiltless
Of all dishonest purpose. We have used it,—
You rather—and the profit has been ours!—

Why, if he pays the money as he proffers,
Why treasure still this paper? More—why hate him?
WARREN. Let it suffice you that I have my reasons!—
And let me tell you, Osborne, that I love not
This sympathy which you show for Norman Maurice.
Beware! who goes not with me is against me!
OSBORNE. I'm in your power, I know—
WARREN. Then let your wisdom
Abate its fond pretension as my teacher!
I'm better pleased with service than tuition;
Will hold you as my ally, not my master!
I have remarked, of late, that you discover
Rare virtues in my cousin! He hath fee'd you;
Employed you as attorney in his cases—
OSBORNE. Not more than other counsellors.
WARREN. No matter!
It is enough that you are mine!
OSBORNE. This jealousy—
WARREN. Is only vigilance! Each look of favor,
Bestow'd on him I loathe, is disaffection
In him that's bound to me.
OSBORNE. This document?—
WARREN. The *real* one,—the *original*—is mine;
The *copy* you will yield him when he pays you;—
That he will do so, now, I make no question,
Though where his money comes from is my wonder.
OSBORNE. The case of Jones & Peters, just determined,
Brings him large fees. Another action,
The insurance case of Ferguson & Brooks,
Secures him handsome profits. Other cases,
Have lately brought him, with new reputation,
Liberal returns of money.
WARREN. We'll have all!
See that you pile the costs—crowd interest—

Expense of service; tax to the uttermost
The value of your silence and forbearance—
Leave nothing you have done without full charges,
While, what has been forborne, more highly rated,
Shall sweep the remaining eagles from his purse.
OSBORNE. What bitterness is yours!
WARREN. Oh! quite ungracious,
Contrasted with the sweetness of your moods!
Once more, beware! Do as I bid you, Osborne,
Or you shall feel me. Yield him up this *copy*,
Which we shall see him, with delirious rapture,
Thrust in the blazing furnace,—little dreaming,
That still the damning scrawl that blasts his honor,
Lies here, in the possession of his foe!
OSBORNE. Will nothing move you, Warren?
WARREN. His funeral only,—
To follow—while above his burial place,
I show this fatal paper,—still lamenting
That one with so much talent should have falter'd,
When virtue cried "Be firm!"—Oh! I will sorrow,
So deeply o'er his sad infirmity,
That they who come to weep above his grave,
Will turn from it in scorn. But, get you ready;—
You'll sup with me; and afterwards we'll seek him.
We must look smiling then as summer flowers,
Nor show the serpent crouching in the leaves. [*Exeunt.*

SCENE III.

Evening: Chestnut-street. Enter Maurice with Clarice.

MAURICE. Thou'rt mine, my Clarice.
CLARICE. Wholly thine, my husband.

MAURICE. Now let the furies clamor as they may,
That the capricious fortune which had mock'd
Our blessings with denial, has been baffled
By the true nobleness of that human will,
Which, when the grim necessity looks worst,
Can fearlessly resolve to brave its fate.
Thou'rt mine, and all grows suppliant in my path
That lately looked defiance. We are one!—
This is our dwelling, Clarice:—let us in.
[*They enter the house of Maurice.*

SCENE IV.

The parlor of a dwelling in the residence of Maurice, handsomely and newly furnished. Enter Warren and Osborne.

WARREN. I am amazed.
OSBORNE. 'Tis certainly a change
From his old lodging-house in Cedar-street.
WARREN. His run of luck hath crazed him, and he fancies
The world is in his string.
OSBORNE. He's not far wrong!
His arguments have made a great impression;
Their subtlety and closeness, and the power
Of clear and forcible development,
Which seems most native to his faculty!
He was born an orator! With such a person—
A voice to glide from thunder into music,
A form and face so full of majesty,
Yet, with such frankness and simplicity,—
So much to please, and so commanding—
WARREN. Pshaw!—
You prate as do the newspapers, with a jargon

Of wretched common-place, bestuffed with phrases,
That, weighed against the ballad of an idiot,
Would show less burden and significance.
We'll spoil his fortune—

OSBORNE. Hark! He comes.

WARREN. Be firm now!
See that you do it manfully—no halting.—

OSBORNE. You still persist, then?

WARREN. Ay! when I have him here. [*touching his breast.*]

Enter Norman Maurice.

MAURICE. Be seated, sirs.
You bring with you the paper? [*To Osborne.*

OSBORNE. It is here, sir. [*Giving copy of document.*
And here the separate claim—the costs and charges.

MAURICE. 'Tis well! This first!—I pay this money, sir,
In liquidation of this wretched paper,
To which my hand appears, and, for which writing,
The world, unconscious of the facts, might hold me
A most unhappy criminal. Your knowledge
Includes this person's agency—my cousin—
As still, in moments of insidious fondness,
It is his wont to call me.

WARREN. Norman, nay!

MAURICE, [*impatiently to Warren.*] Awhile, awhile, sir! we shall deal directly!—
I said [*to Osborne,*] your knowledge of this boyish error,
Betrayed the agency of Robert Warren,
Which does not here appear. He made *that* guilty
Which in itself was innocent. These moneys,
Procured by him upon this document,
Were all by him consumed. You were his agent,
Perhaps as ignorant of his vicious deed,
As I, who am its victim. Was it so, sir?

OSBORNE. I sold for him the bill, sir, knowing nothing,
And still believed it genuine.

MAURICE. He will tell you,
That, what I utter of his agency,
In this insane and inconsiderate act,
Is true as Holy Writ! Speak, Robert Warren!

WARREN. I have admitted it already, Norman.

MAURICE. [*To Osborne.*] Be you the witness of his words hereafter.
Here is your money,—and I take this paper,
The proof of boyish error and misfortune,
But not of crime, in me. Thus, let it perish,
With that confiding and believing nature,
Which gave me to the power of one so base! [*putting it in the fire, and placing his foot on it while it burns.*

WARREN. Norman! Cousin!

MAURICE. You cozen me no more!
And if your agent has the wit to gather
A lesson from your faithlessness to me,
You will not cozen him. Take counsel, sir,
And never trust this man! [*To Osborne.*

WARREN. Norman Maurice!

MAURICE. [*To Osborne.*] Our business ends! Will it please you, leave us now!

[*Exit Osborne: Warren is about to follow when Maurice lays his hand on his shoulder.*

MAURICE. Stay *you!* There must be other words before we part,
Not many, but most needful.

WARREN. Let me pray you,
To fashion them in less offensive spirit.

MAURICE. Why, so I should, could I suppose one virtue,
A life to leaven a dense mass of vices,
Remain'd within your bosom. You *shall* listen
Though every syllable should be a sting!

'Twould not offend me greatly, Robert Warren,
If, as I brand thy baseness on thy forehead,
Thy heart, with courage born of just resentment,
Should move thee to defiance! It would glad me,
In sudden strife, to put a proper finish
To thy deep, secret, foul, hostility.

WARREN. You have no reason for this cruel language.

MAURICE. Look on me as thou say'st the monstrous falsehood;
But lift thine eye to mine—and, if thy glance
Can brazen out the loathing in mine own,
I will forgive thee all! Thou dar'st not do it!
No reason, say'st thou?—Thou, whose arrant cunning,
Hath taken the profits of three toilsome years
To pay thy wage of sin,—and smutch'd my garments,
That else had known no stain!

WARREN. Have I not
Confess'd that wrong and folly?—

MAURICE. Wert repentant,
When making thy confession—

WARREN. So I am!

MAURICE. Traitor! I know thee better! Thy confession
But followed on detection! While thou mad'st it,
The busy devil, dwelling in thy heart,
Was framing other schemes of crime and hatred,
Outbraving all the past. Ev'n while my pity
Was taking thee to mercy, thou wast planning
New evil to my fortunes!

WARREN. Never, Norman!
By heaven! you do me wrong.

MAURICE. Pure Innocent,
The very angels look on thee with sorrow,
To see such virtue suffer such injustice!—
But hearken, while I paint another picture:
The fiends exulting in thy ready service,

A voluntary minister of evil,
As, with a spirit born of hell and hatred,
Thou pluck'st the flower of hope from happiness,
To plant the thorn instead.
WARREN. What crime is this?
MAURICE. I heard thy plea for mercy! I believed thee,
And, as thou wert the child of that dear woman
Who called my mother, sister, I forgave thee,
Most glad to listen to thy deep assurance
Of shame for each sad error. So, I took thee,
Once more, to confidence—my bosom open'd,
And show'd thee, shrined within its holiest chamber,
The image of the being that I loved!—
I led thee to her—taught her to behold thee,
My friend and kinsman; and, misdoubting never,
Still saw thee bend thy footsteps to her dwelling,
Nor dream'd that to the flowers that made my Eden,
Myself had brought the serpent!
WARREN. What means this?
MAURICE. What! Thou know'st nothing? Thou hast no conjecture
Of what the serpent sought within the garden!
Why, man, he whispered in Eve's innocent ears,
The oiliest nothings,—mingled with such slander
Of him who sought to make himself her Adam,
That—
WARREN. 'Tis false!—I swear! I never did this mischief!
MAURICE. Liar! The oath thou tak'st is thy perdition!
Behold the evidence that proves thy blackness,
In contrast with its purity and truth!
Clarice! Come forth! My wife, sir!

Enter Clarice from within.

WARREN. Damnation! [*Warren rushes out.*

MAURICE. Thus fled the fiend, touch'd by Ithuriel's spear,
Even from the reptile rising to the fiend,
And speeding from the Eden that his presence
Shall never trouble more. Henceforth, dear wife,
Our paradise shall still be free from taint;
A realm of sweetness unobscured by shadow,
And freshening still with flow'rs that take their beauty,
As favor'd still by thine. From this blest moment,
Our peace shall be secure!
CLARICE. And yet I fear,
This bold, bad man.
MAURICE. Bad, but not bold! Fear nothing!
I've pluck'd his sting! Thou know'st the cruel story;
I told thee all,—suppressed no syllable—
Of his perversion of a simple paper,
Wherein, in vain display of penmanship,
I gave him power for practice which he seized on,
Exposing me to ruin. In those embers,
The fatal proof lies buried. I am free;—
And in the freedom I have won from him,
And in the bondage I have sworn to thee,
I write the record of my happiness!
This day I feel triumphant as the hunter,
Who, on the wild steed that his skill hath captured,
Rifle in grasp, and bridle rein flung loose,
Darts forth upon the prairie's waste of empire,
And feels it all his own!
CLARICE. I share thy triumph—
Would share that waste with thee and feel no sorrow,
For all that love foregoes.
MAURICE. I take thy promise—
Will try thy strength, thy courage and thy heart,
As little thou hast fancied! Clarice, dear wife,
With dawn we leave this city.

CLARICE. How! to-morrow?
And leave this city, Norman?
MAURICE. Dost thou fail me?
CLARICE. No! I am thine! My world is in thy love;
I wish no dearer dwelling-place—would ask
No sweeter realm of home! Go, where thou wilt,
I cling to thee as did the Hebrew woman
To him who had his empire in her heart.
MAURICE. I bless thee for this proof of thy affection!
This is the city of thy birth and mine,
But that's our native land alone which suffers
That we take root and flourish;—those alone,
Our kindred, who will gladden in our growth,
And succor till we triumph. Here, it may be,
That, after weary toil, and matchless struggle,
When strength subsides in age, they will acknowledge,
That I am worthy of my bread,—may bid me,
Look up and be an alderman or mayor!—
And this were of their favor. The near neighbors,
Who grew with us, and saw our gradual progress,
Who knew the boy, and all his sports and follies,
Have seldom faith that he will grow the man
To cast them into shadow. We'll go hence!—
CLARICE. Whither, dear Norman?
MAURICE. Whither! Dost thou ask?
Both in God's keeping, Clarice—thou in mine!
I'll tender thee as the most precious treasure,
That city ever yielded wilderness.
CLARICE. I know thou wilt;—but what thy means, my husband
Thou told'st me thou wast poor.
MAURICE. Means! I have manhood!
Youth, strength, and men say, intellect—
CLARICE. You have! You have!
MAURICE. A heart at ease, secure in its affections,

And still the soul to seek each manly struggle!
Wide is the world before me—a great people,
Spread o'er a realm, along whose verdant meadows
The sun can never set. I know this people—
Love them—would make them mine! I have ambition
To serve them in high places, and do battle
With the arch-tyrannies, in various guises,
That still from freedom pluck its panoply,
Degrade its precious rites, and, with vain shadows,
Mock the fond hopes that fasten on their words.
CLARICE. Could you not serve them *here?*
MAURICE. No! No!
CLARICE. Wherefore not?—
And oh! they need some saviour here, methinks!
MAURICE. Ay! They do need! But I am one of them,—
Sprung from themselves—have neither friends nor fortune,
And will not stoop, entreating as for favor,
When I would serve to save! They lack all faith
In him who scorns to flatter their delusions,
And lie them to self-worship. In the West,
There is a simpler and a hardier nature,
That proves men's values, not by wealth and title,
But mind and manhood. There, no ancient stocks,
Claim power from precedence. Patrician people,
That boast of virtues in their grandmothers,
Are challenged for their own. With them it answers,
If each man founds his family, and stands
The father of a race of future men!
Mere parchment, and the vain parade of title,
Lift no man into stature. Such a region
Yields all that I demand—an open field,
And freedom to all comers. So, the virtues
Flourish according to their proper nature;
And each man, as he works with will and courage,

Reaps the good fruitage proper to his claim ;—
Thither, dear wife!

CLARICE. I'm thine!

MAURICE. Thy ready answer,
Completes my triumph! Wings are at my shoulders,
And more than eagle empires woo my flight!
Yet, do I something fear,—Clarice—

CLARICE. What fear?

MAURICE. *Thou*'rt not ambitious.

CLARICE. But for thee, Norman;
If that, in service at thy shrine of glory,
Thou dost not lose the love—

MAURICE. Be satisfied
That, when my state is proudest, thou shalt be
The one, whom, most of all, these eyes shall look for,
This heart still follow with devoted service.
But, to thy preparations: I will follow;—
Before the dawn we shall have left this city. [*Clarice going.*
That reptile— [*musingly.*]

CLARICE. [*returning.*] Norman!

MAURICE. My Clarice! [*embracing her.* [*Exit Clarice.*
His fangs are drawn!—
Yet, somehow, he is present to my thoughts,
As if he still had power. But, let him dare,
Once more to cross my path, and he shall feel
His serpent head grow flat beneath my heel. [*Exit within.*

END OF ACT FIRST.

ACT II.—SCENE I.

Scene: Missouri. A room in the cottage of Norman Maurice. Enter Maurice and Clarice.

CLARICE. Oh! Norman, this is happiness.
MAURICE. 'Tis more,—
Security in happiness. Our blossoms
Fear not the spoiler. On your cheek the roses
Declare a joyous presence in the heart,
That makes our cottage bloom.
CLARICE. You triumph too,
In favor as in fortune. On all sides
I hear your name reëchoed with a plaudit,
That fills my bosom with exulting raptures
I never knew before.
MAURICE. Ah! this is nothing,
Dear heart, to the sweet peace that crowns our dwelling,
And tells us, though the tempest growls afar,
Its thunders strike not here. The fame I covet
Is still in tribute subject to your joys;
And, these secure—you, happy in my bosom—
My pride forgets its aim! Ambition slumbers
Nor makes me once forgetful of the rapture,
That follows your embrace. [*Knock without.*
CLARICE. The widow Pressley.
MAURICE. Quick, welcome her.—Poor woman, we will save her.
CLARICE. I joy to hear you say so.—Come in, madam.

Enter Widow Pressley and Kate.

MAURICE. Welcome, dear madam; you must needs be anxious;
But still be hopeful. I have brought the action,

And doubt not, from my study of your case,
That we shall gain it—put the usurper out,
And win you back some portion of your wealth.
The truth is on our side,—the evidence
Sustains your claim most amply. We shall gain it!

WIDOW. Alas! sir, but the power of this bad man—

MAURICE. Need not be powerful here.

WIDOW. You know it not;—
His wealth, his violence—

MAURICE. Will scarce prevail.

WIDOW. He buys or bullies justice at his pleasure;
No lawyer here would undertake my case
Lest he should lose a friend or make a foe;
And thus, for fifteen years—

MAURICE. He buys not me,
And scarce will profit by an insolence,
That hopes to bully here.

WIDOW. Oh! sir, I tremble,
And cannot help but doubt. I know your talents;
All people speak of them,—and yet I fear!
With hopes so often lifted and defeated,
How should I dream of better fortune now?
The widow and the orphan find small favor,
In struggle with the strong and selfish man;
And this success you promise—

MAURICE. None may take
The sovereign accent from the lip of Fate
And say—this thing is written certainly—
But, if I err not, madam, better promise,
Of the clear dawn and the unclouded sunshine,
Ne'er waited on the night. I trust the Jury.
They have no fears to nurse, and seek no favors,
As do that class of men, the mean ambitious,
Who, for the lowly greed of appetite,

Or hungering for a state they never merit,
Cringe with a servile zeal to wealth and numbers,
And nothing show but baseness when they rise.
My faith is in the people.

WIDOW. Mine in you, sir.

MAURICE. I will deserve your confidence. This person,
Who robb'd you of your fortune, would but vainly
Attempt to bully me. I am no bully,
But something have I in my soul which strengthens
Its courage, when the insolent would dare
Usurp the rights that I am set to guard.
Be hopeful, madam. Take no care for the morrow,
Though, with the morrow, our great trial comes!
God and his angels keep the innocent,
And, in his own good season, will redress
Their many wrongs with triumph.

WIDOW. Sir, I thank you;—
And this poor child, the child of bitterness,
If not of wrath, shall bless you in her prayers,
That nightly seek her mother in the heavens!

MAURICE. [*kissing the child.*] Your name is Kate, they tell me—a sweet name!
You'll pray for us to-night, Kate. With the morrow,
If my heart's hope do not deceive my heart,
Your prayers shall all be answer'd.—I'll think of her,
And of her sweet and innocent face to-morrow,
When striving with her enemy.

KATE. I'll pray, sir,
As if you were my father.

WIDOW. She has none, sir.

MAURICE. Losing or winning, daughter, still in me,
Look for a father who will cherish you.

WIDOW. Farewell, good sir, I have not words to thank you.

MAURICE. You have a heart that overflows with speech,

And swells into your eyes! No more, dear madam:
Be hopeful and be happy. [*Exeunt widow and child.*
We must gain it.
The proofs are clear—I cannot doubt the issue,—
And still a prescient something at my heart,
Awakes its triumph with assuring accents
That never spoke in vain. But, who are these?
[*Enter Col. Mercer and Brooks.*
Welcome, gentlemen.

MERCER. We trust, sir, that you see in us your friends.

MAURICE. Such, since our brief acquaintance, you have seemed, sir,
And mine's a heart preferring to confide;
That still would rather suffer wrong of faith,
Than not believe in man.

MERCER. You'll find us true;—
And thus it is, that, sure of our good purpose,
We come to counsel with you as a friend.

MAURICE. As friends, I welcome you. Be seated, sirs.

BROOKS. We do regard you, sir, as one to help us,—
In public matters. From our knowledge of you,
We've said among our friends, this is our man;
And, looking still to you to serve our people,
We hear with grief that you are in a peril
Whose straits, perchance, you know not.

MAURICE. Peril, sir?

BROOKS. You have brought action for the widow Pressley,
For the recovery of a large possession,
Withheld by Colonel Blasinghame—

MAURICE. 'Tis true, sir,

MERCER. You do not know this man.

MAURICE. I've heard of him.

MERCER. But not that he is one whom men find prudent
To pass with civil aspect, nor confront

With wrath or opposition. He has power,
Such as few men possess, or dare contend with—
Has wealth in great abundance—is a person,
Most fearless and most desperate in battle,
Who better loves the conflict with his fellow
Than any gifts that peaceful life can bring;
Endow'd with giant strength and resolution,
And such a shot, from five to fifteen paces,
As still to shatter, wavering in the wind,
The slenderest wand of willow.

MAURICE. Famous shooting!

BROOKS. It were not wise to wake his enmity!
We look to you to serve our cause in Congress—
Make him your foe, and he opposes you;
His wealth—his popularity—the terrors,
His very name provokes,—all leagued against you—
You still a stranger.

MAURICE. Patiently, I hear;
And though I feel not like solicitude
With that you show for me, am grateful for it!
And now, sirs, let us understand each other.
I am a man who, in pursuit of duty,
Will hold no parley with that week day prudence
Which teaches still how much a virtue costs.
Of this man, Blasinghame, I've heard already,—
Even as you both describe him. It would seem,
Lest I should fail in utter ignorance,
He took a patient trouble on himself,
To school me in his virtues. Read this letter. [*gives letter.*

MERCER. BROOKS. } His hand!—his signature! [*they read.*

MAURICE. Well, gentlemen, you see it written there,
What are my dangers if I dare to venture
This widow's cause against him. Favor me,

And read the answer which has just been written.

MERCER. [*reads aloud.*] Sir:—The suit of Pressley *vs.* Blasinghame will be prosecuted to conclusion, without regard to consequences, with the best strength and abilities of

NORMAN MAURICE.

MAURICE. It is brief, sir.

BROOKS. 'Tis a defiance, Maurice!

MAURICE. 'Twas meant so, gentlemen. I am a man,
Or I am nothing! This poor widow's cause,
The very insolence of this Blasinghame,
Hath made my own! I'll die for it if need be.

MERCER. Art principled 'gainst the duel?

MAURICE. Rather ask,
If, when my enemy takes me by the throat,
I do oppose him with an homily.
No man shall drive me from society!—
I take the laws I find of force, and use them,
For my protection and defence, as others
Employ them for assault.

MERCER. You've practised then?

MAURICE. Never shot pistol.

BROOKS. Nor rifle?

MAURICE. Scarcely!

MERCER. You are very rash, sir!

MAURICE. Ay! but rashness, sir,
Becomes a virtue in a case like this;
And the brave heart, untaught in human practice,
Finds good assurance from another source
That prompts its action right. This letter's written,
And goes within the hour. Let Blasinghame
Chafe as he may, and thunder to the terror,
Of those who have no manhood in themselves;—
He thunders at these portals still in vain!
To-morrow comes the trial—after that!—

But let the future wear what look it may,
I'll find the heart to meet it—as a man!
MERCER. Then you are firm?
MAURICE. As are the rocks,
In conflict with the sea.
MERCER. We joy to find you thus!
We'll stand by you through danger to the last.
BROOKS. Ay, Maurice, we are with you.
MAURICE. Friends, your hands!—
I am not used to friendship, but I love it,
As still a precious gift, vouchsafed by heaven,
Next best to love of woman! For this danger,—
Fear nothing! we shall 'scape it! Nay, 'twill give us,
Or truth is not of God, new plumes for triumph!

SCENE II.

The law office of Richard Osborne. Osborne discovered writing. Enter Warren.

WARREN. We're on the track at last, Look at that letter;
It comes from our old comrade, Harry Matthews,
And tells us miracles of Norman Maurice!—
Our worthy cousin has the run of fortune;—
She seems to crown him with her richest favors,
As some old bawd, grown hackney'd in the market,
Adopts a virgin passion in her dotage,
And yields to her late folly, all the profits
That follow'd the old vice. He's growing finely;
But I shall dock his feathers.
OSBORNE. [*reading.*] In Missouri.
WARREN. Ay, in St. Louis, that great western city,

Our worthy cousin, Norman, has grown famous!
You read what Matthews writes. In one short twelvemonth
He springs above all shoulders.

OSBORNE. I look'd for it!
He's not the man whom fortune can keep under.

WARREN. What! you forget our precious document?

OSBORNE. You will not use it *now?*

WARREN. Ah, will I not then?
If ever useful, *now's* the right time for it!
See you not that he rises like an eagle,
Already is in practice with the ablest,
Wins popular favor without working for it,
And stands i' the way of better politicians?
They fit his name to music for bad singers,
To whom none listen save at suffrage time.—
We'll spoil the song for him.

OSBORNE. What would you do?

WARREN. You are dull, Dick Osborne! Have I yet to tell you
That, over all, conspicuous in my hate,
This minion of Fortune stands. His better luck
Hath robb'd me of the prize which most I treasured—
His better genius trampled mine to dust,—
Humbled my pride when at its height, and crush'd me,
Until I learn'd to loathe myself, as being
So feeble in his grasp.

OSBORNE. He crushes you no longer!

WARREN. Can I forget the past? This memory
Becomes a part of the nature o' the man,
And of his future makes a fearful aspect,
Unless he cures its hurts. My path is where
My enemy treads in triumph! I shall seek it,
And 'twill be hard if hate, well leagued with cunning,
Is baffled of his toil. I seek St. Louis!

OSBORNE. Beware! You'll make him desperate!

WARREN. I hope so!

OSBORNE. It brings its perils with it! Norman Maurice
Will rend his hunter!—

WARREN. If he be not wary!
But, fear you nothing. You shall go with me,
And see how deftly, with what happy art,
I shall prepare the meshes for my captive.

OSBORNE. Me! go with you?—and wherefore?

WARREN. A small matter!—
While I shall drive the nail, you'll clinch the rivet.
I'd have you there to prove this document!

OSBORNE. Spare me this, Warren!

WARREN. I can spare you nothing.

OSBORNE. I do not hate this man! He hath not wrong'd me,
Cross'd not my path, nor, with a better fortune,
Won from me aught I cherish'd.

WARREN. Enough! Enough!—
Me hath he robb'd and wrong'd—*me* hath he cross'd—
His better fortune still a fate to mine!—
My injury is yours! You love me, Osborne,—
Will do the thing that I regard as needful,
The more especially as you have secrets,
No less than Norman Maurice. We shall go,
Together, as I fancy, to St. Louis!

OSBORNE. This is mere tyranny, Warren.

WARREN. Very like it!
Guilt ever finds its tyrant in its secret,
And, twinn'd with every crime, the accuser stands,
Its own grim shadow, with the scourge and torture.

OSBORNE. A dark and damnable truth! Would I had perish'd
Ere I had fallen, and follow'd, as you bade me!

WARREN. Spare the vain toil to cheat a troubled conscience,
And to your preparations. By the morrow,
We'll be upon the road.

OSBORNE. But, for these papers?
WARREN. Confound the papers! They will wait for us,
But opportunity never! Get you ready,
And hush all vain excuses. If my sway
Be somewhat tyrannous, still it hath its profits:—
Be you but true, and from the Egyptian spoil,
There shall be still sufficient for your toil. [*Exit Warren.*
OSBORNE. I'm chain'd to the stake! He hath me in his power!—
How truly hath he pictured my estate!—
Thus he who doth a deed of ill in youth,
Raises a ghost no seventy years can lay!
I must submit; yet, following still his lead,
Pray Providence for rescue, ere too late:—
'Tis Providence, alone, may baffle Fate! [*Exit Osborne.*

SCENE III.

The house of Mrs. Jervas in Walnut-street. Enter Mrs. J. and Robert Warren.

MRS. J. Art sure of what you tell me?
WARREN. Never doubt it!—
Matthews, who writes me, is an ancient friend
Who knows this Maurice well. He sees him often,
Though it would seem that Maurice knows not him.
His rising fortunes favor you! 'Twere well
You sought your niece. You are her kinswoman,—
The nearest,—and the loss of all your fortune,
By failure of the bank—
MRS. J. But Maurice likes me not!
WARREN. Natural enough! You still opposed his passion;
But things are alter'd now. You've but to show him

'Twas for your niece's good, in your best judgment,
That you denied his suit. But, go to her ;—
He's doing well—is popular—grows wealthy ;
And now that Fortune looks with smiles on him,
He well may smile on you ! You'll live with them,
And we shall meet there.

MRS. J. We ? Meet ?

WARREN. Did I not love her ?

MRS. J. Ah !—

WARREN. And should *he* die ?—Should accident, or—

MRS. J. I see ! I see !

WARREN. You are my friend, and you will show her—

MRS. J. Ah ! trust me, Robert Warren—

WARREN. That's enough !
We understand each other. You will go,—
Her only kinswoman—to seek her out.
You have but her in the world ! Say you have err'd ;
It was because you loved her that you strove,
'Gainst one, who, whatsoe'er his worth and talent,
Was not o'erbless'd by Fortune ! He may frown,
But cannot well deny you ; and, for Clarice—
She will not, sure, repel her mother's sister.

MRS. J. I'll go ! I need the succor of my kindred.

WARREN. We'll meet then ; but you must not know me there !
'Tis not my policy to vex my rival,
Provoke suspicion, move his jealousy,
Or startle her by any bold renewal,
Of pleadings late denied. Should you discover
That he who, in their presence, stands before you,
Is other than he seems, you will know nothing ;
Since that may spoil your game as well as mine.

MRS. J. You are a deep one !

WARREN. When I have your counsel !
This Maurice thought but humbly of your judgment.

He knew you not as I do. He was blinded
By his own proud conceit and arrogance,
And held himself an oracle. 'Twere wise
If still you suffer'd him to fancy thus—
Check'd him in nothing—never counsell'd him—
For still I know he holds your wisdom cheaply,
And scorns the experience which might rise against
His own assured opinion. Such a person
Needs but sufficient cord—

MRS. J. And he shall have it!

WARREN. I'll seek your counsel soon, and you shall teach me
What is our proper action. You will find me
More ready to confide in your experience,
Than him whose cunning seem'd to baffle it.
Farewell then, madam, till we meet again. [*Exit Warren.*

MRS. J. Farewell, sir! A most excellent young man!
This Maurice shall not carry it at will,—
He scorns me,—does he? He shall feel me still! [*Exit.*

SCENE IV.

The hall in the cottage of Norman Maurice. Time—midnight. Enter Maurice in night-gown, as just started from his couch. His hair dishevelled—his manner wild and agitated—his whole appearance that of a man painfully excited and distressed.

MAURICE. That I should be unmann'd! That a mere dream,
The blear and frightful aspects of a vision,
Should rouse me to such terror,—shake my soul
From the strong moorings of a steadfast will,
And drive it, a mere wreck, upon the seas,
No hand upon the helm! Ah! my Clarice. [*Enter Clarice.*

CLARICE. My husband—
MAURICE. I would thou had'st not seen me thus, Clarice.
CLARICE. What means this terror—wherefore did you cry?
MAURICE. Surely I did not.
CLARICE. Yes, a terrible shriek,
As one who rushes desperate on his foe!
MAURICE. No mortal foe has ever from my lips,
Sleeping or waking, forced acknowledgment,
That humbles me like this—
CLARICE. What dost thou mean?
What fear?
MAURICE. What answer shall I make to thee?—
How tell thee, my Clarice, 'twas a mere dream,
That filled me with that agonizing fear,
Whose shriek thou heard'st. Yet, such a dream, my wife,
As still pursues me with its hideous forms,
And shakes me yet with terror. That a man,
Conscious of strength and will, with conscience free,
Should, in a mere disorder of his blood,
In midnight sleep, feel all his soul unsinew'd,
And sink into the coward!
CLARICE. Thou art none!
MAURICE. Yet such a vision—and methinks I see!—
Hist,—is there nothing crawling by the hearth,
Crouching and winding, and with serpent folds,
Preparing its dread venom?
CLARICE. There is nothing, husband—
The hearth holds only the small jar of flowers.
MAURICE. The reptile ever seeks such crouching place,
And garbs his spotty hide with heedless blossoms,
That know not what they harbor. Fling it hence!
'Twas on the hearth it crouch'd. But, hear me, wife;
That dream! 'Twas of a serpent on our hearth,
Thou heedless, with thy hand upon the flowers,

Disposing them for show. Unseen and soft—
It wound about thee its insidious coil,
And, at the moment when I first beheld,
Its brazen head was lifted, its sharp fang
Was darting at thy heart! 'Twas then I shriek'd
And rush'd upon the monster thus, and smote!—
[*Dashing the vase to pieces.*
Heedless of every sting, I trampled it;
But, even as it writhed beneath my heel,
Methought, it lifted up a human face
That look'd like Robert Warren!
CLARICE. What a dream!
MAURICE. I cannot shake it off. Did'st hear a sound
Most like a hiss?
CLARICE. Nay, nay! 'twas but a dream!
Come—come to bed.
MAURICE. Why should I dream of him?
CLARICE. You think of him, perchance.
MAURICE. And, as a reptile!
The terrible image still before me crawls—
Oh! that I might, with but a bound and struggle,
Though still at life's worst peril, trample him!
CLARICE. Yet wherefore?
MAURICE. There are instincts of the soul,
That have a deep and true significance,
And, though no more in danger from his malice,
I feel within me that he works unsleeping,
In venomous toils against me.
CLARICE. But, in vain.
Come, Norman, come to bed. You frighten me.
MAURICE. Forgive me! There! I have thee at my lips,
I strain thee to my bosom with a joy
That leaves no rapture wanting—yet, methinks,
I hear a sound of hissing, and still see

Glimpses of folding serpents that, behind,
Crawl after us—

CLARICE. My Norman!

MAURICE. I grieve thee!
I will forget this vision in the blessing
This grasp makes real to rapture. Let us in.

[*He folds his arm about her, and they leave the apartment, he still looking behind him suspiciously—she looking up to him.*

SCENE V.

The edge of a wood. A cottage in the distance. Enter Robert Warren, Osborne, and Harry Matthews. The former disguised with false hair, whiskers, &c.

MATTHEWS. [*pointing to cottage.*] Look!—you may see it now!

WARREN. There, then, he harbors?
A goodly cottage—he's a man of taste,
Not yet too old for sentiment, it seems;
Loves flowers and shade trees, and around his porches
I fancy that we see some gadding tendrils,
That wanton, with full censers, in his homage!
He should be happy there!

MATTHEWS. Why, so he is.

WARREN. You think so?

MATTHEWS. There's every thing to make him so. He's young—
Is on the road to fortune and to fame,
And has a handsome wife.

WARREN. The landscape's fair,—
Looks bright beneath the sunshine and exhales
A thousand delicate odors rich in life;
But, sometimes, there's a tempest in the night,
And where's your landscape then?

MATTHEWS. Be this his case,
It shall not cost me one poor hour of sleep,
For all the coil it makes. This man's our foe,—
Goes with our enemies in politics,
And will, though now he knows it not himself,
Be run, against our crack man, for the Senate.
WARREN. Who's he?
MATTHEWS. Ben Ferguson.
WARREN. Plain Ben?
MATTHEWS. Colonel Ben!
'Tis only when the man's a favorite,
We take the formal handle from his name
And sing it short for sweetness.
WARREN. Is he able?
MATTHEWS. We thought him so till this your Maurice came;—
Since then our favorite loses in the race.
Ben is a lawyer in first practice here
And had the field to himself since I have known him,
Till now—
OSBORNE. Maurice and he have grappled then?
MATTHEWS. To Ferguson's defeat.
OSBORNE. Before the jury?
MATTHEWS. Ay, every way—before the judge and jury,—
In court and out of court. At public meetings
They were in opposite ranks, and, with each issue,
Maurice hath risen still in popular favor,
While Ferguson declines. It will rejoice us,
If, as you say, you have some history
To floor this powerful foe!
WARREN. You need not doubt it.
But who are friends to Maurice, here,—the people?
MATTHEWS. Were it the people only, it were nothing.
They have not yet arisen to self-esteem,
And, kept full fed on vanity, are heedless,

Hugging their shadows, how they lose the substance.
Here, all their sympathies are held by others;
Men of much wealth and some ability,
Who, gladly, in this Maurice find an ally,
And join with him to use him. There's a party
Who long have lacked a leader. Norman Maurice
Brings them the head they seek. He guides their councils,
And, with such prudent skill and policy,
That still they fancy he is but their mouth-piece,
Even while he gives the breath of life to them.
I know that they will run him for the Senate.

WARREN. Can they elect him?

MATTHEWS. It is somewhat doubtful.
They never yet succeeded with their man,
Not having had the man to make success.
What they can do *for him* is not the question,
So much as what he may achieve *for them.*
I tell you, though not fearful for the issue,
It makes us something anxious. Now,—this secret—
If it be true, indeed, that,—

WARREN. Be you ready;—
I'll see your friends to-morrow. We'll sleep on it.
To-night, I'll fathom Maurice if I can,
And see how he enjoys his Western life.
Enough! I have him in my power! To-morrow!—

MATTHEWS. But what's the secret?

WARREN. It will keep till then.
Be sure, that when your game is to be play'd—
When Norman Maurice, at the height of favor,
Waits but the will to rise up Senator—
A single word shall damn him down to ruin,
And stifle every voice that shouts his name.

OSBORNE. Yet, once more, Warren, ere it be too late,
Let me entreat and counsel—

WARREN. You are doting!
Go you with Matthews, and, should I be missing,
You both can tell whither my steps were bent,
And what my power upon him.

OSBORNE. [*aside to W.*] Why incur
This danger,—for you too must see the danger,—
To feed this foolish malice?

WARREN. [*aside to O.*] Is it foolish?—
Not when the profit's yours, the pleasure mine;—
And I, if fortune mocks me not with fancies,
Shall find a pleasure in the game I play at,
That you may never dream of! Be you easy—
There's little danger! I've securities
'Gainst *him* in *you*, and in his secret fears,
Not less than in the policy I use;
Besides, my habit, does it not disguise me?

OSBORNE. He has the eye of an eagle!

WARREN. Pshaw!

OSBORNE. Beware!—
His genius—you yourself confess it, Warren—
Hath always, when the final issue came,
Soar'd over you triumphant!

WARREN. Oh! Good night.
We'll meet again to-morrow! [*Exit Warren.*

OSBORNE. He'll pay for it!
He runs on ruin!

MATTHEWS. Not his own, methinks!

OSBORNE. His own, though now it seems not. I've an instinct
That tells me Maurice cannot be o'erthrown.
Baffled he may be;—you may torture him—
Deny him his just place and high position,
One or more seasons; but he'll rise at last,
So firmly, that the very hands that struggle
To tear him from his throne, will help to build it.

There are some men to whom the fates decree
Performance,—and this man is one of them!
What was his prospect when I knew him first?
He had no friends,—he had no fellowships,
No heedful care of parents—no tuition;—
He stood alone i' the world—unknown, unhonor'd—
Nay, something hated, as I hap to know,
For that he had some innate qualities,
Of pride, of strength, of soul and character,
That would not let him stoop! In spite of all,
He hath struggled through the strife and the obstruction;
Won friends; won homage; high position won;
And still hath grown, the more erect and noble,
At each assault upon his pride and fortune!
I *feel* that he *must* triumph!

MATTHEWS. You speak well,
The promise of our enemy! You differ,
Somewhat, from Robert Warren; yet, you know
This secret.

OSBORNE. Ay—as Warren's; and I know,
The rise of Maurice is his overthrow! [*Exeunt.*

SCENE VI.

The interior of the cottage of Norman Maurice. A table spread as if supper were just concluded. Maurice and Clarice discovered seated. Maurice balances a spoon upon the cup. Clarice watches him.

CLARICE. You muse, my husband.

MAURICE, [*pushing away the cup.*] 'Tis with happiness!
Know you, Clarice, that fifteen months have pass'd
Since we were married?

CLARICE. Is it possible!
I had not thought it!

MAURICE. Time is wing'd with pleasure,
When that the heart, reposing where it loves,
Finds strength for fresher love in faith secure!
The world would seem to smile on me at last!
'Till we were wedded, such had been my fortune,
I question'd still the sunshine when it came;
And, in its sudden and capricious beauty,
Still dreaded something sinister and hostile.
But now I feel secure! With you beside me,
A fair, free world before me, and employment,
Grateful at once to intellect and feeling,
Affording thought due exercise for triumph,
Methinks, I have from fate a guaranty,
That she foregoes at last her ancient grudges;
And, it may be, despising our ambition,
Thus easily satisfied with love and quiet,
Turns her sharp arrows on some nobler victim,
Whose young audacity offends her pride!
Sure, Clarice, this is happiness.

CLARICE. It is more!
Such happiness as well might task the fancy,
To wing with words of sweetest poesy.

MAURICE. Then sing for me. I'm in the mood for music;
My heart is glad; my thoughts would wander freely;
Commercing with the indistinct, but sweet.

CLARICE. Nay, Norman, nay: I'm selfish in my gladness;
You sing not; but a something more than music
Swells in the verse that gathers on your lips;—
And this reminds me of the little ballad
You promised me,—once half recited me,
And fain would have me think your heart conceived it
When first it grew to mine!

MAURICE. And I said truly!
Thoughts passing fair had floated through my fancy—
Thoughts born of warmest tastes and pure affections,
Which yet had found no name! I had strange visions
Of grace and feminine beauty, such as never
The world had shown me living. Then I met thee,
And, on the instant, did they take thy image;—
And thus I first knew how, and whom, to love!
These fancies did I body forth in verses,
As one records a vision of the midnight,
That fills his soul with marvels; and the hour,
That brought me first acquainted with thy beauties,
Taught me what name to write above my record,
Which, until then, had none.

CLARICE. Norman—*was* it mine?

MAURICE. Thine, only, my beloved one!

CLARICE. Now, the verses,
In thy best manner, Norman.

MAURICE. What! repeat them?—
Wouldst ruin me, Clarice, in public favor;
Sap my distinction, lose me my profession,
Draw down the vulgar laughter on my head,
And make grave senators and learned statesmen
Shake reverend brows in sorrow at my folly?

CLARICE. Nay, you mock me now?

MAURICE. Wouldst have a lawyer,—
Subtle, and stern, and disputatious, still,—
Full of retorts and strange philosophies;
Whose dreams by night are of the close encounter
With rival wits and wary adversaries,—
Whose thoughts by day are still upon indictments,
Flaws, fees, exceptions, old authorities,
And worldly arguments, and stubborn juries,—
And all the thousand small details that gather,

Like strings about the giant Gulliver,
Dragging and fettering down to lowly earth
The upsoaring mind that else might scale the heavens!—
Wouldst have him in the vagrancy of fancy,
Possess his soul with spells of poesy;
Having no fear that, lurking at his threshold,
His neighbor Jones or Jenkins, Smith or Thompson,
Some round and fat, but most suspicious client,
Bringing great fees,—his heart upon his action,—
Seeking the sourest aspect in his lawyer,—
Stands, rooted, with strange horror, as he listens
To most ridiculous rhymes, and talk of flowers,
Moonbeams, and zephyrs—all that staple sweetness,
That makes the fancies of young thoughtless bosoms;—
When most he hoped to hear of *Chose in action*,
Trespass, *assumpsit*, *action on the case*,
And other phrases, silly as the rhymester's,—
But that they sound in money, not in music!
No! No!—no poesy! 'Twere loss of client!

CLARICE. Nay, Norman, but you jest now! Speak the verses,
If need be, in low accents.

MAURICE. Lest Jones or Jenkins
Should turn about, possess'd with holy horror,
And seek some other lawyer! You shall have them!
They are yours, Clarice, for, truly, they embody
What still meseem'd the virtues of your nature;—
Tastes, sweet and delicate as evening glories
That tend upon the passage of the day,
And, twinn'd with gleam and shadows, through the twilight,
Betoken, as it were, the unknown beauties,
That make a happier future in the far.

CLARICE. You describe the verses!

MAURICE. It needs I should!
They take a mystic tone and character,

And ask the key-note. You will hardly like them :
Thoughtful, not lyrical, nor passionate,
They need that you should pause upon each accent,
Or they will lose their due significance !
But, next to the grave folly of such doing,
Is the grave preface that still pleads for it.
You lead me erring, Clarice, to these trifles—
You, and the exulting feeling at my heart,
That deems this happiness sure !—Ha ! That knock !
[*Knock at the door—he starts.*
Methinks it hath a meaning ! A sharp instinct
Tells me that evil at our threshold lurks. [*Whispers.*

CLARICE. Evil, my husband ! Let me open it !
[*Goes toward the door.*

MAURICE, [*interposing.*] You, Clarice ! You mistake me.—
There's an instinct,
That, though it speaks of evil, hath no fear !—
Who's there ? [*Aloud.*]

Voice without. A friend !

MAURICE, [*throwing open the door.*] Enter, friend !

Enter Robert Warren as before, with valise in his hand.

WARREN. Pardon me this intrusion, but I'm wearied,—
I've travell'd far,—the last seven miles afoot,
Having lost my horse by the way.

MAURICE. You're welcome, sir,
To our poor fare, and shelter of our dwelling
'Till you recover. Clarice, see to it.
[*Maurice points her to the supper table. She turns and leaves the room,—Warren follows her with his eye, while that of Maurice observes him.*

WARREN. I thank you, sir.

MAURICE. Meanwhile, sit down and rest.
Give me your burden. 'Twill require some minutes

To get your supper, make your chamber ready;
'Till then, forget your travel.

WARREN. You are kind!
How far, sir, are we from St. Louis, here?

MAURICE. Four miles only.

WARREN. You, perhaps, can tell me
Something of persons living in St. Louis;
I'm a collector from an Eastern city,
And have a claim upon one Harry Matthews.

MAURICE. [*His brow slightly contracts.*] *Harry* Matthews!

WARREN. Or *Henry* Matthews: is he good, sir?

MAURICE, [*coldly.*] It may be, sir; I know not!

WARREN. You know the man?

MAURICE. I have seen him often, sir, but know him i

WARREN. The house I represent has had suspicions;—
A Philadelphia house.

MAURICE. Of Philadelphia!

WARREN. A famous city, sir; but you have seen it?

MAURICE. I know it well, sir. [*Catches the eye of Warren, whic. suddenly drops at the encounter.*

WARREN. Ah! you've travell'd thither?

MAURICE. Have *lived* there, sir; and, now I think of it,
It may be you can answer *me* of persons,
Whom once I knew there;—there was Mrs. Jervas—

WARREN. A widow, sir, who lived in Walnut-street?

MAURICE. The same!—

WARREN. I've heard of her. She lost her fortune lately
By failure of the bank.

MAURICE. Indeed!

WARREN. And has left the city,
'Twas said, to seek her kindred in the West.

MAURICE. [*To Clarice, who reënters.*] Hear you that, Clarice?

CLARICE. Is it possible?
It cannot be she means—

MAURICE. Perhaps. 'Tis like.

WARREN. She has a niece and nephew in the West—
'Twas so reported—who have sent for her,
They being very wealthy, she in want.

MAURICE, [*with a smile.*] Indeed!

CLARICE. She has no nephew living, sir.

WARREN. [*smiles.*] Ah! you know her, then?

MAURICE. She is this lady's aunt, sir;
And, it may be, this excellent Mrs. Jervas
Comes hither to her niece, who is my wife, sir.
I suppose, that, as the husband of the one,
I may be held a nephew to the other;
And loving, too, makes kindred. Well, Clarice,
You'll make the good lady welcome if she comes,
Which, *now*, I scarcely question.—Tell me, sir,
Of other persons in that goodly city;—
There was a mute, I knew, one Nicholas Foster,
Whom much I fancied—

WARREN. A rare machinist,
Though few conceived his talent.

MAURICE, [*aside.*] Yet, *you* knew it!

WARREN. He's well as ever.

MAURICE. Sully, the master-painter,
A pure, good man, whose exquisite art endows
The beauty with a charm beyond her own,
Caught from his delicate fancy.

WARREN. He's still famous.

MAURICE. I would you could say fortunate as famous,
As still his art deserves.—I know not why,
But these inquiries sadden me, and yet—
There was one Richard Osborne—

WARREN. An attorney—

MAURICE. A most obscure one, though of certain merits,
Who might have been distinguish'd, having powers

To raise him into something high and worthy,
But for his evil genius—

WARREN, [*quickly.*] Ah! sir! He?—

MAURICE. Were you a student—an anatomist
Of character—instead of a collector;—
But—

WARREN. Yet would I hear, sir.

MAURICE. *He*, sir, I mean,
Were one whom it were well to analyze,
Did one design a new philosophy,
And sought in strange anomalies to embrace
The opposite things in nature. Fancy a creature,
Having the external attributes of man,—
The capacious brow—the clear, transparent eye—
The form erect—the voice most musical—
Quick talent, ready art, and specious language,
And something winning in his natural manner,
Beguiling still the unwary to belief—
Yet, as if made in mock of heaven's own purpose,
Having, in place of heart, a nest of vipers;
Whose secret venom, mastering all his powers,
Taints ever his performance—makes his doings,
When most they favor virtue, tend to vice—
Corrupts the word he utters, makes him false,
When most the truth should be his policy,—
And keeps him ever lothely in pursuit
Of purposes most loathsome. Know you, sir,
One Robert Warren? [*Laying his hand on Warren's shoulder, and eyeing him closely.*

WARREN, [*shrinking and stammering.*] Me, sir—Warren? No!

MAURICE, [*flinging him away and rising.*] Liar and reptile, as thou still hast been,
'Twere thousand times more hopeful to endow
The serpent with the nature of the dove,

To graft the fruit of Eden on the tree,
That, with its bitter, blights the Dead Sea shore—
Appease the tiger's thirst—the leopard's spots
Pluck from his side, and bind him with a straw—
Than change the designing devil at thy heart!

WARREN. What mean you, sir?

CLARICE, [*seizing his arm.*] Oh! Norman, wherefore this?

MAURICE. What! See you not? Hath sense of happiness
So totally obscured the sense of wrong,
That memory lacks each faculty, and nature,
Losing the subtle instinct which still counsels
The innocent of his peril, stoops to wanton
With the fang'd viper in his villainous coil.
The dream! the dream! my Clarice. Get thee hence!
Leave me to deal with him. Away!

CLARICE. What's he?

MAURICE. What! do his looks not answer as the reptile's,
That speak his subtle snare and silent venom!
Doth not his coward crouching show his nature,
As now I stretch the arm of vengeance o'er him?
Must I confer a name upon the victim,
Even in the moment when I strike the blow,
Lest, in their ignorant blindness, men should fancy
This were a kinsman whom in wrath I slew!

WARREN. Beware!—this violence! [*Snatches a knife from the table.*

MAURICE. Is justice only—

CLARICE, [*interposing.*] Norman! Husband!

MAURICE. What! See'st not still!

CLARICE. I see! I know!—and yet—

MAURICE. And yet, and yet, and yet! is the child's wisdom!
Shall we not be secure—never find refuge!
Shall hate pursue, and vengeance turn not on him!
Must we be driven from each world of peace,

To burrow with the hill fox and the wolf,
When but a stroke is needful—

CLARICE. Oh! thou must not:
He shares our hospitality—our shelter!

MAURICE, [*hurling the table over.*] He hath not touch'd the bread and sacred salt,
He shall not claim the Arab's privilege,—
He dies!—

CLARICE. For my sake, Norman, spare him!
Let him go hence; the past is over now.

WARREN. She counsels wisely, Norman. Lift no hand
Against me, for I come to you in peace.

MAURICE. In peace! In peace! And wherefore this disguise?
Thy fraudulent tale of travel—this false semblance,
False hair, false speech—unless with heart and purpose
False as of old! Didst think, that I, who knew thee,
By such damn'd treachery as thou still hast shown me,
Could be deceived by wretched arts like these?—
My blindness and my confidence so perfect,
That I should sleep and dream, while at my pillow
Thou crep'st at midnight, from the hearth that warm'd thee,
To fasten on my heart! Thou com'st, an outlaw!—
What hinders that I slay thee?—that I take thee,
Thus, by the throat, and, stifling fear and feeling,
Slaughter thee, as a bullock at the altar,
Thy blood would still profane!

CLARICE, [*interposing.*] Norman! Norman!
Oh! must thy Clarice plead to thee in vain?
Spare him, if but in gratitude to heaven,
For that we prosper in his hate's despite.

MAURICE. 'Tis for that very reason I should slay him!
He comes to blight our brief prosperity,
To compass all our sunshine with his cloud,
And taint our flowers with poison.

WARREN. Yet, beware!
She counsels thee with wisdom, Norman Maurice;
I am not friendless here. Did aught befall me,
Here, in thy dwelling, to my mortal hurt,
'Tis known that I came hither—'tis known farther,
That I have that to speak against thy fame,
Shall blacken it forever.

MAURICE. Ha, say'st thou that!
Well thou wouldst something more!

WARREN. Only a word—
And lest thy prudence should not check thy passion,
My providence—[*showing pistol.*]

MAURICE. What! thou hast weapons then!
Now, by my hopes—if it were possible,
To find thee but one moment flush with manhood!—
Look on me, villain, as I now confront thee,
But, lift thine eye to mine, and let thy aim
Be deadly as thy malice! Wretched coward—
Thus do I mock thy impotence. [*Rushes upon him and wrests the weapon from his hand.*

WARREN. Spare me, Norman!

CLARICE. Husband, let him live!

MAURICE. Outlaw! that masks him with deliberate purpose—
[*Takes Warren by the throat.*

WARREN. Mercy, Norman!

MAURICE. That seeks by night my dwelling with a lie!—

CLARICE. Husband—dear husband!

MAURICE. That lifts his deadly weapon 'gainst my bosom—

WARREN. Thou stranglest me!

CLARICE. Have pity, Norman!

MAURICE. For thy sake, I spare him!—

WARREN. Thanks—oh, thanks!

MAURICE. Yet feel how better 'twere to crush him now,
Than suffer him—

WARREN. I swear!

MAURICE. Oh!—if thou durst
Take name of God in vain to do hell service,—
I'll slay thee with a certainty of vengeance
That leaves no limb unhurt. For well I know
Thy heart is never then less free from malice,
Than when thy lips declare thy innocence.
Hence, ere I change my purpose. I will spare thee,
And fling thee from my threshold, but to show thee
How much I still forbear. [*Hurls him out headlong.*

CLARICE. Oh, how I thank thee!

MAURICE. If evil follows on this mercy, Clarice,
Thine is the fault.

CLARICE. Oh, Norman, this man's hate—

MAURICE. While we can tear the falsehood from his brow
Is nothing, but—

CLARICE. Why should he follow us?

MAURICE. Oh! for some hellish purpose. But go in;
Leave me awhile.

CLARICE. Wilt thou not close the door?

MAURICE. Let it stay wide all night.

CLARICE. You go not forth?

MAURICE. One sleeps not when the wolf is in his close,
Lest that his howl should scare his infant's sleep—
And when I doubt if ill is at my threshold,
'Twere base to sleep upon the pillow of doubt.
But, go you in, dear wife!—you must not hear
The voice in anger you have heard in love.
Leave me awhile. This thing still troubles me,
But should not trouble you. Go to your prayers,
And leave the watches of the night to me.
God still presides o'er all. I see not yet,
The evil that this evil spirit brings,
But trust that we shall lack no help of angel,

Whene'er the struggle comes.

CLARICE. Norman.

MAURICE. Dear wife!

CLARICE. Forget not that my life is in thy hands.
Oh, do not rashly purpose.

MAURICE. Never fear! [*Embrace. Ex. Clarice within.*

MAURICE. What can he mean! That paper is destroy'd;—
Why should I fear his malice? Yet, so truly,
I know his equal baseness and design,
I feel that he hath purposes of mischief,
Which, if he lack'd the agencies of evil,
He ne'er had underta'en. No sleep for me,
When that the dark suspicions in my soul,
Engender still the foe. I must go forth!— [*Looks out.*
Oh! God, how beautiful the calm o'er earth,—
How soft the night, that, with a veil of brightness
Wraps all the subject creatures—peace and sleep,
Sharing the dreamy blessing, as if evil,
Sped not malignant spirits through the air,
And never flower of earth had cover'd reptile! [*Goes forth.*

END OF ACT SECOND.

ACT III.—SCENE I.

A chamber in the dwelling of Harry Matthews, in St. Lo
Robert Warren and Richard Osborne discovered.

OSBORNE. I warn'd you of the peril.
WARREN. Yet your wisdom
Had scarcely fancied that his glance could fathom
Disguise so good as mine!
OSBORNE. I said his eye
Was like an eagle's. It were hard to say,
What, with his mind once roused into suspicion,
It could not penetrate.
WARREN. 'Twould better please me,
If one, who should be in my service only,
Could find my foe less perfect.
OSBORNE. And, to do so,
Should prove himself less true.
WARREN. Oh! your truth,
Were better shown in service than opinion!
My habit was good; and I had been secure,
But that, to sound him, I unseal'd myself;
And, like a witling, answered all his questions,
Of persons whom we once had known together.
OSBORNE. Be sure, he first suspected ere he question'd.
WARREN. 'Tis like enough! At all events he floor'd n
Disgraced me as he still hath done before
In frequent strife. The mask is thrown aside;
He knows me, here, his enemy; and now—
The open conflict!
OSBORNE. What is now the game?

The open conflict he would never shrink from!
Why, when his hand was fix'd upon your throat,
Did you forbear the weapon?

WARREN. Ask me rather,
Why one is still superior to his fellow;
Why one is brave, another impotent;
Why I am feeble just where he is strong;—
And why, with will to compass his destruction,
My heart still fails me in the final effort!
Such still hath been the sequel of our issues!
He still hath master'd me with such a will,
My spirit droops before him, and I shudder,
To feel, that, with a hate so fix'd and fearful,
I lack the heart to drive the weapon home!—
But I shall do it yet!

OSBORNE. And why the conflict,
Thus ever urged with fate so full of peril?
Now, while you may forbear, and pause in safety,
Forego the struggle, which hath still been hopeless;
Give him repose, and leave yourself at peace.

WARREN. Peace! with these passions!

OSBORNE. They will wreck your own!
A something tells me such must be the issue,
In any strife with Maurice.

WARREN. Vain the counsel—
I cannot leave the conflict!

OSBORNE. Why?

WARREN. *Will* not do so!
While still my hate must go unsatisfied—
My pride,—to say no more of other passions.

OSBORNE. This woman—

WARREN. Not a word of her!

OSBORNE. Smiles she,
That still you prosecute this doubtful struggle?

WARREN. She may, perchance, when she is duly tutor'd,
That, on my whisper, hangs her husband's honor.

OSBORNE. This is your purpose, then?

WARREN. You do not like it?

OSBORNE. I am your slave,—the creature of your mood,
More at your mercy far than Norman Maurice,
Since he is innocent and I am guilty;—
What matter what I like?

WARREN. Why, that's well said!—
Enough for you I must pursue my victims,
While hate conceives a hell for him, or passion
Dreams still of heaven from her! This day, when Maurice
Leaves for the city, I shall seek his dwelling.

OSBORNE. Again! untaught by late experience!
You seek his wife then?

WARREN. Why, not exactly.—
Perhaps you do not know that Mrs. Jervas
Arrived last night at midnight.

OSBORNE. How can she
Assist you in this mad pursuit? You tell me
That Maurice still suspects her.

WARREN. Never matter—
She is my ally;—but, here's Harry Matthews:
He comes to take me to the secret council,
Where other plans mature against our foeman.

OSBORNE. You will not breathe this secret to these people?

WARREN. I will *but* breathe it.

OSBORNE. And withhold the proof?

WARREN. As suits my purpose. It is very likely,
I shall not call on you till the last hour,
When all is ready for his overthrow!
Of this be sure, Dick Osborne: I will pamper
My several passions as I can, and stint them,
In nothing, that may gratify their rage.

Enter Harry Matthews.

MATTHEWS. Art ready, Warren?

WARREN. Will be in a moment!

MATTHEWS, [*to Osborne.*] You'll go with us?

OSBORNE. Excuse me.

WARREN, [*aside to Osborne.*] Why not go?

OSBORNE, [*aside to W.*] Sufficient, as they tell us, for the day
Its evil; when I can no longer 'scape it,
I'll mix in this conspiracy;—till then,
Let me go idle.

WARREN, [*aside to Osborne.*] Hark you, Richard Osborne,
No faltering when the moment comes to speak;
The rod that does not yield to me, I break!

[*Ex. Matthews and Warren.*

OSBORNE. And no escape! I dare not run on ruin,
And face the shame with which he threatens me;
Yet, with a tyranny so terrible,
That plies me with its torture night and day,
'Twere better throw increase of weight on conscience,
And, by embrace with deeds of deadlier aspect,
At least secure escape from sway like this!
Had I the heart for it! Could I find the courage!
'Twere but a blow!—a blow! I'll ponder it. [*Ex. Osborne.*

SCENE II.

An apartment in the house of Col. Ferguson. Ferguson, Blasinghame, Matthews, Warren, and other persons discovered.

BLASINGHAME. The matter then resolves itself to this—
We know for certain, now, that this man, Maurice,

Will be the opposition candidate:—
Ben Ferguson is ours.

FERGUSON. And why not you?

BLASINGHAME. For the best reasons. No! my private business
Needs careful nursing now. This woman, Pressley,
Is like to give me trouble.

MATTHEWS. Her new lawyer
Is stubborn, then?

BLASINGHAME. He seems to be a man;
And we shall suffer him to prove his manhood!
I wrote him of the merits of my case,
Concluding, with a civil exhortation,
As he was young, and but a stranger here,
That he should spare his teeth, nor peril them,
On nuts too hard to crack.

MATTHEWS. What said he then?

BLASINGHAME. Oh! with an answer bold enough, I warrant.

MATTHEWS. He did not know his customer, I fancy.

BLASINGHAME. I think not; and to lesson him a little,
One of my lambs was sent to him this morning—
Joe Savage!

FERGUSON. Joe's a rough teacher, colonel.

BLASINGHAME. As God has made him, Joe. He'll do our business
As tenderly as if it were his own.

FERGUSON. But was there not some whisper of a secret
Touching this Norman Maurice, which, if true,
Would render any messages of honor,
Impossible, to him!

BLASINGHAME. I did not hear;—
Unfold your budget.

FERGUSON. Harry Matthews, there,
Speaks of a secret in his friend's possession,
That's fatal to this man!

BLASINGHAME. Ha! out with it!
'Twill save a monstrous trouble in our wigwam;
For, to say truth, this man is popular,
Grows every day in strength in the assembly,
And, I confess to you, I have my fears,
Touching the game before us. Our new members
Are not what I would have them; and old Mercer,
Catesby and Brooks, gain daily influence,
Under the cunning counsel of this Maurice.
If we can crush this fellow, who has talent,
And shows more stubbornness than I can relish,
'Twere better done before we lose our headway.
This man disposed of, they can find no other
To take the field with Ferguson.

MATTHEWS. Speak, Warren!

WARREN. There *is* a secret, gentlemen; a dark one
Which, told, *were* fatal to this Norman Maurice!
I will *not* tell it *now;* but wait the moment,
When, over all, conspicuous most, he stands,
With triumph in his prospect, and his spirit,
Exulting in the state he deems secure!
Then will I come between his hope and triumph;
Then show the guilty secret that degrades him,
Confound him with the proofs which now are ready,
And hurl him down to ruin, the more fatal,
For that I suffer'd him to rise so high.

BLASINGHAME. But why not now? The man is high enough!

WARREN. The secret's mine, sir. When I'm done with it,
I'll bury it as did the Phrygian barber,
Where every reed that whistles in the wind
Shall make it into music for his ear.
Be sure of this, I'll yield it you in season,
Ere Maurice sits a Senator in Congress!

MATTHEWS. Well—that's sufficient!

BLASINGHAME. Yes! Let him do that!
Meanwhile, there is a way to save himself.
This Maurice has my message—

MATTHEWS. He'll not fight!

BLASINGHAME. If he would—

MATTHEWS. His honor would be rescued by his death?

WARREN. Scarcely; since 'tis for me to keep the secret,
Or free it, if I please! But, let me tell you,
That Maurice will not shrink from any combat!
I know him well. He is mine enemy,
But let me do him justice. He will fight,
Though all the devils of hell stood up against him.
Look to it, sir; [*to Blasing.*,] your reputation's great,
But Maurice is no common opponent;
And you will need your utmost excellence,
To conquer him when once he takes the field!

BLASINGHAME. Well! that's good news! My lamb is with him now;
We'll hear from him by noon.

FERGUSON. Before we part,
'Tis understood we put our troops in motion;
The strife will be a close one! Blasinghame
Hath truly spoken of this new assembly;
It puzzles me to fathom it. This Maurice,
Is, questionless, a man of wondrous power;
And, though I much prefer that we should beat him,
In a fair wrestle, with the usual agents,
Yet this is not so certainly our prospect,
As that we should forego this fatal secret,
That makes our game secure.

WARREN. You shall have it.

BLASINGHAME. We meet to-night at Baylor's.

MATTHEWS, [*to Warren.*] You'll be with us?
It may be that your fruit will then be ripe.

Blasinghame. Ay, come, sir, with your friend.

Warren, [*to Matthews.*] Perhaps! We'll see;—
There may be other fruits upon that tree.

[*Exeunt several ways.*

SCENE III.

An apartment in the house of Norman Maurice. He appears seated at a table with books and papers before him. After a pause, he closes his books, folds and ties the papers in a bundle, pushes them from before him and rises.

Maurice, [*solus.*] It is the curse of insecurity,
That cruel doubt that hangs upon possession
Glides with the midnight to the sleepless pillow,
And, with the laurel wreath that crowns the triumph,
Sows thick the thorns that make the brow to ache!
Did the endowment not imply the service,
Were we not each enjoin'd with a commission,
The task decreed, the struggle thrust upon us,
Making it manhood to comply with duty;
How better far—the treasure in our keeping,
Love at our bosom, peace upon our threshold,
When bliss can never hope increase of rapture,
And fear begins to dream of unknown danger,—
To fly the world—the conflict,—nay, the triumph,
And, bearing off the trophy we have won,
Hush the ambitious spirit in our hearts
That whispers, "Life hath more!" Have I won nothing,
That I should toil, as unrequited Labor
Still hoping yet to win? Am I a beggar,
Who, perilling nothing in each fearful venture,
Stakes all his hopes on change? With goods so precious,

Should I still venture in the common market,
Where Malice stands, with gibe of cruel slander,
And Envy lurks in readiness to steal?—
When the still shelter of the wilderness,
The depth of shadow, the great solitudes,
Beckon the heart with promise of their own,
Still singing, "Here is refuge!"
Wretched folly!—
As if the serpent could not find the garden;
As if the malicious Hate, by hell engendered,
Had not an equal instinct, how to fathom
The secret haunt where rapture hopes to hide!
Hate bears a will as resolute as love,
A wing as swift, an eye as vigilant,
And instincts, that, as still they keep it sleepless,
Prompt the keen search when Rapture stops for rest!
A sad presentiment of coming evil
Stifles each generous impulse at my heart,
That ever spoke in confidence. This Warren
Is here for mischief; with what hope to prosper—
That single proof destroy'd—I now divine not.
This woman, coming close upon his footsteps,
Confirms my apprehensions. They are allies—
She false as he, but feeble—his mere creature,
To beat the bush, while he secures the game!
Well! I must watch them with a vigilance
Due to the precious treasure in my trust;
And, swift as justice in avenging mission,
With the first show of evil in their purpose,
Crush them to earth, and———Well? [*Enter servant.*

SERVANT. Major Savage, sir.

MAURICE. Show him in. [*Enter Sava*

SAVAGE. Your name is Maurice?

MAURICE. 'Tis sir. Yours?

SAVAGE. Mine is Joe Savage,—Major of militia.
You got a letter, sir, a week ago,
From Colonel Blasinghame.
MAURICE. And answer'd it!
SAVAGE. That answer did not please him, Blasinghame.
MAURICE. I'm sorry for it, sir; but you'll believe me,
When I assure you, that, in penning it,
I never once conceived it necessary
To ask what were his tastes.
SAVAGE. Eh, sir: you did not!
Well, let me tell you, those who know him better,
Are something curious never to offend him.
But you, sir, are a stranger—do not know him
So well as others, born here in Missouri—
And so, he sends me to enlighten you.
MAURICE. I thank him, sir.
SAVAGE. Well, you have need to do so;
He does not use such courtesy in common,
But usually the blow before the word!
MAURICE. I'm lucky in his new-born courtesy.
SAVAGE. You are, sir! He's a rough colt, Blasinghame.
MAURICE. Kicks, does he?
SAVAGE. Kicks, sir! Why do you say kicks?
MAURICE. Surely, no act more proper to a colt.
SAVAGE. You are something literal, sir. I'm glad of it,
Since 'twill be easier to be understood!
Well, sir, I come to you from Blasinghame.
You know not, sir, in taking up this case
Of mother Pressley's, sir, that you are doing
That which, until your coming, not a lawyer
Had done here in Missouri.
MAURICE. Shame upon them!
SAVAGE. Shame, say you? Wherefore, when the right of it
Is all with Blasinghame!

MAURICE. Or with his cudgel!

SAVAGE, [*laughs.*] Something in that, too. Well, sir,—I say!—

MAURICE. Well, sir!

SAVAGE. Now, as you something seem to know already
Of my friend's mode of managing his case,
I need not dwell upon the policy
Of stopping all proceedings ere the trial;—
In which event I'm authorized to tell you
That Blasinghame forgives your insolent letter,
And spares you as a stranger.

MAURICE. Merciful,
As he is powerful! But what if—having
No such afflicting terror of this person,
So terrible to his neighbors, in mine eyes—
I do reject this liberal grant of mercy.

SAVAGE. Then, sir, I bear his peremptory challenge,
Which leaves you, sir, without alternative,
Takes no apology, no explanation,
And only seeks atonement in your blood. [*Gives challenge.*

MAURICE. Or his!

SAVAGE. Or his! But that's no easy matter, sir;
He's fought some thirty duels in his time,
Wing'd nineteen combatants, and slew the rest,
Nor had a scratch himself.

MAURICE. Why, we may say,
As Thumb, in the great tragedy—"Enter Thumb,
And slays them all!"

SAVAGE. You mock, sir!—

MAURICE. Not a bit, sir!
I marvel only, after hearing you,
That still I have the courage to resist.

SAVAGE. You will not, sir?

MAURICE. I fear me that I shall!

SAVAGE. What! you accept the challenge, then?

MAURICE. I'll keep it, sir, until this trial's over.
SAVAGE. Beware, sir, of evasion.
MAURICE. You, in turn, sir,
Beware of insolence. You have my answer;
When I have gain'd this suit of Widow Pressley,
I'll see to that of Colonel Blasinghame.
SAVAGE. I must have your answer now, or—
MAURICE. The door, sir,—
Unless, indeed, you should prefer the window.
SAVAGE. Well! You're a man, that's certain! Give us hand.
I'm a rough beast, and like you not the less,
Because you keep a muzzle for the bear;
I *feel* that you will meet with Blasinghame,
And I shall see it. [*Shakes hands.*
MAURICE. Very like you will! [*Exit Savage.*
The game becomes of interest! [*tap within.*
Clarice! [*Opens to her, she enters.*
CLARICE. Art busy, Norman?
MAURICE. Have been. But,—this lady?—
CLARICE. Will you not see her?
MAURICE. Not if I can help it.
CLARICE. She is my only kinswoman, my husband—
You will not drive her from me?
MAURICE. Your only!—
You were *my* only, Clarice—I *your* only,
Until her coming! *Only* to each other,
Was the o'erprecious bond that most endear'd you
To my affections, wife. I cannot suffer
That she should pass between your heart and mine—
She who loves neither.
CLARICE. Nay, Norman!
MAURICE. Nay, Clarice!
This cold, coarse, selfish, this dishonest woman,

Who strove to keep us separate—
CLARICE. Her error,
She pleads, was but, in a mistaken fondness,
To find a suitor, for her favorite niece,
With better hope of fortune than yourself.
MAURICE. Who broke the sacred seal upon our letters,
Mine read,—yours hurried to the flames, unsent—
And would have sold you to this Robert Warren,
My enemy—
CLARICE. She confesses all, and weeps!
MAURICE. Tears of the crocodile! Believe them not.
Plead for her nothing more! I tell you, Clarice,
I cannot hold my table sure and sacred,
With one so false beside me at the board!—
I cannot yield my home, now pure and peaceful,
To such a treacherous heart as that she carries.
My home is not my home, when doubts of safety
Haunt still my thoughts by day, my dreams by night.
She must go hence!
CLARICE. Oh! husband, pardon her!
She urges abject poverty!
MAURICE. More falsehood still!
But we'll provide her;—she shall never suffer,
From cold, or thirst, or hunger, my Clarice.
I will to-day seek lodgings in St. Louis;
To-morrow—
CLARICE. But, should her pride?—
MAURICE. She has no right
To nurse her pride at peril of our peace!
No more! I will not mock her poverty,
Offend her pride, reproach her evil doing—
Will speak her kindly, and will care for her,
So long as I have strength for any care;—
But will not suffer, for a single moment,

Her shadow on the sunshine of my house. [*Knock without.*
Come in!

Enter Cols. Mercer and Brooks.

Friends, welcome!
[*Clarice curtsies as they bow, and is about to retire.*
MERCER. If we be welcome,
Your lady need not leave us.
BROOKS. That which brings us,
Is business of your own, no less than ours,—
A grateful business still, we trust, to you—
Which, doing honor to your worth and virtue,
It may be grateful to your wife to hear.
CLARICE. If such its burden, I were glad to linger.
MAURICE. Do so, Clarice!—we, gentlemen, are one!
Marriage, with us, fulfils its ample mission,
Making a mutual need for both our hearts;
Whose sweet dependence knows no other refuge,
Than that which each bestows. It is our fortune,
To have no kindred which may pass between us,
To take from either heart the sweet possession
We hold in one another. But, be seated.
MERCER. Court now in session, sir, your time is precious,
And this great case of yours, 'gainst Blasinghame,
Comes on to-day?
MAURICE. It does.
MERCER. A moment then?
Our friends, sir, conscious of your great endowment,
Assured of your just principles and conduct,
Your sense of public trust and public duty,
Have, with unanimous voice, in a full caucus,
Deputed us to bear you their request,
That you will be our candidate for Senator,
In the next Congress.

BROOKS. And we now entreat you,
Suffer this nomination.
MAURICE. Friends, believe me,
I feel with proper sense, this compliment;
And, if my own desire, my young ambition,
Were the sole arbiter to shape my conduct,
Then would I say to you, with hearty frankness,
My wing and eye are set upon the station,
To which your accents now implore my flight.
But, though 'twould give me pride to serve our people,
In any station where their rights are vested,
I have some scruples—
MERCER. Pray deliver them.
MAURICE. To be a candidate in common usage,
To take the field and canvass with the voter,
To use or sanction fraud—to buy with money,
Or other bribe, the suffrage of the people—
Is to dishonor them—degrade myself!
BROOKS. We ask not this.
MERCER. It needs not.
MAURICE. Hear me, sirs.
Our liberties are in the popular vote,
Their best security, the popular heart,
Their noblest triumph in the popular will,—
And this can never be expressed with safety,
Until the unbias'd voice of public judgment,
Flinging aside each intermediate agent,
Rises, with proper knowledge of its person,
And cries—"Behold our man!"
MERCER. You are our man!
Such is already what is spoken loudly
By thousands in Missouri.
MAURICE. I'll not deny it—
If I had one ambition o'er another,

One passion, prompting still a search for power,
'Twas for a station such as this you show me,
Where, standing on the platform of the nation,
I might stand up for man! And so, my studies,
The books I read, the maxims I examined,—
The laws I conn'd—the models set before me,—
All had some eminence like this in view,
That, with my training, should the occasion offer,
I might be ready still! But, in my progress,—
The better knowledge I have learn'd from men—
My doubts increase—my scruples grow—and now,
A sense of duty prompts me to declare,
Though each fond idol of the ambitious nature,
Be, from its pedestal, forever thrown,
I will not seek for office on conditions
Adverse to right and manhood. I will never
Become the creature of a selfish party—
Never use wealth or fraud to rise to power,—
Never use power itself to keep in power,
Nor see in him who favor'd my ascent,
A virtue not his own! Nor can I offer
One tribute to the vulgar vanity!
I will not bow, nor smile, nor deference yield,
Where justice still withholds acknowledgment.

MERCER. We feel the justice of your sentiments.

BROOKS. They're needful to us now, when all's corruption.
Oh! could we but inform the popular mind.

MAURICE. This can be done where virtue is the teacher,
No students learn so quickly as the people.
They have no cliques to foster—no professions,
Whose narrow boundaries, and scholastic rules,
Frown on each novel truth and principle,
And, where they can, still hunt them down to ruin.
They take a truth in secret to their hearts,

And nurse it, till it rises to a law,
Thenceforth to live forever!
  BROOKS. We are agreed—
The people must be taught—what should we teach the
  MAURICE. In politics, to know the proper value
Of the high trusts, the sacred privileges,
They do confide their statesmen. Show to them,
On these depend their liberties and lives,
The safety of their children, and the future!
To yield such trusts to smiling sycophants,
Who flatter still the voter's vanity,
At the expense of his most precious fortunes,
Is to betray the land's security;
To sell the wealth most precious in our keeping,
And, for the thing most worthless, yield to fortune,
What fortune cannot purchase! We must teach,
That he who cringes meanly for the station,
Will meanly hold him in the nation's eye;
That he who buys the vote will sell his own;—
That he, alone, is worthy of the trust,
Who, with the faculty to use it nobly,
Will never sacrifice his manhood for it.
If, with these principles and these resolves,
Thus freely shown you, and invincible,
Our people, through their representatives,
Demand my poor abilities,—'twill glad me,
To yield me at their summons. This implies not
One effort of my own. You, sirs, may make me
A Senator, but not a Candidate.
  MERCER. This suits us well. On your own terms we take y
We feel with you, a stern necessity
To check the abuse of the elective franchise!
  BROOKS. But should we call a meeting to enlighten
The people, in respect to public measures

You'll not refuse to meet them?

MAURICE. No, sir, surely!
I still have done so, upon all occasions,
Whene'er a novel principle demanded
Discussion.

MERCER. Thanks, sir! There will be to-morrow
A general meeting at the Capitol,
Without respect to party.

MAURICE. I will be there!

BROOKS. Our quest is satisfied to our desire.

MERCER. We will no longer trespass. Farewell, madam,
Farewell, sir. We shall meet again at court.

[*Exeunt Mercer and Brooks.*

CLARICE, [*embracing him.*] Husband, you triumph! There should be no care
Upon your forehead now! Last night, you slept not.

MAURICE. And now, *you* dream! But clouds *will* come, Clarice,
Still, with the morrow! Care that flies the forehead,
Still finds a secret shelter in the heart!—
That timid knock! [*Knock without.*

CLARICE. It is the widow Pressley.

MAURICE, [*opening.*] Come in, madam!

Enter Widow Pressley and Kate.

WIDOW. Oh! sir, the day has come!

MAURICE. That brings you back your property, I trust.

WIDOW. Alas! sir! You encourage me to hope,—
And yet I fear!

MAURICE. It is that we are liable to fear,
That we must hope. If judgment be not erring
No less than justice, madam, mine's a hope
That grows the bolder with each hour of thought.
Be of good heart, dear madam. Check these sorrows,
That wear such needless furrows in your cheeks.

WIDOW. They're old ones, sir, plough'd twenty years ago.
MAURICE. Renew them not!
WIDOW. And yet, if what I hear!—
Oh, sir! they tell me that this cruel man
Hath sworn a horrible oath against your life,
If he should lose his case.
MAURICE. Ah! swears he then!
That looks as if he felt some cause of fear!
WIDOW. Do not make light of it, I do entreat you!
He's a most desperate ruffian when he's thwarted,
And has the blood of many on his hands!
'Twas said he left the army for his murders,
And in his duels—
MAURICE. Let me see,—" of thirty,
Wing'd nineteen combatants, and slew the rest!"
CLARICE. Oh! horrible! How can you jest upon it?
MAURICE. I jest!
CLARICE. In truth, you smile not!
MAURICE. Do not fear!
I do not think that he will murder me.
CLARICE. Yet be not rash, my husband; take precautions,
This weapon— [*hands him a small dagger.*
MAURICE. What! your dagger, my Clarice,
This pretty Turkish trifle from your bodice,
The blade mosaic—handle wrought in pearl—
The sheath of exquisite morocco, dropp'd
In gold and green! This ornament for masking,
Were a frail weapon for a man's defence!
Nay, keep your dagger, child, I shall not need it.
CLARICE. Be not so confident.
MAURICE. Be not so timid!
Who looks for danger surely happens on it!
My papers there! You go with me, dear madam. [*To widow.*
WIDOW. Thanks, sir!

There was a time I kept *my* carriage!

MAURICE. Be hopeful: you shall keep it once a

[*Aside to Clarice.*] I feed this hapless woman with

Such as it glads me to indulge myself,—

Yet, should I err in judgment?

CLARICE, [*aside.*] Oh! should you fail!

'Twould break her heart.

MAURICE. 'Twere something worse than death!

[*Aside to Clarice.*

But we'll not fail! [*aloud.*] The courage born of virtue

Hath still a holy sanction for its hope;

And he who strives with justice on his side,

May boldly challenge fortune for success,

If he be true himself!—*We will not fail!*

The carriage there! Come, madam—for the Court-house!

[*Exeunt.*

END OF ACT THIRD.

ACT IV.—SCENE I.

A garden in the rear of the house of Norman Maurice. Walk through a thick shrubbery. Enter Robert Warren and Mrs. Jervas.

WARREN. So! So! You heard it all, then?

MRS. J. Every syllable.

WARREN. Glorious! But how did you conceal yourself?

MRS. J. An ante-room conducts us to the hall
Where they were secretly at conference;
Thither, when she descended from my chamber,
I softly follow'd. The convenient key-hole
Gave me the means, at once to hear and see them.

WARREN. Your foresight shames my thought! And so, this Maurice,
Denies that you shall harbor in his dwelling?
But this you must do! Your security
Lies in his household only! He might promise you
Your lodging in St. Louis,—board and clothing—
Ample provision for your state in future—
But once you free his household of your presence,
He whistles you down the wind. No obligation
Would bind him to the care of you hereafter!

MRS. J. What then? He's very stubborn in his spirit!

WARREN. Why, to be sure! The very thing, dear madam—
Your sickness will not suffer your removal:
Fatigue of travel, grief, anxiety,
Will have their penalties; and your prostration
Is such, that all the world would say 'twas monstrous
To drive you,—you, a stranger in the country,—

The home of the one kinswoman that's left you!
Your notion is a good one! Norman Maurice
Is not the man to urge the matter on you—
An invalid,—with feeble frame,—hot fever—
Confined to bed,—mind somewhat wandering!—
You're right! Methinks you need no counsel, madam.

MRS. J. I see! 'Twill do!

WARREN. 'Tis excellent! So, Maurice
Accepts the Senatorial nomination,
Though still his pride revolts at working for it.
Well! He's not Senator yet. The widow's case
Will bring its perils too; and, at the finish,
I'll interpose to blight his growing glories,
And show him———Hark! a footstep—

MRS. J. Here she comes!

WARREN. Auspicious! Here, away; and, while you leave us,
I'll open a brief conference with her.
Meanwhile, 'tis well you put your scheme in progress;
Take to your bed, and get your nostrums ready;
Spare not your groans and sighs—a little faintness
Might well arrest you suddenly in your speech!
And—but enough. The thicket! Here, away!

[*They retire behind the copse.*

Enter Clarice.

CLARICE. Now all my sorrows sink into the sea,
Since Norman rises to such noble height,
The first in his desert and his desire!
Methinks, till now, I doubted of his fortune,
Nor ever felt secure from sad mischance;
The gibe of envious tongues, the jeer of malice,
The snares of bitter foes, and those dark meshes,
That still the treacherous hands of Warren spread!
These do not fright me now, and, though his presence,

So apt with coming hither of my aunt,
Would seem to shadow forth some evil purpose,
Yet can I not esteem it cause of fear,
Since it were vain for such as he to struggle
Against the noble fortunes of my husband.

WARREN, [*coming out behind her.*] Indeed! and yet the shaft that slew the lion,
Was but a reed beside the sedgy stream!

CLARICE, [*seeing him and starting.*] Ah!

WARREN. The little scorpion issuing from the rock,
First slew the steed whose skull he 'habited.

CLARICE. Thou here again!

WARREN. If but to teach thee in philosophy!—
A pebble in the hand of shepherd slinger,
Smote, so we learn from Sacred History,
The proudest giant in Philistia's ranks.

CLARICE. And he whose presence still offends a woman,
But little dreams what champion she may call.

WARREN. I knew *your* champion absent ere I ventured.
Your highest pitch of voice, and greatest need,
Would never bring him timely to your succor.

CLARICE. What means this threat?

WARREN. It is no threat, Clarice;—
You will not need a champion when I'm near you.

CLARICE. And if I did, methinks, in Robert Warren
I should be loth to seek one! Why come hither,
My husband's foe, pursuing still his fortunes,
And mine, with bitter malice!

WARREN. *Thee* with love!

CLARICE. Who wrongs the husband, cannot love the wife!

WARREN. Clarice, 'twas in my passionate love for thee,
First grew the passionate hate I bear thy husband!
'Till thou, with fatal beauty, came between us,
He was the twin companion of my pleasures.—

My first associate in each boyish frolic,
We still together went, by hill and valley,
Beside the stream, and through th' untrodden forest,
Having no faith but in our youthful friendship,
No joy, but in the practice shared together.
'Twas thou that changed my kinsman to a rival—
'Twas thou that changed our friendship into hate;
We fell apart, suspecting both, and loathing,
When first our mutual hearts inclined to thee!

CLARICE. He did not hate thee—had no jealousy,
But still confided to thee, even his passion;
And thou—alas! audacious that thou art,
How canst thou still forget that I too know thee,
A traitor to his trust!

WARREN. Have I denied it?
I would have won thee from my dearest kinsman.
My treachery to him was truth to thee!

CLARICE. And yet 'twas fruitless! Was it not enough
That thou shouldst fail? Why now—

WARREN. Enough!
Was every passion to be wreck'd forever,
In that which had denial in thy scorn?
With love denied, was vengeance—

CLARICE. Vengeance! Ha!
Is it his life thou aim'st at now, or mine?

WARREN. Neither!

CLARICE. What then? We're separate forever,—
Our lots are cast apart,—our lives divided,—
Why, when no profit comes to thee—no pleasure,
To us, at this dark crossing of our footsteps—
Why art thou here?—Why vex us with thy presence,
To thy own deep defeat?

WARREN. In your own thoughts,
Look for the answer to this teeming question.

You know me well—enough of me to know,
Whate'er my vices or deficiencies,
I am no simpleton, but have a cunning
That scarce would keep me profitlessly working,
Still drawing fruitless waters in a sieve!
That I should press upon your husband's footsteps,
Would prove I still had hope of my revenge!
That I should seek thee in thy secret bower,
Would show me still not hopeless of thy love!

CLARICE. Oh! vain and insolent man!

WARREN. Hold, a little!
If hopeful still of you, 'tis through the prospect
Of vengeance on your husband.

CLARICE. Face *him* then!

WARREN. You but increase my eager thirst for vengeance,
When you remind me of the frequent struggle,
Which ended in my overthrow and shame.

CLARICE. Is't not enough, thus baffled and defeated?—
Why thus encounter still the shame and danger?

WARREN. And if my hope lay only in my fortune—
If still my triumph waited on my strength,
And, to the skill and vigor of mine arm,
I looked to win the vengeance that I covet—
I should forego the conflict, as you counsel,
And leave your world in peace, concealing mine!

CLARICE. Well, sir—you pause!

WARREN. I would have had your thought
Supply the words of mine; but, as it does not—
Know that I look to other means of vengeance;
Not through my strength, but in his feebleness—
Not in my virtue, but your husband's vices!

CLARICE. Oh! hence!

WARREN. Yet, hear me! at this very moment
Your husband seeks the pinnacle of power;

He stands conspicuous in the public eye;
The highest place awaits him in the state—
The highest in the nation! At a word,
I can o'erthrow him from his eminence,
Can make his name a by-word and a mock,
Degrade him from his rank, and, with a secret—

CLARICE. Shallow and impotent, as base and worthless!—
Hence with your secret! Me can you delude not,
Though you delude yourself. I know this secret!

WARREN. What! Your husband's forgery?

CLARICE. *Your* forgery?
Think not to cheat me with your foul contrivance.
You prated of his skill in penmanship—
Defied it,—placed examples in his eye—
And he, confiding—dreaming not that one,
The kinsman who had shared his home and bosom,
Could meditate a falsehood or a crime—
Wrote, at your bidding, sundry names of persons;
And, with these names, without his privity,
Your hand devised the drafts which got the money—
Your hand expended what your guilt procured,
On your own pleasures, in his grievous wrong—
And he hath paid the debt. The fatal papers,
Which might have been a means of his undoing,
Were burned before mine eyes!

WARREN. Your eyes deceived you.
I'll not deny your story of the fraud;
But, for the papers—let me whisper you—
They were *not* burn'd—they live for evidence—
Are now in my possession—damning proofs,
For the conviction still of Norman Maurice.

CLARICE. Oh, false as hell! These eyes beheld them burning.

WARREN. Hark, in your ear! What you beheld destroyed,
Were but the copies of originals,

The neatly written forgeries of forgeries:
The originals are mine!
  CLARICE. Have mercy, heaven!
What will you do with them?
  WARREN. What you determine.
  CLARICE. What mean you?
  WARREN. What! can you not conjecture?
  CLARICE. No, as I live!
  WARREN. What should I do with them?
Appease my hatred, pacify my vengeance,—
Wait till this still triumphant enemy
Puts foot upon the topmost ring of the ladder,
Then cut away the lofty props that raise him,
And let him down to scorn and infamy.
Another day would make him senator,
But that I step between, and show these papers,
And then the thousand voices in his honor,
Pursue him with their hiss!
  CLARICE. Hellish malice!
Oh, if there be a human nature in thee,
Forbear this vengeance.
  WARREN. If it pleases thee!
  CLARICE. How, if it pleases me?
  WARREN. See you not yet?
The alternative is yours to let him perish,
Or win the eminence that still he seeks.
  CLARICE. Tell me!
  WARREN. Be mine!
  CLARICE, [*recoiling.*] Thine!
  WARREN. Ay! for nothing less
Than the sweet honey dew that lines thy lips,
The heaven that heaves in thy embracing bosom,
Will I forego this vengeance.
  CLARICE. God have mercy!

Yet no! I'll not believe this cruel story;
Thou hast no papers! I must see—

WARREN. Thou shalt!
Meet me, Clarice, at sunset, in yon thicket.

CLARICE. I dare not. In yon thicket—

WARREN. Dare you, then,
Behold your husband perish?

CLARICE. You but mock.

WARREN. Wilt have me swear?

CLARICE. What oath would bind a wretch
So profligate in sin? I will not come!
My husband's honor still defies your arts,
And mine defies your passion.

WARREN. You have doom'd him!

CLARICE. Oh, say not so! You would not have me madden.

WARREN. I swear it! what I tell you is the truth.—
I have these papers, own this fearful power
Upon his fame and fortune, and *will* use it—

CLARICE. And—if I come? [*Looking vacantly.*

WARREN. And yield you to my passion,
The papers, with the fatal evidence,
Shall all be yours.

CLARICE, [*aside.*] Be resolute, my soul!
Heaven help me in this strait and give me courage.
[*Aloud.*] Bring you the papers, Robert Warren; and—

WARREN, [*eagerly.*] You'll come?

CLARICE. If I have strength and courage, I will come.
[*Exit Clarice, slowly.*

WARREN. Then mine's a double triumph! Fool!—these papers
Shall serve a twofold purpose: win the treasure,
And yet confound the keeper when he wakes!
[*Exit Warren.*

SCENE II.

The porch of the Court-house of St. Louis. Norman Maurice about to enter, accompanied by the Widow Pressley and Kate, is detained by Mercer upon the threshold.

MERCER. A word with you, if you please.
MAURICE. Go in, madam,
And find yourself a seat until I come:
I'll follow soon. [*Widow and child enter.*
MERCER. This case will keep you late,
And we this evening hold a conference,
Touching the course of the debate to-morrow;—
Were it not better you took bed with us,
And, in the mean while, lest your wife grows anxious,
Advise her, by a billet, of your purpose?
MAURICE. Well thought of. I will do so. [*going.*
MERCER. Something farther:
Catesby here tells me—but he comes: here, Catesby.
What's this of Savage? [*Enter Catesby.*
CATESBY, [*to Maurice.*] You've won the Savage heart.
It seems that Blasinghame misdoubts your courage,
And, as you gave no reference on his challenge,
Inclines to violence; and has bid his lambs
Gather about him to behold the sport.
MAURICE. Ah, sport!
CATESBY. And this in utter scorn of Savage,
Who counsell'd patience till the time is over,
Fix'd by you for your answer. Blasinghame
Growls sullen, and shows Savage a cold shoulder:
'Twas he himself advised that you be watchful.

MAURICE. I thank him, and feel grateful to the Savage.
As for this Blasinghame, he'll have need to growl,
When we have done with him. But farther—Catesby—
Be you convenient, and, when court is over,
Meet us at Mercer's.

CATESBY. I shall stay the trial.

MAURICE. Good. Let us in then. [*Exeunt within.*

Enter Blasinghame, Savage, and others.

BLASINGHAME. That's enough, Joe Savage.

SAVAGE. Ay, if it answers.

BLASINGHAME. Answers or not, I tell you, still enough.
Your counsel's something quite unlike yourself.

SAVAGE. And, for that very reason, may be wisdom.

BLASINGHAME. Perhaps!—but I'm not used to sudden changes.
I will take farther counsel with myself.

SAVAGE. Doubtless, to find the way to wise conclusions.
I wash my hands of the business.

BLASINGHAME. Pray do so!
But, see you Ferguson?

SAVAGE. He follows us,
Yonder, with Matthews and the stranger, Warren.

BLASINGHAME. Well, if all fails to bring this Maurice down,
That fellow hath a secret.

SAVAGE. What is it?

BLASINGHAME. Why, something that should please you,—quite pacific—
For final overthrow of this man, Maurice;
But let us in. I should be rather anxious,
Having at stake a fortune on this trial. [*Exeunt within.*

Enter Ferguson with books and papers, accompanied by Warren.

WARREN. You have it all, sir. At the public meeting
You boldly challenge him with forgery,

Call on me to produce the fatal papers,
And summon Richard Osborne to confirm them.

FERGUSON. We'll crush him at a blow.

WARREN. 'Till then, nothing!
The shame must be complete, beyond recovery.
Let him stretch forth his hand to gain the station,
In sight of all, then, in remediless ruin,
Hurl him down headlong.

FERGUSON. You are sure of him—
Your facts—your proofs, your persons?

WARREN. Sure as fate!

FERGUSON. You will not fail us?

WARREN. Would you have me swear?
Have I been wrong'd, and do I hate this Maurice?
Will hate forego the prospect of revenge?
Revenge reject the draught that quenches thirst,
And he who long has dream'd of hidden treasure,
Turn from the golden prize, at last his own?
Not, if the hell that feeds this passion fiercely,
Bestow the needful resolution for it!

FERGUSON. And this man, Osborne?

WARREN. He has had his lesson—
He'll answer when you call him.

FERGUSON. All then is true?

WARREN. As true as need be for a lawyer's purpose,
As for a foe's.

FERGUSON. 'Tis very pitiful—
For, though I like him not, this Norman Maurice
Is still a man of wondrous qualities;—
But for this lapse from virtue he had been
Most perfect.

WARREN. It is well he is not perfect,
Or he had put humanity to the blush,
By showing, in rough contrast, to her shame,

The meaner value of the coin she carries.

FERGUSON. I do not like this business, but our need
Will not permit that we discuss its merits;—
We'll see you with the morrow.

WARREN. With the hour,
That hears your accusation!

FERGUSON. Good! [*Exit Ferguson within.*

WARREN. Ay, good!
It could not well be better for our purpose.
The mine is sprung, the victim still approaches,
Unconscious, and my hand must fire the train!
But here comes Osborne. I must speak him sternly;
He cannot silence me with womanish scruples,—
He shall not!—Well, our scheme works famously.

Enter Osborne.

OSBORNE. *Your* scheme; not mine!

WARREN. When will your wisdom, Osborne,
Conceive that scheme of mine is scheme of yours,—
Or should be? Now, then, hear our present purpose.
Ferguson brings the charge!

OSBORNE. What! you have told it?

WARREN. Only to him; and he will keep it safely,
'Till comes the proper moment for explosion.
When our young senator, in public meeting,
Rises to answer to the public summons,
And take the coveted laurel to his brow,
Then will we loose our thunderbolt, whose bursting
Tears him to atoms.

OSBORNE. What am I to do, then?
What wretched part must I play in this business?

WARREN. A minor one, 'tis true, but quite important.
You'll be my echo. When I give the signal,
Confirm my statement and complete our proofs.

OSBORNE. Are you not under pledges to his wife,
To yield her up these proofs?

WARREN. Ay, on conditions.

OSBORNE. Well!

WARREN. What of that? Another means of vengeance!
See you not that I strike him, through her virtue,
But not the less denounce him to the public.
I'll wheedle *her* with a promise to my arms,
Then mock the easy confidence that listen'd
To one she dared despise.

OSBORNE. Oh, Warren! Warren!
Whither would you carry me—where go yourself?

WARREN. To hell, if need be, so I gain my object!—
Achieve the conquest that to me is heaven,
Comprising, as it must, in equal measure,
At once the joys of passion and of hate!
For you—remember, Osborne—no more scruples!
You are mine—soul, body, thought and feeling, mine—
And these shall ply as still my passions counsel,
Or woe betide the rebel.

OSBORNE. Better slay me!

WARREN. Nay, you're not fit to die yet; nor could serve me
Hereafter, half so usefully as now.
At dusk, I keep the meeting with our beauty,
And thence with Matthews to a secret meeting.
Look for me home at midnight; and to-morrow—
Remember! no evasion. Fix'd as fatal,
My will nor brooks dissuasion nor defeat. [*Exit Warren.*

OSBORNE. Had I the heart to perish, 'twere less pain,
Than bend beneath this scourge and bear this chain.

SCENE III.

An apartment in the dwelling of Norman Maurice. Enter Clarice, reading a note.

CLARICE. Not with me till to-morrow! 'Tis an age!
The first night separate since we were married.
Yet better thus. How could I meet my Norman,
Having this deep concealment in my heart,
Nor shudder with a weight of shame, whose crimson
Would set my cheeks on flame! How stifle feeling,
To cling in fondness to his manly bosom,
Nor speak the terrible purpose in my heart,
That said, would stifle his! 'Tis better thus!
Enough, that when I meet him—meet him—yes!—
When his dear voice is sounding in mine ears,
Full of the conscious triumphs that await him,
I then may fling myself upon his breast,
And show the dire necessity that made me
The thing I dare not name,—and plead with him,
For each prompt sacrifice of feminine feeling;
The nerve that rose above the woman weakness,
As still the tribute to his fame and safety.
He will forgive—will bless;—and if he does not!—
Should he recoil from my embrace, and show me
The crimson proof of shame upon my garments,
And cry, "thy hands, that once were white and spotless,
Are red with guilt:"—but no—I dare not think it.
Let me not look that way. Impossible!
Shall I not, while they threaten, steel my heart,
Against this dread necessity, nor tremble,

Though on the altars of his fame and glory,
I bathe this white and innocent hand in crime!
I shudder, yet I shrink not. Give the power,
God, to this heart, against the coming hour!

SCENE IV.

Open space before the Court-house of St. Louis. Groups of Lawyers and Citizens.

1st Lawyer. Didst hear the speech of Maurice in this case?
2d Lawyer. 'Twas terrible!
1st Lawyer. I never heard the like!
And when he did discourse of Blasinghame,—
His first wrong to the widow—his denial
Of the poor orphan's right—his violence
To those who strove to serve her interests—
The picture that he painted was so monstrous,
That every heart grew cold.
3d Lawyer. And Blasinghame,
Himself—didst note him?
2d Lawyer. 'Twas another picture!
1st Lawyer. He sat a spectacle of ghastly fury,
That had moved pity, could we have forgotten
His looks at the beginning of the case.
At first, how bold he seem'd—with what defiance;
Next, with what doubt; then follow'd his dismay—
And last, his fury; while, with impotent rage,
And something, as it seem'd, of shame and horror,
In his own spite at what the other drew,
He crouch'd at last beneath the terrible scourging,
And half escaped from sight.

2D LAWYER. I saw him clutching
The panel that he lean'd on, as for help,
While, beaded on his forehead, the big sweat
Still gather'd as it fell; and, on his lips
The stain of red that mingled with the foam,
Show'd how he had even bitten through his lips,
In his great agony, and knew it not.

1ST LAWYER. The judge has charged the jury?

2D LAWYER. He was charging
Just when I left. I could not stand it longer—
As much exhausted at the stern excitement,
As Blasinghame himself.

1ST LAWYER. For Ferguson,
The up-hill work was pitiful. To follow,
With such a case, a speaker such as Maurice,
Was quite as killing to himself as client.
Nobody heard, or cared to hear, his pleading—
Not even the jury.

2D LAWYER. What will be the verdict?

1ST LAWYER. Why, who can doubt? The insuppressible groan,
That broke from every breast—the gaze of fury
That blazed in every eye, when, pointing slowly,
And shaking with such dire significance,
The hand of Maurice fix'd on Blasinghame,
As still, with holy horror in his accents,
He spoke his wonder, that, with guilt so hideous,
He still could brave the gaze of man and justice!—
That groan and glance declared the popular judgment,
And such will be the verdict.

2D LAWYER. Hark! that cry—

1ST LAWYER. Declares it.

[*Shouts in the porch as the people rush out of the Court-house.*]

1ST CITIZEN. Hurrah for Norman Maurice!

2D CITIZEN. The widow's friend!

3D CITIZEN. The people's man forever!
2D LAWYER. There speaks the popular heart.
1ST LAWYER. A glorious voice,
That makes him senator.
2D LAWYER. Hark! he comes forth.

Enter Maurice, with widow Pressley and Kate, followed by Mercer Brooks, Catesby, and others. Shouts.

WIDOW. Ah! sir. God's blessing on you,—make us happy,
And take the half of all you've got for us!
MAURICE. Not for the world, dear madam! I'll not forfeit
The pure delight I feel in serving virtue
For its own sake! In lifting the down-trodden,
For sake of wrong'd humanity! No more. [*People shout.*
1ST VOICE. Hurrah for Norman Maurice!
2D VOICE. The widow's friend!
3D VOICE. The people's man forever!
MAURICE, [*to Mercer.*] Let us get hence.
Dear madam, take my carriage,
And bear the grateful tidings to my wife;
Remain with her to-day while I am absent;—
To-night, as still it's like, I shall be absent,
Rejoice her with our triumph. She expects you!
WIDOW. I have no thanks—no words,—my tongue is frozen.
MAURICE. 'Tis that the thaw is wholly at your heart!
Go hence. Escort her, Mercer, to the carriage.
[*Exeunt Widow, Kate, and Mercer.*
CATESBY, [*whispering to Maurice.*] Look to it, Maurice—here comes Blasinghame!

Enter Blasinghame with others.

BLASINGHAME. Where is he! Let me see! Ha, give me way!
[*Forces through the crowd, rushes upon Maurice, striking him with a stick.*

Villain, my blows make answer to thy speech!

MAURICE. A blow—and I no weapon! But it needs none—
When, with such powerful passions in my heart,
I feel my sinews fortified with strength,
To drag a thousand tigers to my feet.
Thus, monster, that hast trampled on a people,
Defied their virtues—at their sufferings mock'd—
Thus, with my foot upon thy stubborn neck,
I trample—I degrade thee to the dust! [*Seizes Blasinghame by the throat, hurls him to the ground, and stands upon his neck. Shouts of the people.*

1ST CITIZEN. Hurrah for Norman Maurice!

2D CITIZEN. The people's friend!

3D CITIZEN. The champion of the widow!

CATESBY, [*interposing.*] Enough, sir. Let him rise. I'll whisper him
Where he can find us.

MAURICE. Now, within the hour!

[*Catesby and Savage lift Blasinghame.*

CATESBY. Colonel Blasinghame!

BLASINGHAME. Where is he? Give me way!

MAURICE, [*confronting him.*] Here!

SAVAGE, [*interposing.*] Enough of this!
I see! You'll be at Mercer's. [*To M.*]

MAURICE. Ay, now!

SAVAGE. No more! Come, Blasinghame.

BLASINGHAME. You, Joe!
Well, you are true, boy, and I did you wrong.
Forgive me! You will see to this. This man
Hath had his cursed foot upon my neck!
You saw it!—ha! You saw it!

SAVAGE. He will meet you!

BLASINGHAME. Ha, Joe! Your hand. But when?

SAVAGE. Within the hour!

BLASINGHAME. Good! See to it. Ha, ha. Methinks—

SAVAGE. No more!—
Away with me at once; you must not linger.

BLASINGHAME. Methinks I could drink blood. I'm very thirsty.

[*Exeunt Blasinghame and Savage.*

CATESBY. Come, let us get in trim. Are you a shot?

MAURICE. No!

CATESBY. Ah! that's unfortunate!

MAURICE. You think so?—
Never you matter, Catesby: I will kill him!

END OF ACT FOURTH.

ACT V.—SCENE I.

A chamber in the house of Col. Mercer. Norman Maurice and Catesby discovered.

CATESBY. The challenge comes from Blasinghame. This gives us
Advantages, which we should rightly use,
'Gainst one so old in practice.

MAURICE. We shall use them:—
The weapon for example. Mine's the small sword.

CATESBY. The small sword! Blasinghame expects the pistol.

MAURICE. We have the right in this and other matters;—
I waive the rest; but this we must insist on.
'Twas still my fancy, upward from my boyhood,
That, next to lance and spear, the proper weapon
For honorable combat is the sword;—
Admitting grace of movement and decision,
Allowing still discretion to the champion,—
Obeying all the changes of his temper,
And, as the enemy betrayed his purpose,
Giving him power to spare or slay at pleasure,
Or simply to draw blood and to disarm.

CATESBY. You've learn'd to use the weapon?

MAURICE. But a little!
Some confidence, at least, in eye and motion,
Grew from my youthful practice; and a passage,
With the bright rapiers flashing in the sunlight,
Was ever such a pleasure to my spirit,
That I am half content to risk the duel,
For the excitement of the keen dispute!
'Tis long since I have exercised, but nature

Hath so endow'd me, that a play acquired,
I never yet have lost. 'Tis fortunate,
That I have made provision for this practice,
And have with me two reeds of Milan steel,
In all respects so equal, that a swordsman
Would linger long to choose.—But here comes Savage!

Enter Savage.

SAVAGE. Save you, gentlemen.
MAURICE. Your hand, sir. We are ready:
We know your business. Here is Captain Catesby,
Who will discuss with you the needful matters.
CATESBY. Our policy demands the immediate issue,
Lest friends or officers should interpose.
Within the hour,—or, at the least, by sunset,
This meeting should be had.
SAVAGE. You cannot have it
Too soon for Blasinghame. You know the man!
Well! what the weapon?
CATESBY. We shall choose the small sword.
SAVAGE. The small sword! Why—'tis not the usual weapon.
MAURICE. As much as any other. France and Poland—
Indeed, most countries of the continent,
Where'er society allows the duel,—
Employ it—
CATESBY. And, you know, in Louisiana?—
SAVAGE. The pistol's the more equal.
CATESBY. Were Blasinghame,
Or Maurice, feeble, and the other strong,
That were, perhaps, an argument, but—
MAURICE. And, if the question's courage, Major Savage,
As I am told your friend is pleased to make it,
Somewhat at my expense, then, let me tell you,
Cold steel will better try the manly bosom,

Than any decent distance with the pop-gun.
If I remember, Colonel Blasinghame
Hath served in the army, worn the soldier's weapon,
And will not scruple at its use in season.

SAVAGE. Your words decide it:
You have the right—the small sword be it then.

MAURICE, [*giving swords.*] Here are two noble weapons—better never
Play'd in the spiral and conflicting circle,
Above the head whose life was made the forfeit
In the delirious conflict. Take them with you;
Your friend can choose from them, or note the measure
Of that which I employ.

SAVAGE. At sunset, then.

CATESBY. The place?—

MAURICE. If you will suffer me—there is,
By Baynton's meadow, a sweet bit of copse,
East of it, through which runs an Indian trail:—
It leads us to a patch of open lawn,
Level, and smooth, and grassy—a fit place
For one to fight, or sleep on!

SAVAGE. Be it there, then.
And now I leave you, gentlemen: an hour
Remains for preparation ere we meet! [*Exit Savage.*

CATESBY. You are the coolest person—for a person
That never was in combat. You will kill him!

MAURICE. Not if I'm cool enough! I fain would spare him,
Now, that I see him not. But when before me,
And I behold in him the insulting tyrant,
That robs the feeble and defies the strong
I feel a passionate anger in my heart,
That makes me long to trample him to dust!

CATESBY. What more, but seek the surgeon and the carriage!

MAURICE. I'm ready when you please.

CATESBY. Within the hour! [*Exit Catesby.*

MAURICE. My poor Clarice! she sits beside the window,
And with a vacant spirit still looks forth,
Unthinking, yet still dreaming that I come.
What a long night to both—and that to-morrow!
Well! it will chide her tears, and soothe my sorrow.
[*Scene closes.*

SCENE II.

The entrance of a thick wood near the dwelling of Norman Maurice. Sunset. Robert Warren discovered.

WARREN. The sun is at its set, and yet she comes not.
Can she have faltered—what doth she suspect,—
What fear! It sinks, and hark—her footstep.
Now comes our triumph—now! [*Retires into the wood.*

Enter Clarice.

CLARICE. Oh, if I err,
I that am feeble, and though feeble, loving,—
Devoted, where the sacrifice is needful,—
Willing to die for him whose dear devotion,
Hath made it my religion still to love him—
Oh, God have mercy on the hapless error,
That grows from love's necessities alone!
If in my death his triumph may be certain,
My breast is ready for the knife. I need
No prayer, no prompting to the sacrifice,
That saves him from the wreck of all his hopes,
And honor with them. Let me now not falter!
Forgive me, Heaven, in pity to the weakness
That knows not how to 'scape. If it be crime,—
The deed, which I have brooded o'er, until

My shuddering fancy almost deems it done—
By which I do avoid the loathlier crime;
Let not the guilt lie heavy on my soul,
As solemnly I do profess myself,
Most free from evil purpose, and most hating
That which meseems the dread necessity
That shadows all my fortune! God have pity,
And show the way, that still unseen before me,
Lies open for my rescue! Ha, 'tis he!

WARREN, [*reënters.*] Methinks, Clarice, you come reluctantly.
Your husband's fate—the dangers that await him,
That do appear so terrible to me,
Would seem to touch you not.

CLARICE. I'll not believe it!
I tell you I must see these fatal papers—
Must feel them—spell and weigh each syllable,
Ere I believe you!

WARREN. Said I not you should?

CLARICE. Show me them. I'm here.

WARREN. Come hither, then.

CLARICE. What! in the deeper darkness of the wood?
No! Here!

WARREN. What! dost forget my recompense?
Wouldst thou the naked heaven behold our pleasures?

CLARICE. Oh, Heaven! sustain me! Let me not go mad;
That I may hear unmoved this foul assailant,
Nor show, to baffling of my hope and purpose,
The loathing that I feel! [*Aside.*

WARREN. The proof is ready—
Wherefore dost thou linger?

CLARICE, [*eagerly.*] Ha! then thou hast it—
Here, in thy bosom—here, in yonder wood.

WARREN. Even as thou sayest—here, within my bosom;
But 'tis in yonder wood that thou shalt see it.

Behold! [*Takes the papers from his bosom and waves her to the wood.*

CLARICE. Give me to see them.

WARREN. Yes!

CLARICE. But here!

WARREN. No—there! [*Waving papers and retiring.*

CLARICE. Show me! I come! [*Following.*

WARREN. Yet farther. Follow me!

By yon red oak, where the dark thicket spreads,
Where silence, and her twin, security,
Brood ever, and declare for loving hearts
Their meet protection in this lonely shade.—
Thither, Clarice! [*Retires from sight, beckoning with the papers.*

CLARICE. Thither, then; I follow thee!

Thou dost implore thy fate! I follow thee
Where shadow and silence both invoke with speech,
Too potent for my feeble prayer and plaint,
A shadow and a silence yet more deep!
They awfully declare a hideous worship
Where Horror sits supreme, and summons me
To make befitting sacrifice. My soul,
Be firm of purpose now. Nerves, do not falter,
When that I do demand your resolute office.
I dare not call on Heaven to help my weakness,
But from the indulgent mercy, born of Heaven,
Implore the saving grace I may not merit.

WARREN, [*within.*] Clarice!

CLARICE. Ha, then, I come to thee.

Fool! thou entreat'st a Fury to thy arms,
And not a woman. Thou wouldst have my love—
Partake of my embrace—my kiss—thou shalt!
My husband—'tis for thee!

WARREN, [*within.*] Clarice!

CLARICE. He calls me!

I do but answer to his summons! Ha!
Another voice is sounding in mine ears,—
And many voices! One of them is Norman's,—
He calls!—he, too, implores me to the wood!
There will he meet with Warren. If he meets him,
I know what then must happen. I must thither.
His voice again. It sinks into a murmur—
Mix'd murmurs follow of a crowd! What is it,
That rolls so dully in my brain, and makes me
Uncertain of my footstep? Oh! the horror
Of this strange weakness! Ha!

WARREN, [*within the wood.*] Clarice!

CLARICE. He calls!

Thrice! Thrice! It is decreed. I come—I come! [*Exit within: a moment after a cry of agony, and then a sound as of a falling body. Reënter Clarice with papers in her hand, and garments all bloody.*

CLARICE. Ha, ha, I have them! I could laugh! Ha! ha!—
But for this horrible silence. Yet, I have them!
He would have kept them from me—he. Ha, ha!
But would I suffer him when he threaten'd Norman,
My husband, with dishonor—my brave husband,
That even now is rising in the nation,
Among the great, in the high places of power,
Rank'd with the men most eminent. Dear Norman!
Ha!—ha! I'm very happy now. I have the papers,
The proof, and Norman is made Senator,
Spite of this wretched liar! He'll lie no more.
He wish'd for my embrace, and sure he had it!
Such close embrace, so sharp, so sudden, sweet,
It made him shriek and shrink with such a pleasure,
As men endure not twice. [*Groan within.*
God! what is that!
A footstep! He pursues me for the papers. [*Thrusts them into her bosom.*

He shall not have them. No—I have no papers.
He comes! Home—Norman—Home! Home! Home! my Norman!

[*Exit wildly, looking behind her as she departs.*

SCENE III.

The wood behind Baynton's meadow. Enter from opposite sides, Norman Maurice, Catesby, Surgeon; and Colonel Blasinghame Savage, Surgeon.

SAVAGE. Can nothing reconcile our parties, Catesby?

CATESBY. The invitation to the field is yours:
Yours still must be each overture for peace.

SAVAGE. What will content you, Blasinghame?

BLASINGHAME. His blood!

SAVAGE, [*to Catesby.*] I'm sorry, but you hear?

CATESBY. To business, then!
Maurice is at his post; so, place your man.

[*Maurice and Blasinghame confront each other.*

MAURICE. Art ready, sir?

BLASINGHAME. For vengeance! You have foil'd me—
Disgraced me in the eyes of all our people,
So, look to it, for by the God that made me,
I'll write my living tortures on your heart!

MAURICE. Your blood upon your head!

[*They fight. Maurice disarms him.*

BLASINGHAME. Curse on the weapon!

MAURICE. Curse not the weapon!—curse the hand, the heart—
The cause,—which have betrayed you;—not the weapon!
Your life is at my mercy!

BLASINGHAME, [*folding his arms.*] Take it, then!
I would not live dishonor'd. You may slay me,

But cannot conquer me.—My breast is open!

MAURICE. I will not slay you. I *will* conquer you.
Your life is mine. I give it you. Live on,
A wiser and a better man hereafter.

BLASINGHAME, [*tottering and turning away.*] My strength is gone from me; my heart is crush'd.
Look, Savage,—these are tears, and not of blood.
Come with me, for I falter. [*Going.*

SAVAGE, [*to Maurice.*] You're a man
Among ten thousand, Maurice. Now, forgive him.
He weeps. The strong man weeps.—I must go with him,
But know me for your friend.

[*Exit Savage following Blasinghame.*

CATESBY. 'Twas nobly done.
When I consider Blasinghame's career,
His brutal murders, his long tyrannies,
The provocation you have had to slay him—
I marvel that you spared him. Sir, your triumph
Is now without alloy.

MAURICE. I'm glad you think so,
Yet deem the merit of forbearance small.
Had he been bolder, I had never spared him;
But could not strike him when, with folded arms,
He stood to meet the stroke. But—let's to Mercer.

[*Exeunt.*

SCENE IV.

The chamber of Richard Osborne. Enter to him Harry Matthews.

MATTHEWS. Where's Warren?

OSBORNE. I've not seen him.

MATTHEWS. Not since when?

OSBORNE. Noon yesterday.
MATTHEWS. Indeed. 'Twas then we parted.
He promised to meet with me last night at Baylor's.
OSBORNE. And came not?
MATTHEWS. No. 'Twas probable his business—
For you must know his hands are full at present—
Was quite too grateful and too full of profit,
To make him leave it soon. I marvell'd not
That he should fail us *then;* but now, this morning,
When, by agreement, he should breakfast with us—
And here's the hour—that he should still be absent,
Seems something strange. He must be at the meeting,
Or we are done forever.
OSBORNE. What's the meeting?
MATTHEWS. One of both parties, meant for caucussing,
Popular wholly in its character,
Whose temper will determine our Assembly
As to its choice of Senator in Congress.
OSBORNE. Ay,—indeed.
MATTHEWS. You'll be there?
OSBORNE. Yes; I promised him.
MATTHEWS. Who? Warren?
OSBORNE. Yes.
MATTHEWS. I must go look for him.
We must not risk our fortunes by delay.
His voice may help to make our Senator. [*Exit Matt.*
OSBORNE. Would he were dumb or I! Alas! these murmurs,
How feeble—since the fetters are about me,
And but one way remains—to curse and perish. [*Exit.*

SCENE V.

The open street. Ferguson and Matthews.

FERGUSON. What quest was that, I pray?
MATTHEWS, [*smiling.*] I must not tell it—
A lady's in the secret.
FERGUSON. Keep it then.
But give yourself no farther care for Warren.
His last words, when we parted yesterday,
Implied his absence till the latest moment.
He'll be with us to-day, when we are ready.
MATTHEWS. 'Twill do no harm at least to hurry him.
FERGUSON. Have you seen Blasinghame?
MATTHEWS. This morning? No.
FERGUSON. You know not he and Maurice fought at sunset?
MATTHEWS. Indeed! How did they fight?
FERGUSON. With swords.
MATTHEWS. What then?
FERGUSON. Why, Maurice had him at his mercy!
MATTHEWS. And spared his life?
FERGUSON. He did, but had been much more merciful
To have taken it,—for he has crush'd the other!
MATTHEWS. How! Blasinghame!
FERGUSON. Has wither'd in a night.
MATTHEWS. Good Heaven! Impossible! What! Imbecile!
FERGUSON. He stares in vacancy—his hair's grown white,—
He trembles as with palsy, and he weeps,
Even as an infant!
MATTHEWS. What a change is this!

FERGUSON. He's useless to us now; and Savage grows
More friendly now to Maurice than to me.
MATTHEWS. This Maurice wrecks us all.
FERGUSON. But, in an hour,—
Let Warren be but faithful to his pledges,
And we shall see his vessel in a tempest,
Such as no bark can weather.
MATTHEWS. Be it so—
My breath shall not be wanting to the blow! [*Exeunt.*

SCENE VI.

The interior of the City Hall of St. Louis. A raised platform in the centre. Citizens crowding about it. Chairman presiding and seated with other distinguished men. On one hand, Ferguson and others—opposite, Norman Maurice, Mercer, Brooks, &c. Norman Maurice discovered speaking.

MAURICE. Thus have we, sir, discuss'd the several questions
Involved in this upon the Constitution—
I trust that, on this instrument, I speak
The doctrines of Missouri. I would have it
A ligament of fix'd, unchanging value,
Maintain'd by strict construction,—neither warp'd,
Nor stretch'd, nor lopt of its now fair proportions,
By the ambitious demagogue or statesman,
Who, with the baits of station in their eyes,
Still sacrifice the State! Our policy,
Should hold ours as a linkéd realm of nations
Where each one sits secure, however feeble,
And, pointing to the sacred written record,

Finds in it her Palladium. Government,
We hold to be the creature of our need,
Having no power but where necessity,
Still under guidance of the Charter, gives it.
Our taxes raised to meet our exigence,
And not for waste or favorites—our people
Left free to share the commerce of the world,
Without one needless barrier on their prows!
Our industry at liberty for venture,
Neither abridged, nor pamper'd; and no calling
Preferr'd before another, to the ruin,
Or wrong of either. These, sir, are my doctrines!
They are the only doctrines which shall keep us
From anarchy, and that worst peril yet,
That threatens to dissever, in the tempest,
That married harmony of hope with power,
Which keeps our starry Union o'er the storm,
And, in the sacred bond that links our fortunes,
Makes us defy its thunders!—Thus, in one,—
The foreign despot threatens us in vain.
Guizot and Palmerston may fret to see us
Grasping the empires which they vainly covet,
And stretching forth our trident o'er the seas,
In rivalry with Britain. They may chafe,
But cannot chain us. Balances of power,
Framed by corrupt and cunning monarchists,
Weigh none of our possessions; and the seasons
That mark our mighty progress, East and West,
Show Europe's struggling millions, fondly seeking,
The better shores and shelters that are ours.
Enough, sir—I have yielded my opinions,
Freely deliver'd, frankly argued, fairly,
With deference to the learning and the wisdom,

Shown by my opponent! The rest is yours.
CHAIRMAN. You have heard, citizens; what farther order
Is it your pleasure, that we—
MERCER. Sir, it needs not!—
The ample range that this debate hath taken,
The spacious grasp of argument upon it—
How well discuss'd the questions—how complete
And clear, the several reasons which concluded,—
Leave none in doubt of what should be our judgment.
Methinks there's but one matter now before us,
And this decided, stays the whole discussion,—
By showing, in our preference for the man,
What still hath been our thoughts upon his measures.
Well have the advocates on both sides spoken,
Not equally, but well! For Ferguson,
His eloquence honors his experience past,
And ancient reputation;—but, methinks,
That none who listen'd to the speech of Maurice,
But must have yielded to his clear opinions;—
Enforced by illustrations near and foreign,
Such full analysis, such profound research—
Statements so fairly made,—objections battled
So fearlessly—and arguments sustain'd
With so much equal truth and eloquence!
His views are mine—are those of this assembly!
Nay more—I boldly challenge in their favor
The voices of Missouri! What remains—
But that we speak to her assembled wisdom?
This day they choose a Senator in Congress—
Whom shall we name to them of all our people?
1ST VOICE. Why, Norman Maurice!
2D VOICE. Who but Norman Maurice?
3D VOICE. The widow's friend—the champion of the people!

BROOKS. Such is the popular will!

FERGUSON. A moment, sir!
If eloquence and talent, just opinion,
Were the sole requisite, for this high station,
I should be silent here, or probably,
Join with you in the shout for Norman Maurice.
But truth and virtue claim a place with talent,
And he who serves, our Senator in Congress,
Must know no smutch of shame upon his garments.

MAURICE. Ha! shame, sir?

FERGUSON. That was the word, sir.

MAURICE. Shame of mine?

FERGUSON. Of thine!

MAURICE. Speak, sir; I listen.

FERGUSON. It is charged, sir,
That Norman Maurice, ere he sought St. Louis,
Was once a resident of Philadelphia;
That there he forged a paper on a merchant,
Well known, by which he gain'd two thousand dollars!

MAURICE. A falsehood! false as hell! As God's in heaven,
I never did this thing!

FERGUSON. The proof is here!

MAURICE. The proof! What proof?

FERGUSON. Know you one Robert Warren?
Ha! you are silent, sir—you start, you redden!—

MAURICE. With scorn and indignation, not with terror!
I do know Robert Warren; that base reptile
Whom thrice I spared the scourge. Set him before me,
And you shall see whose tremors speak the guilty,
And whose the innocent, aroused to vengeance!

FERGUSON. Have then your wish! Accuser! Robert Warren!
Stand forth and answer! [*Pause.*

MAURICE. He dare not!

FERGUSON. He will!

MAURICE. Shout for your man again. Set him before me.

FERGUSON. Call at the door, there—call for Robert Warren.

VOICE WITHOUT. Ho! Robert Warren, Robert Warren! Ho!

Enter Harry Matthews hastily, and in great agitation.

MATTHEWS. Who calls for Robert Warren? He is murder'd,—
Stabb'd with a dagger, and was found a corse,
Within the wood behind the house of Maurice.
Here is the dagger, found upon the body,
And crusted with his blood. [*Showing dagger.*

MAURICE. Murder'd! Give it me! [*Seizes the dagger, looks at and drops it.*
Great God! 'tis hers! [*Aside.*]

MATTHEWS. Behold the murderer!
He staggers! It is he hath done the deed!

FERGUSON. Ay, truly,—who so like to do the deed,
As one who needs to silence such a witness.

MAURICE. Thy bitter jealousy and hate delude thee,
And make thee but a liar. I convict thee,
Out of the mouths of thine own witnesses.—
When saw you Warren last? [*To Matthews.*]

MATTHEWS. Noon yesterday:
He left me then to seek *your* house.

MAURICE. *My house!*
What would he at my house?

MATTHEWS. I do not know.
But know that from that hour until the present,
When now we find him by your house a corse,
He has no more been seen.

MAURICE. 'Tis fortunate,
That we may get the truth from fraud and cunning,
Even when it makes against them. Noon yesterday

Found me in public court-house, on a trial,
Before a thousand eyes, till four o'clock!

FERGUSON. But after that?

MAURICE. My witness here is Mercer.

MERCER. From that hour
Till sunset, he continued at my house,
Then left with Captain Catesby, to return
With dark, and to remain with us all night,
Most part in consultation with our friends,
Who did not separate until near the dawn.

FERGUSON. Then, till this hour?

CATESBY. With me! We slept together!

MAURICE. Man of a bitter malice, art thou answer'd?

FERGUSON. Thou 'scapest the murder, not the forgery.
Warren was not the only evidence;
Where's Richard Osborne?

OSBORNE, [*coming forward.*] Here!

FERGUSON. All do not fail us!
Your name is Richard Osborne! You know Maurice,
And know the crime which Warren charged upon him?
He named you as his witness.

OSBORNE. He did wrong, then!
I know of no offence of Norman Maurice—
Yet know him well, and all I know of him,
Hath still approved him, to my sense and judgment,
The noblest, as he is the first of men!

1. PEOPLE SHOUT. Hurrah for that!

2. PEOPLE SHOUT. Hurrah for Norman Maurice!

FERGUSON. Confusion!

MATTHEWS. I'm off. [*Exeunt Matthews and Ferg*

PEOPLE, [*with cries and hisses.*] Away with Fergusor .

MERCER, [*to Maurice.*] Your triumph is complete!

BROOKS. All's well!

MAURICE. Tell me that!—
All's well!—You spoke! Did you not say, my wife?
What of her—speak!

MERCER. You're ill! Your lips are very pale!
But courage, all your trial's over now.

MAURICE. Art sure of that? Let me but understand it!—

MERCER. 'Twould seem so!—What a foul conspiracy,
So fatally arrested. For this murder—

MAURICE. What of it?

MERCER. 'Tis very strange!

MAURICE. Very strange indeed!

MERCER. But stranger still the audacious charge against you.
Who was this Warren?

MAURICE, [*with an effort.*] Who? but here is one,
To put you in possession of the story.
He knows how dexterously a lie was founded,
Most monstrous, on the basis of a truth,
By this same Warren, to my injury. [*Osborne comes forward.*
Osborne, I thank you for your ready answer,
And good opinion.

OSBORNE. It was but your right.

MAURICE. What is that cry? my fears— [*Noise without.*

Enter Kate, followed by Mrs. Jervas.

KATE. Oh! Sir! Your wife!

MAURICE. My wife! Be still my heart. What of my wife?

KATE. She's sick! Oh! very sick!

MRS. JERVAS. She's broke blood-vessel!

MAURICE, [*with a cry.*] God! thou hast sent
This Terror, like a fate into my house,
And wreck'd the hope that nestled there in peace!—
Hence, woman, from my sight!
My wife! My wife! [*Rushes out.*

MERCER, [*to Catesby.*] Follow him with a surgeon.

BROOKS. What a day's history of storm and sorrow!
There is some cruel mystery in these doings,
Which we must fathom! This conspiracy,
For such it clearly shows, makes for our party;
Let's hasten to the use of it. They'll never
Hold up their heads again. The people's with us,
The assembly waits us and will crown our triumph!

SCENE VII.

A chamber in the house of Norman Maurice. Clarice reclines upon a couch. The widow Pressley stands at a little distance watching her.

WIDOW. Dear lady, you will die.

CLARICE. Do not come near me!

WIDOW. You bleed! You suffocate!

CLARICE. And still he comes not.
You promised me to send for him. Oh, God—
Should they behold these papers. Ha! I hear him.
Do you hear nothing?

WIDOW. Nothing!

CLARICE. I hear! 'Tis he!

MAURICE, [*without.*] Clarice! my wife!

Enter Norman Maurice.

MAURICE. Speak! Tell me! Where!—Clarice. [*Seeing her.*

CLARICE. Oh! now you come! Heaven bless! I'm dying, Norman!

[*Raises herself feebly to his arms.*

MAURICE. Dying!

CLARICE. I feel it; but——

MAURICE. The surgeon! God of heaven!—

CLARICE. He cannot help me now. Too late! no succor,—
I've but the words for blessing and farewell!—
I'm sinking;—but you're safe! Safe! Oh! the rapture,
To know it, and to whisper in your ears,
With the last loving words. He would have crush'd you—
Made infamous your name, my noble husband;
But stoop,—your ear—he'll trouble us no more.
He's silent—and I have the fatal papers;—
No copies—all the originals.—Ha! Ha!—
They're here—now take me,—closer—to your heart;
I leave you—lose you—Norman. Ah! your lips,—
How cold, but sweet, my Norman—cold—sweet—Norman! [*Dies.*

MAURICE. Now sink my soul!—since the bright star is gone,
That made thy life and glory from the heavens—
That stored thee with all blessings. I am crush'd!
Ha! what are these! (*lays her down gently—the papers fall from her bosom.*
Oh, God! I see it all.
Oh, bloody wretch, whose nature was a lie,
This was thy work,—not hers. 'Tis plain before me.
My poor Clarice! how faithful unto death,
Shielding me at the peril of thyself,
And, in the seeming dread necessity,
Doing the deed that from its delicate props,
Shook the fair fabric of thy innocent life!
My wife! My wife! [*Sinks down.*

[*Noise and voices without.*]

PEOPLE. Hurrah for Norman Maurice!

Enter Mercer, Brooks, and others.

MERCER. Maurice, my friend, we triumph. You are Senator

For the next term, in Congress, from Missouri.

MAURICE. Couldst wake her with thy tidings!

MERCER. God! This is death!

MAURICE. It lies upon her silent lips like snow.
Oh! do not speak—she hears not! why should I?
Nor sorrow, nor joy shall fill these frozen eyes,
That see not me. She would have listen'd once,
How gladly,—and found music in the triumph,
That now can bring me none. My wife! My wife!

THE END.

ATALANTIS;

A STORY OF THE SEA.

> " 'Tis not vain or fabulous,—
> Though so esteem'd by shallow ignorance,—
> What the sage Poets, taught by th' heavenly Muse,
> Storied of old in high immortal verse,
> Of dire chimeras and enchanted isles,
> And rifted rocks."—Milton.

The first edition of "Atalantis" was published in 1832. It has been subsequently revised, and, I trust, amended. I am not satisfied that the dramatic form was appropriately adopted, since it leads to expectations which the character of the poem will scarcely satisfy. The advantage of the dialogue consists simply in permitting that diversification of the descriptive portions, which, in a work so purely fanciful, would seem necessary to prevent monotony.—This poem, with those pieces which follow it, belongs to a class, the standards of which are almost entirely imaginative. The reader who looks here for the merely human sentiment, will find himself at fault. The province of poetry is too various for the application of laws derived wholly from individual tastes; and he who opens the pages of an author must always be prepared to ascend that mount of vision from which he has made his survey. The highest regions of the ideal, are unquestionably such as belong to the spiritual nature. To this nature, exclusively, verse which is solely imaginative must commend itself. It is not the less human, though it may be more remote and foreign, than that which simply appeals to mortal passions, and the more earthly purposes of man and life.

PERSONS OF THE POEM.

ONESIMARCHUS, *a King of Sea-Demons.*
COUNT LEON, *a noble Spanish Knight.*
MENDEZ CELER, *Captain of the Arragon.*
OGRÉ, *a slave of Onesimarchus.*
Mariners, Demons, &c., &c.

ATALANTIS, *a Princess of the Nereids.*
NEA, *her attendant.*
LADY ISABEL, *sister to Count Leon.*

ZEPHYR-SPIRIT.
TININA,
CARETA,
NANITA,
LOLINE, } *Fairies.*

ATALANTIS.

ACT I.—SCENE I.

An Islet of the Atlantic Ocean.

ATALANTIS AND ONESIMARCHUS.

Atal. Get thee hence, monster, I defy thee now,
As late I scorn'd thee. Thy base threats are vain,
And thy lures idle. All in vain thy prayer,—
And, in thy promise, do I nothing see
To move my spirit;—nothing to misguide
My firm persuasion, that so foul a thing
Should have no thought of mine.
Onesi. I prithee, hold!
Be charier of thy feèlings;—have a care,
If thou dost love thyself and wouldst be free!
Beseems thee not this proud authority,
In such condition as I hold thee now.
Look round thee, lovely Atalant!—Survey
My wondrous power, and heed the prison house,
Most fit for thee to flutter in,—not fly!
Thou art my captive, maiden, bound by spells,
Potent as night, that, struggle as thou mayst,
Mock thy best effort, and defy thy hopes.
Atal. Foul tyrant, I despise thee and thy power,
And laugh at all thy threats. I know thee well,

Thy strength, thy spells, thy hatefulness, and all
That makes thee what thou art!—

ONESI. Dost know thyself?

ATAL. Ay, my own weakness, now,—yet nothing fear
Thy greater strength in this my overthrow.

ONESI. Thou fear'dst not this?

ATAL. I did not; yet I knew,
Even ere the moment of captivity,
That thou hadst power for this. 'Twas in my scorn,—
In the full feeling of my pride and strength,
Mocking thy gross dominion,—that I grew
Improvident of caution.

ONESI. Yet, beware!
Lest a new lesson counsel thee to fears
Thy scorn believes not now.

ATAL. Oh! get thee hence!
Think'st thou I am so shallow, not to know
Thy close impassable limit? Am I not,
Thrice guarded in myself, with power mine own,
Match'd unto thine, and know I not that thou—
Howe'er in captive bound thou keep'st me now,
Having robb'd me of the wand that serves my will,
By a foul trickery worthy of thyself,—
Hast not the might—unless I do forget
My better nature and give way to thine—
A wretched madness, most impossible!—
To graze with licensed breath the idlest hair,
That wantons from my shoulder. Get thee hence,—
I dread thee not, thou monstrous impotence!

ONESI. Hold! or thou wilt impel me unto wrath,
When I would love thee!

ATAL. Do I fear thy wrath?
And prat'st thou of thy love, thou crooked game-make,
Thou gross deformity!—how I could laugh

At thy rough gambols in an element
Made for pure spirits, and the delicate grace
Of the angelic youth and morning beauty,—
But that a prison laugh is seemly sad,
And turns into a sorrow.

ONESI. So shall thine,
If thou bethink not oft'ner of thy bound!
Thou art a sprightly and most pleasant child,
But all unlearn'd by crude adversity,
Else wouldst thou teach thyself another mood,
And reason in the guise of circumstance.
Wert thou array'd in panoply of war,
With all thy armies on the equal field,
Naught wanting to thy might, the spoken taunt
Were not unseemly;—now, it hath an air
That ill becomes thy lip and present state.

ATAL. And wouldst thou teach, oh! rare philosopher,
The prudence of compliance with the law,
Of that worst fate, a base necessity?
Why, thou'dst disfigure truth, and all distort
The fairer argument into the foul,
Make right a truckler to expediency
And conjure virtue with the spells of fear,
Till she grows common, a base thing of time,
Having but present office. Thou hast err'd,—
For, but suppose me ignorant of good,
Untutor'd in truth's excellence, and all
That virtue wills to beauty,—*thee* I know,
And know to hate the lesson thou wouldst teach.

ONESI. Thou'rt rash, fair damsel, rash and ill advised!
Beware of what thou say'st—to prudence hold;
Remember, when thy spirit would offend,
Thou art the captive to my greater power.

ATAL. Thy greater cunning—thy dishonest guile!

ONESI. And that is greater power, thou simple child;—
And, as thou art a captive, let thy speech
Mate with thy fortunes. I deny thee now
A farther range than suits my jealous mood;
And I shall guard thee well, and watch thy steps,
And check thee when thou trippest. On thy paths,
My slaves, that never close the eye, attend,
And, though thou seest them not———

ATAL. I see them not!—
Thou dost forget my nature and my power;—
Let me but wave my hand thus, with a will!—
What call you this blear imp?

[*She waves her hand, and Ogré becomes visible.*

ONESI. Ha! thou base whelp?
Did I not warn thee?—wherefore didst thou lurk,
Thus nigh, to feel her spells?—but thou shalt learn.
Shall I not have obedience where I rule?
Ho! Runa! Merla! take this sodden slave
And bind him to his pits against the rock,
Till midnight—let the scourge be well applied,
While his shrieks wake the drowsy mariner,
Filling his head with storms, for which they make
Fit music, and foretell!

OGRE. Master, oh, spare!
The day grows dark, and the night rushes on,
Long ere the accustomed hour. The cruel scourge
Will torture, and the wrath upon the wave,
Will dash me into madness 'gainst the rocks.

ONESI. Take him hence! away!

OGRE. Spare me,—'twas my zeal
To serve thee, that o'erstepp'd. But pardon now,
I err not thus again. Be pitiful!
Merla doth own for me a silent grudge,
And will outstretch thy order. He will bind

Both hands and feet, and, with a double thong,
Will tear my flesh, then mock me with keen gibes,
Until I faint, while the cold cavern waves
Do creep about and wrap me!

ONESI. Not in vain:
Though he doth punish thee as thou hast said,
Thou shalt not perish. Hence with him. Ye stand
As if ye did delight in his discourse,
Insolent with himself.

ATAL. Oh! thou art stern—
A tyrant 'gainst all nature, that will spurn
The kneeling wretch, but for excess of zeal
Doing thy bidding truly.

ONESI. 'Tis for thee
I punish him, fair Atalant.

ATAL. For me!

ONESI. Hath he not hung too closely on thy steps,
Intrusive, watching thee most narrowly
Beyond my will? Shalt thou not be secure
From what offends thee?

ATAL. 'Tis thou offend'st me!
Make me secure from thee, and 'gainst thy slave
I shall have instant remedy.

ONESI. Still thus!

ATAL. Ay, ever!—while the light lasts of my life,
Thought, feeling, best affection. 'Tis for me
That thou wouldst punish him?—then set him free;—
The wrong that he has done is done to me,
And I forgive it him.

ONESI. It fits thee well,
This ready spirit of mercy which conceives,
And grants the boon ere spoken. Not so me,
'Twere a poor state, and brief the power, if thus,
O'er-zealous though it be, each slave should leap,

His bound unchasten'd. Hence with him, away!
The scourge shall lessen his o'er-ready zeal,
And midnight seas, and colds, and biting airs
Shall teach him penitence. [*Ogré is led off.*

ATAL. Thou cruel king!
Hadst thou by other qualities of grace
Master'd the heart that feels for thee but scorn,
This merciless act of thine had set it free;
Had robb'd it of persuasion of thy worth
In every office; and, from virtuous meed,
Had pluck'd all fair deserving, that had else
Been yielded by just tribute.

ONESI. Thou wrong'st me;—
And chid'st too harshly the o'ercoming sway,
Which keeps dominion safe, and makes it strong.
Wouldst thou not master? Is the woman heart
Unfriendly to the pleasant tastes of power?
I know thee better,—better know thy sex—
Esteem thee as the rest,—born with the love
Of measureless rule,—the will to reach afar,
Plucking down station, putting strength aside,
Till, in the midst, alone, o'er all thou stand'st,
All fearing, all adoring!

ATAL. How thou soar'st!
And this thy aim, how fruitlessly thy rule
Is wasted on the wretched slave that cowers,
Hopeless and still submissive, to his lord.
Onesimarchus, I despise thee more,
That I have seen thee in the wid'st extent
Of thy dominion.

ONESI. 'Tis well! But thou shalt feel,—
So shalt thou better know,—how great the power
Thou mock'st at, in thy ignorance and pride!
And though, unless by wanton will of thine,

I may not gain possession of thy form,
Yet shall I so constrain thee by my arts,
So work upon thy weakness—so forbid
All bent of inclination,—all desire,—
Curtailing every thought that does not tend
To the fierce satisfaction of my want,—
That thou shalt yield thyself in very dread,
Though thy heart loathe me in its secret mood,
And every sense grow outraged at the fate
To which thou still submit'st.

ATAL. Oh! shallow slave!
This is thy precious scheme! And there thou stand'st,
With thy red gloating eye stretch'd 'yond its sphere,
Glaring with foul and fiend imaginings—
Thy lip, that quivers with voluptuous rage,
Thicken'd with vicious fury,—thy scant brows,
Retreating wide and back, with wool o'erhung,
That links thee with the sooty African
Who wallows in thy worship;—there thou stand'st,
Blinded with beastly hope, that thou canst will
A spirit so pure as mine to leave its sphere,
And come, untended and unlighted, down,
From its bright mansions, to thy pool and cave!
Till now, my thought had been that, with thy power,
There was a sense to give it dignity,
And marshal thy gross attributes with state
Into considerate order. But not now,—
When I look on thee, so incapable,—
So wanting in that art, which, when it lacks,
Strength is a toiling giant up the hills
That never wins the summit—all my hate
Subsides into a feeling less than scorn,
Which cannot yet be pity. Prithee, go,—
Thou dost but move me to unseemly mirth,

Which yet I would not.

ONESI. Nay! give it vent and words!
Thy wit is lively; thou hast eloquence;
I feel that thou might'st chafe me, were it not
That there will be a season too for me,
When I may answer thee.

ATAL. What canst thou more?
Thou hast done all in stealing me away
From mine own kingdom with thy felon arts:
And this shall find its punishment ere long,
For, even now, in Mergevan, my town,
I do, by precious instincts, see the array
Of thousands, whom my brothers, to the war,
Will haste with meet decision. Thou, methinks,
Hast proved their arms before;—a little while,
The proofs shall be renew'd,—and what shall then
Be thy fond refuge, when their mighty powers
Descend on thee to battle?

ONESI. Let them come!
I shall be ready then—am ready now!
Thou speak'st with a rare confidence, but know,
I took thee not, thus boldly, from thy realms,
Till I had meetly, with commission'd force,
Prepared for all thy battles. Thou forget'st
The strength I bring—the powers that, in a trice,
From farthest ocean I can call at once,
Where the deep thickens to a bed of reeds;
And from the kings that o'er the whirlpools sway,
Gather'd to my allegiance, by a blast
Upon the shell I bear within my hand.
Thou seem'st to have forgotten too, methinks,
That, by my single arm, thy mother's first,
And thy own brother, fiercest of them all,
Fell, like an infant, impotent, o'erthrown!

What though I lost the conflict, did ye gain?
Was not your city of the rocks destroy'd
By the wild waves, which, in my wanton mood,
O'erwent and left them prostrate;—while thyself,
An infant then, rock'd in a purple shell,
'Twixt two obedient billows, scarce preserved,
Wast borne away, affrighted, in the arms
Of thy most humble follower. This, methinks,
Thy memory lacks, and I repeat it thee,
Not for the glory of mine own exploit,
But to remind me of the groundless hope
On which thou build'st for safety.

ATAL. It is well!
Thou hast chosen for thy wooing a fit style,
And most judicious, when that thou relat'st
Thy bloody traffic with thyself and mine.

ONESI. Thyself hast moved me to 't.

ATAL. I blame thee not,
Rude monster, for the evil thou hast done,
And sought beyond thy utmost power to do!
'Tis in thy nature. There is on thy front
The character of the beast. Thy savage eye,
Fix'd in thy bloated and unmeasured face,
From which it glares like some red, baleful star,
Upon a dismal, dusk, unspeaking blank,—
Hath mark'd thee strongly. Labor as thou mayst—
Speak, like thy shell, in music—let thy words
Be like the honey dews, that, on the rocks,
Nursed in the hollows, nightly fall from heaven,
A solace for the storm-bird and the gull,—
Yet art thou fatal to the spells thou hast,
And bafflest thine own art. Thou canst not change;
The beast is high o'er all, a monstrous mock,
In contradiction of itself and strength—

So that the very sweets that thou mayst own
Grow poisonous in thy use.

ONESI. Oh, thou dost well,
And wisely, urging me to anger thus,
Till thou dost dissipate that kindly sense,
At variance with my spirit, which my love,
Bids live in thy behalf. Dost thou not fear,
That, vex'd by thy sharp mock and wanton speech,
My love shall grow to hatred?

ATAL. Be it so!
I heed thee not—thy anger scorn, not fear;—
Thou art of those, being the foe to truth,
That are, when friendliest, most inimical,—
And dost most harm in doing seeming good,
And art most hateful, most injurious,
When most professing love! I fear thee not,—
Though by an active cunning—and yet less,
By active cunning than mine own neglect,—
Gaining the advance upon us, thou hast made
A prisoner and dire enemy of one,
Who, in another chance, and other time,
Had never made so little of her thought,
To waste it on thee.

ONESI. Wilt thou nothing, then,
To gain thy freedom? Thou wilt surely smile,
Look pleased in some small sort, and speak him well,
Whose power alone can free thee.

ATAL. Trust not that!
I shall be free by other means, and soon!
I barter not my grace for mine own right;—
Lest that the gift, misused, grow valueless!—
Thou hast no boon in all thy store and might
Which I can give thee thanks for. In myself
The means of freedom rest.

ONESI. [*aside.*] Ha! in herself!
I snatch'd from her the powerful wand which made
The elements do her bidding. What remains?

ATAL. A power, which as it teaches me to know
The secret thought thou speak'st not, cannot be
Wrench'd from my firm possession.

ONESI. We shall see!
Thy instincts may declare my thought, but cannot
Avail to give thee freedom. All in vain
Thy hope, whether within thyself it be,
Or in the armies which thy brothers raise—
Here, powerless in the conflict, useless all;—
For, in the air, I've thrown a circling spell,
Borrow'd from night and silence,—which, being gross,
Far grosser than the elements which make
Your finer tempers, ye may not withstand!
This will resist them! Into this, who comes,
Not fitted like ourselves to meet its power,
Blinded and shorn of strength, falls feebly down,
And straight is thrall'd forever. All around
Our island limit, where the ocean breaks,
This element is scattered;—like a wall,
Shutting out all invasion,—closing all,
Within, from commerce with the realm without!
Thus art thou girdled now. Denied thy wand—
Which, in yon rock, within a mystic frame,
Moulded by midnight spells, in halls where rule
Thousands of spirits dethroned, I have encased
And seal'd with magic, and the mighty word
Given me at creation as a spell,
That consummates my will;—thou canst not break
The narrow circle of thy prison bound,
And taste the finer element, whose breath
Might bring thee to thy power.

Atal. Thy prudence well
Hath counselled thee of dangers thou must dread—
Dangers best studied in thy strong defence
And wily combinations. But thy art
Is shallow like thy power. A little while,
Watch as thou mayst, the wand is mine again,
And whatsoe'er its faculty, be sure
It shall be raised against thee. Thou shalt be
O'erthrown when most secure; and, like the bird,
Slain by its stronger fellow, as thou saw'st
Upon the morn I fell thy prisoner,
Even from thy topmost pinnacle struck down,
Thy fall shall mate thy arrogance of flight,
Beneath the lowest, low. How should my soul,
Strong among giant spirits, hark or heed
Thy profferings or thy threats? What canst thou do
To bend my purer nature unto thine,
In base extremity, unless I yield,
Wanton, and shorn of the true woman strength,—
Which finds best nutriment in innocence,
And lives mature in its own delicate essence,
A power in due degree with chastity,—
To meet thy brutal want and foul desire,
Thou that art foulest! Thou hast 'vantage won,
And when I slept thou waked'st; and I now,
For a brief season, suffer that I slept,—
That the condition of all negligence,—
When, with a subtle and dishonest foe,
Such as thou art, in certain neighborhood,
We should have watch'd with armament prepared,
And every weapon bright, and high rock lit,
Kindled with sea-spar into ruddiness!
So hadst thou shrunk away, scared by the blaze,
Cowering, with backward terror, till the sun,

Thy nature's dread, thy great antipathy,
Leaping from off his billowy bed at morn,
No cloud about his brow, and strong from sleep,
Drives thee, with glittering shafts that never fail,
Blinded and bellowing to thy marshy gulfs.

Onesi. Dost thou exult, and is my fate so sure,—
And shalt thou have thy liberty so soon,
As thou dost fancy? Then, a gentler speech
Had better graced thy lips as conqueror,
Over the feeble foe thou canst not fear.
But let me win thee to some fair constraint
Of seeming amnesty. A truce awhile,
To this so keen and profitless retort,
Which keeps us thus asunder. Let us each
Heed reason from the other. Thou hast said,
With hope 'yond expectation, that thou look'st
For soon and certain help. I see not this
Present or in far prospect; nor beyond,
In the imperfect future, can I frame
The aid thou look'st for from thy tribute realms.
These things affright me not as once before,—
My kingdom as it is, all well prepared
To keep its own, and conquer, right or wrong.
Its barriers shut out hope from thee, unless
Thou swerv'st my settled feeling, which thou mayst
By seasonable yielding—so shall both
Our anxious purpose win;—thy freedom thou,
And I, the sweet accomplishment of that
Which flames desire within me! Well I know
My power can go no farther than thou will'st,
In this so dear condition,—but thou art,
My prisoner still—and that may move thy wish,
Not capable of liberty unless
My will shall break thy fetters. Hear me then,

Since this our opposition.

ATAL. Speak! I hear!

ONESI. Become my bride,—nay, patiently!—smile not—
My queen, if better lists thee. On my throne,—
Thou hast beheld its state,—of emeralds made,
Each one a crowning and a marvellous gem,
Set round the spacious bosom of a shell
Torn from a fierce sea-monster—one who bore
The miracled wonder on his glittering back,
And battled for it as became its worth,
Nor lost it ere his life;—thy hand shall wield,—
Fit hand for such a rule!—a sceptred wand,
Pluck'd from an ocean cave of farthest Ind,
By ancient giants held,—a pillär'd spire,
Of holiest sapphire, which at evening burns
Deeper than ever sunlight, and around
Lights up the sable waters many a league,
From sea to shore, till the scared 'habitants
Fly to their cover in the wood, nor dream
How sportive is the sway of that Sea-Queen,
Who rides the waves and makes them smile by night.

ATAL. Oh! wonderful! most wonderful!

ONESI. Dost scorn?—
But let me not be anger'd. Hear me still.—
These are but shown thee to declare the fruit,
The effect, perchance, but not the source of might,
So fertile as is mine. But thou shalt know,
That, of the full division of these seas,
One part of which thou hold'st, the great'st is mine;
My realm the wid'st; and, of the numerous powers
That hold dominion in these provinces,
Most are to me as tributary bound,
Sworn to my bidding, subject to my will,
Compell'd for peace and war! These, if I bid,

I gather such array, as leaves my power
Unmatchable by all the tribes that swarm
Thy cities, when the starlight wakes the dance.

Atal. I know not that! The kingdom which I hold
Though in extent less spacious, is not less
Proportion'd to the incidents of war!
Thou hast wide realm of sea, but scatter'd tribes;
Canst gambol hugely when the waves are smooth,
With uncouth legions; but when sounds the gong,
Struck sharply on our headlands, they go down,
Sudden, in search of shadowing slime and reeds,
Forgetting all their state and mocking thine,
Indifferent where they hide. Thou mayst o'ercome
The sluggish monster, that, upon the deep,
Slumbers at noonday,—winning, with his life
The useless glitter of his cumbrous shell;—
But, for becoming enemy, thou hast
But little armament of serious force,
Save, as I said, in fraud and stratagem.
Art answer'd?

Onesi. Wouldst thou more?

Atal. Oh! say thy thought!

Onesi. Meetly indulgent for a captive maid.—
I will proceed, and leave thee to decide,
Whether, a free and queenly mistress, thou
Ascend'st a monarch's throne and shar'st his rule,
Strong in sustaining majesty and pride,
Or, vainly chafing at thy prison bar,
Rav'st for the freedom that but mocks thy sight,
In gleams of blessed sky, or sudden breath
Of zephyr from the seas, or glimpse of wing,
Lustrous in noonday sunlight, that thou see'st
Disparting the white clouds!

Atal. Go on! Go on!

ONESI. Three princely cities own my single rule,—
Hamlets unnumber'd,—homes that, scatter'd wide,
Hath each a mighty circle for a court,
Might clasp your utter empire. Plain and cave
Are thus made rich in dwellings for a tribe.
Each rock hath its high palace. Not a wave
Spans its receding billow but o'erswims
Some golden habitation; where the light,
A mitigated splendor, like the moon,
Without its chill and solitude, comes down
From empires where a thousand suns abide,
Struggling with rival splendors to inflame
A thousand realms like ours. There, subtle gems,
With glories such as starlight flings on earth,
Adorn the innoxious serpents, that for aye
Through the long hours, with toil that mocks fatigue,
Nightly replenishing their founts of light,
Trail through the giant groves, and meet in vales
Whose lavish wealth, in absence of the sun,
Still recompense his beams. There shalt thou see
Rocks, in their own gifts marvellous, at stroke
Of wondrous masters, spring to palaces;
And, at a word, as thou hast cause to know,
Fair islands, flush with flowers, and rich in airs
Of most persuasive odor, break the deeps,
And gather in the sunlight. And again,
Even at the will of him whose sovereign power
Thou mock'st at in thy mood, evanishing,
Forget they had existence;—cheating thus
The gaze of simple mariner, who dreams
That, towards evening, he beholds the land
And cries it to his fellows,—who straight cheer
The hungering hope within them, while they spread
The broad and yellow sail, and urge their prows,

To find at last,—so wills my cunning art—
Some hazy cloud, that hangs with mocking skirts
Where slept the wooing land as night came down.

ATAL. Ay, thou art all a cheat! 'Tis like thyself
To mock the weary heart, and still to vex
The sick soul's expectation. But thy power,
As thou describ'st it in thy fairest speech,
And most imploring aspect, moves not me,
And wins me not in wonder or in love.
The simple mariner who needs the barque,
Which, in their reckless mood, the waves may wreck,
And wanton winds destroy, affords, methinks,
But little trophy, with his bleaching bones,
On desert sands, and isles beyond thy gulf,
To him who conquers thus, even by a will,
Without the joy of conflict. Spare, I pray,
Thy farther story. Breathe, and let me breathe,
Some purer air than that which from thy lips
Assails each wholesome sense with sickliness.

ONESI. Wilt thou not hear me?

ATAL. Can I else than hear,
Close girt as my poor fortunes find me now?
Wer't in my will, thou shouldst play orator
To things of thy own fashion, not to me!
Thy jewel-headed serpents, the huge beast
Thou rid'st to war, and whom, when met by foes
Thou canst not baffle here, thou send'st to land,
To trample down the cities of the tribes
That only wet their feet within thy waves,
To bring down ruin on them. Go to these,
And tell them of thy prowess and thy wealth!—
Nor these, nor thee I heed, and would not hear.

ONESI. Thou bind'st thy fetters faster with each word!—
But ho!—That signal breaks my farther speech.

Here are new captives. Prone upon our isle
Comes some adventurous barque that must be stay'd,
And punish'd for its crime. We must not have
Thy presence mock'd with such vile things of earth,
That know not of the rarest beautiful,
Such as adorns thy virtues—makes thy form
Itself a virtue of the beautiful,
That spells all best affections at a glance,
And makes them slaves forever. I must speed
And save thee from these wretches, who shall taste
That power which thou defy'st. But now look forth,
And see the great ship shatter'd into foam;
Fierce, rending wings among its cloud broad vans,
And mounting billows darting up its sides
To drag it down to ruin. Lend thine ear
To the wild music of men's cries;—their shrieks
That the storm mocks, and the ascending seas
Stifle in their own murmurs!—It will need,
Fair Atalant, I leave thee:—yet, ere day
Hath fully, in the chambers of the deep,
Ta'en off his pinions;—ere this gentle eve,
With eyes of ever-dropping dews, hath shut
The sweet unmurmuring flowers,—and bade the night
Summon upon her realm the spirit airs
That all subdue to silence—the voiced things
Of myriad elements and agencies,
That breathe beneath the moon—I shall return
To seek thee with a hope;—ah! not in vain,—
Eager for fitting answer to that prayer
That else must be the stern authority
Of will that breaks resistance. Till that hour,
Thou hast for calm reflection;—let it teach
A sweet response of sympathy to mine,
And love as yielding soft as mine is fond—

Else, let thy fear ———

ATAL. Thou know'st I have no fear!
Get thee hence, monster, to thy work of dread,
Since prayer may never move thee. Thou'st no art
To work upon my terrors. My spirit is made
Of essence far more confident than thine.
Rather thou tremble, that, as I am pure,—
For so the ruler that we all obey
Hath will'd it—and most haply will'd it too—
I may command to use the spirits who rule
O'er the unclouded seasons—those who glide,
Through the illumined mansions of the night,
Teaching the stars their watches—those who sway,
With melodies of power, all elements—
And of the zephyr from the south and west,
The voice that comes with morning, and declares
The hour when day shall droop,—can call a spell
To dissipate the darkness, and dispart
Thy blackest shapes of storm.

ONESI. When thou art free!

ATAL. Alas! that I were free,—then should'st thou feel,
And fly, and learn to spare!

ONESI. Now, I despise
And, as you speak their agencies, defy
The entire realm of air, the stars, and all,—
Your spirit of the south and of the west,
Your voice of night and morning, and their spells;—
Your tiny tribes, your coral queen—the hosts,
Myriads of lesser power and feebler wing,
That make your choice dominion—all I scorn!
And, but that mine own want would have thee grace
With milder seeming this same prayer of mine,
I should devote thee, heedless of the youth,
The glory and the beauty of thy form,—

Which, to mine eye, foul as you deem its make,
Stands up a rich perfection, born to shine,
In any world of loveliness, the first—
To the same ruin and destruction sure
Thou hold'st for the most hateful enemy.
I love thee not to pleasure thee, or give
A satisfaction craved. I please myself,
And nothing care for others. I play not
The wary hypocrite, but speak my thought,—
My will, even as it rises to my thought;—
Nor seek I for thy love, but only seek
For such equivalent as may suffice,
In love's own absence, my enamored sense.
Thou hear'st me?—and thou know'st me! It is well!
Be wise while thou art wary. I depart. [*Exit Onesi.*

Atal. Ay, go, thou loathsome! Thou hast fill'd the air
With foulness, and my breath is scarce more free
Than the poor form thou hast fetter'd by thy fraud!
Thou, as thy menace, from my thought depart:
I scorn thee and defy thy utmost power!
Thou hast no art to win me to thy will,
And, until I, forgetful of myself,
Do so declare me, thou canst never bend
My spirit to thy purpose. I behold,—
Though in what shape it come I may not see,—
My liberation sure. Awhile, awhile!
Sweet patience in my circumscribed bound,
Give me thy succor. Ere the moon shall soar
Thrice from her saffron chamber—ere the winds,
Sporting thrice round the red embodied day
Shall win him into smiles with melodies—
And, ere the wing'd stars, through the misty vault,
Gleam thrice upon the troubles of the night—
I shall be free this monster's pestilence.
Come hither to me, Nea. Thou, at least,

Art spared me, and he knows not—shallow king!
That knows not his own power, and little dreams,
Of captive but the one. Hither to me,
And let my sad eyes freshen with the sight,
The picture of the gentler clime and race,
In thy perfections, damsel. Wake thy shell,
And with a sweet song from its purple depths,
Call up the happier fancies that preside
O'er the dear hopes we see not. Let me lose
The turbulent thought within me!

SCENE II.—*The same.*

Atalantis, Nea.

NEA. Mistress, here!

ATAL. Thy sweetest song, my Nea,—
Such as he sings, the spirit of the shell,
That brooding in his billows never sleeps,
For longing of his home, and still who hears
Its voices, breathing ever sighs of love,
In echo to his own, by ocean's marge,
Telling of purple islets in the deep,
Where first he won his wings and whence his voice.

SONG OF THE SHELL-SPIRIT.

I.

I am of the sprites of ocean,
  Dweller there, the gentlest one,
And I take my airy motion,
  When the day is done;
It is mine, the voice that rouses
  All the lovely tribes of sea,
From their tiny coral houses,
  Glad to wake with me.

II.

When the sun, in ocean sinking,
  Leaves to fairy power the earth,
When the night stars, slowly winking,
  Bid the winds have birth:
Gently o'er the waters stealing,
  Mine's the song that sweetly flies,
Wooing to one common feeling
  Ocean, earth, and skies.

III.

Loveliest of the zephyr's daughters,
  Born to breathe in bloom and shine,
I can still the angry waters
  With a breath of mine.
Not a stronger spirit rideth
  O'er the rolling waves than I;
Not a lovelier shape abideth
  'Neath the tropic sky.

ATAL. Sweet is the air thou sing'st! Ah! would 'twere true!
Would that our spirit of the shell had power,
Such as thou brag'st of;—it were easy then,
Flung by our billows on this sultry isle,
To conjure up a service at his wings,
Might give us present freedom. Thou hast themes,
Might better suit our state than this, which mocks
Our hearts' best wishes. One of these, my girl,—
Some ditty of old romance, such as our realm—
A spacious province, where the wand'ring thought
And wilder'd fancy, erring, may be lost—
Owns without limit. Thou canst meetly sing
Of bearded-white Ogrear, the giant king,
Who, with the music of his magic horn,
Subdued, and to his pastures midst the rocks,

Guided the monster first, which, in itself,
Is a huge mountain, rolling on the deeps,
Unconscious of his load, though on his back,
Rode the old wizard's tribe—his giant sons
And daughters, an unnumbered family,
That sung in concert to the old man's horn,
Until the monster, drowsing in his path,
Yielded himself, as fast fix'd as an isle,
Through the long summer's day. This were a theme,
Might make us half forgetful that we weep
As fettered as was he. And other themes,—
The gloom that hangs above the prison-house,
Might challenge something from thy memory,
More kindred to the touch of mournful thoughts.
Let thy song teach us of the coming hour,—
Sad time,—when on the perillous journey bent,
We pass the untravell'd valley, till we find,
That other province of delay,—that home,
Of temporary refuge, dark or bright,
As suited to the service we have done,
In past conditions;—other seas, perchance,
Unvex'd by contact with rebellious power,
Such as offends us here;—a happy realm,
Whose provinces are lit by countless smiles,
From the benignant presence of a God,
Whose will is born of love!—or, saddest thought,
Descending from our grade, in baser shape,
Doom'd in the mansions of sea-weed to dwell,
Thence only darting, under cruel impulse,
And chasing, with a terrible agony,
The wild and staring mariner, grown weak,
And hopeless of the shore, his straining balls
Shall never more encounter.

NEA. None of these!—

Too sad thy fortunes now for themes so sad.—
But I would rather from my memory call,
Some of those ditties sung in happier days,
Which thou hast bid me thrice and thrice repeat,
And ever with the tear within thine eye,
Which spoke thy pleasure—when, upon the close,
Thou didst, unconscious, with mine own chime in
The murmurs of thy melancholy voice,
Till the vex'd waters, wroth with overflow,
Subdued their sullen crests, in service rapt,
And, at thy feet, in murmurs like thine own,
Grew captive to our song. There is one strain
Methinks might glad thine ear, of Coraline—
One of those gentle damsels of the groves,
Whom sometimes we see sporting on the isles,
Amidst the flowers, when first upon the sky
The moon's bright sickle glows. She taught it me;—
It tells of love, and how they love, and speaks
So truly of the passion, that meseems,
It must have first been wrought within our cells,
And borrowed by these warblers of the wood.

ATAL. Sing, if it speaks of love. Such song, methinks,
Must only make more hateful our constraint,
Upon this loathsome isle. I hearken thee.

SONG OF CORALINE.

I.

Be at my side when the winds are awaking,
  Each from his cave, in the depths of the night;
Fly to our groves, till the daylight comes breaking,
  Fresh from the east with his tremulous light.
When the stars peer out in the blue deeps of even,
  When the crowd is at rest, and the moon soars apace,

Silent and sad, through the watches of heaven,
  Be thou, beloved, at the love-hallow'd place:
  Come in thy beauty and lightness,
    Bright-eyed and free-footed, oh! dearest one, come,
  Filling the dark wood with brightness
    And crowning the green hill with bloom;—
Such bloom—the heart-chosen for thousand sweet groves,
As is dear to the wood-nymphs and born of their loves.

II.

In the spirit of beauty, bewitchingly tender,
  Fly to my bosom, beloved of my heart;
Thy lip bearing sweetness, thine eye giving splendor,
  Thy smile shedding rapture wherever thou art;
And while the pale moonlight is round and above thee,
  While the leaves twinkle soft in the breeze o'er thy
Hear, dearest rose of my heart, how I love thee,
  And treasure, sweet spirit, my vow.
  Come! while the night-gems are glowing,
    Each in his orb, over forest and sea,
  Less glory, though bright in their beauty, bestowing
    Than that which now hangs about thee.
Fly to me, blest, in this gentlest of hours,
Outshining the planets, outblooming the flowers.

ATAL. Thy song delights me not—nay, not thy song
That fails, the softness of thy linked words,
Or melody of thy music;—in my heart,
Lies the defect of sweetness—which comes not
To take the shadow from our prison-house.
It is the captive's spirit that complains,
Not Atalantis.

NEA. Would I could cheer thee, mistress.

ATAL. Thou shalt, my Nea.—Speed thee round this isle,
And mark what thou behold'st. 'Tis not in thee
To shrink from contact with the heavy earth,
Its damp and vapor. But to us, who are

Wrought of more delicate matter, all is gross
That yields this monster tribute.
NEA. We've some range,
Sweet mistress! and I prithee wend with me,
As near we may, the borders of the sea,
Looking towards our province. Better airs
Methinks, will come to cheer us into smiles,
From waters that we loved; and newer hopes,
As we look out upon the waste beyond,
Will freshen us with strength. Along the sea,
Some little range is left us. There we may
Call up sweet fancies from our dreams of hope,
And feel the wayward spirit wake to life,
Surveying the blue waters and our home!
ATAL. I'll go with thee! I pine for the sweet airs
Of my own Mergevan.
NEA. They'll seek us out,
With loving consciousness of that we seek.

ACT II.—SCENE I.

The Ocean: the islet of Onesimarchus in the background—a ship in the distance, approaching. The Zephyr-Spirit rides upon the billow.

ZEPHYR-SPIRIT. It is a gallant vessel, and it bends,
To the new islet of Onesimarch;—
That bigot and most brutal arbiter
Of eighty leagues of ocean. He hath rear'd,
In the past day, these undetected rocks,
Whose subtle currents, by his strategy,
Will suck the unconscious vessel to the snare;
Baffling the untutor'd mariner, whose skill
Might vainly hope escape, within the jaws
Of this dread artifice. Now, in the deep,
Will I dispose myself; and, by my art,
Conceal'd in folding billows, in the guise
Of green-hair'd maid of the waters, with a song
Still gently studied to invade his sense,
Will teach him of the danger he may 'scape
By seasonable flight. A human voice
'Tis mine to mingle with these ocean tones.
And, by a sweet mysterious sympathy,
That ever still its benefit declares
To the unslumb'ring instinct, will I teach
The error of his prow. Haply, by this,
His way he may regain, and newly trim
His prone and headlong sail, that, steering thus,
Must soon encounter with the treacherous rocks,

That hunger for their prey. And, to my wish
Of swift concealment from his eager sight,
A sudden cloud is spreading o'er yon heap
Of crested waters. There will I imbed
My many folds of form, while, with my voice,
I frame a music for this mariner,
Not to beguile him with fresh fantasies,
But wake him to the peril in his path.

[Scene changes to the deck of the ship. Count Leon musing at the side.

LEON, [*solus.*] I have been drowsing sure,—yet what a dream,
So strange to earth, so natural to romance;—
And such wild music;—hark!—it comes again.

SONG OF THE ZEPHYR-SPIRIT.

I.

I have come from the deeps where the sea-maiden twines,
  In her bowers of amber, her garlands of shells;
For a captive like thee, in her chamber she pines,
  And weaves for thy coming the subtlest of spells;
She has breathed on the harpstring that sounds in her cave,
  And the strain as it rose hath been murmur'd for thee;
She would win thee from earth for her home in the wave,
  And her couch, in the coral grove, deep in the sea.

II.

Thou hast dream'd in thy boyhood of sea-circled bowers,
  Where all may be found that is joyous and bright,—
Where life is a frolic through fancies and flowers,
  And the soul lives in dreams of a lasting delight!
Wouldst thou win what thy fancies have taught to thy heart?
  Wouldst thou dwell with the maiden now pining for thee?
Flee away from the cares of the earth, and depart
  For her mansions of coral, far down in the sea.

III.

Her charms will beguile thee when noonday is nigh,
The song of her nymphs shall persuade thee to sleep,
She will watch o'er thy couch as the storm hurries by,
Nor suffer the sea-snake beside thee to creep:
But still with a charm which is born of the hours
Her love shall implore thee to bliss ever free;
Thou wilt rove with delight through her crystalline bowers,
And sleep without care in her home of the sea.

LEON. Most sweet indeed, but something in the spell
Proclaims it cold. Even were the precious love
Such as this music speaks of, 'twere enough
To palsy passion in the human heart,
And make its fancies fail.—My Isabel.

Enter Isabel.

ISABEL. What wraps you thus, sweet brother? Why so sad,
When thus so trimly speeds our swanlike bark
O'er the smooth waters? But a few days more,
We tread the lovely island that we seek,
Whose bowers of beauty and eternal spring
Recall the first sweet garden of our race,
Before it knew the serpent. Dost thou sadden,
That thus we near those regions? Art thou sick,
Dear brother, that such vague abstraction creeps
Over your eyes, that seem as 'twere in search
For airy speculations in the deep?
LEON. Thou'rt right!—An airy speculation sure,
Since I can nothing see to speak for it,
And tell me whence it comes.
ISABEL. What is't thou mean'st?
LEON. A moment,—stay! Now, as I live, I heard it
Steal by me, as the murmurs of a lute
From thy own lattice, Isabel.

ISABEL. What heard'st?—
What is it that thou speak'st of?

LEON. A strain of song,—
That crept along the waters from afar,
Softly at first, but growing as it came
To an embodied strength of harmony,
That spoke to all my joys. It bore a tone
Slight as a spirit's whisper, born of love
In aspiration,—such as innocent youth
Acknowledges at first, ere yet the world
Hath school'd it through its sorrows to caprice.
'Twas like thy own sweet music, Isabel,
When out among our Andalusian hills,
We play'd the dusk Morisco for a while,
Grown wanton in the moonlight with the flowers
That seem'd to sing us back. Oh! thou shouldst hear,
To sadden with its sweetness.

ISABEL. Thou hast dream'd!
Whence should such music come?

LEON. Ay! whence indeed,
But from some green-hair'd maiden of the deep,
As still our legends tell us such there be,
That, sitting on the edge of lonely rocks,
Midway in ocean, loose their flowing locks,
And, with strange songs, discoursing to the waves,
Subdue their crests to service.

ISABEL. As the tale
Of Nicuesa pictures. Wouldst thou hear?

LEON. Sing it, my Isabel.

ISABEL. 'Tis something like
Thy fancy,—nay, has been the making of 't,
While thou wert dreaming. But thou didst not dream.

BALLAD.

I.

'Mong Lucayo's isles and waters,
  Leaping to the evening light,
Dance the moonlight's silver daughters—
Tresses streaming, glances gleaming,
  Ever beautiful and bright.

II.

And their wild and mellow voices,
  Still to hear along the deep,
Every brooding star rejoices,
While the billow, on its pillow
  Lull'd to silence, sinks to sleep.

III.

Yet they wake a song of sorrow,
  Those sweet voices of the night;
Still from grief a gift they borrow,
And hearts shiver, as they quiver
  With a wild and sad delight.

IV.

'Tis the wail for life they waken
  By Samana's lonely shore;
With the tempest it is shaken,
The wide ocean is in motion,
  And the song is heard no more.

V.

But the gallant bark comes sailing,
  At her prow the chieftain stands;
He hath heard the tender wailing—
It delights him—it invites him
  To the joys of other lands.

VI.

Bright the moonlight round and o'er him,
And, oh ! see, a picture lies
In the yielding waves before him,—
Woman smiling, still beguiling
From the depths of wondrous eyes.

VII.

White arms toss above the waters,
Pleading murmurs fill his ears,
And the Queen of Ocean's daughters,
Heart alluring, love assuring,
Wins him down with tears.

VIII.

On, the good ship speeds without him,
By Samana's lonely shore;
They have wound their arms about him,
In the water's—ocean's daughters
Sadly singing as before.

LEON. Unhappy Nicuesa!
ISABEL. Such his song,
And, with the ocean murmur in thy ears,
Thy fancy, in thy dream, hath made it thine.
LEON. I did not sleep or dream, my Isabel ;—
I heard this wondrous music, even now,
When first I summon'd thee. I grant it strange
That it should syllable to familiar sound,
Boyhood's first fancies, of fair isles that lie
In farthest depths of ocean,—jewell'd isles
Boundless in but imaginable spoils,
Such as boy-visions only can conceive
And boyhood's faith admit.
ISABEL. And still thou dream'st !—

Thy boyhood's legends and thy boyhood's faith,
Grown fresh beneath the force of circumstance,
And the wild fancies of this foreign world,
Still carry thee away,—till thou forget'st,—
As still the wisest may,—the difference
'Twixt those two worlds,—the one where nature toils,
The other she but dreams of.

LEON. 'Twas no dream!
It comes again! Now hark thee, Isabel—
It is no murmur of the deep thou hear'st!
It hath a voice not human,—not unlike—
And sings, as still a spirit might sing, that wills
To do humanity service. Hark!

ISABEL. I do!—
Yet I hear nothing.

LEON. Sure, I did not dream!
'Twas like the zephyr through a bed of reeds
Sighing as 'twere at cheerlessness of home,
In the approach of winter.

ISABEL. Oh! no more!—
Thou art too led astray by idle thoughts,
Dear Leon;—dost possess thee of the hues,
Shed by the passing cloud, and mak'st thy heart,
Still the abiding place of hopeless fancies
That waste thy strength of will. Thou art too prone
To these wild speculations.

LEON. Hear it now!
My fancy trick'd me not,—my sense was true,—
It comes again, far off, and very fine,
As the first birth 'twixt silence and his dame,
The mother of the voice. Now, Isabel,—
Thine ears are traitors if they do not feel
That music as it sweeps by us but now.

ISABEL. I hear a murmur truly, but so slight—

A breath of the wind might make it, or a sail
Drawn suddenly.

LEON. Art silenced? It is there!

ZEPHYR-SPIRIT.

In the billow before thee
  My form is conceal'd—
In the breath that comes o'er thee
  My thought is reveal'd—
Strown thickly beneath me
  The coral rocks grow,
And the waves that enwreath me,
  Are working thee woe.

LEON. Didst hear it, Isabel?

ISABEL. It spoke, methought,
Of peril from the rocks that near us grow.

LEON. It did, but idly! Here can lurk no rocks
For, by the chart which now before us lies,
Thy own unpractised eye may well discern
The wide extent of the ocean—shoreless all;
The land, for many a league, to th' westward hangs,
And not a point beside it.

ISABEL. Wherefore then,
Should come this voice of warning?

LEON. From the deep:
It hath its demons as the earth and air,
All tributaries to the master-fiend
That sets their springs in motion. This is one,
That, doubting to mislead us, plants this wile,
So to divert our course, that we may strike
The very rocks he fain would warn us from.

ISABEL. A subtle sprite—and, now I think of it,
Dost thou remember the old story told

By Diaz Ortis, the lame mariner,
Of an adventure in the Indian seas,
Where he made one with John of Portugal,—
Touching a woman of the ocean wave
That swam beside the barque and sang strange songs
Of riches in the waters;—with a speech
So winning on the senses, that the crew
Grew all infected with the melody,
And, but for a good father of the church
Who made the sign of the cross and offer'd up
Befitting prayer, which drove the fiend away,
They had been tempted by her cunning voice
To leap into the ocean.

LEON. I do, I do!
And, at the time, I do remember me,
I made much mirth of the extravagant tale,
As a deceit of the reason;—the old man
Being in his second childhood, and at fits,
As wild, in other histories, as in this.

ISABEL. I never more shall mock at marvellous things;
Such strange conceits hath after time found true,
That once were themes for jest. I shall not smile
At the most monstrous legend.

LEON. Nor will I!—
To any tale of foreign wonderment,
I shall bestow mine ear nor wonder more;
And every image that my childhood bred,
In vagrant dreams of fancy, I shall look,
To find, without rebuke, my sense approve.
Thus, like a little island of the deep,
Girdled by perilous seas, and all unknown
To prows of venture, may be yon same cloud
Specking, with fleecy bosom, the blue sky,
Lit by the rising moon. There, we may dream,

And find no censure in an after day,
Throng the assembled fairies, perch'd on beams,
And riding on their way triumphantly.
There gather the coy spirits. Many a fay,
Roving the silver sands of that same isle,
Floating in azure ether, plumes her wing
Of ever-frolicsome fancy, and pursues—
While myriads like herself, do watch the chase—
Some truant sylph, through the infinitude
Of their uncircumscribed and rich domain.
There sport they through the night, with mimicry
Of strife and battle,—striking their tiny shields
And gathering into combat; meeting fierce,
With lip compress'd, and spear aloft, and eye
Glaring with desperate purpose in the fight;—
Then sudden—in a moment all their wrath
Mellow'd to friendly terms of courtesy—
Throwing aside the dread array and link'd,
Each, in his foe's embrace. Then comes the dance,
The grateful route, the wild and musical pomp,
The long procession o'er fantastic realms
Of cloud and moonbeam, through th' enamor'd night,
Making it all one revel. Thus, the eye
Breathed on by fancy, with enlargéd scope,
Through the protracted and deep hush of night,
May note the fairies, coursing the lazy hours,
In various changes, and without fatigue.
A fickle race, who tell their time by flowers,
And live on zephyrs, and have stars for lamps,
And night-dews for ambrosia; perch'd on beams,
Speeding through space, even with the scattering light
On which they feed and frolic.

ISABEL. A wild dream!—
And yet, since this old tale of Diaz Ortis,

That moved our laughter once, is thus made sooth,
Perchance, not all a dream.

LEON. Yet, may we doubt!—
There may be something in this marvel still
Of human practice. Man hath wondrous powers,
Most like a God;—that, with each hour of toil,
Perfect themselves in actions strangely great.
Some cunning seaman, having natural skill,
As by the books we learn hath oft been done,
Hath 'yond our vessel's figure pitch'd his voice,—
With gay deceit of unsuspected art,
Leading us wantonly.

ISABEL. It is not so;—
Or, does my sense deceive? Look, where the wave
A perch beyond our vessel, grows in folds
That seem not like the element. Dost see?

LEON. A marvellous shape that with the billow curls,
In gambols of the deep, and yet is not
Its wonted burden; for, beneath the waves,
I mark the elaborate windings of a form,
That heaves and flashes with an antic play,
As if to win our gaze.

ISABEL. Again—it sings.

ZEPHYR-SPIRIT

I.

By the planet at whose bid,
I must close the heavy lid,
Ere the hour that wings my flight
I unfold me to your sight,
That your wondering thoughts may find,
Wherewith to awake the mind;—
To arouse ye with a fear,
Do I sing and wanton here;

Sing with sorrow lest too late,
Ye awaken to your fate:
Hearken to my voice and fly,
For the danger lurketh nigh.

II.

Deem me not a form of ill,
Free to lure and injure still;—
Mine's the gentler task to save
From the perils of the wave.
When thou feel'st the tempest's shocks,
I send breezes off the rocks;
When the ocean's calm as death,
From me comes the tradewind's breath ·—
For my essence is not made
Of the cold and gloomy shade,
But of gentlest dews of night,
And of purest rays of light.

III.

Heed me then, and turn thy prow
From the rocks that wait thee now;—
Close beneath thee, do they sleep
In the hollows of the deep;
And thy sail is truly prone
Where the yellow sand is strown;
And no human power can save
From the terrors of the wave,
Smooth, and gently gliding, now,
With a whisper, round thy prow;
In an hour and all is o'er—
Thou wilt hear my voice no more.

LEON. 'Tis passing strange, and it were well to rouse
The master to this marvel. What, ho! there!
Hark ye, good Mendez Celer, lend awhile
Your presence here on deck.

Enter Mendez Celer.

MENDEZ. Who summons me?
Ha! brave Don Leon, but thou look'st as wild,
As thou hadst spoke some monster of the deep,
And shipp'd his tidings in a sea of foam.
Hadst thou but weather'd awhile the Indian seas,
As I have done, where, from his fiery steep,
El Norté plunges headlong o'er the seas,
Smiting the billows with his scourge of wings
Till their gray scalps lie flat, methinks thine eyes,
That find a wonder in each hour of change,
Would soon grow slow to marvel.

LEON. It may be,—
Yet there's a marvel here to challenge well
Thy old experience in these wizard seas.
Here swam a voice that spoke to us in song
Of most prevailing sweetness. There it rose—
Even from yon heap of waters, which thou see'st
Still stirring with an action not their own,
Unlike the rest of the ocean. Thou mayst note
Where the sea rises and the billows toss,
Still swelling in strange folds. 'Tis there it moves,—
From thence the music came.

MEN. What said the song?
A ditty of the marvellous love, I ween,
The girl of the ocean bears thee—was it not?

LEON. No, in no wise!—the tones it used were soft,
And the words gentle, and the music sweet,
But yet it spoke no love and ask'd for none.—
It rather told of danger to our barque;—
Of rocks in certain and near neighborhood,
And shoals and sands, that, close beneath our prow,
Are lurking to ensnare.

MEN. Bah! good Don Leon!
'Tis, as we say in Palos, a poor devil
That goes without his brimstone.—A dull cheat
Who when he shows his hook forgets the bait.
Your sea-girl was a young one. Mark me now,
There is no land—no single spot of shore
Whereon a plank or spar might lie at ease,
Within a three day's sail of us. I've been
Some thirty years a mariner, and scarce,
In all that time, have been from off the seas
A month or two, at farthest, at a spell;
And this same route o'er which we travel now,
Comes to me as my nightcap or my prayers—
I put not on the one, nor say the other,
Yet both are done, the thanks to Mary Mother,
And I am none the wiser.

LEON. It is strange
That we should hear this music!

MEN. Not a whit.
I've oftentimes heard from the Portuguese—
I'm rather one myself, belike you know,
My father having stray'd, at a wrong time,
From Lisbon to my mother's house at Palos,
And then it came about that I was born—
(Nothing ill-graced to Lady Isabel;)
And, as I say, it is a standing tale
With the old seamen, that a woman comes—
Her lower parts being fishlike—in the wave;
Singing strange songs of love, that so inflame
The blinded seamen, that they steal away
And join her in the waters; and, that then,
Having her victim, she is seen no more.

LEON. And is it deem'd, the men thus wildly snared
Become a prey and forfeit life at once?

MEN. So must it be; and yet, there is a tale
That they do wed these creatures; which have power,
So to convert their nature, that they make,
As to themselves, the sea their element;
And have a life renew'd, though at the risk
And grievous peril of their Christian souls,
Doom'd thence unto perdition.

LEON. And you then
Think nothing of this warning?

MEN. By your grace,
Surely, I hold it the wild lustful song
Of this same woman. She has lost, perchance,—
Since death must come at last who comes to all,—
Her late companion. Would you take his place?
If not, wax up your ears, and sleep secure,
There's naught to fear, and sea-room quite enough.

[*Shock—the ship strikes.*

God, and thou gracious Mary, what is that?

[*Ship strikes again*

We're in our certain course—what may this mean?

LEON. The vessel strikes—she strikes again and shivers,
Through all her frame, as if convulsed with horror,
She felt herself the pangs we soon must feel!
The devil speaks truth, for once, good Mendez Celer!

MEN. Oh, holy Mary, and thou gracious shield
Blessed Saint Anthony, lend us now your aid;
Speak fairly to the waters—see us through
This sad deceit. Below there—hands aloft!—
Ho, Juan! trim the sail,—out with the lead—
Helm down, Pedrillo—Hernan—luff yet more.
Jesu! She rides again—we yet may swim!

[*Vessel strikes heavily upon the rocks.*

It is all over! To your prayers at once!
There is no longer hope, nor chance of life,

Unless from the good saints and Mary Mother,
We may have mercy and sweet countenance!

[*The master takes a leaden image from his he': and prostrates himself before it. Storm rises.*

Gracious Saint Anthony, for fifty years
We've voyagéd in company, and now,
I pray thee, in this strait, that thou forsake not
Thy ancient comrade. To thy use I vow--
If thou wilt man our yards, and trim our sails,
And lift our ragged keel from off these rocks,—
A box of Cadiz candles——

LEON. Be a man!
Rise, Mendez, to the peril and the storm.
Let us do something for ourselves, nor ask
The smiles of heaven upon our fears alone.
Shall we but crouch and perish, with no stroke
Made for our lives! For shame, sir—ply your men;
Nor with an idle prayer, which the waves mock
And the winds laugh at, show our feebleness.
If there be land so nigh, as by our glance,
The eye may seem to conjure, we may try,
The little we can do, to save our lives.
The boats—get out the boats!

MEN. In vain--in vain;
No boat may live in such a sea as that.
Look at this surf, that chafes like a wild beast,
And ramps, like something mad, upon the rocks.
This is the strangest chance I yet have known:—
By the chart we are in the open sea,
And here we meet with land, where land is none.
A moment since, and the whole sea was calm,
Now boils it like a cauldron—and the winds,
That late were almost breathless, now exclaim
In wrath, and yell like fiends above the sea.

Oh, Mary Mother, in this strait befriend!—
To thee, to Jesu, and the saints alone,
May we now look for mercy!

[*Storm increases. Ship strikes with increasing violenc*

LEON. So we perish!—
The ship is parting! We must try the boat,
Whate'er the peril from the raging sea!
Better, thus struggling in the embrace of strife,
To meet the fatal enemy, than thus,
With idly folded arms and shivering fears
That mock the very passion in our prayer
With broken utterance most unmeet for heaven,
Await him feebly here. Ho! man the boat.

ISABEL. Leave me not, brother, for a moment now!
There's not a pressing danger, or I do
Greatly mistake the courage in your eye,
That hath no touch of terror in its calm,
And looks the strength of safety.

LEON. Yet, there is,
Dear Isabel, a danger of the worst,
Now pressing on our lives with terrible wrath,
That needs the soul's best fortitude and hope
To meet with manhood. We may yet escape,
So, take you heart. Look not with such an eye,
Or I may fail at this most perilous hour,
And sink into the woman. Be all firm,
And like our mother, dearest,—nor grow weak,
When I do tell you that the chances gather
Against our fondest hope.

ISABEL. And is it so?—
And you and I, dear Leon,—both so young,
So fond,—so full of life's best promises,—
Thus sudden cut from all—the loved, the loving,—
And by a fate so terrible!

LEON. Still hope!—
Since combating the fear that ushers death,
We little feel his shaft. Whatever haps,
Be firm, and cling to me. Keep close at hand,
And, with the mercy of God, through every chance,
Dear sister, I devote myself to thee.

ISABEL. I know thou wilt!—I will be at thy side,
Nor trouble thee with my terrors.

LEON. Noble girl!
My safety shall be thine;—and if I fail,
'Twill somewhat soothe the pang of that sad passage
That still we go together. We have lived,
So truly in one another from the first,
And known no sense of pleasure not inwrought,
With twin affection in our mutual hearts,
That 'twill not move our chiding when the fate
Strikes both in one, and with a kindly blow,
Secures 'gainst future parting.

ISABEL. I'll not chide!
I will be firm,—and yet I dread the rage
And rushing of the waters. How they roar,
And lash themselves to madness o'er our bows!
I dread me, Leon, that my senses fail!
Mine eyes grow blind—I see thee not—Here, here!
My brother, leave me not.

LEON. I'm here with thee!

ISABEL. Dost hear me when I speak,—dost hear me, brother?
I cannot hear myself. My voice is gone,
Drown'd in that horrible coil of storm and billow
That fain would wrap us all. That crash!— [*Shrieks.*

LEON. Hither!—
I have thee, poor unconscious!—child of sorrow,
That hast no farther feeling of thy woe!
Make way there.

MARINER. The boat is ready, masters.

[*The vessel parts. The seamen enter the boat. Leon lifts Isabel into it.*

MEN. Delay not now for me—bear off, bear off,—
I go in no new craft—my log's complete.
This is my ninetieth voyage, and the last,
Though not the longest or most fortunate.
I cannot leave the ship—it is our creed—
Till she leaves me. We've sail'd together long—
And if I 'scaped the present, would not much
Survive her reckoning. Bid me well at home,
And say the manner of my death to all.
Tell old Bertiaz, should you ever make
The shore I never more shall touch again,
(He owns the vessel), that the "Arragon"
(Too fine a name for such a fate as this),
Is Arragon no longer. You may say—
'Twill do me good in my grave—I died in her.

[*They leave her—she goes to pieces in their sight.*

SCENE II.—*The Boat.*

MARINER. There, she goes down,—the master still in her;
I see him on a spar, and—now he sinks.
Pull there more freely, boys. The swell she makes
May trouble us greatly. Fiercely, all at once,
Mark you, Don Leon, how the waters leap,
And the seas whiten. Here are ugly rocks.

LEON. The billows rush on madly, as they were
Some battling armies. These are cruel waves,
That, fastening on our sides, still clamber high,

More like the forms of demons, dark and dread,
With fiend malignity and bent on wrath,
Than billows of the ocean. We shall scarce—
Unless good fortune and the blessed saints
Look kindly on us—overcome the space,
Growing as we o'erleap it, that, between,
Now keeps us from yon islet, which I mark,
Dim, in the distance, o'er the swell in front.
Pray ye, strike full your oars and all at once,
Cheerly and bold, becoming fearless men;—
And, if we live, God's blessing on your service,
But lack, ye shall not, your reward on earth.
My arm grows weary with the weight upon 't
Of this most precious burden; while a cloud
Like a thick pitchy wall, right in our way
Rests heavily on the waters, and denies
That I should see beyond. Give way, like men,
And enter the deep darkness unafraid.

[*The boat disappears.*

SCENE III.—*The ocean waste.*

ZEPHYR-SPIRIT. Now, terribly through the waters comes the form
Of that fierce savage and malignant king,
Onesimarch. Behind him gathering rush
Clouds of his brutal followers, clad in wrath,
Howling for prey. Beneath their vexing spells
The deep boils like a whirlpool, and the waves,
So lately still and placid, wrought to rage,
Leap up about the poor ill-fated barque.
Now grappling to her prow, they drag her down,

The billows rushing in ; and, wrapt in each,
Some of the monster's followers, well conceal'd,
With fierce and furious might, impel her down ;—
Now mount her bending sides, now strike with force
Their own, against her weak and shrieking ribs—
Tear up her planks, and rushing through the space,
Rend her broad back, and o'er the flinty rocks
Drag the too yielding keel until it parts.
Onesimarch, himself, a hungry fiend,
With darker powers endow'd, with sulphur arm'd,
Hurls a perpetual lightning, which distracts
And dazzles the weak eye. He shapes their course,
And guides the tribute legions ; working new joys
From out the wrongs he doth, for his own sense,
And for that potentest of all the fiends,
By whom his power is wrought. And now, they chant
A song of terror in the drowning ears
Of the wild seamen, cutting off all hope
That manhood may achieve against its fate.

SCENE IV.—*The same.*

Storm. Flight of Sea-Demons, singing.

I.

Fly ! fly !
Through the perilous sky,
Spirits of terror and tumult on high !
Even as we go,
Working the woe,
Of all that is hatefully happy below !
Speed ! our mission, fierce and fatal,
Is to spoil superior things ;

For, at birth, our planets natal
  Crown'd with blight our demon wings!
Oh! the joy to rob the treasures,
  Hopes of soul and beauty given,
From the race whose purer pleasures,
  Are the special care of Heaven!
Joy, that thus, still doom'd to sorrow,
  We may happier fortunes blight,
And from woe extremest borrow,
  Still the power that yields delight.
To the terror, fiercely wending,
  Speed we, till our work is done,
Still destroying, raging, rending,
  Till the shadow chokes the sun!

II.

Speed! for the meed
Of merciless deed,
Summons us fiercely with clamors of greed;
While the ship glides
Through the treacherous tides,
Break down her bulwarks and rush through her sides!
These are mortals, wretched creatures!
  Yet from doom like ours set free;
Wrought of clay, and yet with features,
  Such as make us rage to see!
Such the haughty sovereign presence,
  That pursued with storm and flame!
From our homes of power and pleasaunce,
  Drove us forth in grief and shame!
Him we dare not face with battle,
  Now, as then, with fearless powers,
But his race of God-mark'd cattle,
  Yields the proper spoil for ours.
In his likeness made, they languish,
  For the wings he hath not given;
And, in trampling on their anguish,
  Wage we still our war with Heaven!

III.

Why, oh! why,
Breathing the sky
Orisons still should they offer on high;
Why should they pray,
Creatures of clay,
Whose faith is a fable, whose life is a day!
Mock the mortals with your voices,
Shouting death and hate and hell;
Fill their ears with horrid noises,
Ring for every soul the knell!
Tell them, while the ocean smothers
Life and hope, that, never more,
Shall the loved ones, wives and mothers,
See the forms so dear before!
Show them Death in grimmest aspect,
Cold, corruption, worms, and night;
And depict the penal prospect
Of the future world of blight,
Endless, for the guilt-unshriven,
Fetter'd fast by tyrant powers,
With no hope to be forgiven,
And a doom more dread than ours!

IV.

Lo! where in sight,
Fierce as in fight,
Rising from ocean, our monarch of might;
With the storm for his steed,
He is here at our need,
The dreadful in strife, and the matchless in speed.
Full our legions,—dread battalions,
Sweep we now the ocean plain;
Cower the golden Spanish galleons,
Cower and sink beneath the main!
Vain the skill and power to stay us,
Vain the prayers that hope to spell

Hate, alone, may soothe or sway us,
And the power that conquers hell!
These we dread not in our mission,
When the victim wrought of clay,
Guilty grown, in his condition,
Yields himself beneath our sway.
Then he forfeits angel keeping,
Which had baffled else our hate;
And the doom of woe and weeping,
Makes him subject to our fate!

CHORUS.

From the regions south, and the regions north,
Mount we, and speed we, and hurry we forth;
From where the sun fails, in the putrid gales,
Launch we afloat on our shadowy sails:
Darkening the sky, oh! how we fly,
Spirits of tumult and terror on high:
The whirlwind we fling abroad on its wing,
And the hurricane speeds to its work, as we sing!
Lo! the skies how they stoop, and the stars how they droop
While the trailing storms follow our flight in a troop;
As downward we sweep, the black billows leap,
To welcome our flight, with a roar from the deep!
We are here, we are there; in the ocean, the air,
With a breath that is death, and a song that's despair!
Ho! for the master! The sulphur balls go!
How sweet is the shriek of the perishing foe!
Ho! for the master! The red arrows fly,
And burst in the blackness of billow and sky!
Papé Sathanas! We work for thee well!
*Aleppé!** There's clucking for triumph in Hell!
Hear'st thou the groans of the victims?—They pray—
Ho! ho! but how vainly!—too late i' the day!

* See Dante, Inferno, Canto vii:—

"Pape Satan, pape Satan aleppe,
Cominciò Pluto colla voce chioccia."

We stifle the prayer, in the breath—and we tear,
The last hope away from the breast of despair!
Ho! for new flights and new victims,—Ho! Ho!
With the tempest for wings, and the lightning we go.
Papé Sathanas! we work for thee well!
Aleppé! There's clucking for triumph in Hell!

SCENE V.—*The Boat.*

MARINER. Master, we strive in vain.
LEON. We can but die.
MAR. Why toil for it?
LEON. As one who strikes his foe,
Though conscious that he battles without hope,
And dies in the brave conflict.—Ha! she stirs.
ISABEL, [*recovering.*] Horrible sounds are rushing through mine ears,
More like the cries of demons, mad for blood,
Than the hoarse billows and the roaring winds.
They dart into my brain, and seem to shout,
Triumphant, oh, my brother, o'er our fate;—
Speak of the sorrow in our father's halls,
That, with an anguish, far too great for speech,
Grows dumb and scorns expression. Could we live—
But live to see him once!—oh, bear me up;—
Desert me not, dear Leon, but entwine,
Closely, thy arm around; nor let these waves,
That seem impatient of their midnight feast,
Suck me into their black and ravenous jaws.
LEON. Doubt me not, Isabel, in this dark hour!
Think'st thou I could desert thee, precious sweetness,
To whose frail nature and too delicate youth
Sweet elements should minister with love,

Not hunt with hate. I have thee in my arms;
Will hold thee, while they have their hold in life,
And I have thought and sense to will the struggle
That wards the final danger from thy breast.
But, cling to me, my sister.

ISABEL. Will I not?
Why should we think of death?

MAR. It comes! It comes!

[*The boat strikes and goes to pieces.*

LEON. Isabel,—sister!

ISABEL, [*faintly afar off.*] Here, Leon, here!

LEON. Oh, Jesu! lost!

[*Scene closes.*

SCENE VI.—*The Ocean waste.*

ZEPHYR-SPIRIT. 'Tis done! The strife is over. Hope is none!
These cruel demons triumph, with a rage
That mocks at mortal strength. Prone to the deep,
I watch'd that hungry slave, Calemmia, seize,
Conceal'd in a dense billow, on the prow;
And, all despite the seaman's sturdy stroke,
The helmsman's firm direction, and the cheer
Of that strong human impulse, which did grow,
Upon the sight of land, into a hope,
Drag her among the sharp rocks, while the surfs
Beat her to pieces. She is scatter'd far—
A spar floats on the wave—a single oar,
Cast high among the sands, alone has reach'd
The mocking shores that wreck'd them. Yet, not so!—
I mark a floating form that struggles still,
With a most human love of life, afar.
Him may I succor, and, with safety now;—

The legions of Onesimarch, being done
Their toil of terror, have, for newer spoils,
Wrapt in a gathering cloud, departed hence,
Leaving all calm again. Curl'd in this wave,
I will beneath him glide, and bear him up;
Till, on the shore, beyond the ocean's swell,
He rests in safety. I can do no more—
Since, in gross contact with the heavy earth,
I lose the subtle power that makes my gift,
And forfeit, of the light ethereal nature,
The buoyant spirit that supplies its wing.

ACT III.—SCENE I.

The islet of Onesimerchus.

Atalantis, Nea.

Atal. This islet hath no quality of joy,
Fair to the sight, or fragrant to the sense,—
No beauty that upon its surface glows,
No treasure that within its bosom sleeps;—
It is the foul'st deception—all is gross,
And tainted with that sinborn leprousness
That marks the soul who will'd it into birth,
And raised its treacherous rocks along the deep.
No innocent beast hath dwelling in this clime,
No valley blooms with verdure. Not a flower
Gems the bleak sands, that, barrenly spread out,
Pain the unsatisfied and wandering eye,
That, seeing naught else, grows weary. Not a bird,
But, as he flies above, subdues his voice,
And, panting in his silence, quickens his wing,
Having a nameless terror. The foul taint
That poisons all things in this tyrant's sway,
Takes from them all their virtue. Not a shrub
Breathes fragrance to the breeze, whose whisper'd plaint
Would woo it still to fondness. Not an air
Enters these bounds, but flags and settles down
Clumsy and wingless; and the very stars
Do seem to leave their places in the heavens,
Looking down on it. Even we, who are
Of a tenacious temper, yielding naught,—

If that our hearts be pure and souls be firm
To the capricious influence,—we lose
Something of that refined and subtler sense,
Which gives us power to meet and match the sway
Of his low cunning and detested art.
How heavy is this silence! What a spell
Comes with the sullen muttering of the winds,
Now sweeping from the waters; and, how sad
Are the faint murmurs of yon moaning sea,
In the far distance chiding, as in grief,
For some new stroke of sorrow! All things yield—
So it would seem—a something to the spell,
That makes his power, and keeps us captive here;
Wrapping us in a circle, not to move,
Or strive, lest it undoes us. The shrill scream
Of one poor gull, that, o'er the whiten'd foam,
Hung with gray wing suspended, breaks no more
Fitfully on the ear;—and all of life
Seems resolute to pay its offering now
To that dread silence, which, in human sense,
Makes up the all of death!

NEA. Even as thou say'st!—
'Tis a sad spot, fair mistress; sad for us,
That have been wont, in finer element,
To drink the nurture of a better lot.
Ah! how unlike the sweet life of the light,
Blessing the fair dominion thou hast lost;—
Lost for a season only,—yet too long,
Since such a dwelling as we find perforce,
Subdues the heart to sorrows not its own,
Which still must bide in memory. I feel
How dreary is the labor of restraint,
This watching, waiting,—when my wonted use,
Would have me winging an unlicensed flight,

Now in the embracing air, now through the deeps,
Disparting their white billows night and morn,
With no more pause than to adjust my plumes,
Ruffled by zephyrs; then, with fresh device,
Soaring in wilder progress,—sea and sky,
Our ample field, and the delighted tribes,
Their habitants, come forth to share the chase.

ATAL. And lack'st thou now all wonted qualities—
Thy dance, thy song, whose melodies can make
The mad seas sleep when wildest, while the winds
Fold up their cloudy vans to hear thy lay?
Hast thou no strain to fit these drowsy hours
With wings of light and fragrance, while the thought
Grows wanton and forgetful of the grief
That burden'd it with gloom? Methinks, my girl,
'Twere in thy happy spells of verse to find
Some carol of our own domain, to take
The impatient soul, and in delicious dews
Steep the fine sense to sweet forgetfulness.
Sing me some ditty from our Mergevan,
While every flower, in gardens of the past,
Our hands have ever gather'd, the young page,
Whose name is Memory, faithful to his task,
Shall bring anew to joy us in our need.
Give me the song the Flower-Spirit once framed,
When through our gardens, far beneath the sea,
Wall'd in by wildest waters, we pursued,
For the first time, the summer festival.

SONG OF THE FLOWER-SPIRIT.

I.

I am the spirit that sleeps in the flower,
Mine is the music of fragrance that flies,

When silence and moonlight are dressing each bower
  That blooms in the favor of tropical skies:
I win the bird with new melody glowing,
  To rise with the zephyr, and warble his strain;
And mine is the odor, in turn, that bestowing,
  The minstrel is paid for his music again.

II.

Sorrow comes never where I am abiding,
  The tempests are strangers, and far from us rove;
I woo the zephyrs too hurriedly riding,
  And gently they linger and fill us with love.
They pause, and we glow in their winning embraces;
  They drink our warm breath, rich with odor and song;
Then hurry away to their desolate places,
  And look for us hourly, and mourn for us long.

III.

We were born of the dews, and our destiny found us,
  Embraced by a sunbeam, all budding and bright;
On its wing, came from heaven the glory that crown'd us,
  And the odor that makes us a living delight.
And when the warm blessings of summer stream on us,
  Our winglets of silk we unfold to the air;
Leaping upward in joy to the spirit that won us,
  And made us the tenants of regions so fair.

ATAL. The ocean hath no calm like what is here—
And, if the waters might unfold to us,
There hath been fearful strife upon their waves.
Here come its tokens. These are broken spars
From some tall ship, that lately sped along,
As oft-times I have seen them, with a grace
And majesty becoming in a queen
Ruling a thousand seas. It is a game
Onesimarch delights in, to destroy

The goodly creatures that do dwell in them—
Shaped like ourselves, though little taught to cope
In knowledge with ourselves. Inferior things
Of lower grade, who, when we have become
The tenants and possessors of a realm
Now far beyond our state, shall rise to ours,
As we enjoy it now. But what is here,
Grasping a shaft, and lifelessly spread out?
[*Seeing the body of Leon.*

NEA. One of the creatures of that goodly barque,—
Perchance, the only one of many men,
That, from their distant homes, went forth in her,
And here have perish'd.

ATAL. There is life in him;—
His bosom swells, methinks, beneath my hand,—
With fitful pulse—most faint—now here—now gone!
Alas! I fear it may not come again.
How very young he is—how beautiful!—
Made with a matchless sense of what is true
In manly grace and mortal elegance;
And features, rounded in as soft a mould
As our own, Nea.

NEA. His eye unfolds.

ATAL. Ah!
Stand aside, girl, and let me look on him.
I see not that he wakes.

NEA. But now he did.

ATAL. Alas! he sleeps in death! How pitiful
That one so young, and princely in his port,
Should fall so soon a victim. He hath been,
I doubt not, a great noble with his people.
How should it be that such a form as this,
So lovely and commanding in its aspect,
Should rank below the people of our race?

Methinks he is a creature, that, in life,
Might stand compared with any of our chiefs.

NEA. At least, in outward seeming.

ATAL. And this speaks,—
Where still the brow is lofty, and the form
Familiar, in erect and graceful carriage,—
For that which guides within.

NEA. He looks well;—
Yet may he be a thing of seeming only,
Wanting in all that higher sense of soul,
Which makes the virtue of true excellence.

ATAL. Oh! I am sure there is no want in him;
The spirit must be true, the sense supreme,
The soul as far ascending, strong and bright,
As is the form they do inhabit in.
Breathe on him, Nea; fan him with thy wing
And rouse him, if thou canst. Oh! could I bring
The life into his cheek. Stay, yet awhile;—
Now, while his senses sleep, I'll place my lip
Upon his own—it is so beautiful!
Such lips should give forth music—such a sweet
Should have been got in heaven,—the produce there,
Of never-blighted gardens. [*Kisses him.*

LEON, [*starts.*] Cling to me—
Am I not with thee now, my Isabel! [*Swoons again.*

ATAL. Oh, gentle sounds—how sweetly did they fall,
In broken murmurs, like a melody,
From lips, that waiting long on loving hearts,
Had learn'd to murmur like them. Wake again,
Sweet stranger! If my lips have wrought this spell,
And won thee back to life, though but to sigh,
And sleep again in death,—they shall, once more,
Wake and restore thee.

NEA. You arouse him not.

ATAL. Alas! should life's string, overstrain'd, be crack'd,
No more to be reknit, I forfeit peace
Forever,—never more to hope for joy
In any life that follows.

NEA. Oh! my mistress,
This passion of grief—

ATAL. Nea, now at last,
I feel that I do love! The sudden fire
Kindles at last, where never yet before
Its spark found nurture. If it be in vain!—
I, that had scorn'd the suppliant before,
I too, must be the suppliant for a love
That's born without a hope. The lesson comes
Too late, and I have but to weep o'er dreams
That have no waking promise for the heart,
And leave it but to tears. Alas! Alas!

[*Throws herself upon Leon.*

NEA. Oh! yield not thus, my mistress, to a passion
That never can be blest. The best of love
Still teaches sorrow as his natural gift,
More sure than precious.

ATAL. Know you aught of Love?

NEA. As of a power that's best esteemed in fancy,
In which he more abides than in the heart.
Love's but an artful tyrant. He first wins
By the most servile flatteries. He can stoop
The better to ascend; and pliant grows,
When most the secret purpose in his soul,
Makes him unyielding. Pleasant is his prayer;—
He will discourse you in the dove's own note,
Cooing and plaining, with such murmur'd sweets,
That pity learns to take the place of doubt,
And paves the way for trust. But, wait awhile,
And soon his habit changes. He grows apt,—

Learns the new lesson his condition makes,
As readily as the old; and, sure of power,
Firm, with free footing walks, where late he crept.
Then, see you heed the master;—who will now
Claim, for his right, that which he lately sued,
As the poor meed of charity; and thus
Step by step upward, with insidious art,
And cunning most unequall'd, doth he rise,
Until you find your neck beneath his foot,
And you become his slave, who once was yours.

ATAL. Oh! terrible,—where heard you this of Love?

NEA. From many teachers.

ATAL. Did they know him well?
They slander him, methinks.

NEA. They suffer'd first!
Our minstrels note him thus!—Our maidens, taught
By many a hapless lesson, thus describe
His art and empire. They do further tell,
Beyond his tyrant habits, that his sweets
Are few and failing. Painful, do they say,
Are even the creature's pleasures, since they wake
Such doubts and dread misgiving for their loss,
As even their joys can't equal. The sick soul,
That grieves with Love's delusions, evermore dreams
Dreading its losses. It forever makes
A sombre cloud to gather in the sky,
And glooms the spirit. Looking far beyond
The glory in its gaze, it sadly sees
Countless privations, and far-coming storms,
Shrinking from what it conjures. Let them say
Green youth and greener maidens, as they may,
Of Love and of his raptures:—for my part,
I hold him a disease—a very ache,
And ague-fever, sore and troublesome;

Apt caller forth of tears, and wails, and plaints,
And then of colds, and heats, and fantasies—
Realities most mournful, and, forsooth,
Imaginings, whose strange complexions be
Not a whit kinder. Love's a sorry slave,
And a sad master. As a slave, he steals
The jewel of our nature, and its lights,—
The heart and its affections;—which, having got,
He straight assumes the master:—they, in turn,
Being his willing instruments and doom'd,
When that the tyrant of his play grows sick,
To be the creature's victims at the last.
Atal. I cannot think this truly said of Love!—
The minstrels do belie him, much, methinks,
For envy of his conquests; and, the maids—
They only do complain, whom he doth slight.
They never knew his nature. They, perchance—
Since what is winning still hath counterfeits—
Have seen some subtle semblance of his form,
His true spirit all being wanting; and were made,
Haply, the victims of some wanton art,
That hath betray'd them. It were wisdom poor,
And a most sad philosophy, to scorn
The blessing, as in nature's exigence,
It might grow forfeit. Better, with this rule,
Not live, since in the end we all must die.
Though there be doubts that love may yet be lost,
Still let me love;—the very doubt but shows
The worth of the possession. Not for me
The sway of kingdoms only. In my heart
There still hath been a void—a vacant place,
That ever seem'd to crave some image there,
Set up for worship. Till this happy hour,
The shrine hath been unoccupied and cold;

Now doth the warmth of a divinity
Suffuse the reluctant nature, and I glow
In the superior consciousness of hopes
That fill me with devotion. Here is one
Might teach me wherefore this.

NEA. He breathes again;
There's life within him yet.—His lips, they part
In murmurs:—he will live. Shall we now leave him?

ATAL. Leave him, dost thou ask? alas! my Nea,
I cannot if I would. His image takes
Possession of the waste place in my soul,
And fills me with himself. Whether I go,
Or stay,—the fates forbid that we should part;—
And known, perchance, and loved too late, he still
Hath grown to such a presence in my thought,
That, though I lose him in the hour that finds,
I lose him not from love. Now, let us call
The life into his cheek. Some water bring,
Scoop'd out from yonder fountain near the sea.
There, fan him with thy pinions. See, his lips,—
Again they part, how sweetly!—and again,
I stoop to press them with my own that burn
With a strange fervor never felt before.
He wakes!—Ah me, he wakes! His eyes unclose
With a dim beauty. As they open, mine
Sink to the sands. I feel his glances now,
Stealing and searching through my throbbing heart,
Until it hath no secret. Doth he speak?
What says he, my sweet Nea?

LEON, [*struggling to his feet.*] Nay,—no more!—
Ah! sister, is it thou? That terrible thought
That thou wert swallow'd in the ravenous sea,
And the waves over thee! I saw thee sink—
Beheld thy outstretch'd arms—heard thy wild cry

For succor, that I strove in vain to give,—
And, struggling in the surf, 'gainst cruel hands,
That kept me from thee in the fearful hour,
I yielded thee as lost.—I have thee now—
We shall not part again. [*Embracing Atalantis.*

ATAL. Ah!—

LEON, [*discovering her.*] Who art thou?
Where is my sister—give her to my arms;
Why dost thou keep her from me when I call?

ATAL. Oh! look not thus upon me, gentle youth:
I have not done thee wrong.

LEON. My sister?

ATAL. She—
I know not.—

LEON. Alas! alas! for me!—I am alone.

ATAL. Oh! not alone, for though we know not her,
The sister thou hast lost, we'll seek for her,
And strive to bring her to thy love again.
We too will love thee, if thou'lt suffer us,
And claim thy love in turn.

LEON. Where am I then?
Oh! tell me, noble lady, tell me true,
What is the shore we stand on—where the ship
That bore us—the old master, and the men,—
And over all of these, the precious maid,
My sister, whom I swore to save from harm,
While strength was in my arms to strive for her.
Alas! that I am here, with life and strength,
And she—thou look'st as thou hadst love and truth,—
Spare me these pangs—withhold her not from me,—
I shall not sink into an agony,
Joy-troubled at her sight. I'm strong to bear
This happiness, if thou hast it to bestow,
And take my blessing for it. Give her me!

ATAL. Alas! thou plead'st to me, dear youth, in vain;
I know not of the gentle maid you seek.
Thou only, of the creatures of the ship,
Hast found the refuge of the shore.

LEON. She's gone,—
And I survive her! How can I survive?
With what a terror she entreated me,
Never to leave her; and I pledged my soul,
If I had power to save, she should not sink,
Or I should share her fate. My Isabel!
I could not save, and cannot now survive;—
I come to thee,—I come! [*Rushes towards the sea.*

ATAL. Forbear! Forbear!
Oh! be not thus the murderer of thyself,
When heaven's own voice hath order'd thee to live.
For my sake as for thine! I kneel to thee.
Do not this wrong unto thyself, I pray,
Nor to the memory of the maid thou griev'st,
Who, if she loved thee, never could be blest,
At this, thy woeful sacrifice. Oh! hear!
Let me implore. Thy sister yet may live,
Cast on some other isle, as thou on this.
We'll seek her hence together, with a hope
That we may find her on the yellow sands,
And win her back to life.

LEON. Oh! sweet thy words!
I will believe thee, lady, with a hope
That comes on golden pinions; for thine eye
Tells of a true sense prompting thee to speak,
In mercy, with a blessing won from truth;
While in thy voice a delicate music lies,
Spelling all sympathies that fill the heart.
Say, who art thou?

ATAL. My name is Atalantis.

I am a Princess of the ocean waste,
But now a prisoner on this cruel isle,
Which, raised by magic from the hidden deep,
Wreck'd thee and fetters me. I have the sway
Of a large ocean empire which, in sight,
Extends beyond the sight, and far beneath
In winding ways and valleys of the sea.
I keep no state, but, as a captive, pine
In sight of my own kingdom, in the power
Of a dread monarch of the demon race,
A mighty potentate who keeps me here,
Seeking my love.

LEON. How fell you in his power?

ATAL. 'Twere a long speech to tell you of our realms,
The sway that's mine and his respectively,
And the slight space betwixt us; or to dwell
On the opposing powers we each possess:
It is enough, sweet youth, that yestermorn,
I and this maiden, o'er the quiet sea,
Idly disporting in our innocence,
Pass'd from our own dominions into his;
When, straightway he,—being ever on the watch,
And all unmatch'd for cunning—raised this isle,
At once, beneath us. In this sudden strait,
Frighted, I cast aside my magic wand,
Without which, I am nothing; and, with joy,
Knowing its powers, this monster seized it then,
And keeps me now his captive, close fenced in
By thickest spells, which, circling all this isle,
And having with our fine sense deadly hate,
We may not pass, unless he wills it so,
Or I regain my wand. Could that be done,
Its power is such that I could sink this isle,

And, with one stroke in air, undo the spells
Of his foul-brew'd enchantment.
  LEON. It is strange!
Methinks I wander in the Arabian tale,
And wear the enchanted ring.—This demon king—
Where is his castle where he harbors now?
I would behold him, and do battle for you.
I am a knight of Spain, well known in arms,
And wear the honors of the noblest courts,
Shining in Christendie.
  ATAL. The arms you wield,
In fight with such as he, would nothing serve:
He deals in subtlest magic, and receives
Spells from gigantic spirits. 'Twas his power
Aroused the storm that overthrew your bark;
And now, on like employment bent, he speeds
Afar upon the ocean, with a host
Of most malignant followers in his train,
Rank for destruction. Could I get my wand,
In which a power of mightiest strength abides,
I'd battle him myself, and drive him back,
And whelm the barren isle which keeps us now!
Nay, more than this,—if that thy sister sleeps
Beneath the waters,—though I may not win
Her spirit back to life—with that same wand,
We both may penetrate the tumbling waves,
Without or hurt or harm,—with vision free,
To find her gentle beauties where they rest
On quiet beds of flowers beneath the deep.
There, with our magic art may we enwrap
Her fragile beauty in protecting spells,
That still her eyes shall shine as when in life,
Her cheeks still glow with love's own red,—her lips,
Though they no more with many a tone of joy,

Made soft by feeling, whisper in your ears,—
Still look the sweetness they have ever worn,
Keeping the wonted freshness that they knew,—
When first they grew to thine. This shall we do,
And more, that nothing that thy sense may seek
Shall lack to make her lovely.

LEON. Gentle Queen,
If this be so,—do with me as thou wilt,—
I am thy slave,—thy slave!

ATAL. Rather I thine!
If thou wilt love me, this will I perform;
Nay, though thou love me not, I still will do it,
For love I have for thee.

NEA, [*aside.*] No more a Queen!
How doth she yield herself unto this power,
Forgetting her dominion.

LEON. Gentle Princess,
Shall we not get possession of this wand?
Methinks that I could do 't. But let me hear;
Teach me the way!—I shall not fear to meet
This monster, though with magic panoplied
And all foul arts. Trust then the toil with me,
I am a soldier of the holy cross,
And do defy the fiend and all his works.

ATAL. 'Tis a brave spirit, but here can little do,
Save to adventure.—This, indeed, is much!—
Magic must baffle magic. 'Tis for thee,
Still to procure this wand, which thou canst win,
When I have arm'd thee with some little power;
Thou being of earthly essence, with no fear
From contact with the all-infectious spell
Girdling the island round. Within yon rock,
That hangs precipitous above the deep—
That should be far beneath it—by him raised,

With sudden conjuration, at a word—
Seal'd in with spells, and in a curious vase,
Itself a spell, the treasure lies enshrined.
These charms, to me, were naught, could I but reach
The chambers where they lie; for, with this ring,
Which now upon thy hand I place from mine,
I may command all seals, and bid them break.
Onesimarch knows this, and trusts them not;
But placing an earthborn taint upon the air,
He doth restrain my footstep.

LEON. Let me go—
I will achieve the adventure, or will die.

ATAL. Not yet—it were in vain that you would pass,
With your enfeebled strength, the threatening gulfs
Of leaping waters, that, between this isle,
And the high rocks you aim at, spread themselves.
We must seek other aid—and, what are these,
Auspiciously, that gather on the sands,
In the fine haze of moonlight?

NEA. Fairy tribes,
That, sporting in the moonbeams, saw below
This new creation of Onesimarch,
And straight came down, still glad in what is new,
To keep their revels on it.

LEON, [*aside.*] Wonders grow,
Fruitful as things of nature.

ATAL. [*To Nea.*] This is well;—
Meet to our purpose, at the needful hour,
When they might succor us. We must persuade
The aid and office they will scarce deny
To one who holds them of a kindred race,
Though of another element. Away!
Seek their chief, Nea. Show him all our strait,—
Declare our want, and for his service now,

Pledge our good office at another time.
We wait thee here. [*Exit Nea.*] Alas! sweet youth, thou look'st
With such a sadness on me!

LEON. Not on thee;—
'Tis on my fate I look!

ATAL. I am thy fate!
And thou wilt hate me for it! Oh! forgive!—
If I have won thee now against thy will,
To this wild venture, I do free thee from 't;—
I would not have my freedom, did it bring
A moment's grief to thee.

LEON. Thou little know'st,
Sweet Princess, of the lessons of my youth,
The training of my people, and the laws
Which make it still our duty as our pride,
To stake the issues all, of life and death,—
All that we pleasure and can peril most,—
In cause of love and beauty. I rejoice
That it is mine to combat thy mishap.
This is a venture of my heart's own choice,
Too precious to be yielded,—and, forgive,—
But little know'st thou of Spain's chivalry,
When thou believest that its valor shrinks
From any odds with fortune. 'Tis with me
A pride to seek for peril; and we hold,
Taught in our schools of faith and courtesie,
That, to the soul, no life is worth a care,
Lock'd up from noble deeds, lapsing away
Like a scant brook, beneath a sunny sky,
Scarce murmuring as it wanders to be lost,
In the embrace of the o'erwhelming sea.

ATAL. Oh! noble, brave philosophy!

LEON. We fight,
That insolence should meet check and overthrow,

The weak find succor, and the innocent
Be always sure of shelter from the base;—
And, when the peril is sought for one so fair,
Then do our masters teach us, it is one
On which the heavens look down approvingly
And the bright angels cheer.

ATAL. And yet thou griev'st;—
The sorrow grows to dews upon thy lids,
Even while thine eyes flash fire.

LEON. My grief, alas!
Mark'd in my face, is from the wretched fear,
Now coursing through my brain, that she I seek,
The gentle girl, companion of my youth,
Bland as the moonlight, wooing as the shade,
And sweet as fairy music, deeply lies
Buried in these wild waters—never more,
To bless me with the music of her voice—
The magic of her smile—the calm delight
Of her not troublesome, devoted love!

ATAL. Oh! I have tears to share with thee for her!—
I may not give her back to thee, nor bid
The voice to that young lip, where, like a bird,
That had its life in music with the flowers,
It lapsed in long and loving melodies;
But I will toil in thy service, glad to be,
For thy bereavéd heart and fever'd brain,
Most like to her thou grievest. I will strive,
That thou shalt so esteem me. Not a tone,
Fashion'd by love's own mood, and most like hers,
But I shall teach my language;—not a look,
Worn by her gentlest features, but shall mine
Skilfully take from summer skies and flowers,
Requiting thy sad heart.

LEON. Oh, sweetest maid—

Thy form is kindred to thy purposes,
And half restores me.

ATAL. All will I restore—
All thou hast lost,—and more. Believe me then—
And stay thy sorrows. I will all replace,
Of thy fond fancies, and, with love as true,
Coupled with better power to serve its hope,
I'll be to thee far more than she thou grievest,
Though her affection, from the innocent hour
Of thy confiding childhood and pure dreams,
Boundless as ocean, like the Mexique waves,
Knew but one course, and ever ran to thee.
Believe me, dearest, thou shalt nothing lose
Of the known raptures. Thou shalt many win,
Not in thy wealth before. Thou shalt not think,
Ere I shall know and satisfy thy thought.

LEON. Too generous maid.

ATAL. And,—hear me, gentle prince!—
If to thy sleepless, striving memory,
There be some marks, some moods, some images,
Some sweet tone, some fond action, some dear song
Of childhood, or some innocent prank you've known
Together, roving amid natural bowers,—
Teach me the trick of it all;—teach me the tone,
The dear song, the fond action, the gay prank,
Known to thy happiest childhood;—show me the art,
That nothing may be wanting—that I may take
A presence like to hers upon thy sight,
And make thee rich again, possessing her.

LEON. Thy words are queenliest, like thyself, sweet maid,
And balsam my deep wound,—if not to cure,
To soothe and stay its throbbing. Thou hast said,
In sweet tones, sweetest words, that soften much
The temper of my sorrows.

ATAL. I am glad,
To offer to thy aid, to chide thy grief,—
LEON. Yet, for this sweet and undeservéd love,
If I look coldly, unbecomingly,—
As feeling not its ministry, nor yet,
Beholding my own lack that makes it dear—
Impute it not, I pray, a crime in me.
I am not cold because my hope is so,
Nor yet ungrateful that I do not joy;—
I shall learn better to requite thy love,
In warmest language, when the pang is gone
Of this sad trial—if it ever goes.
ATAL. What do they call thee?
LEON. Leon is my name.
ATAL. I'll call thee Leon;—call me Atalant,—
Thy Atalant,—for shall I not be thine?
Ah me! no longer may I be mine own!
LEON. Beautiful Atalant!—
ATAL. But here they come,
Nea, and with her all the tricksy tribe,
That ride on beams, and travel with the stars;
And sing in place of speech; and fly to walk;
Now here, now gone; garb'd cunningly with flowers,
They know to seem at pleasure; and still bless'd,
With that which were our sorrow—constant change.

SCENE II.—*The Same.*

Enter Nea with Fairies. They circle the Princess and Leon singing.

CHORUS OF FAIRIES.

I.

Lo, we come, we come, we come,
  On the glassy moonbeams riding,
While no cloud, with eye of gloom,
  Looks down on us chiding—
Where the silver sands spread out,
  Fit for spirits gayly moving;
Tossing fruits and flowers about,
  We are ever roving.

II.

Lo, we fly, we fly, we fly,
  All the world about us viewing,
Now in sea and now in sky,
  Still our sport pursuing.
Where the moon is shining clear,
  Where the winds are met together,
Do we daily gather there,
  In the summer weather.

III.

Lo, we dance, we dance, we dance,
  On the land, and o'er the ocean;
Seizing on each happy chance,
  With a glad commotion.
Where the summer's leaves are green,
  Where the early birds are singing,
And the flowers are soonest seen,
  We are with them springing.

IV.

Lo, we come, we come, we come,
On our wings of light descending;
Wings that breathe, like flowers in bloom,
Perfumes never ending.
On the shining sands we meet,
In the bright and gentle weather,
Each with something new and sweet,
Dancing all together.

ATAL. Oh! ye are glad to-night, ye merry ones,
With a fresh spirit, methinks. What pleasant hap,
New privilege, or wild inheritance,
Works on your wings such fine delirium?
I somewhat marvel at your happiness,
Though happy always; yet your wont is dull
To the extravagant rapture of your mirth,
And your free song to-night.
NANITA. Extravagant!
Our mirth, fair Queen, is very soberness;
We are the modestest fairies of the wild,
The gravest, quietest, best of little bodies,
That ever made mischief in a neighbor's fold,
And laugh'd to find our own. Why, people call us
The very prudes of faerydom. We shake
Our heads with gravity o'er state affairs,
And sit in council with old Oberon,
Who, when Titania wakes his jealousy,
Will straight prefer our wisdom to his own;—
As, at such times, indeed, he wisely may.
ATAL. Oh! pray you then forgive me! Now I see
That you are sober and quiet as you claim,
Having but little mirth, and, at no season,
Extravagant in its utterance. Your excess
Lay only in my sadness. 'Twas my grief

That made your joy extreme. Your mood,
Thus born of freedom, little sorts with mine,
That grows with my captivity, and glooms
With the dread aspect of my prison-house.

LOLINE. Yet is there much to gladden us to-night.
Have we not newly added to our realms
A goodly island, gracious in extent,
Whose beauteous sands, drawn out in lavish scope,
Persuades the moon's best smile upon our revels.

ATAL. If you knew all,—the story of this isle!—
Yet is there something more, or I mistake ye,
For which ye joy to-night.

CARETA. There is! There is!
Rightly you spoke, fair Princess, when you deem'd
Our joy unwonted. We are bless'd to-night,
Beyond our usual measure. You shall hear.
Perchance you know Zelina,—of our tribe,
The sweetest, merriest creature—full of fun,—
But glad to serve, and, with the happiest art,
To make the service pleasant as the will,
That prompts it to compliance. She is here—
Just freed from a captivity like yours;
Since in her sport, by some undreampt mischance,
She smote Titania's favorite nonpareil,
And broke its gossamer wing. The angry Queen,
For this, our little sister's innocent deed,
Doom'd her a prisoner in the zephyr's shell,
Till the first flowers that blossom in the spring
Should speak her into freedom. Till this time
Her fate was pitiful:—to use no wing,
Murmur no more, and mingle not, in song—
See none to comfort—hear no voice of love—
Dance no capricious revel on the sands,
But, with an unresisting sense, to float

On the tumultuous billows, night and morn,
Until the birth of that same flower of spring!
Found on the pleasantest shore beneath the sun,
Where first he soars in brightness from the seas,
We hail'd its presence, and have set her free;
And, from her prison, with delighted wing,
She soars with us to-night.

LOL. Nor is this all—
Another captive hath to-night been freed,
We had deem'd lost forever to our sports.
This wanton fairy, sporting in the breeze,
Last moon, alone, was taken prisoner
By that same tyrant-king, Onesimarch,
That locks you in; and, 'twere a fit revenge,
That we should join with you, for these same wrongs,
To punish him in turn. Within yon rock,
He seal'd her up in crystal. By some chance,
Not yet discover'd, all her bonds were broke,
And she is here with us. Tinina!—here!
Behold the maiden, Princess. She knows all
The secrets of this tyrant's ocean-towers,
And, for your wand's recovery, will do
Aught that will seem most needful.

ATAL. [*To Tinina.*] Fit a barque,
And make thy wing its sail, to waft this Prince
To the same rock that was thy prison late.
Himself will do the rest. 'Tis there, I learn,
My sceptre is sealed up.

TININA. The barque is here,
Even with a whisper, and my wing is ready;
Will 't please you go, my Prince?

ATAL. [*timidly.*] Wilt thou go, Leon?

LEON. 'Twill please and make me proud.

LOL. Tinina, hence!

I give thee winds, and waters, and a star,—
I spell thee with a talisman of safety,—
And crown thee with a will and wing of strength;
Go hence in courage, and be bless'd in service;
And when thy task is done, regain our course,
Which now we take toward the Hundred Isles,
That smile in the Southern Cross. We wait thee there.
Princess, we gladden that our offices
Seem worth thy tasking, and shall find delight,
If that they prosper 'neath thy hope and ours.
Wings, be ye up and wheeling—up, I say!

FLIGHT OF FAIRIES, AND CHORUS.

We are they who fly by night,
When the maiden moon is bright,
And the silver beach is spread,
Out on ocean like a thread,
Meetly for a fairy's tread:
When the air of heaven is balm,
When the ocean waves are calm,
And the flowers of earth grow bright,—
We are they who fly by night!

[*Exeunt Fairies.*

Atal. Now, Leon, if the task before thee seem
Unsuited to thy human strength,—
Leon. No more!
Hold me, I pray thee, Princess, as a man
That better loves the struggle that proves manhood,
Than the base sleep that stagnates all his soul.
I seek the adventure.
Atal. Then, this sylph will guide;—
Will bear thee safely o'er these tumbling gulfs,
To yon tall rock, now beetling black and vast
Above the whiten'd billows. Boldly speed,

Nothing misdoubting, howsoever strange
The thing that rises threatening in thy path.
The mystic ring that wraps thy finger round,
Hath, in itself, a wondrous faculty,
To shield the wearer from the unlicensed power
Of spirits of evil.
  LEON. Atalant, I go,
Having a better talisman of safety,
In service which is noble, and in prayer
To him who checks and may subdue all spirits,
Than in this hoop of magic. See, this cross,
Which crowns the mortal weapon that I wear,
As life is over death!—this is my shield,
As, in the blade, I find my ample sword;
With these I go unfearing.
  ATAL. Would thou went'st
With brow serene—with happier thought than now.
  LEON. Heed not the mood of this most heavy heart,
That clouds the brow thou look'st on. Some few days
Will hush the impatient grief that murmuring cries,
Seeking a loved one lost. When I return,
And thou hast led me where my sister lies,
Though she beholds not as I weep beside her,
Still will I strive to thank thee with a blessing,
Whose eyes shall look but love!
  ATAL. Till then I live not!

Tinina sings.

The wind is on the wave, and the billow rolls away,
  And the star that is the guide to the voyager is bright,
But the fickle wind may change, should the voyager delay,
  And the star beneath the demon cloud may perish from the sight.
The will, and the wing, are both ready while I sing—
  And the service that makes music as for love it labors still,

Hath no murmur for the ear, though it whispers still of care,
  And implores that the season be not forfeit to the will.
Then away, then away, ere we meet the coming day,
  For the dewy haze is rising like a curtain o'er the sea;—
I have winds and waves and star, but they serve us not in war,
  And the present bears the flower that's most precious unto me.

LEON. The delicate song is sung in my behalf,
A counsel spoke in sweetness, as should be
All counsel for the loved one;—fairy, thanks!—
I'm with thee!—sweetest princess, fare thee well!

ATAL. I dare not bid thee go, but if thou wilt,
My heart has but one bidding—soon return.
[*Exeunt Leon and Tinina.*

NEA. Sweet mistress!—

ATAL. Come with me to ocean's edge,—
That we may soonest hail his coming back,
Made happy in his safety.

NEA. This is love! [*Exeunt.*

SCENE III.

The Rock and Tower of Onesimarchus. Ogré chained at the base.

OGRÉ. Shall I not have revenge—shall he not feel,
This wanton wrong that he hath put on me,
In his unmeasured wrath? Must I submit
To wear the chains about my limbs, as now;
Still fearing, that, for every erring deed,
I may not 'scape the villain penalty,
But bend my shrinking back to meet the scourge,
When 't suits a fellow-slave to place it there!
I'll be revenged.—Already have I done

Something towards it; for, throughout the hour,
When that his storms were raging o'er my limbs,
Chafed into madness, the dismember'd rocks
I hurl'd into his secret halls above,
And the repeated crash gave token sure
Of a wild mischief—and I rest not here!
He cannot punish me more than he has done,
And, let the tyrant will it so or not,
I leave his service when my limbs are free.
Ha! What are these? How now! What seek you here?

Enter Leon and Tinina.

What is it that you lack? Speak, ere I strike,
And hurl you into pieces with this rock.
LEON. Thou monstrous slave, what is it that thou sayst?
Dost threaten too? Stand by, and let me pass,
Or thus, I thrust my weapon to thy heart.
TININA. Forbear! Thou wert an infant in his grasp,
And he would crush thee at a single stroke.
Show him thy spell of power—but lift thy ring!
See, now, he trembles: keep it thus in sight,
And we shall pass. No strength is in his arm,—
He cannot hurt us now. [*They ascend and enter the rock.*
OGRÉ. Terrible power!
How has it fetter'd me, and taken away
Each nerve once strung for action. Lo! they come,
And bearing off my master's instruments.—
Well, let them go! I glad me he hath wrong!
I would that he were fetter'd in my place,
And I were free and had no master then;
How would I revel in all goodly things!—
What lusts would I delight in,—food and drink,
Until my senses swim, and sleep i' the sun,
Doing no service more! Ah! here they come.

Enter Leon and Tinina.

LEON. Slave, wouldst thou have thy freedom, and escape
The tyranny that tramples in this wise,
Loading thy limbs with chains, while the salt sea,
Enflames the galling tortures of the scourge?

OGRÉ. That would I, mighty prince.

LEON. Thou hast it then.
Throw by the chain thou wear'st and follow me.

OGRÉ. I'll fling it in the sea. Shall I do more?
Bid me upheave this rocky battlement,
Wherein he keeps his magic, I'll not pause;—.
Do thou but say the word.

LEON. Nay, heed it not!
If she I serve do thus decree, thou mayst,—
Not else.

OGRÉ. How now! you are no monarch then?
Whom serve you?

LEON. The fair princess, Atalantis.

OGRÉ. I do remember that she spoke for me,
And would have saved me from this scourge and rock.
A goodly princess—I will worship her.

Tinina sings.

The bark is on the sea, and the breeze is in the sail,
And the star to guide us onward is now gleaming o'er the steep;
We have won the prize we sought, and the whisper of the gale
Would counsel us, the treasure, we have haply won, to keep.
Then away, then away, ere the tyrant seeks his prey,—
There's a murmur of the ocean that's unfriendly to our flight;
And the cricket at mine ear has a chirrup full of fear,
That but lately sung in music of a confident delight.

LEON. Even as thou wilt, sweet maiden; let us hence
To her who waits in hope and innocence.

SCENE IV.

The Ocean between the rocks and the Islet.

Atalantis, Leon, and Nea. Onesimarchus approaching with his Legions.

ONESI. Ha! what is here—what fearful change is this?—
The rock of spells o'erthrown, and Atalant,
Again with wand restored, and, at her side,
The lowly instrument of her release.
I did not guard against a thing of earth,
And he hath wrought this ruin of my hopes.
She smiles upon him too—perchance she loves—
Hell!—that I cannot blast her with a look,
And him, the minion, that hath won her love!—
He shall not live, to triumph in that love,
Enjoying raptures still denied to me.
Rise waters—lift your heads—mount up and soar,
Engulfing all that may not ride upon ye;
And thou, dismember'd shore, again descend,
Down to the oozy depths from whence thou cam'st—
I need thee nothing farther—sink, I say.
[*He waves his wand and the island descends.*

ATAL. Now, Leon, place thy hand within mine own;
Fear not the billows—hearken not their roar,—
They cannot harm thee, thus accompanied.

LEON. And ye, fair skies, farewell. Thou fatal isle,
Which robb'd me of my best beloved, farewell!
I sorrow not to see thee downward go,
Troubling no mariner hence. One long last look,
Ye bright clouds, that remind me of my home—

My country, all, farewell. Oh, never more
Shall my eyes gladden with your glimpse again.
Now Isabel, I come!

Atal. Thou hast no fear,
Dear Leon, from this danger?

Leon. Little now,
Since, in the wonders that are shown to me,
I yield me to the fullest faith in all
That thou hast promised me.

Atal. Thou soon shalt see,
How, as to me, these waters shall become
Familiar to thy nature. Thou wilt glide
Unharm'd between their billows, which shall lift
Thy form, with friendly succor, as thou will'st,
Making their arms thy servants.

Leon. I believe,—
And round thy waist, sweet Atalant, I twine,
Fearless, my confident arm and murmur not.
I would not look upon the skies again,
That witness'd my late ruin; and the seas,
That wrought it all, beget no terrors now.—
We do not sink.

Atal. Not yet!—Behold afar,
Where, gathering, grow vast legions—angry forms,
Gigantic, that in masses, or alone,
Dart onward, with a glittering panoply
That flames the crests of ocean far and wide,
While roll the constant thunders of the gong,
That calls them still to rise.

Leon. I see! I see!

Atal. These are the armies of my own domain,
Led by my gallant brothers. They go forth,
To fight and conquer this Onesimarch,
Who, strong in trick and artifice alone,

Will never meet them in the open field.
Already, see, he shrinks ;—his hosts retire,
And his fierce rule departs.
LEON. The land is gone!
ATAL. Yes, down we sink, and thou art all mine own:
I bear thee on the waters, for a while,
To prove the power I have to succor thee.
Now for the calm retreat, by ocean girt,
And stormy waves protected—now with me!
There in the sunny hours that lapse away,
Like angel messengers, and leave no pain,
Thy heart shall grow to gladness. Life shall be
A sweet, rich, gracious time,—a pure estate,
Beyond the strifes that trouble it with man:—
Free from controlling crowds—free from the jar,
The heat, the noise, the dust of human care.
Nature shall blight thee never, nor disease
Bind thee in loathsome sheets; nor tempests rise
To blasts thy fields, dispute thy fondest hope,
And, from thy wearied and exhausted heart,
Drink the sweet life-blood of thy innocent joy.
The breeze shall rather soothe thee with a breath,
Robb'd from celestial gardens. The blue waves,
Shall roll their tribute honors to thy feet;
Upon their bosom, many an offering placed,
Of fruits, fresh wafted from far Indian isles
Wooing thee with their fragrance. In the air,
Nature shall cast her odors, and thine eye
Shall never ope but to behold some new
And most luxuriant freshness in her form;
And, I shall love thee too, and toil untired
To give thee back the maiden whom thou seek'st.
LEON. Ah! if thou couldst!—but no! The hope is vain,
And the wish idle. Yet the love thou givest,

Might well compensate, to this baffled heart,
The loss which still it weeps.

ATAL. Oh! do not weep.
I'll love thee in all fortunes. At the morn,
I'll lead thee through our waters, 'mid our caves,
Where, in unconscious brightness, cluster gems
Had set your world on fire. There shall you mark
Glad sea-maids that, attending on our steps,
Fill their deep shells with song; and, when the sun
Shines burningly at noon, in coral groves,
Thy head well pillow'd on my happy breast,
I'll sit and watch thy slumbers, blest to soothe
Thy ever beating pulse, and kiss thy lips,
When, murmuring in thy sleep, thou speak'st the name,
Of her thou still hast loved.

LEON. No more of her.
I go with thee, sweet Atalant.—We sink!

Chorus of Sea-Nymphs as the island descends.

THE CASSIQUE OF ACCABEE;

A LEGEND OF ASHLEY RIVER.

A FEW words, by way of preface, will save us the necessity of burdening with notes the little story which follows. Accabee is the well-known name of a lovely, but neglected, farmstead, in the neighborhood of Charleston, on Ashley River. It was in earlier periods applied to a larger district in the same neighborhood. Keawah is the aboriginal name of the Ashley. The tribe of Accabee was probably of the same family with the Yemassees, the Edistos, and other groups, inhabiting the lower country of South Carolina. The Gaelic Chief spoken of in the text was Lord Cardross, who made a settlement at, or near, Beaufort, which, after a brief existence of four years, was destroyed by an incursion of the Indians and Spaniards.

It was a night of calm—o'er Ashley's waters
Crept the sweet billows to their own soft tune,
While she, most bright of Keawah's fair daughters,
Whose voice might spell the footsteps of the moon,
As slow we swept along,
Pour'd forth her own sweet song,
A lay of rapture not forgotten soon.

Hush'd was our breathing, stay'd the lifted oar,
Our spirits rapt, our souls no longer free,
While the boat drifting softly to the shore,
Brought us within the shades of Accabee;—
"Ah!" sudden cried the maid,
In the dim light afraid;
"'Tis here the ghost still walks of the old Yemassee."

And sure the spot was haunted by a power,
To fix the pulses in each youthful heart;
Never was moon more gracious in a bower,
Making delicious fancy work for art;
Weaving, so meekly bright,
Her pictures of delight,
That, though afraid to stay, we sorrow'd to depart.

"If these old groves are haunted"—sudden then,
Said she, our sweet companion—"it must be
By one who loved, and was beloved again,
And joy'd all forms of loveliness to see:—
Here, in these groves they went,
Where love and worship, blent,
Still framed the proper God for each idolatry.

"It could not be that love should here be stern,
Or beauty fail to sway with sov'ran might;
These, from so blessèd scenes, should something learn,
And swell with tenderness and shape delight:
These groves have had their power,
And bliss, in bygone hour,
Hath charm'd, with sigh and song, the passage of the night."

"It were a bliss to think so;" made reply
Our Hubert—"yet the tale is something old,
That checks us with denial;—and our sky,
And these brown woods that, in its glittering fold,
Look like a fairy clime,
Still unsubdued by time,
Have evermore the tale of wrong'd devotion told."

"Give us thy legend, Hubert;" cried the maid;—
And, with down-dropping oars, our yielding prow
Shot to a still lagoon, whose ample shade
Droop'd from the gray moss of an old oak's brow:
The groves, meanwhile, lay bright,
Like the broad stream, in light,
Soft, sweet as ever yet the lunar loom display'd.

"Great was the native chief,"—'twas thus began
The legend of our comrade—"who, in sway,
Held the sweet empire which to-night we scan,
Stretching, on either hand, for miles away:
A stalwart chief was he,
Cassique of Accabee,
And lord o'er numerous tribes who did with pride obey.

"War was his passion, till the white man came,
And then his policy;—and well he knew,
How, over all, to plan the desperate game,
And when to rise, and when to sink from view;
To plant his ambush well,
And how, with horrid yell,
To dart, at midnight forth, in fury arm'd with flame.

"His neighbors by the Ashley, the pale race,
Were friends and allies 'gainst all other foes;
They dwelt too nearly to his royal place,
To make the objects of their commerce blows;
But no such scruple staid
His wild and cruel raid,
When, by Heléna's Bay, the Gaelic hamlet rose.

"And moved by Spanish wile that still misled,
Our chieftain, in one dark November night,
With all his warriors, darted from his bed,
And drove the Gaelic chief from his, in flight:—
Scalplocks and other spoils,
Rewarded well his toils,
And captives graced his triumph after fight.

"But, when the strife was wildest, and the fire
Play'd fiercest on the roofs of bough and leaf,
A fair-hair'd child, misdeeming him her sire,
Rush'd headlong to the arms of the red chief:—
'Twas not his hour to spare—
His fingers in her hair,
And tomahawk, lifted high, declared his savage ire.

"But, in the light of her own blazing home,
He caught the entreaty in her soft blue eye,
Which, weeping still the while, would wildly roam,
From him who held, to those who hurried by;—
Strange was the emotion then,
That bade him stay his men,
And, in his muscular arms, lift that young damsel high.

"He bore her through the forest, many a mile,
With a rude tenderness and matchless strength;
She slept upon his arm—she saw his smile,
Seen seldom, and reached Accabee at length;
Here, for a term, he kept
The child, her griefs unwept,
With love, that did from her a seeming love beguile.

"Daughter of ancient Albyn, she was bright,
With a transparent beauty; on her cheek,
The rose and lily, struggling to unite,
Did the best blooms of either flower bespeak;
Whilst floods of silken hair,
Free flowing, did declare
The gold of western heavens when sinks the sun from sight.

"Our chief had reached his thirtieth summer—she
Was but thirteen; yet, till he saw this maid,
Love made no portion of his reverie:
Strife was his passion, and the midnight raid;
The dusky maids, in vain,
Had sought to weave their chain,
About that fierce wild heart that still from all went free.

"But, free no longer, they beheld him bound
By his fair captive; strife was now unsought;
The chase abandon'd; and his warriors found
Their chief no more where fields were to be fought;—
He better loved to brood
In this sweet solitude,
She still in sight, who thus her captor's self had caught.

"She little dream'd her conquest, for he still
Maintain'd her as his child, with tenderness;—
As one who seeks no farther of his will,
Than to protect and with sweet nurture bless;
Such love as sire might show,
Did that dark chief bestow,
When, with a gentle clasp, he met her child-caress.

"She grew to be the blossom of his sight—
For her he snared the fawn,—for her he brought
Gay gauds of foreign fabric;—her delight
Being still the sweetest recompense he sought;—
And, when her feet would rove,
He led her through the grove,
Show'd her its devious paths and all its secrets taught.

"She grew apace in beauty as in years,
And he the more devoted:—until now
His eye beheld her growth and had no fears,—
But soon a shadow rose above his brow;—
That shadow, born of doubt,
Which finds love's secret out,
And, o'er its sunniest bower, still spans an arch of tears.

"This shadow had its birth with our dark chief,
When to his home, one eve, returning late,
He saw, with passion still subdued by grief,
A stranger with his beauty, in his gate;—
One of the pale white race,
Whose presence, in that place,
Brought to his heart a fear that troubled it like fate.

"Yet was he but a pedlar,—he who came,—
Thus troubling waters which had slept before;
He brought his glittering wares, and did but claim
To show them, and night's lodging to implore:
And, o'er his pack, with eyes
Of eager, glad surprise,
Stoop'd our young maid when stept the chief within his door.

"His stealthy footsteps stirr'd no single sound;
They knew not of the eyes upon them set—
She, the gay thoughtless girl, in thought profound,
Deep in such wealth as had not tempted yet;
While his—the stranger's—gaze,
In a most pleasant maze,
Scann'd her bright cheeks, unseen, from eyes of glittering jet.

"A handsome youth, of dark and amorous glance,
Showing a grateful consciousness of power,
Yet thoughtless, in that moment of sweet trance,
How best to woo and win the forest flower;
Even at that moment, stood
The red-man from the wood,
Gazing, with instinct grief, that had its birth that hour.

"Quickly he broke the silence and came forth,
While the fair girl, upstarting from her dream,
Hurried his search into such stores of worth,
As did on eyes of young Aladdin gleam:—
Clipping his neck with arms
That spoke of dearer charms,
The maid Othello loved might she that moment seem.

"And, with a pleased, but still a sinking heart,
He yielded to her pleading: he had stores,—
Such treasures as the red-man might impart,
Of precious value, borne to foreign shores;
Spoils in the forest caught,
By tribute hunter brought,
Soft furs from beaver won by snares of sylvan art.

"Sadly, the indulgent chief—but with a smile,—
Gave up his treasure at his ward's demand;
The precious gauds which did her eyes beguile,
Soon clasp'd her neck, or glitter'd in her hand.
All had she won—but still
There was a feminine will,
That led her glance astray beneath that stranger's wile.

"Their eyes commerced beside the blazing fire,
Hers still unconscious of the erring vein;
The chief beheld, in his, the keen desire,
And his heart swell'd with still increasing pain;
Yet, though the sting was deep,
His passion, made to sleep,
Look'd calm through eyes that seem'd a stranger still to ire.

"His board was spread with hospitable hand,
Crisp'd the brown bread and smoked the venison steak;
An ancient squaw, still ready at command,
Pour'd the casina tea, their thirst to slake;
Then, as the hour grew late,
With calm and lofty state,
The chief himself, with care, the stranger's couch did make.

"At sunrise they partook the morning meal,
And then the white man went upon his way;
Not without feeling—teaching her to feel—
How sweet to both had been his still delay:—
The nature, long at rest,
Rose, pleading, at her breast,
For that pale race from which, perforce, she dwelt astray.

"She long'd for their communion,—for the youth
Had waken'd memories, not to be subdued,
Of that dear home, and friends whose tender ruth
Possess'd her still in that sweet solitude;
And, saddening with the thought,
Her secret soul grew fraught
With hopes, with doubts, with dreams, o'er which she loved to brood.

"The chief beheld the trouble in her eye,
He felt as well the trouble in his heart,
And, ere the morrow's sun was in the sky,
He bade her make her ready to depart;—
He had a wider home,
Where love might safely roam,
Nor fear the stranger's foot, nor tremble at his art.

"Cassique among the Edistos, he bore
His treasure to the river of that name;
He sought the forests on its western shore,
Millions of acres he alone might claim;
Where the great stream divides,
He cross'd its double tides,
Still seeking denser empires to explore.

"At length, he paused beside a little lake,
A clear sweet mirror for the midnight star;
'Soon, weary one, thy slumbers shalt thou take;
In sooth, to-day, our feet have wander'd far;
Yet look, and thou shalt see,
The wigwam smokes for thee,—
Those fires that gleam through woods show where our people are.

"'Here shalt thou have fond service—here the clime
Is sweet and healthful;—buskin'd, with thy bow,
Thou'lt wander forth with me, at morning's chime,
And I to snare or slay the game, will show:
Broad are the sheltering woods,
Bright are the streams, the floods,
And safe the realm that hence thy youthful heart shall know.'

"Thus counselling, he led her o'er the plain,
Down the smooth hill, beside the lakelet clear;
They tread the gloomy forest paths again,
Till sudden, the whole landscape opens fair;
'Look! weary one,' he cries;
'Our realm before us lies,
Far spread as bird can fly, or speeds by day the deer.'

"In sooth, to one whose heart is all at rest,
With not a human care to call it thence,
It was a home that rapture might have bless'd,
Lovely to sight and dear to innocence;
Great trees, a welcome shade,
Of beech and poplar made,
Fortress of peace that love might deem his best defence.

"Long groves of pine and cedar led through wastes
Made lovely by wild flowers of every hue;
Through arching boughs and vines the river hastes,
Still with the song of birds that wander too;
A fresh green realm, unbroke
By plough, or woodman's stroke,
Rich in savannahs green, and lakes of skyey blue.

"His was the realm, and at his bidding came
The tribes that peopled it; beneath his sway
They framed their rude society;—his blame,
Or praise, sufficient guide to shape their way;
Still, with the falling leaf,
The signal of our chief
Prepared them for the chase and counsell'd their array.

"And thus, for many a moon, within that shade,
Dwelling 'mongst vassals rude but loyal still,
Remote, but not in loneliness, our maid
Had all that love could sigh for, but its will;
Submissive still she found
The gentle tribes around,
The squaws received her law, the warriors too obey'd.

"No censure check'd her walks—no evil eyes
Darken'd upon her childish sports at eve;
If o'er the chieftain's brow a trouble lies,
'Tis sure no fault of hers that makes him grieve;
For her he still hath smiles,
And, in her playful wiles,
He finds a charm that still must artlessly deceive.

"Her wild song cheers him at the twilight hour,
As, on the sward, beside her sylvan cot,
He throws him down, meet image of a power
Subdued by beauty to the vassal's lot;
With half unconscious gaze,
His eye her form surveys,
And fancies fill his heart which utterance yet have not.

"She had expanded into womanhood
In those brief years of mild captivity,
And now, as 'neath his glance the damsel stood,
Nothing more sweet had ever met his eye;—
Fair, with her Saxon face,
Her form a forest grace
Had won from woodland sports of rare agility.

"Her rich blue eyes, her streaming yellow hair,
The soft white skin that show'd the crimson tide,
And perfect features—made her beauties rare,
That well the charms of Indian race defied;—
Her motion, as of flight,
Tutor'd by wild delight,
Brought to her form a grace at once of love and pride.

"And, as he gazed, with rapture ill suppress'd,
Inly the chief resolved that she should be
The woman he would take unto his breast,
Ere the next moon should ride up from the sea;
His child no more,—he felt
His soul within him melt,
To hear her voice in song, her thought in fancy free.

"She felt at last her power upon his heart,
As she beheld the language in his eye;
And, with this knowledge, came a natural art,
Which bade her glances unto his reply;
Made happy by her look
His soul new poison took,
her to his breast, nor seem'd she to deny.

"'I shall go hence,' quoth he, 'the Hunter's Moon—
These sticks shall tell thee of the broken days;
When all are gone, I shall return,—and soon
The beauties that I hold within my gaze,
Shall bless, if thou approve,
This heart, and the fond love
That knows thee as the star the ocean stream that sways.'

"And she was silent while he spake—her head
Sunk, not in sadness, and upon his breast;
Fondly he kiss'd her—other words he said,
And still, in dear embrace, her form caress'd;
Then parting, sped afar,
Led by the Hunter's Star,
Where the bear wallows in his summer nest.

"She had no sorrow to obey the will
That ruled a nation: true, he slew her sire,
But he had been a gentle guardian still,
Baffling each danger, soothing each desire;
The power that he possess'd
Was grateful to her breast,
And warm'd with pride the heart, that lack'd each holier fire.

"That night there rose an image in her dreams,
Of the young trader seen at Accabee;
His fair soft face upon her memory gleams,
His keen, dark, searching eye, still wantonly
Pursues her with its blaze;
And she returns the gaze,
And thus her heart communes with one she cannot see.

"It was as if the chief, by the same word
That told his own fond purpose, had compell'd
The image of the person she preferr'd,—
And, seeing him in dreams, her soul was spell'd
With fancies that, in vain,
She strove to hush again—
She saw their shapes by day, by night their voices heard.

"Saddened by this communion, she withdrew
From those who sought her; in deep forests went,
By lonely streams and shades, from human view,
Nursing a vague and vexing discontent;—
For the first time, a care
Hung on her heart like fear—
The shadows from a soul not wholly innocent.

"There is a fate beside us day and night,
Obedient to the voice within our hearts;
Boldly we summon, and it stands in sight;
We speak not, and in silence it departs;—
'Twas thus with her, as still
She roved with aimless will,
Beside the swamps through which the Edisto still darts.

"She spoke aloud, or did not speak, his name,
Whose image was the sole one in her breast;
But, suddenly, from out the woods he came,
And mutual glances mutual joy express'd:—
'Ah! sought so long before,
I fear'd that, never more,
Mine eyes should see the form that kept my soul from rest.

"'How have I search'd for you in devious path,
Forgetful of the mercenary trade!
And now, though perill'd by the redman's wrath,
I seek you in forbidden forest shade;
For never, since that night,
When first you met my sight,
Hath beauty on my heart such sweet impression made.'

"They sat beneath the shade of silent trees,
Close guarded by a thicket dense and deep;
There, onward, stole the river at its ease,
And, through the air, the birds made easy sweep;—
Those bowers were sweetly dight
For safety and delight;—
The stranger won the prize the chieftain still would keep.

"He came, the dark-brow'd chieftain, from the chase,
Laden with precious spoils of forest pride;
His heart exulting as he near'd the place
Where the fair Saxon waited as his bride:
But who shall speak the grief
That shook that warrior chief,
When they declared her flight with yester-eventide.

"He had no voice for anguish or regret;—
He spake not of his purpose—but went forth,
With a keen spirit, on one progress set,
Now on the southern stream side, now the north;
Following, with sleuthhound's scent,
The way the lovers went,
Tracking each footfall sure, in leaf, in grass, and earth.

"Nor did he track in vain! They little knew
The unerring instinct of that hunter race;
A devious progress did the twain pursue,
Through streams and woods, to baffle still the trace;
But how should they beguile
The master of each wile,
Each art pursued in war or needful in the chase?

"In fancy safe, and weary now with flight,
The lovers lay at noonday in the shade;
Soft through the leaves and grateful to the sight,
The sun in droplets o'er the valley play'd;
But two short leagues, and they
Should leave the perilous way,
On Keawah secure, in home by squatter made.

"Thus satisfied, with seeming certainty,
Won by the hour's sweet stillness, did the pair,
Shelter'd beneath the brows of an old tree,
Give freedom to the love they joy'd to share;
His arm about her press'd,
She lay upon his breast,
Life's self forgot in bliss that left no room for care.

"They little dream'd that, lurking in the wood,
A witness to the freedom of their bliss,
The fiery chieftain they had baffled stood,
Fierce, with envenom'd fang and fatal hiss;
The lord of death and life,
He grasp'd the deadly knife,
And shook the tomahawk high but rarely known to miss.

"But, ere he sped the weapon to its mark,
His heart grew gentle 'neath a milder sway;
True, they had left his dwelling lone and dark,
But should he make it glad were he to slay?
Nor, if the man he slew,
Could he again renew
The trust he gave the maid as in his happier day.

"Nor could he strike, with stern and fatal blow,
Her whose fair beauties were too precious still;
A noble purpose came to soothe his woe,
And crown, with best revenge, a generous will;—
Forth strode he from the wood,
And ere they knew, he stood,
With weapon bared, and look still resolute to kill.

"As one who at the serpent's rattle starts,
Sharp, sudden sounded in the covert nigh,
They heard his voice, and both their guilty hearts
Sunk, hopeless, 'neath the expected penalty;
But, stifling his deep grief,
With few stern words, the chief,
Declared, though worthy death, the guilty should not die!

"O'erjoy'd at respite scarcely yet believed,
The girl had risen and rush'd to clasp his knees,
But he whose faith had been so much deceived,
No homage now could pacify or please;
Calm, but with gloomy face,
He checks the false embrace,
And still, the crouching youth, with scornful eye, he sees.

"He bade them rise and follow where he led,
Himself conducted to the dwelling near;
Here, till the dawn, each found a separate bed;
With morning o'er the Keawah they steer;
Still guided he the way,
And, ere the close of day,
Once more the three to shades of Accabee repair.

"'Here,' said he, 'is your future dwelling-place,
This be, my gift, your heritage of right;
The holy man, of your own foreign race,
Shall, with the coming day, your hands unite;
And men of law shall know
That I these lands forego,
For her who still hath been the apple of my sight.

"'See that you cherish her with proper faith;—
If that you wrong her, look for wrong from me:
Once have I spared you, when the doom was death;
Beware the future wrath you may not flee;
Mine eye shall watch for hers,
And if a breath but stirs
Her hair too rudely,—look for storms on Accabee.'

"He did as he had promised; they were wed
By Christian rites,—and legal deeds convey'd
The heritage;—without a word then sped
The chief into his forests, seeking shade:
Months pass'd—a year went by,
And none beheld his eye, [stray'd.
Where still his thought, with love, through these sweet places

"He grew to be forgotten by the twain;
Or if not wholly by the woman, she
Ne'er spoke of him,—ne'er look'd for him again,
Though much it might have gladden'd her to see;
For love had lost its flower,
And soon there came an hour,
When all her young heart's pleasure grew to pain!

"The first sweet flush of summer dalliance gone,
The first most precious bloom of passion o'er,
Indifference follow'd in the heart that won,
And scorn found place where rapture woke no more;
No kindly nurture bless'd
With love her lonely breast,
And soon even peace had fled the home so glad before.

"And scorn grew into hate, and hate to wrath,
And wrath found speech in violence;—his arm
Smote the unhappy woman from his path;—
Submission could not soothe, nor tears disarm,
The cruel mood, the will,
True to past passions still,
Which Love and Beauty now, no more sufficed to charm.

"The profligate husband, reckless of her woe,
Her meek submission and her misery,
Prepared, in secret, still another blow,
And bargain'd for the sale of Accabee;
Already had he drawn
The fatal deed—had gone,
Resolved, in other lands, remote, his wife to flee.

"He little knew that eyes were on his flight,
That long had mark'd his deeds;—his way led through
The umbrageous groves of Eutaw:—long ere night
His footsteps to the white man's clearings drew;—
Exulting in the dream,
Successful, of his scheme,
He hails the cottage-smokes of him who bought, in sight.

"But now a voice arrests him as he goes—
Forth starts the red chief from the covering wood;
At once he knew him for the worst of foes;
Guilt quell'd his courage, terror froze his blood;
The horse is stay'd—in vain,
He jerks the extended rein,
Vainly applies the spur, and showers his flanks with blows.

"Stern was the summons—in a single word—
'Down!'—and he yielded to the vigorous hand;
'I gave thee all!' were then the accents heard—
'The woman from my bosom, and my land;—
I warn'd thee, ere I went,
Of wrath and punishment,
If hair upon her head, in wrath was ever stirr'd.

"'I know thee, and thy deeds; and thou shalt die!'
'Mercy!' implored the profligate in vain.
Vainly he struggles—vainly seeks to fly—
Even as he strives, the hatchet cleaves his brain.
Quivering, he lies beneath,
While, from his leathern sheath,
The warrior draws his knife, and coldly scalps the slain.

"Another night, and on the Accabee,
Softly the moon was smiling through its grove;
Yet sad the woman hail'd its light, for she
No longer warm'd with hope, or glow'd with love:
Grief, and a wan despair,
Reign'd in her soul of care,
Whence love, expell'd by wrath, had long been forced to flee.

"She crouch'd beside the hearth in vacant mood,
Silence and woe close crouch'd on either hand,—
Life's hope all baffled,—all the innocent brood
Of joys, that once had crowded at command,
Dead—gone like summer flowers;
Desolate all her hours,
Her life was now one dread, one deathlike solitude.

"With dreary gaze she watch'd the flickering fire,
Nor mark'd around the thickening growth of gloom;
She sees, unheeding, the bright flame expire,
Nor marks the fearful aspect in her room;
Beside her rest the brands—
'Tis but to stretch her hands:
Alas! her desolate soul for light hath no desire.

"But lo! another form, beside her own,
Bends to the task;—sudden, the resinous pine
Flames up;—she feels she is no more alone;
She sees a well-known eye upon her shine,
And hides her face, and cries—
'The Chief!' His silent eyes
Still saddening o'er the shape too long and dearly known.

"'The man whom thou didst wed, will never more
Lay angry hand upon thee—he had sold
Thy land, and fled thee for another shore;
But that I wound him in the serpent's fold,
And took from him the power
That had usurp'd thy dower;
In proof of what I tell thee,—lo! behold!'

"Thus speaking, he, beside her, on the floor,
Cast down the white man's written instrument;
Sign'd, seal'd, and witness'd; framed with legal lore;
Conveying—such the document's intent—
All these fair groves and plains,
The Accabee domains,
To one, of kindred race, whose name the paper bore.

"And she had sign'd it, with unwilling hand,
Ignorant of its meaning, but in dread;
Obedient to her tyrant's fierce command,
While his arm shook in threat'ning o'er her head;
'Twas in that very hour,
His blow, with brutal power,
Had stricken her to the earth, where long she lay as dead.

"He little dream'd that the avenger near,
Beheld him, and prepared his punishment;
You ask, Why came he not to interfere,
And stay, ere yet was wrought the foul intent;
Enough, the red man knows
His time to interpose:—
Sternly his hour he takes, with resolute will unbent.

"Unerring, we have seen him in pursuit—
Unsparing, we have seen him in his blow;—
His mission was not ended; and, though mute,
He stood surveying her, who, cowering low,
Crept humbly to his feet,
As seeming to entreat,—
He had another task, which found the warrior slow.

"But he was firm:—'This paper is your own,—
Another proof is mine, that you will be
Safe from the blows of him so lately known;
He hath his separate lands henceforth from me;
Ample the soil I gave,
Beside the Eutaw's wave;
In token of my truth—this bloody scalplock see.'

"Then shriek'd the unhappy woman with affright,
Revolting at the trophy, dripping yet,
That, down upon the paper, in her sight,
With quiet hand, the haughty chieftain set;
'Spare me! Oh, spare!' she cries:
And crouching, with shut eyes,
Backward she crept, as if she safety sought in flight.

"'Fear nothing!' said the chieftain; ''twas for thee,
I brought this bloody token of my truth,
To show thee, from this moment, thou art free
To the possession of thy life and youth;
Still hast thou beauty; still
Thy heritage—thy will;
Go, seek thy kindred pale, secure of love and ruth.

"'From him, who, in thy thoughtlessness of heart,
Thou mad'st a master over thee, I save;
I slew thy father—I have done his part,
And give thee wealth more ample than he gave;
Henceforth, thou wilt not see
The Chief at Accabee;
Beware again lest passion make thee slave.

"'I leave thee now forever!' 'No!' she cried:
'Oh! take me to thy people;—let me dwell
Lone, peaceful, on the Edisto's green side,
Which, had I left not, I had still been well:—
Forgive me, that the child,
With heart both weak and wild,
Err'd, in not loving, where she might have loved with pride!'

"'I had believed thee once; but now, too late!
Henceforth I know thee, only to forget.'
'Thou canst not!'—'It may be, that thus my fate
Hath spoken; but my resolute will is set,
In manhood,—and I know,
Though all of life be woe,
Thus better—than with faithlessness to mate.'

"She crouch'd beneath his feet, incapable
Of answer to that speech; and his sad look,
As if his eyes acknowledged still a spell,
One long, deep survey of the woman took;—
She still unseeing aught,
Of that sad, searching thought,
Which, speaking through his eye, her soul could never brook.

Sudden as spectre, waving wide his hand,
He parted from her presence :—He was gone,
Into the shadows of that forest land ;
And, desolate now, the woman lay alone,—
Crouching beside the hearth,
While thousand fears had birth,
Haunting her thought with griefs more fearful than the known.

"Our story here is ended. Of her fate
Nothing remains to us, but that she sold,
Of Accabee, the beautiful estate,
And sought her shelter in the city's fold;
The purchaser, meanwhile,
Made the dark forest smile,
And crown'd its walks with works most lovely to behold.

"A noble dwelling rose amidst the trees,
Fair statues crown'd the vistas—pathways broke
The umbrageous shadows,—and sweet melodies,
Among the groves, at noon and morning woke ;—
And great reserves of game,
In which the wild grew tame—
And pleasant lakes, by art, were scoop'd for fisheries.

"Here pleasure strove to make her own abode;
She left no mood uncherish'd which might cheer;
Through the grim forests she threw wide the road,
And welcomed Beauty, while expelling care :
Wealth spared no toils to bless,
And still, with due caress,
Honor'd the daily groups that sought for pastime there.

"But still the spot was haunted by a grief;—
Joy ever sank in sadness:—guests depart;
A something sorrowful, beyond belief,
Impairs the charms of music and of art;
Till sadly went each grace,
And, as you see the place,
Gradual the ruin grew, a grief to eye and heart.

"The native genius, born in solitude,
Is still a thing of sorrow; and his spell,
Whatever be the graft of foreign mood,
Maintains its ancient, sorrowful, aspect well;—
Still reigns its gloomy lord,
With all his sway restored,
Lone, o'er his barren sceptre doom'd to brood."

Slow sped our skiff into the open light,—
The billows bright before us,—but no more
Rose love's sweet ditty on our ears that night;—
Silent the maid look'd back upon the shore,
And thought of those dark groves,
And that wild chieftain's loves,
As they had been a truth her heart had felt of yore.

ALBERT AND ROSALIE

I.

She sat beside the lattice and look'd forth
Upon the waters. A smooth stream went by,
Playfully murmuring, and along its banks
Making a pleasant music. 'Twas the hour,
When, shooting through the light wave, his canoe
Bore him that loved her; when, in other days,
Her own love, deeply hallow'd by its truth,
Was sanctified by hope and trust in heaven—
In heaven and him! It was the hour, and there,
The waters lay in light—the silvery light
Of the May moon, that gliding through the trees,
Pour'd down her rich smile on them. A sweet breeze
Came from the opposite shore, and would have borne
The birdlike streamer of his little bark,
And made her sail swell out, as if it knew
And felt the love-assignéd office. 'Twas the hour,
But still he came not. A sad servitor
That ever watch'd her heart, and had a look
Of frowning sorrow, and was named Despair,
Rebuked her eyes that look'd for him in vain,
And bade her hope not. Wherefore look'd she then,
Thus ever, and still earnestly with hope,
That seem'd but a sweet sorrow? Who shall tell
If thought was in that fondness?—if the mind

Went with the unconscious eye; and, in that glance
Of sad abstraction, if the expression strong,
Had reason for its guide? It was, alas!
But the sad habit of her form that now
Kept her a watcher. Her fond eyes look'd forth,
Unmonitor'd by mind, from memory!—
She saw not the bright waters—not the moon—
Not the fair prospect!—All was vacancy,
To that unheeding mourner! She had gazed
Till all grew dark before her!—She had thought,
Till thought had swoll'n to madness!—She had felt,
Till feeling, like some fever, ate away
The heart it fed on.

II.

'Twas a cruel tale,
Told by the villagers, of an early love,
And childish indiscretion:—such a tale,
As erring but fond natures, aptly leave
In every valley where warm spirits dwell,
And sunny maidens. Rosalie was young—
Lovely as young. A childish excellence,
Infantile grace, with archness intermix'd,
Play'd in her look, and sparkled in her eye,
Which glow'd with ravishing fires, from a dark orb,
That had a depth like heaven! A cheek, fair
And delicate as a rose-leaf newly blown;—
A brow like marble—lofty and profuse,
With the rich brown of her o'ergathering hair!—
These were her beauties—nor through these, alone,
Was she held worthy to be sought of love
In frequent worship. The rich, rosy lips,
That play'd and parted ever with a smile,
Becoming, with mix'd dignity and love,—

Had music there a dweller. Many a night,
Her wild song, o'er those waters, silenced them,
And their rough murmurs, to the spell-bound ears
Of her enamor'd hearers. She would sing,
As if song were an element, and she,
The gay, glad bird, just fitted to extend
Her bright wings o'er its bosom and go forth,—
Bringing rich notes to earth from the high heaven,
To which sweet echoes ever bore them back!
And in her rustic home, and, with the crowd
That came about her ever, 'twas a sway,
Queen-like and undisputed, which she bore,
And which they gave her;—nor, in this abused;—
The power she wielded had its spells in love,
And gentleness, and true thought—never in scorn,
Or any wayward impulse or caprice,
Solicitous to humble or deny:—
The queen of loveliness, she was no less
The queen of modesty and maiden grace,
Unchallenged in each subject's heart, and there,
Having a home or palace, at her will.

III.

What wonder, then, if many lovers came
To woo that maiden? Never maiden yet
Had sway like hers in the secluded vale,
Where stood her dwelling. From afar and near
Came the tall rustics in their Sunday garb
To see and seek her. From the distant hills,
Where fame and fond report had made her known,
They came on mix'd pretences. Having seen,
Their feet grew fasten'd, and their amorous hearts
Dissolved away to weakness, while they bow'd,
And spoke their several loves,—but spoke in vain.

Not proud, nor coy, the maiden yet was choice,
And sought a kindred spirit for her own,
When she should give her heart,—and him she found—
So thought she fondly—for the youth was fair—
A gentle youth, to whom a better sphere,
And an occasional travel in far lands,
Had taught the polish of the citizen,
Subduing the rude manners, and bestowing
The grace of social life—the symmetry
Of movement and expression, while it takes
The sharp, rough edge from language, and refines,
To unobtrusive sweetness, the discourse,
That soothes the ear it never should assail.
He had departed from his native home,
Leaving his father's hills in early youth,
When Rosalie—herself a native there—
Was yet a child. Returning, she was then
A child no longer. With the rest he saw,
And, with a better fortune than the rest,
He sought her out and wooed her. 'Tis a tale—
A chronicle of sorrow, not of shame,
Sacred in memory, in the heart secure,
And sweetly dear, though sad!

IV.

We linger now,—
We would not hasten in our narrative,
To its sad close. But on their early loves,—
The hours when they were happy—with no thought
To promise the thick sorrow that o'ercame
And tore their hearts asunder—let us pause.
She loved but him of all the valley round,
She saw but him of all the suitors there,
She heard but his discourse, knew but his form,

And had no thought, no feeling for the rest!
The sunset hour still brought him o'er the lake,—
The sunset hour still found her watching there,
Where now we see her. From the opposite shore,
Her eye could note his little, light canoe,
When first emerging from the reedy banks,
It broke the quiet waters into smiles.
She saw him trim his sail, and every change
Of movement she discerned; and, through her heart,
Seeing, as through a glass, where every hope
Had lent some light, and every love gave power,
She thought the very smile upon his lips
Grew visible to her gaze. Thus, day by day,
For months, in a sweet silence of discourse,
They moved and met each other with their hearts,
Having no other speech. But the time came,—
Too soon, perchance, though slow to youthful hope,—
When love should shape his language. 'Twas an hour,
In early spring—Love's season and the flowers',
Season of budding eyes, and blessing hearts!—
Nature was in her sweet virginity,
When they walk'd forth i' the garden. Lovely buds,
Clustering in leafy cells, gave promise meet
Of untold fruitage—brightly the sun shone,
Yet inoppressive, for his slanting rays
Came broken through the forest. All around,
Young flower and humming insect, bird and breeze,
Partaking of youth's happiest harmonies,
Murmur'd in gladness to the delicate sense
That flowed in its fresh feelings. Rosalie
Hung on her lover's arm, yet undeclared
His passion for her. The young maiden's heart
Gush'd with its sweet o'erfulness, while the tear
Of an unstudied joy upon her cheek,

Trembled in light, and then exhaled away
In odor,—till he grew a worshipper,
Yet had no words, save in his eloquent eyes,
Which spoke that language of sublimer love,
Too pure for common syllables, too like
The high devotion of an innocent heart,
Looking through gentle fears, and blessing hopes,
As to its God! Together they walk'd on,
Till the groves thicken'd, and the silent trees,
Closed round them like a dwelling; with no eye
To peer into that holy home of love,
Scaring its trembling, tried inhabitants!
He spoke—he spoke at last! He spoke of love,
And the breeze echoed him, and murmur'd "love;"
And every flower and leaf had a sweet name,
Love-written, upon them; and a print of hearts,
United, grew, like flower and leaf together,—
And Rosalie and Albert, thence, were one!

V.

Silent before so long, their prison'd souls
Then gush'd in mutual language, and pour'd forth,
In homage to each other, the fond thoughts,
The dreams by night, the fancies through the day,
Which had possess'd and purified them long.
Their thoughts were so much music, and they spoke,
In sweetest measures;—even as the bird just 'scaped
From the close caging of some gentle dame,
Showing its freedom's consciousness in song
Not less than flight. Love was their monitor—
Love their companion—Love their pleasant charge.
In Rosalie it spoke in gentlest sighs,
A broken language,—in a start of song,

Capricious, wild, that suddenly came forth,
Even as the playful robin from the brake,
As suddenly retiring into shade,
And trembling at his own audacity.
She was a sweet dependant, and her arm
On Albert's, hung so fondly—and her head
Droop'd with her joy, like some dew-laden flower
Upon his bosom; and he loved the more
For such dependence. Noble and erect,
He clasp'd her to his heart, and his eye gleam'd
With pride and pleasure while surveying hers.
His sweet, melodious voice, deep, organ-like,
Went to her heart at every utter'd word,
Making his love a power, whose sway, secure,
And conscious of its own security,
Forbore to wrong, and with exaction sweet,
Solicited the boon, as 't were a boon,
When, in her heart, the spelling passion there
Proclaim'd it his own right. He was a man
Among the thousand! Unassuming, he
Might yet assume, unquestion'd. Gentleness,
And a strange strength—a calm, o'erruling strength,
Were mix'd within him so, that neither took
Possession from the other—neither rose
In mastery or in passion; but still grew
Harmoniously together.—In his strength,
The mighty oak had likeness—while gentleness,
Wound round him like the rosy parasite,
The flush spring gives it, wreathing its great might
With sweetest color, and adorning grace.
His soul, refined beyond the rustic world,
Had yet no city vices. He had kept,
Its whiteness unprofaned, and he could lift

His heart to heaven in faith—his eye on man,
Having no fear—his hope to Rosalie,
As to an object of abiding love,
Without one taint of base or sinful thought.

VI.

True joy, still born of heaven, is bless'd with wings,
And, tired of earth, it plumes them back again,
And so we lose it. A sad change came o'er
The fortunes of that pair, whose loves have been
Our theme of story:—a sad change, that oft
Comes o'er love's fortunes in all lands and homes,
Nor spares the humblest. Rosalie was young
In fancy, as in years. Truly she loved,
And yet not wisely. Had her heart replied
To any question of its love for him,
To whom she pledged it, she had warmly spoke
For its devotion; but her fancy, quick,
Roving, and playful, was not yet subdued
To that sweet-tempered, fond exclusiveness,
Which shuts out every object from the thought,
Save of that one to whom all thought is given.
The early train of her admirers gone—
The crowd that flatter'd her with looks and words,
That gave her homage, and pronounced her praise,
In sweet eulogium, vanish'd,—she grew sad.
The praises of her lover were in looks,
And constant, sweet devotion—seldom in words:—
And sometimes, too, he spoke her chidingly,
Though still in truest love. He spoke to her
As one who lived forever in his thought,
A part of him and it—the dearest part;
But yet he spoke her truly,—with no burst
Of fraudulent praise, that runs away with truth,

And gives habitual error place for sway,
In the deluded bosom. Calm, serene,—
His thoughts were clear and honest; and his words,
Still chosen most gently, were not yet disguised
To please the ear of tingling vanity.
Though loving him beyond all other men,
She would have had him, like the rest that came,
A flattering wooer. His substantial worth,
She valued truly; but, not yet content,
She deem'd it might be mingled with those sweets,—
False sweets that lead to sadness!—which were dear
To youthful fancy and a thoughtless heart;—
And, in the wantonness of her sportive moods,
Still craving this frail incense, she would turn
Capriciously away, when most he sought
Her ear and presence; and, in gayest crowds,
Lose the dear hour so rich in love's esteem,
And barter truest pleasures and noblest thoughts,—
Trifling with feelings which should be secure
As they are sacred,—for the idlest game
That ever butterfly pursued in May.

VII.

Yet did he not reproach her. At the first
He gently pray'd that she might live for him,
And know and love him better. Much he strove
To teach her, that, thus bound for life together,
Her study, like his own, should be to make
Her heart familiar with its offices—
Those offices of sweet domestic love,
Which cannot dream of gay society,
And the insidious flattery of the crowd
Having no fireside duties. Fondly still,
With indirect speech, he told his wishes o'er,

And whisper'd counsels such as love might hear,
And none but love could utter. But her ear
Turn'd from him, with a playful, sad caprice,
And she would leave him,—or, in mood more wild,
Reply in tones impatient,—till at last
The youth grew into sadness, as he fear'd,
When they were wedded, that her love might change
Even into hatred, as he could not bring
His nature to a level with the herd
Whose flatteries so misled her. He grew sad,
And yet he sought her; still entreating her
With his own love, which was all earnestness,
Not to make forfeit of the better faith,
The substance for the shade, and sacrifice,
For the capricious freedom of the hour,
The holy, hopeful, best security,
That grows in heart of confidence alone.
Oh! very earnest was he in these prayers;
His soul, the very safety of his being,
Were treasured in that passion! Few his friends,—
An orphan without kindred;—slight the ties
That bound him to all others. None of strength
Did he acknowledge, save the one with her;
And that was his whole life. Wonder not, then,
He trembled at her sad infirmity:—
The loss of Rosalie was loss of all.

VIII.

One night there was a bridal in the vale,
A rustic bridal. Mirth and pleasant cheer,
veet music and gay lights, laughter and glee,
ssembled young and old. All that could make
A dear occasion dearer, mingled then,
And the vale rang with joy. Our lovers came,

And revell'd with the rest. Never before
Had Rosalie look'd lovelier. 'Mid the crowd,
She was beheld of all the crowd alone—
She was the bright star to which every eye
Seemed turn'd as in devotion—the gay light
Of every fancy—the fair queen who sway'd
O'er every heart, even then, as in the time
When all were wooers, and no heart, preferr'd,
Had bound her to itself. In her sweet song,
They gather'd round, and had fond memories
Of hours when hope was theirs. They praised her strains
And watch'd the eloquent pleasure in her eye
That said their praise was sweet. From song to song
They led her with beguiling flatteries,
And when the dance began, they crowded round,
Contending for her hand.
There was one dance,
Brought from a foreign land—a winning dance,
Whose sweet voluptuous twinings witch the heart
Into a sad forgetfulness, and arouse
Strange fevers and wild fancies in the blood.
'Twas from a land where vice, in many a form,
Had sapped society, and torn away
The pillars of religion; where the name
Of wife is but another name for all
Of shame and prostitution; where the pride
Of virtue is unknown; where character
Is but a thing of barter and stale use,
And fashion makes a crime necessity.

IX.

"You will not mingle, dearest Rosalie,
Among these waltzers?" It was thus he spoke,
As he beheld the suitors for her hand

Crowding around, impatient to enwrap
Her form in the impassion'd, free caress
Of that voluptuous motion.
"And why not?".
Straightway she answer'd.
"Was it not your thought,
No less than mine, dear Rosalie, that this dance
Better belong'd to races like th' Italian,
Than a frank, earnest people such as ours,
In whom simplicity, the soul of virtue,
Forbids the goad of passion, lest we drive
The blood to fearful phrensies! Didst thou not
Join with me in the thought, that the pure heart
Must shrink from the embrace with stranger forms;—
Embrace so free as this—as if each touch
Took something from its purity;—for virtue
Is like the down upon the peach;—the flush
Of beauty on the flower;—the golden lustre
That flecks with delicate variety
The slight wing of the butterfly;—one touch
Being fatal to the excellence, whose glory
Lives in its very unapproachableness.
The barriers of opinion in a people,
Belong to their necessity and nature—
Subject them to the abuse of foreign custom,
And we make forfeit all security.
Custom makes barriers still for chastity,—
O'erthrow these barriers, idle though they seem,
And Passion saps the citadel.—Dear Rosalie,
Thou wilt not join these waltzers?"
"But I will!"
Thus the capricious damsel, to the youth,
Who earnestly besought her, still replied—
As, turning from him, she bestow'd her hand

On one who seized it with triumphant joy,
Having the victory—for he had urged
The cause of that fond movement; and, to her,
The pledged wife of another, had discuss'd
The question of that nice propriety,
Which woman must not argue, and yet feel!
"But I will dance it, Albert, as I please,
Or not, if so it please me. And why not?—
I am not yet a bond-woman methinks,
And such constraint as this, would best beseem
A petty household tyranny,—the rule
Of modern Blue Beard, than the free regard
Of one who seeks for sympathies, not slaves."
And, with these words, she join'd the whirling group,
While Albert turn'd away and left the hall.

X.

Next morning came a letter to the maid,
And this its language:
"Dearest Rosalie,—
Still dear, though, from this moment, I resign
All claim to call thee so exclusively—
I leave thee. When this scrawl thou read'st, my feet
Shall be beyond these mountains—other climes
Will soon receive me, and on distant waves,
The foreign bark shall bear me,—still from thee.
Farewell—farewell.
"Oh, it had been my thought,
That, from the moment thou didst give thyself
To my fond pleadings, I should cease to be
What I am now—a weary wanderer!
"That hope is gone forever. Thou hast said
The words which have unlink'd our mutual hearts,
They being no longer kindred. Thou hast broken

The flowery twines of love, in thoughtlessness—
Ah! may it be a sorrow but to one!
"And I must bear that sorrow. Thou to me,
Wast all—art all! I may not hope again,
To find thee in another—and I dare not
Seek for another in thee. Those cruel words—
Why didst thou speak them!—they have doom'd us both
To isolation;—me, to the worse doom,
Of hopelessness. 'Tis nothing now I live for—
Yet never heart could love thee, as did mine.
And still I love thee—love thee recklessly,
As loving thee in vain. Henceforth, I live,
As one denied. I cannot love another—
I would not pray such freedom. I have not
The elastic temper of the froward boy,
To change capricious with the monthly moon,
Nor share the blight with each sweet star that sets.
My mind is too subdued—my character,
Too fix'd—too firm! I must be resolute
In love, as in all other qualities,—
Having no changing moods—earnest in all,
Unvarying as the needle, and as true,
Though the storms howl. Such is my nature now.
Vicissitude has tried me—poverty
Counsell'd, and taught me due stability—
Affliction chasten'd; travel, here and there,
'Mong strangers in far wilds and realms unknown,
Taught me their several sorrows, and prepared me,
To better love the quiet walks of home!
"I have no home. It had been in thy heart,
But thou denied'st it lodgment—better pleased
To make a tenant there of idlest moods,
Enjoyments light and worthless, when in mine,
Thou hadst a temple—pure, inviolate,

Sacred to love—and strong—sacred to thee!—
Would thine had been to me but thus devote,
I then had been a hermit. In its cells,
My thoughts and feelings had been saintly forms,
Filling each several niche. Morning and night,
Had found me there a doting worshipper,
And I had hung it round with sweetest store,
The dearest flowers of love—the purest sweets
That follow young enjoyment, and that make,
For twin hearts, of the gloomy caves of earth,
A happy home like heaven.

"Thou hast decreed,
And all these dreams are vanish'd. I would be
Thy tyrant, Rosalie!—ah, happy she
Who loves the gentle tyranny of truth.
Thou wouldst not be a bond-woman!—dear to me,
The sweet bond-service I had pledged to thee.
Thou'dst do or not, as so it pleasured thee—
Ah, me! how different from thy thought was mine!
To do thee pleasure—ay, at mine own pain,—
Was sure to be my sweetest pleasure still;—
And to make slaves of my best sympathies,—
Slaves in thy service,—seem'd to my poor heart,
Their happiest office.

"We have differ'd much—
Too much for love! If these be thoughts of mine,
And thou dost scorn them, having thoughts unlike,—
We are not fit for each other! We must part—
And it is wisdom! When I gave my love,
And pledged my best affections unto thee—
I pledged thee what, next to thy sacred love,
I valued more than all the world beside.
Thou hast not so esteem'd my offering—
Thou hast not so esteem'd my principles,

Nor yet maintain'd thine own, as that we should
Keep bound with true respect, and mutual pride:—
'Tis well we part.
"Yet think not, Rosalie—
The wayward, sad caprice of the last night,
Sole cause of my resolve. I might have sigh'd
And sorrow'd o'er that error, yet forgiven:—
The sin lies deeper. When thou show'st another,
That difference grows betwixt thy heart and mine,
Thou dost invite a foreign arbitration—
Thou makest our secret thought a public thing,
And to the prying eye, and busy tongue
Of peevish envy, and a tattling scorn,
Thou dost unveil the sacred, vestal fire,
Which the mysterious love design'd for us—
For those who love alone!
"If, in my heart,
Or in my deed, or language, I had done
A wrong to thee or thine—where shouldst thou seek
Arbitrament?—where carry up thy cause,
In fond appeal?—where clamor for redress?—
Where, but in *my* heart!—in our secret shade,
In sacred moments, when, to love devote,
We met in mutual fondness! There, hadst thou come,
And said, as late in public thou didst say,
'Thou art my tyrant—thou wouldst 'slave me quite,
Make me thy bond-woman, and of sympathies
Generous and freely given, make wretched slaves!'—
Ah, Rosalie! hadst thou but thought of this,
I had not now—but let it pass—no more,—
It is all idle now!
"Once more, farewell!
Be happy, and forget me, Rosalie;—
And shouldst thou love another, let my words

Sink in thy memory, so that thou shalt say
Nothing in rashness—so that ye may keep
The troth between ye as a sacred thing,
Beyond the gaze of the herd, beyond its speech,
Beyond its judgment!—value it beyond
The moment-pleasure always, till thy heart,
Shall grow into a kindred life and thought,
With him to whom thou giv'st it.
"And I pray,—
'Twill be no wrong to him, dear Rosalie—
That, in thy happier moments, when with him,
Thou joy'st in life's most dear realities,—
The pleasant fireside, the cheerful friend,
The gladsome child, and the indulgent lord,—
Thou wilt bestow me one sad memory—
One blessing—and forgive me, that, in thus
Tearing myself away from thee and life,
Perchance, I wound thy pride, or touch thy heart,
With unavoidable pain. Forgive me this,
And other errors, as, this dreary night,
When all is sleepless sorrow at my heart,
I do forgive thee, who art cause of all!
Farewell—farewell." And thus the letter closed.

XI.

She had no tears—no language. From her lips
There broke no sound of sorrow, but her eye,
As if her sense yet lack'd the news it brought,
Did reperuse that fatal messenger,
In fear and hope. A little while she paused,
And then she sought her chamber, with no word
To those around. She had no strength for speech,
And did not dare, in the uncertain mood
Of her sad spirit, to look up and meet

The curious eyes that watch'd her. Much they sought,
By various questions and inquisitive glance,
To learn her secret;—for the tale was known—
How soon love's errors and misfortunes grow
The pastime of the cold and common crowd!—
That Albert had departed from the vale,
In foreign journey. And she turn'd away—
She sought to be alone with her own heart,
And long and sad their secret conference.
  Her heart rebuked itself, her mind rebuked,
And all her feelings, self-retributive,
Reproach'd her with her error. Long the strife
They waged within her bosom, till she sank
In prayer, self-humbled—prostrate on the floor,
In true contrition.
                    "In a heedless hour,"
'Twas thus she murmur'd—"in a heedless hour,
My erring spirit, with a fond caprice,
Hath sported with its happiness too much;—
Father, forgive me—be the punishment
Forborne in mercy—teach him to forgive,
And, oh, restore him to me. In my grief
I do not heed the shame of such a prayer.
Restore him—teach him also to forgive."
  When she came forth again, her look was changed—
Her heart had been subdued. She had been weak,
She was now strengthen'd; yet her sorrow grew
From that same strengthening; for the scales were gone
That dimm'd her vision; and the full extent
Of her own loss grew clear and palpable!
Her error had been one of wantonness—
The last that love hath ever yet forgiven,
True love, that worships with a lofty heart
And even mood. She felt that she had erred,

And fear'd that he—the man of all the world
Whom most she loved—calm, true, and resolute,
Might prove inflexible. No trifler he,
Capricious with sweet feelings and fond ties,—
But stern, unbending in his principles!
His rigid purpose, noble and severe,
Tenacious pride, and changeless character,
Had been her boast, and best security!
It was her joy that no caprice of mood,
No passing influence of the idle time,
No popular show, no clamor from the crowd,
Could move him, erring, from the path of right,
Love's path and hers,—those sacred principles,
Which make all happiness, or make it naught!
How could she hope a change in such a man,
How love him still, if so that he could change,
Even to pity her? Her thought approved,
Though her heart grieved, his rigor and resolve.

XII.

"Ah, sweet," cried he,* who, of a thousand sweets,
Hath sung most sweetly—"sweet, when winter frowns
And folds his ice-chain round us—sweet to dream
Of spring's enamoring charms, and gentle reign!
The hopeless heart thus cherishes the form
Of that which was a hope; even as we seal
The ashes of the loved one in an urn
We keep beside us, till we half forget
That it is ashes. Memory thus endows,
Even as a god, the insensate clay with life,
And hallows to the lone one, in a dream,
The old sweet faith, the perish'd love, and all,
That made earth worthy to its worshipper!

* Rousseau.

But if hope come not, in alliance close
With that creative genius, till we think
The past may be the future—if it be
That memory comes alone!—no guardian she,
But a stern tyrant, taught in cruel arts,
And sleepless as the agony of guilt."
It was a sweet hope, counsell'd her to hope
Against conviction.
"He will come again,—
'Tis but awhile—he cannot long forbear—
He must forgive me, as, so help me heaven,
I had forgiven him even crueller wrongs,
And harsher words, than these."
He did not come!—
That night—the next—the next—and weeks, went by,
Till hope grew sad and sicken'd in her heart,
And on her face a visible hand was laid,
As of a burning grief, a sleepless woe,
That would not be appeased.
And soon her friends
Beheld the change upon her, and they spoke
Harshly of Albert: then she chided them
Most sadly into silence, and forbade
That they should speak again upon her griefs.
Still was she not ungrateful for the care
That sought to comfort; and, as day by day,
Her face grew paler and her step more slow,
Her heart became more gentle than its wont,
And with a meekness, dovelike, and from heaven,
She won a fresher love from all that knew.

XIII.

And what of him—so sudden and so stern,
So quick of apprehension, so resolved,

So little merciful to his own heart,
So stern a judge of hers—what now of him?
What art may paint his feelings to the sense,
What eye perceive them, as, that fatal night,
He fled the insensate revel! He felt crush'd,
And the devoted feelings of his heart,
So long her homagers, now all recall'd,
Came home rebellious from that sweeter realm,
Where they had spent the hours so joyously.
They came to torture, and he fled with them,
Even as a fugitive—he fled *from* them,
Or strove to fly; but they pursued him close,
And tore him as he fled! In foreign lands
He made himself a home—if that may be
A home, which is a prison-house and scourge!
He made himself new comrades, day by day,
And fled from each in turn. He still went on,
And sought new dwellings, only to behold
Smiles change to frowns—seeking new friends and flowers,
To find the one grow cold—the other die.
The curse of hopelessness, and a premature blight,
Clung to him in his journey, and the doom
Of desolation was unchanged to him!—
In crowds, in camps, in cities, and in fields,
Where'er he fled, whatever home he sought,
'Twas written still, and Albert was alone.

XIV.

A bloody war waged in a neighbor land,
And the perpetual strife in his own mood
There led him, as if seeking sympathy,
To fields of danger. In the ranks of war
He soon became a leader. Fierce his ire,
Hot his pursuit, impetuous in assault,

Desperate in daring, and in perilous strife
Fatal his muscular arm. His men grew fond,
And joy'd in such a leader. Rash, not bold,
He hourly sought new dangers. Numbers stood
Between him and his aim. He counted not
The dense array, but, striking right and left,
He plunged where foes were thickest. Walls arose,
High, steep, and massive—ranging cannon poured
The rattling shot, like hail, upon his path,—
But did not stop him. Soon the walls were gained,
The banner of the foe beneath his foot,
His voice in victory shouting.
                                        Where was death?
The foe he struck could answer, but the chief,
Who sought for the grim enemy in vain,
Went through the strife unharméd. The sharp sword
Swept by him edgeless—the directed ball,
Fatal, if sent against another breast,
Swerved harmlessly from his,—his doom was still
To live, though thousands perish'd—but alone!
And she!—the news was brought her that he fought
The battles of the Texians. That he stood
Upon the Alamo's walls, when the fierce tribes
Of Mexico, in numbers overspread
And crowded down the defenders—it was said,
That, striking to the last, each stroke a death,
The gallant chief was slain by many hands,
O'erpower'd, not conquer'd;—and the tale was told
By one most thoughtless, in a sudden tone,
That went even like an ice-bolt to her heart,
And froze its hope forever. From that hour,
The last sad change, foretelling all the rest,
Came o'er the maiden. Much they strove to cheer,
Or chide, her prisoner-mood, but all in vain.

They led her to the revel, with fond hope,
By change to cheer her; but she sicken'd there!—
The idle song of love, which fill'd her ears,
Was then a sadness! It reminded her
Of those she once had sung, when he was by
A listener in the moonlight. From the dance
She shrank away in horror!—What a throng
Of images most fearful came with it!
New suitors sought her, but they left her soon
As hopeless as herself! Nothing could change
The spirit of that mourner—nothing move
Her sorrow from its deep devotedness!—
Life's harmonies had gone, its strings that once,
Beneath Hope's finger, did discourse so long,
And such sweet music, gave but discord forth,—
Despair, not Hope, the one musician now!

XV.

A little longer, and our strain is done—
The story of love's sorrow is soon told,
A word will tell it always. Rosalie,—
'Twas but a few days when we saw her last,
There, sitting by her lattice, looking forth
Upon these waters. See the lattice now;—
How vacant, and how cheerless it appears.
We seek her elsewhere. But a week ago,
She sat, where last we saw her. It was night,
A soft and mellow evening, calm and clear.
A thousand beautiful forms were in the sky,
Light forms of fleece, that hung around the moon,
Like robes of regal splendor;—a sweet breath
Of perfume fill'd the air, and pleasant sounds,
Of winds and waters meeting, rose aloft,
In harmony to the spirit.

"The guitar"—
Feebly, to one who tended her, she spoke,
"Bring it, I pray thee:"—
And the damsel brought
The well-known instrument, so cherish'd once
When he was by, and yet untouch'd so long.
She play'd a soft, prelusive, pensive air,
And then the notes grew wanton. Fitfully,
Shadows of ancient melodies arose,
And vanish'd from the strings; until her hand
Seem'd resting only on the instrument,
Which sounded with the beatings of her pulse,
Unprompted by her will;—but, suddenly,
Her mood grew firm, and, most commandingly,
A bold and ranging melody she framed,
With nicest variations; and, awhile,
The strain was like the first flight of a bird,
Waking, at morning, with rejoicing wing,
And soaring, soaring upward, even to heaven.
Then, as the high tones of the instrument,
Grew soften'd as by distance, with her voice
She coupled sweetest thoughts, most gently framed
By suited language. Mournfully, she sang
A ditty of the saddest circumstance—
Of fortune long denied, and tenderest love,
That should have been, like some well-treasured flower,
Worn in the genial bosom, left to pale
Its leaves in hopeless blight; and, at the close,
Fondly and gently, thus she spoke of him!
"Yet, will I not reproach thee, though thou hast
Dealt most unkindly, Albert. 'Twas a fault,
A most unmaidenly fault—those words of mine:—
Yet might have been forgiven—should have been
Chidden, and then forgotten. 'Twas a child,

That spoke with little thought :—thou shouldst have known
My heart was with thee.
"But, 'tis over now ;—
Thou wilt forgive me when I am no more,
And, as thy nature is all gentleness,
Even when thy word is sternest, well I know
Thou wilt reproach thyself, that thou hast been
So rigid with me."
A faint cry below,
Broke in upon her speech—a cry of woe—
And, in another moment, through the leaves,
Came darting a strange form—yet not so strange,
When the next glance survey'd him. It was he—
'Twas Albert—and he came all penitent,
And sorrowing for his sternness. In his arms,
She sank most fondly, and yet speechlessly.
"Forgive me, dearest Rosalie!" he cried:
"Too long forgetful of thy worth and claims,
I come to thee at last ;—forgive me all—
I was too rash—too cruel, thou hast been
The sufferer at my hands, and I have wrong'd thee
Beyond atonement,—yet, I pray thee smile :
Look up and say—look up, my well beloved,
And bless me with thy smile—and, with thy words,
Say, thou forgivest me."
The dim eyes unclosed,
The bosom heaved in sighs—a bright smile spread,
From the sweet lips, and from the kindling eye,
Over her pallid face, and then it pass'd,
Even like some soft and rosy cloud at eve,
Suddenly, from the sight.
"I am forgiven!—
That eye hath said it—from those lips it came,
Even though they spoke not,—and this heaving breast,

Sent me its pardon in that gentle sigh.
Yet, speak to me, beloved,—speak to me!—
What means this silence?—speak to me—but once!
But once!—Help, there!—some water—quickly bring,
Or she will die in my arms!—God!—she is dead,
And I have slain her!"
                    Truly, had he said.
The parted breath that would have spoke in mercy,
Had made its way to heaven. He was alone—
The destiny of Albert was not done—
And forth he fled—and still he fled, alone.

A STORY OF GOD'S JUDGMENT.

A LEGEND OF GEORGIA.

I.

A grandam, by the cottage door,
At evening, when the sun
Left hues among the forest trees
That gilded every one,
Thus, in the grandchild's listening ear,
Who gather'd at her knee,
"A tale of God's own judgment, child,
Thy mother tells to thee.

II.

"A tale of God's own judgment, child,
And how the deed was known,
And how they took the murderer,
And punishment was done—
Give ear, and thou shalt hear, my child,
And heedful be thy sense,
For know that crime, or soon or late,
Will have intelligence.

III.

"Will have intelligence, my child,
And find a tongue, whose sound,
Like church-bell in the wilderness,
Will rouse the people round.—

Wouldst hear this cruel tale, my child?"
  The young boy, at her knee,
Upstarted, and, with accent wild,
  Cried, "Gran'am, tell it me!"

IV.

"Once on a time," in good old phrase,
  The dame began the tale;—
"Just where the town of Macon stands
  There ran the Indian trail;—
'Twas there the cruel deed was done,
  There was no Macon then,
And but a single house was there,
  Kept by two aged men.

V.

"These old men in the wilderness,
  They kept the house that stood
Upon the Indian trail that ran,
  For ages, through the wood;
And there the traveller stay'd by night,
  Who journey'd out in quest
Of those rich prairie lands that make
  So famous all the West.

VI.

"Thus bent for Al'bamá, my child,
  A seeking lands one day,
Three strangers to the old men's house,
  Came riding on their way;
Two were rough men, with heavy beards,
  And very coarse of speech,
But the young one was a gentleman,
  And far above their reach.

VII.

"Ay, far above their reach was he,
That gentleman so fair,
With a sweet smile and countenance,
And long and sandy hair,—
He talk'd with them, and freely told
The business that he had;—
For, you see, there was a maiden fair,
Whose smiles had made him glad.

VIII.

"Her smiles had made him glad, my child,
And he was bent to find
A pleasant spot and fruitful lands,
To satisfy her mind—
And they were to be wed as soon
As, finding what he sought,
He should convey the tidings home,
Of lands which he had bought.

IX.

"He had the wealth to buy the lands,
And with never a thought or care,
In evil hour he show'd the bills,
In the wallet that he bare;
Nor mark'd the eyes, so dark with sin,
They fix'd upon the book,
Nor how they suddenly cast them down,
Lest he should see the look.

X.

"He did not see the look, alas!
Else he were much to blame,
To go a-travelling on with them,
When the next morning came.

And on they started by the dawn,—
The twain were first abroad,—
But soon the youthful gentleman
Came riding down the road.

XI.

"And riding down the road so wild,
You would have thought the three,
So frank was that young gentleman,
Were all one company.
And pleasantly enough they went,
Till towards noon they came
To an old Indian settlement—
Chilicté was its name.

XII.

"Chilicté was its name, my child,
But all deserted then—
'Twas by the burial-place alone,
You knew the homes of men;
The woods grew thick about the spot,
And the hills rose darkly round,
And a hush in the air fill'd the soul with fear,
Of the stillness so profound.

XIII.

"But the owl he made his dwelling there,
And as the sun went down,
He hooted aloud to the silent air,
And he claim'd it for his own:
The night-hawk wheel'd, and the bat went round
In his dizzy circles fast,
And the owl drew nigher, with every hoot,
To the road, as the travellers pass'd.

XIV.

"O'er the road he sat, on a blighted bough,
And down he stared as they sped beneath,
And his great eyes gloom'd 'neath his hornéd brow,
With a fearful look of death.
With a stifled breath the three went on,—
The path grew hard to find,
And while the youth rode on with one,
The other dropp'd behind.

XV.

"He dropp'd behind with cruel thought,
And while his comrade spoke,
With heavy arm and loaded whip,
He struck a sudden stroke—
And down the light-hair'd stranger fell,
As quickly and as low
As heavy ox, that swims and reels
Beneath the butcher's blow.

XVI.

"It was a butcher's blow he gave,
And wild the stranger cried,
To spare his life, and let him live
For his young and promised bride.
But they had not a thought for her,
And spoke an idle jest—
Then knelt, and stuck the fatal knife,
Twice, deep into his breast.

XVII.

"Twice, deeply did they stick the knife,
And no more prayer had he:
One blow had been enough for life—
He perish'd instantly.

And from his breast they took the spoil,—
  The money which had bought
Their souls for that old serpent, child,
  That all this mischief wrought.

XVIII.

"The mischief all was wrought, and vain
  To wish it now undone;—
They took the body up, and hid
  The secret from the sun.
And in a hollow of the hills,
  In that old Indian town,
They stript the dead youth silently,
  And dropp'd the body down.

XIX.

"They dropp'd him down, nor buried him,
  But left him bleeding, bare;
Though well they knew, at night, the wolf
  And wild-cat would be there.
And then, with fear that look'd behind,
  They rode upon their way,
And thought they heard upon the wind,
  A voice that bade them stay.

XX.

"A voice that bade them stay, they heard,
  And then a laugh and scream,
And such they heard in after years,
  In many a midnight dream—
But on they rode, nor linger'd then,
  And, day by day, they went,
Till, like the wealth of drinking men,
  The money soon was spent.

XXI.

"The money soon was spent, and so—
(Now years had past)—they thought,
To part awhile, and each pursue
The scheme his fancy taught;
And one went down to New Orleans,
The other, hardier yet,
Took the same road on which, before,
The murder'd youth he met.

XXII.

"The murder'd youth, on that same road,
He met, long years before,
And, with a sinner's hardihood,
The spot he travell'd o'er—
Till as the evening shadows fell,
In glimpses, through the trees,
The reedy-rimm'd Ockmulgé stream,
By Macon town, he sees.

XXXIII.

"By Macon town—'what change is here!
The place is not the same.'
He looks,—a city rises there,
He does not know its name.
The old fort is in ruins too,
He marks the broken guns,
Some tumbled to the very brink,
Where dark Ockmulgé runs.

XXIV.

"He sees the dark Ockmulgé run,
And now he draws him nigh,
But neither boat nor boatman comes,
Although he shouts full high—

Yet, while he looks, a silent skiff
  Shoots outward from the banks,
Where osiers and the matted canes,
  Stand up in solid ranks.

XXV.

"From out their solid ranks, the skiff
  Shoots silent o'er the stream,
The murderer stares—he shuts his eyes—
  He feels as in a dream:
For who should paddle then that skiff
  Upon the swelling flood,
But the same youth, that, years before,
  He murder'd down the road.

XXVI.

"The youth he murder'd down the road,
  The knife stuck in his breast!—
Two cruel wounds, and each a death,
  Yet there he would not rest.
Wild grew the murderer's spirit then,
  And white as chalk his cheek—
And when the boatman's bark drew nigh,
  He had no word to speak.

XXVII.

"He had no word to speak to him—
  The boatman waved his hand;
And with no thought, yet full of fear,
  He came at his command—
And trembled much, though much he strove
  His shiv'ring dread to hide;—
And held the bridle of his steed,
  That swam the skiff beside.

XXVIII.

"The good steed swam beside the skiff,
And though he held the rein,
It were a speech too much to say
He thought of him again.
His thought was of that boatman there,
And of the wicked time,
When, journeying o'er that very road,
He did the deed of crime.

XXIX.

"The deed of crime was in his thought,
And all his limbs were weak;—
He strove in vain—his tongue was parch'd,
And no word could he speak:
A cold wind went through all his bones,—
His hair stood up on end,—
To slay him then, had surely been
The kindness of a friend.

XXX.

"But the kindness of a friend is not
For him who slays, like Cain,
The brother, who, confiding, goes
Beside him on the plain—
And so, the murderer reach'd the shore,
And with a desperate speed,
He dash'd the passage-money down,
And leapt upon his steed.

XXXI.

"He leapt upon his steed and flew,
Nor look'd upon the way;
Nor heeded that remember'd voice
That loudly bade him stay:

'How came ye over the river, friend?'
  Cried one who mark'd his flight,—
'When the boat was swamp'd in the heavy fresh
  And the ferryman drown'd, last night?

XXXII.

"'The ferryman drown'd last night, friend,
  And the boat lies high and dry,—
And well I know no steed can ford,
  When the river runs so high.'
There was fearful sense in every word,
  And the murderer's brain grew wild,
For still he heard, for evermore,
  The cryings of a child.

XXXIII.

"The cryings of a child he heard,
  And a voice of innocence—
Then a pleading note, and a prayer of doom,
  To the awful providence.
And, ever and anon, a crash,
  Of the terrible thunder, came,—
And he shut his eyes, for out of the wood,
  There leapt a flash of flame.

XXXIV.

"There leapt a flash of flame, and so,
  With a blindness strange, he flew,
And the goodly steed that then he rode,
  Alone the pathway knew,—
And the blood grew cold in his bosom, when
  He reach'd the town he sought,—
And down he sank on the tavern steps,
  And he had no farther thought.

XXXV.

"He had no thought, but in a swoon
For a goodly hour he lay;
And the gathering crowd came nigh, and strove
To drive his sleep away.
And while they wonder'd much, he woke,
His eye glared strange with light—
For the face of the murder'd man did seem
Still full before his sight.

XXXVI.

"Still full the eyes of the murder'd man
Peer'd ever as he lay;
And with fury then, the murderer rose,
Like one in a sudden fray—
And he drew from his bosom a deadly knife,
And, with no let, he ran,
And plunged it deep in the breast of him
Who look'd like the murder'd man.

XXXVII.

"He look'd like the murder'd man no more,
For as with the stroke he fell,
The madness fled from the murderer's sense,
And he knew his own brother well.—
'Twas that same brother, who with him slew
The youth, many long years gone;
And the fearful doom for that evil deed
Will now be quickly done.

XXXVIII.

"'Twill soon be done, for the judge is there,
And he reads the doom of death,—
And the murderer told of his evil life,
With the truth of a dying breath.

They hung him high where the cross roads meet,
  Close down by the gravel ford;
And they left his farther doom, my child,
  To the ever blessed Lord."

XXXIX.

Upstarted then the listening boy,—
  "Now tell me, oh, tell me, dame,—
And what of the sweet young lady,
  And what of her became?
Who told her, then, of the gentle youth,
  And how, in that savage glen,
The knife was stuck in his bosom,
  By the hands of those cruel men?"

XL.

"Out, out, my child,—was it right to tell
  Such a tale to the maiden true?—
They had no name for the murder'd man,
  And the story she never knew.
And they had no word to comfort her,
  And paler her cheek grew, day by day,—
Till the cruel grief, ere a year had gone,
  Had eaten her heart away."

THE LAST FIELDS OF THE BILOXI;

A TRADITION OF LOUISIANA.

The Bay of Pascagoula is a lovely and retired spot, lying at nearly equal travelling distances between the cities of Mobile and New Orleans. It has long been famous among persons of taste in those cities for its quiet beauties; but more so on account of a very singular and sweet superstition which pertains to it. A remarkable, and most spiritual kind of music, is heard above and around its waters, from which it is supposed to issue. The sound is fitful, occurring by day and night, at all hours, sometimes with more or less strength and fulness, but always very sweet and touching in its strains. Some compare it to the wind-harp, which, indeed, it sometimes most wonderfully resembles. Others liken it to the humming of an insect of great and curious powers. The Indian tradition explanatory of this music,—which no philosophical speculation has yet ventured to disturb,—is one of a beauty not often surpassed. The story goes that the whole Southwest was once controlled, and in the possession of a people called the Biloxi; that these people had attained a very high, if not a perfect civilization—that they were versed in various arts, profound lovers of music, and were finally enervated by the arts which they possessed. They were overrun and conquered by the fiercer tribes coming from the West. They made a last stand on the borders of the sea, by Pascagoula, when driven from all other positions. Here they erected a fortress, the ruins of which are still said to be seen; though the work so described as theirs was probably erected by some of the roving bands of Spanish and French who first brought European civilization into the country. The last struggles of the Biloxi were protracted, as became the efforts of a brave nation fighting for life and liberty. But they fought in vain. Famine came in to the assistance of their enemies, and unconditional submission or death were the only alternatives. They chose the last; and men, women, and children proceeded to the sacrifice—which was as solemn, and perhaps more touching, than that of the citizens of Numantia under like circumstances. Throwing open the gates of their fortress, at a moment when the assailants were withdrawn, they marched down to the waters of the bay, singing their last song of death and defiance. With unshaken resolution they pressed forward until the waters finally engulfed them all. None survived. The strange spiritual music of the Bay of Pascagoula is said to be the haunting echo of that last melancholy strain. * * Such is one of the traditions respecting this mysterious music; and the one which we most prefer. Another legend is agreeably reported by Mr. Gayarré, in his late work on the picturesque and romantic in the history of Louisiana. It is due to the reader that he should be put in possession of this other version of the story. Gayarré describes the music as occurring mostly at the mouth of the Pascagoula River, and as seeming to float upon the waters, particularly in a calm moonlight. "It seems to issue from caverns or grottoes in the bed of the river, and sometimes oozes up through the water, under the very keel of the boat which contains the inquisitive traveller, whose ear it strikes as the distant concert of a thousand æolian harps. On the banks of the river, close by the spot where the music is heard, tradition says there existed a tribe different in color and in other peculiarities from the rest of the Indians. Their ancestors had originally emerged from the sea, where they were born, and were of a light complexion. They were a gentle, gay, inoffensive race, living chiefly on oysters and fish, and they passed their time in festivals and rejoicings. They had a temple in which they adored a mermaid. Every night when the moon was visible, they gathered round the beautifully carved figure of the mermaid, and with instruments of strange shape, worshipped that idol with such soul-stirring music as had never before blessed human ears.

"One day, a short time after the destruction of Mauvila, or Mobile, in 1539, by Soto and his companions, there appeared among them a white man, with a long gray beard, flowing garments, and a large cross in his right hand. He drew from his bosom a book, which he kissed reverentially, and he began to explain to them what was contained in that *sacred little casket*. Tradition does not say how he came suddenly to acquire the language of those people when he attempted to communicate to them the solemn truths of the Gospel. It must have been by the operation of that faith which, we are authoritatively told, will remove mountains. Be it as it may, the holy man, in the course of a few months, was proceeding with much success in his pious undertaking, and the work of conversion was going on bravely, when his purposes were defeated by an awful prodigy.

"One night, when the moon at her zenith poured on heaven and earth, with more profusion than usual, a flood of light angelic, at the solemn hour of twelve, when all in nature was repose and silence, there came, on a sudden, a rushing on the surface of the river, as if the still air had been flapped into a whirlwind by myriads of invisible wings sweeping onward. The water seemed to be seized with convulsive fury; uttering a deep groan, it rolled several times from one bank to the other with rapid oscillations, and then gathered itself up into a towering column of foaming waves, on the top of which stood a mermaid, looking with magnetic eyes that could draw almost every thing to her, and singing with a voice which fascinated into madness. The Indians and the priest, their new guest, rushed to the bank of the river to contemplate this supernatural spectacle. When she saw them, the mermaid tuned her tones into still more bewitching melody, and kept chanting a sort of mystic song, with this often-repeated ditty:—

'Come to me, come to me, children of the sea,
Neither bell, book, nor cross, shall win ye from your queen.'

"The Indians listened with growing ecstasy, and one of them plunged into the river, to rise no more. The rest, men, women, and children, followed in quick succession, moved, as it were, with the same irresistible impulse. When the last of the race disappeared, a wild laugh of exultation was heard; down returned the river to its bed with the roar of a cataract, and the whole scene seemed to have been but a dream. Ever since that time is heard occasionally the distant music which has excited so much attention and investigation. The other Indian tribes of the neighborhood have always thought that it was their musical brethren, who still keep up their revels at the bottom of the river, in the palace of the mermaid. Tradition further relates that the poor priest died in an agony of grief, and that he attributed this awful event, and victory of the powers of darkness, to his not having been in a perfect state of grace when he attempted the conversion of those infidels. It is believed, also, that he said on his death-bed, that those deluded pagan souls would be redeemed from their bondage and sent to the kingdom of heaven, if, on a Christmas night, at twelve of the clock, when the moon shall happen to be at her meridian, a priest should dare to come alone to that musical spot, in a boat propelled by himself, and should drop a crucifix into the water. But, alas! if this be ever done, neither the holy man nor the boat are to be seen again by mortal eyes. So far, the attempt has not been made; skeptic minds have sneered, but no one has been found bold enough to try the experiment."

The reader has now both the leading traditions before him, and can choose between them. It will be seen, that, in the narrative which follows, I prefer the former version of the legend. The Poet is supposed to be a spectator of the scene,—one greatly ravished with the quiet and sweet beauty of the landscape, and beguiled by it into a long train of dreamy speculations, which insensibly conduct him to the state of mind when he shall be most susceptible to spiritual influences. It is then that he is suddenly made aware of the awakening murmurs of the mysterious music. The reflections which precede the revelation are designed as a natural prelude to the strain.

THE LAST FIELDS OF THE BILOXI.

I.

Beautiful spread these waters 'neath mine eye,
Glassy and bright, with myrtles overhung;
Blue stretch the heavens above them—in their depths,
Far down reflected—arch more beautiful,
Seen through the mellowing medium of the wave,
Than in its native empire,—spann'd above,
Blazing, all cloudless, with the noonday star.
I wander by the islets near the sea,
That, from the Mexique bay, a tribute deep,
Rolls in on Pascagoula. There it sinks,
And sleeps with faintest murmurs; or, with strife
Brought from more turbulent regions, still bears on,
With threatening crest, and lips of whitening foam,
To battle with Biloxi. Short the strife!
Feebler at each recoil, its languid waves
Fling themselves, listless, on the yellow sands,
With a sweet chiding, as of grief that moans,
Oblivious not in slumber, of the strife,
That slumber still subdues. A dream of peace
Succeeds, and all her images arise,
To hallow the fair picture. Ocean sleeps
Lock'd in by earth's embrace. Her islets stand
Gray sentinels, that guard her waste domain,
And, from their watch-towers station'd by the deep,

Survey the midnight legions of the Gulf,
Numberless, wild, in their blue armor clad,
Forever bent on spoil. A sweet repose
Hangs o'er the groves, and on the sloping shore
And the far ocean. Not a murmur chides
The sacred silence. From the lone lagoon,
The patriarch of the ancient pelican,
Leads forth his train; though not with plashy wing
Break they the glassy stream, whose buoyant wave
Maintains each breast, and still reflects each form,
Without a riple on its face to mar
The perfect image. Gliding thus, they steer
To islands of green rushes, where they hide
In sports most human;—in white glimpses seen,—
Or by the light tops of the reeds that stoop,
Divided in the press of struggling forms.
But rapture hath a reign as short as peace—
The wild fowls' sports are ended. They repose
By the still marge of lakes, that, in the embrace
Of groves of cane and myrtle, steal away,
And crouch in sleep secure; while through the Gulf
Rolls the black hurricane. The summer noon
Prevails. A universal hush
Absorbs the drowsy hours, and Nature droops
With sweetness; as upon the listless eyes
Of beauty, steal the images of dreams,
Made up of star-crown'd hopes and truest loves,
And joy's own purple prospects. The still air
Falters with perfume of delicious fruits;—
The orange flings its fragrance to the seas,
Wooing the zephyr thence; and lo! he comes
Fresh from the toiling conflict with the deep,
Upon whose breast, subduing and subdued,
He snatches fitful rest. The glassy wave,

Smooth and serene as heaven, is broken now
Into complaining ripples. Now, his breath
Sweeps the rush islands, while the tall reed stoops
Its feathery crest to ocean. The gray sands,
Whirl'd suddenly beneath his arrowy tread,
Pursue his flight in vain;—and now he glides
Over the sacred bay, whose clear serene
Is whimpled by his wing. Anon, he stirs
The orange blossoms,—drinks full surfeit thence,
And sleeps among their leaves.

II.

I lay me down
In the sweet keeping of the wilderness,
Listless and blest as he! No wild to me,
Though lonely, all the silent groves and streams,
That slumber in my glance. For I have been
A wanderer, and denied all human ties:—
I made my friends among the hills and streams
Least loved or sought by man. To me, they wear
Aspects of love and kindness. Voices call,
And fair hands beckon me from alleys green,
Amidst a world of shadow;—solitudes
That woo the thoughtful footstep, and persuade
To realms of pensive silence,—beautiful groves,
Sad only, as their beauty blooms unsought.

III.

These win me from my path. I turn aside;
My heart drinks in the sweetness of the scene
I gaze on;—and how lovelier grows the spot,
To him who comes in love! I bow my head—
Where still she holds her matchless sov'reignty—
To all endowing Nature. Here she sits

Supreme, in tangled bower, and sunny mead,
And high umbrageous forest. At her feet,
Broad lakes spread forth their bosoms to the skies,
Whose beauties still they bear. Sweet fountains swell
From loneliest depths, among the hidden dells,
That, crouching 'neath the sway of sullen hills,
Yet send their crystal sorrows down the stream,
In secret channels; that the world may seek,
And free them from their darksome prison-place.
Tree, flower, and leaf, consorting with her mood,
Impress their calm on mine. I lay me down,
Within her solemn temple. Altars rise
About me, of green turf; and tufted beds,
Of grassy and blue flowers, beneath my head,
Pillow it gently. Mightiest subjects stand
Around me, grouped, and bending still, to serve—
Thick-bearded giants, that spread wide their arms,
And shield me from the burning shafts of noon.

IV.

Now, sweeter than the soft recorder's voice,
Or lute of ravishing syren, in mine ear,
This gentle diapason of the woods—
This sacred concert,—airs with bending pines,
Whose murmurs melt to one, and part again
With new accords,—with now a catch of song,
From bird that starts and sleeps. The fancy glows
In spiritual converse, as I dream
Of the old fated men of these sweet plains,—
Departed—all their dwelling-places waste,
And their wild gods grown powerless!
Powerless?—No!
They have a spell for fancy, and a charm
To waken echoes in the dreaming heart;

And from the prompt and sleepless sympathies,
Extort unfailing homage. For the Past,
They live, and live forever! That which speaks
For the sole moral of the faded race,
Dies not when it hath perished. Song will speak,—
Tradition, and the venerable groves,
With mounds, and fragments of old implements,
Even for the heathen;—as in temples, books,
Old columns, and the echoes of deep strains
From Phœbus-smitten minstrels, still survive
The proofs of mightier nations—godlike proofs,
That challenge human toil, the tooth of time,
And speak when he is voiceless. These connect
Races which mingle not; whose separate eyes—
By years and ocean separate—never saw
Their mutual aspects; yet, by sympathies,
Born of like trials, strifes, and mightiest deeds,
Yearn for communion,—yearn to see and love;
And when the earthquake threatens, bear, in flight,
Each glorious token of the transmitted race.

V.

Thus lives the savage god. Here, still, he roves
Among his hills made consecrate. Here, still,—
By this broad glassy lake, among these groves
Of yellow fruits and fragrance,—o'er yon isles,
The limit of his reign,—his old gray eye
Still ranges, as if watchful of the trust
His sway no more may compass.

——Yet, no more
Gather the simple tribes that bow'd the knee,
In love, or deprecation of his wrath;—
No more from plain to hill-top glows the pile
Fired in his sacrifice;—and, to glad his ear,

Rolls the deep strain of forest worshippers,
A wild and antique song of faith and fear,
No more! no more!

VI.

——'Tis sure a dream that stirs
These sounds within my soul; or, do I hear
A swell of song,—sweet, sad, upon mine ear,
That, like a wayward chant from out the sea,
Rises and floats along the yellow sands!
A note most like the wind-harp, hung in trees
Where the coy zephyr harbors. Still it comes,
In more elaborate windings; with a tone
Most human, and a fitfulness of sound
That speaks for various woes, as if it link'd
The deep, despairing, still defying cry,
From man in his last struggle,—with the shriek
Of passionate woman, not afraid to die,
Though pleading still for pity,—and the scream
Of childhood, conscious only of the woes
It feels not, but beholds in those who feel,
Unutterable still! A long-drawn plaint,
It swells and soars, until the difficult breath
Fails me;—I gasp;—I may not follow it
With auditory sense! It glows—it spreads—
'Till the whole living atmosphere is flush
With the strange harmony; and now it sinks,
Sudden, but not extinguished! A faint tone
Survives, in quivering murmurs, that awhile
Tremble like life within the flickering pulse
Of the consumptive. Losing it, we hush
Our breathing; and suspend the struggling sense,
Whose utterance mars its own; and still we hear
Its mellow and lone cadences, that float,

Prolong'd, and finally lost, as the deep sounds
Superior rise, of winds and waving trees!

VII.

It is a sweet tradition of these shores,
Told by the Choctaw, that, when ages gone,
His savage sire descended from the west,
A dark and desperate hunter,—all these woods,
From the rich valleys where the Missouri bounds,
To mix his turbid waters with the streams
Of him, the Sire of Waters,*—to the blue hills
Of Apalachia,—dwelt a numerous race,
Named "The Biloxi." Towns and villages,
Cities and colleges, and various arts,
Declared their vast antiquity. They were proud—
More proud than all the living tribes of men;
Wiser, and versed in many sciences;
And, from their towers of earth, that sought the skies,
In emulous mountain-stretches, watch'd the stars,
In nightly contemplation. With a skill
Wondrous, by other tribes unmatchable,
They rear'd high temples, which they fill'd with forms
Of love and beauty. In their thousand homes,
Joy was a living presence. There they danced
At evening; while the mellow song went forth,
Married to fitting strains, from instruments
Of curious form, but fill'd with strangest power,
That, when the savage hearken'd, half subdued
His bloody thirst, and made the reptile's fang
Forget his venomous office. By these arts
Were they at last betray'd. They soon forgot
The vigorous toils of manhood, and grew weak,
Incapable of arms. Voluptuous joys,

* The Mississippi.

Morning and evening in their courts, surprised
The strength of their young people, till they grew,
Like the rank grass upon the bearded plain,
Fit for the fire and scythe.

VIII.

——The Choctaw Chief
Look'd, from his dusky hills, upon their vales,
Exulting. When he heard their songs of love,
That floated upward on the perfumed air,
And saw, below, their loose, effeminate forms
Link'd in voluptuous dance,—he shouted loud
His scornful satisfaction; while he bade
His warriors nigh, to look upon their homes,
And mark their easy victims. They, below,
By happiness made deaf and arrogant,
Heard not the mighty discord, which, above,
Mock'd their soft harmonies. Their dream went on;
The midnight dance and revel; the sweet song
Of love and gold-eyed fancy; and the prayer,
Unbroken, of true genius, in his cell,
Toiling, with pen or pencil, to prepare
His triumph for the adoring eyes of day!

IX.

But with day came the conflict. The fierce tribes,
With hellish shout, that shook the affrighted walls
Till the high temples quaked, rush'd down the vale,
Smiting with heavy mace; or, from above,
Shooting their poison'd arrows at each mark,
Unerring. Though surprised, the Biloxi fought
Fiercely, and with an ardency of soul
Superior to their strength. The savage press'd
More resolute when baffled. Day by day,

Some citadel was won—some lovelier town
Despoil'd by the barbarian. Thousands fell
In conflict; yet the thousands that remain'd
Breathed nothing but defiance. With each loss,
Rose a new spirit in their hopeless breasts,
That warm'd them with fresh courage; and they swore
A terrible oath, with link'd hands, each in each,
And all, to their old deities, to yield
Life first, and freedom never! Well they kept
Their sacramental pledges. They could die,
But could not conquer. Yielding sullenly
Each foothold, they departed from the towns
They could no more maintain; and, fighting, fled;
Till from the hills of Memphis—from the springs
Of Loosahatchie—from the golden ridge,
Where the gay streams of Noxabee arise,—
Contented captives that complain not oft
Against the rocks, that, from the western streams,
Bar their free passage—gradual still they fled—
Still turning, still at bay, and battling oft
The dread pursuer.

X.

——To this spot they came—
They pitch'd their tents where Pascagoula flows,
Through shallows of gray shells, and finds its way
To the embraces of the purple Gulf.
"Here!" said the Prince—his subjects gather'd round—
"Make the last stand! The land beneath our feet
Slips rapidly, and farther flight is none,
Save to the ocean. We must stand and die!"

XI.

Sad were their hearts, but fearless. Not a lip
Spoke for submission. Soul and arm were firm;

And here, in resolute silence, they threw up
Their earthen ramparts. On the narrow walls
Of their rude fortress, in that perilous hour,
Ranged their few champions. To the hills, their eyes
Turn'd ever, till the savage rose in sight.
Then took they up their weapons. Flight no more
Was in their choice; but, in its place, there came,
From hopelessness, resolve—and such resolve,
As makes man terrible as fate. They stood,
Silent, with lips compress'd. No answering shout
Admonish'd the invader of the strength
Thus newly found; and down his warriors rush'd,
As to an easy conquest. But they shrunk,—
And wonder'd whence should come the singular might,
So sudden, of a race so feeble late!
Days, weeks, and months, and the Biloxi fought,
Invincible. Their narrow boundary grew
More strong and powerful, in the invader's eyes,
Than had been their sole empire. Spring, at length,
Put on her flowers. Green leaves and blossoming fruits
Declared for mercy; but the barbarian tribes,
Strengthen'd by fiercer thousands from the west,
Maintain'd the leaguer. Rescue there was none;
Despair had no more strength, for famine sapp'd
The hearts of the Biloxi.

XII.

One bright noon
Beheld them met in council—women and men;
The mother newly made, with the young babe,
Unconscious, striving at her bloodless breasts;—
For all are equal in the hour of woe,
And all are heard, or none!—

It needed not

That they should ask what doom awaited them!
They saw it in the tottering march—the face,
Pinch'd by lean famine;—the imperfect speech,
That falter'd with the syllable prolong'd;—
The hollow eyes from which a spiritual glare
Shot out like death. They saw it in all sights,
And sounds, that fate, in that protracted term
Of struggle and endurance, still vouchsafed;—
And there was silence—a long, dreary pause
Broken by feminine sobs. Then spoke the Prince,
Last of a line of kings!—
—— "Shall we submit
To bonds and probable torture, or go forth,
Made free by death?"
Brief silence follow'd then:—
In that brief silence, memories of years,
And ages, crowded thick. Years of delight—
Ages of national fame! They thought of all
The grace of their old homes,—the charm, the song,
Pure rights and soothing offices,—and pride,
Made household, by the trophies, richly strown,
Through court and chamber, of creative art;—
All lost!—and then the probable doom of bonds,—
The only slavery,—the superior race
Bow'd to the base and barbarous!—and one voice
Proclaim'd the unanimous will of all—to die!

XIII.

That eve, while yet within the western heavens,
Linger'd the rosy sunset—while the waves
Lay calm before them in the crystal bay,
And the soft winds were sleeping—and a smile,
As of unbroken peace and happiness,
Mantled the glittering forest green, and far,

Sprinkled the yellow beach with glinting fires,
That shone like precious gems;—the destined race
Threw wide their fortress gate. Thence went they forth
In sad procession. At their head, the Prince,
Who still had led their fortunes;—then, the chiefs,
And soldiers—few, but fearless;—the old men—
Patriarchs, who still remain'd,—memorials
Of the more fortunate past—and, last of all,
The women and the children. 'Twas an hour,
When Nature craved a respite from her toils;
And, from the strife withdrawn, the savage foe
Were distant, in their woodland tents retired.
These started with strange wonder to behold
The solemn march, unwitting of its end
And glorious aim; nor strove they to disturb
The rights which they divined not. On they went,
That ancient nation. Weapons bore they none;
But with hands cross'd upon their fearless hearts,
The warriors led the way. The matron clung
To her son's arm, that yielded no support.
The infant, hush'd upon its mother's breast,
Was sleeping; but the mother's sobs were still
Audible with her song;—and, with her song,
Rose that of thousands, mingling in one strain!
The art which in their happier days had been
Most loved among them, in spontaneous voice,
Unsummon'd, pour'd itself upon the air,
As, slowly, but with steps unfaltering still,
March'd the pale band, self-destined to the deep!
Never had Ocean in his balmiest hours,
Look'd less like death—less terrible, less wild!
An infant's slumber had not been more free
From all commotion. Beautiful and bright,
In the declining sunset, lay the scene

That witness'd the sad sacrifice; and sweet,
Like the fair prospect, was the united song,—
That epicedium o'er a nation's fate,
Self-chanted, which went with them to the waves,
And still survives them—breathing, from their graves,
The story of their empire,—of its fame,—
Its fall, and their devoted faith that knew
No life unbless'd with freedom. Sweetest strain!—
Once more it rises into sounds, that grow
Human in strength; and now, it floats away,
Subdued and sinking, as in that sad hour
When its last breathings from the warrior's throat
Stopp'd suddenly; and through the desolate air
Went a more desolate hush that told the rest!

THE HUNTER OF CALAWASSEE;

A LEGEND OF SOUTH CAROLINA.

I.

WHEN bites, in bleak November, the blast that rives the tree,
And scatters wide the yellow leaves, so sweetly sad to see,
Its voice's moaning murmur, borne through the trembling wood,
Awakes the heedful hunter up, and stirs his drowsy blood;—
In ancient times a summons meet,* for all who struck the deer,
He will not be the last to heed, who's still the first to hear;
He plucks the rifle from its rest, he winds the yellow horn,
And sweet the music of the sound through all the forest borne.

II.

'Way down where ghostly cypress and dodder'd oaks spread free,
By the winding fen of Calawass, and on to Ocketee,
The mellow notes go searching far, the bloodhound's bay is full,—
Shame light upon that hunter now whose bosom's beat is dull!
There's life within that bugle note, steeds snort and riders shout,
And life, in every bound they take, is gushing gladly out;
A spirit rends the thicket,—upstarts the couchant deer,
Shakes from his sluggish flanks the dew, and bounds away in fear.

III.

"Now sound your horns," cried Kedar, "and let the hunt be up,
And bring me, ere we start, my boy, a strong and stirring cup;

* The fall of the leaf was always the signal for ancient hunting.

The air is keen and searching, and sadly, in my breast,
The blood, that should be bounding still, lies lazily at rest;
Not long to rest, for, by my soul, and all the saints! I swear,
This day I perish, or I kill the buck that harbors here,—
That one-horn'd buck;"—"Nay, swear not so, dear master," thus he cried,
The aged slave, who then drew nigh and stood by Kedar's side.

IV.

"Now, out upon thy coward soul!" cried Kedar to the slave;
"Thou wast a man upon a time,—my father thought thee brave;
But age has dull'd thy spirit—thy limbs have need of rest,
This air's too keen for such as thou—go, harbor in thy nest;
Fool-fears have quell'd thy manhood, and, in this buck I seek,
Thou find'st a foe whose very name 'twould white thy lips to speak;
But though he be the fiend himself, and stand before my eyes,
This day I hunt him down, I say, and deer or hunter dies!"

V.

Then sadly spoke that aged slave—"Oh, master, swear not so—
Leave hunting of this one-horn'd buck, that's like no beast we know;
He makes no slot,* no entry* leaves, though through the closest brakes
Of bush, or cane, or thicket swamp, his headlong course he takes:
Still bears the same erected port, and never frays a head;—*
Two seasons have you hunted him, and still with evil sped;

* Old Lauto is somewhat more learned in his terms than most of the *drivers* of the southern country; and, for the sake of his brethren, some little explanation may be given here. These are all terms of the chase in ancient English hunting; and are furnished to me, at second hand, from Gascoigne's "Commendation of the noble Arte of Venerie." The *slot* is the print of a stag's foot upon the ground; *entries* are places through which deer have lately passed, by which their size is conjectured; *frayings* are the pillings of their horns; and a deer is said to "fray a head" when he rubs it against a tree to cause the outer coat to fall away in the season of renewal. These nice traits

Some grievous chance hath ever happ'd when on his scent v
The first"—"Now, fool," then Kedar cried, "be still for very s

VI.

"Sound, hunters, ere this idle tale arrest the sluggish blood,
And lend to braver hearts than his yon aged dotard's mood;
It is my oath this day to track that buck unto his den,
And we shall see if he or me shall live for hunt again;—
Two seasons hath he baffled us, 'twere shame if still he may,
And I am sworn, and heed my oath, to end the toil to-day;
And Lauto, you shall stay behind—I would not have you drive;
If such the fears that fill your heart, the hunt can never thrive."

VII.

"I'll go, my master," cried the slave, with sorrow in his tone,
"If fears are in old Lauto's heart, they're fears for you alone;
Here, Willow, Wand, and Wallow!"—three dogs of famous breed,
That had a boast from Rollo's pack, the Norman's, to be seed:—
He sounded then most cheerily, that aged slave, and cried,
'Till, from the kennel, all the pack, came bounding to his side;
He took the route his master bade, and with a heavy heart,
That shook with fears he could not name, did Lauto then depart.

VIII.

'Twas standing in a cypress grove, that, by the Ocketee,
Kept crowding shadows that forbade the searching eye to see,
Young Kedar waited long to hear the music of the hounds,
That told the hunt was up, and fill'd the wood with cheering sounds;
No sound he heard, yet, on his sight, that one-horn'd deer arose,
As speeding on, he left behind, in secret, all his foes:—

of the hunt, by which the hunter learns all that is desirable to know of the game he seeks, form, however, but a small number of those in the collection of the experienced in this "noble arte."

"But me he shall not baffle thus," cried Kedar as he came—
And lifting up his rifle then, he stood with ready aim.

IX.

Three strides the buck hath taken, his single horn on high,
And then he stay'd his forward flight, and look'd with steady eye;
He look'd upon the cypress grove where Kedar watching stood,
Then, turning, took his easy way toward the distant wood.
This madden'd Kedar then to see, and to his steed he gave
Free rein and rashing spur, and went as if some devil drave;
With shriek and shout he bounded on, and wonder'd to behold
How easy was the gait he went, that deer, along the wold.

X.

And still nor horn nor hound he heard, and nothing did he see,
Save that one deer that, fleeing, seem'd as not to care to flee;
This vex'd young Kedar to behold—a madness fill'd his blood,
And shouting as he went, he flew, with fury through the wood;
He heeded not for stop or stay—he look'd not once behind,
His soul was in that fearful chase—his spirit on the wind;—
A twilight shade came o'er the earth, and through the wood a moan,
Yet nothing did he see or hear, but that one deer alone!

XI.

The cypress groves he leaves behind, where, with impatient heart,
Three goodly hours he watch'd that day, from all the rest apart;
The long pines gather round him now, and now the thicket stays,
Yet on, with headlong haste, he goes, through wild and rugged ways;—
The deer, still wiling as he wends, keeps ever in his sight,
Yet indirect his forward course, as careless still of flight;—
More furious grew that hunter then, to see his mocking pace,
And feel at last, his noble steed was failing in the race.

XII.

No warning sign like this he heeds, but with his oath in mind,
Young Kedar, in that keen pursuit, is striving with the wind;
The rowel tears his charger's flanks until they glisten red,
The thong now smites his burning sides and now his aching head;
Yet docile still, in all his pain, though fainting with the chase,
He strives, that noble beast, to keep, unfailing, in the race;
The madness grows in Kedar's soul, and blinds his thought and will,
Such madness as must vex the heart of him that's doom'd to ill.

XIII.

And he that has no eye to see his weary charger's pain,
As little heeds the baffling wood through which his feet must strain;
The giant pines have faded far—the knotted thicket shakes
Its purple berries round his brow at every bound he takes;
The swamp is nigh, the horse's hoofs in ooze are plashing fast,
God save him, if he mean to save—such chase can never last!
The river's edge is nigh, and dusk, its solemn shadows rise,
And what a heavy silence hangs and broods along the skies.

XIV.

Before him sleeps the sluggish swamp that never sees the day,
And through its bosom, bounding on, the deer still keeps his way;
Another leap he gains the stream—another effort more—
And deeply in the charger's flanks, the rashing rowel tore;—
A sound is in young Kedar's ears—his hounds are close behind—
And 'tis old Lauto's cry that cheers upon that sudden wind;—
A warning cry that vainly seeks to drive the spell away,
And check the fiend that lies in wait and hungers for his prey.

XV.

Mad shouts from Kedar answer'd then old Lauto's kindly cry,—
"Ha! ha! I have him now!" was still the hunter's wild reply;

"I have him now—that one-horn'd buck—our path lies fair and free,
He sinks—he can no farther run—he lies by yonder tree;—
Upon him, Cygnet!—he is ours—one goodly effort more,
By death and all the saints, he's mine!—ha! ha! our hunt is o'er!"
And still the noble steed obeys, and through the swamp he goes,—
The swamp is past, and, round his feet, the dark Che-che-see flows.

XVI.

The dark Che-che-see flows along, in tribute to the main,
But stops not Kedar's rash pursuit—he spurs his steed again;
And breathing hard, the patient steed now takes the gloomy stream,
While roll'd the thunder cloud above, and sunk the westering gleam.
Old Lauto reach'd the river's edge, with dim and straining eye,
And something like a struggling steed, a moment did he spy;
But soon the waters closed above—he look'd beyond, and there
Still went, a failing shadow now, with easy pace, the deer!

THE SHIP OF THE PALATINES.

The tradition upon which the following legend is founded, is still, at the present day, somewhat current in the "Old North State." Within the last twenty years, indeed, we have seen in the newspapers a statement of the reappearance of the spectre ship of the Palatines, "all a-fire," and have been edified with the affidavits of good citizens, so solemnly impressed with the truth of the apparition, that they have not scrupled to make oath to the fact before the magistrates. The tradition—it will hardly escape the literary reader—is somewhat like that upon which Dana founds his poem of the "Buccaneer;" but it is of simpler structure, and not the less suitable, perhaps, because of its simplicity, for metrical purposes. I have treated it according to the tradition, without seeking to graft upon it any of my own inventions.

A shaft of sudden light, as if a glance,
Shot from the fiery eyes of sinking day,
Lights the green edges of the western wave,
And purples it with beauty. Yet the sun
Now flames on Asian summits. Midnight sways
His abdicated realm upon our shores,
And his successor, the pursuing moon,
Hath vanish'd in his wake. A cloudy veil
Hangs o'er her mansion, and the twiring stars
Grow dim along her track. Once more that blaze,
A sulphury column o'er the midnight waste,
Darts upward and prolongs a fitful glow,
Leaping from wave to wave.
"A ship on fire,
Crowd sail, and let us reach it!"
Thus the cry
Ran through our vessel, and each straining eye,
Piercing the solid depth of dark between,

Beheld—through fancies that with quicken'd birth,
Peopled all the scene with persons at their need—
The wreck'd and perishing wretches,—the strong man,
And trembling woman, and unconscious child,
As, hanging o'er the eternal precipice,
They cried to Heaven for succor,—cried and sank!—
Preferring the sure sentence of the deep,
To that dread doom, that, darting on their steps,
With thousand forkéd, fiery tongues pursued!
One moment of deep terror!—but the hand
Touch'd not the cordage. The uplifted voice,
Of order, lapsed in silence. It was gone,
That sudden blaze, as suddenly; and night,
A vast and shapeless shadow, frown'd in place.
Yet was the semblance, to each eye that saw,
A burning vessel, a majestic barque,
Limm'd in consuming flame—erect, yet doom'd—
From gunwale up to top, from stem to stern,
In fiery lines articulate and clear,
Each spar, and shaft, and lineament a-blaze,
Glorious in ruin!
Thus, in western wilds,
The traveller, in belated journey, sees
A vision of destruction,—not like this
A vision only; but reality,
So wildly, terribly beautiful, as takes
Possession of all senses. The tall wood
Is traversed by a tempest of bright flame,
That, coursing far, on seraph wing, defies
Restraint; leaps up to the inflammable pine,
And fastens, like a tiger, on its heart.
The monarch tree, with sky achieving spire,
And limbs spread out like patriarchal arms,
Exchanging all its garniture of green,

Is clothed in fiercest crimson—kingly shroud
For more than kingly shape. The mighty shaft,
Consuming, yet unshrinking!—the broad limbs
Blazing, but still extended—while the vine,
Supported long on those paternal arms,
Crackles, and curls, and shrivels, in the flame,
Like cordage on the vessel lately gone.
  There is a deep and serious faith in man,
Nursed in his secret soul, and strengthen'd there,
By numerous stern and solemn instances,
That finds a latent but close sympathy,
Betwixt his own and that mysterious world
To which our shadows hasten. Earth may cloud,
Not wholly darken, that superior light
Which burns within us. This, immortal hands
Trim nightly; and upon our startled ken,
Purged of its sullen and unfruitful humors,
Betray brief glimpses of the thing that was,
And thing that may be. Purposes of dread,
To us, obscure and wondrous—not for us
To fathom or examine—in HIS will,
Whose will is monarch over all that lives,
Life's single source and Sov'reign,—rise in forms
That soothe, or awe, or waken—shake with fright,
Or startle into meritorious deed
And righteous duty. Innocence o'erborne,
Finds succor when most fearful; wan Despair
Grows hopeful, though the gleam upon his eye,
That wins him, with new confidence, to life,
Be germined by the vaporous fogs that rise
From ancient charnels and forbidden graves,
Where rot the unknown race;—and crime that lurks,
Ever in dread, a thing of hate and fear,
Is dragg'd to make confession of his guilt

By some inexorable shade,—some shape—
That moves the unwitting tongue, the unwilling hand,
In inauspicious moment, to betray
The one dread secret. Murder will come out,
And find a voice, and challenge scrutiny,
Though seas roll o'er the victim, and long years
Brood o'er the terrible hour that saw the deed!
There is a wild tradition of these shores,
Still told by ancient men,—who, in such blaze
As that which lately dazzled and withdrew,
See but a phantom beacon, set by heaven,
To mark the period and the place of crime.
Familiar to their eyes that spectral light,
With each returning year; and learned scribes
Have set their hands and signets to the tale
In solemn record.
Once upon a time—
Thus runs the story—ere our fathers yet
Flung off the sway of British sov'reignty,
A little band of German Palatines,*
Having fond hopes from change—it may be, lured
By vague, wild dreams of freedom,—left their homes,
And charter'd a frail vessel, which they fill'd
With wives, and sons, and daughters,—all their wealth
Of family and treasure. But the last
They screen'd from curious eyes, and, meanly garb'd,
No other seem'd than helpless destitutes,
Bless'd if the pittance, needful for the day,
Were, by the hand of charity, bestowed.
Thus habited—thus lowly in the sight
Of strangers they embark'd. They cross'd the seas,—
God smiled upon their voyage, till the shores

* So called, as they came from the Palatinate.

Of Carolina, gathering on their gaze,
Rose up in welcome, on the ocean's marge.
Then joy was in their hearts. The smiling sun
Look'd on them from blue summits. Green, the groves
Woo'd them with promised shelter; while the fruits,—
Fragrant and purple, that, in southern lands,
Spring, undemanding labor, at the word
Of sweet and sovereign nature,—to their glance
Made all one Eden. Joy, in every heart,
Burst forth from tongue and eye;—and children all,
Thus gladden'd, they forgot the prudent cares
That garb'd them late in seeming poverty.
The peril of the seas was at an end—
Their world before them. They had homes to build,
And time was precious;—wherefore then delay?
They brought their stores to light. Their eager hands
Unveil'd their treasures. Little family gauds,
Of gold and jewels, hidden through the past,
Long centuries of danger and distress,
Display'd by happy hands—on heaving hearts,—
And cups of silver in more precious grasp
Of dearest children. Confident, at last,
Of fortune,—in the hope that, baffled long,
No more could be denied—they yielded them
To every sweet assurance.
"With the morn,"
Thus rang their eager voices in all ears,
With iteration fond, rehearsing hope,—
"Our feet shall tread these shores—our fingers pluck
Their fruits—our forms beneath yon sacred shade
Of forests, that have felt no hand but heaven's,
Catch precious dews of slumber. Heaven be praised,—
For its dear mercies—for this best of all!"
Thus, like fond children, full of fresh delights,

In little groups, they throng'd the vessel's deck,
Each glad with pleasant purposes—his toils,
His petty schemes of future happiness—
Where build, what plant, what hours to care devote,
And what to recreation—what the flowers
Of this new world;—and—these were maiden thoughts—
How sweet, when garlanded with blue and pink
The evening dance beneath the spreading oak,
Love darting keenest glances from the grove,
And, in its shadow, weaving subtlest charms
To soothe and still subdue half-willing hearts!
Thus dreaming each, with some particular joy
To feed on, as the soul's best nutriment,
They mused together; framing at the last,
For absent dear ones in the father-land,
Glowing dispatches, in whose bright details
Hopes in a moment grew to certainties—
With fond entreaties to the ancient sire,
And timorous grand-dame, doubtful of the seas,
To follow, and their forest-homes partake.
Noon pass'd, and evening came, and courtly night,
With all her proud, but pale patrician throng,
Sweet, but how stately! Lingering to the last,
While yet the shores lay visible to sight,
Our blue-eyed wanderers hung with eager eyes
Upon the yellow sands, the green-plumed pines,
Tall warriors, set as watchers on the deep,
In close array and serried rank and file.
But, with the darkness they withdrew—with hearts
How joyful—with a thousand hopes in one,
And that how full of child-significance,
In the one word—"To-morrow!"
But to them,
That morrow, with its wealth of promises,

Came never! Fatal was their sad mistake—
That vain display of treasure, shown to eyes
Which gloated, with an eager, fierce delight,
On the bright vision. In the master's heart
Rose up the hungry fiend of avarice;—
A greedy pang, a lust that had no fear,
Work'd fearfully within him. In his eyes
Glitter'd the secret thirst, that might have taught,
Meet prudence to his simple passengers,
Had they been vigilant watchers with their eyes,
Less greedy than their hearts. But they had grown
Suspicionless beneath prosperity;
Saw not the malice—had no instinct dread
Of that so sudden passion which should work,
Even in the moment of their sweetest hope,
For their destruction. From their eyes he shrank,
The master—sought his cabin—conn'd his charts—
Fled from temptation—but his brooding thought
Clung to the one possession. Through the day,
A single image glanced before his gaze,
Of all those golden spoils within his grasp,
Blinding and dazzling; baffling the better nature
Stifling the pleading conscience, and with iron,
Of heated avarice, searing Pity's eyes.
He had no other thought. Within his ears,
Ever a single voice was whispering—
So softly, so soliciting!—that said,—
"Midnight will hide the deed—an hour is all—
Wherefore thy terror—thou shouldst be a man,
And make thyself forever!"

'Twas enough!

The demon triumph'd. Then the master sought
His crew, and with like argument o'ercame
The germ of mercy in their stubborn souls.

They swore, with linkéd hands, a horrid oath,
Fidelity, in blood, to one another—
And hell,—and then they whisper'd o'er their plans
Of cruelty and safety. With the night,
When darkness fill'd the close abode where slept
Their wearied victims,—silently they stole,
Each to his hateful task. With stealthy care
The fatal knife was lifted o'er the breast
Of each strong sleeper. At a signal given,
They struck, and struck together,—but one blow—
And writhing, but scarce shrieking in his pain,
The sleeper slept forever. One hoarse cry,
Stifled in utterance,—one spasmodic fling
Of upward striving arms,—and all was hush'd
In burdensome silence;—so oppressive then,
That the fierce criminal, shuddering at his post,
Paused, hopeful, that his victim still might groan,
And half implored the mercy of the struggle,
That he might feel the deed was yet undone!
But brief cessation from their bloody toils
Claim'd terror. Conscience flung aside and hush'd—
Then follow'd the last dreadful sacrifice!—
Women and children—shrieking innocents,
Pleading and clinging to their murderers,
And wondering that the father came not nigh—
The husband, brother,—while the threat'ning blade,
Blood-dripping gleam'd above their dying eyes.
All perish'd—prayer and supplication vain—
Mammon to Moloch made his sacrifice,
And, elbow-deep in blood, the murderers,
Stood cowering within the darkness, half afraid,
Lest, through the hold, the innocent starry eyes
Summon'd to look by each escaping soul,
Might pierce, in passing, and lay bare the deed.

A moment, and in contemplation brief,
The criminals found resolve. With hurried toils,
They gather'd up the wealth, whose fatal lures,
Had won them to the guilt of bloody hands,
And, with their ill-got treasure made secure,
They hasten'd to their boats. But first, to hide
All traces of their footsteps and their crime,
They plied with busy care the blazing brand;
And in the bowels of the fated ship,
Left flaming torches. Speeding to the shore,
They watch'd the fierce destruction. From the hold,
Shot up, in thousand tongues and jets of fire,
The raging flames ascended. On the masts,
The deck, the gunwale, spars and sails, they seized,
With sudden fury. All a-blaze, the ship
Darted along the deep, a form complete,
Complex in lineament, but subtly wrought
In lines of blazing light. And thus she sped—
No wind impelling—close beside the shore,
Where stood the gasping criminals—their eyes,
Wide-staring on that wond'rous spectacle.
Thus, to and fro, the livelong night she went,
They watching still, incapable of flight.
By day, a charr'd and dismal skeleton,
She frown'd upon them, as, in restless drift,
She floated slowly by the yellow sands—
Now gone from sight, now suddenly, once more,
Gliding above the self-same dreary spot
Which saw the deed most dark and damnable!
All day, as by some awful spell enchain'd,
They linger'd by the shore. Now, in the wood,
Hiding their trembling forms—now, peering forth,
With the deceitful hope that, from their eyes,
The dreaded sight was gone,—beneath the wave,

Hiding their secret. But when night once more
Swept with starr'd train along the accustom'd march,
Again the spectre vessel heaves in sight;—
The bright flames darting upwards, spreading fast
O'er sails, spars, cordage! Blazing as before,
Yet unconsuming still, the phantom barque
Bears right for shore. Too terrible the sight
Upon the eyes of those most wretched men.
They fled,—and in the forest wilderness,
'Mongst beasts of prey, and tribes more savage still,
Buried their heads, their secret and their hopes—
Never their fears! Years, generations pass'd:—
The living are the dead! What fate befel
These hapless and still hopeless criminals,
The chronicles reveal not;—but the tale,
Still told by wise and venerable men,
Declared they went unpunish'd, save by God,—
And that the spectre vessel, still a-blaze,
Upon that fearful anniversary,
Appears with night, and still must re-appear,
Until, upon each man child, from the loins
Of those most bloody men, the avenger's hand
Hath fatally fallen,—when the spectre ship,
Her work complete, all blazing as she goes,
Shall lay her aching ribs in ocean's caves!

THE TRYST OF ACAYMA.

I.

Fair 'fall the Indian maiden, who sits by yonder stream,
For, though her eyes are full of tears, she dreams a happy dream;
She waits Panaco's coming,—he left her for the shore,
Where, bursting through the Darien rocks, Atrato's waters roar;
A poison'd javelin fill'd his hand, a knife was by his side,
And countless were the valiant chiefs beneath his arm that died;—
A brave among the bravest, the first to lead was he,
When down the mountain warriors sped to meet the Caribbee.

II.

A fear is in Acayma's heart, and yet that heart is glad,
For, bless'd with brave Panaco's love, it could not well be sad;
Three moons ago he sought her tent,—"Where is the maid?" said he,
"I seek but one of all the tribe that wanders by the sea."—
His eye is on Acayma,—she dares not look on high,
Though well she knows, that happy hour, she stands beneath his eye,—
His hand is on the maiden's hand,—she felt her bosom heave;—
He kept the willing heart and hand, she had no power to give.

III.

'Twas by the rapids of the stream that down the mountain fell,
Just where Biloxi's iron head looks o'er Senonee's dell;
"I'll watch these babbling waters, and they shall speak for thee;"
The maiden cried,—"and tell me why thou lingerest by the sea;—

I know thou dost not love me."—Then lightly did he reach,
And, sprinkling with the falling drops, he stay'd her idle speech;
Then laughing long, and looking back, he bounded down the steep,
And, in her very joy of heart, the maiden could but weep.

IV.

But weary grow the lengthening hours, and shadows of distress
Now haunt the heart, that, in its love, still finds its loneliness;
The tears of joy that fill'd her eye when first Panaco went,
Are dry—but down the silent rocks her gloomy glance is sent;
A thousand fears are in her thought—she plucks and rends the flowers,
And anxious looks, where, in the sky, a heavy tempest lowers;
Though none may better guide the bark or trim the sail than he,
Still swells within her heart the hope he be not on the sea.

V.

Too rash and too resolved his soul, too prone to rove afar,
To launch the boat, to lead the hunt, to urge the tribe to war;
She weeps to think, to meet her wish, and win her love, he speeds
Where yellow waters boil in rage among the cavern weeds:
He promised ere he left her, to bring for her that day,
The brightest pearl that ever slept 'neath the gulf of Urabay;
To rob the sea-maid of her shells, and from the snake-god's home,
Tear the green gem that lights his crest, and rend his crystal foam.*

VI.

The noontide hour is going fast,—she lingers still and sighs,
For thicker yet the shadows crowd, and gather on her eyes;

* The tradition is, that there is a great sea-snake of the Gulf, which the Indians call the king-snake, or god-snake, whose head is one entire emerald which lights the ocean for many leagues; that he sleeps in a cavern of the purest crystal, which is beautiful, in fantastic forms, like the combing foam of the sea when petrified.

A shadow o'er her spirit steals, more darkly, deeply dread,
Than that which closes now in storm above the mountain's head;
Yet watches she the falling wave, and, to her trembling ears,
A murmur, like an omen comes—what is it that she hears?
'Tis sure Panaco's voice,—but no!—ah, sweet, delusive dream,
'Twas but some loosen'd rock above that tumbled down the stream.

VII.

She knows not of her sorrow yet,—she chides at his delay;
Oh! would she thus reproach him, if she knew what made him stay?—
Could she dream that while she blamed him, he battled for his life,—
Could she see the Spanish foeman, and Panaco 'neath his knife?
Alas! for thee, Acayma,—what though thy lover swore,
He will not come to bless thee now,—he lies by yonder shore;
And though thy tears were torrents, like those adown yon glen,
They cannot move Panaco,—he will never come again.

VASCO NUNEZ;

OR THE PROPHECY OF THE ASTROLOGER.

A LEGEND OF DARIEN.

The reader needs no information in respect to the renowned Vasco Nunez de Balboa, the discoverer of the Pacific, and one of the most noble of all the cavaliers that followed in the footsteps of Columbus and Hernan Cortes. Of the astrologer, Micer Codro, less is known; but the pathetic facts in his career, as far as we possess them, may be found in the pleasant and instructive volume of Irving, which he devotes to the companions of Columbus. The legend which follows supplies its own facts, and needs no further introduction.

I.

Triumphant on a peak of Darien,
The eagle conqueror that, in one bold flight,
Had scaled each high impediment of cloud,
And stood above the summits of the storm,—
Balboa,—on the topmost crag that crown'd
The narrow isthmus, which between two seas
Spread barrier walls, denying their embrace,—
Rose, silent, with his eye uplift to heaven,
A moment, as in prayer and thankfulness,
Then, hopefully, he cast his glance below,
And trembled in his rapture.
'Neath him roll'd
The broad Pacific, never yet before
Unveil'd to European! What were then
Th' emotions of that conqueror, in whose toils
Such courage, with such great endurance mix'd,
Were the best proofs of virtue. Who shall tell
The struggling, glad sensations of the soul,

So highly reaching, when,—to crown at last
The hope so fruitful in great enterprise,
And noble consummation—on his eyes
Burst forth that mighty prospect—that deep sea,
In the virginity of its pure waves,
Unrifled of a charm—for the first time
Won to a mortal's arms!—or, who conceive,
When on the summit of that isthmus throned,
Higher than sovereign, and on either hand
Ranged the two sister seas, for the first time
Given to each other; he, that gallant chief,
Most noble and most valiant of the sons
Spain sent on this great service, stood alone,
And look'd upon his conquest? Who shall tell
The melancholy pride of his great soul,
When the achievement, long withheld, and won
Only by toil at last—the fearless toil
Of true adventure and achievement great,
That greater grew from trial—was his own;
And, to a spirit as aspiring, he
Added a name and triumph, scarce below
That of the "Admiral," who led the way,
First, in this path of glory!—
With glad eye,
And soaring sense, and spirit almost drunk,
In its excess of rapture, dumb he stood,
And gazed upon the waters. Were these, then,
The billows of that Indian sea, which clasps
In its capacious bosom, those broad isles
Of boundless, unimaginable wealth,
In gold and gems o'erflowing, locking in
The spices and the perfumes of the East—
The world of spoil, the field of enterprise,
Meet for that ocean chivalry, to whom

The sea and land, the wild, and wilder yet
The savages that sway them, have no bar?
Was this that glorious sea—or, prouder still,
Had fortune yielded to his daring aim
Some lonely, lock'd-up ocean of the wild,
Some savage realm of water, undisturb'd,
Save by the Indian's bark, when, at the dawn,
He plunges through its silvery depths, unscared,
For the pearl oyster, and at eve returns,
Laden and glutted with its precious spoils,
To his lone wigwam by the reedy shore?
Proud were the thoughts of that young conqueror,
But with a due humility, that taught
Meet homage to the Deity who gave
The genius for the conquest, and laid bare
The portals of the empire and the deep!
Tears glitter'd in his great eyes, while he gazed;
His gleaming sword was laid upon the heights,
And his strong hands uplifted; while his knees,
Taught by the gratitude swelling in his heart,
Bow'd at that primitive altar of the rock,
That glow'd in day's first sunshine. Thus, alone,
A moment, pray'd Balboa. No one shared
The spectacle that gladden'd his fond eyes,
Or felt the secret sentiment of pride
That in his heart taught worship—till he bade
The host ascend the summits which his feet
Had singly scaled, and gather at a glance,
The marvellous empire hidden in the waste,
Whose secrets thus were won.
They came, they saw;
Like him, the host sank prostrate on their knees,
While audible hearts of worship breathed in prayer,
And one strong shout from that fierce chivalry

Spoke all the dark devotion of their race,
As, at the bidding of their chief, the cross,
Hewn from the tallest pine, was lifted up,
A symbol of their service and their faith,
In triumph o'er their heads. Then every eye
Grew pregnant with its tears—some upward turn'd
To heaven in thanks and gladness—others again,
In wonder not to be appeased, and love,
That had its source in wonder and delight,
To the broad realm of ocean at their feet.

II.

'Twas midnight, and the stars were in the heavens,
Each the proud centre of a countless host,
Each with a world of glory in its glance
Such as the orient knows not. Not a cloud
Dull'd their profusion; and upon that sea,
Soft, with a billowy rising, and a swell,
Like the voluptuous heavings, in the breast
Of some warm princess of the passionate East,
They flung their emulous and repeated lights,
With a most profligate glory. From the south,
Where, all day, it had wander'd seeking flowers,
And whence, with wing embarrass'd still with spoil,
It came diffusing odor, stole the wind,—
That robber of the close that feeds the waste,
And stirr'd with gentlest ripplings the great sea,
Until, with musical murmurs to the shore,
It roll'd its little billows to the reeds,
That straightway took a voice most like their own,
And join'd the natural concert;—sweet, sad tones,
The music of that spirit whose brooding wing
Ever gives tone to earth's vast provinces,
Her seas, and sloping shores, and the great heights,

Her mountains, vast world-citadels, that need
The blue wings of such spirit to subdue
Their rudeness, and such voices as it knows,
To harmonize, and with due sympathies,
Blend meetly, the wild aspect of the crag
With valleys, and the swelling tides of sea!
'Twas midnight, but the chieftain did not sleep!
Still, as he lay upon the summit crag,
Glided on the gradual hosts of starry eyes,
Sweet smiling in his own; and to his ear,
Still upward rose those voices of the wave,
Bidding him welcome; and around the heights,
With song of winds in commerce with the pines,
Such music of the wilderness as best
Persuades the sense to rapture, while the dream
Finds ever a shape of beauty for the eyes,
And still a ravishing feeling for the soul,
That sweetly takes possession of a thought,
Then wholly given to nature. There he lay,
Fond listening to those tones of land and sea,
With speech mysterious to the worshipping sea,—
Voices to voices calling, hill to hill,
And ocean to old forests, through still hours,
Keeping up a solemn chorus, and soft chant,
Such as soothes solitude on lonely heights,
And takes away the sorrow from the waste.

How could he sleep? The creature of his dreams,
That for so long had brought him wakeful hours,—
The vague conceit, the great expectancy,
The wondrous fond illusion, the wild hope,
The quenchless thirst, the matchless passion, all,
That show'd him ever glimpses of great heights
Attain'd, and empire won, and fame secure,

For the all worshipping future,—all the dreams
That wrought his soul's ambition from the hour
He first had dream'd of glory,—were his own !—
The prize of a long dream was his at last !
The crown of a long strife was realized !
That hour had changed him, and possession won,
He was no more the creature he had been,
When boyhood was a season of delight,
And hope had many a semblance. When, amid
The festive throng, for mirth and music bent,
At evening by the waters, or attuned
To a more fell employment, he was found
Rashly adventurous, daring still the first,
Where all were daring—in the tented field,
Join'd in close combat with the tawny Moor,
A kingdom on his arm. The ruthless mood,
Indifferent to aught but valorous deed
And bloody retribution—all were gone !
And, in their stead, a loftier spirit came,
Keeping him watchful. His adventurous mind
Felt its own wing, and knew its strength at last
And soar'd into the heavens ; and, eagle-like,
He brooded 'mong those mountains through the night,
And meditated, with the matin chime,
His flight across the waters ;—where to lead
He knew not ; but his dreams, his waking dreams,
Peopled the wilds beyond, with glorious forms
And empires of the sun. He too would give
To Castile and to Leon a new world ;
And more than he, the mighty Genoese,
Another ocean with its tribute wealth,
And uncomplaining waters.

He would yield
His country such a treasure, and a realm,

Of such unbounded wealth and eminence
As should eclipse each jewel in her crown,
The gift of former sons. Thus mighty souls
Commune with their own purposes. Their pride,
That seeks the conquest, sees the hour beyond,
When, with a generous, free magnificence,
They fling the golden guerdon they have brought,
On shrines which still embody to their souls
A power for love and worship. Sovereigns thus
Find loyalty, faith, and sweet humility;
And beauty, the fond homage of a heart
That never dared to breathe its passionate love,
Yet yearn'd the while to bless and to endow.

Thus, on the rocks of Darien, lay the chief,
Brooding with sweet, proud fancies, while the stars
Lapsed overhead above, and still below
Lay his exhausted followers, wrapt in sleep,
That knew no dream like his. At last, a voice
Aroused him, and the weight of a strong hand,
But not in anger, on his shoulder fell.
He started from his trance. Beside him stood
One of the wise men of that dreaming age,
A fond, self-mortified spirit,—one who sought
Its thoughts in realms forbidden—an old man,
Whose spirit, through long abstinence and toil,
Deep study, musings vast and infinite,
And rigorous penance, in its age had grown
Familiar with the stars. To him they were
Not less than wizard lights, and presences,
Of soul and speech. To him they bared the seals
That held the future, and they laid the past
Before him as an open scroll, writ full
Of all familiar characters. Unveil'd to him,

All time grew present;—and, in rocky cells,
In ruin'd castles, and secluded caves,
By seas, in lonely forests, and afar
From human converse, still he conn'd the page,
Nightly, of mortal story. He could read
All futures. He could conjure shapes at will,
Into the speaker's presence;—so his fame
Ran 'mongst the Spanish host;—and such as he
Was ever sought and honor'd by the chief
That toil'd in wild adventure. Thus they made
Apparent, the large glory in their search;
Their wild, ambitious reachings, and the dream
That still ennobles conquest, with the thirst
For something, which the world may not bestow.
Such was the aged man, who, on that night,
Stood by the musing conqueror, as he lay
Upon the mountain peak of Darien.
He rose, and they together look'd below,
Where, flashing ever out beneath the stars,
Gleam'd the calm waters, the Pacific plain,
Repeating all the glories in the heavens.
Thus look'd they both in silence for awhile,
Till the young chief, with gladness in his tones,
Cried to the aged man:

"Hast thou no voice,
My father, for this triumph? Here, at last,
We have laid bare the secret of the West,—
New worlds,—new oceans,—people—countless lands,
And empires yet to win. What toil was ours!
Yet vainly have these perilous heights and wilds
Opposed us in our march—vainly our fears,
Striven to retard—vainly these barbarous tribes
Raised their red spears, or hurl'd their feathery shafts.
These have we overcome, and Balboa now

May vaunt his conquests on the kindred page
That glows with Colon's glory. Have I not
Given a new ocean to our sovereign's rule,
A tributary world, a myriad race
Of subjects, and a vast and nameless wealth,
Not to be number'd? Have I not outspread
Here, to the embraces of a foreign breeze,
That blossoms in its odor, borne afar,
Doubtless, from gardens of the orient realm,
Hard by to Ophir—his unconquer'd flag;
And, on this rock, beheld from either sea,
Planted the sacred standard of our faith,
The hallow'd cross; in token that the wild
Is now the care of Christ, henceforth to be
The creature of his people? These are deeds,
Good father, that shall never be forgot;
And Balboa's name, when he shall be no more,
Shall have its chronicler to spell the ear,
And on the lips of story sound as well,
As any in the record. How will 't read,
With "Vasco Nunez de Balboa," to write
"Colon the Admiral"—"world-finders both:"

The Magian paused a space, and to his eye—
Where brightness, strangely mingled up with gloom,
Wore an appalling lustre, not unlike
Such as our dreams for spirit forms provide—
A darker shade, a deeper, sadder hue,
And, it might be, a large but single tear,
Gather'd unbidden. Calmly then he spoke.

"My son, at Palos, by the convent walls
Of La Rabida, your old mother dwells:
I saw her, when we last departed thence,

On this adventure. Not to me unknown,
The future, as you found it. You were then,
Already, known to glory—so men call
Words from their fellow-men—and 'twas her pride
To speak of you as all the country spake.
I could not check the current of her speech,
Nor were it kind to do so ; but, aroused,
And ravish'd with the subject, when she grew
Wild with imagined triumphs and great spoils,
And all the gauds of fortune—in my heart
I sorrow'd for her strange simplicity.
I did not tell her that her eyes in vain
Would, till the sunset, o'er the waves look out
For her son's caravel. I did not say,
What, well persuaded, I might well have said,
That all your triumphs were to end at last
In a base dungeon and a bloody grave,
And ignominious scaffold—

"Ah ! you start !

But 'tis my grief, as 'tis thy destiny,
That I should mourn for that I must foresee,
And thou escape not. Hearken, then, awhile.
Thou wilt remember, on our voyage out,
I traced thy fortune. Thou didst seek of me
Its features ; but thy quest I still withstood,
As aiding not thy service to be known,
And, haply, moving thy too soaring thought,
Too much to dwell upon it. But with me
It grew a settled study. From my art—
Of which in praise I speak not, when I say
It has not fail'd me oft—I linger'd o'er
Thy varying fortunes. Every step thou took'st,
Whether in peace or war, in court or camp,
In ease or peril, I beheld at large.

I saw thee trace thy journey to the wild—
Thy each reverse—thy final, full success,
Until the mighty waters, which now roll
Incessant to our feet, proclaim'd thy fame;
And to the daring soldier gave the praise
Of calm forethought, deliberation wise,
And an intelligent sense that all confirms
In this thy conquest. Here then are we now—
So far, the fortune I have traced is true!"

"What more, what more?" impatient, then, the chief
Ask'd of the aged man. "Let me know all—
I do esteem thy art, and well believe
Thou lovest me as thy son. Thou wilt not speak
What 'twere not well to hear; and well I know,
Thy wisdom, if ill fortune do betide,
May guide my wilder'd bark, and bring it safe.
Speak then at once, nor think that at thy speech,
Though fearful be its form, my soul shall quake,
Or my knees tremble. Let me know it all,
That I may battle boldly with my fate,
However vain the struggle, as becomes
A son of Spain, a warrior of the wild,
A spirit prone to combat with the seas,
And brave them at their wildest. Speak, old man;
Give thy thought words, and let my fortune stand
Before me on the instant."

The magian spoke:
"When in the gather'd stars thy fate I read,
In one remote and solitary light,
I saw its bane, and baleful influence.
A single star, thus quarter'd in the heavens,
Teem'd with malicious auguries, and shook

All fires malign upon thee. It was then
I sought its secret power, and early read,
That, while afar, in the extremest east,
It kept its foreign station, thou wert safe;
But when, with daring wing, it took its way,
And, where the evening hangs her golden lamp
O'er the sun's chambers, shook its lurid fires,
That hour to thee was perilously dark,
And death, a bloody, ignominious death,
Was gather'd in its verge. That hour's at hand!—
Look forth into the west. Behold, apart,
From all communion with its fellow lights,
Where, with audacious blaze and angry beam,
That fate casts forth its fires. Redly it burns,
And, as exulting in the near approach
To the destruction of its victim, takes
A subtle halo round it. There are stars,
That to the eye of mortals seem but stars,
Yet are they evil spirits. Such is this.
They are not of the class with which they roam,
Their lights are not like those which burn around,
Nor have they the like genial influence;
They hold a fearful power o'er earthly things,
Man, and the worlds about him. O'er the earth,
And on the waters, they still exercise;
They have their moods, and, bitterly at war
With all God's works, they seek for their annoy;
Impede their fortunes, or attend them on,
Even to success, as, with thee, this hath done,
That, when they hurl them down to the abyss,
The height shall be a perilous one they leave.
The gentler lights of heavenly providence
Shrink from their foul contagion, till they stand
Apart, and from the rest all separate.

Some they precipitate from their high spheres,
Leaping into their places; the dethroned,
Extinguish'd in the deeps of all their light,
Find there a dwelling-place, to their new life
More apt and fitting. Such powers have these
O'er men and stars, as these do err and shoot,
Out from their proper places. Over thee
Yon planet hangs its spell, and thou art mark'd
Its victim, surely—all thy triumph naught—
Thy spoils for other spoilers, and thy deeds
Naught valued, nothing doing for thy life,
But all against thee. Jesu be thy shield!"

Brief was the respite;—a short season pass'd,
The omen was complete;—the augury
Had its fulfilment! He who, at that hour,
Beheld himself—by all the world beheld—
Successful—born for conquest and renown,—
Died on the block; the moral rounded well
To closing of a mighty history,
Such as too commonly sculptures mortal glory,
Where Shame sits watchful how to mock the triumph,
And Hate despoils the conqueror! In the grasp,
The full possession of his matchless heights,
The power pass'd from him to his enemy's hands;
And he who built the altar, was the first
To shed his blood on it in sacrifice,
Yet hopeless of atonement. The base spirit
Triumph'd above the noble; as the viper
Crawls to the bosom of the sleeping lion,
And stings him where he lies. Thus overcome,
Among his foes at Acla, Balboa died,
A hero's glory and a felon's doom
Closing a perilous life of many toils

And true adventure. The magician's speech
Was sooth—and he, whom worlds could not contain,
So vast his spirit—whose far-darting soul
Saw, from its skyey pinnacle, the new
And boundless shores he conquer'd—he, the brave—
The noblest in renown, where all were brave—
Perish'd, unheard, unheeded—not an eye
To weep his fortunes; not a single arm
To do his nature justice, and redress
The wrongs of men and nations. Thus he died—
The world he conquer'd yielding him—a grave.

THE SIOUX BOY;

AN INDIAN LEGEND.

Deep hidden in the forest wild,
  Where yet the savage wander'd free,
A manly Sioux Boy beguiled
  The hours beneath a tree;
And gayly, in his native tongue,
Mix'd lay of love and war he sung.

Yet, to himself, for none were near,
  Nor chief, nor maid, to list the strain,
And, save mine own, no other ear
  Might know his pride or pain.
Yet, subject to his secret thought,
This ditty for himself he wrought.

"O! soon upon the Pawnee's trail,
  Sweet Manné, will thy Ontwa go;
And I shall hear his woman wail,
  And meetly use the bended bow,
And hurl the spear, and bare the knife,
And win, or lose, the forfeit life.

"I glad me that the time is come
  To win among the tribe a name,
And, in thy tent, no longer dumb,
  To tell thee of my flame;
How much I'll love,—how bravely do,
To teach thee how to love me too.

"I'll make thy home of sheltering reeds,
And store it with each forest prize;
For thee, the red deer bounds and bleeds;
For thee, the spotted panther dies;
Soft furs shall frame thy couch by night,
And gentlest steeds shall bear thy flight.

"Oh, 'mongst our people thou shalt be
Made glorious by thy Ontwa's love;
I'll triumph in the fight for thee,
And win the spoils of field and grove;
And when they see how brave my hand,
They'll make me leader of the band.

"There shall be songs in other days,
Of what thy Ontwa's strength hath done,
And chiefs to come shall speak with praise,
Of scalp-locks from the Pawnee won;
And they shall tell of thee, as blest,
The young fawn at the warrior's breast.

"'Neath summer sky, o'er sunny plain,
Together, fearless, shall we speed:
I'll house thee from the winter rain,
In spring to pleasant pastures lead;
And thou shalt see me, with the bow,
Pursue, and slay the buffalo,

"And bring thee from the morning chase,
Unhurt, the meek and spotty fawn;
And proudly at thy feet I'll place,
The skin from panther drawn;
Torn from him with a warrior's art,
While yet the life is at his heart.

"And thou shalt shape the moccasin,
  And well repay thy warrior's deeds,
When thou shalt work the red deer's skin,
  Gay with thy many color'd beads,
Meet for a chief, when at our home
An hundred braves his guests become."

Thus mused the boy beneath his tree,
  Of love's delights, and warrior's pride,
A long and gladsome reverie,
  Where he the chief, and she the bride,
Swept through the sylvan future still,
A realm of love, and free from ill.

With very joy at last he slept,—
  He dream'd of bliss, and had no fear
That nigh the hateful Pawnee crept,
  Like serpent, close beside his ear;
He wakens only into life
To feel within his heart the knife!

One moment's consciousness he knew,
  Before the fatal blow was sped;
The red blade flashes on his view,
  He feels it circling round his head;
And dies;—his fancy not more sooth
Than that which cheats the white man's youth.

THE SYREN OF TSELICA;

A TRADITION OF THE FRENCH BROAD.

THE tradition of the Cherokees asserts the existence of a Syren, in the French Broad, who implores the Hunter to the stream, and strangles him in her embrace, or so infects him with some mortal disease, that he invariably perishes. The story, stripped of all poetry, would seem to be that of a youth, who, overcome with fatigue and heat together, sought the cool waters of the river, and was seized with cramp or spasms; or, too much exhausted for re-action, sunk under the shock. It does not much concern us, however, what degree of faith is due to the tradition. Enough that such exists, and that its locality is one of the most magnificent regions, for its scenery, in the known world. Tselica is the Indian name of the river.

'TWAS in summer prime, the noontide hour,
Sleep lay heavy o'er the sunny vale;
Droop'd the sad leaves 'neath the fiery vapor,
Droop'd and panted for the evening gale.

Gloomy, lonely, and with travail weary,
Down the mountain slopes the stranger came;
Droop'd his eyes, and in his fainting bosom
Lay the pulsing blood, a lake of flame.

Oh, how cool in sight the rushing river,
With its thousand barrier-rocks at strife,
All its billows tossing high their foam wreaths,
As if maddening with the impatient life.

Wild, with ceaseless shout they hurried onward,
Laughing ever with their cheerful glee,
O'er the antique rocks their great limbs flinging,
With a frantic joy was strange to see.

They, of all, possess'd the life and action,
  Silence else had sovereign sway alone,
All the woods were hush'd, and the gray mountain
  Look'd with stony eyes from crumbling throne.

Sad the youth sank down in the great shadows,
  Close beside the waters as they ran,
Very hopeless was he of his travail,
  Very weary since it first began.

Friends and fortune he had none to cheer him,
  And the growing sorrow at his heart
Wrought the bitter thought to bitter feeling,
  And he yearn'd to perish and depart.

"Why," he murmurs, "still in toil unresting,
  Should I strive for aye in fruitless strife;
Where the hopes and loves that used to glad me,
  When I first began the race of life?

"Where's the pride of triumph that was promised,
  That should crown me with the immortal wreath;
Where the fond heart that in youth embraced me—
  Gone, forever gone—and where is Death?

"Give me peace, ye skies and rocks: ye waters,
  Peace yourselves ye know not, but your flow
Tells of calm and rest beneath your billows—
  Coolness, for the fiery griefs I know."

Thus, with languid soul beside the river,
  Gazed he sadly as that hour he lay;
Gloomy with the past, and of the future
  Hopeless,—hence his guilty prayer that day.

Brooding thus, and weary, a song rises,
  From the very billows, soft and clear;
Such as evening bird, with parting ditty,
  Pours at twilight to the floweret's ear.

Wild and sweet, and passionate and tender;
  Now full, now faint; with such a touching art,
His soul dissolves in weakness, and his spirit
  Goes with the throbbing sweetness at his heart.

He looks with strain'd eyes at the lapsing waters,
  And gleaming bright beneath the billows, lo!
Flashes white arms, and glides a lovely damsel,
  Bright eyes, dark locks, and bosom white as snow.

He sees, but still in moment glimpses only,
  Gleams of strange beauty, from an eye all bright,—
As when some single star, at midnight, flashes
  From the cold cloud, above the mountain's height.

As raven black as night float free her tresses,
  Outflung above the waves by snowy arms,
Now o'er her bosom spread, and half betraying,
  While half concealing still her sunny charms.

And then again ascends her song of pleading—
  "Ah, but thou failest with the noonday heat,
Thy brow is pale with care, thine eyelids drooping,
  Thy soul is sad, and weary-worn thy feet.

"Oh! come to me, and taste my waves of cooling;
  I'll soothe thy sorrows; I will bring thee rest;
Thy fainting limbs grow strong in my embraces,
  Thy burning cheek find pillow on my breast.

"Oh! come to me!" was still the loving burden,
  With charm of such a sweetness in its swell,
That every fancy in his bosom kindled,
  And every feeling woke to work the spell.

Wild was the dreamy passion that possess'd him;
  Won by the syren song, and glimpsing charms,
He leapt to join her in the wave, but shudder'd
  At the first foldings of her death-cold arms.

Fiercely against her own she press'd his bosom;-
  'Tis the ice-mountain whose embrace he feels;
Within his eyes she shot her dazzling glances:
  'Tis Death's own stony stare the look reveals.

He breaks away, the shore in horror seeking;
  But all too late,—the doom is in his heart:
He sinks beside the fatal stream, and dying,
  Deplores the prayer that pleaded to depart.

His dying sense still hears the fatal Syren;
  She sings her triumph now, her love no more:
A fearful hate was in the eldritch music,
  And terror now, where beauty sway'd before.

No more the pleasing wile, the plaintive ditty:
  He strives in vain the wizard strain to flee;
"Death," ran the song,—no more of peace and pity,
  "To him who madly seeks embrace with me!"

THE CITY OF THE SILENT.*

WHEN, in the twilight hour and pensive mood,
Thought seeks repose, and Passion sleeps subdued,
Why doth the eye with mournful fondness rest,
On the dark shadows gathering in the west?
Why doth the soul delight to follow fast,
O'er that dim realm from which the sun hath pass'd?
No more his smiles persuade the upward eye,
No more his glories gladden in the sky;
The rainbow tints, the children of his beams,
Dear to our sight as music to our dreams,
That hung around, pavilioning his throne
With hues and gleams more lovely than his own,—
That closed his eyes, that caught their dying sign,
And soothed, with office sweet, his sad decline,—
Themselves, in shadowy folds of cloud and dun,
Depart, like mourners, following still the sun;
Forego the glorious empire which, awhile,
Glow'd in the sweetness of his dying smile,
And all their happy heritage of light
Yield to dusk eve and pall-enshrouding night.

* Delivered at the Dedication of the Grounds of Magnolia Cemetery, near the city of Charleston, on the 19th day of November, 1850.

Yet, still we gaze,—and, through the gloomy waste,
Pore, with fond search, for all the realm they graced;
Our living cares and purposes forgot,
Our wealth unvalued, or remember'd not,
Why do we thus, with eager vision strain,
And strive with thoughts themselves that strive in vain?
Why grasp at each bright mirage that no more
Can cheer the fancy which it charm'd before?

'Tis that an image from the heart is cast,
That shows how rich our empire in the past!
There, twins of rapture, Hope and Memory strive
Our skies to brighten, and our joys revive;
These, when the clouds about our vision roll,
Bestow the beauteous prospect on the soul,—
There still we grasp the beings loved and lost,
There shield our flowers, uninjured, from the frost,—
There shrine each feature in whose smile we felt
The fancies kindle, and the feelings melt,
The hope grow warm, the impulsive passion rise
That caught its sunlight from the loved-one's eyes,—
And still, in dreamy consciousness of bliss,
Feel Love's last hour of rapture sweetening this.
Thus link we still, with shadows that depart,
Dear aspects always shining in the heart,
Soothe the keen sorrow which their loss deplores,
By fondest search through memory's haunted stores,—
By dreams, that freshen to the soul, by night,
What day and care would ever take from sight.
These paint them, sweet and smiling as of yore,
And all the virtues teach they taught before;
Their forms unseen, with memory's help we trace,
Still fresh, the beauties of each well-known face,
The genial blessings which their presence brought,

And all the dear delights they yielded thought;—
Thus do they soothe the pangs their parting gave,
And, through their memories, gladden from the grave,
Even as the flowers their odors still unfold,
Where long before they perish'd, through the mould;—
Thus still they bloom around the silent hearth,
Thus make a sacred altar-place of earth,
Thus help us shrine the dear ones pass'd from day,
And catch their smiles long after their decay.

The thoughtful wanderer thus, while musing lone,
O'er realms whose ruins speak for empires gone,
With reverent search the temple still explores,
Copan re-peoples, and Palenque restores;
Bends, in mute homage, at each mouldering shrine,
And broods o'er altars once believed divine!—
No sun-shaft kindles now the sacred height,
Where spake the Prophet once in words of might;
No holy chant ascends from virgin choirs,
From golden censer, now, no cloud aspires;
The song is hush'd—the prayer is dumb,—and still
That heart whose humbler faith survived its will;
No passion strives, no virtue lifts its eye,
And all is fled that might have told us why!
Silence, alone, with finger on cold lips,
But shows the nation through its drear eclipse,—
Eclipse that smote, with power decreed to crush,
Pride's mighty heart, and all its voices hush!
Vainly the Pilgrim, from the Past implores
The curious legend of these speechless shores,
What races fill'd their cities,—what the Fate,
That found them weak, and left them desolate?—
What deeds were theirs—what mighty works they wrought?
What Faith they cherish'd?—what their toils of Thought?

From the bleak ruin comes no answering tone:
Realms of the silent! still they sleep unknown!

Yet, not the less, with reverent awe we glide
Through each dark portal, once of power and pride;
A human sense and sympathy, with spell
Of thought and worship still, the soul compel:
With what a speech these crumbling piles declare,
How stern the rule,—the realm how rich and fair!—
What various fortunes sped their march of state,—
How Wealth grew prodigal and Genius great;
What ages pass'd, of virtues crown'd with sway,
How slow their steps from conquest to decay;
How subtly stole the conqueror on their sleep—
Their dream how soothing, and their doom how deep!
Here man hath been Heaven's minister—and foe!
Hath felt, like us, the tides of joy and woe;
Hath, like our living races, known his hour
Of hope and triumph, and strode on to power;
In fond fruition of each earthly bliss,
Hath found his sole sufficient world in this;
Scorn'd the sage counsels of the reverend sire
That taught the moderate aim and meet desire,
Defied the seer who show'd the scourge and yoke,
Nor fear'd the danger, till he felt the stroke;
In pride of place hath mock'd the blessings given,
And lost Earth's gifts, despising those of Heaven!

In these memorials, silent though they stand,
We read the dangers of each living land;
They teach the moral to our shrinking hearts,
That, with our virtue's loss, our strength departs;
That the proud empire, wallowing still in crime,
Must lose, at last, the power to cope with Time;

Must drink the dregs of bitterness and blight,
And veil its glories all in gloom and night!

'Tis even for this, with reverent sense we tread
These silent dwellings of the unknown dead;
'Tis that the echo from their lonely towers,
Speaks for the fate that yet may fall on ours;
Recalls such histories as we feel our own,
And shows the skeleton behind the throne!—
Their homes are ruins, but they once were bright,
With living beauty bursting on the sight;
Here, in the dance, while music gush'd in air,
Swam the gay groups insensible to care;
These groves, now silent, heard each whispering voice,
Whose low fond accents bade some heart rejoice;
And song, that seem'd to bring the heaven it sought,
Was here to soothe the wearied brain of Thought!
The purple trophies of their golden state,
'Tis ours, in fancy, thus to re-create;
Evoke their hero-aspects, chiefs of fame,
And point old morals with each new-born name;
Their Bards arouse,—their Sages,—as they speak,
With voices wise and powerful, like the Greek,
And strain all senses, gazing into night,
Still, for the glorious phantoms gone from sight!

Yes! here they toil'd—here triumph'd—here they won
A glorious height of empire like the sun,
Here set, like him, in clouds—perchance, to rise,
With him, triumphant still, in other skies!
Even through the shroud about their empire cast,
We catch faint glimpses of their wondrous past;
The spirit of ancient days, if good or great,
Gilds even the ruins of its former state;

With pleasing sadness we explore each shrine
Our kindred races once esteem'd divine;
The horizon dark, still keeps some sacred gleams
That all our living instinct crowds with dreams,—
Dreams that to human consciousness appeal,
And teach those truths Time never can reveal!
Here, living, breathing, burning souls, in strife
That led to mightiest conquests, sprang to life,
With fierce ambition pluck'd the crown of Fame,
And left a monument, without a name!—
Their altars sacred, though obscure their faith,
Their labors living, though themselves in death,
We bend in awe beneath each mournful shade,
And yield our worship where the God hath sway'd.
We know their might, their faith, the soul, the will,
In the great shrines their Fate hath left us still.
These were their temples,—noble, vast, and high,—
They honor'd thus no lowly Deity!
For sure, the ambition which can nobly raise,
Must crave a sovereign worthy all its praise,
And each conception greatly born of Thought,
Finds still a kindred God for him who wrought.
The grand achievement thus declares a flight,
That seeks its ideal on the loftiest height,
And where, of worship, it avows the need,
Demands a God superior to its deed.
Thus the Egyptian Magian, working well
To make his temples grand and durable,
With sleepless aim and subtle hope aspires
To a far future worthy such desires,
And taught his soul, with eager sense, to lift
The wing and eye to her immortal gift!
So the Athenian, exquisite in taste,
In wisdom strong, in great conception chaste,

Still felt that earth was not alone the sphere
To his soul's want compatible and dear.
Each virtue found its God, each fancy grace,
Each Deity his fitting shrine and place:
But *one* was wanting yet, superior still
To all that soothed his sense, or sway'd his will;
His mind, unsatisfied by all below,
He raised one shrine to HIM he did not know;*
Taught by etherial Plato still to crave,
That hope, o'er all, which soars but from the grave.

The vast but ruin'd piles of these unknown,
Demand meet temples for the state and throne;
And not in vain our search—around us start
The halls of learning, and the homes of art.
This was the Senate House—the Forum there,
Where plebeian thousands came to feel and hear;
And still, on fancy's ear, the living swell
Of eloquence, omnipotent to spell,
Shakes with electric fires that thrill and dart,
With seraph-mission, through the nation's heart.
With patriot prescience it declares the fate—
That last, perchance, which left them desolate!—
Still summoning up, the State to save at last,
All that was glorious in the grateful Past!—
Their prophets well foresaw the approaching storm,
And bade their revels cease, their warriors arm;
Show'd the dark speck, no larger than a hand,
Destined to shroud in blackness all the land,
Yet show'd in vain;—Cassandra-like, decreed
To speak the truth, with none the truth to heed:
They danced, they slept—untimely slept—and woke

Acts xvii. 23: "To the unknown God."

To feel the ruin, and to wear the yoke,
To fly their homes, to crouch in them as slaves,
Or find—last hope of freemen—freemen's graves!

The truth that teaches nothing of the race,
Which, in its ruins, shows how proud its place,—
That writes no record on its mighty towers,
At least assures us of a life like ours:—
Shows us the very yearnings that we know,
Still to achieve, and leave a name below:
A fond ambition, struggling 'gainst decay,
To wrench from Time the sceptre of his sway,
Still to assert, though we no more may see,
O'er future souls, the soul's proud sovereignty,
To challenge worship, though our sun be set,
And win that homage that pursues us yet!

Thus build we shrines of marble—towers, whose height
Declare our pride of aim and people's might,
Rear temples, columns, and inscribe on each,
Names that shall yet lend eloquence to speech,
And life to language,—with a voice sublime,
Pealing, through wrecks of years, o'er tracts of Time!
All nations feel this yearning—thus they raise
The tower and tomb for future love and praise,
Heedful of memories that shall fondly keep
A filial watch o'er their ancestral sleep,
Recall each virtue precious as their own,
And make with pride the sire's great actions known.

That fond solicitude that makes them strive
Their names and triumphs thus to keep alive,
Moves still a care more sacred, at the close,
Which shrines their ashes in supreme repose.

The frail, decaying form which once enshrined
The immortal spirit, the imperial mind,
Thus, by its trust, made sacred, too, we store
As the dear casket which the jewel bore :—
Not worthless now, because no more we hear
Its voice of soul and sweetness on the ear;
Not honor'd less, because no more our sight
Glows in the beauty of its kindred light;—
But cherish'd still, and treasured to the last,
For its dear memories in the haunted past.

With eyes that weep to see, yet weep to lose,
We yield the loved one to his long repose;
With reverent hands the kindred dust we bear,
To sacred shadows of the wood repair,
Far from the crowded mart, the world whose strife
Still mocks at death, and seldom honors life,
There lay we down the form that cannot know
How fond our homage, and how great our woe.
With tender love,—with tearful eyes,—we trace
For his last dwelling some selected place,
Some shady copse, or isle—some spot of green,
By oak and elm secure with leafy screen;
Where the Magnolia towers—where tribute vines
Steal up to clamber o'er supporting pines;—
Some spot most precious to the musing hour
Of him whose relics cold we thus embower;—
Some sunny bank, whence, gazing on the west,
His living eye with all the landscape blest,
It was his wont, from friendship still to crave,
The spot he couch'd on might be made his grave;—
A spot to heart subdued, and cheer'd by faith,
To make the spirit half "in love with death,"—
Peace in the prospect, peace upon the sea,

And sunny smiles about each guardian tree,
No voice of man to vex the solitude,
But breezes softly whispering through the wood.

The filial love that honors thus the dead,
And shrines the form from which the soul hath fled,
Wide as the world, and various as the race,
Howe'er remote the time, or far the place,
Alike in all, acknowledges the same,
How dear to love the loved-one's precious frame;—
How dear to pride the ashes once so bright,
With all that hope could warm, or joy delight.—
To natural instincts true, the heart requires
Meet shrines and emblems for departed sires;
Feels well the alliance 'twixt the soul and clay,
That makes us shrink to see the last decay,—
Moves us to cherish the delusive thought,
That, with the one, the other still is fraught—
That, of the living spirit, lately ours,
With sense so keen, and will of wondrous powers,
So quick to feel and glow, so prompt to hear
Love's wooing accent, and bewitching prayer,—
All is not lost, and we shall yet behold
The form arise, the eye grow bright and bold,
The soul return and fold its wandering wing,
And the cold arms embrace us while we cling.

Even with such dream, so vague but precious still,
The ancients honor'd death with pomp and skill,
Forgot no rite to pride or worship dear,
And spread meet flowers and emblems on the bier;
Bade music sound, with dirge-becoming woe,
And lighten'd Death's sad brow with state and show;
The grave became a temple, grand in gloom,

And lamps sepulchral shone within the tomb,
Symbols of that pure element of light
That Earth may dim, but not extinguish quite!
Back, through the vista of five thousand years,
How simply sad each varied rite appears;
How strangely same, yet multiplied, the plan
Which shrined and honor'd the remains of man!
The Egyptian rear'd his pyramid, which shows
At once his monarch's pride, and people's woes;
With precious unguents pluck'd from Time his prey,
And kept the loved-one's features from decay;
Through plates of glass the unconscious visage show'd,
And framed, in mightiest cells, the last abode;
Circled the sleeper with the pomps of art,
Dear to his fame, or grateful to his heart:
Thus, o'er the gloomy walls, the painter spread
The storied progress of the conqueror-dead;
Each great achievement of his pride or might,
His towers of state, his triumphs won in fight;
How, with keen lust, he tore, with savage hand,
His bloody trophies from each neighboring land;
What myriads march'd to swell his despot train,
What nations battled, and what hosts were slain!
Lofty in chariot, arm'd with wrath, we see
His onward stride to death or victory;
Trace him, with Fire and Famine in his wake,
Through the red surges which his battles make;
Behold the tower go down, the city flame,
And join the rabble shout that calls it fame;
For one wild moment, reckless still of life,
Share in the wild delirium of the strife;
The rush of steeds, the wreck of spears, the dread
Lock of the victor-living with the dead!
So well, portraying all the powers of ill,

The servile painter shows the courtier's skill;
Enslaved by power, and scarcely true to art,
Heedless of all that's precious to the heart,
On brows of Guilt, the laurel crown bestows,
And makes us glory still in human woes;
These, following fast upon his march appear,
But neither wake the pang, nor force the tear;
Though, in procession sad, the captive crowd
Leash'd at his heels, still cry their griefs aloud,
We yield no pity, but in pride elate,
Turn, where the conqueror sits and sways in state.

With ruder pomp, in more barbaric taste,
His burial rites the Abyssinian graced;
Like the Egyptian, striving 'gainst the worm,
With costly balms preserved the mortal form;
But not with numerous swathings wrapt the dead,
His fancy counsell'd to unveil instead:
Most heedless, in his vanity, of shame,
Transparent amber clothed the naked frame;
Thus, to all eyes reveal'd, his farther rite,
Raised on high pillars, placed the corse in sight;
Thus, mocking Life with Death, and Time with Fate,
He left the loved one in his hideous state,
The sun still daily shining, but in vain,
On eyes that never smile on sun again!

In better taste, with tribute more refined,
The Etrurian chief his sepulchre design'd;
That wondrous race, of whom the little shown,
Reveals such promise in the vast unknown;
Kin to the Egyptian, father to the Greek—
If true the legend and conjecture speak—
In arts and arms that gloriously achieved,

And still survive the worship they believed;
That left to Rome their gods, without their faith,
And live in marble, though they sleep in death;
A night of twenty centuries, like a spell,
Oppressing Genius that achieved so well,
Denying History, curious still to pierce
The purple pall that hangs about her hearse,
And, hush'd on every theme that might have taught,
Still speaking vaguely, wondrously, to Thought!

How, as with pick and axe, exploring deep
In vaults that shelter well their ancient sleep,
We break through caves of marble that reveal
What pride hath wrought, and Time would still conceal—
How do we start, as on our vision rise,
Perfect as when their children closed their eyes,
Stately in helm and armor, robes and gold,
Their Lucumones as they sway'd of old!—
Princes and chiefs, whose deeds of answering fame
Thrill'd through their world, yet have for ours no name!
The weight of earth, for near three thousand years,
Press'd on the marble vault that hides their biers,
Preserving well from touch, and rude decay,
The haughty forms of manhood and of sway.

There he reclines,* as when he sought the strife,
Clad in bright armor, looking as in life,
The proud Lucumo!—They have scarcely gone,—
'Twould seem—who laid and seal'd him up in stone!
What awe pervades the soul, as thus we gaze
On this life-seeming state of ancient days!
No cunning effigy, the work of art,

* See the "Sepulchres of Etruria," by Mrs. Hamilton Gray.

Wrought in the marble, wanting sense and heart,
But the once powerful chieftain as he shone,
By nations honor'd, and to thousands known;—
Himself, at length, his limbs composed, his breast
Expanding, as with happiest slumbers bless'd.
Even as we gaze, life seems to stir beneath,
The bosom heaves as with returning breath;
We look to see him rise,—we pause to hear
His trumpet peal of battle from the bier!
But death is in the movement;—'tis the light
That heaves the frame, and stirs him to the sight;
Smote by the insidious air, the unwelcome day,
The crumbling corse sinks sudden to decay;
Time, mock'd so long, upon his subject darts,
The clay dissolves, the linkéd armor parts;—
The sceptre-grasping hand, the helméd brow,
And the mail'd breast that perfect seem'd but now,
Subside to dust, and mock the fond surprise,
That hail'd the vision late with awe-struck eyes.

We glide below: with curious search we gaze
On these proud mansions of ancestral days;
Here wealth and care have vainly striven to prove
How proud their homage, and how fond their love;
What toils they used, what precious unguents brought,
With what sad skill the funeral garments wrought;
What sacrifice of gold and pomp was made,
For the great chief whose relics here they laid!
Art spared no service! On the walls behold,
How fresh the colors twenty centuries old;
How rich the painting—with what free design,
Warm in each tint, and bold in every line;
A wondrous story, which reveals a faith
That sees the soul escaped, surviving death;

Shows the group'd forms, in long procession led,
Surrounding fond, or following slow, the dead.—
There, stately still, the enfranchised ghost survey,
Led, by the rival Genii, into day—
The day that lets in judgment on the past,
Bright with great joys, or dread with clouds o'ercast.
There the good Angel, seeking still to save,
Receives and guides the freed one from the grave;
Beckons with smiling hope that soothes the fear,
And shows his "Esar"* merciful and near.
Not so the Evil Genii, who withstand
The gentle guidance of his guardian hand;
They bar the way to mercy, and, with thirst
Of eager malice, hoping still the worst,
Declare, of evil deeds, the dark account,
That should deny the ambitious soul to mount.
The painter leaves in doubt the fearful strife,
Whose issue broods with doom or glorious life,
But, of his aim and hope enough are shown,
To prove his promise not unlike our own,
Show that his faith still sought an upward goal,
And challenged wings for each immortal soul!

The Greek! The Roman! At each mighty name,
How glow the great stars on the towers of Fame!
What triumphs crown'd their arms, their arts refined,
And lifted theirs o'er all the works of mind;
To gods raised mortals—for the mortal wrought
A refuge sure in deathless realms of thought—
From thought evoked philosophy, and wove
Bright laurels for the academy and grove!
That *they* should perish, should succumb, at length,

* Esar;—the Supreme Being of the ancient Etrurians.

Spite of their ardent souls and matchless strength,
Perhaps was needful, lest, defying Fate,
They should forget how mortal was their state,—
Forget their subject destiny, and prove
Ungrateful rebels to the power of Jove!

Their arts, their subtle tastes, refined and proud,
Still mock'd the worm, and shudder'd at the shroud:
Still strove against corruption, and decreed
The fire their flesh, and not the grave, should feed.
Should earth, o'er which, in matchless might, they trod,
Lords of the world that trembled at their nod—
Should earth, the lowly, hide, as if in shame,
The imperial aspect and majestic frame?—
Should filial homage so forget the sire,
His pride, his fame, each deed and each desire,
Nor seek to cherish still, with ceaseless care,
The dust of one so precious, proud and fair?—
Preserve each vestige of the great, and shrine
In during gold the relics deem'd divine?

They dress the pyre with frankincense and spice,
Woods of rich perfume, and of rare device;
Slay the white oxen on the pile, and spread
With fat of sheep and lambs, the honor'd dead;
Gather the slaughter'd victims to the pile,
With flagons crown'd of honey and of oil;
Libations red, from golden bowls they pour,
Then from their brows the amber tresses shore;
These strew the dead. The corse upon the pyre,—
They light the scented torch, and feed the fire;
Watch through the night until it sinks from view,
Then, with ambrosial wines, the flames subdue.
This duty done, with reverent hands and care

They take the sacred ashes from the bier;
These, in a golden vase inurn'd, they hide,
By household love and worship deified;—
Nor kept in vain, since destined to receive,
In time, the ashes of the fond who grieve;
All, at the last, each honor'd one in turn,
May hope to mingle in the self-same urn,
In death unite the hearts, which, true in life,
Kept faith, unbroken still, by storm or strife!

These rites, barbarian still, with all their state,
Were but false tributes to the good and great.
Better our Christian rule, whose simple trust
Confides the dust, with tears, to kindred dust;
Holds in meet reverence still, the sacred clay,
The soul's fair mansion in its mortal day;
But builds its home from human homes apart,
Nor mocks corruption with the toys of art;
To the fresh earth, with meek and holy rite,
Conveys the shrouded clay from common light;
Midst sacred gloom of trees, midst shadows meet,
That mingle well the solemn with the sweet;
Where banks of thyme and daisy scent the ground,
While waters murmur nigh with slumberous sound;
Where the light hangs with mild autumnal ray,
And makes a sabbath of the livelong day;
As sacred here, by Etiwando's wave,*
As Mamre's plain, or old Machpelah's cave.

Even as we watch, with sad and wistful eye,
Where each gay phantom leaves the twilight sky,—
Through glooms material seeking still to trace

* Etiwando, the Indian name of Ashley River.

Each sweet expression, and beguiling grace;
From "cold obstruction" striving still to wrest
The features once so precious to the breast;
So, through the shadowy doubt of mortal gloom,
Through the grave's shroud, and through the marble tomb,
We trace the immortal spirit in its flight,
And hail its shining progress through the night;
Glow with new life, as on each rising wing,
We mark the colors of eternal spring,
And, for ourselves, find better strength to rise,
As thus we trace its passage through the skies!

Even as we muse, with homage that is prayer,
O'er each gray ruin once a temple fair,
And read the tale of empires through the shroud
That wraps the Genius once so strong and proud—
Grope through their vaults, explore with awe the rite
That makes their dead still sacred in our sight;—
The past grows subject to our present need,
And all the future blossoms as we read!—
If precious thus the nation's grave, unknown,
How, to our children, dearer still our own!
How fit the care that guards the holy place,
Crowns it with trees, and shapes its walks with grace;
Removes each noxious weed,—with tracts of green,
Soothes the sad eye, and solaces the scene;
Decrees, that hallowing peace shall still persuade
The living hearts that loved us, to its shade!

Here will they come, when wearied in the strife,
And gain, from walks of death, the strength for life;
Here fondly read each record that declares
To what bright virtues they become the heirs;
What patriot sires have done, to crown with fame,

The son's, the citizen's, the nation's name;
How Moultrie fought,—the scene beneath our glance,—*
In our first struggle for deliverance;—
Trace, with sweet tears of homage, mix'd with pain,
The mournful legend of the martyr'd Hayne;†
Turn, still obedient to the patriot spell,
To read how, rashly brave, young Laurens fell;‡
And, field and forum, equally in sight,
The shrine of Rutledge hail on loftiest height!
How, from the sea, returning to our shores,
Each kindred eye this sacred realm explores;
Reads at a glance, and reading still, reveres
Our State's proud record of two hundred years;
Sees, in each tomb, a tale of generous strife,
That crown'd our name with pride, our land with life;
And, from each shaft that rises o'er the steep,
Tells where the hero and the statesman sleep;
Cries, breathless, to his comrades, as he sees
There rest the Pinckneys, Gadsdens, Rutledges;§
Yon column honors Marion,§—and the spire,
White-shafted, 'neath the sun that glows like fire,
Our city rear'd in sadness, but in pride,
To one who, battling, in his harness died,
Late for *his* glory,—for *our* peace too soon,
The wondrous man of statesmen, our Calhoun!

Yet, not to these alone, the gifted, great,
Our sacred shrines and shades we consecrate;

* At Magnolia Cemetery, you look out and see Fort Moultrie, whence the British were beaten in the Revolution.

† Executed by the British in the war of the Revolution.

‡ John Laurens, the Bayard of the Revolution.

§ Well-known patriots of the Revolution.

Their tombs, the landmarks to the patriot eye,
With great historic names that cannot die,
Command the homage justly due to fame:—
But other loved and lost ones have their claim.
Not to our wonder, but our love, they plead,
With quiet virtues and unwritten deed;
This realm a city, where the humblest stand,
In place with those, the loftiest of the land;
Not great, but good; not raised to glory's height,
But dear to love, and precious in its sight;
By memory cherish'd when their toils are done,—
In hearts still warm, though hidden from the sun;
Bewept with tears, that soften as they fall,
And sought with prayers, though still beyond recall.
Their lowlier tombs in sacred groves shall rise,
Where Grief, unwatch'd, may watch with shrouded eyes!
Hither shall Love repair, in future hours
To dress and deck the cherish'd turf with flowers;
Here linger fond, while slowly sinks the day,
And fancy still a voice that pleads to stay.
Hither shall Reverence come,—the son, the friend,—
Mute with dear memories, and devoutly bend;
Here Contemplation veil her lofty brow,
Passion deplore, and meek Repentance bow;
Hope, from old ashes, light her torch anew,
And Duty learn what pathways to pursue.
The Sire, decreed to see his first-born fail,
Stricken, like the flower in wild autumnal gale,
Here, by the fractured column which he rears,
Find still a soothing virtue in his tears.
Hither, the Mother, widow'd in the hour
When Love was joyous most in bloom and flower,
Her orphan brood shall bring; and, by the sod
Where sleeps the Sire, describe the ways of God;

Train their young hearts to tenderness, and chide,
By sense of mortal loss, their mortal pride.

All, from the shrines of grief shall strengthen faith,
All gather lessons from the lips of death;
In fields of silence, find best gifts of speech;
Through worlds of darkness, worlds of brightness reach;
Grow strong with wrestling at the tomb with Thought,
And there win triumphs never won unsought!
Arm'd with the Cross, and glad beneath its weight,
There matchless Love shall conquer matchless Hate;
From sin the victim pluck, from wrath the doom,
From death the living—glory from the gloom!—
Grave, where thy victory now?—O Death, thy sting?—
Lo! the freed spirit on triumphant wing!
Joyous in conquest, hark! the white-robed train,
The Prince of Peace that welcome to his reign:
His trump of victory sounds—his legions rise,
Myriads of might, in congregated skies;
By Mercy led, they gather fast to save,
Time has no sway, no prison now the grave;
Glad eyes unclose, the bonds of Death are riven,
And white-wing'd Faith, with Love, ascends to Heaven!

THE END.

POEMS

DESCRIPTIVE, DRAMATIC, LEGENDARY

AND

CONTEMPLATIVE

BY

WILLIAM GILMORE SIMMS, ESQ.

IN TWO VOLUMES

VOL. II.

I. SOUTHERN PASSAGES AND PICTURES
II. HISTORICAL AND DRAMATIC SKETCHES
III. SCRIPTURE LEGENDS
IV. FRANCESCA DA RIMINI

REDFIELD
110 & 112 NASSAU-STREET, NEW YORK
1853

SOUTHERN PASSAGES AND PICTURES.

FLIGHT TO NATURE.

Sick of the crowd, the toil, the strife,
Sweet Nature, how I turn to thee,
Seeking for renovated life,
By brawling brook and shady tree!

I knew thy rocks had spells of old,
To soothe the wanderer's woe to calm,
And in thy waters, clear and cold,
My fev'rish brow would seek for balm.

I've bent beneath thy ancient oak,
And sought for slumber in its shade,
And, as the clouds above me broke,
I dream'd to find the boon I pray'd;

For light—a blessed light—was given,
Wide streaming round me from above,
And in the deep, deep vaults of heaven,
There shone, methought, a look of love.

And, through the long, long summer hours,
When every bird had won its wing,
How sweet to think, amidst thy flowers,
That youth might yet renew its spring;—

That sacred season of the heart,
  When every pulse with hope is strong,
And, still untaught by selfish art,
  Truth fears no guile, and love no wrong.

And who, but nature's self, could yield
  The blessing in the prayer I made,
Throned in her realm of wood and field,
  Of rocky realm and haunted shade?

Who, but that magic queen, whose sway
  Drives winter from his path of strife,
Whilst all her thousand fingers play,
  With bud and bird, in games of life!

With these a kindred life I ask,—
  Not wealth that mortals vainly seek;
But, in heaven's sunshine let me bask,
  My heart as glowing as my cheek;—

An idle heart, that would not heed
  That chiding voice, when duty comes,
To drag the soul, but freshly freed,
  Back to cold toils and weary glooms.

No lure she finds in mortal schemes,
  Which wiser fancies still reprove,—
Far happier in her woodland dreams,
  With one sweet teacher, taught by love!

Thou, Nature, that magician be,
  Restore each dream that taught the boy,
That warm'd his hope, that made him free,
  While wisdom took the shape of joy;

And I will bless thee with a song,
  As fond as hers, that idle bird,
That sings above me all day long,
  As if she knew I watch'd and heard.

THE BROOKLET.

A LITTLE farther on there is a brook,
Where the breeze loiters ever. The great oaks
Have roof'd it with their arms and affluent leaves,
So that the sunbeam rifles not its fount,
While the shade cools it. You may hear it now,
A low faint murmur, as through pebbly paths,
In soft and sinuous progress it flows on,
In streams that make division as they go,
Still parting, still uniting, in one song,
The sweetest mortals know, of constancy.

Thither, ah, thither, if thy heart be sad!—
That song will bring thee solace. Or, if hope
That may not yet find name for what it seeks,
Inspires thee with a dream whose essence brings
Fruition in its keeping,—still, the strain
That's murmur'd by yon brooklet, is the best,—
Having a voice for fancy at its birth,
That keeps it wakeful on its own sweet wings.
And thou wilt gather, for whatever mood
That makes thee fond or thoughtful, a sweet tone
Beguiling thy best sympathies, and still
Leaving in thy keeping, as thou seek'st thy home,
A kindlier sense of what is in thy path.

Beside these banks, through the whole livelong day,
Ere yet I noted much the flight of time,
And knew him but in ballad books and songs,
Nor cared to know him better,—I have lain,
Nursing delicious reveries that made
All being but a circle of bright flowers,
With love the centre, sov'ran of that realm,
And I a happy inmate, with the rest.
There, with sweet thoughts, all liquid like the stream
That still inspired their progress, clear and bright,
I lay as one who slept, through happy hours,
Unvex'd by din of duty, unrebuked
By chiding counsellor to youthful cares,
That ever seeks to plant on boyish brow
The winter that has silver'd all its own.
And thus, in long delight, with the rapt soul
Shaping its own elysium of the peace
That harbor'd in the solitude, the eye
Grew momently familiar with sweet forms,
That offer'd to the genius of the place,
Making all consecrate to gentleness.
How came the thrush to whistle as he drank,
Heeding not me, and darting through the copse,
Only to bring his loved one on his wing,
To gather like refreshment? Squirrels dropt
Their nuts adown the bankside where I lay,
And, leaping to recover them, ere yet
They rolled into the brooklet and away,
Swept over me, and with fantastic play
Drew up the feathery brush above their heads,—
And their gray orbs, with bright intelligence,
Cast round them, while from hand to hand they frisk'd
The prize, which none might covet but to feed
Such nimble harlequins. The dove at noon

Couch'd in thick bristly covering of the pine,
Sought here its sweet siesta, wooing sleep,
By plaintive iteration of sad notes,
That might be still a sensible happiness:—
And sometimes, meek intruder on my realm,
Through yonder thick emerging, half in light
And half in shadow, stole the timid fawn,
That came down to the basin's edge to drink,
Now lapping, and now turning to the bank,
Cropping the young blade of the coming spring
And heedless, as I lay along unstirr'd,
Of any stranger—sauntering through the shade,
Even where I crouch'd,—having a quiet mood,
And not disturbing, while beholding mine.

Thou smil'st; and on thy lip the speaking thought
Looks still like censure—deems my hours misspent,
And saddens into warning. A shrewd thought,
I will not combat with an argument,
But leave the worldly policy to boast,
That such an errantry as this life of mine,
Hath found its fit sarcasm, well rebuked.
And yet there is a something in the life
Thou mock'st, as idle still and profligate,
Something to life compensative, and dear
To feelings that are fashion'd not by man.
Ah! the delicious sadness of the hours,
Spent by this brooklet—ah! the dreams they brought,
Of other hopes and beings—the sweet truths,
That still subdued the heart to patientness,
And made all flexible in the youthful will,
That else had been most passionate and rash.
I know the toils that gather on my path,
And I will grapple them with a strength that shows

A love for the encounter, not the less
For hours thus wasted in the solitude,
And fancies born of dreams—and 'twill not more
Impair the resolute courage of my heart,
Wrestling with toil, in conflicts of the race,
If still, in pauses of the fight, I dream
Of this dear idlesse,—gazing on that brook
So sweet in shade, thus singing on its way,
Like some dear child, all thoughtless, as it goes
From shadow into sunlight and is lost.

SABBATH IN THE FOREST.

1. FREEDOM OF THE SABBATH.

LET us escape! This is our holiday—
  God's day, devote to rest; and, through the wood
  We'll wander, and, perchance, find heavenly food:
So, profitless, it shall not pass away.
'Tis life, but with sweet difference, methinks,
  Here, in the forest;—from the crowd set free,
The spirit, like escaping song-bird, drinks
  Fresh sense of music from its liberty.
Thoughts crowd about us with the trees—the shade
  Holds teachers that await us: in our ear,
  Unwonted, but sweet voices do we hear,
That with rare excellence of tongue persuade:
They do not chide our idlesse,—were content,
If all our walks were half so innocent.

FLOWERS AND TREES.

MARCH is profuse in violets—at our feet
They cluster,—not in pride, but modesty;
The damsel pauses as she passes by,
Plucks them with smiles, and calls them very sweet.
But such beguile me not! The trees are mine,
These hoary-headed masters;—and I glide,
Humbled, beneath their unpresuming pride,
And wist not much what blossoms bud or shine.
I better love to see yon grandsire oak,
Old Druid-patriarch, lone among his race,—
With blessing, out-stretch'd arms, as giving grace
When solemn rites are said, or bread is broke:
Decay is at his roots,—the storm has been
Among his limbs,—but the old top is green.

3. THE SAME SUBJECT.

THE pine with its green honors; cypress gray,
Bedded in waters; crimsoning with bloom
The maple, that, irreverently gay,
Too soon, methinks, throws off his winter gloom;
The red bud, lavish in its every spray,
Glowing with promise of the exulting spring;
And over all, the laurel, like some king,
Conscious of strength and stature, born for sway.
I care not for their species—never look
For class or order in pedantic book,—
Enough that I behold them—that they lead
To meek retreats of solitude and thought,
Declare me from the world's day-labors freed,
And bring me tidings books have never brought.

4. RELIGIOUS MUSINGS.

THE mighty and the massy of the wood
  Compel my worship: satisfied I lie,
  With naught in sight but forest, earth, and sky,
And give sweet sustenance to precious mood!—
'Tis thus from visible but inanimate things,
  We gather mortal reverence. They declare
  In silence, a persuasion we must share,
Of hidden sources, spiritual springs,
Fountains of deep intelligence, and powers,
  That man himself implores not; and I grow
  From wonder into worship, as the show,
Majestic, but unvoiced, through noteless hours,
Imposes on my soul, with musings high,
That, like Jacob's Ladder, lifts them to the sky!

5. SOLACE OF THE WOODS.

WOODS, waters, have a charm to soothe the ear,
  When common sounds have vex'd it. When the day
  Grows sultry, and the crowd is in thy way,
And working in thy soul much coil and care—
Betake thee to the forests. In the shade
  Of pines, and by the side of purling streams
  That prattle all their secrets in their dreams,
Unconscious of a listener—unafraid—
Thy soul shall feel their freshening, and the truth
  Of nature then, reviving in thy heart,
Shall bring thee the best feelings of thy youth,
  When in all natural joys thy joy had part,
Ere lucre and the narrowing toils of trade
Had turn'd thee to the thing thou wast not made.

6. POETRY OF THE FOREST.

These haunts are sacred,—for the vulgar mood
Loves not seclusion. Here the very day
Seems in a Sabbath dreaminess to brood:
The groves breathe slumber—the great tree-tops sway
Drowsily, with the idle-going wind;
And sweetest images before my mind
Persuade me into pleasure with their play.
Here, fancies of the present and the past
Delight to mingle, 'till the palpable seems
Inseparate from the glory in my dreams,
And golden with the halo round it cast;
Thus do I live with Rosalind, thus stray
With Jacques; and churning o'er some native rhyme,
Persuade myself it smacks of the old time.

THE LOST PLEIAD.

I.

Not in the sky,
Where it was seen
So long in eminence of light serene,—
Nor on the white tops of the glistering wave,
Nor down, in mansions of the hidden deep,
Though beautiful in green
And crystal, its great caves of mystery,—
Shall the bright watcher have
Her place, and, as of old, high station keep!

II.

Gone! gone!
Oh! never more, to cheer
The mariner, who holds his course alone
On the Atlantic, through the weary night,
When the stars turn to watchers, and do sleep,
Shall it again appear,
With the sweet-loving certainty of light,
Down shining on the shut eyes of the deep!

III.

The upward-looking shepherd on the hills
Of Chaldea, night-returning, with his flocks,
He wonders why his beauty doth not blaze,
Gladding his gaze,—
And, from his dreary watch along the rocks,
Guiding him homeward o'er the perilous ways!
How stands he waiting still, in a sad maze,
Much wondering, while the drowsy silence fills
The sorrowful vault!—how lingers, in the hope that night
May yet renew the expected and sweet light,
So natural to his sight!

IV.

And lone,
Where, at the first, in smiling love she shone,
Brood the once happy circle of bright stars:
How should they dream, until her fate was known,
That they were ever confiscate to death?
That dark oblivion the pure beauty mars,
And, like the earth, its common bloom and breath,
That they should fall from high;
Their lights grow blasted by a touch, and die,—
All their concerted springs of harmony
Snapt rudely, and the generous music gone!

V.

Ah! still the strain
Of wailing sweetness fills the saddening sky;
The sister stars, lamenting in their pain
That one of the selectest ones must die,—
Must vanish, when most lovely, from the rest!
Alas! 'tis ever thus the destiny.
Even Rapture's song hath evermore a tone
Of wailing, as for bliss too quickly gone.
The hope most precious is the soonest lost,
The flower most sweet is first to feel the frost.
Are not all short-lived things the loveliest?
And, like the pale star, shooting down the sky,
Look they not ever brightest, as they fly
From the lone sphere they blest!

FIRST DAY OF SPRING.

Oh! thou bright and beautiful day,
  First bright day of the virgin spring,
Bringing the slumbering life into play,
  Giving the leaping bird his wing.

Thou art round me now in all thy hues,
  Thy robe of green, and thy scented sweets,
In thy bursting buds, in thy blessing dews,
  In every form that my footstep meets.

I hear thy voice in the lark's clear note,
  In the cricket's chirp at the evening hour;
In the zephyr's sighs that around me float,
  In the breathing bud and the opening flower.

I see thy forms o'er the parting earth,
  In the tender shoots of the grassy blade,
In the thousand plants that spring to birth,
  On the valley's side in the home of shade.

I feel thy promise in all my veins,
  They bound with a feeling long suppress'd,
And, like a captive who breaks his chains,
  Leap the glad hopes in my heaving breast.

There are life and joy in thy coming, Spring,
  Thou hast no tidings of gloom and death,
But buds thou shakest from every wing,
  And sweets thou breathest with every breath.

BALLAD.

By the brooklet, grove and meadow,
  Where together once we stray'd,
Do I wander, fond as ever,
  Haunting still each secret shade;
And, that thus content I wander,
  Where such precious joys were mine,
Do I know that thou art with me,
  And my spirit walks with thine.

In the murmur of the brooklet,
  Still thy well-known voice I hear,
And the whisper in the tree-top,
  Tells me that thy form is near;

Thou hast left me, at departing,
All that earth could never take,
And, still comforted, I wander
Through these shadows for thy sake.

Were I guilty of a passion
Which thy beauty could survive,
Still I feel thy gentle presence
Must the earthly fancy shrive;
And, discoursing with thy spirit,
Oh! I feel that earth has naught
To compensate the forgetting
Of the sweetness thou hast taught.

SONNET.—BY THE SWANANNOA.

Is it not lovely, while the day flows on
Like some unnoticed water through the vale,
Sun-sprinkled,—and, across the fields, a gale,
Ausonian, murmurs out an idle tale,
Of groves deserted late, but lately won?
How calm the silent mountains, that, around,
Bend their blue summits, as if group'd to hear
Some high ambassador from foreign ground,—
To hearken, and, most probably, confound!
While, leaping onward, with a voice of cheer,
Glad as some schoolboy ever on the bound,
The lively Swanannoa sparkles near;—
A flash and murmur mark him as he roves,
Now foaming white o'er rocks, now glimpsing soft through groves.

TO TIME.

Gray monarch of the waste of years,
Mine eyes have told thy steps in tears,
Yet yield I not to feeble fears,
  In watching now thy flight:
The pangs that follow'd still thy blow
Have lost their edge with frequent woe,
And stronger must the courage grow
  That's fed by constant fight.
The neck long used to weighty yoke,
The tree once shiver'd by the stroke,
The heart by frequent torture broke—
  These fear no later blight.

Oh! mine hath been a mournful song,—
My neck hath felt the burden long,—
My tree was shiver'd,—weak and strong,
  Beneath the bolt went down!—
The Fate that thus took early sway,
Hath spared of mine but little prey,
For old and young were torn away,
  Ere manhood's wing had flown;—
I saw the noble sire, who stood
Majestic, as in crowded wood,
The pine—and after him, the brood,
  All perish in thy frown.

So, count my hopes—so, tell my fears,
And ask what now this life endears,
To him who gave, with many tears,
  Each blossom of his love;

Whose store in heaven, so precious grown,
He counts each earthly moment flown,
As loss of something from his own,
In treasures shrined above.
Denied to seek—to see—his store,
Yet daily adding more and more,
Some precious plant, that, left before,
The spoiler rends at last.
Not hard the task to number now
The few that live to feel the blow;
The perish'd,—count them on my brow,
With white hairs overcast.

White hairs—while yet each limb is strong
To help the right and crush the wrong—
Ere youth, in manhood's struggling throng,
Had well begun his way:—
Thought premature, that still denied
The boy's exulting sports—the pride,
That, with the blood's unconscious tide,
Knows but to shout and play;
Youth, that in love's first gush was taught
To see his best affection brought
To tears, and woe, and death,—
While yet the fire was in his eye,
That told of passion's victory,
And, in his ear, the first sweet sigh,
From beauty's laboring breath.

And manhood now,—and loneliness,—
With, oh! how few to love and bless,
Save those who, in their dear duresse,
Look down from heaven's high towers;
The stately sire, the gentle dame,

The maid who first awoke the flame,
That gave to both a mutual claim,
   Soon forfeited, as ours—
And all those dearest buds of bloom,
That simply sought on earth a tomb,
From birth to death, with rapid doom,
   A bird-flight wing'd for fate:
How thick the shafts!—how sure the aim!—
What other passion wouldst thou tame,
Oh! Time, within this heart of flame,
   Elastic, not elate?

Is't pride?—methinks 'tis joy to bend;—
My foe—he can no more offend;—
My friend is false;—I love my friend;—
   I love my foeman too!—
'Tis man I love;—nor him alone,
The brute, the bird,—its joy or moan,
Not heedless, to my heart hath gone—
   I feel with all I view.
Wouldst have me worthy?—make me so,
By frequent bruise and overthrow;—
But spare on other hearts the blow,
Spare, from the cruel pang, the woe,
   My innocent—my bright!
On me thy vengeance! 'Tis *my* crime
That needs the scourge, and, in my prime,
'Twere fruitful of improving time,
   Thy hands should not be light.

I bend me willing to the thrall,
Whate'er the doom will bear it all,—
Drink of the bitter cup of gall,
   Nor once complain of thee;

Will poverty avail to chide,
Or sickness bend the soul of pride,
Or social scorn, still evil-eyed?—
  Have, then, thy will of me!
But spare the woman and the child!—
Let me not see their features mild
Distorted,—hear their accents wild,
  In agonizing pain—
Too much of this!—I thought me sure,
In frequent pang and loss before;—
I still have something to endure,—
  And tremble, and—refrain!

On every shore they watch thy wing,—
To some the winter, some the spring,
Thou bring'st, or yet art doom'd to bring,
  In rapid-rolling years:
How many seek thee, smiling now,
Who soon shall look with clouded brow,
Heart fill'd with bitter doubt and woe,
  And eyes with gathering tears!
But late, they fancied,—life's parade
Still moving on,—that, not a shade
Thou flung'st on bower and sunny glade,
  In which they took delight:—
Sharp satirist—methinks I see
Thy glance in sternest mockery;—
They little think, not seeing thee,
  How fatal is thy flight;—
What feathers grow beneath thy wing,
What darts—how poison'd—from what spring
Of sorrow, and how keen the sting,—
  How cureless still the blight.

Enough !—the cry has had its way,
As thou hast had !—'tis not the lay
Of vain complaint,—no idle play
  Of fancy-dreaming care :
A mocking bitter like thine own,
Wells up from fountains, deep and lone,
Where sorrow, by sepulchral stone,
  Sits watching thy career.
Thou'st mock'd my hope and dash'd my joy,
With keen rebuke and sad alloy—
The father, son—the man, the boy,
  All, all ! have felt the rod :—
Perchance, not all thy work in vain,
In softening soul, subduing brain,
If, suffering, I submit to pain,—
  That minister of God.

THE TRAVELLER'S REST.

For hours we wander'd o'er the beaten track,
A dreary stretch of sand, that, in the blaze
Of noonday, seem'd to launch sharp arrows back,
As fiery as the sun's. Our weary steeds
Falter'd, with drooping heads, along the plain,
Looking from side to side most wistfully,
For shade and water. We could feel for them,
Having like thirst ; and, in a desperate mood,
Gloomy with toil, and parching with the heat,
I had thrown down my burden by the way,
And slept, as man may never sleep but once,

Yielding without a sigh,—so utterly
Had the strong will, beneath the oppressive care,
Fail'd of the needed energy for life,—
When, with a smile, the traveller by my side,
A veteran of the forest and true friend,
Whose memory I recall with many a tear,
Laid his rough hand most gently on mine own,
And said, in accents still encouraging:—

"Faint not,—a little farther we shall rest,
And find sufficient succor from repose,
For other travel: vigor will come back,
And sweet forgetfulness of all annoy,
With a siesta in the noontide hour,
Shelter'd by ample oaks. A little while
Will bring us to the sweetest spot in the woods,
Named aptly, 'Traveller's Rest.' There, we shall drink
Of the pure fountain, and beneath the shade
Of trees, that murmur lessons of content
To streams impatient as they glide from sight,
Forget the long day's weariness, o'er steppes
Of burning sand, with thirst that looks in vain
For the cool brooklet. All these paths I know
From frequent travail, when my pulse, like yours,
Beat with an ardor soon discomfited,
Unseason'd by endurance. Through a course
Of toil, I now can think upon with smiles,
Which brought but terror when I felt it first,
I grew profound in knowledge of the route,
Marking each wayside rock, each hill of clay,
Blazed shaft, or blighted thick, and forked tree,
With confidence familiar as you found
In bookish lore and company. Cheer up,

Our pathway soon grows pleasant. We shall reach—
Note well how truly were my lessons conn'd,—
A little swell of earth, which, on these plains,
Looks proudly like a hill. This having pass'd,
The land sinks suddenly—the groves grow thick,
And, in the embrace of May, the giant wood
Puts on new glories. Shade from these will soothe
Thy overwearied spirit, and anon,
The broad blaze on the trunk of a dark pine
That strides out on the highway to our right,
Will guide us where, in woodland hollow, keeps
One lonely fountain; such as those of yore,
The ancient poets fabled as the home,
Each of its nymph ; a nymph of chastity,
Whose duty yet is love. A thousand times,
When I was near exhausted as yourself,
That gash upon the pine-tree strengthen'd me,
As showing where the waters might be found,
Otherwise voiceless. Thanks to the rude man—
Rude in the manners of his forest life,
But frank and generous,—whose benevolent heart—
Good kernel in rough outside,—counsels him,
As in the ages of the Patriarch,
To make provision for the stranger's need.
His axe, whose keen edge blazons on the tree
Our pathway to the waters that refresh,
Was in that office consecrate, and made
Holier than knife, in hands of bearded priest,
That smote, in elder days, the innocent lamb,
In sacrifice to Heaven !

"Now, as we glide,
The forest deepens round us. The bald tracts,
Sterile, or glittering but with profitless sands,

Depart; and through the glimmering woods behold
A darker soil, that on its bosom bears
A nobler harvest. Venerable oaks,
Whose rings are the successive records, scored
By Time, of his dim centuries; pines that lift,
And wave their coronets of green aloft,
Highest to heaven of all the aspiring wood;
And cedars, that with slower worship rise—
Less proudly, but with better grace, and stand
More surely in their meekness;—how they crowd,
As if 'twere at our coming, on the path!—
Not more majestic, not more beautiful,
The sacred shafts of Lebanon, though sung
By Princes, to the music of high harps,
Midway from heaven;—for these, as they, attest
His countenance who, to glory over all,
Adds grace in the highest, and above these groves
Hung brooding, when, beneath the creative word,
They freshen'd into green, and towering grew,
Memorials of his presence as his power!
—Alas! the forward vision! a few years
Will see these shafts o'erthrown. The profligate hands
Of avarice and of ignorance will despoil
The woods of their old glories; and the earth,
Uncherish'd, will grow barren, even as the fields,
Vast still, and beautiful once, and rich as these,
Which, in my own loved home, half desolate,
Attest the locust rule,—the waste, the shame,
The barbarous cultivation—which still robs
The earth of its warm garment and denies
Fit succor, which might recompense the soil,
Whose inexhaustible bounty, fitly kept,
Was meant to fill the granaries of man,
Through all earth's countless ages.

"How the sward
Thickens in matted green. Each tufted cone
Gleams with its own blue jewel, dropt with white,
Whose delicate hues and tints significant,
Wake tenderness within the virgin's heart,
In love's own season. In each mystic cup
She reads sweet meaning, which commends the flower
Close to her tremulous breast. Nor seems it there
Less lovely than upon its natural couch,
Of emerald bright,—and still its hues denote
Love's generous spring-time, which, like generous youth,
Clouds never the dear aspect of its green,
With sickly doubts of what the autumn brings."

Boy as I was, and speaking still through books—
Not speaking from myself—I said: "Alas!
For this love's spring-time—quite unlike the woods,
It never knows but one; and, following close,
The long, long years of autumn, with her robes
Of yellow mourning, and her faded wreath
Of blighted flowers, that, taken from her heart,
She flings upon the grave-heap where it rots!"

"Ah! fie!" was straightway the reply of him,
The old benevolent master, who had seen,
Through thousand media yet withheld from me,
The life I had but dream'd of—"this is false!—
Love hath its thousand spring-times like the flowers,
If we are dutiful to our own hearts,
And nurse the truths of life, and not its dreams.
But not in hours like this, with such a show
Around us, of earth's treasures, to despond,
To sink in weariness and to brood on death.
Oh! be no churl, in presence of the Queen

Of this most beautiful country, to withhold
Thy joy,—when all her court caparison'd,
Comes to her coronation in such suits
Of holiday glitter. It were sure a sin
In sight of Heaven, when now the humblest shrub
By the maternal bounty is set forth,
As for a bridal, with a jewell'd pomp
Of flowers in blue enamel—lustrous hues
Brightening upon their bosoms like sweet tints,
Caught from dissolving rainbows, as the sun
Rends with his ruddy shafts their violet robes,—
When gay vines stretching o'er the streamlet's breast
Link the opposing pines and arch the space,
Between, with a bright canopy of charms,
Whose very least attraction wears a look
Of life and fragrance!—when the pathway gleams,
As spread for march of Princess of the East,
With gems of living lustre—ravishing hues
Of purple, as if blood-dipp'd in the wounds
Of Hyacinthus,—him Apollo loved,
And slew though loving:—now, when over all
The viewless nymphs that tend upon the streams,
And watch the upward growth of April flowers,
Wave ever, with a hand that knows not stint,
Yet suffers no rebuke for profligate waste,
Their aromatic censers, 'till we breathe
With difficult delight;—not now to gloom
With feeble cares and individual doubts,
Of cloud to-morrow. It were churlish here,
Ungracious in the sovereign Beauty's sight,
Who rules this realm, the dove-eyed sovran, Spring!
This hour to sympathy—to free release
From toil, and sorrow, and doubt, and all the fears
That hang about the horizon of the heart,

Making it feel its sad mortality,
Even when most sweet its joy—she hath decreed:
Let us obey her, though no citizens.

"How grateful grows the shade—mix'd shade of trees,
And clouds, that drifting o'er the sun's red path,
Curtain his awful brows! Ascend yon hill,
And we behold the valley from whose breast
Flows the sweet brooklet. Yon emblazon'd pine
Marks the abrupt transition to the shade,
Where, welling from the bankside, it steals forth,
A voice without a form. Through grassy slopes,
It wanders on unseen, and seems no more
Than their own glitter; yet, behold it now,
Where, jetting through its green spout, it bounds forth,
Capricious, as if doubtful where to flow,—
A pale white streak—a glimmering, as it were,
Cast by some trembling moonbow through the woods!

"Here let us rest. A shade like that of towers,
Wrought by the Moor in matchless arabesque,
Makes the fantastic ceiling,—leaves and stems,
Half-form'd, yet flowery tendrils, that shoot out,
Each wearing its own jewel,—that above
O'erhangs; sustain'd by giants of the wood,
Erect and high, like warriors gray with years,
Who lift their massive shields of holiest green,
On fearless arms, that still defy the sun,
And foil his arrows. At our feet they fall,
Harmless and few, and of the fresh turf make
A rich mosaic. Tremblingly, they creep,
Half-hidden only, to the blushing shoots
Of pinks, that never were abroad before,
And shrink from such warm instance. Here are flowers,

Pied, blue, and white, with creepers that uplift
Their green heads, and survey the world around—
As modest merit, still ambitionless—
Only to crouch again; yet each sustains
Some treasure, which, were earth less profligate,
Or rich, were never in such keeping left.
And here are daisies, violets that peep forth
When winds of March are blowing, and escape
Their censure in their fondness. Thousands more,—
Look where they spread around us—at our feet—
Nursed on the mossy trunks of massive trees,
Themselves that bear no flowers—and by the stream—
Too humble and too numerous to have names!

"There is no sweeter spot along the path,
In all these western forests,—sweet for shade,
Or beauty, or reflection—sights and sounds—
All that can charm the wanderer, or o'ercome
His cares of travel. Here we may repose,
Subdued by gentlest murmurs of the noon,
Nor feel its heat, nor note the flight of hours,
That never linger here. How sweetly falls
The purring prattle of the stream above,
Where, roused by petty strife with vines and flowers,
It wakes with childish anger, nor forbears
Complaint, even when, beguiled by dear embrace,
It sinks to slumber in its bed below!
The red-bird's song now greets us from yon grove,
Where, starring all around with countless flowers,
Thick as the heavenly host, the dogwood glows,
Array'd in virgin white. There, mid the frowns
Of sombrous oaks, and where the cedar's glooms
Tell of life's evening shades, unchidden shines
The maple's silver bough, that seems to flash

A sudden moonlight; while its wounded arms,
Stream with their own pure crimson, strangely bou
With yellow wreaths, flung o'er its summer hurts,
By the lascivious jessamine, that, in turn,
Capricious, creeps to the embrace of all.

"The eye unpain'd with splendor—with unrest
That mocks the free rapidity of wings,
Just taught to know their uses and go forth,
Seeking range but no employment—hath no quest
That Beauty leaves unsatisfied. The lull
Of drowsing sounds, from leaf, and stream, and tree
Persuades each sense, and to forgetfulness
Beguiles the impetuous thought. Upon the air
Sweetness hangs heavy, like the incense cloud
O'er the high altar, when cathedral rites
Are holiest, and our breathing for a while
Grows half suspended. Sullen, in the sky,
With legions thick, and banners broad unfurl'd,
The summer tempest broods. Below him wheels,
Like some fierce trooper of the charging host,
One fearless vulture. Earth beside us sleeps,
Having no terror; though an hour may bring
A thousand fiery bolts to break her rest.

"How natural is the face of woods and vales,
Trees, and the unfailing waters, spite of years,
Time's changes, and the havoc made by storm!
The change is all in man. Year after year,
I look for the old landmarks on my route,
And seldom look in vain. A darker moss
Coats the rough outside of the old gray rock;—
Some broad arm of the oak is wrench'd away,
By storm and thunder—through the hill-side wears

A deeper furrow,—and the streams descend,
Sometimes, in wilder torrents than before—
But still they serve as guides o'er ancient paths,
For wearied wanderers. Still do they arise,
In groups of grandeur, an old family,
These great magnificent trees, that, as I look,
Fill me with loftiest thoughts, such as one feels
Beholding the broad wing of some strong bird,
Poised on its centre, motionless in air,
Yet sworn its master still. Not in our life,
Whose limit, still inferior, mocks our pride,
Reach they this glorious stature. At their feet,
Our young, grown aged like ourselves, may find
Their final couches, ere one vigorous shaft
Yields to the stroke of time. Beneath mine eyes,
All that makes beautiful this place of peace,
Wears the peculiar countenance which first
Won my delight and wonder as I came—
Then scarcely free from boyhood,—wild as he,
The savage Muscoghee, who, in that day,
Was master of these plains. His hunting range
Grasp'd the great mountains of the Cherokee,
The Apalachian ridge—extended west
By Talladega's valleys—by the streams
Of Tallas-hatchie—through the silent woods
Of gray Emuckfau, and where, deep in shades,
Rise the clear brooks of Autossee that flow
To Tallapoosa;—names of infamy
In Indian chronicle! 'Twas here they fell,
The numerous youth of Muscoghee,—the strong—
Patriarchs of many a tribe—dark seers renown'd,
As deeply read in savage mystery—
The Prophet Monohöee—priest as famed,
Among his tribe, as any that divined

In Askelon or Ashdod;—stricken to the earth,
Body and spirit, in repeated strife,
With him, that iron-soul'd old chief, who came
Plunging from Tennessee.

"Below they stretch'd,
In sovran mastery o'er the wood and stream,
'Till the last waves of Choctawhatchie slept,
Subsiding, in the gulf. Such was the realm
They traversed, in that season of my youth,
When first beside this pleasant stream I sank,
In noontide slumber. What is now their realm,
And where are now their warriors? Streams that once
Soothed their exhaustion, satisfied their thirst—
Woods that gave shelter—plains o'er which they sped
In mimic battle—battle-fields whereon
Their bravest chieftains perish'd—trees that bore
The fruits they loved but rear'd not;—these remain,
But yield no answer for the numerous race,—
Gone with the summer breezes—with the leaves
Of perish'd autumn;—with the cloud that frowns
This moment in the heavens, and, ere the night,
Borne forward in the grasp of chainless winds,
Is speeding on to ocean.

"Wandering still—
That sterile and most melancholy life,—
They skirt the turbid streams of Arkansas,
And hunt the buffalo to the rocky steeps
Of Saladanha; and, on lonely nooks,
Ridge-barrens, build their little huts of clay,
As frail as their own fortunes. Dreams, perchance,
Restore the land they never more shall see;
Or, in meet recompense, bestow them tracts

More lovely—vast, unmeasured tracts, that lie
Beyond those peaks, that, in the northern heavens,
Rise blue and perilous now. There, rich reserves
Console them in the future for the past;
And, with a Christian trust, the Pagan dreams
His powerful gods will recompense his faith,
By pleasures, in degree as exquisite
As the stern suffering he hath well endured.
His forest fancy, not untaught to soar,
Already, in his vision of midnight, sees
The fertile valleys; on his sight arise
Herds of the shadowy deer; and, from the copse,
Slow stealing, he beholds, with eager gaze,
The spirit-hunter gliding toward his prey,
In whose lithe form, and practised art, he views
Himself!—a noble image of his youth
That never more shall fail!

"We may not share
His rapture; for if thus the might of change
Mocks the great nation, sweeps them from the soil
Which bore, but could not keep—what is't with us,
Who muse upon their fate? Darkly, erewhile,
Thou spok'st of death and change, and I rebuked
The mood that scorn'd the present good—still fond
To brood above the past. Yet, in my heart,
Grave feelings rise to chide the undesert,
That knew not well to use the power I held,
In craving that to come. Have these short years
Wrought thus disastrously upon *my* strength,
As on the savage? What have I done to build
My better home of refuge; where the heart,
By virtue taught, by conscience made secure,
May safely find an altar, 'neath whose base

The tempest rocks in vain? The red-man's fate
Belong'd to his performance. They who know
How to destroy alone, and not to raise,
Leaving a ruin for a monument,
Must perish as the brute. But I was taught
The nobler lesson, that, for man alone,
The maker gives the example of his power,
That he may build on him. What work of life—
The moral monument of the Christian's toil—
Stands, to maintain my memory after death,
Amongst the following footsteps? Sadly, the ear
Receives his question, who, with sadder speech,
Makes his own answer. Unperforming still,
He yet hath felt the mighty change that moves,
Progressive, as the march of mournful hours,
Still hurrying to the tomb. 'Tis on his cheek,
No more the cheek of boyhood—in his eye,
That laughs not with its wonted merriment,
And in his secret heart. 'Tis over all
He sees and feels—o'er all that he hath loved,
And fain would love, and must remember still!
Those gray usurpers, Death and Change, have been
Familiar in his household, and he stands,
Of all that grew around his innocent hearth,
Alone—the last! And this hath made him now
An exile,—better pleased with woods and streams,
Wild ocean, and the rocks that vex his waves,
Than, sitting in the city's porch, to hear
The hurry, and the thoughtless hum of trade!

"The charm is broken and the 'Traveller's Rest!'
The sun no longer beats with noonday heat
Above the pathway, and the evening bird,
Short wheeling through the air, on whirring wing,

Counsels our flight with his. Another draught—
And to these pleasant waters—to the groves
That shelter'd—to the gentle breeze that soothed,
Even as a breath from heaven—to all sweet sights,
Melodious sounds and murmurs, that arise
To cheer the sadden'd spirit at its need—
Be thanks and blessing; gratitude o'er all,
To God in the Highest! He it is who guides
The unerring footstep—prompts the wayward heart
To kindly office—shelters from the sun—
Withholds the storm,—and, with his leaves and flowers,
Sweet freshening streams and ministry of birds,
Sustains, and succors, and invigorates;—
To Him, the praise and homage—Him o'er all!"

THE MOCK-BIRD.

What has winter left for thee,
That, within the ancient tree,
Thou dost linger, in thy gray,
  Sober vestments, like some friar,
Haunting still the old abbaye,
  Wasted by the strife and fire?
Wherefore house thee thus alone,
When the other tribes have gone?—
With them to the forest speed:
  Leave to human heart the grief,
That in woe and dusky weed,
  When winter twilight's cold and brief,
Walks sad with hooded Thought, through perish'd wood and leaf.

Sure I know thee!—thou art he,
That, with reckless minstrelsy,
Lately sung—while all the grove,
By the spring-buds won to joy,
Bathed in fragrance, breathed of love—
Ditty of a wild annoy;
Mocking all with scornful strain,
Till the passion grew to pain,
And each humbler warbler fled,
Silent, in his shame and fear,
Thou the while, with wing outspread,
Sweetly voiced in spite of sneer,
Throned on the topmost bough, or darting wild through air.

Thou hast pleasures. I have seen,
When the buxom spring was green,
How thy nest was tended—how
Thou didst gather straw and blade,
And, within the ancient bough,
Sit, the stem and leaf to braid.—
Patient was thy watch, and stern
Lesson might the serpent learn,—
Crawling where thy young ones lie,
With his cruel, keen desire,—
From thy eagle-raging eye,
Showing all thy soul on fire,
While talon, beak and wing declared the warrior's ire.

Patient, as thy young ones grow,
Use of feeble wings to show,
How, to glide from bough to bough,
How with gradual flight, to bear,
Poised on spreading pinion now,
Through the yielding heart of air;

And, when free of wing, and high,
Winging, singing, through the sky,—
Then, with thy triumphant strain,
Matchless in unmeasured might,
As if born of madden'd brain,
Ecstasied with deep delight,
Whirling in voice aloft, in far, capricious flight.

Why the cynic temper?—why
Still that strain of mockery?
Art thou truer? Dost thou sneer,
As thou haply know'st that none
Of the love songs spring must hear,
Speaks fidelity but one?
Thou art constant—that I know—
To thy young ones,—to the foe,—
To thy mate, and to the tree,
That beside my window-sill,
Many a year, has been to thee
Cottage-home and empire still,—
Thou wast the sovereign there, and ever hadst thy will.

Still maintain it—thou alone,
Of the birds, when summer's gone,
Keep'st thy dwelling, hold'st thy place,
As if in thy breast there grew
Something, which, to human race,
Kept thee dedicate and true.
Cynical thy song, but mine
Might be cynical like thine,
Could I deem with thee, that all
Of the vows in spring we hear,
Were forgotten by the fall;—
But I shrink from doubt so drear;—
I yield my heart to faith, and love when thou wouldst sneer.

AUTUMN TWILIGHT.

There is a soft haze hanging on yon hill,
Tinged with a purple light. How beautiful,
And yet, how cold! 'Tis the first robe put on,
With gloomy foretaste of a gloomier hour,
By the sad Autumn. Well may she repine,—
With heavy dread of winter at her heart,
Adverse to present sweetness as to hope,
Which never cheers her fortunes. She is doom'd—
Survivor of a race that left no heirs,
And she, the mourner of the beautiful,
Whose treasure, in the past to which she glides,
Was but a bright decay, a perishing bloom,
The bounty of a love whose dearest gifts
Best show in desolation. The sweet green,
The summer flush of love—the golden bloom
That came with flowers in April, and brought sweets
Whose purity might teach a faith that life
Were also in their breathing—all are gone!
The green grows pallid—the warm, virgin flush,
That was in summer's eye, and on her cheek,
A glory all too precious for a dream,—
Too precious far for mortal certainty—
Fleets all—as keen, the breezes from the hills
Sweep icily o'er the meadows. All the bright hues,
That graced the flowers and hemispheric crowns
Of trees grown haughty in a birthday dress,
Seem vanishing with the sunset. The last rays
That drink their purple brightness with their lives,
Fade upwards through the forest—a sad flush,
That lothly leaves the twilight, and a while
Lingers upon the hill-tops, as surveying

The empires that it forfeits. Now the winds,
Slow rising as from caverns of the night,
With trailing robes of darkness, and broad arms,
Stretched out, in action suited to the dirge
That speaks the mournful ruin of their homes,
Wail heavily through the branches; while the leaves,
Saddest of mourners! flung on summer's grave,
Lament her in the silence of true grief!
Ah! mock me not that thus I mourn with them;
The sad heart's wisdom is to weep enough!—
I hear your lesson, but of what avail?
Since, while it teaches worthlessness of grief,
It still acknowledges the pregnant cause
That, in the very uselessness of tears,
Compels our tears most freely. You discourse,
To feeling, with a counsel that prevents
All feeling; and unless you stifle her,
You teach most idly. Never yet was grief
Fit moralist,—and that philosophy,
Which will not take its color from the heart
It seeks to fortify against the cloud,
Reaches no sacred chord of sympathy,
Responsive with sweet echoes. All your laws
Teach sorrow when you teach her hopelessness.
To bid the sacred current cease to flow,
'Tis needful first you freeze it; and what gain,
To him with dear affections, o'er whose grave,
He still encourages dear memories,
That feeling should be made secure from hurt,
By gross and cold insensibility?
Foregoing nature, what do we acquire
But forfeiture? As well persuade the flower
To grow to stone, lest, rifled by the storm,
Its premature bloom shall perish. If unwise

To yield to sorrow the sole sovereignty,
As little wise to substitute for this,
The apathy, that, still rejecting grief,
Grows ignorant of all rapture. You declaim—
With the grave studied eloquence of books,
Writ by cold monks in the ascetic cell,
That life is full of changes.—Be it so!
These changes ever are from joy to woe,
And woe to joy again. To conquer one
Is scarce to know the other. In your calm,
'Tis easy to declare that things of life,
By the inevitable laws of things,
Are also things of death; but not the less
Find we a sacred certainty of grief,
Even in this very knowledge. Death, you say,
Still harvests forms that love, not less than forms
That simply live; and folly 'tis to mourn,
That the dear life whose presence was a joy
And fragrance, that forever brought us joy,
Is destined to as sure an apathy
As the poor flowers we tread on.

Happy he,
Perchance—and yet I think not—who can thus
Prose calmly over nature, and the fate
Of her dear offspring in whatever fields.
But mine is not this happiness;—nor mine,
The thought that happiness may light her fire,
From such dry chips of doctrine. The rich sap,
May from the wounded tree gush forth in tears,
The green rind feel its hurts, and something lose
Of verdure in the injury which it feels.
But teach the bough, how better were it lopt,
And flung into the fire, than suffering thus,
From the keen hurts of the too wanton axe

The wound will heal. You point me to the scars;
But while it still hath rind for newer hurts,
And fresh sap still to flow from other wounds,
The scars are but in proof of strength to bear,
As well as hurts to suffer. Tears, for me,
Bring sweet relief for what is lost or borne,
As teaching still of sensibilities
For future feeling; whether joy or woe,
Or gain or loss;—and, in this consciousness,
One finds a better solace for the past,
Than in that cold philosophy which stills
The too susceptible pulse, lest it should throb,
Some day, with fever. Yet, that fever throb,
Itself, declares the warm vitality
Still looking forth with hope.
And still you chide,
That grief should waste upon inferior things,
Leaves of the forest, flowers of the summer day,
Fruits of a season's tribute, and frail fancies
Born of the dew and sunshine, for the hour,
The sorrows that might find excuse, if given
For loss of human treasure—forms and greatness,
Which fill society with sense of virtue,
And still commend to love that fierce ambition
That makes even love a sacrifice in turn!
Alas! we know not what is worthy, what is great,
And weep from fancy, rather than from law;
And fancy is a law, and in our feelings
Hath charter'd rights, and shapes them at her pleasure,
To make us weep, if need be; tears and sorrows
Being as much her proper properties,
As sunshine and gay laughter, sport and flight.
Yet have I something of a plea beyond,
In the condition which has shut me out

From much, that, in the common social life,
Commends itself unto humanity,
As only worth its care. Mine was a lot
Peculiar in its loneliness of aim,
If not distinction. Childhood found me first
A sad bewilder'd orphan—one who stood
Alone among his fellows,—and when wrong'd,
Knew not the lap in which to hide his head,
Nor friendly ear in which to pour complaint.
I had no parent's tendance. Never mine
A sister's lips have hallow'd while they press'd;—
No brother call'd me his;—no natural ties
Embraced, and train'd, and cherish'd my wild youth,
Which still went erring into devious ways,
Sorrowing as much as sinning, in a mood
That craved love only for its guide to goodness;—
And this alone it found not—or in vain!—
And thus, with strong affections, still in exile,
Denied where they sought favor, I have turn'd
To the inanimate, unspeaking creatures,
That grew about or wanton'd in my path—
Having no scorn or hatred in their hearts—
Having no voice of censure on their tongues—
For that most needed sympathy of nature,
Which answer'd best the hunger in my heart.
Thus were my footsteps won into the forest,
Thus did I seek these groves as if in worship,
With regular tendance, and a meek observance,
That suffer'd not the chant of winds, the sighing,
That seem'd most human, in the pine's great branches,—
The fall of leaf, the shadows of the thicket,
Or flutter of the gay bird o'er the pathway,—
To 'scape me;—moralizing at each motion,
Something, that as it soothed the troubled feeling,

Was surely not philosophy. My rambles
Still brought me what I sought;—and these pale flowers,
And the green leaves, now yellow, at our feet,
Were something more to me than leaves and flowers.
They were my kindred. Now, that they are gone,
I weep them as a loss of family,
And tread among them with a cautious step,
A sad, slow motion, and with trembling heart,
As I were reading, in some ancient church-yard,
The names of dear ones precious to my childhood.

BALLAD.

Oh! bury him quickly, and utter no word
  Of the memory sadden'd by sorrow so long;
But when the cold stranger shall say that he err'd,
  Then tell the dark tale of his crueller wrong.
We may not approve, but when others condemn,
  'Twere crime that defence of his heart to forbear,
And show that his faults were all prompted by them,—
  They could goad him to danger, then fly from him there

You saw him for many long days ere he fell,
  In chains and in solitude, sad but serene;
'Tis grateful to know that he battled it well,
  While his spirit grew strong in the gloom of the scene.
They thought him all callous to feeling and shame,—
  Ah! little they knew him;—the spirit he bore
Once aim'd at, and sigh'd for, as lofty a fame
  As shines on the pages of history's lore.

But pile the dank sod which no stone shall adorn,
No hand ever freshen with shrub or with flower;
We bury him coldly—we leave him forlorn—
And midnight was never more dark than this hour.
It is but a year since all proudly he stood,
Brave, bright, unassuming—the sought, the preferr'd—
Upheld by the strong, and beloved by the good—
Now—bury him quickly, and utter no word!

HAST THOU A SONG FOR A FLOWER.

I.

Hast thou a song for a flower,
Such as, if breathed in its ear,
Would waken in beauty's own bower
The spirit most fit to be there?
Then, minstrel, I challenge thy power—
Such song, if thou hast, sing it here!—
Here, where the breeze o'erwearied,
With his travel o'er ocean creeps,
And on the green leaf by her lattice,
Sinks languidly down and sleeps.

II.

For her the sweet music thou bringest
Must in a true spirit be wrought,
And the passion of mine thou singest
Must be pure as the child's first thought.
If none such within thee springest,
Away, for thy presence is naught.

Far better the breeze, at waking,
  Should tell her that hopeless I come,
With itself, to the leaf at her lattice,
  And laid me down, dreaming but dumb.

ENIGMA.

I AM most potent of all earthly powers,
Save one. I penetrate the loftiest towers,
As freely as the cottage, in all hours;
I paralyze the strongest with a spell;
Soothe the most suffering; shut the fatal knell
From out the ears of misery; beguile
The saddest mourner to a hopeful smile;
Bring cheerful guests into the solitude,
That minister unto the sufferer's mood,
So that he straight forgets what gave him pain,
And wins the strength and hope of youth again.
No will can combat mine, no might withstand;
And man before me bows throughout the land,
As at a tyrant's progress; yet with joy,
For that I sway to succor, not destroy.
Yet, do I arm myself with terrors still,
When they are needful. I can bring the thrill,
Of fear or horror, to the guilty soul,
And make him hear the far-off thunders roll,
As at his feet; can swift around him group,
Even at a whisper, a most terrible troop
Of his assailing enemies. My spell,
Most strong when softest, is invincible.
You strive with me in vain. I stretch a wing,

Unseen above you. In your ears I sing,
In most unnoted accents. Round your neck
I weave such subtle chains as never break,
Save with my satisfied purpose. Your white breast,
You do unfold me, whether as a guest,
Obtrusive, or implored and much caress'd.
You may not shut from me your secret thought,
Your passion or your guilt. Unask'd, unsought,
You whisper to me your best hope and fear,
What you endure of grief, what joys endear,
And whom you love and hate. And I, who hear.
Still keep your secret;—to your service bound,
Still faithful, still unbidden, I am found,
Whene'er the season calls me, or the place;
An angel you may hold me, or a grace;
Devoted as the first, and as the last,
Still blessing—though the sights I bring may blast!
My bond of service never shall be broke,
Till I no more may spell, or thou invoke,
Then, when perforce I leave thee, I resign
Thy charge to one, a kinswoman of mine,
Of greater powers, but hostile still to thine.

SONNET.

SYMPATHY BETWEEN THE PAST AND FUTURE.

Would we go forward boldly, and gain heart
For farther progress, we must pause a while,
And gaze upon the path, for many a mile,
We follow'd when we first grew bold to start;—
That so much has been traversed, is a goad

To fresh endeavor; and the eye grows bright,
With expectation, as the baffled sight
Would vainly compass all the o'er-trodden road;—
The pathways of the future will grow clear,
When the first fresh beginnings of the march
Lie bright beneath the broad and sheltering arch;
And, repossess'd of childhood, we are near
Heaven's sources,—for the true humanity
Keeps past and future still in either eye.

TO THE BREEZE.

AFTER A PROTRACTED CALM IN THE GULF OF MEXICO.

I.

Thou com'st at last! Our sorrow is at end;
Thou com'st, and hast our blessing, pleasant breeze.
Yet where hast thou been wandering, fickle friend?
Where, when the midnight gather'd to her brow
Her pale and silent minister, wast thou?
On what far, sullen, solitary seas,
Piping the mariner's requiem, didst thou tend
The home-returning bark,
Curling the white foam o'er her plunging prow,—
White, when the rolling waves about her all were dark?

II.

Ah! thou didst woo her sweetly as she lay,
Still idly rocking on the unconscious deep;
Thou sought'st her with a breath
Of spicy odor from Sonora's vales;

And, with the sweetest of imploring gales,
That seem'd like life to death,
Filling her yellow sails,
Beguiled her on her way.
With sudden voice, like that of mountain bird
Singing, thou wok'st her from her dreary sleep,
Until her every pulse of life grew stirr'd:
Her fluttering pennant was the first to fly,
Then the great vans swell'd out delightedly,
And, with the song of land he loves to hear,
Thou bad'st the mariner cheer!

III.

Oh! well thou know'st the mission that is thine,
And, when in sluggish bonds old ocean slept,
Making of life no sign,—
While the faint moaning o'er his breast that crept
Seem'd like the breathings of eternity
Above the grave of the unburied Time,—
Then didst thou clothe thyself in wings of prime,
Then speed thy work of mercy.—How the tar,
His form reclined along the burning deck,
Stretch'd ever more his eager eye afar,
Still watching for thy coming—for the speck,
Marking thy shadow, from some giant steep,
Down darting to the embraces of the deep!

IV.

Late, but not faithless to thy charge, thy flight
Soon came to bless his sight.
So long a fond and watching worshipper,
He knew to hail thy coming, nor to err,
No matter what thy shape, or whence thy wing.

Thou wert his passion. By the dearest names
He did implore thy presence: "My sweet breeze,
Whither! oh whither!"—I have heard him sing
Rudely, but with a strength that feeling tames
To fondness in rough natures—"My delight!
Where art thou—where, oh! beauty of the seas,—
My breeze, my pleasant breeze!"

V.

Were all the charms by mortal passion sung
As worthy of the tongue!
Ah! breath of life to nature, thou art sure
The image of that ever young and pure,
Superior spirit, which, when all was dim,
Ere yet creation sang her choral hymn,
And darkness brooded o'er the stagnant deep,
Moved on the waters, waking them from sleep,
And rousing them to purposes of Him
For whom all wings have flight!
Born in the solemn night,
Ere skies had birth in bright,
With uncreated watchers for the sight,—
Thine was the music, through the firmament
By the fond nature sent,
To hail the happy birth,
And guide to sea and earth
The glorious wing, the blessing eye of light!

VI.

Music to us no less,
Thou com'st in our distress,
To ope the pathway, all made clear by thee,
Through the wide waste of sea!

Soothing, thou bring'st to him who goes alone
Unwatch'd and unremember'd o'er the wave,
Perchance his grave!
Should he there perish, to thy simple moan
What hope to add, from human tenderness,
One fond imploring tone!

VII.

I bless thee, gentle breeze!
Sweet minister to many a fond desire,
Thou bear'st me to my sire,
Thou, and these rolling seas!
What, O dear God of this great element,
Are we before thee, that its breath is sent,
Obedient to young love and eager hope?
But that its pinion with our path is blent,
We had been doom'd, blind, weak, and dark, to grope,
Where plummet's cast is vain, and human art
Lacking all chart!

LYRICAL BALLAD.

If the fruit of the tree was delicious,
  Yet how keen was the bitter it brought;
As the zephyr, though sweet, is capricious,
  With blight as with luxury fraught:
Who roves in a garden, ungrateful
  For the tendance that nourish'd its bloom?
Better fly to the wilderness hateful,
  Where nothing is false but the gloom!

We are still the vain creatures of vision,
Where the eyes only torture the soul;
Our worship still meets with derision,
And we gain, but by flying the goal.
He dreams not, the victim, self-banish'd
From the shrine which has mock'd at his prayer,
That 'tis only when pleasure has vanish'd
He safely may harbor with Care!

The doubt that still hangs o'er the dreaming,
Spoils the rapture that follows its show;
As the flash of the lightning, whose gleaming
Reveals the deep blackness below:
The spirit of Love, thus, in flying,
Still glooms the sad Being it woos,
And finds its best solace in sighing,
With a doubt of the heart it subdues!

THE NEW MOON.

"Bend thy bow, Dian! shoot thy silver shaft
Through the dark bosom of yon murky cloud,
That, like a shroud,
Hangs heavy o'er the dwelling of sweet night!"

And the sky laugh'd,
Even as I spake the words; and, in the west,
The columns of her mansion shone out bright!
A glory hung above Eve's visible brow,
The maiden empress!—and she glided forth
In beauty, looking down on the tranced earth,

So fondly, that its rivulets below
Gush'd out to hail her, as if then first blest
With the soft motion of their voiceless birth.
A sudden burst of brightness o'er me broke—
The rugged crags of the dull cloud were cleft
By her sharp arrow, and the edges left,—
How sweetly wounded!—silver'd with the stroke;
Thus making a fit pathway for her march
Through the blue arch!

FOREST REVERIE BY STARLIGHT.

The night has settled down. A dewy hush
Hangs o'er the forest, save when fitful gusts
Vex the tall pines with murmurs. Spring is here,
With breath all incense, and with cheek all bloom,
And voice of many minstrels. Balmy airs
Creep gently to my bosom, and beguile
Each feeling into freshness. I will forth,
And gaze upon the stars—the uncounted stars—
Holding high watch in heaven—still high, still bright,
Though the storm gathers round the sacred hill,
And shakes the cottage roof-tree. There they shine,
In well-remember'd youth. They bear me back,
With strange persuasiveness, to the old time
And happy hours of boyhood. There's no change
In all their virgin glory. Clouds that roll,
And congregate in the azure deeps of heaven,
In wild debate and darkness, pass away,
Leaving them bright in the same beauty still,
Defying, in the progress of the years,

All change; and rising ever from the night,
In soft and dewy splendor as at first,
When, golden footprints of the Eternal steps,
They paved the walks of heaven, and grew to eyes
Beckoning the feet of man. Ah! would his eyes
Behold them, with meet yearning to pursue
The holy heights they counsel! Would his soul
Claim kindred with the happy forms that now
Walk by their blessed guidance—walk in heaven,
In paths of the Good Shepherd! Then were earth
Deserving of their beauty: then were man,
Already following, step by step, their points
To the One Presence—at each onward step
Leaving new lights that cheer his brother on,
In a like progress. Happily they shine,
As in his hours of music and of youth,
When every breath of the fresh-coming breeze,
And every darting vision of the cloud,
Gleam of the day and glimmer of the night,
Brought to the craving spirit harmony,
And bless'd each fond assurance of the hope
With sweetest confirmation. Still they shine,
And dear the story of their early prime—
And his—the conscious worshipper may read
In their enduring presence. Happiest tales
Of innocence and joy, events and hours,
That never more return. These they record,
Renew and hallow, with their own pure rays,
When blight of age is on the frame—when grief
Weighs the vex'd heart to earth—when all beside,
The father, and the mother, and the friend,
Speak in decaying syllables—dread proof
Of worse decay!—and that sad chronicler,
Feeble and failing in excess of years,

Old Memory, tottering from his mossy cell,
Stops with the imperfect legend on his lips,
And drowses into dream. No change like this
Falls on their golden-eyed veracity,
Takes from the silvery truths that line their lips,
Or stales their lovely aspects. Well they know
The years they never feel; see, without dread,
The storm that rises and the bolt that falls,
The age that chills, the apathy that chokes,
The death that withers all that blooms below,
Yet smile they on as ever, sweetly bright,
Serene, in their security from all
The change that troubles man!

Yet, hill and tree
Change with the season—with the alter'd heart,
And weak and withering muscle. Ancient groves,
That shelter'd me in childhood, have given place
To gaudy gardens; and the solemn oaks,
That heard the first prayers of my youthful heart
For greatness, and a life beyond their own—
Lo! in their stead, a maiden's slender hand
Tutors green vines, and purple buds, and flowers,
As frail as her own fancies. At each step
I miss some old companion of my walks,
Memorial of the happy hours of youth,
Whose presence had brought back a thousand joys,
And images that took the shape of joys—
The loveliest masquers, and all innocent—
That vanish'd with the rest. I would recall,
But vainly, each lost presence; and the sigh
That mourns the dear memorials now no more,
Counsels desires that to the mortal eye
Commend no mortal images. The thought

Grasps vainly, right and left, whereon to hold,
And droops, as one grown hopeless of support,
That once, with native strength for every strife,
Scorn'd succor from without. The earth denies
Her bosom for repose—the shade is gone
That offer'd grateful shelter to the eye;
And the dear aspects, which had each its birth
Twinn'd with some proud affection,—they depart,
In mournful robes of shadow that disguise
Each lineament of love.

Ah! not with these,
The perishing things that suffer from decay,
Seek we the sweet memorials of our youth—
The youth that seem'd immortal—youth that bloom'd
With hues and hopes of heaven,—firing its heart
With aspirations for eternal life,
Perpetual triumphs, and the ambitious thirst
Still for new fields and empires of domain!
In tokens of the soul—that craving thirst
That earth supplies not—in the undying things,
That man can never change—that mock his fate
With never-changing sweet serenity,
Assured of a security that builds
Upon the steadfast rock, 'gainst which the storm
Beats through successive ages, but to prove
How fast its bulwarks—how eternally
Sunk in the innate principle of things,
It draws, as to the inevitable heart,
Its growth from all the rest!—to these we turn
For the memorials precious to our youth:—
That season when the Fancy is a god—
Hope a conviction—Love an instinct—Truth,
The generous friend that ever by our side,

Hath still the sweetest story for the ear,
And wins us on our way!

Ah! stars,—though taught,
That ye too, in the inevitable doom,
Must perish like the rest—grow dim and fade,
Having no eyes of beauty for the eyes
That look to ye in beauty—yet your light
Brings back all boyhood's blessings! In my heart
Stand up the old divinities anew.
I hear their well-known voices, see their eyes
Shining once more in mine, and straight forget
That I have wept their loss in many tears,
Mix'd with reproaches—bitter, sad regrets,
Self-chidings, and the memory of wrongs,
Endured, inflicted, suffer'd, and avenged!

As I behold ye now, ye bring me back
The treasures of my boyhood. All is mine
That I had once surrender'd. Scarce a scene
Of childish prank or merriment, but comes,
With all the freshness of the infant time,
Back to my recollection. The old school,
The noisy rabble, the tumultuous cries—
The green, remember'd in the wintry day,
For the encounter of the flying ball—
The marble play, the hoop, the top, the kite,
And, when the ambition prompted higher games,
The battle-array and conflict—friends and foes
Mix'd in the wild melée, with shouts of might
Triumphant o'er the clamors of retreat!

These, in their regular seasons, with their deeds,
Their incidents of happiness or pain,

In the revival of old memories,
Your lovely lights restore: nor these alone!
The chroniclers of riper years ye grow,
And loftier thoughts and fancies; when my heart
First took ye for sweet counsellors, and loved
To wander in your evening lights, and dream
Of other eyes that watch'd ye from afar,
At the same hour—and of another heart
That gush'd in yearning sympathy with mine!
And, as the years flew by—as I became
Warier, yet more devoted—fix'd and strong—
Growing in the affections and the thoughts
When growth had ceased in stature—then, when life,
Wing'd with impetuous passions, darted by—
And voices grew into a spell, that hung,
Through the dim hours of night, about the heart,
Making it tremble strangely;—when dark eyes
Were planets, having power upon the soul,
As fated, dimly, at nativity;—
And older men were monitors too dull
For passionate youth,—and all our oracles
Were still mysterious counsellors to love,
And faith, and confident trust for all who brought
The meet credential of a faith like ours,
Gushing with sweetest overflow, and fond
Of its own tears and weaknesses.—Ah! then,
How precious was your language! What dear strains
Of promise ye pour'd forth,—in sounds that made
The impatient soul leap upward into flight,
The skies stoop down and yield to every wish,
While earth, embraced by heaven, instinct with love,
And blessing, had forgot all fears of death!

The brightness of your age, in every change,
Mocks that which palsies man. Dim centuries
That saw your fresh beginnings with delight,
Are swallow'd in the ocean-flood of years,
Or crowd with ruin the gray sands of Time,
Who still, with appetite and thirst unslaked—
Active but unappeased—voracious still,
Must swallow what remains. Sweet images,
Whose memories wake our song—whose forms abide—
The heart's ideal standards of delight—
Are gone to people those dim realms of shade,
Where rules the Past—that sovereign, single-eyed,
Whose back is on the sun!

Ah! when all these—
The joys we have recorded, and the forms
Whose very names were blessings—forms of youth,
Of childhood, and the hours we know not twice,
Which won us first, and carried us away
To strange conceits of coming happiness,
But to be thought on as delusions all,
Yet such delusions as we still must love!—
When these have parted from us—when the sky
Hath lost the charm of its ethereal blue,
And the nights lose their freshness—and the trees
No longer have a welcome shade for love—
And the moon wanes into a paler bright,
And all the poetry that stirr'd the leaves,
And all the perfume that was on the flowers—
Music upon the winds—wings in the void—
The carpeted valley's wealth of green—the dew
That morning flings on the enamell'd moss—
The hill-side, the acclivity, the grove—
Sweeter that Solitude is sleeping there!—

Are gone, as the last hope of misery :—
When the last dream of a deluded life
Hath left us to awaken—not to feel
The golden morning, but the appalling night,
When sight itself is weariness, and hope
No longer rifles from the barren path
One flower of promise!—when disease is nigh,
And every bone is racking—and the thought
Is of dry, nauseous, ineffectual drugs,
Which we must painfully swallow—but in vain—
And not a hand is nigh to quench the thirst
With one poor cup of water,—or our prayer
Is answer'd with indifferent mood, that shows
The moderate service irksome—when the eye
Strains for the closing heavens, and the fair sky
Which it is losing,—and dread images,
Meetly successive, of the sable pall,
The melancholy carriage, and the clod,
Make us to shudder with a stifling fear ;—
When we have bade adieu to earthly things,
Fought through that long last struggle, still the worst,
Wrestling with self,—and winning that best boon,
Of resignation to the sovereign will,
We may no longer baffle or delude,—
And offer'd up our prayer of penitence,
Doubtful of its acceptance, yet prepared,
As well as our condition will admit,
For the last change in an unhappy life!—
Oh ! then methinks 'twould still rejoice mine eyes,
Would they throw wide my casement, and permit
A last fond gaze upon the placid sky,
And all the heavenly watchers which have seen
My fair beginning, and my rising youth,
And my tall manhood. Oh ! dear friend that hear'st

This chant—thy office may be soon to ask,
How shall I soothe the suffering which I see?—
With what sweet service to the friend I love,
But have not power to save, prepare his couch,
And robe him for his rest? Think of this song,
And of thy own sweet thoughts and sympathies.
Give him to see the blessed skies—the Night—
Her azure garments glowing with great eyes,
That look on him with love;—and, at the hour
Which brings thee to thy parting, it will glad
Thy heart, in that sad struggle, to behold
Their sweet serene of smiles. 'Twill bear thee back,
With all the current of thy better thoughts,
To the pure practice of thy innocent years.—
Repentant, then, of errors, evil deeds,
Imaginings of darkness, thou wilt weep
Over thy recollections; and thy tears,
The purest tribute of thy contrite heart,
Will be as a sweet prayer sent up to heaven!

INSCRIPTION FOR THERMOPYLÆ.

STRANGER! thou stand'st upon Thermopylæ!
The pass that led into the heart of Greece,
But gave no passage save through greater hearts:
They keep it still.—Their graves are at thy feet.

BY THE EDISTO.

River, that still go'st brightly,
Though sweeping to the sea,
And chantest daily, nightly,
Thy own dirge-melody;
Methinks thy murmur strengthens
The purpose in my soul,
And, as thy progress lengthens,
I seem to see my goal.

I seek, as thou, the ocean,
Great sea of human life,
Won by its wild commotion,
And striving with its strife:
Vainly, we fondly linger
Where green shades woo our stay;
We both obey a finger
That points us on our way.

Yet, downward as thou rovest,
How glad thy waters make
The green banks which thou lovest,
And the zephyrs where they wake!
They wake among thy willows,
And they laugh with welcome still,
As thy downward-lapsing billows
Lift their lilies with a thrill.

The blue-bird stoops to carol,
As thy glittering streams go by,
And the bay-tree and the laurel
Bend above thee with a sigh;

But the sigh is of a pleasure
  That may take no wilder voice;
And the great pines share the treasure,
  And, to welcome thee, rejoice.

If thus my course may gladden
  While I hurry to the deep,
Sure my heart shall never sadden
  When 'tis swallow'd up in sleep;
I, too, shall hear sweet voices,
  That requite me as I run,
And the pleasant thought rejoices,
  I shall only grieve when gone.

THE APPROACH OF SUMMER.

Now, darting through green leaves, and bringing flowers,
Fresh blooming, borrow'd from a thousand bowers
Where nature fills her lap with fruits, and gleams
The carpet of the prairies, stars and streams,—
Comes forth, all wantoning in joyous dreams,
With eye that laughs in beauty, golden hair,
Curling and floating o'er a neck as fair
As the young moon, when in the dusky vale
She lifts her virgin crescent, soft and pale,—
The flush'd and revelling Summer. At her glance
Sinks the old wizard, Winter, into trance;
No more the mighty potentate, who shook
His icy sceptre over field and brook,

But, tottering into apathy, that goes,
Soulless and sad, to polar home of snows;
The realm usurp'd made glad in his decline,
Made free to bourgeon in its flower and vine;
The steel-bound waters rescued where he lay,
And leaping, flashing, to the smiles of day,
With all their little billows out at play;—
Birds gladsome singing round the cottage tree,
And hope and heart, for once, at liberty,
Mingling in joyous anthems which make air
All musical with love, that might be prayer.

Give the heart freedom! Let the soul take wing
With the soft promise of the golden Spring;
From book and study, forth;—uplift the eye
To the blue beauties in the morning sky;
Forget that Toil hath had his task decreed,
The daily labor, for the daily need;
Give Hope new charm in respite from its chain,
Thought fresher impulse in unlaboring brain;
No duty rules that Drudgery shall not find
Some moments grateful to the unfetter'd mind;
The heart's sweet Sabbath must not be denied,
Now, when boon Nature smiles on all beside!
Where the winds play,—where great green branches wave.
And lilies softly lapse upon the wave,—
Forth with the Sun, with heart that sings within,
In sense of joy that hath no taint of sin;
A song of Summer born, that feels, instinct,
How near with Earth the soul of man is link'd,
And thus through earth with heaven, that still foreshows,
In bright, sweet symbols, how the future glows,
How freshly, gladsomely, and purely Bliss
May yet, in man's true life, atone for this!

Spirits of holiest gift have been at range,
O'er stream and forest, to effect this change;—
What potent spells, what breath of balm, they brought,
By which the magic of this birth was wrought;—
How did they whisper on the bankside, where
Lurk'd all the hooded flowers, in shame and fear;
Hush'd through long months of winter, while the sway
Of that cold tyrant threaten'd still his prey,
'Till that warm whisper to the clod which hid,
Brought each sweet virgin to unclose her lid,
And won the nun-like daisy from her cell,
In sweet obedience to the grateful spell,—
Blessing the shrine that shelter'd her so well!
What legions of bright angels, far and wide,
Have sped, that earth should waken up in pride;
A single breath, one short sweet night—the moon
Of April only watching through its noon—
And, with the dawn, how wondrous was the show
That hail'd the sun from thousand plains below;
With song,—though faint, how sweet!—and scents so rare,
As if the flowers were wedded to the air,
That nothing did but drink of the delight,
With wings diffused in never-resting flight,
As conscious, in the rapture of such taste,
Of no fatigue, in all that world of waste.

Oh! with a range as wide as his, we speed
To each fair empire of the newly freed;
With hearts as free as any of the race,
That glow and gladden in the sun's embrace.
How spreads the various picture as we go!
Hills greenly stretch aloft, and vales below;
The mountain wears no more the brow of age,
And nature flies her gloomy hermitage,

Now desolate no longer,—to abide,
With birds and blossoms, by the brooklet's side;
How prattle the glad waters, as she brings,
Her gayest buds to nurture at their springs;
Pleased with the song of kindred, which declares
Her joy in these, and all her beauties theirs!
Banks, on each side, slope down with fringe of green,
To kiss the silvery waves that sing between,
Sing with fit chant to the cathedral trees,
Through which, still sleepless, trolls the thoughtless breeze,
With music most like that of swarming bees!

The song is still an echo to the toil,—
The heart is tutor'd when the sinews moil;
Mere song were something vicious,—but the strain
That tells of solace for the limbs and brain—
Which call for respite for due service done,
In fields of meet succession with the sun,—
This brings a healthful nurture, and, if right
The duty done, we look for the delight.
The charm that still beguiles us at the close
Of the day-labor, freshening its repose,
Is the sweet nourishment for strength anew,
The future toil, or conquest, to pursue.
Thus sings the earth at seasons,—thus we hear
The bird and insect joyous far and near;
A choral hymn the nation's toil preludes,
And the glad creature frolics ere it broods.
Full of a sweet and wise intelligence,
Not simply fashion'd for the idiot's sense,
The voices that we hear from plain and grove,
They speak in gladness, for they breathe of love;
And love is the great duty which implies
Toil for the drudge and study for the wise;

Both earnest ever in the fond pursuit,
That, in the very tillage, finds the fruit!
Earth has a labor in her womb below!—
The watchful ear may catch the murmuring flow
Of mingling strifes and sounds,—the strifes of toil,
Of those who sing and serve, for those who moil.
The mighty mother, with mysterious art,
Hath fashion'd well each agent in her mart;
Various in product, as in office, still,
Each, without murmur, follows at her will;
No void unfill'd beneath her searching eye,
No realm unwatch'd, of water, earth, or sky;—
There runs the lizard o'er the freshest flowers,
As death gives shadow to our sunniest hours;—
There, the gay butterfly, on varied wing,
Pursues the insect that it cannot sting;—
There goes the coiling serpent, with raised crest,
And warning rattle, to his slimy nest,—
Vex'd by pursuit he slowly wins his way,
Nor seems unwilling to prolong his stay,—
Too closely press'd he would not shun the strife,
And he who takes, must battle for, his life.

Turn where the dove,—meet contrast!—with his mate
Just won, delighted with his new estate,
Lingers beside the path a fearless thing,
Nor claims the succor of his idle wing.
Nature endows him with the season's sense,
Where all is breathing hope and confidence,—
And, heedful of her interest, man decrees
His safety from the fowler. Thus we seize
Our sweetest lessons of preserving good,
From the dumb nature and unthinking mood,—

For it were base to wrong the faith implied,
Which seeks our steps, nor hurries once aside,
Though life is dearer now, so full of love,
And fear is the first instinct of the dove!

NIGHT STORM.

This tempest sweeps the Atlantic!—Nevasink
  Is howling to the Capes! Grim Hatteras cries
Like thousand damned ghosts, that on the brink
  Lift their dark hands and threat the threatening skies;
Surging through foam and tempest, old Román
  Hangs o'er the gulf, and, with his cavernous throat,
  Pours out the torrent of his wolfish note,
And bids the billows bear it where they can!
Deep calleth unto deep, and, from the cloud,
  Launches the bolt, that, bursting o'er the sea,
Rends for a moment the thick pitchy shroud,
  And shows the ship the shore beneath her lea:—
Start not, dear wife, no dangers here betide,—
And see, the boy still sleeping at your side!

"WELL," SANG A BLUE-EYED DAMSEL.

I.

"Well," sang a blue-eyed damsel, half hidden by a wood
Of bearded oaks, that on the banks of Etiwando stood;
"Give me such days of beauty forever by these shores,
Such glimpses of this noble stream as to the sea it pours;

The palm, the pine, the song of birds, and this gay realm of flowers,
That sweetens now, with smile and scent, this ancient home of ours;
And not your Texian world of wealth, your wild and wondrous
gleams,
Your giant herds, your mighty birds, your silver-bedded streams;
No, nor the glimpse of golden spoils, that tempt the eager eye,
As half display'd, in Mexique vales, with scarce a guard they lie,
Shall move me to repine with thoughts that pomp and wealth
bedeck,
No more, with rich and jewell'd pride, our Carolina's neck.

II.

For, stately in her beauty still, and stainless in her fame,
She rises like a queen of grace, while others sink in shame;
The wealth so dear in other eyes, the bribe that wins the rest,
Shows basely in her matron glance, moves scorn within her breast;
True to her proud example still, her sons pursue their way,
And wisdom gives their counsels weight, and virtue yields them
sway:
Ah! shall her daughters heed the prize of selfish, stranger lands,
Nor all prefer, which she bestows, whose nobler worth commands?
What though her sons no wealth declare when they approach to
woo,
Yet sprung from noble stocks they come, and like their sires are
true;
With one of these, but build for me my cottage on these shores,
And all the wealth of Mexico, and Texas too, be yours."

NATURE'S FAVORITE.

Some men are Nature's favorites; they were born
Beneath the canopy of trees in May,
When Beauty fills the sky, and from the bud
Breathes the fresh odor; when the merry birds
Go singing through the air, and whirls aloft,
In maddest paroxysms of delight,
The wanton mimic of a thousand tongues,
Pouring a torrent of impetuous song
That stuns the grove to silence. She has been
The gentle mother, leading them away
From the immure of the unnatural town,
To the free homestead of the ancient trees;
Bestowing them the life that there alone
Makes life a dear romance. They have gone forth
And brought her flowers, and fill'd her lap with them;
And she has told them, of the life of each,
Most ravishing stories. Oh! how very sweet
Thus to be taught! No musty books—no rules,
In dull, damp dungeons, shutting out the sky,
And drudging the free fancy with a weight
That leaves it wingless after.—'Tis my joy
That I have thus been tutored! Nature came
And took me for her charge when I was young,
And brought me up herself. I was not taught
Vain histories of schoolmen—men of cloud
And vapor, with philosophies of straw,
That strive in bubble-hunting. Ancient tongues
That, having answer'd for their day, had gone
Into forgetfulness, ne'er tortured mine!
Destined for life—the present and the real—

Condemn'd to its necessities, and full
Of all its glorious conquests—its new truths
And coming victories—I was not vex'd
With frigid phantoms of philosophy
At midnight in my chamber—ghosts of doubt
And speculation, that, in all their eyes,
No speculation wore—when the broad heavens
Were hung with forms of rare intelligence,
Teachers of heart and fancy—twiring forms,
The herds of eyes, the numerous flocking stars,
Gazing down on me, and imploring mine!
The present was my own! I made it mine,—
Enjoying it, the past was mine as well;—
I lived the life of the world, as still the world
Has render'd life to the living—yielding man
Experience of his father in his own;
Trod the same ground that they had travell'd o'er,
The sage and soldier of dim ages gone,
In the same company.—What did I need,
With the same feelings and affections fill'd—
For I drew milk from breasts which they had drawn—
To toil through their adventures? They were mine,
Already in my progress. I was taught
By the same tutor—happy that I was!

SONNETS.—DAWNINGS OF FANCY.

I.

Voices are on the winds!—I hear them now
  Foating around me, musical and sweet
  As are the waves of ocean when they meet,
Combing and flashing round some sunny prow;—

Then, as if seeking softer melody,
  Back shrinking from the lately sought embrace;
Even as the new-won virgin, bashfully,
  Love in her heart, but fear upon her face!
How exquisite, and yet how sad withal,
These murmurs, that fond meeting, and faint fall!
They swell upon my spirit's ear by night,
  And morning brings them on her purple wings,—
  Oh, Fancy!—as if feeding at thy springs,
They took from thee all voices of delight.

II.

Nor only of delight! The music swells
  To sorrow, as the rosy day declines;
  And folding up his wing among the vines,
The wandering zephyr of his garden tells
By the Euphrates.—Exiled from its flowers,
His wing is weary—he forgets its powers,
  And his heart sinks with the decaying light,—
Most wretched, the Capricious! three long hours!
  Ere dawn he plumes his wing for fresher flight,
Dreams of enduring joys in other bowers,
  And wild his song of rapture that same night!
Rapture in sadness finds his fit repose,
  As toil in sleep; and Fancy's self rebels,
Denied her evening bower and brief repose.

III.

Whoso denies this wholesome, natural want,
  Endangers her existence! She must bask
  Among the woods she rifles,—free from task,
The master's eye, and hard command,—and nap,
Where nature yields her groves and matron lap;—

Where birds sing slumber, and the hunted doe,
Assured of safety, stops a while to pant!
Thus resting she arises, prompt and strong,
  With eye all vigor,—wing prepared to go,
Rapt, heavenward, in the upward-gushing song!—
Poised like the great sea-eagle in his state,
  Sovereign 'mongst rolling clouds, careering free,
Or, like the meeker lark, at heaven's own gate,
  That, in her love, proclaims her liberty.

SONNETS.—POPULAR MISDIRECTION.

I.

How went the cry in Greece, an ominous sound,
  When Elatea fell—disaster dread,
  Presaging Chœronea! Is the tale read—
Is there no moral in the history found,
That we grope on, with tidings each day brought
  Of outposts lost to the enemy—our foe
That saps our liberties through the popular thought,
  And in our stupor, brings our virtue low.
Yet may we not despair—a nation sleeps
  Not always:—she may need repose for strength,
  And, at the perilous moment, break at length
Her bonds, as from his lair the lion leaps
To conquest, in the pride of all his powers:—
Ah! Chœronea never shall be ours!

II.

We are no more a people of the free;
  A change is on our fortunes—we forget

The high design that made our liberty
  A thing of hope and wonder, and have set
Our hearts on earthly idols, vanities,
  The childish wants of fashion, and a crowd
  Of sordid appetites that clamor loud,
The eager ear of emptiness to please.
The nobler toils that only to high thought,
  Patience and inward struggle yield the prize,
  Are ours no longer;—we no more devise
Conquests of self and fortune;—all unwrought
That glorious vein our fathers struck of yore,
Which, left unwork'd, but makes us doubly poor.

III.

Sudden, the mighty nation goes not down,
  There is no mortal fleetness in its fate;
Time,—many omens—still anticipate
  The peril that removes its iron crown
And shakes its homes with ruin! Centuries
  Fleet by in the long struggle; and great men
Rush mounted to the breach where victory lies,
  And personal virtue brings us life again!
Were it not thus, my country!—were this hope
  Not ours,—the present were a fearful time;
Vainly we summon mighty hearts to cope
  With thy oppressors,—vanity and crime—
These ride thee, as upon some noble beast,
The scoundrel jackal, hurrying to his feast.

IV.

Would we recall our virtues and our peace?
  The ancient teraphim we must restore;
  Bring back the household gods we loved of yore,

And bid our yearning for strange idols cease.
Our worship still is in the public way,—
  Our altars are the market-place;—our prayer
  Strives for meet welcome in our neighbor's ear,
And heaven affects us little while we pray.
  We do not call on God, but man, to hear;—
Nor even on his affections;—we have lost
  The sweet humility of our home desires,
  And flaunt in foreign fashions at rare cost;
Nor God our souls, nor man our hearts inspires,
  Nor aught that should to God or man be dear.

THE FIRST DREAM OF LOVE.

I.

Soft, oh! how softly sleeping
  Shadow'd by beauty she lies,
Dreams, as of rapture, creeping,
  Smile by smile, over her eyes;
Lips, oh! how sweetly parting,
  As if the delight between,
With its own warm pulses starting,
  Strove to go forth and be seen.

II.

'Tis Love, born newly of fancy,
  Brushing her heart with his plume,
That wakes, with his necromancy,
  On the tale-telling cheek the bloom;—

Ah! long as a fancy gladden,
  Sweet Love, the delighted heart,
Nor ever with passion madden,
  Nor ever with hope depart.

HAUNTED WOODS.—A FRAGMENT.

THESE woods have all been haunted, and the power
Of spells still harbors in each tree and flower;
The groves still keep, and hide, a various race,
Whom we should vainly labor to displace;
Nor were it wise, so long as we deplore
The failing virtues that we knew before;
Those precious sympathies that loved to find,
In speechless nature, voices for mankind:
That still acknowledged spirits in the beam,
Gnomes in the mountain, undines in the stream;
Dryads in woods, not near so wild as these,
And sweet, sad nymphs, that hide in ancient trees!
Here, to my faith, they still abide, and crown
The dark deep groves with beauties not their own:
Still, 'midst the sacred ring, in doubtful light,
The tricksy elves go dancing through the night;
Meet the capricious fairies, where they glide,
Sparkling in moonlight, by Saluda's side,
And, join'd in mimic battle, or in sport
More genial, find the happy night too short!
Thus the sad Indian, ever as he flew
O'er these smooth waters in his birch canoe,
Beheld afar, in light of summer eves,
Wild forms and faces glimmering through the leaves:

Bright, star-like eyes flash'd out from thickest shades,
And, softly sudden, laugh'd ascending maids;
Strange antic shapes, half mingled with the pine,
Shriek'd out, as baffled in some foul design;
Shook their fierce torches at each flitting grace,
And stamp'd in fury o'er their trysting-place;
Trampled on flowers to fairy fingers dear,
And flouted joys they had not soul to share;—
Then fled to genial swamps and thickets dark,
Where the faint glow-worm shrouds her little spark.
An envious tribe, that, ere the white man came,
The dusky savage well had learn'd to name;
Mischievous elves, that charm'd his sylvan bow,
Warp'd the shaft, erring, sent against his foe;
'Wilder'd his footsteps in the search of prey,
And led his dog aside, the scentless way;
Still, when the day was done, beside him crept,
And fill'd his dreams with horror while he slept;
Nor gave him respite, till, with hallowing rite,
His priests, with incense, soothed the demon's spite!
In these the red-man's faith was no less strong
Than that which Allegmania kept so long:
A realm as various peopled, in his creed,
As Albion recognized, and knew indeed;
With native instincts, conscious of a tie,
'Twixt earth and air, that lifts humanity,
Supplying still a void between our race
And that we dream of in the world of space;
Showing faint glimpses, shapes of cloud and light,
Of fancy born, yet precious to the sight,
And still appealing, when we droop or dream,
To worlds and hopes which thus bestow their gleam;
A light, though faint, to show us where to rise,
And wings, though feeble, which may pierce the skies.

Ah! from these woods they do not yet depart,
They win our worship still, they soothe our heart:
The ancient fancies still as strongly glow,
And still the antic shadows come and go;
Strange aspects haunt the forests, to our eyes,
As fill'd the red-man's home with mysteries;
We hear the wild chant of the eldritch race,
And see them flitting in their midnight chase:
They live for us as them. Our woodman sees,
Even now, quaint masks that lurk behind the trees;
Possess with spells that haunt him as he speeds,
Inspire his terrors, or arrest his deeds;
Until his soul grows full of faith, for which
His reason finds no answer and no speech:
He deems all true the red-man taught of spells,
Still loathly lingers where the demon dwells,
And still imagines that the charmed song,
Among the pines, will harbor in them long;
Not simply winds, communing with the boughs,
But sounds of brooding myriads, as they drowse.

THE STATESMAN.

Well, if it be that Fortune's sun is setting,
  And friends that cheer'd thee in thy happier day
Turn from thy griefs, thy glorious gifts forgetting,
  And faithless prove when faith had been thy stay:
Thou art thine own mind's master, though forsaken
  Of those who came and crouch'd while all was bright;
Thou bear'st a soul that storms have never shaken,
  And resolute will to tread the path of right.

And this is still to conquer, though we perish!
'Tis no defeat, when, steadfast in our hearts,
We yet, o'er all, the sacred purpose cherish,
Though every hope that grew with it departs;—
The will that moves us to the strife unquailing,
Still keeps the faith unchanging it believes;
Though in the hope that dream'd of conquest failing,
The future still avenges and—retrieves!

And, to thyself thus true in every fortune,
The very foes must honor who o'erthrow:
Calm, steadfast, firm—oh! why shouldst thou impórtune
The fate whose seasons ever come and go?
Thou hast no loss in ever-losing struggle,
For that thou strivest still in Duty's cause;
Rejecting still the bauble and the juggle,
True to thyself, the virtues and the laws.

SLEEPING CHILD.

My little girl sleeps on my arm all night,
And seldom stirs, save, when with playful wile,
I bid her turn, and lift her lip to mine,—
Which, even as she sleeps, she does; and sometimes then,
Half muttering in her slumbers, she declares
Her love for me is boundless. Then I take
The precious promise closer to my arms,
And, by my action—for, in such a time,
My lips can find no utterance for my heart—
Give her assurance meet that she is there

Most treasured of my jewels. Thus, tenderly,
Hour after hour, with no desire of sleep,
I watch above that large amount of hope,
With eyes made doubly vigilant by their tears,
Until the stars wane, and the yellow moon
Walks forth into the night.

THE GRAPE-VINE SWING.

Lithe and long as the serpent train,
Springing and clinging from tree to tree,
Now darting upward, now down again,
With a twist and a twirl that are strange to see:
Never took serpent a deadlier hold,
Never the cougar a wilder spring,
Strangling the oak with the boa's fold,
Spanning the beech with the condor's wing.

Yet no foe that we fear to seek
The boy leaps wild to thy rude embrace;
Thy bulging arms bear as soft a cheek
As ever on lover's breast found place:
On thy waving train is a playful hold
Thou shalt never to lighter grasp persuade;
While a maiden sits in thy drooping fold,
And swings and sings in the noonday shade!

Oh! giant strange of our southern woods,
I dream of thee still in the well-known spot,
Though our vessel strains o'er the ocean floods,
And the northern forest beholds thee not;

I think of thee still with a sweet regret,
As the cordage yields to my playful grasp—
Dost thou spring and cling in our woodlands yet?
Does the maiden still swing in thy giant clasp?

SONNET.—THE OLD MASTERS.

I REVERENCE these old masters—men who sung
Or painted, not for love of praise or fame;
Who heeded not the popular eye or tongue,
And craved no present honors for their name;
Who toil'd because they sorrow'd! In their hearts
The secret of their inspiration lay;—
When these were by the oppressor's minions wrung,
The terrible pang to utterance forced its way.
And hence it is, their passionate song imparts,
To him who listens, a like sensible woe,
That moves him much to turn aside and pray
As if his personal grief had present claim;—
Thus Danté found his muse,—the pride and shame
Of Florence;—Milton thus, and Michael Angelo!

SEASIDE SOLITUDE.

How, in this castled battlement that stands
A grim and ghastly giant o'er the sea,
As if to guard the subject smiling lands,
Safe kept in meet subjection, and so free,—

How, with a silent sadness do I love,
  When night winds all unfetter'd fly abroad,
And the pale moon, in peerless car above,
  Moves onward like some melancholy god,
    In very sadness of sublimity,
Bemoaning the great state which makes him lone;
How do I love to watch above the deep,
To hear winds whistle and the surges sweep,
And share the sadness and the silence then,
More full of speech for Thought than crowds of men;—
  And drink in lessons of the great expanse,
    That teaches still the far Eternity;
The world itself laid bare beneath the glance,
  And all made subject to the soul and eye:
While still with choir of storm the great sea rolls
Its anthem, fitting conflicts of great souls;
A mighty heart of passion; even in sleep
Heaving with saddest moans, that show the strife how deep.

MENTAL SOLITUDE.

The bells are gayly pealing, and the crowd,
The thoughtless and the happy, with light hearts,
Are moving by the casement:—I can hear
The rude din of their voices and the tramp
Of hurrying footsteps o'er the pavement nigh,
And my soul sickens in its solitude.
  Each hath his own companion, and can bend,
As to a centre of enlivening warmth,
To some abode of happiness and mirth;—

Greeted by pleasant voices,—words of cheer,
And hospitality,—whose outstretch'd hand
Draws in the smiling stranger at the door.
They go not singly by, as I should go,
But hanging on fond arms. They muse not thoughts
Of strange and timid sadness, such as mine;
But dreams of promised joys are in their souls,
And, in their ears, the music of kind words
That make them happy.
I, alas!—alone,
Of all this populous city, must remain,
Shut up in my dim chamber,—or, perchance,
If I dare venture out among the crowd,
Will be among, not of, them; and appear—
For that I have not walk'd with them before,
Nor been a sharer in their festivals—
As some strange monster brought from foreign climes
But to be baited with the thoughtless gaze,
The rude remark, cold eye and sneering lip,
Till I grow savage, and become, at last,
The rugged brute they do behold in me.

Talk not to me of solitude!—thou hast
But little of its meaning in thy thought,
And less in thy observance. It is not
To go abroad into the wilderness,
Or dart upon the ocean;—to behold
The broad expanse of prairie or of wood,
And deem,—for that the human form is not
A dweller on its bosom,—(with its shrill
And senseless clamor oft, breaking away
The melancholy of its sweet serene,
That, like a mantle, lifted by the breath
Of some presiding deity, o'erwraps,

Making all mystery and gentleness,)—
That solitude is thine. Thy thought is vain!—
That is no desert, where the heart is free
To its own spirit-worship;—where the soul,
Untainted by the breath of busy life,
Converses with the elements, and grows
To a familiar notion of the skies,
Which are its portion. That is liberty!
And the sweet quiet of the waving woods,
The solemn song of ocean—the blue skies,
That hang like canopies above the plain,
And lend their richest hues to the fresh flowers
That carpet its broad bosom,—are most full
Of solace and the sweetest company!
I love these teeming voids,—their voiceless words,
So full of truest teaching. God is there,
Walking beside me, as, in elder times,
He walk'd beside the shepherds, and gave ear
To the first whisper'd doubts of early thought,
And prompted it aright. Such wilds to me
Seem full of friends and teachers. In the trees,
The never-ceasing billows, winds and leaves,
Feather'd and finny tribes,—all that I see,
All that I hear and fancy,—I have friends,
That soothe my heart to meekness, lift my soul
To loftiest hope, and, to my toiling mind,
Impart just thoughts and safest principles.
They have a language I can understand,
When man is voiceless, or with vexing words
Offends my judgment. They have melodies
That soothe my heart to peace, even as the dame
Soothes her dear infant with a song of sounds
That have no meaning for the older ear,
And mock the seeming wise. Even wint'ry clouds

Have charms for me amid their cheerlessness,
And hang out images of love and light,
At evening, 'mong the stars,—or, ere the dusk
That specks so stilly the gray twilight's wing,
With many colors sweetly intermixt:—
And, when the breezes gather with the night,
And shake the roof-tree under which I sleep,
'Till the dried leaves enshroud me, then I hear
Voices of love and friendship in mine ear,
That speak to me in soothing, idle sounds,
And flatter me, I am not *all* alone.
  Darting o'er ocean's blue domain, or far
In the deep woods, where the gaunt Choctaw yet
Lingers to perish;—galloping o'er the bald
Yet beautiful plain of prairie,—I become
Part of the world around me, and my heart
Forgets its singleness and solitude.
But, in the city's crowd, where I am one
'Mongst many,—many who delight to throw
The altar I have worshipp'd in the dust—
And trample my best offerings—and revile
My prayers—and scorn the tribute, which I still
Devoted with full heart and purest mind
To the all-wooing and all-visible God,
In nature ever present—having no mood
With mine, nor any sympathy with aught
That I have loved;—'tis there that I am taught
The essence and the form of solitude—
'Tis there that I am lonely!—'mid a world,
To feel I have no business in that world;
And when I hear men laughing, not to join,
Because their cause of mirth is hid from me:—
To feel the lights of the assembly glare
And fever all my senses, till I grow

Stupid, or sad and boorish;—then return,
Sick of false joys and misnamed festivals,
To my own gloomy chambers, and old books
That counsel me no more, and cease to cheer,
And, like an aged dotard, with dull truths,
Significant of nothings, often told,
And told to be denied, that wear me out,
In patience, as in peace;—and then to lie,
And watch the lazy-footed night away,
With fretful nerve, that sorrows when it flies!—
To feel the day advancing which must bring
The weary night once more, that I had pray'd
Forever gone! To hear the laboring wind
Depart, in melting murmurs, with the tide,
And, ere the morn, to catch his sullen roar,
Mocking the ear, with watching overdone,
Returning from his rough lair on the seas!
If life be now denied me;—if I sit
Within my chamber when all other men
Are revelling;—if I must be alone,
Musing on idle minstrelsy and lore—
Weaving sad fancies with the fleeting hours,
And making fetters of the folding thoughts,
That crush into my heart, and canker there;—
If nature calls me to her company,
Takes up my time, teaches me legends strange,
Prattles of wild conceits that have no form,
Save in extravagant fancy of old years,
When spirits were abroad;—if still she leads
My steps away from the establish'd walks,
And, with seducing strains of syren song,
Beguiles my spirit far among the groves
Of fairy-trodden forests, that I may
Wrestle with dreams, that wear away my days,

And make my nights a peopled realm which steals
Sleep from my eyes, and peace;—if she ordains
That I shall win no human blandishment,
Nor, in the present hour, as other men,
Find meet advantage:—she will sure provide,
Just recompense—a better sphere and life,
Atoning for the past, and full of hope
In a long future;—or she treats me now,
Unkindly, and I may not help complaint.

"SUCH, O BEAUTY!"

Such, O Beauty! the amorous strains
  Sung in thy praises in happier hours;
Then the free spirit rejoiced in chains,
  But only because they were framed of flowers;
When they grew strong, with flight of years,
  To fetter the heart of the youthful rover,
The spirit felt troubled with many fears,
  And the time for laughing in chains was over.
        Beauty, yes!
The spirit felt troubled with many fears,
  And the time for laughing in chains was over.

And yet, O Beauty! thy chains, though breaking,
  And sterner grown in the strifes of men,
A look, or a lay of thine will waken
  A rapture such as they kindled then;
And sad, in its very freedom sighing,
  The spirit will turn for thy smile and say,

Ah! better far in her bondage lying,
  Than cheerlessly thus waste life away;
        Beauty, yes!
Better far in thy bondage lying,
  Than cheerlessly thus waste life away.

SONNETS.—THE CAPRICE OF THE SENSIBILITIES.

I.

True,—love hath its perils and denials—takes
  Its color from the cloud; and, with a will,
Born of capricious fancy, sometimes aches
  With its own raptures, wild and wilful still;—
Is pleased to grieve o'er griefs that may not rise,
  And finds a tempest in serenest skies;—
Suspects where it should worship, and grows cold
  When most the mutual fire is warm and bright,—
  And is, self-doom'd, a stranger to delight,
When most the entwining arms of truth would fold
The estranged one in the happiest heart-embrace!
  But these are natural aspects in the strife
Of nature, worn by all of mortal race,
  And prove far less of suffering than of life.

II.

It is, indeed, the nature that acquires,
  Even from these changing aspects, a new birth;
Caprice is but the sleep of the desires,
  As sadness is the sweet repose of mirth;—
  And all the dear variety of earth

Is so much fuel to renew her fires!
The eye that saddens now, unknowing why,
  To-morrow, with as little consciousness,
Will blaze with freshest lustres,—as the sky,
  Late sorrowing with a cloudy, cold distress,
Anon, in all her bright of blue appears!—
  Love puts on strangest aspects, that confess
A nature, not a will; and in her tears
  The very hope is born whose birth alone can bless!

III.

Not such are love's true sorrows;—in her fate
Lie deeper perils—dooms more desolate!—
Hers are the worst of fortune, since they grow
  From the excessive exquisite in life,
  She perils in the field of human strife;—
The sensibilities—the hopes that flow
From those superior fountains of the soul,
  Where all is but a dying and a birth,
A resurrection and a sacrifice;
  Which, though it happen on the lowliest hearth,
Is yet the breaking of a golden bowl,
  Still destined to renewal,—for new ties
And other sunderings,—and that mortal pain,
To know that death and birth alike are vain!

IV.

That stroke which shatters the devoted heart,
  Its faith in the beloved one—the sweet trust,
  That felt him genial and believed him just,
And rudely rends the linkéd souls apart,
Denied the old communion—is the blow
Most mortal, that the mortal meets below!

The death of the affections—the true life
   That from humanity pluck'd the cruel sting,
Which, born of its first faltering, doom'd the strife
   Heal'd only by the true heart's minist'ring!—
There is no other sorrow, born of love,
   Which love itself can heal not;—and for this,
'Twere idle any ministry to prove,—
   Since love, in loss of faith, hath lost all right to bliss!

V.

Thus is it that the heart which other woe
   But strengthens with new tendrils,—when it shakes,
Doom'd to the lightning terrors of this blow,
   Sinks, shivering with the bolt, and sudden breaks.
Fibres knit close as tendrils of the vine,
Lock'd fast and clinging to the upholding pine,—
Even as the faith is rent, which was the tree,
   Fix'd steadfast and high-towering o'er all,
   To which the affections clung, nor fear'd to fall,—
So perish all the hopes and sympathies:—
A thousand veins, and ruptured arteries
Lie sunder'd at the stroke, all bleeding free;
Wasting their precious streams upon the roots
Of the great tree that never more bears fruits!

VI.

No fruits, no life!—what matter if the tree
   Still lifts a brow erect against the sky,
Great shaft and mighty branches,—if there be
   No blossom, in his season, for the eye—
   No green of leaf, no gorgeous pageantry,
Wooing the prolific and embracing air
   To harbor in the noontide, and to brood

Still murmuring music in his slumberous mood,
While birds sit swinging with their young ones there:
Their life a summer day or less—not long,
But still a life of blossom and of song,—
The blossom and the song being each a birth,
Born only of the fruit, and born of earth,
For earth, that still love's promise might be fair!

MOTHER AND CHILD.

The wind blew wide the casement, and within—
It was the loveliest picture! a sweet child
Lay in its mother's arms, and drew its life,
In pauses, from the fountain,—the white round,
Part shaded by loose tresses, soft and dark,
Concealing, but still showing, the fair realm
Of so much rapture, as green shadowing trees
With beauty shroud the brooklet. The red lips
Were parted, and the cheek upon the breast
Lay close, and, like the young leaf of the flower,
Wore the same color—rich, and warm, and fresh:—
And such alone are beautiful. Its eye,
A full, blue gem, most exquisitely set,
Look'd archly on its world—the little imp,
As if it knew, even then, that such a wealth
Were not for all;—and with its playful hands
It drew aside the robe that hid its realm,
And peep'd and laugh'd aloud, and so it laid
Its head upon the shrine of such pure joys,
And laughing, slept. And while it slept, the tears
Of the sweet mother fell upon its cheek—

Tears, such as fall from April skies, and bring
The sunlight after. They were tears of joy;
And the true heart of that young mother then
Grew lighter, and she sang unconsciously
The silliest ballad-song that ever yet
Subdued the nursery's voices, and brought sleep
To fold her sabbath wings above its couch.

COME, WHEN THE EVENING INTO SILENCE CLOSES.

I.

Come, when the evening into silence closes,
When the pale stars steal out upon the blue;
And watchful zephyrs to the virgin roses,
Descend in sweetest murmurs, bringing dew;
Come to the heart that sadly then declining,
Would need a soothing day has never known;
Come, like those stars upon the night-cloud shining,
And bless me with a beauty all thine own.
Beauty of songs and tears,
And blessed tremulous fears—
Beauty that shrinks from every gaze but one:
Ah! for the dear delight,
The music of thy sight,
I yield the day, the lonely day, and live for night alone.

II.

It is no grief that in the night hour only,
The love that is our solace may be sought;
Day mocks the soul that is in rapture lonely,
And voices break the spell with sorrow fraught;

Better that single, silent star above us,
  And still around us that subduing hush,
As of some brooding wing, ordain'd to love us,
  That spells the troubled soul and soothes its gush;
    Shadows that still beguile,
    Sorrows that wear a smile,
Griefs that in dear delusions lead away—
    And oh! that whispering tone,
    Breathed, heard, by one alone,
That, as it dies—a wordless sound—speaks more than words can say

---

SONNETS.

OBJECTS WHICH INFLUENCE THE AMBITIOUS NATURE.

I. TROPHIES.—HOW PLANTED.

The trophies which shine out for eager eyes,
  In youth's first hour of progress, and delude
  With promise dearest to ambition's mood,
Lie not within life's limits; but arise
Beyond the realm of sunset;—phantoms bright,
  Glowing above the tomb; having their roots
  Even in the worshipper's heart;—from whence their fruits,
And all that thence grows precious to man's sight!
Thence, too, their power to lure from beaten ways
  That Love hath set with flowers; and thence the spell,
  'Gainst which the blood denied may ne'er rebel,
That leads to sleepless nights and toilsome days,
And sacrifice of all those human joys,
That, to the ambitious nature, seem but toys.

II. WHERE PLANTED.

It is the error of the impatient heart
   To hope undying gifts, even while the strife
Is worst;—and, struggling 'gainst its mortal part,
   The glorious Genius, laboring still for life,
Springs even from death to birth! 'Tis from his tomb
   The amaranth rises which must wreathe his brow,
And crown his memory with unfading bloom!—
   Rooted in best affections, it will grow,
Though water'd by sad tears, and watch'd by pride
Made humble in rejection! Love denied,
Shall tend it through all seasons, and shall give
   Her never-failing tenderness,—though still
   Be the proud spirit and the unyielding will,
That, through the mortal, made the immortal live!

III. TRIUMPH.

The grave but ends the struggle! Follows then
   The triumph, which, superior to the doom,
Grows loveliest, and looks best, to mortal men,
   Purple in beauty, towering o'er the tomb!
Oh! with the stoppage of the impulsive tide
   That vex'd the impatient heart with needful strife,
   The soul that is Hope's living leaps to life,
And shakes her fragrant plumage far and wide!
Eyes follow then in worship which but late
   Frown'd in defiance;—and the timorous herd,
   That sleekly waited for another's word,
Grow bold, at last, to bring,—obeying Fate,—
   The tribute of their praise, but late denied,—
Tribute of homage which is sometimes—hate!

IV. GLORY AND ENDURING FAME.

Thus Glory hath her being! Thus she stands
  Star-crown'd—a high divinity of woe:
Her temples fill, her columns crown all lands,
  Where lofty attribute is known below.
  For her the smokes ascend, the waters flow,
The grave foregoes his prey, the soul goes free;
  The gray rock gives out music,—hearthstones grow
To temples at her word—her footprints see,
  On ruins, that are thus made holiest shrines,
Where Love may win devotion, and the heart,
  That with the fire of Genius inly pines,
May find the guidance of a kindred art—
And, from the branch of that eternal tree,
Pluck fruits at once of death and immortality!

THE SWALLOWS.

With no signal of their coming,
  With no promise of the spring,
With the dawning hark their humming,
  And, across the window-pane,
  See each gayly flashing wing,—
As delighted to discover,
While about the eaves they hover,
  That all's safe at home again!

Such a merry, screaming clatter,
  Such a chorus of delight;—
Something more must be the matter,
  Than the simple certainty

Of the savage winter's flight,
And their ancient homes secure;
Still upon the slender ashes,
Hanging free their calabashes,*
And still wide each aperture!

Friend of pigeon and of chicken,
Lately trembling at the hawk,
Well may that old ruffian sicken,
As he, slowly circling, sees
Those who come his sports to balk,—
Those that swift on arrowy pinion,
Drive him from his dread dominion,
And arrest his butcheries.†

Modest champions of the feeble,
Thus content in dwellings rude,
Joyful, and with happy treble,
Singing still in gladsome mood,
Ever happy, ever busy,
Whirling still in circles dizzy,
Making gay the solitude;—

Ye are welcome!—at your coming,
With your motion wild and glad,
Still rejoicing with your humming,
Hearts but lately all so sad;

* The gourd or calabash, hung upon ash or cypress poles, being, as every one knows, the home usually assigned to the swallow at all Southern farmsteads.

† The swallow is cherished, as he protects the chicken from the hawk. This he does by darting *above* him, and descending rapidly, with flapping wings, above the eyes of the outlaw.

Tidings sweet ye bring to me,
Singing ever—Winter's flying,
Spring is nigh our buds supplying,
And the birds and blessings free!

SONNET.—DEATH IN YOUTH.

They tell us—whom the gods love die in youth!
'Tis something to die innocent and pure;
But death without performance is most sure
Ambition's martyrdom—worst death, in truth,
To the aspiring temper, fix'd in thought
Of high achievement! Happier far are they
Who, as the Prophet of the Ancients taught,
Hail the bright finish of a perfect day!
With fullest consummation of each aim,
That wrought the hope of manhood—with the crown
Fix'd to their mighty brows, of amplest fame—
Who smile at death's approaches and lie down
Calmly, as one beneath the shade-tree yields,
Satisfied of the morrow and green fields.

SUNSET PIECE.

All day had we been gliding o'er the seas,
With swan-like motion; for the skies were fair,
The waters smooth, or by a winning breeze,
But rippled into beauty far and near;
Our bark shot onward with a glad career,

Like a brave steed with motion swift and free;
And now, as to the growing land we near,
Its headlands rising into majesty,
The mighty sun prepares to seek the embracing sea.

It is a sovereign's burial! O'er his brow
Hangs the imperial crown, a golden sphere;
While dark, in sullen majesty below,
The waters gathering in their mighty lair,
Rise, swelling into mountains! Far and near,
Mellow'd to soften'd twilight, a repose,
Sweet as the mild breath of the autumn air,
Is down upon the earth at evening's close:
No light too strongly beams, no breath too rudely blows.

But all above and all around,—the all
That links the visible to humanity—
Wound to a pleasant and seductive fall,
Woos the worn heart and wins the weary eye;
A pale star o'er yon steep acclivity,
Beckons the modest evening to her side,
Ere yet the dying monarch has thrown by
His purple, and, with glance of love and pride,
Sends peace throughout her empire, far and wide.

A freshness in the breeze, a pleasant breath,
As of a living odor, late from vales
Undimm'd by shadow, undeprived by death,
Of greenest verdure or of sweetest gales—
At fits it swells aloft, and then exhales
Away in music,—while a muttering sound,
As of the ocean when the tempest wails,
Breaks through the yielding tree-tops—all around
The day droops faintly clear, but purples still the ground.

Far off, the tall rocks, in his latest glance,
Glow like Vesuvius! On each rugged brow
Capricious fires ascend, recede, advance,
Down sinking, then up rushing, as the flow
Of waves that seek the beach when seas are low,
Fond of old places! His sweet smile subdues
Their harsher aspects; warms with godlike glow,
The cold he may not conquer; 'till they lose
The aspects harsh and wild that still our steps refuse.

Love in his dying purpose, he relieves
The gloom of parting: thus, the cloud that far
Still follows on his footstep, now receives
His smile; and made all radiant like a star,
Glows in soft crimson and around his car
Curtains his couch as downward still he hies;—
Tempering the glorious light it may not mar,
The lovely drapery closes o'er his eyes,
Yet keeps his latest gift, his robe of thousand dyes.

Leap the wild billows round him as he goes,
Reddening their edges as in noonday pride;
Still struggling, as the giant girt by foes,
And failing but still fighting, eagle-eyed,
With full unfailing heart and sovereign stride,
Till the prevailing waters with wild roar,
Do homage to the glories they defied,—
Their realm of waste with fresh lights purpled o'er,
Borne far, from wave to wave, along the receding shore.

He sinks and in the heavens another star
Glides forth to her that beckon'd from the blue;
And the young moon in pearly-cinctured car,
Rides up where ocean's barriers bind the view.
Silvering the cloud she cannot quite subdue,

Soothing the strife she may not hope to sway,
Her chaster livery chides the purple's hue,
And drapes the glare that made the garish day:
Thus Love doth Glory spell to choose her milder way.

SONNETS.—TO MY FRIEND.

I.

Ambition owns no friend yet be thou mine!—
I have not much to win thee,—yet if song
Born of affection may one name prolong,
My lay shall seek to give a life to thine.
Let this requite thee for the honoring thought
That has forgiven me each capricious mood;
Dealt gently with my phrensies, school'd my blood,
And still with love my sad seclusion sought.
And when the gray sod rises o'er my breast,
Be thou the guardian of my deeds and name,
Defend me from the foes who hunt my fame,—
And, when thou show'st its purity, attest
Mine eye was ever on the sun, and bent,
Where clouds and difficult rocks make steep the great as

II.

Thou wilt remark my fate when I am dead;
Let not fools scoff above me and proclaim
That I had vainly struggled after fame,
'Till the good oil of my young life was shed,
And I became a mockery, and fell
Into the yellow leaf before my time;
A sacrifice, even in my earliest prime,
To that which thinn'd the heavens and peopled hell!

How few will understand us at the best,
  How few so yield their sympathies, to know
What cares have robb'd us of our nightly rest,
  How stern our trial, how complete our woe,—
And how much more our doom it was than pride,
To toil in devious ways with none who loved beside!

FLOWERS IN AUTUMN.

I.

Sweet roses! that alone beneath the sky,
The mellow sky of autumn, are, of all
Life's and remember'd nature's blandishments,
Purest and sweetest,—ye shall haply fall
Into a yellow sickliness and die!
The gentle heart that knows your luxury,
And deems ye sweetest pilgrims of the wood,
And found ye always gracious in your mood,
Bringing to Fancy its most precious food,
Such fate might well appall,—
But that your purple hues and delicate scents
Have taken fast abode in memory,
She will not lose ye, will not let ye fly!

II.

Upon each broken stalk,
Drooping in autumn's tears all desolate,
Sadly, in wild but well-accustom'd walk,
She mourns your hapless fate,
The beauty of your youth, the shortness of your date!
No charm is lost ye had for her when first
Your little petals into blossom burst!

Well she remembers, when in early spring,
The swallow won his wing,
How she hath sought in thought-imprison'd mood,
Your nun-like sweetness in your solitude,—
Glad to commune, unhooded monitors,
With such as wore a sorrow sweet like hers!

III.

And ye repaid her, well repaid, in kind;
For where, in what sweet vale
Of Yemen or of Trebizond,—
Or lands yet far beyond,
Decreed to beauty and the joys of earth,
When summer's infant warbler, from a throat
Bursting with joyous song and attic note,
Pours to the blossoming year his garrulous tale—
Could she have stray'd to find
Such beauty as ye 'herited from birth,
Such sweetness as ye lavish'd on the gale
At the warm wooing of the southern wind?

IV.

Life was a joy to ye forever, yet
Ye shudder not to die;
Your leaves are pale, but with a sweet regret,
That half persuades a faith that every sigh
Of parting hath its pleasure. Ye betray
No anguish, offer up no prayer to stay;
With feeble yearnings striving to oppose
The blight that o'er ye blows.
Sure some true instinct bids ye moralize,
And fits ye to restore to the pure skies
The sweets we know ye by.
So meekly to your doom
Ye bend to meet the summoning of death,

And, with no murmuring breath,
Yield beauty, sweet and bloom!

V.

Happy, thrice happy, perishing in sweet,
While yet the bloom is on ye and the scent
Is soft about ye, and the birds repeat,
At parting, the same songs of love and joy
That hail'd your budding from the firmament.
Death may destroy
Your being—not your beauty or your bliss—
And solace lives in this;
For thus ye know not that ye fade and fall,
Melting, as 'twere, into the sleep of all,
With a sweet prelude calm that shows like heaven!
No tender strings are riven,
Ye know not pangs—ye feel no venom'd dart
Go griding through the heart!
Ah! happy thus to part!
To go from life—its little hopes, its toys,
The idle of its promise and its noise—
Calmly as into slumbers that desire
No counsel of the awakening and the dawn,—
As bright flames in the hearth at night expire,
Nor say when they are gone!

VI.

Pale flowers, ye teach the lessons that I feel,
And, with a pictured gaze, lingering I look
Upon your parted leaves as in a book,
Which doth most pure philosophies reveal.
Your beauty hath not spoil'd ye, to deny
Your sweetness to the fond and hungering sense;

Ye bloom to glad the heedless wanderer's eye,
And ask no recompense.
Ye serve with meekness as with sweet, and go,
Even as ye came, in silence, nor complain
That they who loved ye, whom ye gladden'd so,
Would have ye still remain.

THE LAND OF THE PINE.

I.

THE land of the pine,
The cedar, the vine,
Oh! may this blessed land ever be mine;
Lose not in air
Breezes that bear
Blossoms and odors, the song and the prayer.

II.

Take not from mine eye
The blue of its sky,
Bid not the soul of its loveliness die;
Still let me see
The bloom on its tree
Still bring its blossoms and blessings to me.

III.

The mountain, the vale,
Each hath a tale
Of valor that shrunk not in days of our bale—
Valor that stood
Fearless, though blood
Stream'd from his gushing veins, free, like a flood.

IV.

And oh! may the song
The burden prolong,
That told of our solace in days of our wrong;
Woman's sweet strain,
Rising o'er pain,
Cheering her warrior to combat again!

THE INUTILE PURSUIT.

Labors he then for naught, who thus pursues
What you misdeem a vision? Does he build
Vain fancies only, warm delusions, up,
And profitless chimeras;—still deceived,—
Cheating himself with hopes which haply cheat
None other than himself? Are these his toils?—
And you who work in more substantial ways,
And vex the seasons, man, all elements,
In multiplying gains—you are more wise,
And laugh to scorn the fool whose idle aim,
Like the warm painter of his own bright hues
Enamor'd, would impart to things around,
The glories that are growing in his heart
And kindling up his fancy into flame.

His are vain follies, but can yours be less,
And what are their delights? I will not ask—
But yon wild dreamer gazing on the stars
As if they were his kindred, what are his?
He gazes on them long, with musing mood
That thinks not once of earth. His spirit flies

Afar, on eagle pinions—he hath lost
The world which is around him—he hath gain'd
The world which is above him; and he feels
A mightier spirit working in his soul
Than thou hast ever dream'd of. He hath thoughts
That yield him strength and life—a treasury
In which thy gold is dross; and couldst thou give
Thy thousands in the barter, they could buy
No portion of the empire he hath won
In the fond thought he strives in. He hath felt
That life should have due play, and every nerve
Susceptible of consciousness, should do
Its separate function, ministering to the whole,
Or you have never lived, or lived in vain—
Having quick feelings, generous taste and blood,
At waste or rioting, or unemploy'd,
And damming up the system they should move.
You see no charm in those mysterious lights,
He follows evermore with eyes of thought,
And hold the worship madness which bestows
No worldly profit. Thou hast yet to learn
The things of highest profit to the heart
Are never things of trade. 'Twould be thy shame,
Star-gazing like yon dreamer, to be seen
By brother tradesmen. They would jeer thee much
With alehouse humor; and their truculent wit
Would bring the creature blood into thy cheeks,
And thou wouldst feel among thy brother men
As thou hadst done some crime, and for a while
Would shrink from the relation of thy deeds.

He thou rebukest in no kindly wise
Hath no such shame within him. In that star
He hath survey'd this hour, he joys to think

He looks on God's own handiwork and deems,
So far as he may venture on such theme,
The structure of that planetary light
Marvellous as his own, and born to shine
When he and thou, and all of us are dead!
Thence doth he draw a hope—a glorious hope—
That this poor struggle—thou, for earth's goods and gear,
And he, as thou hast thought, grappling at naught,
But fancies and a shadow—will not be,
What his quick spirit teaches him is life.
The difference 'twixt his hope and thine is great,
If thou hast never tutor'd thus thy heart,
Nor felt of these delusions. He, indeed,
Lives on them ever—is made up of them,
And glories more in that thou think'st thy shame,
Than any Greek who won a hecatomb,
Or Roman with his triumph. Nor in this
Alone, he gathers fuel for the mood
That lessons his wild spirit. In all things,
For the vain labor thou dost so deplore,
Mind hath its compensation. Ideal worlds,
Where spirits of departed myriads roam,
Are in the poet's fancy. He surveys,
In every leaf, each waving tree and bush,
Wild ocean or still brooklet, rippling down
Through twigs and bending osiers night and day,
The form of some enjoyment—some true word
From never-swerving teachers, building up
The moral of his faith into a pile,
Its apex in the heavens. Nor, in this work
Of self-perfection and self-eminence,
Lacks he for aid and fellowship. They come—
Spirits and whispering shades, that in the hush,
The stillness of deep forests, are abroad,

Obedient to his beck, whose lifted heart
May see them, and demand their services,
And make them slaves or teachers at his will.

Mock not the dream you may not understand,
Nor laugh to scorn the spirit whose pursuit
Stands not within the custom of the crowd.
The God who, to the offices of trade
Impell'd your aim, to him, perchance, assign'd
A duty—not like yours and yet not less
A duty—and he but pursues it now,
Even as assign'd him. The still flower that hides,
With speckled leaf, secure beneath yon cliff,
Gives odor to the breeze that cheers the heart
Of the consumptive—not less blest in this
Sad office, than the tree whose inner ring
Yields the small pouncet-box from which you feed
That nose you turn up, with so wise an air,
At the poor gazer on the journeying stars.

SONNETS.—THE SOUL IN IMAGINATIVE ART.

I.

Methinks each noble purpose of man's heart,
  Declared by his performance, crowns his works
  With a becoming spirit, which still lurks
In what he builds, nor will from thence depart,
Though time bestows it on the solitude,
  The solitude on Ruin, and her gray,
  In moss and lichen honoring decay,
Makes her a refuge where a nobler mood

Had rear'd a temple to diviner art,
  And based its shrines on worship. In the stone
  Dismember'd, sits that guardian shape alone,
Twin-being with the precious trust whose birth
  Brought down a wandering genius to a throne,
And gave him thence a realm and power on earth.

II.

Thy thought but whisper'd rises up a spirit,
  Wing'd, and from thence immortal. The sweet tone,
  Freed by thy skill from prisoning wood or stone,
Doth thence for thine a tribute soul inherit!
When from the genius speaking in thy mind,
  Thou hast evolved the godlike shrine or tower,
That moment does thy matchless art unbind
  A spirit born for earth, and arm'd with power,
The fabric of thy love to watch and keep
  From utter desecration. It may fall,
  Thy structure,—and its gray stones topple all,—
But he who treads its portals feels how deep
A presence is upon him,—and his word
Grows hush'd, as if a shape, unseen beside him heard.

III.

At every whisper we endow with life
  A being of good or evil,—who must thence,
  Allegiance yield to that intelligence
Which, calling into birth decreed the strife
Which he must seek forever! The good thought
  Is born a blessed angel that goes forth,
  In ministry of gladness through the earth
Still teaching what is love, by love still taught!
The evil joins the numerous ranks of ill,

And, born of curses, through the endless years,
'Till Time shall be no more, and human tears
Dried up in judgment,—must his curse fulfil!
Dream'st thou of what is blessing or unblest,
Thou tak'st a God or Demon to thy breast!

THE SHADED WATER.

When that my mood is sad, and in the noise
And bustle of the crowd I feel rebuke,
I turn my footsteps from its hollow joys
And sit me down beside this little brook:
The waters have a music to mine ear
It glads me much to hear.

It is a quiet glen as you may see,
Shut in from all intrusion by the trees,
That spread their giant branches, broad and free,
The silent growth of many centuries;
And make a hallow'd time for hapless moods,
A sabbath of the woods.

Few know its quiet shelter,—none like me,
Do seek it out with such a fond desire,
Poring, in idlesse mood on flower and tree,
And listening as the voiceless leaves respire,—
When the far travelling breeze, done wandering,
Rests here his weary wing.

And all the day, with fancies ever new,
And sweet companions from their boundless store,

Of merry elves bespangled all with dew,
  Fantastic creatures of the old time lore,—
Watching their wild but unobtrusive play,
I fling the hours away.

A gracious couch,—the root of an old oak,
  Whose branches yield it moss and canopy,—
Is mine—and so it be from woodman's stroke
  Secure, shall never be resign'd by me;
It hangs above the stream that idly plies,
Heedless of any eyes.

There, with eye sometimes shut but upward bent,
  Sweetly I muse through many a quiet hour,
While every sense on earnest mission sent,
  Returns, thought-laden, back with bloom and flower
Pursuing, though rebuked by those who moil,
A profitable toil.

And still the waters trickling at my feet,
  Wind on their way with gentlest melody,
Yielding sweet music which the leaves repeat,
  Above them, to the gay breeze gliding by,—
Yet not so rudely as to send one sound
Through the thick copse around.

Sometimes a brighter cloud than all the rest
  Hangs o'er the archway opening through the trees,
Breaking the spell that, like a slumber press'd
  On my worn spirit its sweet luxuries,—
And, with awaken'd vision upward bent,
I watch the firmament.

How like—its sure and undisturb'd retreat,
  Life's sanctuary at last, secure from storm—

To the pure waters trickling at my feet,
  The bending trees that overshade my form;
So far as sweetest things of earth may seem
Like those of which we dream.

Such, to my mind, is the philosophy
  The young bird teaches, who, with sudden flight,
Sails far into the blue that spreads on high,
  Until I lose him from my straining sight,—
With a most lofty discontent to fly,
Upward, from earth to sky.

AT A CHILD'S GRAVE.

SLEEP, dear one, in thy lowly bed,—
  We strew thy grave with flowers,
Yet know that happier dawns shall shed
Such brightness round thy infant head,
  As never gladden'd ours!

Not long thy sleep!—a summer night,
  And then the eternal day,
All joy;—for sin hath brought no blight
To check thy free and happy flight
  To bowers where all is gay.

Gay in the sinless thought, and dear
  With pure delights, that grow
Still, in the eternal sunshine there,
To music, such as mortal sphere
  May dream, but never know!

Already, on thy infant face,
The soft repose would seem
To shadow forth the dawning grace
Of an ethereal hope and place,
Heaven's opening gates and gleam.

Ah! happier thus, and vain the tears
That vex thy sweet repose;
Why should thy hopes awake our fears,
Thy growing glories prompt our cares,
Thy raptures move our woes?

Thou'st 'scaped the cell—hast broke the chain,
Already wear'st thy wings;
Wilt never feel the grief again,
Wilt never know the guilt, the pain,
That vex all mortal things!

Already, at heaven's gate, with songs—
Thy angel gift at birth—
Proclaim'st to glad and greeting throngs,
Thy freedom from the woes and wrongs
That gloom'd thy home on earth!

That gloom it still to guardian eyes,—
That move their tears,—that wrest
From the strong bosom of man the sighs,
And wring with woe the soul that lies
Deep down in woman's breast.

Yet why the woe? For thee? And thou,
Afar and joyous!—Shame!—
Wouldst bring thee back, thus heavenward now,
To pangs of heart, to clouds of brow,
Long sorrows, strifes and blame!

Why heart so sad? fond eyes why weep?
   Cease mourners! Would ye wake
This little dreamer from the sleep,
That seems so beautiful and deep,
   His weary eyelids take?

REMINISCENCE.

Whose is the heart that never beat,
   With all it fancied yet of joy,
Returning to that blest retreat
   Where he so fondly roved a boy;
When, after years of wandering grief,
   Pursuing phantoms sweet but vain,
His wearied spirit seeks relief
   In dear but homely haunts again?
When the old roof-tree fresh appears,
   The lowly cottage-thatch and dome,
Which shelter'd well his boyish years,
   And taught the virtues sweet of home.
The well-known plain, the ancient grove,
   In all unchanged, as when he sped,
By Fate or Fancy taught to rove,
   To worlds that gave him naught instead!

Ah! sicklied in the wasting chase,
   By idlest hopes misled no more,
How fondly doth his thought retrace
   The scenes that fill'd his heart before!
Here still the oak whose spreading arms
   Gave shelter from the noonday heat;—
Here still the maid whose childish charms

His childish fancy felt were sweet;
Here still the mead whose ample grounds
Gave scope to boyhood's eager flight;
And there the "old-field school," whose sounds
Spoke less for study than delight.

How natural do they all appear,
By time untouch'd, by age unbent;
The maiden still more bright and fair,
More wise and yet as innocent;
The oak scarce lustier in its might,
With bearded moss well-known of old,
And groves that gladden green in sight,
With song-bird gay and squirrel bold!

How swift the backward glance which runs
O'er thousand memories still as new
As if, unchanged by thousand suns,
The heart were fresh and changeless too!
What loves, what strifes, what hopes and fears
Grow thick about the laboring thought,
Until, unconscious of its tears,
The eye no longer sees the sought.
Memory, triumphant o'er the past,
Restores each dear possession gone;
And the world's orphan, long outcast,
Deems each lost treasure still his own!
Oh! stay the dream! Let Memory sway,
Nor all too soon the truth unfold,—
The cottage roof-tree in decay,
The sire, the friend, the maiden cold!

EVENING BY THE SEA-SHORE.

How, with a spell of sweetness all her own,
  The dew-eyed evening hallows the broad land!
She rises like a sovereign to her throne;
  Earth sleeps; the waters murmur on the strand;
A breathing calm descending from the skies,
Wraps her wide realm in happiest harmonies.

There is no ruder breath than stirs the flowers,
  Winning their proffer'd odor;—earth and air,
The sea,—even down amid the coralline bowers,
  Seen through the perilous waters,—all is fair;
God's spirit, like a spell-word sent abroad,
Subdues earth's strife, makes sweet each gift of God!

The little wavelet breaking on the shore,
  Brings with it kindly mission from the deep:
Its strifes at rest, its angry terrors o'er,
  It feels the calm of brightness o'er it creep;
Shares in the kindred blessing of the skies,
And hallow'd like the land, in holiest beauty lies.

The winds that travell'd on its breast all night,
  And rock'd their own great cradle till they slept,
Have caught up sweetest odors in their flight,
  From the soft Haytien gardens;—they have swept
Fruit forests, where the generous tribute grows
Unheeded, and in vain its wealth on earth bestows.

What tidings doth such mournful truth convey
  Of savage and regardless nature there!
Still the wild man, untutor'd to obey,
  Makes foul the realm that Heaven hath made most fair:

The heart that is not gentle hath no eyes
For beauty, and esteems no loving harmonies.

His mood is in the dark; he loves the night
  Even in its stormier aspects;—skies, to him,
Which God hath robed in sweet, give no delight;
  The moon herself might just as well be dim;
Breezes of bliss that sweep the placid sea,
Sing in his ears no song of sweet humanity.

Ah! dear their several voices in my breast,
  Teaching the moral loving faith makes strong;
There is a hope that will not be repress'd,—
  The strifes of earth shall cease and human wrong
Be but a theme for fiction—of a race
That lived in barbarous times, nor had the means of grace.

I feel it in the picture round me spread;
  Earth link'd with heaven; old ocean won to calm,
And glassy smooth, as for an angel's tread;
  Winds musical and zephyrs full of balm;
And the wild passions of my soul, they rest:—
There is not now a wrong within my breast.

I do forgive mine ancient enemy;—
  I would that he were nigh to hear my prayer;
God's light be shining now upon his eye,
  God's blessed voice, in mercy, reach his ear:
Hath he a child—may it be blest as she,
The one whom Heaven hath spared, of all my flock, to me.

These winds have blessings in them; they have come
  From happiest realms where sorrow never dwells;
They rouse the languid nature to new bloom,
  The thought expands, the soul in triumph swells;

Ah! for the power this feeling to impart,
To tell these raptures rising in my heart!

The affections that have slumber'd in the strife,
  Sweet charities that human strifes subdue,
And virtues, that man seldom keeps through life,
  Return once more, to prove his nature true:
Still may the soul its fondest hope maintain,
When such as these come back to strengthen love again.

Oh! precious ministry of Eve, whose peace
  Thus still commends the harmonies that soothe;
Still with thy stars in the great vault increase,
  Still with thy breezes freshen hope with youth;
Breathe calm upon the hearts that strive with hate,
And smile on homes by wrong made desolate.

CONGAREE BOAT-HORN BY MOONLIGHT.

I.

As a bird leaving some desolate shore,
  Slowly unclosing his vans for the flight,
Then upward cleaving the sky that before,
  Softly reposing, lay sweet in the night;
Thus gently soaring from Congaree's stream,
  Swelling and spreading through forest and bay,
A pinion exploring in search of a beam,
  Soothing and shedding a bliss on its way!

II.

Luscious in sadness and lovely in light,
  Melting while swelling and failing when won,

Tears of a gladness that, born of a flight,
  Weeps the rebelling that leaves her undone!
Oh! that a billow thus swelling and fair,
  Should ever subsiding steal off from the bright;
Music its pillow and rapture so rare,
  Ever more gliding through dreams of its night.

III.

Wings that, ascending, still bear me away,
  Lose me not, falling from rapture's own sphere;
With my thought blending its happiness sway,
  As a voice calling through measureless air;
Still, with these daughters of Congaree's stream,
  Born of thee only in moonlight and song,—
Still o'er these waters ascend with a gleam,
  'Till with the lonely thou leavest a throng.

SONNETS.—INVOLUNTARY STRUGGLE.

I.

Not in the rashness of warm confidence,
  Too vainly, self-assured that I was strong,
To struggle for and reach that eminence,
  Around whose rugged steeps such terrors throng;
Did I resolve upon the perilous toil
  Which calls for man's best strength and hardihood,
Ere he may win the height and take the spoil;—
  But that a spirit stronger than my mood,
Stood ever by and drave me to the task!—
Oh! not in vain presumption did I choose

The barren honors of the unfruitful Nine,
Sure that no favor from them did I ask;
Small resolution did it need of mine,
To bind me to the service of the Muse!

II.

Even as the boy whom the stern prophet sire
Devotes, in some deep forest, with a vow—
So, with no thought of mine, and no desire,
Was I constrain'd to seek and sworn to bow
At altars, whose strange gods did never tire
Of service, but commanded night and day!
I knew no sports of comrades,—when in play
My young companions shouted, I was sad;
Fill'd with strange yearnings,—summon'd still away
To that lone worship—watchful, yet not glad!
Shall it be deem'd a voluntary mood
That leads the boy from boyhood,—sports he loves,—
The merry games of comrades,—still to brood,
While others laugh, in melancholy groves?

TO THE MOCK-BIRD,

SINGING GAYLY IN MY ROOF-TREES THE NIGHT AFTER THE DEATH OF ONE OF MY CHILDREN.

The grief that is at riot in my heart
Would harshly chide to silence thy sweet song,
Vain minstrel, that beside my window sing'st,
Couch'd in thy guarded nest, of all its joys,—
Its peace secure from spoiler—its delights,
That spring from mutual souls, with mutual wings,
That know one course for flight, and seek no more;

Thus linking, through the long, long summer day,
Their happy, idle songs.
Thy rapture brings
My grief. Thou mock'st me, though thou little know'st,
With hopes I cannot feel, and loves that now
Shall make me blest no more. Go, make thy nest
In gardens, where the thoughtless ear of joy
May list thee,—and the idle lips of youth
Give thee meet welcome, in a strain as loud,
Though not so sweet as thine. Beneath my tree
Sits Sorrow. At her feet her treasure lies—
Her young! Go, tremble in thy peaceful nest,
And know, no innocence is so secure
That Death presumes not. Happiest songs like thine,
Caroll'd above that young bird at its birth;
And oh! what joyful dreams were in the hearts
Of the fond pair that watch'd it. Idlest dreams,
Of sweetest summer days, when all their toil
Should be to guide its little wings in flight,
And hearken to its callow song of love,
That now can never rise. Leave this lone tree!—
Sing not those wild and vagrant notes that make
The sad heart loathe thy accents. Other groves
Will give thee shelter, where no spoiler comes,
Or latest comes. Grief claims this home for hers,
For solitude and mourning. Here she craves
More fit companionship with ghostly thoughts;
Shadows that might be smiles, but for the cloud
About them; and the tenderest loves that grew
To sorrows, in the morning of their day,
And so were hallow'd. 'Tis no home for thee!—
When thou hast lost thy brood—when the hawk strikes
Thy fledgling, come thou back and take thy rest,
As thou hast done of old, within thy tree;

And sing, if sing thou canst. I will not chide,
For then, methinks, thy strain will, like mine own,
Tell of thy treasure—of its loveliness,
Bright, dazzling eyes, and of its little chirp,
All sweetness, but which never swell'd to song.

SONNETS.—DESPONDENCY AND SELF-REPROACH.

I.

Oh friend, but thou art come to see me die!
I parted from thee as I think in tears,
Alas! in tears that we should meet again:
Yet have they been my proper property,
And not for me to boast their needful pain,
Since 'twas my wilful, sad perversity,
That made them mine in my unreasoning years!
Yet if thou com'st for solace, give me thine,
For sympathy with sorrow still endears;
Grief seeks her happiest medicine in grief,
And, doom'd no more in silence to repine,
Finds in the kindred fortune best relief!
Ah! weeping thus, in such sweet company,
Methinks this sorrow is not wholly mine!

II.

Hadst thou come sooner! But 'tis not too late
To soothe, though late to save! Thou canst not know
The profligate waste of hope, the scorn of fate
Which brings me now to this unmeasured woe!
The bitter birthright of unreckoning will,
The much too perfect freedom of my youth—

Oh privilege! to youth so perilous still,
  Given by a fate as void of love as truth!
To these I owe this sorrow, and to these
  The ruin that awaits my little bark,
Driven with too docile breezes on the seas
  Till on the rocks, when skies grew sudden dark,
Foundering, she darted high, to sink as low
As hate might joy to see, as guilt and grief may go.

III.

Ah! *thou* didst use to steer her chartfully,
  But when we parted, wilful on the deep,
  I launch'd, too bold the modest shore to keep,
Considering not the storm-conceiving sky,
The wind's caprice; that still a music gave,
  As for an infant's slumber; nor the rocks,
That, fraudulent lurking, hush'd their wonted roar,
And buried their white heads along the shore,
  Till, in their gripe, their keel-destroying shocks
Wreck'd me forever! Thou art late to save;
  But thou wilt raise a beacon on the steep,
That other wrecks will happen here no more;
And if thou build it from this wreck of mine,
Even though it shame my grave, 'twill honor thine.

STANZAS IN APRIL.

A FEW light drifts of fleecy snow,
  And all the skies are bright again,
While gusts of March subdued, now blow
  In murmurs only o'er the plain;

They speak of milder guests at hand,
  And gentler powers that take the sway,
Sweet nymphs of Spring, a joyous band,
  That dance around the maiden May!

Ah! precious flowers, that to the heart
  Appeal with promise long to cheer;
Beneath my feet I see ye start,
  In token of the awakening year;
Even while the snow-drift sweeps the plain,
  Your leaves of blue are gleaming low,
Above the very spot again,
  Which made your graves a year ago.

Ye had your mission for a while,
  And served as teachers sweet of love,
As infant souls appear to smile,
  Then flee, to tempt our souls above;
A thousand seasons hence, when I
  Within a grave like yours recline,
My children shall your blossoms spy,
  And muse with grateful thoughts like mine.

A LAST PRAYER.

I.

SWEET be the laughing skies around,
  And sunny flowers be seen,
And let a carpet strew the ground,
  Of summer's richest green—
Thus, when the weary strife is o'er,
  Should still our parting be;

I would not have one heart deplore
When it remembers me.

II.

Lay me in pleasant earth's embrace
When all things smile around,
When eyes of gentleness may trace
Sweet blossoms on the ground—
When merriest birds delight to sing,
And chirping insects swell
A gracious note of early spring,
O'er the spot wherein I dwell.

III.

Not that, when slumbering in its shade,
My 'wilder'd soul may dream
That I shall hear one cricket's chirp,
Or wandering mock-bird's scream ;
But, at a time when all are glad,
If the dead may solaced be,
I would be sure if aught was sad,
It was not so through me.

IV.

I would not have a stone to mark
The place of my repose,
Nor, chronicled in clumsy verse,
The story of my woes—
My virtues, such as are my own,
In some true heart will bloom—
My vices, when I'm dead and gone,
Should moulder in my tomb.

V.

There let the summer's leaflets blow,
  And blossom 'neath the morn,
And primrose buds and daisies grow,
  The moment spring is born—
And let the hours, a sweet serene,
  Around my dwelling throng—
While birds and bees with vocal hum,
  Make merry all with song.

VI.

And if in life there be one heart
  That song or speech of mine,
Counsell'd by erring sympathies,
  Hath tutor'd to repine—
Let not that gentle heart upbraid,
  With eye or aspect dim,
The father of the wayward verse
  When it remembers him.

VII.

Or, if the latest prayer be vain,
  And some fond heart shall weep,
And pour above his grave a strain
  Of memories, sad and deep;
Let the tear fall in loneliness,
  I would not crowds should see
The dear but silent intercourse
  Such heart shall hold with me.

ZEPHYRS, THAT WAIT ON MY LADY.

A SOUTHERN AREYTO.

I.

Zephyrs, that wait on my lady,
Plumes, that still soothe her to rest,
My spirit grows jealous already,
Lest in blessing ye too should be blest;
Yet lift ye the curls of her tresses,
And bend to her lips at each sigh,
And fold her in fondest caresses,
That these may be mine when ye fly;—
Sweet zephyrs,
These bring me whenever ye fly!

II.

I know why ye tend on the showers,
I know why ye glide to the deep,
And watch by the side of the flowers
To rifle their lips as they sleep;
Their freshness and odor ye carry
To woo the fair maiden to rest,
And then at her lattice ye tarry,
Like blessings to rob from her breast:
Sly zephyrs!
Would, like ye, I could also be blest!

SUMMER-NIGHT WIND.

How soothingly, to close the sultry day,
Comes the sweet breeze from off the murmuring waves,
That break away in music!—and I feel
As a new spirit were within my veins
And a new life in nature. I awake
From the deep weight of weariness that fell,
Pall-like, upon my spirit as my frame,
Making the sense of helplessness a pain,
Even to the soul;—a fresher pulse of life
Throbs quickly through each vein and artery,
And a new wing, a livelier nerve and strength,
Kindle the languid spirit into play.

Oh! generous nature, this is then thy boon,
These airs that come with evening—these sweet spells
That glide into the bosom with the embrace,
Whose very touch is life, and on the frame,
O'erborne and humbled by the oppressive weight
Of this fierce August atmosphere, bestow'st
A sense as precious as the boon that takes
The captive from his dungeon, and provides
The wings for his departure to free realms
Where no oppression harbors. Oh! I lift
My brow, as with a consciousness of power
I had not known before. I drink a joy
Most like a rapture, from each gushing air
That rustles and ruffles over the green shrub
And the gay orange, late so motionless,
That half obscure my window. Precious airs,
Full of delicious affluence, flow on

With wings that beat the drowsy atmosphere,
Until, in emulous murmur like your own,
It mates with ye in anthem, such as thrills
The Atlantic, till each billow takes a voice,
And echoes the deep chant.
Ye come! I feel
Your wings in playful office all about me,
Lifting the moisten'd hair upon my brows,
As if some spirit fann'd me. Is it not
A spirit, thus wrought from subtlest elements,
Child of the storm, perchance of ocean born,
But with commission sweet to check its sire
And soothe his rage to fondness? Thou persuad'st
His passions to repose beside the sea,
And chid'st his billows. With a sportive play
Thou steal'st the freshening vigor from his waves,
And bear'st it to the fainting on the waste
Where other wings are fire, and nature droops
Amidst her richest treasures.
Ah! how sweet
That fervent gush that shook apart the boughs,
And made the orange quiver beneath the eaves,
Even to its odorous roots.
Had I the voice
To mingle with that mighty chant, and grow
With its caprices flexible—now borne
A torrent through the void, and now a sigh,
Drooping with folded wing beside the couch,
As glad but gentle in the duteous office,
That soothes even while it stirs! Again the strain
Swelling in gradual volume, till the burst
Mocks the cathedral anthem, and rolls on,
Precursor of new billows of proud song
That grow to mountains on the beaten beach,

Suddenly to subside in the great deeps
That sent them first abroad. How lowlily
The murmurs waken now, and now the voice
Sinks audibly, with seeming consciousness:—
As one, a maid, that falters in her sports,
Steals back with sweet timidity of step,
As fearing that, in very guilelessness,
Her play hath been too wild; and now, as bold,
By truer thought, that forward glides again,
Renewing dance and song, surpassing still,
With each fresh effort, the repeated grace.
How wild that sudden gust—how sweet that breath
That seem'd to borrow music from the groves
Of Paphos, kindling to an amorous mood
The sense so lately dull! Alas! it shrinks!
The breeze's virtue is not constancy!—
What gay caprice!—but hence its secret fervor,
The charm that piques to renovate the heart,
And cools to fan its fires. It shrinks away
To gather up new strength. Subdued and awed,
It wantons forth at moments—a soft breath,
That whispers at the lattice—then creeps in
As doubtful of permission:—to be seen
Swelling the shrinking drapery of the couch,
Then melting into silence. Now, again,
It comes, and with a perfume in its breath,
Caught up from spicy gardens. The fair maid
Whose roses thus yield tribute to the march
Of that wild rover, guesses not the thief,
Whose fierce embrace thus robs them of their youth,
And virgin treasure—leaving them at morn
To weep that eager, fond soliciting,
They knew not to resist. Yet I rejoice
That they are thus despoil'd. 'Twere an ill wind

That brought to none its treasure. Is it not
A loving providence that thus provides
With blessing such as this, the unfavor'd one
Who else had never known it? In my cot,
Who sees the precious flowers of foreign growth,
From whose unfolding bosoms, this wild thief
Drinks the aroma to bestow on me?
My lordly neighbor's palace frowns me down,
His walls shut out my footsteps—his great gates
Open not to bid me enter, and mine eyes
Catch but faint glimpses of that prisoner realm,
His floral Harem, where his flowers but fade,
Having no proper worshipper. Yet in vain
His stone precautions and his iron gates,
Against my Ariel, my tricksy spirit,
That comes to me again with sweets so laden
As half to check his flight.
My precious breeze,
Misfortune well may love thee. Thou hast fled
The gayest regions. The high palaces,
Fair groves and gardens of nice excellence,—
The pride of power—the pageantry and pomp
That gild ambition and conceal its cares,—
Could not detain thee! Thou hast fled them all,
And, like an angel, still on blessing bent,
Hast come to cheer the lonely. It is meet
Thy welcome should be lavish like thyself.
Thou art no flatterer, and thou shouldst not creep
Through a close lattice with but half thy train,
When I would gather all of thee, and wrap
Thy draperies about me, as a robe
Dear as the first dews of the embracing spring
To the young buds of nature.
Sweet, oh! sweet,

Thy play about my brows. Thy whispers tell
Of songs in tree-tops when the forest pines
Give shelter, 'neath their ample and green boughs
In dark and mighty colonnades, to airs
That had no refuge else. They whisper me
A music such as glads the o'erladen heart,
Subdued, yet sleepless, fever'd with the heat
Of the long day in summer. Dear the dream
Thy service brings me. The still vexing care
Of body sleepless, that still troubles mind,
And makes one long commotion in the brain,
Grows soothed beneath thy ministry; and now,
Slumbers so coy, and woo'd so long in vain,
Are wrapping me at last. I will lie down
Beneath my window. There shall be no bar
To thy free entrance. Thou wilt linger here,
And with thy wings above my wearied brow,
Will put aside the masses of my hair
With a mysterious kindness—'till my sleep
Shall seem to me, in dreams which thou wilt shape,
Hallow'd by Love's officious tenderness,
And watch'd by one, the heart's ideal beauty,
Whose smile shall be a treasure like thine own,
Though never, in the experience of the day,
It finds the mortal match for my desire.

SONNETS.—PROGRESS IN DENIAL.

I.

"Yet, onward still!" the spirit cries within,
'Tis I that must repay thee. Mortal fame,
If won, is but at best the hollow din,
The vulgar freedom with a mighty name;
Seek not this music—ask not this acclaim,
But in the strife find succor;—for the toil
Pursued for such false barter ends in shame,
As certainly as that which seeks but spoil!
Best recompense he finds, who, to his task
Brings a proud, patient spirit that will wait,
Nor for the guerdon stoop, nor vainly ask
Of fate or fortune,—but with right good-will,
Go, working on, and uncomplaining still,
Assured of fit reward or soon or late!

II.

Thousands must perish in this hopeless strife,
And other thousands, withering as they stand,
Grow old in the long conflict waged for life!—
The conflict not for homes, or gold, or land,
But the rare privilege of rule,—command
Over the meaner spirits that surround—
And worship while they mock—that starry band,
They call ambitious! Rivalry and Blame
Attend their footsteps,—envy, and the host
Of reptile passions that delight to wound
The spirits whom their hatred honor's most,—
And worse, Ingratitude!—that still from fame
Plucks its best laurel, as if loth to know
How much it owes and cannot help but owe.

BALLAD.

GIVE me thy song of sorrow;
  Its 'plainings touch the heart,
First born of melancholy,
  And not of mortal art:
It strengthens though it saddens,
  A love-commission'd thing;
Oh! sorrow's song is holy,
  And thus, I pray thee, sing!

Sing while the shadows deepen
  Upon yon hill whose brow
Wears still the flickering sunlight,
  But whence 'tis flitting now;
Sing of the fading beauty,
  Sing of the coming night,
And as our eyes grow tearful,
  Methinks they must grow bright.

Let him who has not sorrow'd
  With loss of things most dear,
Exult in music's triumph,
  And joy in Hope's career;
But he who weeps the parting
  That made each blessing brief,
Will seek from music only
  The song that wakens grief.

IMMORTALITY.

I.

Beside me, in a dream of the deep night,
Unsummon'd, but in loveliness array'd,
Stood a warm, blue-eyed maid;
And the night fled before her, and the bloom
Of her eternal beauty from my sight
Dispell'd the midnight gloom.

II.

She stood beside me, and her white hand fell,
A touch of life and light upon my brow,—
That straightway felt the freshening waters flow,
As from a heart whose tides had sudden might
In the bright presence of some holy spell,—
Whose smile at once brought strength with new delight.

III.

And in her voice a winningness prevail'd,—
A music born of waters that go free
Through forests gladden'd in their greenery,
And lapsing through their leaves, as in a play
Of song and bird, by flower and beam regaled,
Whose pastimes are not ended with the day.

IV.

Hers was a voice of wings;—the linnet's note,
The lark's clear morning song of upper skies,
The dove's sweet plaint of tenderness and sighs;—
And the unparallel'd life within her own,
Made these a happier music than they brought
Unchorus'd, when they caroll'd forth alone!

V.

Her eye was its own music,—its own flight,—
As if, commercing ever with the spheres,
It strove for harmonies to mate with theirs,
And wings to pass from star to star at will;—
To shun the province yielded up to night,
For realms of brightness still!

VI.

The living speech upon her lips, in fire
Rose swelling like a soul;—while in her eye
The truth that blossoms with divinity,
Ray'd out with golden brightness, and awoke
Within my heart a pulse of new desire,
That burst each ancient yoke.

VII.

Then, in my rapture, I had lain my head
Upon the soft swell of that happy round,
That rose up like a white celestial mound,—
As saying,—"bring your gifts to this one shrine;"
But that her brow's clear will soon banishéd
The fond resolve from mine!

VIII.

I did not quail or tremble at her glance,
For still it seem'd as she were there to bring
New loves to crown my hope, a newer wing,
And open better provinces of life;—
Within her smile I saw deliverance,
And broad new realms for strife.

IX.

Yet broken was my speech, and forth I stood
Despairing, though immersed in certain bliss,
Lest I should lose, in my soul's feebleness,
The embrace that now seem'd needful to content;
And tears were all that the impetuous blood
Vouchsafed, of all it meant!

X.

Then sweeter grew the smile upon her face,
As conscious of my suffering and my truth,
Her heart for mine was sudden smit with ruth;
And she made answer, not with human word,—
But in her smile, and the intelligent grace
Of motion, was she heard.

XI.

"Thy wish is thy performance," said she then;—
"And thou wilt take me to thy arms anon
When thou hast put thy loftier nature on,
And made me the sole passion in thy heart;
But not for thee, when we shall meet again,
To be what now thou art!

XII.

"And 'tis for thy soliciting to say,
Whether my form will show to thee as now;—
It may be thou wilt shrink to see the brow,
Which, though in loveliness it now appears,
May so affront thee, thou wilt turn away
In terror and in tears!

XIII.

" If that the passion thou hast felt for me
Live in thy future memory, thou wilt raise
Thy altar and thy anthem in my praise;
And I will light thy fires and wing thy strain;—
But if I lose thee from my love, for thee
My presence must be pain.

XIV.

" 'Tis written, we shall meet;—'tis written more,
Thou shalt be mine, I thine; and we must go
Forever link'd through ages that still flow
From founts of time eternal, to no end,
Save one of toil, which we may both deplore,
Or covet, as thy single wishes tend.

XV.

" Our future is performance! Worlds are placed
Around us for possession; and, in these
We make our separate mansions as we please,
And choose the separate task that each fulfil;
In these, or happy and blest,—or low debased,—
Must wait upon thy will.

XVI.

" And thus, in a brief vision of the night,
I show thee what I am, that thou mayst see
How great the blessings that still wait on thee,
Even at thy pleasure:—Could I show thee more,
Then should thy wonder grow with thy delight,
At what is in my store.

XVII.

"I come not with denial, though I now
Deny thee my embrace;—thy head shall lie
Upon this bosom—on thy doubtful eye
This form shall rise at last, whate'er thou beest;
For thee to say, how fair shall be the brow,
How bright the eye, which, in that day thou seest.

XVIII.

"Oh! 'tis to all my charms that I entreat
Thy coming;—thou shalt have my crown and wings;
For thee, the bird that late and early sings,
When hope is at the entrance, shall appear;
And we will glide, with pinions at our feet,
To tasks by Love made dear!

XIX.

"Come to me then, beloved one, with thy heart
Made pure in my remembrance—with thy thought
By hope of triumph in mine forever taught
To seek the unnamed condition of delight;—
So shall I meet thee, fond as now thou art,
Thou me, as now I seem unto thy sight!"

XX.

Rapture, oh rapture!—wherefore wert thou born
So soon to perish?—thou, a part of death,
Art lost to being with thy first sweet breath,
And lifelong then we mourn thee, with an eye,
Turn'd outwards, inwards—with the look forlorn—
Too happy, if it seeks for thee on high.

EVENING AT SEA.

Day sinks in rosy vestments that, afar
Spread o'er the billows, as with guardian office,
To shelter his decline. Gorgeous in gold
And purple, fall the curtains of the west,
In the same gracious duty;—his repose
Screening from vulgar gaze of those who late
Had flourish'd in his favor. Now they fleet,
Those clouds of glorious garniture and shade,
Changing their apt varieties of form,
No less than hue and loveliness, to lines
That melt even while they linger, in the embrace
Of the fast-rising Night; who, like a mother,
Takes all within her fold. A little while,
And darkness sways the ocean, whose great waves
Grow sullen as they murmur through the gloom,
Resentful of its shadows.—But anon,
Comes forth the maiden Moon,—her sickle bent
For service in these fields; a glorious blade,
Of silver, that subdues them at a stroke,
Leaving the keen reflection of its edge
On every heaving hillock as she goes!
How rare the hush that follows! Not a wave
Lifts its rebellious head; but, lawn'd in light,
Subdues itself most willing to the embrace
Of that perfecting beauty which makes all
Her tribute objects precious, though obscure!
How sudden sinks the wind, that, but a while,
Took a capricious play upon its vans,
And shook our streamers out! The heavenly things

Seem brooding o'er our path ; the great abyss
Of deep and sky, flush'd with intelligent forms,
The herds of eyes, the numerous flocking stars,
Gazing in wonder on the serene march.

WHERE BY DARRO'S EVENING WATERS.

I.

Where by Darro's evening waters
  Hang the weeping willows low,
There they sat, the twilight's daughters,
  Ever beautiful with woe :—
Murmuring songs of fitful sorrow,—
  Sorrow mingled with such sweetness,
  That it would not know completeness
But for softening tears that borrow
  From the yielding heart compliance ;—
  And such touching, fond reliance
On the rapture of the morrow,—
That the hearer weeps for pleasure,
  As the music o'er him creeps,
And he finds increasing measure,
  In his pleasure, that he weeps !

II.

Sleeps he then beside the waters,
  By that twilight song oppress'd ;
Softly gliding then, the daughters
  Steal beside his rest ;—
Three young maids of touching sweetness,

Born of dew, and light, and air,
Mourning still the life of fleetness,
That belongs to birth so rare!—
Yet, so human still their 'plaining,
In his heart strange pangs arise,
And a new life they are gaining,
From the drops that fill his eyes.
Reason good for sorrow's power,
In that sad and dreaming hour—
Far beyond their hapless plight,
Is his own and kindred birth;—
Born of air, and dew, and light,
He is also born of earth!

SOUL-FLIGHT.

I.

What checks the eagle's wing—what dims his eye,
Turn'd upward to the sky?
Doth the cloud cumber the ascending flight
Of that which is all light?
Fruitless, indeed, were such a frail defence
Against intelligence;
And all in vain the chains of earth would bind
The disembodied mind!

II.

Glorious and unrestrainéd on its way,
It seeks the endless day;
It drinks more deeply of the intenser air,
That streams with being there;

A thing of sense and sight, it early learns,
And sees, adores, and burns;
Claiming, with every breath from out the sky,
Its own divinity.

III.

From world to world, from gathering star to star,
Its flight is fast and far;
As through an ordeal, it prepares in each
Some higher form to reach;
From the small orb that lights the outer gate
Of that all-nameless state,
To that which burns before the eternal throne,
Fearless it hurries on.

IV.

Dread mystery, that to the mortal sight,
Seems all one shapeless night,—
Wild with unbidden clouds, that flickering haste
Still o'er a pathless waste,
Without one intellectual planet's ray
To yield a partial day;
Will death reveal the truth to sons of men?—
Shall we explore you then?

V.

I would not be the creature of the clay,
Mouldering with time away,
Nor hold, for my soul's hope, the awful thought
That death is all, life naught!—
That all this soaring mind, this high desire
Still upward to aspire,
Is but the yearning of some painted thing
That would not lose its wing.

THE CHILD-ANGEL.

It is our blessing that her lot was fair—
The precious birthright of the dew and air,
The green and shade of woods, the song of birds,
And dreams too bright for words—
All that makes moonlight for the innocent heart,
And love, that, in its bud, is still its crowning part.

The sadness of the spring-time in the shade
Of dusk—the shadows of the night array'd,
By stars in the great forests, as they look,
Glistening, as from a brook;
And stillness in the gloom, that seems a sound,
Breathed up, unconscious, out from nature's great profound.

Fancies, that go beside us when we glide,
Still seeking no companion—prompt to guide
Even where we would not, to the saddest grove,
Where one still weeps for love,—
Still nursing ever a most sweet distress,
That through our very sorrow seems to bless;—

These, since the child's departure, still declare
Her precious birthright in the dew and air—
And I, that do inherit them from her,
Do feel them minister,
As with new voices never felt before,
To love that in my heart still groweth more and more.

CAPE HATTERAS.

"Ah! by these breezes—(how unlike the airs
That clipp'd us when we sought our berths last night!)—
These languid breezes, and the odorous breath
That sweeps to us from forests of green pines,
I know that we have pass'd the stormy Cape!"

Exclaiming thus, when, waking at the dawn,
I hurried from the cabin to the deck,
And there—his wrath subdued, his winds at rest—
Lay the fierce god of cloudy Hatteras,
At length upon the deep. Our vessel ran
Beside him fearless, and the eyes that oft
Had trembled at the story of his storms
Look'd on him without dread. Yet, in his sleep,
The sun down blazing on his old gray head,
There was a moody murmur of his waves
That spake of ruthless powers, and bade us fly
To our far homes, with wings of moving fear
Not less than hope. We might not loiter long,
Like thoughtless birds, improvident of home,
And wandering, by the sunshine still seduced,
O'er treacherous billows. No half despot he,
To spare in mercy in his wrathful hour.
A thousand miles along his sandy couch
The shores shall feel his wakening, and his lash
Resound in thunder. Brooding by the sea
He lurks in waiting for the passing bark,
And every year hath its own chronicle
Of his exactions—of the fearful tribute

He takes from all alike. Cruel the tale
Of friends that here pay forfeit with their lives
For the o'erweening faith that trusts his calms;—
Whilst the beloved ones, watching by the port,
Look vainly for their coming. Sad the tale
Of the poor maiden, shrieking in despair,
Grasp'd in his rude embrace, and borne away
To unreturning caverns of the deep,—
Which, with an aspect obdurate, behold
The precious lamp of life put sudden out
Even its kindling glow. Yet are there hours
When the true spirit of love defies his rage;
And, in one night of terror and of storm,
When his wild seas were wildest—and the ship
Strove, sinking 'neath them,—and all living souls
Were all distraught—all hopeless, purposeless,
Struggling against each other as with death—
Blind, knowing not the kinsman or the friend,—
Calling on God, with but a half a prayer,—
And him forgettingly;—one voice, o'er all,
Was heard amid the clamor and the storm,
Firm, crying for the woman who had lain,
Until that fearful hour, upon his breast,
And now was sunder'd from him by the night,
Unconsciously:—"Oh! where art thou, my wife!"
That loving cry was heard above the storm;—
The winds grew moment still;—the tumbling waves
Lifted their heads as in a grim surprise,
And paused in their huge gambols! Ah! too soon
To rush to their renewal. The fond cry
Was stifled ere it rose into the heavens,
But not before the wife made answer sweet,
That, through the midnight blackness, seem'd a voice

To waken life in death;—"I come to thee,
Where art thou, dearest husband? Let me come!"*

She sprang to join him, and the sullen seas
Closed over them forever. 'Tis my prayer
That, ere he perish'd, she had wound her arms
About him, and had press'd her lip to his:—
And it were seemly, if, beneath the waves,
They sleep encircled in the same embrace;—
Her cheek upon his bosom, and his arms
Wrapt round her in the holy grasp of love;
Secure from storm, and, best assurance yet,
Secure from separation evermore!

SONNET.—THE AGE OF GOLD.

THESE times deserve no song—they but deride
The poet's holy craft,—nor his alone;
Methinks as little courtesy is shown
To what was chivalry in days of pride:
Honor but meets with mock:—the worldling shakes
His money-bags, and cries—"My strength is here;
O'erthrows my enemy, his empire takes,
And makes the ally serve, the alien fear!"
Is love the object? Cash is conqueror,—
Wins hearts as soon as empires—puts his foot
Upon the best affections, and will spur
His way to eloquence, when Faith stands mute;
And for Religion,—can we hope for her,
When love and valor serve the same poor brute!

* The incident, as related in the text, really happened. The facts, known by survivors, were subsequently adduced in evidence in a court of justice, and constituted the point upon which the direction was given to the estates of the parties.

BILLOWS.

Gently, with sweet commotion,
Sweeping the shore,
Billows that break from ocean,
Rush to our feet;
Slaves that, with fond devotion,
Prone to adore,
Seek not to stint with measure,
Service that's meet;—
Bearing their liquid treasure,
Flinging it round,
Shouting the while the pleasure
True service knows,
Then, as if bless'd with leisure,
Flung on the yellow ground
Taking repose!

FALL OF THE LEAF.

I.

The leaves, the pleasant and green leaves that hung
Abroad in the gay summer woods, are dead;
They do not hear the morning carols sung
By the sad birds that miss the blooms they shed;
They know not of the vacancy they leave,
The cheerlessness of trees to which they clung—
How even the winds for their departure grieve,
How birds grow silent; how the groaning boughs
Rock sorrowful, the sport of every breeze;

And as a nun that takes the proper vows,
How nature hoods her beauty in her woe,
And silent walks beneath the naked trees,
Much wondering that she still survives the blow.
With such a silent sorrow on each tongue,
I marvel that their last dirge be not sung!

II.

Shall not the vagrant and light wooing breeze,
Fresh from its native seas
In the Pacific, wandering with the sun,—
While hurrying onward through the well-known trees
That now no more, as in sweet days of yore,
Yield shade and comfort to the desolate one,—
Prepare his dirge, and on the midnight gale
In token of his perish'd luxuries,
Pour forth his wail!
And yield, in very ecstasy of grief,
One fond lament above the perishing leaf!

III.

He hath not stay'd his flight,
But, tracking the lone land bird, he hath bent
His insusceptible wing throughout the night,
Far as the fancy's sight
Might trace the dim lines of the firmament—
And, ere the gray dawn from his ocean-bed
Rush'd to the visible heaven, hath turn'd his plume
To where the flowers, in a sweet tremulous bloom
Were wont to yield perfume,—
And, as an exile o'er whom hangs the doom,
He comes to find them dead.

IV.

And hath he then no wail?—
And folding round him not his mourning wing,
Will he forbear to sing
The melancholy anthem and sad tale?
Shall he not say, he, who forever grieves,
The story of the leaves?
And, with a tone to match the sad complain,
And desolate aspect of the world around,
Shall he not pour along the waste that strain
Of wild and incommunicable sound,
Such as in Mexique gulf the seaman hears,
Like scream of unknown sea-bird in his ears,
Vexing the black profound?

V.

He hath a voice for sorrow as delight;
For death as life; for night as for the dawn:
He sings the ruin which is in his sight,
He wails the perish'd beautiful and gone!
The plaint he pours, though cold to human sense,
And wild and vague, hath yet a magic tone
For the dumb nature full of competence,
And dear to her alone:
Yet, even to human thought it still must wear
The semblance of a moan,
The wild gush of a heart, that, in its woe,
First finds its voice: one asks not words to show
The speech of anguish; and, as now we hear,
The Fancy readily deems, that while he grieves
His home all desolate, his soul all drear,
The wanderer wails the leaves.

VI.

"Never—oh! never more,
Unburied honors of the pilgrim year,—
In glossy and bright garb of innocent green,
With crispéd veins from nature's palmy print,
And each sweet scent and lovely tinge and tint,
Shall ye appear,
The roving sense to charm, the eye to cheer·
The time—sweet time!—that ye and I have seen,
Is o'er, forever o'er!
Ye feel me not—I press ye—never more;
My early joy, your loveliness,—how brief!
I may forget ye on some happier shore,
But, on your fruitless now, and scentless bier,
I leave my tear!"

VII.

Away! away!
Far in the blaze of the descending day,
After that brief lament he spreads his wings—
Now that the summer charm that led astray
The licensed rover of wild Indian seas,
No longer clings
With blossoming odor, wooing his wild flight—
And, but the ruin of the leafless trees
Is there in token of the common blight!
Ah! who hath not been hopeless like the breeze?
Whose leaves and flowers, secure against the doom,
Hav: ever, through all seasons, kept their bloom,
Nor perish'd in a night?

THE EUTAW MAID.

The battle of the Eutaw Springs, one of the most brilliant events of the Revolution, is well known in the history of the partisan warfare carried on in the southern department.

I.

It was in Eutaw's covert shade, and on a hill-side stood
A young and gentle Santee maid, who watch'd the distant wood,
Where he, the loved one of her heart, in fearful battle then,
Had gone to flesh his maiden sword with Albion's martial men:
Untaught in fight, and all unused to join the strife of blows,—
Oh! can there be a doubt with her how the deadly battle goes?

II.

And wild the din ascends from far, and high in eddying whirls,
Above the forest trees and wide, the sulphur storm-cloud curls,
And fast and thick upon her ear the dreadful cries of pain,
The groan, the shriek, the hoarse alarm, run piercing to her brain:
She may not hope that he is safe when thousands fall around,
But looks to see his bloody form outstretch'd upon the ground.

III.

There's a cry of conquest on the breeze, the cannon's roar is still,—
She dares not look, she does not weep, her trembling heart is chill:
The tramplings of the victors come in triumph through the glade,
She hears the loud note of the drum, the clattering of the blade:
Perchance that very blade is red with the blood of him, her love;—
The thought is death, and down she sinks within the woodland grove.

IV.

But, a gentle arm entwines her form—a voice is in her ear,
Which, even in death's cold grasp itself, 'twould win her back to hear;

Her lips unclose, her eyes unfold once more upon the light,
And he is there, that gallant youth, unharm'd, before her sight!
Now happy is that Santee maid, and proudly blest is he,
And in her face the tear and smile are strangely sweet to see.

ALF-SONG.

I.

The sunbeam darting to the stream,
The birth that glows in dying,
Love's meeting hour and beauty's gleam,
And raptures born when flying;
How, if we speed o'er summits fair,
Just at each fountain dipping,
And pause to rest, in valleys rare,
Their single blisses sipping!

II.

The cup that flows for us must take
Its color from the fountain,
In whose embrace the blue skies wake,
Still dreaming of the mountain;—
We ask no better boon for us
While yet the bead is gleaming,
To snatch its single blessings thus,
Though all the rest be seeming.

III.

And still the leaf that skims the lake,
Shall satisfy our seeking;
And still the bird-note in the brake,
Be ample for our speaking;—

And still the dream at morning-tide,
When April buds awaken,
Shall welcome bring, though from our side
The other self be taken.

STANZAS.

Silent with all her vassal stars as ever,
Night in the sky,
Here, by this dark and lonely Indian river,
Scarce moaning by;—
Our spirits brood together in communion
Too deep for speech;
Thought wings its way to thought, and in their union
'Tis love they teach.

And yet how deep the mock to this condition!
That dream of youth,
Whose night-stars tremble over waves Elysian,
Whose day is truth—
Whose hope, with angel wings, to consummation
Speeds from its birth,
Whose joy, unfettered at its first creation,
Bends heaven o'er earth.

Hast thou not felt the cruel world's denial,—
Art thou not here;
Exiled and tortured, ere thy soul had trial
Of hope and fear;
Unknown and unconsider'd, thy devotion
Denied a shrine;—
Methinks, these waters speak for thy emotion,
And echo mine.

The love that blesses youth is none of ours—
No smiles, no tears—
A sky that never moved the earth to flowers,
In earlier years:—
But the deep consciousness, still speaking only,
Of the twin woe,
That finds fit music in these waters lonely,
That moan and go!

HEADS OF THE POETS.

I.—CHAUCER.

—— CHAUCER's healthy Muse
Did wisely one sweet instrument to choose,
The native reed; which, tutor'd with rare skill,
Brought other Muses* down to aid its trill!
A cheerful song, that sometimes quaintly mask'd
The fancy, as the affections, sweetly task'd;
And won from England's proud and *foreign*† court,
For native England's *tongue*, a sweet report—
And sympathy—till in due time it grew
A permanent voice that proved itself the true,
And rescued the brave language of the land
From that‡ which help'd to strength the invader's hand!
Thus, with great patriot service, making clear
The way to other virtues quite as dear
In English liberty—which could grow alone,
When English speech grew pleasant to be known;

* The Provençal—the Italian. † The Norman.
‡ The French.

To spell the ears of princes, and to make
The peasant worthy for his poet's sake.

II.—SHAKSPEARE.

—— 'Twere hard to say
Upon what instrument did Shakspeare play—
Still harder what he did not! He had all
The orchestra at service, and could call
To use still other implements unknown,
Or only valued in his hands alone!
The Lyre, whose burning inspiration came
Still darting upward, sudden as the flame;
The murmuring wind-harp, whose melodious sighs
Seem still from hopefulest heart of love to rise,
And gladden even while grieving; the wild strain
That night-winds wake from reeds that breathe in pain,
Though breathing still in music; and that voice
Which most he did affect—whose happy choice
Made sweet flute-accents for humanity
Out of that living heart which cannot die—
The catholic, born of love, that still controls,
While man is man, the tide in human souls.

III.—THE SAME.

—— His universal song
Who sung by Avon, and, with purpose strong,
Compell'd a voice from native oracles,
That still survive their altars by their spells—
Guarding with might each avenue to fame,
Where, trophied over all, glows Shakspeare's name!
The mighty master-hand in his we trace—
If erring often, never commonplace;
Forever frank and cheerful, even when woe
Commands the tear to speak, the sigh to flow;

Sweet without weakness—without storming, strong,
Jest not o'erstrain'd, nor argument too long;
Still true to reason, though intent on sport,
His wit ne'er drives his wisdom out of court;
A brooklet now, a noble stream anon,
Careering in the meadows and the sun;
A mighty ocean next, deep, far, and wide,
Earth, life, and heaven, all imaged in its tide!
Oh! when the master bends him to his art,
How the mind follows, how vibrates the heart!
The mighty grief o'ercomes us as we hear,
And the soul hurries, hungering, to the ear;
The willing nature, yielding as he sings,
Unfolds her secret and bestows her wings,
Glad of that best interpreter, whose skill
Brings hosts to worship at her sacred hill!

IV.—SPENSER.

It was for Spenser, by his quaint device,
To spiritualize the passionate, and subdue
The wild, coarse temper of the British Muse,
By meet diversion from the absolute:
To lift the fancy, and, where still the song
Proclaim'd a wild humanity, to sway
Soothingly soft, and, by fantastic wiles,
Persuade the passions to a milder clime!
His was the song of chivalry, and wrought
For like results upon society;
Artful in high degree, with plan obscure,
That mystified to lure; and, by its spells,
Making the heart forgetful of itself,
To follow out and trace its labyrinths,
In that forgetfulness made visible!

Such were the uses of his Muse; to say
How proper and how exquisite his lay—
How quaintly rich his masking—with what art
He fashions fairy realms and paints their queen,
How purely—with how delicate a skill—
It needs not, since his song is with us still!

V.—MILTON.

The master of a single instrument,
But that the Cathedral Organ, Milton sings
With drooping spheres about him, and his eye
Fix'd steadily upward, through its mortal cloud
Seeing the glories of eternity!
The sense of the invisible and the true
Still present to his soul; and, in his song,
The consciousness of duration through all time,
Of work in each condition, and of hopes
Ineffable, that well sustain through life,
Encouraging through danger and in death,
Cheering, as with a promise rich in wings!
A godlike voice, that through cathedral towers
Still rolls, prolong'd in echoes, whose deep tones
Seem born of thunder, that, subdued to music,
Soothe when they startle most! A Prophet Bard,
With utterance equal to his mission of power,
And harmonies, that, not unworthy heaven,
Might well lift earth to equal worthiness.

VI.—BURNS.

——Thither at eve,
Where Burns still wanders with his violin song;
A melancholy conqueror, in whose sway
His own irregular soul grew dark and fell,

Incapable to spell, with resolute will,
The capricious genius that, o'er all beside,
Held perfect mastery. 'Twas here he went,
A man of pride and sorrows, weak yet strong,
With still a song discoursing to the heart,
The lowly human heart, of all its joys,—
Buoyant and cheerful, yet with sadness too,
Such sadness as still shows us love through tears.

VII.—SCOTT.

—— Not forgotten or denied,
Scott's trumpet lay of chivalry and pride;
Homeric in its rush, and, in its strife,
With every impulse brimming o'er with life,
Teeming with action, and the call to arms;—
A robust Dame, his muse, with martial charms,
To strive, when need demands it, or to love;—
The Eagle quite as often as the Dove.

VIII.—BYRON.

—— For Byron's home and fame,
It needed manhood only! Had he known
How sorrow should be borne, nor sunk in shame,
For that his destiny decreed to moan—
His muse had been triumphant over Time
As still she is o'er Passion: still sublime—
Having subdued her soul's infirmity
To aliment; and, with herself o'ercome,
O'ercome the barriers of Eternity,
And lived through all the ages; with a sway
Complete, and unembarrass'd by the doom
That makes of Nature's porcelain common clay!

IX.—A GROUP.

—— As one who had been brought
By Fairy hands, and as a changeling left
In human cradle—the sad substitute
For a more smiling infant—Shelley sings
Vague minstrelsies that speak a foreign birth,
Among erratic tribes. Yet not in vain
His moral, and the fancies in his flight
Not without profit for another race!
He left his spirit with his voice—a voice
Solely spiritual—which will long suffice
To wing the otherwise earthy of the time,
And, with the subtler leaven of the soul,
Inform the impetuous passions!
With him came,
Antagonist, yet still with sympathy,
Wordsworth, the Bard of the Contemplative—
A voice of purest thought in sweetest music!
—These, in themselves unlike, together link'd,
Appear in unison in after days,
Making progressive still the mental births,
That pass successively through rings of time,
Each to a several conquest, most unlike
That of its sire; yet borrowing of its strength,
Where needful, and endowing it with new,
To meet the fresh necessities which still
Haunt the free progress of each conquering race.

—Thus Tennyson and Barrett, Browning and Horne,
Blend their opposing faculties, and speak
For that fresh nature, which, in daily things,
Beholds the immortal, and from common forms

Extorts the Eternal still! So Baily sings
In Festus—so, upon an humbler rank,
Testing the worth of social policies,
As working through a single human will,
The Muse of Taylor argues—Artevelde,
Being the man who marks a popular growth,
And notes the transit of a thought through time,
Growing as still it speeds. . . . .
Exquisite
The ballads of Campbell, and the lays of Moore,
Appealing to our tastes, our gentler moods,
The play of the affections, or the thoughts
That come with national pride; and, as we pause
In our own march, delight the sentiment!
But nothing they make for progress. They perfect
The language, and diversify its powers—
Please and beguile, and, for the forms of art,
Prove what they are, and may be. But they lift
None of our standards; help us not in growth;
Compel no prosecution of our search,
And leave us, where they found us—with our time!

SONNET TO THE PAST.

Thy presence hath been grateful—thou hast brought
Toil and privation, which have tutor'd me
To strength and fit endurance; set me free
From vainest fancies—and most kindly wrought
On the affections which had else run wild,
Untrain'd by meet denial of their thirst.
What though I held thee yesterday accurst,—

Believe me not the vain and erring child
Still to remember chastening by its pain,
  More than its uses;—True, that to my home
  Thou hast brought grief, and often left it gloom;—
But that I do not of thy deeds complain,
Is proof that they have done no bootless part—
Have hurt my house, perchance, but help'd my heart.

STANZAS.

Ah! not that song, nor any song:
  Thy music mocks the heart
With memories cherish'd still too long,
  That will not now depart;
For me, o'er whom a blighted past
Will still its withering trophies cast,
  There is no heaven in art:—
The strain that cannot hope restore,
But makes me feel the lost the more.

I ask not music's power to show
  What earth has once possess'd;
Nor does it need that all should know
  My heart has once been bless'd:
The tear thy song has made to start,
Betrays the secret of my heart,
  The pang that will not rest;
But wakes to instant strength and sting,
When memory spreads her dusky wing.

That night-bird, with its chant, still nigh,
  A sad, mysterious tone,

Recalling, with its boding cry,
  The ghosts of glories gone;
Bends o'er me with each human strain,
Restores that *hour*, with all its pain,
  Dark hour, I could not shun;
Brings back the full soul's trial then,
Which left me desolate 'mongst men!

They tell me that thy song is sweet,
  And eyes that look delight,
Follow, with silent love, thy feet,
  And gladden in thy sight;—
It needs not proof like this—thy strain,
That brings the perish'd back again,
  The musical, the bright,—
May well persuade me of thy grace,
In pure white soul and angel face.

Enough—thou hast her charm divine,
  To kindle and to move;
On others let thy beauties shine,
  In others waken love;
Perchance—and it is sure my prayer—
Life's joys alone, and not its care,
  Thy future fate may prove;
Enough, resembling her, I see
Her virtues, not herself, in thee.

THE WESTERN EMIGRANTS.

An aged man, whose head some seventy years
Had snow'd on freely, led the caravan ;—
His sons and sons' sons, and their families,
Tall youths and sunny maidens—a glad group,
That glow'd in generous blood and had no care,
And little thought of the future—follow'd him ;—
Some perch'd on gallant steeds, others, more slow,
The infants and the matrons of the flock,
In coach and jersey,—but all moving on
To the new land of promise, full of dreams
Of western riches, Mississippi-mad!
Then came the *hands*, some forty-five or more,
Their moderate wealth united—some in carts
Laden with mattresses ;—on ponies some;
Others, more sturdy, following close afoot,
Chattering like jays, and keeping, as they went,
Good time to Juba's creaking violin.

I met and spoke them. The old patriarch,
The grandsire of that goodly family,
Told me his story, and a few brief words
Unfolded that of thousands. Discontent,
With a vague yearning for a better clime,
And richer fields than thine, old Carolina,
Led him to roam. Yet did he not complain
Of thee, dear mother—mother still to me,
Though now, like him, a wanderer from thy homes.
Thou hadst not chidden him, nor trampled down
His young ambition ;—hadst not school'd his pride
By cold indifference ; hadst not taught his heart

To doubt of its own hope, as of thy love,
Making self-exile duty. He knew thee not,
As I, by graves and sorrows. Thy bright sun
Had always yielded flowers and fruits to him,
And thy indulgence and continued smiles
Had made his pittance plenty—made his state
A proud one in the honors which thou gav'st,
Almost in's own despite. And yet he flies thee
For a wild country, where the unplough'd fields
Lie stagnant in their waste fertility,
And long for labor. His are sparkling dreams,
As fond as those of boyhood. Golden stores
They promise him in Mississippian vales,
Outshining all the past, compensating—
So thinks he idly—for the home he leaves,
The grave he should have chosen, and the walks,
And well-known fitness of his ancient woods.
Self-exiled, in his age he hath gone forth
To the abodes of strangers,—seeking wealth—
Not wealth, but money! Heavens! what wealth we give,
Daily, for money! What affections sweet—
What dear abodes—what blessing, happy joys—
What hopes, what hearts, what affluence, what ties,
In a mad barter where we lose our all,
For that which an old trunk, a few feet square,
May compass like our coffin! That old man
Can take no root again! He hath snapp'd off
The ancient tendrils, and in foreign clay
His branches will all wither. Yet he goes,
Falsely persuaded that a bloated purse
Is an affection—is a life—a lease,
Renewing life, with all its thousand ties
Of exquisite endearment—flowery twines,
That, like the purple parasites of March,

Shall wrap his aged trunk, and beautify
Even while they shelter. I could weep for him,
Thus banish'd by that madness of the mind,
But that mine own fate, not like his self-chosen,
Fills me with bitterer thoughts than of rebuke;—
He does not suffer from the lack of home,
And all the pity that I waste on him
Comes of my own privation. Let him go.

There is an exile which no laws provide for,
No crimes compel, no hate pursues;—not written
In any of the records! Not where one goes
To dwell in other regions—from his home
Removed, by taste, or policy, or lust,
Or the base cares of the mere creature need,
Or pride's impatience. Simple change of place
Is seldom exile, as it hath been call'd,
But idly. There's a truer banishment
To which such faith were gentle. 'Tis to be
An exile on the spot where you were born;—
A stranger on the hearth which saw your youth,—
Banish'd from hearts to which your heart is turn'd;—
Unbless'd by those, from whose o'erwatchful love
Your heart would drink all blessings:—'Tis to be
In your own land—the native land whose soil
First gave you birth; whose air still nourishes,—
If that may nourish which denies all care
And every sympathy,—and whose breast sustains,—
A stranger—hopeless of the faded hours,
And reckless of the future;—a lone tree
To which no tendril clings—whose desolate boughs
Are scathed by angry winters, and bereft
Of the green leaves that cherish and adorn.

FIRST PURPOSELESS STRIVINGS OF THE IMAGINATION.

A SICKNESS at the heart that ever pines
For solitude, and baffled in the prayer,
Swells sometimes to a passion like despair!
Jealous of eyes—suspecting all designs,
And trembling for a secret which the heart
Grasps not itself;—still searching, as a life
The soothing of another, yet at strife
With him who first assumes the soother's part,
Nor trusting till too late!—A resolute will
To pine, and be alone, and desolate still;
By day in wood and wild, with vexing thought,
Removed from human converse; and by night
Striving in dreams, and, at the morning's light,
Looking, as with an angel we had fought.

STANZAS.

I.

THE love that won thee did not speak,
The grief that mourns thee has no tear;
To paint thy virtues both were weak,
To lose them neither well can bear.
In boyhood's hours, 'mid childhood's glee,
And through the long succeeding years
The same,—thy presence were to me
What weeping memory still endears.

II.

Let those with mood more calm than mine,
Describe thy virtues as they will;
It is enough that they were thine,
I've lost them yet I love them still:
I love them still, though now no more
Their presence blesses mortal eye;
They dwell within my bosom's core,
And never sleep and cannot die!

III.

When all of earth that well could fade,
And beauty's sweetest blandishment,
The eye might deem, that then survey'd,
Immortal as omnipotent;—
Were crowded into earth,—there stood,
From all that weeping train apart,
One victim of a hopeless mood,
One keeper of a maddening heart.

IV.

To him the boon of memory came,
The young, the lovely, to restore
Warm, tender, as his bosom's flame,
Immortal as the love it bore!
But vain, though sweet, the boon it brings,
Unless it bids the buried live;
It gives him gleams of heavenly things,
But weeps o'er that it cannot give!

THE DECAY OF A PEOPLE.

This the true sign of ruin to a race—
It undertakes no march, and, day by day
Drowses in camp, or, with the laggard's pace,
Walks sentry o'er possessions that decay;
Destined, with sensible waste, to fleet away;—
For the first secret of continued power
Is the continued conquest;—all our sway
Hath surety in the uses of the hour;
If that we waste, in vain wall'd town and lofty tower!

THE TEXAN HUNTER.

I.

Oh! wilt thou be, dear maiden,
The Texan hunter's bride,
And tend his forest bower
By Colorado's side;
Thy childhood's home forgetting,
That newer home to prize,
Near where the sun is setting,
But where our sun must rise?

II.

I bring no wealth to woo thee,
But, in my grasp, I bear
The weapon, at whose sudden speech
The forest nations fear;

The wild Camanché flies the track
  That I have blazed for thee,
And when I wind this yellow horn
  The cougar seeks his tree.

III.

Of all the wild steeds of the West,
  No one is better graced
Than this I bring to bear thy form
  Across the prairie waste;
As little feels the infant,
  Within his cradled height,
The waving of the slender bough,
  As thou his easy flight.

IV.

And gay with richest flowers,
  And green with leafy shade,
Shall be the forest bowers
  Which Love for thee has made:
No high and haughty palace,
  But, smiling through the green
Of waving, sea-like valleys,
  Our snow-white cot is seen.

V.

Sweet groves and soft savannahs,
  A clime of calm, it woos
With blossoms of the rainbow born,
  And fruitage of its hues;
Broad seas asleep in meadows,
  With ranks of cane that rise
Like plumed and painted warriors,
  To sink before our eyes.—

VI.

But if within thy bosom
  There burns a nobler life,
As dames in knightly days could share
  The rapture of the strife;
Then, by my steed and rifle,
  Let Mexic towers beware,
The eye that cheers my cabin now
  Shall light my spirit there.

SONNETS.

I. THE APPROACH OF WINTER.

Comes winter with an aspect dark to me,
  Harried with storms so long? Are his brows stern?
Speaks he a language of asperity,
  Unfit for him to speak or me to learn?
And do I shrink from the impending stroke
  That follows his keen chiding? Would I fly
The terror of his presence, and that yoke
  Borne with so long and so reluctantly?
No! from its prison-house of care and pain
  My spirit dares defy him. Well inured
To trial,—I have borne it—not in vain,
  Since conquer'd is the destiny endured—
Endured with no base spirit! I have grown
Familiar with the future in the known.

II.

Yet bitter were the lessons of that past,
  When life was one long winter! Childhood knew

Nor blossom nor delight. No sunshine cast
The glory of green leaves about mine eye;
No zephyr, laden with sweet perfumes, blew
For me its Eastern tribute from a sky
Looking down love upon me; and my mood
Yearn'd for its kindred—for the humblest tie
To human hopes and aspirations true!
Sickness, and suffering, and solitude
Couch'd o'er my cradle: cheerless was the glance
That watch'd my slumbers in those feeble hours
When pity, with her tears, her only powers,
Might have brought hope, if not deliverance.

III. CHILDHOOD.

That season which all other men regret,
And strive, with boyish longing, to recall,
Which love permits not memory to forget,
And fancy still restores in dreams of all
That boyhood worshipp'd, or believed, or knew,—
Brings no sweet images to me—was true,
Only in cold and cloud, in lonely days
And gloomy fancies—in defrauded claims,
Defeated hopes, denied, denying aims;—
Cheer'd by no promise—lighted by no rays,
Warm'd by no smile—no mother's smile,—that smile,
Of all, best suited sorrow to beguile,
And strengthen hope, and, by unmark'd degrees,
Encourage to their birth high purposes.

IV. YOUTH.

Why should I fear the winter now, when free
To meet and mingle in the strifes of man;
The danger to defy which now I see,
The oppressor to o'erthrow whom now I can!

Childhood! the season of my weaknesses,
  Is gone!—the muscle in my arm is strong;
No longer is there trembling in my knees,
  And my soul kindles at the look of wrong,
And burns in free defiance!—never more
  Let me recall the hour when I was weak,
To shrink, to seek for refuge, to implore;
  When I was scorn'd or trampled, but to speak,
When anger, rising high, though crouching low,
Should, like the tiger, spring upon his foe.

V. STRUGGLE.

Yet, in recalling these vex'd memories,
  Mine is no thought of vengeance! If I speak
  Of childhood, as a time that found me weak,
I utter no complaint of injuries;
These tried, but did not crush me; and they made
My spirit rise to a superior mood,—
  Taught me endurance, and meet hardihood,
And all life's better energies array'd
  For that long conflict which must end in death,
Or victory!—and victory shall yet be mine!
  They cannot keep me from my right—the spoil
  Which is the guerdon of superior toil—
Devotion that, defying hostile breath,
Ceased not to "watch and pray," though stars refused to
    shine!

VI. MANHOOD.

Manhood at last!—and, with its consciousness,
  Are strength and freedom; freedom to pursue
The purposes of hope—the godlike bliss,
  Born in the struggle for the great and true!
And every energy that should be mine,

This day, I dedicate to its object,—Life!
So help me Heaven, that never I resign
The duty which devotes me to the strife;—
The enduring conflict which demands my strength,
Whether of soul or body, to the last;
The tribute of my years, through all their length,—
The future's compensation to the past!—
Boy's pleasures are for boyhood—its best cares
Befit us not in our performing years.

THE SHADE-TREES.

God bless the hand that planted these old trees,
Here, by the wayside. While the August sun
Sends down his brazen arrows on the plain,
They give us shelter. Panting in their shade
We gaze upon the path o'er which we came,
And, in the green leaves overhead, rejoice!
Far as the eye may reach, the sands spread out,
A granulated blaze, pain the dim sense,
And vex the slumberous spirit with their glare.
Like some o'erpolish'd mirror, they give back
The sun's intenser fires. The green snake writhes
To run along the track—the lizard creeps,
Carefully tender, o'er the wither'd leaves,
And shuns the wayside, which, in early spring,
He travell'd only;—while, on the moist track,
Where ran a small brook out, a shining group
Of butterflies fold up their wearied wings,
Mottled with gold and purple, and cling close

To the dank surface, drawing the coolness thence
Which the gray sands deny. A thousand forms,—
Insect and fly, and the capricious bird,
Erewhile that sang so gayly in the spring
To his just wedded partner,—forms of life,
And most irregular impulse,—all seem press'd,
As by the approach of death ; and in the shade,
Hiding in leafy coverts and dense groves,
Where pines make natural temples for fond hearts,
And hopeless mourners,—seem in dread to wait
Some shock of nature. Summer reigns supreme,
With power like that of death ; and here, beneath
This most refreshing shelter of old trees,
I hear a murmuring voice from out the ground,
Where work her agents ; like the busy hum
From out the shops of labor, or, from far,
The excited beating of an army's pulse,
Mix'd in some solemn service.

'Twas a thought
Of good, becoming ancient patriarchs,
Of him who first, in the denying earth,
Planted these oaks. Heaven, for the kindly deed,
Look on his errors kindly ! He hath had
A most benevolent thought to serve his kind,
And felt, in truth, the principle of love
For the wide, various family of man,
Which is the true religion. Happy, for mankind,
Were such the better toil of those who make
The sacred text a theme for bitterness,
Who clamor more than pray, vexing the heart
With disputation. Better far, methinks,
If seated by the wayside, they beheld
The sorrows of its pilgrims ; raised the shade
To shelter in the noonday ; show'd the way

To the secluded fountain; and brought forth
The bread, and bless'd it to the stranger's want,
Who might, even then, be on his way to heaven!—
How fortunate for him who succor'd then!

THE SACRIFICE UPON OUR ALTARS.

OUR very passions leave us—our best tastes
Subside, as do our pleasures, and depart;
The moss and ivy grow about the heart,
And a cold apathy and dulness wastes
Our virgin fancies. We grow old apace,
While every flower that boyhood loved keeps young,
As if in bitter mockery of our pride!
And this it is to run ambition's race,
To lose the pulse of hope, youth's precious tide,
And through strange regions, and with unknown tongue,
As vain as Edward Irving's, wander wide,
Seeking our solemn phantoms,—things of air,
Thin, unsubstantial, which our hearts still grace
With homage, and our eyes still fancy bright and fair.

OH! WELCOME YE THE STRANGER.

OH! welcome ye the stranger,
And think, if e'er you rove,
How sweet in foreign lands must be
The voice that proffers love!
How sweet when sad delaying,
Where Fate compels to roam,

If stranger lips should welcome give
  And sweetly sing of home.

Oh! welcome ye the stranger,
  For still, whate'er his gain,
How much, in dear ones lost to sight,
  Must be his spirit's pain!
His smiles but ill betoken
  The heart within his breast,
That silent beats with hopes deferr'd
  And fears that will not rest.

Oh! welcome ye the stranger,
  To whom your hearth shall bring
The image of his own, and show
  Each dear one in the ring;
And as your song ascending
  Wakes memories sweet of yore,
He'll think of her he left behind,
  Whose song hath bless'd before.

CHILDRENS' EVENING GAMBOLS.

I.

Hear you not the merry sound?
Gather to the fairy round,
  'Tis the hour, 'tis the hour,
When the gentle signs abound,—
    When the bud begins to flower,
    When the moon, with placid power,
Soothes and lights the happy ground.

II.

Leap you not to that array,
Purest hearts in pleasant play?—
  Would you lose, would you lose,
Aught of such a holiday,—
  While the songs of such a muse,
  Lead the chain'd soul where they choose,
Far, in boyhood's world, away?

III.

Sweet to watch that pleasant game,
Chaste but lovely, free from shame;
  Childhood sweet, childhood sweet,—
Eyes of fire you would not tame;—
  On the floor the rapid beat
  Of the music-mocking feet,
The free laugh and wild acclaim!

IV.

Oh! this future on the floor,
How it doth the past restore!—
  In our eye, in our eye,
Stands the maid we loved of yore,—
  When, like him, the urchin nigh,
  First we learn'd to love and sigh,
As we love and sigh no more.

THE MINIATURE.

I've thought upon it long, and to mine eyes,
Howe'er my feet have wander'd, it hath been
The sweet star that hath guided through the night,
And brought me home again. I've worshipp'd it,

Even as the Hindoo maiden her gay boat
Of flowers, her heart's first fond experiment,
Sent down the Ganges. I regard it now—
Though all my flowers have wither'd, and my boat
Been baffled nigh to shipwreck—having loss
Of what the waters give not forth again—
With a beseeming reverence. And 'tis all,
So valued, but an image—one that needs
No color from the artist's brush, to raise
In features sensible. They have been touch'd
In more intense embodyings. Pearl and gold
Are but slight gear, its riches to secure,
And honor by their setting. Wouldst thou see?—
It is the picture of a delicate love,
Fair lady, and I've set it in my heart—
There, couldst thou look, thy own unwitting lips
Would murmur, with misgivings, to thy self,
"Where sat I to this painter?"

BEAUTY'S SPRING-TIME.

I.

VAINLY thou tend'st thy bower,
  Vainly thou deck'st the vine,
And joy'st in the richest flower
  That doth upon Ashley shine;
Thou nigh, though spring advances,
  Who seeks for her sunny train?
We do but glow in thy glances,
  And the garden blossoms in vain.

II.

Spring is in thee, bright creature,
  Thou bringer of songster and rose;
In thine is the blossoming feature,
  Whence the life that is loveliness flows.
A glimpse of the bow descending,
  The purple light on the sea,
A wing with the sunset blending,—
  Oh! these have spoken for thee.

III.

And thus, when the gray-footed morning
  First beats up the fleecy plain;
Ere the stars have had their warning,
  And close their sad eyes in pain;
My heart grows glad in the promise
  Of a holier reign to be,—
And, seeking the soul hid from us,
  I find its flower in thee!

THE UNQUIET SPIRIT.

Midnight!—and I am watching with the stars!
Can ye not let me slumber for a while,
Ye roving thoughts—and thou, unquiet mood,
Still active, wandering through infinity,
All times and nations, changes, destinies,
With sleepless soul, and discontented gaze,
Finding no place of rest? Can ye not spare,
To the o'erwearied votary, one pause
From the sad spirit's vigil? Must he still

Climb the precipitous height, and, with no guide
Save the sad watchers brooding in the heavens,
And the stern instinct, into which resolved,
Ye do compel the labor, hurry him on,
Weary, and with no recompense, to gain
The solitary chaplet of sad flowers,
But little valued, which a stranger hand,—
When I am dead, and those who knew me once
Miss me no longer from the crowded way,—
Will place, perchance, upon my humble grave?

This is the trophy, and for this I toil!—
Yet am I proud among my fellow-men,
And strive with him whose aim is greatly bent
For the sole column;—and with marvellous dread
Shrink from each middle perch of eminence.
And, in my chamber, when the world is still,
And those who were most ready in the strife,
Have sunk to sweet repose,—wakeful, I ask,
Doth my ambition, then, but strive for this
Poor honor,—which no present hand bestows,
And the far future, like some tardy steed,
Brings, when too late, and only brings in vain!
And is it such poor victory which now
Keeps me from slumber—makes the violent pulse,
And the full veins upon my forehead, swell
With aimless tumult, while the unsettled heart,
Now bounding with keen hope, desponding now,
Yearns for some other state, some wider range
For action, and some truer sympathy?
Is it for this, I ask, ye gentler sprites
Which tend upon the discontented soul,
That the still night, with its sad, twiring stars,
Still rises on my gaze, while all besides

Are, in the dwellings of sweet dreams, at rest;
And even the bird that, pendent from my roof,
Murmured, erewhile, at intervals, his song
In wandering catches, wild, and more than sweet,
Hath sought his cover in the mazy wood?

My feeling and my reason are not one,
They do rebuke each other. With the one
The world is full of glowing images,
And life abounds in honors, and strong hearts
Bend to the lofty sway, and gentle eyes
Look forth a pure encouragement, more dear,
And it may be, though not so thought by men,
More full of worth and value than the rest.
'Tis thus that fancy, ever won with dreams,
Portrays its triumphs—until wisdom comes,
And with stern accents and unbending brow,
Experience at her side, proclaims them all
Shallow and profitless—things far beneath
The sober and strong estimate of thought.

I fear me she is true. I have not lived
Untaught by my own being, and the toil,
The battle for existence. Yet, I feel
There is a victory beyond reason's scope,
And out of her domain. The spirit feels
Its urgent nature, which, though dash'd with care,
Knows still a medicine that "physics pain"—
A golden draught, more potent than of old
The alchemist through years of toil pursued,
Wearing out life in idle search of that
Which should preserve it. If I must look forth,
Watching yon sad but lustrous galaxy,
Counting its many and divided lights,

Dispatching thought on missions unto them,
And lingering for response,—I shall not fear,
Thus, in the eye of heaven, to urge my claim
To those same thick-sown fields of glorious life,
My heritage—on which my spirit turns
With a most natural instinct, which approves
Its right, and justifies its high demand—
Our future dwelling-place, to which my soul,
Like one unjustly disinherited,
Still looks, though vain, and cannot cease to look.

SONNET.—REPROACH AND CONSOLATION.

Well said the master,—" The worst grief of all,
  Is to remember, in our hours of woe,
  How blest we have been !"* It were rightly so,
If, like Adam's memory of his wretched fall,
To the keen thought of pleasures ever gone,
  There be the sting of self-reproach, to say,
  " The seed is of thy planting—go thy way,
And let the curse be on thy head alone !"
This is the bitterer truth,—but it is one,
  In bitterness thrice blessed, if it brings
  Repentance, that, with healing on its wings,
Will cheer the future, and the past atone:
It were a grace to pray for, night and day,
In ashes,—while the world is out at play.

* " Nessun maggior dolore,
Che ricordarsi del tempo felice,
Nella miseria."

BALLAD.

I.

HARK! the trumpet's note through all our valleys;—
  Red, the plains are weeping with the strife;
The song and dance have fled our peaceful alleys,
  And the young warrior leaves the drooping wife;
But will she cling to homes by love forsaken?—
  Not long she droops when from her side he goes;
In boyhood's guise, the weapon she hath taken,
  And, all unknown, she fights against his foes!—
      She hears the cry, "To arms!"
      No fear her soul alarms,
As still, with lance in rest, she seeks the thick array;
      Beside him, as he flies
      From foe to foe, she plies
The eager steel, and shares the glory of the fray!

II.

Hark! the trumpet's note from fight recalling,
  Night is in the deep with solemn eye;
Sad the starlight on the red plain falling,
  Shows the wounded soldier where to die!
In the mournful bivouac beside him
  She hath crouch'd in silence,—not to sleep;
But, above the slumbers not denied him,
  With fond thought, a patient watch to keep!
      Is it her name she hears,
      That, borne to eager ears,
Glides from his sleeping lips her soul to bless?—
      Ah! with what idle part
      Would she subdue her heart!
Love triumphs still, and he awakes in her caress.

SUMMER WEST WIND.

I.

From what dear island in the Indian seas
  Com'st thou, sweet spicy breeze ;—
The freshness of the morning on thy wing,
  And all the bloom of spring ?—
Ah ! ere thy flight was taken,
  The rose and shrub were shaken ;
Thou stol'st to many a bower of bloom and bliss,
  Giving and taking many a balmy kiss !
Ah ! happy, that in flying, thou not leavest
  Aught that thou need'st or grievest ;
Thy spirit knows not fetters, though subdued,
  For a long time, thy mood ;—
Yet, let the west implore thee,
  The sweet south smile before thee,
The murmur of their fountains meet thine ear,
  And thou, anon, art there !
The lone one will forget her loneliness
  As thou uplift'st her tress,
Kissing, with none to check,
  The whitest neck,—
She blushing, with fond fancies, that repine
  For other lips than thine,—
Ah ! why not mine !

II.

Methinks from thy sweet breath and tender motion,
  Thy last flight was from caves in southern ocean,
Spar-gemm'd and lustrous ;—there, thy form has crept
  To the pale Nereid as she sighing, slept !
Ah, wanton !—thou hast toy'd with tangled hair,

And bent o'er beauties rare;
Seal'd up bright eyes with kisses, that anon,
When sleep and thou wert gone,
Wept at the hapless waking which destroy'd
The sweetest world of void!—
Thou might'st have linger'd in thy watch secure,—
Thy kisses, though they waken'd her, were pure;
Nay, on her lips thou might'st impress the seal
Her cheeks still blush to feel;
Her sea-shell, meanwhile, suiting with sweet notes,
Till slowly, through its purple winding, floats
Love's fondest plaint,—
The saddest dear'st effusion of her saint;
Touch'd to the soul with such a tenderness,
She may no more express,—
Her only grief, her joy in such excess,
No words may well declare, no music paint!

III.

Canst thou desert her, vain one!—wilt thou fly,
With sunset, when the purple billow glows,
As with new passion 'neath the western sky?—
Thy flight hath borne with it her dear repose;—
That music, as it goes,
Robs her of life with love;—unless it be
She still can fly with thee;—
Borne far with dying day,
A faint but fairy lay,—
That moves her,—following through the fields of air,—
Thee seeking, false one, seeking everywhere!

IV.

Even in his fiercest hour
Thou mock'st the great sun's power,

Thy broad wing o'er the quivering plain below,
Shield'st fondly from his glow,
   And cherishest and cheer'st the drooping flower.
Lo! smiling, the green trees that forward bend
   With thy fast flight to blend;
Lo! the cool'd waves that dimpling ocean's isles,
   Implore thee with a thousand frantic wiles,
Flinging their shells along the yellow beach,
   That thou mayst teach,
With lingering whisper, as thou dartest by,
   To every twisted core, its melody.

V.

Swart labor greets thee from his fields with prayer,
   And bows with dripping hair,
Vest open wide and blue eye that declares
   A gladness born of cares.—
Mother of meekness, child of happy birth,
   Sprung from the sky, yet born alone for earth,—
Glows his broad bosom as he sees thy wing,
   Slow spreading, and with silence hovering,
A purple cloud descending,
Above his green fields bending,
And blessing!—Thou hast cheer'd him with thy breath,
   When all was still as death;
Leaves quivering in the close and stifling air;
   A languor, like despair,
Stretch'd o'er the earth, and through the coppery sky
   That burns the upholding eye;—
Streams fled from ancient channels, and the blade
   Blasted as soon as made—
And the sad drooping of all things that sigh,
   With the dread fear to die!

VI.

Ah! still above our green plains brood, and bring
  Life to their languishing!
Sweet breath and dear protection! go not soon,
  Though, with the rising moon,
The mermaid woos thee to her silvery isle,
  And songs from green-hair'd ocean-maids beguile,
No longer dumb with rapture, waiting thee.
  We may not set thee free,—
Let prayer secure thee for a season, till
  Prayer true as ours gives freedom to thy will!
Then linger not too long, nor all forget
  How fondly, when we met,
Our arms were spread to greet thee,—and each breast,
  Wide, opening for its guest.
Come to us waking—sleeping; do not fear
  To waken, with thy music in each ear,
Music of flowers and of the gentle waves
  That break in moonlight caves,—
Music of youth and hope, which, if it know
  A touch of tears or woe,
Is yet a woe of tenderness, that brings
  Gleams still of sweetest things;—
And, if it tell of night,
  Tells of it only when its stars are bright,
And in the silvery, soft and tremulous air,
  The moon and thou art both commercing there.

THE KINGS IN SHEOL.

PARAPHRASE.—Isaiah xiv.

Hark! the nations take a song
Of deliverance from the strong;—
Still they cry on every hand,
There is freedom for the land;
For the oppressor's overthrown,
And the golden city's down!—
He who smote the world in wrath
Now lies silent in his path;
None so feeble but may stride
O'er the brow they deified:—
God, in vengeance, hath arisen;
He hath broke the captive's prison;
In his smile a freedom bringing,
Which hath set the whole world singing;
All exulting o'er the ruin
Which declares the dread undoing
Of the awful power that made
Earth grow barren in its shade!
The pines, that trembled at his tread,—
The cedars, doom'd to bow the head
Beneath his lordly axe, that won
The grayest brows of Lebanon,—
Now shout triumphant in the blow
That shields them hence from overthrow.
How stands above his open grave,
With words of scorn, his meanest slave!

To his gloomy ghost they cry,
As it shrouds it from the sky,—
Sinking, under doom of woe,
To the awful realm below.

Thou, that lately stood elate,
Hence! to meet a loathlier state,—
Hell, to hail thee, stirs her dead!—
Rising, as they hear thy tread,
Lo! the great ones of the earth
Hail thee with a mocking mirth;
From their thrones of ancient might,
Rise, to welcome thee to—Night.
Thou, with common voice, they speak,
Art become like us, and weak;—
Pomp and music could not save,
All thy pride is in the grave;
'Neath thee winds the worm,—above,
Crawls and clings, with loathsome love!
How art thou fallen! that, like the star,
The son of morning, shone afar,
Flung, midst the glory of thy light,
In darkness from thy mountain height;
Even at the moment when thy aim
Had been the cope of heaven to claim,—
Above the stars of God to rise,
And sway the assembly of the skies!
Lo! where thou sink'st, with mortal dread,
While Sheol closes o'er thy head;—
Grasping her sides with feeble will,
Yet sinking downward, downward still;
How—could they see thee from above,—
The eyes that never watch'd in love,—

How would they cry—can this be he
That made the crowded nations flee,
Did, in his wrath, the kingdoms shake,
And make earth's far foundations quake!

MONNA.

I.

There was an eye, a steadfast eye,
That once I loved,—I love it now;—
And still it gazes on my brow,
Unchanged through all,—unchangingly.

II.

It could not change, though it has gone;—
For 'twas a thing of soul;—and so
It did not with the mortal go
To that one chamber, still and lone.

III.

It had a touch, a winning touch,
Of twilight sadness in its glance;
And look'd, at times, as in a trance,
Till I grew sad, I loved so much.

IV.

For life is selfish, and the tear
In one we love is like a gloom;
And still I wept the stubborn doom
That made a thing of grief so dear.

V.

Through sunny hours and cloudy hours,
  And hours that had nor sun nor cloud,
  That eye was wrapt, as in a shroud,
Such shroud as autumn flings o'er flowers.

VI.

It had a language dear to me,
  Though strange to all the world beside;
  And many a grief I strove to chide
Grew sweet to mine idolatry.

VII.

I could not stay the grief, nor chase
  The cloud that gloom'd the earnest eye;
  But gave,—'twas all,—my sympathy,
And woe was written on my face.

VIII.

'Twas on my face, as in my heart;
  And when the Lady Monna died,
  Whom still I loved,—I never sigh'd,
But tearless saw the lights depart.

IX.

They bore her coldly to the tomb;
  They took me to my home away;
  Nor knew that from that vacant day,
My home was with her in the gloom.

X.

They little knew how still we went,
  Together, in the midnight shade,
  Communing, with wet eyes, that made
Our very passions innocent.

XI.

Born of the cloud, her mournful eye
  Was on me still, as shines the star,
  That, drooping from its heights afar,
Broods ever on eternity.

XII.

It led me aye through folds of shade,
  By day and darkness still the same,
  And, heedless of all mortal blame,
I follow'd meekly where it bade.

XIII.

They watch'd my steps, and scann'd my face,
  And vex'd my heart till I grew stern ;—
  For curious eyes have yet to learn
How sorrow dreads each finger trace.

XIV.

Mine was too deep a love to be
  The common theme for idle tongue,
  And when they spoke of her, they wrung
My spirit into agony.

XV.

I live a lone and settled woe ;—
  I care not if the day be fair
  Or foul,—I would that I were near
The maid they buried long ago.

UR-LIGHT.

Ere, at first, the seals were broken,
And the motive word had spoken,
Earth was but an idiot wonder,
Born in cloud and clad in thunder;
Blindly striving, vainly roaring,
Wildly plunging, feebly soaring,
Whirling with a fretful motion
Like a ship in peevish ocean;—
Graceless all, in grove and fountain,
Shapeless all, in vale and mountain;—
Hopeless, heartless, songless, sightless,
Cold and dismal, soulless, sprightless;—
Little dreaming then of glory,
Which should make so sweet a story
Music-weaving, music-winning,
Closing sweet for sweet beginning;
Borne across the tract of ages,
Still in sweet successive stages,—
In their daily march untying,
Sounds forever thence undying;—
In their daily music, freeing,
Souls, forever thence in being;—
Beauty still, for song revealing,
Love, that finds for beauty, feeling,—
Hope that knows what truth shall follow,—
Truth that hope alone shall hallow!
But a word must first be spoken,
Ere the heavy seals are broken;
And bright clouds of spirits, chosen,—
Watchful, never once reposing,

Hang amid the void, upgazing,
Where the great world's soul is blazing.
Hark! a voice is heard, as calling,
And a star is seen, as falling,
Star of soul, whose spell symphonious,
Makes stars, systems, suns, harmonious!
Oh! that blessed sound, that thrilling
Earth and matter, make them willing!
Hark! the angels join, rejoicing
As they hear that highest voicing;
Stills the ocean, wildly rushing,
As their melody is gushing;—
Lo! the volcan stays his thunder,
And his red eyes ope in wonder!—
Earth, no longer blind, rejoices,
Clapping hands and lifting voices;
While the eastern sky is streaking,—
Hues of white, like lightning breaking,
Lighten ocean up with splendor,
Make the rugged mountains tender,
As still crowding into cluster,
They implore the growing lustre.
Tree and flow'ret, vale and mountain,
Plain and forest, lake and fountain,
Grove and prairie, rock and river,
Give their glories to the giver;—
Win their voices with their seeing,
Find, in light, their fount of being;
And at eve, its smile imploring,
Still, with dawn, begin adoring;—
Ah! by light eternal bidden,
Light shall never more be hidden.

THE LONELY ISLET.

I.

Lift the oar, as silently
By yon sacred isle we pass;
Know we not if still she sleeps,
Where the wind such whisper keeps,
In yon waving grass!
Death's a mocker to delight,
That we know,—and yet,—
There was that in every breath
Of her motion—in the set
Of her features, fair and whole—
In the flashing of her eye,
Spirit joyous still, and high,
Speaking the immortal soul,
In a language warm and bright—
That should mock at death!

II.

Silently!—still silently!
Oh! methinks, if it were true,
If, indeed, she sleeps—
Wakeful never, though the oar
Of the well-beloved one, nigh,
Break the water as before;—
When, with but the sea in view,
And the sky-waste, and the shore,
Or some star that, sinking, creeps,
Between whiles of speech, to show
How sweet lover's tears may flow,—
They together went, forgetting,
How the moon was near her setting,
Down amid the waters low;—

III.

Then no more should lovely things,
Moon or star, or zephyr, stoop,—
But a cloud with dusky wings,
Gloom outgiving, still should droop,
O'er that islet lone:—
And the long grass by the breeze
Sullen rising from the seas,
Should make constant moan!
Silent!—Hark!—that dipping oar,—
Oh! methinks, it roused a tone
As of one upon the shore!—
'Twas the wind that swept the grass!—
Silently, oh! silently,—
As the sacred spot we pass!

SYBILLA.

IN ILLUSTRATION OF A PICTURE.

Her brow is raised, her eye in air,—
The spirit burns and triumphs there!—
Mark the sacred strength that dwells
Where that pure white forehead swells;
Lo! the sacred fire that streams
From that deep eye's sudden gleams,
As a shaft of lightning driven
Through the cloud-veil'd deeps of heaven!

What the passion in that soul,
Thus that bursts and scorns control?
Can it be the lowly birth,—

Passion, which has root in earth—
Which may govern thus, and move,
Soul so high with mortal love?—
No! the feeling in that eye
Finds its birth-place in the sky.

She hath thrown aside the pen,
Which she straight resumes agen:—
Coursing o'er the spotless leaf,
Lo! her heart hath told its grief:
What a sorrow in that tone!
What a passion in that moan!
And the big tear, in her eye,
How it speaks the destiny!

Read the letters;—speak them;—lo!
What a story writ, of woe;
Woe is me, that heart like thine,
Kindling thus, and pure, should pine;
Woe is me, that in thy morn,
Thou shouldst blossom thus forlorn;
Yet the doom is said in sooth,
Thou shalt perish in thy youth:—

Lose the promise at thy birth;
Lose the pleasant green of earth;
Lose the waters, lose the light,
Sweet from sense and fair from sight;
Ere the breaking of thy heart,
From each dear affection part,
Die in spirit, ere the doom
Drags the mortal to the tomb!—

Thus the fearful prophecy
Glares before thy kindling eye;

Thy own fingers pen the word,
Which thy coal-touch'd ear hath heard;
Thou art doom'd to witness all,
Thou hast loved and cherish'd, fall,—
Fall,—the deadliest form of death—
From the friendship, from the faith!

This is worst—for death is naught
To the high and hopeful thought;
'Tis a deeper pang that rends,
In the parting of firm friends;
In the wrenching of that tie
Which links souls of sympathy;
In the hour that finds us lone,
Making o'er the false our moan.

Death she fears not;—but to part,
With each young dream of the heart;
That first hope that brought the rest,
All its sweet brood, to the breast;
Where a virgin in her cares,
Love a mother grew to snares,
Which, with harbor'd vipers strove,
At the last, to strangle Love!—

Yet her sacred soul is strong;
She maintains the struggle long;
In her cheek the pale is bright,
And the tear-drop hath its light;
On the lip the moan that's heard
Is the singing of a bird,
Striving for the distant quire;—
And her fingers clasp the lyre.

She is dying,—dying fast,
But in music to the last;—
Oh! sad swan, thy parting lay
Is the sweetest of thy day;
And it hath a winged might
Bearing up the soul in flight,
Still ascending, seeking place,
'Mong the angels, for a grace.

THE BURDEN OF THE DESERT.

A PARAPHRASE.—Isaiah xxi.

I.

The burden of the Desert,
The Desert like the deep,
That from the south in whirlwinds
Comes rushing up the steep;—
I see the spoiler spoiling,
I hear the strife of blows;
Up, watchman, to thy heights, and say
How the dread conflict goes!

II.

What hear'st thou from the desert?—
"A sound, as if a world
Were from its axle lifted up
And to an ocean hurl'd;
The roaring as of waters,
The rushing as of hills,
And lo! the tempest-smoke and cloud,
That all the desert fills."

III.

What seest thou on the desert ?—
  " A chariot comes," he cried,
" With camels and with horsemen,
  That travel by its side ;
And now a lion darteth
  From out the cloud, and he
Looks backward ever as he flies,
  As fearing still to see !"

IV.

What, watchman, of the horsemen ?—
  " They come, and as they ride,
Their horses crouch and tremble,
  Nor toss their manes in pride ;
The camels wander scatter'd,
  The horsemen heed them naught,
But speed, as if they dreaded still
  The foe with whom they fought."

V.

What foe is this, thou watchman ?—
  " Hark ! Hark ! the horsemen come ;
Still looking on the backward path,
  As if they fear'd a doom ;
Their locks are white with terror,
  Their very shout's a groan ;
'Babylon,' they cry, 'has fallen,
  And all her gods are gone !' "

THE EDGE OF THE SWAMP.

'Tis a wild spot, and even in summer hours,
With wondrous wealth of beauty and a charm
For the sad fancy, hath the gloomiest look,
That awes with strange repulsion. There, the bird
Sings never merrily in the sombre trees,
That seem to have never known a term of youth,
Their young leaves all being blighted. A rank growth
Spreads venomously round, with power to taint;
And blistering dews await the thoughtless hand
That rudely parts the thicket. Cypresses,
Each a great ghastly giant, eld and gray,
Stride o'er the dusk, dank tract,—with buttresses
Spread round, apart, not seeming to sustain,
Yet link'd by secret twines, that, underneath,
Blend with each arching trunk. Fantastic vines,
That swing like monstrous serpents in the sun,
Bind top to top, until the encircling trees
Group all in close embrace. Vast skeletons
Of forests, that have perish'd ages gone,
Moulder, in mighty masses, on the plain;
Now buried in some dark and mystic tarn,
Or sprawl'd above it, resting on great arms,
And making, for the opossum and the fox,
Bridges, that help them as they roam by night.
Alternate stream and lake, between the banks,
Glimmer in doubtful light: smooth, silent, dark,
They tell not what they harbor; but, beware!
Lest, rising to the tree on which you stand,
You sudden see the moccasin snake heave up
His yellow shining belly and flat head

Of burnish'd copper. Stretch'd at length, behold
Where yonder Cayman, in his natural home,
The mammoth lizard, all his armor on,
Slumbers half-buried in the sedgy grass,
Beside the green ooze where he shelters him.
The place, so like the gloomiest realm of death,
Is yet the abode of thousand forms of life,—
The terrible, the beautiful, the strange,—
Wingéd and creeping creatures, such as make
The instinctive flesh with apprehension crawl,
When sudden we behold. Hark! at our voice
The whooping crane, gaunt fisher in these realms,
Erects his skeleton form and shrieks in flight,
On great white wings. A pair of summer ducks,
Most princely in their plumage, as they hear
His cry, with senses quickening all to fear,
Dash up from the lagoon with marvellous haste,
Following his guidance. See! aroused by these,
And startled by our progress o'er the stream,
The steel-jaw'd Cayman, from his grassy slope,
Slides silent to the slimy green abode,
Which is his province. You behold him now,
His bristling back uprising as he speeds
To safety, in the centre of the lake,
Whence his head peers alone,—a shapeless knot,
That shows no sign of life; the hooded eye,
Nathless, being ever vigilant and sharp,
Measuring the victim. See! a butterfly,
That, travelling all the day, has counted climes
Only by flowers, to rest himself a while,
And, as a wanderer in a foreign land,
To pause and look around him ere he goes,
Lights on the monster's brow. The surly mute
Straightway goes down; so suddenly, that he,

The dandy of the summer flowers and woods,
Dips his light wings, and soils his golden coat,
With the rank waters of the turbid lake.
Wondering and vex'd, the pluméd citizen
Flies with an eager terror to the banks,
Seeking more genial natures,—but in vain.
Here are no gardens such as he desires,
No innocent flowers of beauty, no delights
Of sweetness free from taint. The genial growth
He loves, finds here no harbor. Fetid shrubs,
That scent the gloomy atmosphere, offend
His pure patrician fancies. On the trees,
That look like felon spectres, he beholds
No blossoming beauties; and for smiling heavens,
That flutter his wings with breezes of pure balm,
He nothing sees but sadness—aspects dread,
That gather frowning, cloud and fiend in one,
As if in combat, fiercely to defend
Their empire from the intrusive wing and beam.
The example of the butterfly be ours.
He spreads his lacquer'd wings above the trees,
And speeds with free flight, warning us to seek
For a more genial home, and couch more sweet
Than these drear borders offer us to-night.

THE STRUGGLE OF ENDOWMENT WITH FORTUNE.

When thou shalt put my name upon the tomb,
  Write under it, "Here lies the weariest man
  That ever struggled with a wayward ban,
The victim from his birth-hour to a doom
That made all nature war against his will;

Made profitless his toil, its fruits denied
To patient courage and ambition still;
His tasks decreed, his industry decried;
And left him weary of the sun, whose flight
Brought him the gloom without the peace of night.
His toilsome pathway ever was uphill,—
A hill forever growing,—still his draught
Was water in a sieve that could not fill,
And bitter was his cup, or drunk, or left unquaff'd."

MORAL CHANGE.

DARKNESS is gathering round me, but the stars,
Silent and unobtrusive, stealing out,
Lend beauty to the night. The air comes cool
Up from the fountain; and the murmuring breeze,
Gushing through yonder valley, has a song
Spelling the silence to such mystery
As mingles with our dreams. It is the hour
When sad, sweet thoughts have sway;—when memory,
Triumphant o'er the past, waves her green wand,
And bids the clouds roll back, and lifts the veil
That had been closed behind us as a wall,—
And the eye sees, and the heart feels, and lives
Once more in its old feelings. I retrace
The homes of past affections, and dear hopes,
And dreams that look'd like hopes, and fled as well.
This is the spot—I know it as of old
By various tokens, but 'tis sadly changed.—
Men look not as they did; and flowers that grew,
Nursed by some twin affections, grow alone,

Pining for old attendance. Thus, our change
Brings a worse change on nature. She will bloom
To bless a kindred spirit; but she flies
The home that yields no worship. She is seen
Through the sweet medium of our sympathies,
And has no life beside. 'Tis in our eye
Alone that she is lovely—'tis our thought
That makes her dear, as only in our ears
Lies the young minstrel's music, which were harsh,
Did not our mood yield up fit instrument
For his congenial fingers.

It is thus,—
The beautiful evening, the secluded vale,
The murmuring breeze, the gushing fountain, all
So exquisite in nature to the sense,
So cheering to the spirit—bring me naught
But shadows of a gloomy thought that rise
With the dusk memory—with repeated tales,
Censuring the erring heart-hope with its loss :—
Loss upon loss—the dark defeat of all
The pleasant plans of boyhood—promises
That might have grown in fairy land to flowers,
And were but weeds in this. They did but wound,
Or cheat and vanish with deluding glare :
Having the aspect of some heavenly joy,
They also had its wings, and, tired of earth,
Replumed them back for the more natural clime,
And so were lost to ours. Hopes still wrong
And torture, when they grow extravagant—
Youth is their victim ever, for they grow,
With the advancing seasons, into foes
That wolve upon him. 'Tis a grief to me,
Though a strange pleasure still, thus to look forth,
Watching, through lengthening hours, so sweet a scene,

And winning back old feelings as I gaze.
Boyhood had drawn a picture fair like this
On fancy's vision. Ancient oaks were there,
Giving the landscape due solemnity—
A quiet streamlet trickled through a grove,
And the birds sang most sweetly in the trees—
But then the picture was not incomplete,
Nor I alone, as now.

SONNET.—FRIENDSHIP.

THOUGH wrong'd, not harsh my answer! Love is fond,
  Even pain'd,—and rather to his injury bends,
  Than chooses to make shipwreck of his friends
By stormy summons. He hath naught beyond
  For consolation, if that these be lost;
  And rather will he hear of fortune cross'd,
Plans baffled, hopes denied,—than take a tone
  Resentful,—with a quick and keen reply
  To hasty passion and impatient eye,
Such as by noblest natures may be shown,
  When the mood vexes! Friendship is a seed
  Needs tendance: You must keep it free from weed,
Nor, if the tree has sometimes bitter fruit,
Must you for this lay axe unto the root.

THE LAY OF THE CARIB DAMSEL.

I.

Come, seek the ocean's depths with me,
For there are joys beneath the sea,—
Joys, that when all is dark above,
Make all below a home of love!

II.

In hollow bright and fountain clear,
Lo! thousand pearl await us there;
And amber drops that sea-birds weep
In sparry caves along the deep.

III.

A crystal chamber there I know,
Where never yet did sunshaft go;
The soft moss from the rocks I take,
Of this our nuptial couch to make.

IV.

There, as thou yieldest on my breast,
My songs shall soothe thy happy rest,—
Such songs as still our prophets hear,
When winds and stars are singing near.

V.

These tell of climes, whose deep delight
Knows never change from day to night;
Where, if we love, the blooms and flowers,
And fruits, shall evermore be ours.

VI.

Oh! yield thee to the hope I bring,
Believe the truth I feel and sing,
Nor teach thy spirit thus to weep
Thy Christian home beyond the deep.

VII.

'Tis little,—ah! too well I know,
The poor Amaya may bestow,—
But if a heart that's truly thine
Be worthy thee, oh! cherish mine!

VIII.

My life is in thy look—for thee
I bloom, as for the sun, the tree;
My hopes, when thou forget'st thy woes,
Unfold as flowers, when winter goes.

IX.

And though, as our traditions say,
There bloom the worlds of endless day,
I would not care to seek the sky,
If there thy spirit did not fly.

THE MAGIC VOICE.

'Twas a voice that rose in the far blue sky,
The voice of a trumpet melody;
And it woke to joy all the subject things,
And brought to the feeble the strength of wings;

The heart grew glad in the lonely breast,
By the soothing sweet of that voice possess'd;
And the eye flash'd bright, as it look'd to see
The source of so glad a mystery;
While the skies, late gloom'd with the growing nig.
In the dawn of a better hope grew bright!
It floated along, that voice so clear,
And it brought new strength to the soul of fear,
And men grew glad, they knew not why,
As the musical murmurs came floating by;
A mystery lay in each magic tone,
That made the heavens and earth its own;
And the sun was spell'd in his march above,
As brooding fond o'er a realm of love,
While the drooping stars on each lonely height,
Gave echoes back of their soft delight.

Though the summer had gone, though the winter cam.
The tones of that voice were still the same;
And it had a power to make of the cold
But a new spur to the young and old;
The city grew brave in its arts and arms,
And the Court in new virtues put on new charms;
While the reapers look'd up from the sun-ripe field,
Joyous and wild in its wondrous yield;
They saw that wherever that music had been,
The fruits grew ripe, and the fields were green.
Oh! then was the nation's greatness known,
And genius grew stronger than Church and Throne;
Valor went forth, and his spear of light
Bore a fresh laurel from every fight;
And the peaceful, but conquering arts, they wrought
Triumphs more goodly in fields of Thought:
The sculptor, from caverns of rock, bade rise

The Silent Grandeur to human eyes;
And the Painter, with pencil of magic, made
The Beautiful steal from the dusky shade.
Ah! for how long a season came,
The spells of that voice, rejoicing Fame!
Even so long as the nation heard,
Still grew the spells of its potent word;
Still did it prompt and guide to toils,
Great in their grandeur and rich in their spoils;
All that it ask'd was the patient ear,
The heedful heart, and the trustful care;
The Faith, that in every hope believes,
The Love that, in humbleness, still achieves!

But there was a cry of wail by night,
As if for a star that had left its height;
And silence fell on the listening ear,
With a feeling of chill and a spell of fear:
Valor went forth to win no more,
And the Genius now grovell'd that soar'd before;
The arts of the city, the courtly grace,
Fled, as they never there had place;
They had mock'd and banish'd that magic voice,
And the land might never again rejoice!

ELODIE.

I.

A BIRD that had no song by day,
  But crouch'd in sadness in the shade,
As soon as came the evening's ray,
    Took wing and soar'd aloft,

And, with a music soft,
Sweet melodies for all the forest made.
Elodie! Elodie!
Thus evermore the plaintive ditty rose—
Elodie! Elodie!
Subsiding to a murmur at the close,
That grew to silence but was not repose,
And might be tears, for still
The accent seem'd to fill,
As of a heart still bursting to be free—
With evermore that chant—sad chant—of Elodie.

II.

They tell of one denied, who fled
His human to a forest home;
Who laid at last his aching head
Beneath the wood and slept,
While death upon him crept,
And, with a holy word, expell'd his gloom.—
Elodie! Elodie!
Was still the last fond murmur of his breast—
Elodie! Elodie!
And from that moment a wild bird grew blest,
With the sweet burden never more to rest—
For ever, with the night,
Eager in song and flight,
As with a soul still bursting to be free,
His wings swell out with still that chant of Elodie.

NIGHT-WATCHING.

How still is this night's solitude—how calm
All the dim nature round! I hear no voice
From out this populous city—see no light
Beckoning from well-known dwelling of my youth
To some gay hearth and laughing company.
Alone among the stranger, I am sad,
Seeking familiar forms I may not find,
And sorrowing in that bondage of the clay
That checks the spirit's flight to its own home,
Beyond the heaving waters. There, my child
Plays in the summer flowers, that, while they glow,
Have lurking death beneath them. Pestilence
Walks thither in the noonday; and the airs,
Balm breathing, from the bosom of the night,
Are tainted with the fever gale that reeks
From the rank gardens and o'erteeming fields,
That yield the proud man plenty. God of Heaven,
Be with that child in mercy. Guard her well,
With thy o'erwatchful blessings. Shield her breast
From sudden night-winds;—from her red lips drive
The hovering fever. Be thy pitying love
Before her innocent bosom, that, no more,
Her father's arm may shield—his watchful care
Protect by human providence—his love
Die for, if such the sudden need, when wrong
Strikes at the imploring trembler, which it does
When peril seems least present. Here, afar,
My knees are bent to thee—my proud heart sinks
In prayer,—the big tears gather in my eyes,
And, with a deep humility that feels

Its weakness, thinking on that child of love,
My soul implores thy blessings on her head,
In smiles that bring her body health—her mind
Ripeness and purity, that she may bloom,
Worthy of life and happiness and thee.

The city is around me, but its strifes
Are hush'd to silence. What a god is sleep,
That can so chain the faculties of men,
The fearful moods, the restless energies,
So busy and so turbulent a while
Some three hours past, and now so sternly still,
It seems some eastern city of the dead!

Where is the artisan, whose hammer clink'd
On the fire-darting anvil through the day?—
The pedler, who was vaunting o'er his wares,
His worldly wealth about him—rich withal?
The tradesman, conning o'er his daily sales
With eager lip, and eye upon the watch,
Not to be over-bargain'd?—where the youth,
Anxious for honor and distinction, won
By noisy declamation in the crowd
About the forum?—all are sunk in sleep!
Sleep, the subduer of the sick man's pulse,
Bringer of pleasant dreams and airy thoughts,
That while away the fever'd toils of earth,
And give a bounding impulse to the blood,
Distemper'd by the noise-oppresséd brain!
Thou second part of life, that art a death,
Refitting for a newer start in life,
And nerving with a freshness all but me!

In vain I look upon the pensive night,
That hangs her silver crescent in the sky,

Gather'd on fleecy folds, that edge the blue
Of her vast, wild, pavilion'd canopy,
And keeps it, as a warrior doth his shield,
Unstain'd by dark device, or mortal dint,
And pure and spotless as a vestal's heart,
Upon the hour she gives herself to God!
There is no breath to waken up the leaf
That sits within my window—all is still—
And how oppressive grows that stillness now!
I cannot sleep. A spirit at my side,
Though, with the day's fatigue, my form is faint,
Keeps me from slumber. Thought, undying thought,
That dost pervade life's farthest wilderness,
Why may I not repose with those who take
These grateful slumbers? Wherefore, in my soul,
Still wouldst thou sound the silvery cord that trills
With hope of life—the sensible, true life
Of immortality and consciousness,
That is forever present to my dreams,
And bears me with a visible impulse on,
Spite of the rough adventure of the time,
The jostle of far-sighted emulation,
To look beyond myself, and fondly dare
Converse with high intelligence, and powers
Beyond man's frail existence!

Do the stars
Shine forth with fuller loveliness to me,
That thus I wake to watch them? Is the moon
Peculiar in her gaze to-night?—her smile
Sleeps on my very couch, and by my side—
And in the imperfect brightness of her glance,
Fantastic forms and shadows from her light
Glide through the chamber, and, with fancy's aid,

Grow human, and solicit me to speech.
And now, a silvery train is drawn afar,
Like a faint thread upon the utmost verge
Of the dun sky—as if it would unite
The earth I wake on, and the heaven I watch.
It is the star of my nativity—
What wonder I should wake to watch it then,
With a deep fixedness—a strong desire
To gather, from its seeming, all my hope—
Ambition's hope—far fitter gods than men—
Which lives unto the peril of the life
That is my mortal being—wearing away,
Consuming as a night-lamp, dim, untrimm'd,
The frame and sinews of the nerveless form
The forest boor had laugh'd at.—Lo! afar
It shoots along, and sheds in its lone flight,
A rich and tremulous lustre. Doth it wake,
In sympathy with me, alone among
Its starry train of rich intelligences,
As I, among my fellows of the earth—
Restless alike?—and should ambition dwell
So high above the mortal part of life?
Yet was it said, ere this, in ancient time,
When gods were on the earth, in guise of men,
And men, in action, rivall'd the high gods,
That 'twas the quality of heaven, and so
Became transmitted to the humbler race,
With whom they lightly mingled; and to whom
They gave such sad inheritance of pride—
High reaching, strong desire and boundless want,
Love of far rule, undying thirst of praise,
And power that never sleeps, but seeks for sway
Through peril, and foul circumstance and blood—
Heedless that pain and death are in the gift,

Though coupled with high honor!—fatal gift—
That saps the springs of life, of love, of peace,
Eats out the heart with a concealéd fire,
And leaves the desolate frame, self-blasted, thus,
By its own raging spirit overthrown,
Even on the summit of its towering hopes,
The vulture-tortured Titan on his rock!
Oh! what is fame, that I should darken youth—
The fresh attire of morning—the gay sun
Of my young destiny, that shone so fair—
With watching through the night—the sweet, long night
That fills my eyes with gentle drops to see—
Sweet though they flow from out the fount of tears,
Upon my heart, like dews upon the flower
In Hermon's valley! Doth to it belong,
Acknowledgment 'mong men, in words, whose tone,
Like music, offers to the moody soul,
Whose watchfulness is madness?—No, alas!—
Nor Time himself shall evermore retrieve
The life that I have lost! Yet, be this told,
In after years, when at my fireside blaze,
No chair shall be in waiting for my form,
No eye to smile at my unlook'd approach,
No welcome mine;—and from the mossy stoné,
The imperfect characters which love hath traced,
Are trodden out by time—though he hath fail'd
To gain the planet's burning eminence,
With the high fires that he so oft hath watch'd,
The spirit was within him, and he strove,
Unqualified by base desire or deed,
Most nobly, though perchance he reach'd it not.

SONNETS.—RECOMPENSE.

I.

Not profitless the game, even when we lose,
Nor wanting in reward the thankless toil;
The wild adventure that the man pursues,
Requites him, though he gather not the spoil:
Strength follows labor, and its exercise
Brings independence, fearlessness of ill,—
Courage and pride,—all attributes we prize;—
Though their fruits fail, not the less precious still.
Though fame withholds the trophy of desire,
And men deny, and the impatient throng
Grow heedless, and the strains protracted, tire;—
Not wholly vain the minstrel and the song,
If, striving to arouse one heavenly tone
In others' hearts, it wakens up his own.

II.

And this, methinks, were no unseemly boast,
In him who thus records the experience
Of one, the humblest of that erring host,
Whose labors have been thought to need defence.
What though he reap no honors,—what though death
Rise terrible between him and the wreath,
That had been his reward, ere, in the dust,
He too is dust; yet hath he in his heart,
The happiest consciousness of what is just,
Sweet, true, and beautiful,—which will not part
From his possession. In this happy faith,
He knows that life is lovely—that all things
Are sacred—that the air is full of wings
Bent heavenward,—and that bliss is born of scath!

III.

And other lessons of humanity,
  That fill the earth with blossoms—teach to feel
That man is better than he seems to be,
  And he declares himself, and deeds reveal:
Not of good wholly fruitless was the tree
  Whose fruit was death; and, from the crowd apart,
There beckons one, first-born of poesy,
  A gentle power, that from his darkled eyes
Removes all scales, and sets the vision free,
  And teaches mercy for the erring heart,
Not always wilful! We may naught despise
In God's creation! Erring we, not wise;—
Given up to passion,—hateful of the just,—
Prone to blind toils, strange follies, crime and dust.

SUMMER IN THE SOUTH.

Shines in mid-heaven the summer sun,
Green the gay robes which the woods have won,
And far aloft, o'er the snowy fleece,
Of clouds that brood in the realm of peace,
Spreads the great arch, with a deepening blue,
That meetly, with beauty, still bounds the view.
The swallow flits, with a joyous cry,
From the shadow'd eaves to the open sky,
And the vulture stoops, in his eager spring,
'Neath the sudden flash of his arrowy wing.
Oh, freed is the earth from her winter trance,
And the young Summer hath her inheritance;
The surly monarch of storm no more

Darkens the realm he ruled before;
His sceptre, where late he smote the wood,
Lord of the sombre solitude,
Broken, away in his fear he flies,
To the kindred glooms of his northern skies;
And a chirp and a song now cheer the hours,
And the very grave wears a robe of flowers.

She comes, the Summer so blessing, and Earth
Bounds, with a wing, to a better birth;
She breathes o'er the plain, and a thousand eyes
Open at once in a world of dyes;
Blue and purple, the buds unfold,
Happy and bright in their green and gold;
Daisies that speak for the virgin heart,
Lowly but sweet, by the path upstart;
And pinks that promise for hopes of youth,
Blossom with others that speak for truth.

How the enthusiast nature glows,
With that first bound from her long repose;
How, with a shout, she bids arise,
Her messenger-angels of earth and skies!
From height and dell, from brooklet and grove,
Forth they speed on their work of love;
Fanning the faint and warming the chill,
Doing the work of fondness still,
And, with the spells of each winning grace,
Giving new life in each warm embrace.

They come, they come, with the mother spell,
And the tribute children obey them well,
And gladden to hear the call that bids
Each drooping dear one unveil its lids.

The leaf grows green on the agéd trees,
And the blossom is wing'd by the wooing breeze;
The bird leaps free to the sun and air,
And in a new song forgets his care;
While the butterfly sports on his painted wing,
Having no duty to spin or to sing.

Oh, joyous freedom from hostile thrall,
That brings the blessing and bloom to all,
That, on rock and valley, and height, and plain,
Bestows the sun and the smile again;
That only breathes upon Winter's brow,
And breaks his fetters and melts his snow;
That smiles upon Autumn's wither'd bower,
And straightway it glories in fruit and flower,
And but whispers the sons of men, and they seem
Like children bless'd with a joyous dream.

Oh! the glad Summer, how bright her eye,
How sweet her breath, and how soft her sky,
How wondrous her magic power to bless
With the bloom of the garden the wilderness—
To crown the wild thorn with the golden flower,
To bathe the sad earth with the genial shower,
To foster the strength in the breast of Toil,
And hallow with bounty the niggard soil,
Glad the broad fields with the sunripe grain,
Till we dream of the age of Gold again!

HEART ESSENTIAL TO GENIUS.

We are not always equal to our fate,
Nor true to our conditions. Doubt and fear
Beset the bravest in their high career,
At moments when the soul, no more elate
With expectation, sinks beneath the time.
The masters have their weakness. "I would climb,"
Said Raleigh, gazing on the highest hill—
"But that I tremble with the fear to fall!"
Apt was the answer of the high-soul'd Queen,—
"If thy heart fail thee, never climb at all!"
The heart! if that be sound, confirms the rest,
Crowns genius with his lion will and mien,
And, from the conscious virtue in the breast,
To trembling nature gives both strength and will!

THE CAPTIVE.

I.

The Captive crouch'd in his dungeon,
On the floor the sunbeam lay;—
He crept the length of his fetter,
But the sunbeam flitted away:
"Ah! thus hath the cruel fortune
Still mock'd me," the Captive said;
"She came with her sunshine smiling,
But ere I could clasp her, fled.

II.

The Captive slept in his dungeon,
  And a vision of visions spell'd
The sense of his sleeping sorrow,
  The fairest he ever beheld;
A maid at the door stood smiling,
  And she said—"Come hither to me;"
From his wrist his fetters crumbled,
  And his feet and his soul were free.

III.

But with dawn the maiden vanish'd,
  And lo! by the Captive stood
The form of the savage headsman,
  With his axe still dripping blood:—
"Ah! now, indeed," said the Captive,
  "The sense of the dream I see;
The maid was the angel of mercy,
  And 'tis mercy that sets me free."

TWINS IN DEATH.

Shall the true faith, soaring high,
Dreaming still about the sky,
Weep the loved ones who have sought
What hath ever been our thought?—
Better, with a word of cheer,
Send our thoughts to follow, where
Thought 's no more a thing of care!—

Go, ye young twin-hearted,
Whom not even death has parted,

So well ye clung together;—
Ye are free the long campaign,
Marches in the cold and rain,
Hard fight and bitter weather.
Ye shall know no more of trembling,
Weep no more at man's dissembling,
Nor at griefs more dread,
In the cruel, sad defeat
Of the hope, of all most sweet
On which our hearts have fed;—
Fed—fed! as in the solitude
The Hebrew did upon celestial food!

Sweet your future slumbers, where
The young flowers, though soft and fair,
Hide no reptile, nurse no care,—
Where no shaft your hearts may sever!
Sweetest fate was yours,—to mingle
Souls that would unite forever,
Dreading ever to be single!—
God has bless'd your deep repose;
And the union so divine,
Hath a perfume like the rose,
That upon some mountain grows,
Where the clouds ascend not,
Which the tempests rend not,
Where stars of night and day, still twinn'd,
together shine.

Life can wing no after blow,
Ye are safe from mortal woe,
Ye have wings to fly the cloud,
Souls to fling aside the shroud;
Dreading never more the morrow,

With its brow of frown and sorrow;
Free from cruel time's oppressing,
Death himself but brings ye blessing.
Death who soothes even when he blights—
  Where is he stern-hearted?—
Not when thus his hand unites
  What never life had parted!
Ye have ceased your ailing,
There should be no wailing!

GLORY.

I.

'Tis thy first vision of glory;—
Lo! he is sleeping beside thee;
Sweet is the boy in his slumber;
Slumber more beautiful never
Curtain'd the lips of an infant,
Hung on his mouth like a zephyr,
Or from his lips drew a laughter,
Such as an angel might share in!—
Dark are his violet eyelids,
Soft with a tear dewy-glistening;
Red on his cheeks are the blossoms
Of youth and ineffable beauty;
And o'er his brow, how transcendent,
Bright with all colors, and glowing
Lovely as summer's first rainbow,
Circles the halo of heaven.

II.

Madden not, gazing upon him,—
Thus he but sleeps to beguile thee;—

Stoop not to kiss from his eyelid
Those pearly droplets that glisten
Gem-like, as tributes from ocean,
Cast on the gray sand and shining
Bright in the last glance of evening.—
Little thou dream'st of thy peril;—
Lo! where, conceal'd by the roses,
Grasp'd in his hand, and now quivering,
As eager to fly on its mission,
The subtle red shaft of the lightning!—
Look where his head finds its pillow,
Bolt upon bolt, that flash softly,
Tinging, with faintest suffusion,
The tresses of gold that half hide them.

III.

This is no child but an eagle,
Ready for flight with his burden,
Changing his aspect as quickly,
And reckless and stern as the Afrite,
Who, 'scaping from Solomon's signet,
Rose from his urn to a giant,
Stretching from ocean to heaven.
Waken him not in thy madness;—
Sore is the grief he will bring thee;
Hard is the task he will set thee;
Soon, with the daylight beginning,
Late, with the midnight unending;
Toils, that will make thee to weary,
Sinking to die by the wayside,
With an eye and a hand ever stretching
To the lone, unattainable summits.

BALLAD.—WHERE ART THOU?

Oh! where art thou, the dearest
Of all that boyhood knew;—
Oh! where art thou, still fairest
Of all to Memory's view?
Long years have swept above me,
Age silver'd o'er my brow,—
But, if thou live and love me—
Speak! Tell me! where art thou?

I've wander'd long—how lonely!
With one sweet passion fed,
That clung and cheer'd me only,
When other hopes had fled;
That thou, my own one, cherish'd
Still true thy youthful vow—
Alas! if it hath perish'd,—
And thou?—oh! where art thou?

I fled—I left thee weeping,
And bitter tears were mine,
That did not cease when sweeping,
In tempest, o'er the brine;
I saw thee then in vision,
As memory sees thee now,
And dream'd a dream Elysian;—
But where, alas! art thou!

And years of toil and sorrow,
And pain and fear were mine;
My heart could only borrow
Its hope from thoughts of thine:

I strove, that I might measure
  The ocean waste, and now
I come to seek the treasure
  Most loved,—and, where art thou?

And scenes of old rise brightly
  Again on Memory's view;
'Tis boyhood's footstep, lightly
  Trips o'er the fields it knew;
Such dreams of joyous childhood,
  As lift my spirit now:—
There is the cot, the wildwood,
  The hawthorn!—where art thou?

No welcome!—oh! the sorrow
  That shuts yon evening skies!
Vain would they beauty borrow,
  From false and fleeting dyes;
Soft blue,—carnation flushes,
  In mingling tissues glow;
But sad the fear that rushes
  Upon me!—where art thou?

Such silence! oh! the feeling
  Of dread that chills my heart!
Even at my footfall, stealing
  O'er grassy slopes, I start;
Thy voice was full of greeting,
  Why is it silent now?
Thou still wast first at meeting—
  Oh! Mary, where art thou?

The porch! around its column,
  Thou bad'st the creeper twine,

And, with the green made solemn,
  Thy windows wreathed in vine;
Pots, fill'd with purple flowers,
  Stood on long shelves below,—
They're gone—the buds, the bowers,—
  All! all! and where art thou?

And yet, the hearth is blazing,
  As it was wont to burn,
When through thy lattice gazing,
  Thou'st watch'd for my return;
I see, or am I dreaming?
  Thou'rt at the window now!—
'Tis but the sun's last gleaming—
  'Tis gone—oh! where art thou?

I lift the latch!—thy father
  Sits in the ancient chair—
Oh! tears, how thick they gather,
  I scarce can see him there;—
Thy mother! wildly wringing
  Her hands, beholds me now,
Fast to the window clinging,
  She sinks—oh! where art thou?

FANCY.

Would you win from fancy power?—
Woo her in the witching hour,
  When the drooping sun retires,
  And the moon with softer fires
Soothes with dew the drooping flower!

She is free when evening closes,
Fondly veiling summer's roses,
  To pursue, with noiseless flying,
  As the breeze of ocean sighing,
Seeks where zephyr still reposes.

Lo! you trace her airy motion
In the woods and o'er the ocean,—
  By the wing in tree-top whirring,
  By the zephyr sudden stirring,
By the little lake's commotion.

Earth grows fragrant in her power,—
'Tis from her she wins her dower;
  Sigh for sunset, gleam for alley,
  Flush for grove, and voice for valley,
Scent for sun, and beam for flower.

SONNETS.—SPIRIT-FLIGHTS.

I.

Ah me! that sleeping like Endymion,
  Upon a gentle hill-slope flower bestrewn,
  I could be laid to wait the coming moon,
And her fresh smile, as some rich garment, don!
Let the winds gather round me, and the dell,
  That breaks into the valley catch the sound,
  And, with its many voices, speed around
The airy rapture, till the natural spell
  Rouse up the wood-nymphs to delight my sleep;

While she, my mistress, from her ocean cell,
Ascends to the blue summits, with a swell
  Of those sweet noises from the caverns deep,
Where blue-eyed Nereids sport on ocean's shell,
  And to old Triton's conch, in long procession sweep.

II.

Upon the poet's soul they flash forever,
  In evening shades, these glimpses strange and sweet;
They fill his heart betimes—they leave him never,
  And haunt his steps with sounds of falling feet:
He walks beside a mystery night and day;
  Still wanders where the sacred spring is hidden;
  Yet, would he take the seal from the forbidden,
Then must he work and watch, as well as pray!
How work? How watch? Beside him—in his way,—
Springs, without check, the flower, by whose choice spell,—
More potent than "herb moly,"—he can tell
  Where the stream rises and the waters play!—
Ah! spirits call'd avail not! On his eyes,
Seal'd up with stubborn clay, the darkness lies.

YES, LONE WERE MY BOSOM.

Yes, lone were my bosom if liken'd to thine,
And base were my soul if it knelt at thy shrine;
And the heaven we worship were false if it be
More true to the spoiler than thou wert to me.

If the hope that has cheer'd me through danger and death,
Be as easily lost as its owner's frail breath,

Then 'twere meet that my heart in its conflict should fly,
To the succor of him who decrees it to die.

If my hope of the future, as they tell me, be vain,
Thy lures shall not win me to trust it again;
And the evening of life were but anguish to me,
Did I deem its sad sunlight vouchsafed me by thee.

Thou mayst rule o'er the slaves whom thy fortune has made;
I am none, and by me thou canst ne'er be betray'd:
I call for no curse on thy head but the one,
To trust with my trust, and, like me, be undone.

SONNET.—AIMS.

There have been earnest fancies in my soul,
  A wilder summons,—deeper cares than these,
That now possess my spirit and control,
  Subduing me to forests and green trees.
Thoughts have assail'd me in my solitude,
  Of human struggle!—and within mine ear,
  Still and anon, a whispering voice I hear,
That mocks me with my feebleness of mood;
The puny toil of song—the idle dance
Of metaphor, and shadows of romance!
Points to superior struggle—paints the cares
  Of Empire,—the great nation in the toils
Of impotence, that still in blindness dares,
  And what it cannot elevate, despoils.

CHANGES OF HOME.

I.

Well may we sing her beauties, this pleasant land of ours,
Her sunny smiles, her golden fruits, and all her world of flowers;
The young birds of her forest groves, the blue folds of her sky,
And all those airs of gentleness that never seem to fly:
They wind about our forms at noon, they woo us in the shade,
When panting, from the summer heats, the woodman seeks the
glade;
They win us with a song of love, they cheer us with a dream,
That gilds our passing thoughts of life, as sunlight doth the stream;
And well would they persuade us now, in moments all too dear,
That, sinful though our hearts may be, we have our Eden here.

II.

Ah! well has lavish nature, from out her boundless store,
Spread wealth and loveliness around, on river, rock and shore:
No sweeter stream than Ashley glides—and, what of southern
France?—
She boasts no brigher fields than ours within her matron glance;
Our skies look down in tenderness from out their realms of blue,
The fairest of Italian climes may claim no softer hue;
And let them sing of fruits of Spain, and let them boast the flowers,
The Moors' own culture, they may claim no dearer sweet than ours,—
Perchance the dark-hair'd maiden is a glory in your eye,
But the blue-eyed Carolinian rules, when all the rest are nigh.

III.

And none may say, it is not true, the burden of my lay,
'Tis written still in song and sweet, in flower and fruit and ray;

Look on the scene around us now, and say if sung amiss,
The lay that pictures to your eye a spot so fair as this:
Gay springs the merry mock-bird around the cottage pale,—
And, scarcely taught by hunter's aim, the rabbit down the vale;
Each boon of kindly nature—her buds, her blooms, her flowers,
And, more than all, the maidens fair, that fill this land of ours,
Are still in rich perfection, as our fathers found them first,
But our sons are gentle now no more and all the land is curst.

IV.

Wild thoughts are in our bosoms and a savage discontent,
We love no more the life we led, the music, nor the scent;
The merry dance delights us not, as in that better time,
When glad, in happy bands we met, with spirits like our clime;
And all the social loveliness, and all the smile is gone
That link'd the spirits of our youth, and made our people one;
They smile no more together as in that earlier day,
Our maidens sigh in loneliness who once were always gay;
And though our skies are bright, and our sun looks down as then,
Ah me! the thought is sad I feel, we shall never smile again.

THE FOREST GRAVE.

But little heeding where I laid me down,—
For I was worn to weariness by toil
Of a long day of travel in the sun;
I threw myself beneath the thicket's shade,
'Mongst the long grasses of a gentle slope,
And slept unconscious. At my waking, said
My father, who had sate and watch'd the while,
"Thou little know'st what couch hath given thee rest,

Or what thy pillow!" Then I look'd, and found
My form had rested on a Christian grave,
The mouldering cross of wood, beneath mine arm,
Drawn easily down, by motion of my hand,
From its old station at the hillock's head.

"Thou marvell'st," said he, "at a Christian grave,
Here, in this heathen wilderness;—but where
Plants not the foe his trophies? All the earth
Is but Death's garden, where he drills and sows,
That God may find the reapers in his time.
He follows not his craft alone where crowds
Gather for living purposes,—where Pride
Erects his idle palace; and the route
Of Folly, school'd against austerity,
As having not the soul for sad delights,
Meet in licentious revel. But even here,
Where the deer stalk in safety, and the wild,
Unrifled of its rich virginity,
Is glad with simple nature, as at first,
Here, Death hath rear'd his melancholy shrine,
And the slight hillock which hath made thy couch,
Gives proof that he hath claim'd his sacrifice,
Relentless in pursuit as fell in power,
And monarch equally o'er time and place,
The wilderness as city, poor as proud,
Hath bade life render up his trembling staff,
And, like some outlaw, reckless of accompt,
Hath eased him of his burden.

"Shall we ask—
What were thy fortunes, sleeper?—In what part,
Native or foreign, of earth's wilderness,
Didst thou begin thy journey? Was thy life,

Honor'd by gifts of goodness—smear'd by guilt—
Baffled by fortune—hard beset with foes;
Or, cast away in thine own recklessness,
By profligate waste of days?

"All in vain,
This idle quest—yet not to virtue vain,
If, from thy grave, an upward voice might rise,
To give us answer. Nothing may we know
From thy seal'd lips and silent dwelling-place!—
My own blood may have circled in thy heart,
Yet know I naught of thee, and cannot know.

"Yet may the general aspect of thy lot
Be traced in this thy sepulchre! Thy thought
Was one that kept thee sleepless. Thou hast hoped,
With an unyielding, vexing discontent,
For wealth and honors; those delusive gauds,
That dazzle the best eyes, and still defeat
The wisest aims of greatness!—or hast sinned
Beyond forgiveness of thy fellow. God,
The prince of infinite power, if thou hast pray'd,
Will grant what man denied thee. Thou hast striven
Against thy neighbor's greatness. Thou hast dared
Be bold against him, when the power was his
To crush thee with a finger. Thou hast fled
His keen pursuit of vengeance, and the doom
Of exile hath been writ against thy name,
Being thy moral death:—the rest is here!

"I read the story of thy folly here—
Thy folly in thy fortunes. Thou hast wrong'd
Thy fellow, in denying him thy trust!—
Thy nature ask'd for confidence—its laws

Commanded thy dependence. Thou wast bade
Be humble in thine aim, and love thy kind,
Even when it wrong'd thee. Hast thou yielded love,
Or trust, to him that sought it? Didst thou yield
Meet deference to thy betters—to the wise,
Having the nation's rule? Or didst thou shake
Thy bold hand in defiance, and depart,
Calling down vengeance in red bolts from heaven.
To do thee justice in consuming flame?
Would thou couldst answer! It may be, thy tale
Were of the world's injustice—the worse wrong,
That of the many striving 'gainst the one.
Thou couldst unfold a grievance which should bring
A pang to hearts of honor—a cold sweat
On brows, that feel thy argument was theirs—
Thy cause, the cause of freedom. He who stands,
As I, above thy forest-shelter'd sleep,
May read a story in thy dwelling-place.
Thy steps were from thy home of many hours,
From time of youth's first blossoming. Thy grief—
The grief which stretch'd thee on the bed of death—
Came with thy exile. Thou wast banish'd all—
And death that met thee, was a comforter,
To guide thee to a dwelling, and prepare
A couch, and give thee shelter from the night,
Fast coming on, and storm that follow'd close—
Pursuing thee as still the storm pursues
The banish'd and unfriended. Thou hast sunk
To thy last sleep, untroubled by the cares
That throng about the city bed of death—
No idle tramp of men hath follow'd thee;
A hurried hand—perchance a thoughtless heart—
Hath scoop'd thee out a grave some three feet deep,
And left thee in the solitude to God!

"The heart hath better hopes. Humanity
Springs up beside the pathway, like a flower
That takes the blankness from the wilderness,
And sweetens its bleak waters. I have hope
Thou wert not all untended at the last.
Some hand hath smooth'd thy pillow when disease
Kept thee awake through the long dreary night.
Thy birth had friends and parents. Childhood came,
And brought with it a livelier fellowship;
And boyhood gave thee sympathy and sport.
And were there none of all thy fellowships—
Was there no parent in thy last sad hour,
Nor she thou lov'dst in childhood—nor the boy,
Who mated out with thee in roguish play,
The measure of thy laughing pranks erewhile,
Beside thee, when thou groan'dst in agony?
And, in the trying moment, when earth reel'd
Around thee, and the skies began to fade,
And darkness fill'd thy chamber, and gaunt death
Dragged thee about and wrestled with thy frame,
Already overborne—and hurl'd thee down
Never to rise—was it a friend long tried
Who decently composed thy stiffen'd limbs,
And spread thy pall above thee; or strange men
Whom thou hadst never seen, and couldst not see,
To whom thy fortune, most unnatural,
Gave up this mournful office? Did they take
Thy frame, and scooping out a shallow bed,
That gave thee scarce a shelter from the rain,
Consign thee, with a word, unto thy tomb—
With vague conjecture scanning all the while
Thy hopes, thy fortune and thy loneliness?
Had all deserted thee that loved before?
Or was it that thou, in wilfulness of mood,

Self-banish'd, fled the many who had loved,
Deplore thy error still and weep thy loss?
Did none come near to give thee medicine,
Or smooth thy pillow down, support thy head,
Watch by thy midnight couch, and still attend,
With that officious tenderness and zeal,
Which makes the patient smile through every pang,
And bless the malady, however deep,
That brings along with it such pleasant cares?

"And all that infancy and boyhood brought—
Mother and mistress—schoolmate, brother, friend—
Thy fortune took from thee, when most their cares
Had sweeten'd all thy sorrows! Such was not
Thy feeling, when in manhood's health and strength,
Thou fled'st from the great city, with a pride
That made thy errors look like nobleness,
And kept thee in them. In that hour of death,
Feeble and prostrate, what a mockery seem'd
That spirit-exulting, which had led thee forth
Into self-written exile! Thy faint heart
Pray'd then for that humility—that hope—
Thou didst reject in thy vain hour of strength;
And thou hadst given the torturing pride of years,
That fed upon thy heart, and all its hopes,
For one poor hour of love—for those sweet smiles
Of her whose heart look'd out from tearful eyes,
Still hoping for thy soon return, yet sad,
As with a mournful presage of thy fate.

"That fate, perchance, she shared. She fled with thee,
Blind to thy errors, to thy vices blind,
Flying from all beside, and glad to own
A dwelling in thy heart—a lone abode,

Where thou couldst love her. Thou didst build her cot
Beside yon thicket, near yon rippling brook,
And rear'd the jasmine round her cottage door,
And train'd the wild vine o'er it. Thou wast blest,
Deep in the forest, happy in the all,
Rich in the little spoil thou robb'dst from man.

"And where is she? Thy dwelling-place is lone,
The cot in ruins, and the tangled vine
A thicket where the yellow serpent lurks,
And the green lizard glides. Where is the bird
That made thy cottage beautiful—that sooth'd
The desert to thine eye, and fill'd thy heart
With such abundance of her treasured sweet,
That man's hate grew forgotten in her love?

"She did not perish when she saw thee die,
Else had they made her grave where thou art laid,
And that were merciful. No flower is here
Which she hath planted; and the weeds have grown,
Untended, like thy fortunes, thorny and wild,
Meet emblem of thy fate. Methinks,
If there was nothing sweet to bless thy days,—
If youth had no enjoyment—childhood no friend—
Manhood no home—the love of country naught,
To make a venerated shrine a charm,
More sweet to age than all the joys of youth—
If but affliction clung to thee through all—
It had not been a misplaced charity
Of her, or the sad seasons, to have left
One flower above thy grave, poor desolate!"

THOU HAST EYES LIKE STARS.

I.

Thou hast eyes like stars, and sweetness
 Which no fruit of earth supplies;
Thou hast airy grace and fleetness,
 Like some bird of upper skies;—
Let not earthly charms go higher
Than the ones which should aspire;—
 Be thy spirit like thine eyes—
Brightest bounty to them given,
Clothe that too in gifts of heaven.

II.

Bid it bless where now it kindles,
 Let not mocking spirits say,
That thy holy beauty dwindles
 To a common earthly ray;—
Be the wicked speech confounded,
Take the captive thou hast wounded,
 Prove that eyes that so can slay,
Have an attribute the more,
When the stricken they restore.

"LA BOLSA DE LAS SIERRAS."

"La Bolsa de las Sierras,"—the Pocket or Pouch of the Mountains,—is the fanciful title given by the Spaniards to a very picturesque and lovely spot in Texas,—the terminus of the ocean-reach, stretching up towards San Antonio, the mines of San Saba, Chihuahua, and the Rocky Mountains. The scene is one of the rarest loveliness. The meadows are clothed with flowers even in February. The waters spread away among groves that relieve the prospect with a constant variety. Here come, wandering along the margin of lakes and waters, that lose themselves amidst the rich grasses of the slopes, the most wonderful flocks of the flamingo and the swan. But the verses must do the work of description.

Peace woos us here with flowers;—
Peace in the solitude, where Nature still
Looks unpolluted forth from mountain towers,
And takes no shape of ill;
Where, fleet through vales that sleep in lakes below,
The deer leaps free in herds and never dreads the foe.

The swan speeds wild in grace,
Through the sweet lakes that freshen all the vale;
A meadowy sea, far as the eye may trace,
Ripples beneath the trade-wind's soothing gale;
Here woods and groves that never lose their green,
Fringe the fair streams, and crown the heights between.

The gay flamingo there,
Marching with crest erect and footsteps slow,
Looks down to watch his form in waters clear,
Nor heeds the trooping flocks that come and go;
Legions of white-wing'd innocents, that glide,
Or dart, with sense of joy, and mirth, that sweetens pride.

Pensive, the palms arise,
As if o'er cherish'd graves; the mezquite towers

Through the dense chapparal; a thousand dyes
Blend sweetly, and the aroma of the flowers
From thousand shrubs, by ocean zephyrs fann'd,
With music borne afar, makes grateful all the land.

With never-dying song,
The glad winds gather through the blossoming day,
Like truants still, their sportive play prolong,
Forgetful in their pleasures that they stray;
While in the sky the flecking clouds lie calm,
White, soft, as drinking glad from skies below their balm.

Peace! Peace!—the sad heart's cry,
That blossom of security, here finds
Meet echo,—and with voices never high,
Yet absolute in their sweetness, blends and binds
With natural metes her empire, soft as wild,
Takes from the innocent fear, weds rapture to the mild.

Peace! Peace! the peace of Love,
Serene and sure in favor of the skies,—
Waters that lend their voices to the grove,
Groves singing back to waters;—grateful eyes,
From each, that kindle in requited fires,
Blest in the embrace of sanctified desires—

Commerce of kindred things,
Whose instincts find communion and rejoice,
With all that being ever circling brings,—
Each with its power to bless, and each with voice
To answer for the blessing, and requite
The giver in happy song of ever-wing'd delight.

How swells the common strain;
The day-star waking ocean; the gay breeze

That welcomes still the brightness back again,
Skirrs the white beach, and skims among the trees,
Yet whispers to the sea-shell on the shore,
Which thenceforth aye repeats the sweet song o'er and o'er!

Oh! voices of delight,
Wings of my joy, and blossoming stars that gleam,
With still a present fondness for the sight,
That once has gloried in celestial dream;
Here still ye find each dear dismember'd part,
That in youth's first fresh fancies bless'd its heart.

The peace that harbors here
Is that of the soul's infancy,—when first,
Untroubled with to-morrow-haunting fear,
The young affections into blossom burst,
And found in breeze and sky, and earth and sea,
Realms sacred—homes and haunts where Love goes singing free.

Enough for happiness
Is here—where beauty harbors in the shade,
And asks but privilege to tend and bless,
To come in beams and blossoming charms array'd,
And soothe to slumberous sweetness with a strain,
Once heard, that never leaves the happy heart again.

One heart shall grow to mine,
Here in the holy wilderness—shall share
All its sweet treasures, and the peace divine,
That robs the precious rapture of its fear;
Nor sigh for that the mountain in its breast
Holds—which, with lure of hell, would rob our hearts of rest.

Love thus, at last, shall crown
The warfare of long seasons. Born of peace,

She will bring soothing. We shall both lie down
Beneath the slender palm, and feel the increase
That fruitfully belongs to natural joys,
Meet toils, pure thoughts and hopes, delight that never cloys.

SONG IN MARCH.

I.

Now are the winds about us in their glee,
Tossing the slender tree;
Whirling the sands about his furious car,
March cometh from afar;
Breaks the seal'd magic of old winter's dreams,
And rends his glassy streams;
Chafing with potent airs, he fiercely takes
Their fetters from the lakes,
And, with a power by queenly Spring supplied,
Wakens the slumbering tide.

II.

With a wild love he seeks young Summer's charms
And clasps her to his arms;
Lifting his shield between, he drives away
Old Winter from his prey;—
The ancient tyrant whom he boldly braves,
Goes howling to his caves;
And, to his northern realm compell'd to fly,
Yields up the victory;
Melted are all his bands, o'erthrown his towers,
And March comes bringing flowers.

SONNETS.

I. FAERY GLIMPSES.

The spirits that do dress the flowers with dew,
And trip it on the greensward, by the moon,
And play fantastic tricks, both late and soon,
When March with blossoms promises the Spring,—
Have been about me in the merriest ring.
Methought among their forms were some I knew.
They came with hushing laughter,—for I slept
Beneath our willows—slily round me crept,
And prankt my brow with blossoms,—in my ear
Whisper'd the wildest dreams of elfin land,
Then, in a circle, dancing hand in hand,
Sung me a ditty from the Moon's own sphere:—
Starting from slumber, in the dear delight
Of such a vision, it was gone from sight.

II. CHILD FANCIES.

A plague upon your knowledge—books and laws,
Sciences, theories, and doctrines cold,
Maxims and principles, and rules, and saws,
That, propagating nothing, from the old,
Lop off their generations!—Where are now
Those fancies rare, those superstitions wild,
That kept the heart, in wonders, still a child;—
That taught the mind to dream, the soul to glow—
That peopled air with glories—fill'd the mine
With its inhabitants,—fiery-mailéd forms,
That, traversing earth's avenues in swarms,
Met Oberon's light legions, line for line?
Give me these visions of my youth—restore
Its youth, which dwelt in such as these, once more.

MORNING IN THE FOREST.

I.

The voices of the forest! Hear the tale
  Whisper'd, at moments, by the fitful breeze,
That sighing, with a sad but soothing wail,
  Makes sweetest music with the tall old trees;
And blends, with feeling of the dawning hour,
Musings of solemn thought and saddest power.

II.

Such was the birth, the mother-birth, which sung
  The morning of creation:—even so strange,
The first, fresh accents of the infant tongue
  Of nature, moaning through her varied range—
Wild in her desert loneliness of place,
Ere yet she knew her last and noblest race.

III.

Thus moan'd the winds among the giant trees,
  That had no other homage—thus, from far,
Came the deep voices of the sullen seas,
  Striving 'gainst earth, and with themselves at war;—
Night craved the sun, and chaos from her keep
Groan'd with the oppression of her sightless sleep.

IV.

And, in the language of their infant lack,
  They tell their story with each rising dawn;
You hear them when the hour is cold and black,
  Ere yet the feet of day imprint the lawn;
When the faint streakings of the light are seen,
O'er eastern heights, through darkest groves of green.

V.

Each day renews the birth of thousand days,
  Even from the dawn of time :—even now I see,
Amid the gloom that gathers on my gaze,
  Gray distant gleams that shoot up momently—
And hark! a sudden voice—the voice of might,
That hail'd, from infant life, the blessing birth of light.

VI.

The morning grows around me! Shafts of gray,
  Like sudden arrows from the eastern bow,
Rise, through the distant forests, to a ray,
  And light the heavens, and waken earth below ;—
The rill that murmur'd sadly, now sings out,
Leaping, through trembling leaves, with free and gladsome shout.

VII.

I see a glitter on yon glossy leaf,
  Where hangs a silent dew-drop. Hark! a bird
Shrieks out, as if he felt some sudden grief,
  His sleep, perchance, by dream of danger stirr'd :
Wings rustle in the thicket—other eyes
Behold, where, ray on ray, the wings of morning rise.

VIII.

And now the dawn, with eye of glancing gray,
  Comes singing into sight. The trees stand forth,
As singly striving for her brightest ray ;
  And, countless voices, from the awakening earth,
Clamor full-throated joys :—a flapping wing
Prepares, in yonder copse, to take his morning spring.

IX.

A sudden life is round me with the light,
  Voices and wings are in the woods and air ;

Broad vistas open to my travelling sight,
  And hills arise, and valleys wondrous fair—
Even while I gaze, a sudden shaft of fire
Makes yon tall pine blaze up, like some proud city spire.

X.

Oh, beautiful! most beautiful! the things
  I see around me;—lovelier still to thought,
The fancies, welling from a thousand springs,
  The presence of these images hath brought;
The visions of the past are mine this hour,
And, in my heart, the pride of an o'ermastering power—

XI.

A power that could create, and from the dead
  Draw life and gather accents. There are spells,
Known to the unerring thought, which freely shed
  Light round the groping footstep, when rebels
The o'ercautious reason, and the instinct fear
Shrinks from its own huge shadow—they are here!

XII.

This is a spot—if there have ever been,
  As ancient story tells, in legends sooth,
Such forms as are not earthly, earthward seen,
  Having strange shapes of beauty and of youth—
Then do I ween that this should be the spot
Where they should come,—and yet I see them not.

XIII.

Yet have I pray'd their presence with a tongue
  Of song, and a warm fancy that could take,
From many-voiced expression as she sung,
  Her wingéd words of music, and awake

True echoes of her strain to win my quest,
And woo the coming of each spirit-guest.

XIV.

Yet did they come not, though my willing thought
  Grew captive to my wild and vain desire;
And in my heart meet pliancy was wrought,
  To raise the forms, in seeming, I require;—
And in this truant worship I've bow'd down,
Since first night's shadows fell and made the forests brown.

XV.

And sure no fitter spot had spirit sought,
  For the soft-falling of star-pacing feet;
This is the holiest wood, with flowers inwrought,
  Having fresh odors of most heavenly sweet;
Nor in the daylight's coming, then, do these
Cathedral shadows fly, that lurk behind the trees.

XVI.

The wild beast burrows not beneath our hill,
  Nor hide these leaves one serpent. Gentlest doves
Brood in the pines at evening, seldom still,
  With murmur through the night, of innocent loves:
And I have shaken, with no boyish trust,
From my own human feet, the base and selfish dust.

XVII.

And fancy hath been with me, to beguile
  The stubborn reason into faith, and show
The subtle shapes from fairy-land, that while,
  In gamesome dance, the wasted hours below;
Meet lawn of green and purple here is spread,
By nature's liberal hand for fay's fantastic tread.

XVIII.

And memories of old song, the solemn strains
  Of bards, that gave themselves to holiest thought,
And gloried in their wild, poetic pains,
  Were in my heart; and my rapt soul was fraught
With faith in what they feign'd, until my blood
Grew tremulously strong beneath my hopeful mood.

XIX.

And when the dark hours came, the twiring stars
  Seem'd eyes, that darted on me keenest fires;
Earth had her voice, and promised, through her bars,
  To burst the bondage set on free desires—
And not a breath that stirr'd the flowers, but seem'd
The shadowy whisper from some shape I dream'd.

XX.

Yet vainly have I waited!—not in vain!
  What though no fairy won me with her song,
And beckoning finger—'twas a nobler strain
  That struck the ear of thought, and fill'd it long:
A mightier presence yet my soul o'erawed—
He was beside me:—I had been with God!

REPININGS.

"My brother!" said before me a sweet maid,
Who look'd a sister's feeling from her eye,
And thereupon I wept;—for I had none,
Brother nor sister—and my way of life
Hath been among the hills, and where the waste,

Sandy, and like the ocean-plane spread out,
Pains the sick eye with gazing. I, alas!
Have known no brother's, felt no sister's love,
Drank fondly of no blessings, such as make
A cottage fireside seem a home like heaven,
Where all is peace and truth. Yet less I've sought
Of love, than of permission but to love,—
The right to choose, from out the hurrying crowd,
My thing of worship. I have none to love—
None for whose single good my heart may hope—
None for whose choice delight my form may rove,
Bringing home dear enjoyments. Mine hath been
The life of want that sister had supplied—
The other self,—most sweet, most singular,
To whom, as to an altar of high thought,
My heart, when otherwise denied, might turn,
Secure of comfort. You may hold it weak
That thus I wept, hearing that maiden call
The youth who stood beside her. Worlds had I given
Had she but call'd me thus. Had she but placed
Her arm upon my own,—look'd in my face
With that dear smile of confidence, and said
"My brother," I had proudly made her thence
My deity, and she had fill'd my heart,
Its soul and sovereign thence, for evermore!

WONDERS OF THE SEA.

A FRAGMENT.

What I have brought thee is a mystery,
Framed by a wondrous artist—of the sea,—
Of the green mansions, and the sparry caves,
The shells, the sea-maids, and the warring waves;

And stirring dangers;—of the fearful things,
Monstrous and savage, that, from secret springs,
Course, in pursuit of prey; and, all night long,
Keep wakeful but to hear the tempest's song,
And join in terrible chorus!—Would you hear?
Then let your breath be hush'd, and bend your ear,
For he that made it hath the wizard's power,
To call up images that shriek and lower,
From hidden caves, and graves, and dens afar;
His sovereign art commands them, and they are!

IMAGINATION.

I.

He is a god who wills it,—with a power
To work his purpose out in earth and air,
Though neither speak him fair!—
So may he pluck from earth its precious flower,
And in the ether choose a spirit rare,
To serve him deftly in some other sphere;—
And thus it is that I have will'd this hour,
And thou hast heard me, and thy form is here!

II.

Creature of wing and eye,
That, singing, seek'st the sky,
And soar'st because thou sing'st, and singing, still must fly;
Believe me, though I know not mine own voice,
I see thee, and before thee I rejoice;
Thou, precious in both worlds, with thy sole choice
In ours, I bless thee that I knew thee first,

Ere, in the dawn of mortal joys, my heart,
Low-fashion'd by its fond caprice and art,
Had been for thy blest offices accurst;—
Denied the commerce of thy griefs, which bring
The wholesome of Love's sweetness with the sting;—
The love which Sin hath nurst,—
But nursing, could not keep,—
Soothed by delicious dews, the soul that steep,
And circumvent the wing!—
Oh! thou hast heard me;—heard me and com'st down,
Amid the silence and the shade, a gleam;
I see the glimmer of thy golden crown,
I feel thy wing in murmur, and I dream—
Dream of thy pleasant provinces, which lie
Still open to the conqueror, who, no more
May rifle, than resist, thy precious store,
Which grows, the more he spoils, the more beneath his eye!

III.

Oh! thou hast heard me with no jealous grace,—
Hast heard me, and approv'st the daring quest,
Which, heedless of this lowliness of place,
Would build thee here a shrine,—and, to my breast,
Implore thee, that I may be lifted high
To thy vast realms, that still entreat mine eye,
Shining through fields of vision, by the star,
Most sacred, which, at evening and at dawn,
First comes to teach us where the bright ones are,
Each, in his place, upon the heavenly lawn;—
All open to thy wing, that, dusk and day,
Descend'st and risest,—lifting, at each flight,
Some hopeful spirit, that, beneath thy ray,
Grows fitted to a world of more delight!—
Oh! not for thee to censure lowliness,

Save in the soul; which, grovelling as it goes,
Sees not the bright wings that descend to bless,
And will not seek where the true fountain flows!
And he whom man denies,
Hath but to lift his eyes,
Touch'd by thy breath, fresh-parted from the skies,
And the walls tumble outward that did bound,
And, skyward, the blue deepens; and, in air,
A flutter of the happiest wings is found,
Diffusing sweets that earth still finds too rare;—
And faith takes both her wings—
Will, that o'er mortal things
Still sways, as doth the wand o'er hidden springs;
And Love, that, in her trust,
Holds empire over dust,
And lifts to very life the soul to which she clings!
These grow to freedom with thy downward flight,
While the gross earth, bedarken'd in the bright,
That kindles on his sight,
Feels all its pomps grow naught,
Subject to that great thought,
Borne on thy matchless plumes, by which the soul is taught.

IV.

I know my undeserving—know how vain
The poor equivalent of love I bring,
And yet once more I do solicit thee;—
Again! oh! yet again!
Sit by me as thou didst, my beautiful!
When life was but a blossom of the spring,
And thou its zephyr—sit by me and sing.
Thy voice of tears will medicine the gloom
That hangs about my spirit, and set free
That bird of faith that only finds its wing

In thy melodious coming. Chase away
These threatening shapes that cloud my lonely room,
And wrap me in their moody grasp all day!
Come,—for thou only canst,—oh! come and lull,
With the sweet reedy music of thy tone,
The weary spirit left too much alone
By the gay strollers of this idle time;
Yet, deem me not irreverent when I ask!—
With thee, the creature of the wing and eye,—
A bird-flight not a task!—
'Twere easy to adjure, from stars sublime,
Such mighty sorrows, as, through these old walls,
Would leave a thousand echoes gushing free;—
At every trailing of a spirit's train,
Recalling still that strain,
That woke me to thy presence first, when far
Led by a single star,
And following in the wake of fancies sweet,
I wander'd deep into the mountain halls,
And ever, through the flashes of the storm,
Beheld a flitting form;
And heard, when winds grew hush'd, the sounds of falling feet!

V.

I know, with various wing, that thou canst soar
To realms that know no sorrow—that thy flight
Can waft thee to vain regions of delight,
Where wings may rather wanton than explore;—
But not to provinces like these I pray
Thy pinions; nor for me that idle lore,
That only seeks to wile, or win, by art,
The vigilant hours that watch through the long day;—
Those foolish madrigals that chase away,
As old men laugh, time's wrinkles;—the vain joke

That shakes the theatre, while, for the nonce,
The buffoon triumphs in the sage's cloak,
And wisdom, all forgetful of his part,
Grows heedless of the white upon his sconce,
Nor deafens as he shakes his borrow'd bells!—
Nor should you win me when the drama tells
The sportive passions of that wayward god,
Who, riding Libya's lion, yet with craft,
Still wings his wanton shaft,
Subduing mightiest spirits into shame;
Till lowlier men grow scornful of the fame,
That took the name of glory, ere the sport
Of that boy-archer shook their high report!—
As Love is in thy office, let the strain,
That teaches me his affluence, be implored
From the full heart and the sincerest thought;—
As if the captive thus had been restored
To passions of great pride and purest gain,—
Such as, by truth made plain,
Had never partaken of the pernicious fruit
That held the reptile in its core, and brought
Caprice, that ever must the soul imbrute!
Bring me to knowledge of that nobler flame
That never clouds with shame;
That freely may declare its aim and birth,
Nor glow, all doubtful of its proper name,
Impure, unhallow'd, on the hallow'd hearth!
Mine be the creature of a faith that brooks
No fashioning art or offices of man;
But, for its laws and properties, still looks
To the true purpose, first in nature's plan,
Decreed, ere rolling spheres and twinkling orbs began.

VI.

Thine is the night, the cloud, the lone, the far;
Thou bring'st to eve her star:
The cloud from thee receives its wing for flight,
And, clothed in purple light,
Goes sailing, richly freighted, to the sea!—
And thou hast cheer'd the solitude for me;—
Hast borne me, when the fetters of earth had worn
Into the soul its scorpion lash had torn,—
Borne me, triumphant, from my lonely cell,
To freedom, in far empires of the night;—
The freedom of the rugged mountain's height;
The strange companions of the haunted dell;
Great fields of blue, star-lighted,—while the cloud
Lay mantling o'er the city like a shroud,
And all behind was sad, and all before was bright!
Long vistas of the wood were wooing,—gay,
Sprinkt with the droplets which the sun had left,
Fast hurrying, having loiter'd on his way;—
These, in green thick close hid, and rocky cleft,
Made rich the solemn shadows of the wood;
So that the pilgrim, consciously astray,
Might wander still, since all around was good.
Thus night is in thy keeping! Thou alone
Canst take the veil from off her matron brow,
And bid the dreamer gladden in her sight.
Thou mak'st the secrets of her mansion known,
Her mansion, gloomy with excess of bright;—
And, from its wealth, surpassing mortal show,
The starr'd luxuriance of her pillar'd throne,
Thou canst extort her music—a lament,
As if the stars and winds together made
A requiem o'er the glories that must fade,—
Such as might issue, on a god's descent

From some high sphere his presence once had sway'd.
'Tis thine to put a soul into this train,
While earth is sleeping—blasted from her birth
Into unmusical barrenness and dearth,
Such as might move her ne'er to wake again,
Did it not pleasure her vain pride to spoil,
With keen and clamorous coil,
The delicate labors of our secret toil,
To break upon the midnight watch we keep—
Forgetting sleep,
Here, charming night and silence from the deep,
Stars stooping round us ever as they shine,
While wings, from off thy shoulders, grow to mine.

'TIS A LOWLY GRAVE.

'Tis a lowly grave, but it suits her best,
Since it breathes of fragrance, and speaks of rest;
And meet for her is its calm repose,
Whose life was so stormy and sad to its close.

'Tis a shady dell where they laid her form,
And the hills gather round it to break the storm,
While above her head the bending trees
Arrest the wing of each ruder breeze.

A trickling stream, as it winds below,
Hath a music of peace in its quiet flow;
And the buds that are ever in bloom above,
Tell of some minist'ring spirit's love.

It is sweet to think that, when all is o'er,
And life's fever'd pulses shall fret no more,
There still shall be one, with a fond regret,
Who will not forsake, and who cannot forget:

One kindlier heart, all untainted by earth,
That has kept the fresh bloom from its bud and its birth,
Whose tears for the sorrows of youth shall be shed,
And whose prayer shall still rise for the early dead.

SILENCE.

The desert hath its pyramid; but there
Silence is sovereign. Mighty is his throne,
Towering above the waste, and unassail'd
By clamoring subjects. The invader, there,
Is spell-bound at the threshold, and grows fix'd,
Chain'd by the subtle spirit of the Past;—
The dead of thirty centuries, that stand round,
Each with glazed, staring eye, and gloomy smile,
That mocks the intrusive insolence that dares
Ascend to their dread summits; with fond passion
Dreaming of idle conquest in a realm
To silence consecrate. His sovereign spell,
No less supreme than imperceptible,
Holds Thought bewilder'd,—holds the exploring eye
Baffled in mazes that provoke to search,
While mocking it with phantoms. O'er the plains—
Tracts burning with the brightness of a sun
That rears no idle flowers, and needs no streams
To quench the thirst of nature—still he roves,
Forgetting the fierce passion in his aim;—

Subdued himself; and feeling, at each march,
The hand of Fate upon him, and her sway
Superior to the idle boast of Earth.
With speaking finger press'd upon his lips,
He makes sad progress, and at length lies down;—
Sleeps in the shadow of the pyramid,
And dreaming of the sovereign of the place,
Yields up the sway to Silence,—that dread power
That holds the treasures of the sun in fee,
Dumb ever, speaking nothing of his wealth!

He is the saddest despot, with a realm
Older than that of Time; for he was strong,
And had full sway, and all the attributes
Of most unlimited rule, ere Time was born;
And still shall sway, when, from the womb of years,
The universal consciousness shall spring,
Which shall unseal all barriers of the Past,
Making it Present; of the Future, show
The full development; while the periods link'd
Declare the death of Time. Until that hour,
How vainly would we read the histories
Of empire seal'd by Silence! Find the speech
For that great stony Archimage, that sits
Vacant amid the desert; with no voice
To answer for that dread abundant life
That's now lock'd up in shadow,—deep in vaults,
Whose treasured mysteries there, securely kept,
Lie guarded by our fears. We may pursue
The stony labyrinths, and unwind the clues
To vaults of vacancy; we may unfold
The mummied sleeper from his unguent sheets;
Unwind the mystic scroll, and trace, with toil,
The written characters that seem to speak

From ancient fingers. What the Magian wrote,
May rest beneath our eyes; but will they read?
Or what proportion of the needful speech,
To answer for so dread an empire,
Shall we extort from meagre chronicles
And empty tongues like these? The Past is past,—
Not needful to our present, and denied,
Perchance, with proper eye to our best knowledge,
To our too curious search. 'Tis through our past
Alone that we shall penetrate the maze;
Leaving our mysteries in turn for those
Who, with irreverent homage, most like ours,
Shall vex the silence of our vaults in death.
The sovereign who presides above the waste,
Stands the sure guardian of its mysteries;
Not to be won; persuaded by no arts;
Awed by no power; defrauded by no skill,
That boldly tries the entrance to his cell
With cunning office; and, with confident tongue
Cries out "Eureka," at each passage won,
To find himself in a new labyrinth,
Which offers no way out. We must become
True subjects of the Silence sovereign here,—
Ourselves subdued to silence—ere we read
The secrets in his keeping. 'Till that hour
That links the great three periods all in one,
We shall but mock ourselves with wisdom's seeming;
And, with the appetite to sway all kingdoms,
Starve Thought above her scrolls.

But, rising then,
A moving thing of wonder and of life,
Bright in the place of the decaying sun,
This sovereign, speechless now and stony-eyed,

Shall find fit language. From his lips shall fall
The spell that seals them now. With finger lift,
He shall point out the avenues,—unfold
The clues that wind throughout the labyrinth;
Give up the key that locks the mystic scroll,
And solve the enigma. His new song shall wake
Ten thousand other voices, from whose strains
Concurrent, with meet harmonies, shall flow
A second birth of light. The truths, thus won,
Shall speak through myriad voices, but no tongues;
The soul shall drink in consciousness, yet ask
No ears for hearing,—need no breathing words,
Such as are utter'd from elaborate lips,
And by the violent spirit. In his sway
The sense shall gather happiest harmonies;
And, such the symmetry of his perfect tones,
Our dreams shall each have life; each look be speech;
Each flight a revelation; not a wing
Shall speed on mission, but beneath a flood
Of certain light as beauty; eyes shall drink
With joy and gratitude, effortless and fond,
Best knowledge from the gleams in other eyes,
Whose language shall be love! . . . .
. . . . A worship, now,
In this secluded forest of the west,—
(In the cold shadows of the pyramid
No longer,—yet in silence full as deep,—
The silence of a new approaching birth,
Not of a long, and long-forgotten death),—
Shall yet betray to me dim shadowings of
His empire, and the mystic spells that make
His kingdom's secret. Hither, when I rove
At twilight, do the glimmerings lead me on;
And, in a wondrous consciousness, most like

The whisper of a spirit to my soul,
I feel the embodied silence as it grows
To form and feature: a great shadowy form,
That beckons me to follow, till I go
Where the thick woods grow round me to a wall,
And the o'erclosing trees become a roof,
And so, my temple! With bow'd head and heart
I worship! I hear voices, and see forms
That bend above me—echo to my vows—
Receive them; hallow; and, though solemnly,
Smile on me, and unfold their cavernous eyes;
So that I read the mystic in their scrolls,
By supernatural light. There, will they show
Their mysteries; for that there the selfish heart
Comes never; and 'tis only faith that wins
The truth from revelation. Silence there
Possess'd and spell'd me;—sole, in sacred groves
Which held his dim traditions, stood to meet,
And welcomed me to walks of death and ages;
Guiding me as a master, glad to teach,
Yet awing like a god. Solemnly, then,
I bow'd my soul within me, and gave up
The lowlier impulse, and received straightway
The holier spirit. Never yet before
Stood I in such a presence! Thought was nigh,
Brooding, unwhispering; Faith, with orbs uplift,
Drank in great raptures; Hope, beside her, spread
Bright pinions, folding and unfolding vans,
Eager for flight; and Love, with hooded eyes,
Look'd downward, trembling with the quick, sweet beat
Of the awaken'd pulses in her heart.
Oh! the dear fulness of that solitude,
And the rich voices of that sacred speech,
That never broke the silence! Oh! the spells!—

The eternal calm of nature; peace of earth;
Sweet whisperings of the void; the spirit-gleams,
That made the twilight harmony, and crept,
Like wings, all listening, through the tufted tops
Of the great trees, and hung in brooding there,
Filling the vacant world with holy things,
To the fond worshipper; with each a sign,
Making the silence fruitful and divine! . . . .
The glorious fulness of the place o'ercame
My humbled nature; and I bow'd me down,
Even on the little hillock where I stood,
And, as the light winds rose, and, here and there,
Shook down the dead leaf from the bending trees,
I could but deem that Silence—that sad god—
Detach'd, with gentle hand, these faded gifts,
In token of his melancholy sway!

VIA SACRA.

HITHER, with reverent spirit, bend thy steps,
Scarce breathing. We are on the *Sacred Way*
Of Athens, leading out to Eleusis.
A nation's heart is in this dust! Its faith
Lies in these altars! See you not, we move
'Mongst monuments of might, which thus are made
Sacred themselves; deriving honor due
From honors they record? A calm delight
Subdues our awe. We pass through aged groves,
And sense-beguiling gardens, which lead on
By Cephissus' sweet streams, even to the heights

Of Œgaleus, and the sacred plain,
Where all is soul once more!
Oh! we shall dream
Of these hereafter, when, in western lands,
We trace the unnoted forests. Shall *they* have
Such altars? They have names of might like these;
Marble like this of pure Pentelicus;—
Yes, but the Phidias,—the Praxiteles;—
Where is the genius sworn to Fame,—the art
That hallows as it touches, and bids speak
The stubborn marble? We had better ask
For the religion which demands the shrine!
It is the Faith that makes the Priest—he comes
To serve the recognized master, not to make!
The popular heart must *feel* the god—must glow
With his divinity, ere it builds the shrine,
Or summons Priests to service! Patience! patience!
For us, there must be one great labor first,—
First make our sacred way!

THE BARD.

I.

Where dwells the spirit of the Bard—what sky
Persuades his daring wing,—
Folded in soft carnation, or in snow
Still sleeping, far o'er summits of the cloud,
And, with a seeming, sweet unconsciousness,
Wooing his plume, through baffling storms to fly,
Assured of all that ever yet might bless
The spirit, by love and loftiest hope made proud,
Would he but struggle for the dear caress!—

Or would his giant spring,
Impell'd by holiest ire,
Assail the sullen summits of the storm,
Bent with broad breast and still impatient form,
Where clouds unfold themselves in leaping fire!
What vision wins his soul,—
What passion wings his flight,—
What dream of conquest woos his eager eye!—
How glows he with the strife,—
How spurns he at control,—
With what unmeasured rage would he defy
The foes that rise around and threaten life!—
His upward flight is fair,
He goes through parting air,
He breaks the barrier cloud, he sees the eye that's there,
The centre of the realm of storm that mock'd him but to
dare!
And now he grasps the prize,
That on the summit lies,
And binds the burning jewel to his brow;
Transfigured by its bright,
He wears a mightier face,
Nor grovels more in likeness of the earth;—
His wing a bolder flight,
His step a wilder grace,
He glows, the creature of a holier birth;—
Suns sing, and stars glow glad around his light;
And thus he speeds afar,
'Mid gathering sun and star,
The sov'ran, he, of worlds, where these but subjects are;
And men that mark'd his wing with mocking sight,
Do watch and wonder now;—
Will watch and worship with delight, anon,
When far from hiss and hate, his upward form hath gone!

II.

Oh! ere that van was won,
Whose flight hath braved the sun—
Whose daring strength and aim
Have scaled the heights of cloud and bared their breasts of
flame;
What lowly toil was done,—
How slow the moments sped,—
How bitter were the pangs that vex'd the heart and head!
The burden which he bore,
The thorns his feet that tore,
The cruel wounds he suffer'd with no moan,—
Alone,—and still alone!—
Denial, which could smile,
Beholding, all the while,
How salter than the sea were the salt tears he shed;
And over all, the curse,
Than all of these more worse,
Prostrate, before the common way, to bear
The feet of hissing things,
Whose toil it is to tear,
And tramp the glorious creature born to wings!
Ah! should he once despair!—

III.

But, strength from lowliness,—
From patience, power, and pride,—
And freedom ever from the deep duresse!
These, to the one denied,
Still soothe the drear distress,
Brought by the very grief when well defied!
First, grovelling where he lay,
To want and woe the prey,
Unconscious that the darkness led to day;

With eyes from birth still seal'd,
As are the eaglet's ere they dream to fly,
The realm of open empire unreveal'd;—
First came the boon,—the precious boon—to see
That the broad firmament was spread above
A world that yet was free;
And, in the embracing and delicious air,
There hung great wings, whose plumage, bright with love,
Seem'd ever natural to the aim and eye!—
Were these but won!—with these!—
Oh! thence, with fond devotion, rose the prayer
For the one gift that promised such delight,
The single boon of flight!—
A prayer to make the hopeful heart grow wild!—
And, with the hope, still struggling, like the child,
To whom the eager mind the muscle brings,—
Not yet secure of foothold, but erect,
He grew,—in watches of the night, he grew,
When others slept,—in such secure degrees,
He vex'd no jealous view;
And thus the upward progress went uncheck'd;
And thus he put on wings;—
Until, with strength to soar,
He felt the earth no more,
And shook its dust away, and all its reptile things;
The eye and wing together won the height;
And they who mock'd and smote,
Might vainly hiss and roar,
With nothing left them but to dream and dote:
Unless—and this were something of a bliss,
Compensative, from mercy, for their hiss—
To bow, while yet they gaze, and in their shame, adore!

IV.

What if the toil and struggle were with earth?
The purpose of earth's self is for a sphere
In which she has no share;—
And thus it is that she may loathe the birth,
Wherein a spirit so rare
Makes her the rack on which to stretch his wings.
Vainly he loathes and strives;
The victim feels but thrives;
It is appointed he shall still go forth,
If that he neither yields him to her hate,
Nor subjugates his pinion to her snare;
And, it is written, his first passion flings
Her clay off with her fetters, and her stains
With all his immature pains;—
As, in the expression of a joy elate,
With the exulting sense of a new dawn,
One flings away the dreary doubt that pall'd,
With sense of weariness, at close of day,
And, with the merriest strains,
Bids them bring forth his steed upon the sun-bright law
He only hath to wait,—
To wait with confident heart; without complaint,
Endure, whate'er his lowliness of state,—
And, with a spirit resolved and never faint,
To struggle with the griefs that still oppress;
And the appointed moment will unscale
His eye, and he will break from all duresse,
To see the glowing vans, all purple-hued,
Stooping, with gradual waver, to his will;—
At dawn, when happiest dreams his pulses thrill,
To find them freshly to his shoulders glued;
Till, with a sense of upward life, he springs,
Scarce conscious of the motion of his wings,

To flight, and in his flight as all unconscious sings;—
Voice, wing, and eye, being children of a birth;—
Flight of a threefold power, that still implies,
When fairly parted from the enthralling earth,
The song, and sight, and soul, that shape it for the skies!

V.

If, for a moment, he forbears his flight,
Won by seducing siren of the shore,
Self-chidden, he is soon upon his way,
Still, upward, into light!
For, not in the embrace of mortal clay,
Sleeps long the soul of the imperial lyre!
The eye, that is the shoulder of his wing,
Still, in advance, beholds the approaching day,
Long ere the Night, her head on her own heart,
Hath girt her to depart!
And thus doth he aspire,
And thus doth he explore,
And thus he finds his freedom, spite of art,
That would beguile him from his great desire,
And bind him vassal to most lowly will!
'Tis by necessity that he breaks away,
From earth and bondage still!
The soul, that is his substance, warms with ire,
Impatient of each profitless delay;
And, though the song of the siren in his ear,
Works subtly in sweet mazes to his brain,
Yet ever a still voice of sadness tells
Of the past struggle, and the bitter care,
That kept him captive ever and in pain.
Thus warn'd, his better nature soon rebels,
And the false siren glozes still in vain.
Taught that a wing so nerved, need never pause

For rest which humble pinion may require,
He looks to far Parnassus, and takes hues,
Golden and azure, from the endowéd shapes
That linger still above its sacred heights;
And, with the glad persuasion of his song,
An emulous passion stimulates his wing,
So that he passes by the guardian capes,
Triumphant, and, with progress of his own,
He challenges each proud and antique Muse,
By her own altars, to the great delights,
She has made holy:—not that he would wring,
With proud compulsion, sad acknowledgment,
As of the presence of some nobler thing;
But that he fortifies the ancient cause,
Which many, by her own persuasions choose,—
With meet example;—and—her crown reset—
Doth, by his might, her primitive sway prolong.—
He sings, as she hath tutor'd him to sing,
A chant of ages that sustains her throne,
By catholic utterance of the great intent
Which makes her mission hallow'd, and for aye,
And, through a chosen race, o'er all asserts its sway!

VI.

'Twere vain to scan his office, and declare
The power he holds upon the earth and air,
And the sleek spirits that move them to their moods;
He is the sov'ran of the spell that sways
The groves in their spring sweetness—he hath power
To bring a sudden freshness to the hour—
Charm the green leaf, endow the purple flower,
And haunt with such a presence the great floods,
That there shall grow a glory on their banks,
And men shall gather from afar in ranks,

And bend before high altars he shall raise,
And speak with voices only won from him!
He shall bring beauty to the waste, and light
With bloom the wilderness, and so subdue
The terrors of the shade, that it shall be
Made sacred, with a halo, when most dim;
So that its dark, made beautiful to view,
Shall move new passion in the multitude,
To love the shadow whose obscurity
Hath lovelier eyes than haunt the night, and brood
Sad-smiling o'er still fountains that awake,
To fill their cisterns only for her sake!
For it hath been decreed his office still
To summon natural destinies, and invoke,
As with the simple utterance of his will,
The nimble servitors that love his yoke.
So, the devoted Passions hail his sway,
And Joy and Grief, with their link'd torches, glide,
Mute ever, but not heedless, night and day,
Serving his purpose, one on either side.
And hope, which is a feather from his plumes,
Now sinks, now falls, like shooting star through night,
And, even in falling, the abyss illumes,—
As memory of the first joy brings a light
To the sad eyes inhabited by woe—
The waving of a torch o'er mountain lake,
At midnight, while the storm-cloud, stooping low,
Hath iced it with a blackness naught may break.
Nor is he wanting in celestial aid;—
Love being his meekest servitor, with brow
Twined with the myrtle, ever speaking truth,
That never fears the forfeit of his vow,
And, bashful in her bright, but unafraid,
Bearing the rose that symbols innocent youth.

VII.

Not lonely, with the sad nymph Solitude,
Deep in the cover of the ancient wood,
Where the sun leaves him, and the happy dawn,
Stealing with blushes over the gray lawn,
Still finds him, all forgetful of the flight
Of hours, that passing still from dark to bright,
Know not to loiter,—all their progress naught:—
His eye, unconscious of the day, is bright
With inward vision; till, as sudden freed,
By the superior quest of a proud thought,
He darts away with an unmeasured speed;
His pinion purpling as he gains the height,
Where still, though all obscured from mortal sight,
He bathes him in the late smiles of the sun;—
And oh! the glory, as he guides his steed,
Flakes from his pinions falling, as they soar
To mounts where Eos binds her buskins on,
And proud Artemis, watching by her well,
For one,—sole-fortunate of all his race,—
With hand upon his mouth her beagle stays,
Lest he should baffle sounds too sweet to lose,
That even now are gliding with the dews.
How nobly he arrays
His robes for flight—his robes, the woven of songs,
Borrow'd from starry spheres,—with each a muse
That, with her harmonies, maintains its dance
Celestial, and its circles bright prolongs.
Fair ever, but with warrior form and face,
He stands before the eye of each young grace,
Beguiling the sweet passion from her cell,
And still subjecting beauty by the glance,
Which speaks his own subjection to a spell,
The eldest born of rapture, that makes Love,

At once submissive and the Conqueror.
He conquers but to bring deliverance,
And with deliverance light;—
To conquer, he has only to explore,—
And makes a permanent empire, but to spread,—
Though speeding on with unobserving haste,—
A wing above the waste.
A single feather from his pinion shed,
A single beam of beauty from his eye,
Takes captive the dim sleeping realm below,
Through eyes of truest worshippers, that straight
Bring shouts to welcome and bright flowers to wreathe
His altars; and, as those, to life from death,
Pluck'd sudden, in their gratitude and faith
Deem him a god who wrought the miracle,—
So do they take him to their shrines, and vow
Their annual incense of sweet song and smell,
For him to whom their happiness they owe.
Thus goes he still from desert shore to shore,
Where life in darkness droops, where beauty errs,
Having no worshippers,
And lacking sympathy for the light!—The eye,
That is the spirit of his wing, no more,
This progress once begun, can cease to soar,
Suffers eclipse, or sleeps!—
No more be furl'd
The wing,—that, from the first decreed to fly,
Must speed to daily conquests, deep and high,
Till no domain of dark unlighted keeps,
And all the realm of strife beneath the sky
Grows one, in beauty and peace for evermore,—
Soothed to eternal office of delight,
By these that wing the soul on its first flight,
For these are the great spirits that shape the world!

BLESSINGS ON CHILDREN.

Blessings on the blessing children, sweetest gifts of Heaven to earth,
Filling all the heart with gladness, filling all the house with mirth;
Bringing with them native sweetness, pictures of the primal bloom
Which the bliss forever gladdens, of the region whence they come;
Bringing with them joyous impulse of a state withouten care,
And a buoyant faith in being, which makes all in nature fair;
Not a doubt to dim the distance, not a grief to vex the nigh,
And a hope that in existence, finds each hour a luxury;
Going singing, bounding, brightening—never fearing as they go,
That the innocent shall tremble, and the loving find a foe;
In the daylight, in the starlight, still with thought that freely flies,
Prompt and joyous, with no question of the beauty in the skies;
Genial fancies winning raptures, as the bee still sucks her store,
All the present still a garden glean'd a thousand times before;
All the future, but a region, where the happy serving thought,
Still depicts a thousand blessings, by the wingéd hunter caught;
Life a chase where blushing pleasures only seem to strive in flight,
Lingering to be caught, and yielding gladly to the proud delight;
As the maiden, through the alleys, looking backward as she flies,
Woos the fond pursuer onward, with the love-light in her eyes.

Oh! the happy life in children, still restoring joy to ours,
Making for the forest music, planting for the wayside flowers;
Back recalling all the sweetness, in a pleasure pure as rare,
Back the past of hope and rapture bringing to the heart of care.
How, as swell the happy voices, bursting through the shady grove,
Memories take the place of sorrows, time restores the sway to love!
We are in the shouting comrades, shaking off the load of years,
Thought forgetting, strifes and trials, doubts and agonies and tears;
We are in the bounding urchin, as o'er hill and plain he darts,
Share the struggle and the triumph, gladdening in his heart of hearts;

What an image of the vigor and the glorious grace we knew,
When to eager youth from boyhood, at a single bound we grew!
Even such our slender beauty, such upon our cheek the glow,
In our eyes the life and gladness—of our blood the overflow.
Bless the mother of the urchin! in his form we see her truth:
He is now the very picture of the memories in our youth;
Never can we doubt the forehead, nor the sunny flowing hair,
Nor the smiling in the dimple speaking chin and cheek so fair:
Bless the mother of the young one, he hath blended in his grace,
All the hope and joy and beauty, kindling once in either face!

Oh! the happy faith of children! that is glad in all it sees,
And with never need of thinking, pierces still its mysteries;
In simplicity profoundest, in their soul abundance blest,
Wise in value of the sportive, and in restlessness at rest;
Lacking every creed yet having faith so large in all they see,
That to know is still to gladden, and 'tis rapture but to be.
What trim fancies bring them flowers; what rare spirits walk their
wood,
What a wondrous world the moonlight harbors of the gay and good!
Unto them the very tempest walks in glories grateful still,
And the lightning gleams, a seraph, to persuade them to the hill:
'Tis a sweet and loving spirit, that throughout the midnight rains,
Broods beside the shutter'd windows, and with gentle love complains;
And how wooing, how exalting, with the richness of her dyes,
Spans the painter of the rainbow, her bright arch along the skies,
With a dream like Jacob's ladder, showing to the fancy's sight,
How 'twere easy for the sad one to escape to worlds of light!
Ah! the wisdom of such fancies, and the truth in every dream,
That to faith confiding offers, cheering every gloom, a gleam!
Happy hearts, still cherish fondly each delusion of your youth,
Joy is born of well believing, and the fiction wraps the truth.

THE HURRICANE.

With dawn we started on our pilgrimage;
The day was fair at first, with rosy streaks
Suffusing all the east, that, as the sun
Rose radiant o'er the tree tops, grew to gold,
And, softening palely as he soar'd aloft,
Yielded, at length, to the intenser fires
He kindled as he sped. But, ere an hour,
And while the flaming standard he advanced
Flaunted most proudly o'er his eastern towers,
We mark'd a dissonant aspect in the west,
That glow'd adverse—a cloud with sulphurous edge,
Rising with gradual vans that soon diffused
Its murky tints o'er half the western heavens,
Thence stretching to the north. Suddenly fell
A weight upon the atmosphere, that breathed
Wearily, and with moaning, as at night
The giant struggles with the incubus,—
Struggles and sighs but with no power to stir.
Hotly, as from a furnace, came the breath,
That was nor breeze nor zephyr, from the south,
Where denser grew the shape. Shorn of his beams,
Yet burning redly in a vaporous void,
The sun toil'd on in heaven, as dreading still
The encounter that now threaten'd in his path.
Momently grew he paler as he sped,
Then sudden sank from sight,—swallow'd in a sea,
That all his beams extinguish'd. Over all
Hung the gigantic shape that soon became
The pall of the universe; and, settling down,
Shrouded the sky and forest. Thus the mass

Hung brooding, while accumulating clouds
Merged momently within its large embrace,
That still expanded wide. The great pines groan'd
As straining 'neath the burden that they bore,
And shuddering with a something yet to bear
From the great vans incumbent. Slow the day
Creeps on; a deathly silence wraps the scene
As of a terror threatening.

Wer't cloud, or wind,
Or storm of rain and thunder, that impends,
It might be well to hurry on our way
With traveller hardihood, that rates the hours
By miles, and at the measured hostel baits.
But he who dwells beneath a tropic sky,
Knows better in these aspects what to fear.
The lowly cabin of the Borderer,
Close crouching in the shade of yonder hill,
Offers best shelter. Thither, for a while,
Till these great wings, expanding with their blasts,
Collapse in arrowy tempests, that shoot swift
While forests groan, and sink beneath their sweep,
And placid waters, from their valleys roused,
Roll, raging in their terror—roll apart,
To meet again in strife, with angry crests,
That thunder as they meet. The awful hush,—
The sultry atmosphere—the stifling breath
That makes the laboring bosom heave with toil,—
Betoken wrath. This is the Hurricane!
The Vampire of the storm, whose raven wings
Spread, pall-like, o'er the Earth it lulls to sleep,
Till, in the deepest lull of its sad dream
It rouses; and, with ruthless and wild shriek,
Goes raging, rending,—with a power that sweeps

The forest, and upon the eternal rocks
Scores terribly the record of its wrath!

We soon found refuge in the lowly cot,—
A most rude cottage of trimm'd pines, that crouch'd
In safety 'mongst the shadow-keeping hills.
From the piazza—with an anxious gaze,
We watched the approaching terror! Group'd around
Gather'd the simple household,—sire and dame,
And scores of little ones. Too well they knew,
By frequent witness, of that fearful shape,
With its black, brooding aspect. Year by year,
Had they beheld its progress—felt its breath
Of fire,—precursor of its arrowy flight,
And seen the terrible ruin which it wrought
In glorious realms of forest, as it rush'd,
With flight of thousand thunderbolts,—and share,
Ploughing through woods and fields, smiting great heads,
And leaving bald the places which had been
Bless'd with the undulating green of trees
And waving shrubs and blossoms; in their stead—
Those fearful wings gone over it—prostrate forms
Torn, rent and shattered,—indiscriminate piles,
Lying as writhing in their agonies:
A battle-field where none survives—where fate
Sweeps victor and vanquish'd equally; the plain
Sharing the deadly blight of those it bore,
Its green shrubs wither'd, and the desolate earth
Made sterile, with a charm no more in flowers.

"See," said my old companion of the route—
"See where its black brows tower above yon steep,
The shape contracting 'neath it, crouching close,
Keen watching, as it were, with appetite

Raging for blood, like tiger that in tree,
Waits the approaching victim.
We might deem,—
Taught by superior instinct,—that these folds
Lurid and black, like robes that shroud the Fates,
Conceal'd some terrible Demon—some dread power
Commission'd to destroy; even as the Fate
That hung o'er Nineveh in storm and fire,
Nor fled, till o'er its temples went the sea
Of bitumen, and from its thousand homes,
Ceased sudden the long cry of agony,
The work being done forever.
That dread shape
So silent, brooding with the doom it brings,
Hath its own life and mission. It obeys,
With human consciousness the will that bids—
"Go!"—and it goeth. It will plunge anon
A mountain in its might, yet, in its sweep,
Mocking the free wing'd eagle. What a power
To work in such a guise: so ill defined,
So vast and so unseemly to the eye;
So incompact and vague. See, in the south
For many a league outstretch'd, the sluggish form
Lies shapeless—volume upon volume piled,—
Thin robes of gray between,—a melting mist,
That wraps its dusky limbs as in a sea,
Whose farthest waters lose themselves from sight
In deepening folds of cloud. And now the shape
Takes motion: soon that motion will be life!
How terrible the pause that grows between!
Thick vapors close around us, stifling and hot,
Till, with a difficult breath, we pray for storm,—
For the wild tempest in its angriest mood,
That threatens,—rather than the breath of fire

It sends in foretaste of the wrath to come!
Nor pray we long in vain! A wing is felt,
That stirs the masses with a sulphurous gale,
Evolving all their lightnings. Murmurs swell,
Mysterious, low, as rising from the seas;
A hollow voice, that, kindred with their depths,
Takes on the sullen chiding of their caves,
And threatens with their billows. Now, a shaft
Speeds sudden from the bosom of the cloud,
Opening the sable jaws that close as soon,
Just showing the dread gulfs that lie below,
Steaming with thunders. Deeper murmurs flow
From the faint edges of the o'erwhelming mass,
Whose vans are now in motion, wide unroll'd;
But, ever and anon, up-curling still
Their lengthen'd volumes as for newer strength.
Thus the grim serpent, eager for his prey,
Contracts his spiry form in knotted folds,
That he may better fling him forth in ire,
With muscle proper to his venomous will!
Look, where the lighter volumes upward float,
To fill the valleys which the terrible shape
Hath yielded. See them, as they mix, and make
A whirlpool in the sky. The birds fly low,
Screaming for shelter to the stunted copse:—
The vulture hath no longer eye for prey;
A single owl cries hooting from the wood,
As grateful for the darkening sky he loves;—
And the imperial savage who presides
O'er the thin realms of air, with wing less swift
In flight than conflict, bends his eastward way
To some abandon'd summit of the storm!
The horrid pause is o'er! It comes at last,
The shrieking terror, with convulsive bounds,

Solemn but swift, that still before its path,
Sends fearful intimations of approach;—
Even as some mighty host of Attila
Goes singing into battle,—singing of blood,
And striking horrid shields with spears of rage.
How sullenly bend the great boughs of the wood!
The oak scarce breasts the strife, and groans to meet
Its legions. To the roaring in the skies
Ascends the voice of waters. Deep to deep
Is calling—and their mighty concerts make
An awful choir of storm. Behold, where still
The black battalions gather for the charge;—
The wings contract—the rearward masses crowd,
As struggling for the van. A deadlier shape
Shoots outward from the midst; and, breathing now
With pestilent heat along its destined path,
It gives the terrible signal, which begins
The warring of three worlds. With lightnings arm'd,
The fearful spectre hurries on his course,
And the great forests crouch. The mountains heave,
As with the earthquake's labors; and the plain
Is shrouded with his legions. For the sea
They take their arrowy progress. The strong pine
They wring while passing, and with scornful might
Tear from the earth the great well-rooted oak,
And fling it on their path. Sweet fields that lay—
The virgin gifts of summer, by the sun
Bestow'd, when first he look'd on her with love,—
Are plough'd with furrows, such as leave broad scars
For ages on their beauty, and deform!
But reckless, the invader with his scourge
Their lawnéd realms still ravages. An hour
Hath left the blight of centuries. Too late,
Though with such terrible haste, he darts away

For other victories. For the seas he speeds,
With power that grows from progress. Ocean roars
With mortal agonies, as his giant form
Down plunges in its billows. The green waves
Divide in horror! With triumphant shriek
He ploughs the abyss, lays its deep hollows bare,
And shows their ghastly secrets. Then away
He hurries, as if satisfied in rage:—
His lengthening lines still following, howling hoarse,
In train of battle, and his terrible form
Still rending, till the gray void swallows all!

SONG.—THE BREEZE THAT SIGHS.

The breeze that sighs through lemon groves,
  The odor in their gift may bring,
As song from heart that truly loves,
  May soothe the heart that cannot sing.

But what if winds, in progress vain
  Should waste their sweets in empty air,
And hearts should idly breathe the strain,
  For other hearts that will not hear?

Better the breeze had never swept,
  Its sweets to waste, the generous grove;
And still the foolish heart had kept
  The secret close that told its love.

True, they had lost, the grove of sweets,
  The sweetest kiss it ever knew;
And the poor heart, with love that beats,
  Had stored in vain its treasures too.

ON THE DEATH OF AN OBSCURE CITIZEN.

MEN wonder when the planets do go out,
When stars desert their places—when the might
Of the great oak is shatter'd, and the storm
Sweeps the imperial trophy from the brow
Of him who look'd the god in mortal eyes,
And grew so to his own. But ah ! for thee,
So lowly in life's places—with no power
To lift thee into majesty—no grace,
To woo glad eyes in homage to thy walks,
And consecrate thy doings with applause
That cheers to new achievements—with no aim
Of greatness, and but little thirst for life—
Death hath no dignity, and thou hast sunk,
Silent, from out the crowded ways of man,
Into the quiet grave, and art not miss'd!
But nature hath her obsequies for all,
And virtue is remember'd with a tear,
When fame itself grows voiceless o'er the great,
And leaves their shrines to ruin. Thou hast made
Some sweet affections blossom at thy grave,
Which hath befitting flowers, that take on bloom
Ere spring hath made escape from winter cells,
Still pale with cold and terror of pursuit.
Love did not shrink to shelter in thy cot,
Though at the door stood poverty ; and toil,
For evermore within, from dawn to dark,
Had little respite to enjoy the smiles
That warm'd his courage to resolve, and made
The burden easy of the daily care!
But in the very rareness of the joy,
Grows its delicious value ; and thy bliss,

If lowly in condition,—wanting state
In utterance, and significant to thee,
Alone, of all around thee, was not less
The wholesome solace of a life that knew
A cottage empire only. In thy home,
Sate peace, content with lowliness, that gave
New fireside warmth and gladness to thy hearth,
That wore no gauds of grandeur. Love could share
Thy labors, and could lighten them; and truth
Found thee a treasure, that, within thy heart,
Assured of trust, made all a calm delight
That never wept for fortune. Thou wast blest,
To the necessity reconciled, that made
Thy home secure from envy, yet which brought
An adequate beauty to thy homely weeds,
And sweetness to thy threshold; and thy life
Pass'd on as passes the long summer day,
O'er silent forests, making shade and sun,
Equally fruitful of repose and love,
Commercing in rare union with a joy
That if it knows no gushings passionate,
Knows not the storms of passion which but take
The heat of pleasure, all the calm denied,
That makes the pleasure holy and secure.
Thy living and thy dying, both the same,
Safe from the tempest; in the world without
Making no stir. Few were they who knew
Thy virtues; few at thy departure felt
That something which was precious to the day,
Had been despoil'd by night. Yet in thy home,
There hangs a blind sad vacancy, that looks
Through eyes of terror to the lonely seat
Of thy sad widow. If she weeps, her tears
Lack voice, unless to those, her orphan brood,

That hear, through a like consciousness of loss,
And echo with a silence like her own.
Ah! nature hath not one unnoted child:
Some soul still sorrows when the light goes out,
Though feeble, which in poverty's lone cell,
Shone for the humblest; desolate hearts still shrine
The lineaments of care, when thus allied
To love; and precious instincts still discern
The little lowly hiding-place in earth,
Unmark'd by any monument, where sleeps
The form of him whose gifts in poverty
Made poverty's self a treasure, best of all!

ABANDONMENT.

Well, they have all departed,—the false friends,
With all the illusive hopes that led astray,
To dream and madness!—and the struggle ends!
I shall be free, at least the rest o' the day:—
Unloved shall be unflatter'd; and, alone,
Be safe from the poisoner, who feeds the ear
That he may drug the senses with a lie,
Suck'd from most innocent sources. Now they're gone,
I wonder how I suffer'd them so near;
More wonder why I wept to see them fly!
But credulous hearts sleep ever over-late,
And wake to the loss of half their better hours;
See the sun sink, that should be throned in state,
And rage in impotent fury against Fate,
To whom they charge the robbery of their powers,
That simply had been drugg'd by friendly cares,
Mock'd by conceit and credulous length of ears.

THE IMMORTALITY OF THE BELOVED.

None die but the forgotten!—The twin soul
Makes league with an eternal memory,
Whose voice is sleepless, and forever cries,
Through the still watches of the lonely night,
A word that is a spell!—This, when he hears,
Sends the survivor forth!—One only path
He takes,—and at one only altar bends,—
The grave of the beloved one:—a sad joy
Is in his desolate heart; and, stooping down,
With eyes, that, ever-dropping with their tears,
Still blind him to the solemn toil he takes,—
He writes upon the grave—he writes in flowers,
The well-known name; and thus, in death's despite,
Hallows the loved one into life!—What death
So powerful, as can trench upon the fame,
Which grows in true affections?—which springs up,
In greenest gardens of the memory,
Love planting ever his consoling flowers,
And bending gratitude, and weeping faith,
Nursing and tending with devoted watch,—
So that no noxious breath, nor wind, nor blight,
Shall over-pass the consecrated place,
Or rend its blooming tokens;—which, thus kept,
Are trophies,—proudest trophies—that declare
Love's empire over all;—a green amidst
Most cheerless sands;—a marble on the waste;
A bird of light, that, rising from the tomb,
Still leaves it vacant,—yet forever soars
From the same spot; pure emblem of the truth,
That, born of heaven, and with a wing that still
Seeks evermore its home, as if for food,

In the high place of its pure origin,—
Must still return to earth in sympathy,
And share the suffering, and denied to die,
Save, still undying, the sweet memories
Of him it could not save!—

IN ABSENCE.

Oh, wert thou but beside me now,
  Yon cold and cheerless moon would be
A high and purely passing brow,
  That I should joy to watch with thee.

With thee to smile, with thee to cheer,
  To soothe and bless my struggling heart,
This weary night would disappear,
  For all is happy where thou art.

A thousand promised joys should rise,
  In thought and memory, blessing still;
And from thy bright, yet dewy eyes,
  The fountains of mine own should fill.

And that dear pledge!—to me how dear,
  Since first its budding lips became
A smile to charm, a tone to cheer
  Each trembling feeling of my frame:—

Around my neck her clasping hands
  Like blooming tendrils round the tree,
A festive wreath of freshest bands
  That hide the roughness none should see.

To mark her growth, and, day by day,
  Behold her infant mind unclose,
To trim the light, protect the ray,
  Defend the bud and love the rose.

Month after month and year by year,
  To trace her being's rapid growth,
A father's joy, a mother's care,
  The blessing and the pride of both.

Ah! more than sweet is every dream
  My fond and fervent fancy brings—
A wooing breath, a winning gleam
  Of pure and most delightful things.

Fair images that seen before,
  Like angel memories will not part,
And hold their kind dominion o'er
  My weary and o'erburden'd heart.

Oh, come to me, for when thou'rt gone,
  My spirit sad, nor longer free,
Finds nature dull, and cities lone,
  And looks in vain, and weeps for thee.

AT PARTING.

Pray for me at the morning and at eve,
  When downward, lingering, goes the mellowéd sun,
Utter thy prayer that he may always leave
  A smile, a promise, for the wandering one.

Pray for me, though perchance, with mood like mine,
  Forever wayward, wild and obstinate,

All prayer be unavailing—ay, even thine—
  Pray still, and I shall not be desolate.

My heart shall fancy in the pleasant breeze,
  That gathers in the tree-tops, there's a tone
Sweet, sad, like that which comes o'er moaning seas,
  Which thou dost send to cheer the wandering one.

And when I lay me on my noonday bed,
  'Neath the broad foliage of the summer vine,
I'll deem the spirit watching at my head,
  The spirit that has waited long on thine.

Sweet heart! oh, never yet bloom'd sweeter heart—
  Pray for me, and the desert world and wild,
Shall offer tendance, and with gentlest art,
  Hallowing thy prayer, shall bless their erring child.

Sweet airs shall be around me, and though men,
  Not knowing well have wrong'd me—blest by thee,
The elements shall all look kindlier then,
  And doubly grant the boon thou begg'st for me.

MORAL EXILE.

She does not drive me forth with iron hand,
Bared steel, or cruelty yet more acute,
In the stern doom of exile. On her brow
Sits no imperial malice. From her lips
Falls no malignant accent;—but, instead,
Her voice is all melodious, and her smile—
Ah! most deceptive smile that ever mocks
The suffering which it soothes not—shining still,

Would seem to favor the neglected child
She makes her step-son!—
Ah! love not seeks
Smooth smile, soft accent!—love seeks only love;—
Naught less will satisfy its laboring hope,
Appease its hungering longing, or suffice
Its ocean-deep affections! If I sing,
Let the sweet deity that hears my song,
Esteem it sweet; and not, in the dull ear,
Give it cold entrance. If, upon her shrine,
I heap my votive offerings, with a heart
That joins in the hand-service,—let me know
The goddess feels their incense, that my love
Shall relish of her gracious, dear delight.—
But she,—my mother! What seems it to her
That I have sung her beauties? Far aloof
She sits and hears my praises, as some dame,
Proud of position in a royal court,
Sitting as Queen at some high tournament,
That gives indifferent heed to the brave knight
Who battles for her smile. High-prizéd dame,
That makes no count of him whose duteous heart
Beholds no dearer prize;—and coldly takes
His gallant homage as some natural right,
Which is no other than the gift of love—
Love's generous gift, demanding like for like,
Or nothing! 'Tis the bitterest fate of all,
More bitter than the sudden sting of death,
And colder than the black jaws of the grave,
Thus profitless to sue;—thus, hopelessly,
To bend in fruitless labor, still unmark'd
Without reward,—sweet smile of recompense—
Word of encouragement from gracious lips,
Which promise fond remembrance when the toil

Shall be all ended. Let them speak of it,
Whose lot hath thus been cast, and they shall tell
How easier of endurance were the toils
Of poverty in exile;—sweeter far
Its bitter crust and salt draught,—salter yet
By tears that hallow it to hopelessness,
Quenching no mortal thirst!

THE STREAMLET.

I.

Once more in the old places!—and I glow
  Again with boyhood. Once again renew'd,
My wandering feet have found the rivulet's flow,
  My eyes pursue old vistas in the wood;
My heart partakes their consciousness,—I hear
Long lost, but well-known sounds, salute mine ear.

II.

The voices of the forest and the stream,
  And murmuring flights of wind, that through the grove
Come fitfully, like fancies in a dream,
  And speak of wild and most unearthly love—
Such love as hope prefigures to the boy,
Crowning each hillock with a sunbright joy.

III.

There gleams the opening path, and there, below,
  Glimmers the streamlet sparkling through green leaves;
I catch the distant pattering of its flow,
  In sudden murmurs, ere mine eye perceives,

Complaining, as it takes its tiny leaps,
To the scoop'd basin where it sings and sleeps.

IV.

It was my father taught me, when a boy,
The winding way that wins it; and I grew
To love the path with an exceeding joy,
That heeded not the moments as they flew,
So sweetly were they then beguiled—gay gleams
All green and gold, the garments of youth's dreams.

V.

And, sitting by its marge, my father said,
That streamlet had a language for his ear,
Though vainly did I bend my boyish head,
With him, but nothing could I ever hear;
Yet, as we did return, he still would say,
He was a better man, so taught that day.

VI.

Yet, surely was there nothing but the flow
Of idle waters, evermore the same—
A sweet, sad pattering, as they went below—
I never heard them syllable a name,
Though much I strove, for in my father's look
I read the serious truth of all he spoke.

VII.

An hundred streams like this the country knows,
From Santee to Savannah—brooks that glide
Through willow tassels—where the laurel blows
In triumph, and the poplar springs in pride;
A slender thread of silvery white it went,
Winding and prattling in its slow descent.

VIII.

Where, then, the mystery of its voice and whence?
Like other forests those which round it grew;
In what the source of that intelligence,
Denied to me, which yet my father knew?
Change had not touch'd its waters,—'twas that morn
As small as in the hour when he was born.

IX.

He too, like me, had from its yellow bed
Pluck'd the gray pebble, and beneath its wave
Had plunged, in summer noon, his aching head,
Glad of the cool delight that still it gave;—
Then he grew up to manhood,—then became
Agéd,—yet was this little stream the same.

X.

His grave is in the forest, and he sleeps
Far from the groves he loved—his voice no more
Is in mine ear; yet through my memory creeps
Its echo, and the wild and solemn lore
He taught me, when we walk'd beside that brook,
Comes back as now within its waves I look.

XI.

The spells of memory to my side command
The shadowy thought, nor desolate nor lone;—
Faint are the images that near me stand,
Yet are they images of things well known;
Years gather to a moment and inform
The trembling bosom which they fail to warm.

XII.

No longer am I desolate, beside
  These green and sacred borders: in my ear,
As down I bend, where the fast waters glide,
  Murmurs from sweetest fancies do I hear;
Hope takes the swallow's accents, and they bring
To glad the gathering years, a rich and green-eyed spring.

XIII.

And my old sire, he err'd not sure! I feel
  As if I were a listener to the spell
Of one whose voice is power! My senses reel!
  It is his language,—I should know it well,—
He speaks through these sweet waters which he loved
In boyhood, and where still our footsteps roved.

XIV.

I tremble with a joy—my heart is still,
  As, swelling up, the accents break the air;
My spirit, troubled, shrinks, even as the rill
  When leaves disturb the sleeping waters there;—
My feet are fasten'd with a subtle charm,
Soothing but startling—full of sweet alarm.

XV.

The accents gather to familiar sounds,
  And wake anew a lost and well-loved tone,
I hear the sacred words, while silence rounds
  The enchanted circle, and my breath is gone:
They rise melodious, sad, but softly clear,—
My heart receives the music, not mine ear.

XVI.

" I have been when thy father dream'd of thee,
  I shall be, when thou dreamest of thy child;
Thy children shall be listeners to me,
  Whose tones so oft thy father's feet beguiled;
I am thy guardian genius,—from the first
My waters still have slaked thy spirit's thirst.

XVII.

" When thou shall be forgotten I shall be,
  And to the race that shall succeed thee on,
I will repeat my counsel, as to thee,
  And like thy footsteps now, shall theirs be won,
From the thick gathering—from the crowded street
With me, within the solitude, to meet.

XVIII.

" And I shall soothe their spirits, as I now
  Soothe that of him, their sire; my streams shall be
A gracious freshness for each burning brow,
  While my soft voice shall whisper, sweetly free,
Tempering to calm the bosom vex'd and bow'd
By the unfeeling clamors of the crowd.

XIX.

" Go forth, fair boy, and happy be thy years,
  Forget not soon the lessons, long our theme,
Nor, when the growing Time shall teach thee tears,
  Desert these shady bowers—this sacred stream;
'Twill be my care, when man hath taught thee gloom,
To bring thy worn heart back to all its bloom.

XX.

"Look on these waters when thy mood is sad,
  Fly to these groves, when close pursued by power;
These shall restore thee all that made thee glad,
  And bring oblivion of the present hour;
Mine is the stream that must forever roll,
A memory not of earth, but of its soul.

XXI.

"I keep affections pure—I save the heart
  From Earth's pollutions;—treasured in my wave
Is healing, and the power to make depart
  Bad passions, those worst tyrants; and to save
The victim from himself, and still restore
The angel whiteness of the soul once more.

XXII.

"Oh, when the world hath wrong'd thee, seek me then,
  Though, hapless, from thy better self estranged;
Fly to these waters from the strifes of men,
  And gazing in them shall thy heart be changed;
Though years have risen between, and strife and scorn,
Yet shall thy face, once more, be that thou wear'st this morn."

SPRING TIME.

Now's the time when Winter's going
  From the bowers he blighted long;
Now's the time when Spring is glowing,
  Breathing into bloom and song;
When green buds are hourly springing,
  In soft bed and sunny vale;

When the merry birds are singing,
  Fearless, round the cottage pale;
And, a long-expected comer,
  From the gardens of the south,
Swims in sight the blushing Summer,
  Sweet in smiles and warm in youth.

Gladsome notes are floating by us,
  And from earth a murmur steals,
Softly, which must still ally us
  To the clod that breathes and feels.
Life is round us in the breezes,
  In the ground a labor grows,
And the humblest motion pleases,
  That from living fountain flows.
Stagnant now no more, and frozen,
  Lo! the waters flash and run,
And the lake unfetter'd glows in
  The new glances of the sun.

Stoop to earth the ear and listen;
  Hark! the murmur from below;
Lift the upward eyes—they glisten
  With the rich and rosy glow.
Wide and wondrous is the dwelling
  Where the lovely builder works,
And the murmur upward swelling,
  Tells us where her agent lurks.
Prompt and ready at her summons,
  When the signal sounds of spring,
Lo! arise her peers and commons,
  Fleet of foot and wild of wing,
In the mansions long forsaken,
  Free to spin, to build, and moil;

Now they gather, glad to waken,
  Though they waken still to toil.
From their labor grows their treasure,
  Silken robes and honeyed spring;
And their very toil is pleasure,
  Since they fly, and flying sing.

Yet, throughout her vast dominions,
  What unequal forms appear!
Some on gold and purple pinions,
  Seem the princes of the air.
Sweets from others' toils assessing,
  Stooping only to partake
The rich juice and luscious blessing,
  Which they never stoop to make.
Like the lily near the fountain,
  Neither do they toil nor spin,
Yet, in joy and splendor mounting,
  Life and happiness they win:
Flying ever round the summit,
  Heedless of the tribes, that low,
Ply the shovel, dip the plummet,
  Grope in earth, and groping, grow.

'Twere meet answer to repining,
  Did the lowly grub deplore—
"These were made for soaring, shining,
  Shining, singing, as they soar.
When thou wear'st a golden pinion,
  Bright like that which soars so free,
Thou shalt have a like dominion,
  And the grub shall toil for thee."

HISTORICAL LEGENDS.

CAIUS MARIUS.

I.

The Dungeon of Minturnæ.

MARIUS. THE CIMBRIAN.

MARIUS. What art thou, wretch, that, in the darkness com'st,
The midnight of this prison, with sly step,
Most fit for the assassin, and bared dagger
Gleaming in thy lifted grasp!
CIMBRIAN. I am sent by those
Whose needs demand thy death. A single stroke
Sets us both free forever—thou from Fate,
Me from captivity.
MARIUS. Slave, hast thou heart
To strike at that of Marius!
CIMBRIAN. That voice—that name—
Disarm me; and those fearful eyes that roll,
Like red stars in the darkness, fill my soul
With awe that stays my hand. Master of the world,
The conqueror of my people hast thou been,—
I know thee as a Fate! I cannot harm thee.
MARIUS. Go to thy senders, and from Marius say,
That, if they bare the weapon for my breast,
Let them send hither one who has not yet
Look'd in a master's eye. 'Tis not decreed
That I shall perish yet, or by such hands
As gather in Minturnæ. Get thee hence!

II.

Public Hall of Minturnæ.

MAGISTRATES. THE CIMBRIAN. AUGUR.

CIMBRIAN. I cannot slay this man. Give me to strike
Some baser victim, or restore to me
My chains. I cannot purchase, at such price,
The freedom that I covet.

MAGISTRATE. Yet this man
Conquer'd thy people.

CIMBRIAN. He hath conquer'd me!

AUGUR. And he must conquer still!
His hour is not yet come. The Fates reserve
His weapon for their service. They have need
Of his avenging ministry, to purge
The world of its corruptions. I behold
A fearful vision of the terrible deeds
That wait upon his arm. Let him go free.
Give him due homage; clothe him with fresh robes;
Speed him in secret, with a chosen bark,
To other shores. So shall your city 'scape
Rome's wrath, and his hereafter.

MAGISTRATE. It is well:
This counsel looks like wisdom.

AUGUR. It is more!
So the gods speak through their interpreter.

MAGISTRATE. Release him straightway—send him forth in honor;
We give him freedom—let the gods give safety.

III.

Island of Ænaria.

MARIUS. CETHEGUS.

CETHEGUS. Thou hast slept, Marius.
MARIUS. And thou hast watch'd my sleep;
Ah! truest friend and follower, not in vain!
Dismiss that cloudy trouble from thy brows,
Those doubts that vex thy heart; for know that Fate
Still hath me in its keeping, and decrees
Yet other deeds and conquests at my hand,
And still one glorious triumph. I shall be
Once more, in Rome, a Consul! When a child,
Sporting on summer slopes, beneath old hills,
Seven infant eagles, from a passing cloud,
Dropt clustering in my lap. The Augurs thence
Gave me seven times the Roman Consulate.
CETHEGUS. Thou'st had it six.
MARIUS. One other yet remains.
CETHEGUS. Alas! the Fates but mock thee with a dream;
For know that, while thou slept'st, our treacherous bark
Loosed sail, and left the shores.
MARIUS. Gone!
CETHEGUS. Clean from sight.
MARIUS. Ha! ha! Now thank the gods that watch my sleep,
And save me when the might of man would fail!
Courage, my friend, that vessel speeds to wreck,
Rack'd on some lurking rock beneath the wave,
Or foundering in the tempest. We are safe!
CETHEGUS. Thou'rt confident.
MARIUS. As Fate and Hope can make me.
Yet look! there is an omen. We must fly
This place, for other refuge. See the strife

Betwixt these deadly scorpions on the sands.
CETHEGUS. What read'st thou in this omen?
MARIUS. Sylla's soldiers
Are fast upon our heels. Get to the shore;
Some fisher's boat will help us from the land,
And bear us whither the directing Fates
Decree for refuge—safely o'er the seas
That gulf our treacherous vessel.
CETHEGUS. Be it so!
I follow thee whatever be thy fate!
MARIUS. Hark! dost thou hear?
CETHEGUS. What sound?
MARIUS. The tramp of horse;
And lo! the boat awaits us by the shore!

IV.

Marius, alone, seated among the Ruins of Carthage.

Alone, but not a captive—not o'ercome
By any fate, and reckless of its doom—
Even midst the ruins by his own hand made,
There sits the Exile, lone, but unafraid!
What mighty thoughts, that will not be repress'd,
Warm his wild mood, and swell his laboring breast?—
What glorious memories of the immortal strife
Which gave him fame, and took from Carthage life;
That giant-like, sea rival of his own
Proud realm, still challenging the sway and throne;
Doom'd in long conflict, through experience dread,
To bend the neck at last, to bow the head;
To feel his foot upon her lordly brow,
And yield to him who shares her ruins now!

How, o'er his soul, with passions still that gush'd,
The wondrous past with all its memories rush'd!
These ruins were his monument. They told
Of wisest strategy, adventure bold,
Dread fields of strife—an issue doubtful long,
That tried his genius, and approved it strong;
That left him robed in conquest, and supreme,
His country's boast, his deeds her brightest theme;
Written in brass and marble—sung in strains
That warm the blood to dances in old veins;
That make young hearts with wild ambition thrill,
And crown the spirit with achieving will;
That seem eternal in the deeds they show,
And waken echoes that survive below;
Brood o'er the mortal, slumbering in the tomb,
And keep his name in song, his works in bloom,
Till envious rivals, hopeless of pursuit,
Join in the homage, who till then were mute;
Catch up the glorious anthem, and unite
To sing the bird they could not match in flight;
Content to honor where they cannot shame,
And praise the worth they cannot rob of fame.

How, with these memories gathering in his breast,
Of all the labors that denied him rest—
Of all the triumphs that his country bore
To heights of fame she had not won before—
Broods he, the exile from his state and home,
On what awaits thee and himself, O Rome!
Of what thy hate deserves, and his decrees,
Whom thou hast brought unwilling to his knees.
No sad submission yields he to his fate,
So long as solace comes to him from hate,
Or hope from vengeance. In his eyes, ye trace

No single look to recompense disgrace;
With no ambition check'd, no passion hush'd,
No pride o'erthrown, no fond delusion crush'd;
With every fire alive that ever sway'd,
His soul as lordly as when most obey'd,
He broods o'er wrongs, remember'd as his own,
And from his heart hears vengeance cry alone.
Fix'd on the ruins round him, his dread eye
Glares, as if fasten'd on his enemy;
His hand is on the fragment of a shrine
That Hate may henceforth deem a thing divine;
Grasp'd firmly—could the fingers but declare
How dread the oath the soul is heard to swear!
The awful purpose, nursed within, denies
Speech to the lips, but lightens up the eyes,
Informs each feeling with the deadliest will,
But, till the murderous moment, bids "be still!"

Come read, ye ministers of Fate, the lore
That fills the dark soul of the fiend ye bore;
Reveal the secret purpose that inspires
That deadly mood, and kindles all its fires;
Scan the dread meaning in that viperous glance
Fix'd on those ruins in intensest trance,
Which nothing speaks to that it still surveys,
And looks within, alone, with meaning gaze.
Unclose the lip, that, rigidly compress'd,
Stops the free rush of feeling from the breast;
And, on that brow, with seven deep furrows bound,
Write the full record of his thought profound.
What future scene beneath that piercing eye
Depicts the carnage and the victory;
The flashing steel—the shaft in fury sped—
The shrieking victim, and the trampled dead?

Say, what wild sounds have spell'd the eager ear,
That stretches wide, the grateful strain to hear;
How many thousands perish in that cry
That fills his bloody sense with melody?
What pleading voices, stifling as they swell,
Declare the vengeance gratified too well?
What lordly neck, beneath that iron tread,
Strangled in utterance, leaves the prayer unsaid?
What horrid scene of triumph and of hate
Do ye discover to this man of Fate,
Which, while his Fortune mocks the hope he bears,
Consoles his Past, and still his Future cheers?

He hath no speech, save in the ruins round;
But there's a language born without a sound,
A voice whose thunders, though unutter'd, fly
From the red lightnings of the deep-set eye;
There passion speaks of hate that cannot spare,
Still tearing those that taught him how to tear;
One dream alone delighting his desire,
The dream that finds the fuel for his fire:—
Let fancy shape the language for his mood,
And speak the purpose burning in his blood.

V.

Marius. "If thou hadst tears, O Carthage! for the voice
That speaks among thy ruins, it would cheer
The spirit that was crush'd beneath my heel,
To hear the tongue of thy destroyer swear
To live as thy avenger. I have striven
For Rome against thee, till, in frequent strife,

Thy might was overthrown—thy might as great
As Rome's in days most palmy, save in this:
Thou hadst no soul as potent in thy service,
As I have been in hers. And thou, and all—
The Gaul, the Goth, the Cimbrian—all the tribes
That swell'd the northern torrents, and brought down,
Yearly, the volumed avalanche on Rome—
Have sunk beneath my arm, until, secure,
She sat aloft in majesty, seven-throned,
And knew or fear'd no foe. This was my work—
Nor this alone; from the patrician sway,
That used her as the creature of his will,
I pluck'd her eagles, casting down his power
Beneath plebeian footstep. For long years
Of cruellest oppression and misrule,
I took a merited vengeance on her pride,
Debasing her great sons, that, in their fall,
Her people might be men. I loved her tribes,
Since they were mine. I made their homes secure;
I raised their free condition into state—
And I am here! These ruins speak for me—
An exile—scarr'd with honorable wounds,
At seventy years, alone and desolate!

"But the o'erruling Deities decree
My triumph. From thy ruins comes a voice
Full of most sweet assurance. Hark! it cries,
To me, as thy avenger. Thou forgiv'st
My hand the evil it hath wrought on thee,
That the same hand upon thy conqueror's head
May work like ruin. The atoning Fates
Speak through thy desolation. They declare
That I shall tread the ungrateful city's streets,
Arm'd with keen weapon and consuming fire,

And still unglutted rage. My wrath shall sow
The seeds of future ruin in her heart,
So that her fall, if far less swift than thine,
Shall be yet more complete. She shall consume
With more protracted suffering. She shall pass
Through thousand ordeals of the strife and storm,
Each bitterer than the last—each worse than thine—
A dying that shall linger with its pain,
Its dread anxieties, its torturing scourge,
A period long as life, with life prolong'd,
Only for dire, deservéd miseries.
Her state shall fluctuate through successive years,
With now great shows of pride—with arrogance
That goes before destruction—that her fall
May more increase her shame. The future grows—
Dread characters, as written on a wall—
In fiery lines before me; and I read
The rise of thousands who shall follow me,
Each emulous of vengeance fell as mine,
By mine at first begotten. Yet, why gaze
In profitless survey of the work of years,
Inevitable to the prescient soul,
And leave our own undone? I hear a voice
Reproaching me that I am slow to vengeance;
Me, whom the Fates but spare a few short hours,
That I may open paths to other masters,
For whom they find the scourge. They tutor me
That mine's a present mission; not for me
To traverse the wide future, in pursuit
Of those who shall succeed me in their service,
But to speed onward in the work of terror,
So that no hungering Fate, the victim ready,
Shall be defrauded of its prey. I rise,
Obeying the deep voice that, from these ruins,

Rings on mine ear its purpose. I obey,
And bound to my performance as the lion,
Long crouching in his jungle, who, at last,
Sees the devoted nigh. The impatient blood
Rounds with red circle all that fills mine eye;
A crimson sea receives me, and I tread
In billows, thus incarnadined, from nations
That bleed through ages thus at every vein.
Be satisfied, ye Fates! Ye gods, who still
Lurk, homeless, in these ruins that ye once
Made sacred as abodes, and deem'd secure,—
I take the sword of vengeance that ye proffer,
And swear myself your soldier. I will go,
And with each footstep on some mighty neck,
Shall work your full revenge, nor forfeit mine!
Dost thou not feel my presence, like a cloud,
Before my coming, Rome?* Is not my spirit,
That goes abroad in earnest of my purpose,
Upon thy slumbers, City of the Tyrant,
Like the fell hag on breast of midnight sleeper,
That loads him with despair? Alone I come;
But thousands of fell ministers shall crowd
About me, with their service—willing creatures
That shall assist me first to work on thee,
And last upon themselves! The daylight fades,
And night belongs to vengeance. I depart,
Carthage, to riot on thy conqueror's heart."

* The reader will be reminded by this passage of that noble and solemn speech made by the Ghost of Sylla, at the opening of Ben Jonson's tragedy of Catiline: "Dost thou not feel me, Rome," etc.

VI.

Silent once more the ruins—dark the night,
Yet vengeance speeds with unembarrass'd flight;
No fears delay, no toils retard the speed
Of that fierce exile, sworn to deadliest deed;
And thou, O Queen of Empires, now secure
Of state that might be peaceful, were it pure,
Too soon thy halls shall echo with the yell
That summons human fiends to works of hell!
Ambition, long unsated, urged by Hate,
Queen of the Nations, speaks thy mournful fate;
Thy valor wasted, and thy might in vain,
Thy virtues sapp'd to break thy despot's chain!
Long didst thou rule, in simple courage strong,
The guardian friend of right, the foe to wrong;
Great in thyself, and conscious of the sway
That kept meet progress with the march of day;
That, from all nations pluck'd the achieving arts,
Which make sway sovereign in a people's hearts;
Proud on thy heights rose forms to worship dear,
There swell'd the temple's crest, the column there,
Each with its chronicle to spell the soul,
And each most precious to the crowning whole;
A world thyself—a wondrous world—that made
The admiring nations silent in thy shade;
Genius and Art commingling in thy cause,
And gods presiding o'er thy matchless laws.

VII.

But dark the hour impends—the storm is nigh,
And thy proud eagles flaunt no more the sky;
Thou hast not kept thy virtues to the last,
And all thy glories centre in thy past—
Thy safety in thy glories. From beneath
Thine altars swells the midnight cry of death;
The tocsin summons—not to brave the foe,
But to make bare thy bosom to the blow;
From thy own quiver flies the shaft of doom,
And thy own children hollow out thy tomb.
The exulting shouts that mock thee in thy shame,
Were those that led thee once to heights of fame:
The bird that swoops to riot on thy breast,
Is the same eagle that made great thy nest.
Hark! at his shrilly scream the sleuth-hounds wake,
The bloody thirst which in thy heart they slake;
Thy proud patricians, hunted down, survey
The herds they kept, most busy with the prey.
These are the flocks they foster'd from their foes,
And these are first to drink the blood that flows.
Wondrous the arts of vengeance, to inspire
The madden'd son to prey upon the sire!
Wondrous the skill *that* fierce plebeian wields
To make this last the bloodiest of his fields.
Vain all thy prayer and struggle—thou art down—
His iron footstep planted on thy crown;
But in thy fate, 'tis something for thy pride,
Thus self-destroy'd, thou mighty suicide!

BERTRAM:

AN ITALIAN SKETCH.

I.

SCENE: *The Dungeon of Bertram in the Castle of Leoni.*

LEONI. BERTRAM.

LEONI. Thou sleep'st as one who hath no fear—no grief!
BERTRAM. As one who hath no fear; and, for my griefs,
That they permit me sleep at such an hour,
Would show them much more merciful than thou!
LEONI. I, too, am merciful—will bring thee sleep,
So deep, as will shut out all sense of grief
From thy unlaboring senses.
BERTRAM. Be it soon!
LEONI. Is this thy prayer?
BERTRAM. Dost ask?
LEONI. Enough! Then hear!
To-morrow thou shalt have no charge in life—
The fair sky shall reject thee; the bright sun
Lend thee no succor—and the wooing breeze,
That sweeps so sweetly through yon window grate,
Shall only stir the long grass on thy grave!
Dost hear what I have spoken? Thou shalt die!
BERTRAM. 'Tis well!
LEONI. No more?
BERTRAM. What more wouldst have? Thy power

To which I may oppose nor prayer nor pleading,
Needs not my vain acknowledgment of grief;—
And fears I have none.

LEONI. Is all sense of hope
Utterly dead within thee? Does no dream
Rise up before thy fancies, fraught with pleasure,
That life prolong'd may bring thee—happiest hours,
In sunshine or in shade—such as thy bosom
Was once most blest to dream of? Thou hast been
A very bird of the summer, in thy flight,
No less than music. Thou couldst clip the air
With ever-glad embraces; couldst delight
The groves with the spring sweetness of thy song,
And fed'st on all the flowery fields of life,
With never satiate appetite and hope!—
Is thy privation nothing?—the great loss
Of the things visible and glorious, thou
Hast ever sought with such a fresh delight?
The woods and waters—this fair earth and sky,
Glowing in birds and blossoms; and the night
Proud in its starr'd luxuriance; and that moon,
Whose pallid disk looks mournful through yon bars,
As if to yield thee sympathy. A while,
Her beams will gleam upon thy silent grave,
And seek thee through the grasses on its slopes,
And thou know nothing.

BERTRAM. Be it as thou sayest.

LEONI. I tell thee, by the morrow thou shalt sleep
I' the iron grasp of death.

BERTRAM. One word for all!
Time ceased with me to-day—and in *her* grave
Sleep all my earthly morrows.

LEONI. Obdurate!
Yet would a prayer become thee.

BERTRAM. Not to thee!
My prayers are not for life—nor yet for death—
And, if for mercy, but to Him, whose power
Leads through the awful future, in whose shadows
I see no sway of thine! Thou couldst not answer
To any prayer I make thee.

LEONI. Not for life?

BERTRAM. No!
Life were no mercy now. The light which made
My life on earth, now beckons through the gates
Which thou mayst ope, not shut! Thou hast o'erstept
The limits of thy policy. Thy power,
That smote too soon the victim in thy grasp,
Forever lost its sway, in the foul blow,
That rather spoke the madness of thy hate,
Than made its purpose sure. For prayer of mine,
Invoking life for *me*, denied to *her*,
Thou wait'st but vainly. Not to mock thy power
Do I contemn thy mercy; but that blessing
Were now no boon to me. I hear the doom
Thy lips have spoken, and I welcome it!—
Will meet it with no struggle and no prayer,
But, in such meek humility of heart—
Not reft of every hope—which best becomes
These bonds, this weakness—conscious that I breathe
In thy forbearance only. Let the axe
Be sharpen'd and in readiness—the neck
Is bared, and bent already, for the blow!

LEONI. Die in thy pride! I would have wrung the prayer
From thy unnatural bosom, to deny thee;
Would first have moved thee to an abject homage,
That shame, as well as death, might fasten on thee,
Defiling thy past honors; and have shown thee,
Clipping with eager arms about my knees,

While my feet tramp thee to the kindred dust
Which stains thy insolent forehead.
BERTRAM. Oh! I know thee!
LEONI. Thou know'st me! Well! it needs not that I tell thee
Thy doom is written! With the sun, thou diest!

II.

BERTRAM—*solus.*

BERTRAM. I will not shame his brightness! He will blaze
For other seasons. He will bring their fruits,
And cheer to song the throats of merry birds,
And ripen yellow harvests for the race,
In multitudinous lands; and I shall lose
These joys, which never fail'd till now to gladden
This weary heart of mine! But now their sweets
Bring me no hope; nor, with their sweets denied,
Do I feel loss. 'Twas in her love that grew
The season's bounty—and the glorious smile
That bless'd me in the rising of the sun,
And cheer'd me in the music of the bird,
And charm'd me in the beauty of the flower,
And taught me, in the fragrance-blessing earth,
The way to countless blessings, which no more
I find in earth or sky, in song of birds,
Beauty in flowers, or glory in the day!
My day is night: my prayer is for that sleep
That sees no more the day from which is gone
The soul's one beauty, giving charm to all!
Nor is the night which now approacheth fast—
Through which my feet must go—the final night,

Whose coming makes men falter, with a fear
That, in the unknown, still dreads the worst of knowledge—
Without its welcoming light! I have o'ercome
The natural fears of death,—which, in our youth,
Must ever be a Terror! Doubt and dread
Grow passive, in that weariness of soul
When life maintains no hope; and death puts on
The aspect of a friend to him who feels
How toilsome and how endless is the day
Consumed without a quest, through barren realms
That Love hath ceased to brighten with his beams,
Or freshen with his flowers. My woes, that brought
Despair for one dread season, and dismay
That still o'erwhelms my heart, hath also taught
Elsewhere to seek the Comforter! And Fear,
That found on earth but Tyranny, beyond,
Looks upward for protection. He whom Power
Drives from the shelter of the Throne, finds strength
In the more steadfast Altar; and the man,
Who knew no safety with his kindred fellow,
Soon finds the need of Him, who, throned apart,
Repairs the wretched sorrows of the race,—
Rebukes the injustice—from the oppressor plucks
The scourge—and to the victim, soon or late,
Atones for the worst sufferings born on earth.
Oh! Death shall be no pang, though sharp his blow;—
And loss of life, however glad before
In bloom and blossom, bring no sorrow now!

And yet, to tread that passage of thick gloom
Into the world of doubt! To take that plunge,
From consciousness, to the bewildering change
Which may be woe, or apathy still worse,
In loss of that large consciousness, whose hope

Clings to the soul as to its only life,
Secure in joyous certainty of wings,—
High powers, that yield not to the outward pressure,
And, with the will, ne'er-pausing progress keep
To the mind's best achievements! Oh! that doubt!—
Whether, in passage from the state we know,
We rise elsewhere erect, or grow to nothing;
Never know waking—with one pang lose feeling;
Lose, with the sky and earth, all sense and seeing—
The *all* that we have lived for—while the loved one,
Most precious to the heart of all affections,
Lies silently beside us, and we know not!—
Hush'd each divinest instinct that, while living,
Taught us, unseen, of the approaching footstep,
And, with a breath, infusing still the zephyr,
Quicken'd each pulse within the trembling bosom
With intimations of that precious spirit
So natural to our own. Oh! my Francesca!
Where glid'st thou?—through what region, breathing glory—
Through what sweet gardens of delight and treasure,—
That I behold thee not?—and drink no promise
Of what awaits me in the world hereafter,
From the sweet whispers of thy passing spirit,
Stealing beside me? Thou art freed the struggle,
And, in the unlimited province of thy wing,
Why fly'st thou far?—why bring'st me no sweet tidings
To strengthen the dear hope that gave us courage
When we were torn asunder—made us fearless
Of all the tyrant might decree against us—
Assured of that blest future which his power
Might never enter? Wert thou nigh—about me—
Infusing, with thy sweetness, the damp vapor
That chills this gloomy dungeon—I had known it!
My soul had felt thy presence, as one gathers

The scent of flowers that grow in foreign gardens,
Whose blooms he doth not see! Didst thou look on me,
I should not droop this hour. Oh! wouldst thou speak,
I should not feel this dungeon—dread this death—
That, in thy absence from my spirit now—
Thine freed—takes on a shape of during darkness,
That never hopes a dawn! Who comes?

III.

FRIAR. BERTRAM.

FRIAR. My son!
BERTRAM. Art thou mine executioner?
FRIAR. Thy saviour rather—
If I might execute upon thy pride,
Thy sinful thoughts and passions, and thy fears,
By bringing thee, in penitence and sorrow,
To the white feet of Him who came to save,
And perish'd, for thy safety, on the cross!
O son! the moments leave thee. A few hours
Is all the remnant of the time allow'd thee.
I would prepare thee for the terrible change
The morrow brings thee—would entreat thy prayers—
The meek repentance of thy evil passions,
And not less evil thoughts—and such confession
Of each foul secret festering in thy soul,
With the due sorrows which should follow it,
As may commend thee to the Saviour's grace,
And make thee fit for the Eternal Presence!
BERTRAM. Behold me then most guilty. Pride was mine,
And sinful thoughts, and dark imaginings,
And reckless passions, and ungracious fancies,

And all the thousand tendencies to evil
Which ever urge the impatient soul of man
To heedless forfeiture of Heaven's sweet mercy.
What need the dark detail—the nice relation—
The name and character of each offence,
Too numerous quite for name, for recollection—
Too foul for the now blushing consciousness
To summon into sight, or give to speech!
Enough, that I have sinn'd—that, in my sorrow,
I could weep tears of blood; and that I perish
Forgiving all mine enemies—imploring
Of all forgiveness—and of God, o'er all!—
Most doubtful of his mercy, as well knowing
How great mine undesert.

FRIAR. Alas! my son,
This will not answer thee. Thou must disburden
Thy heart of each dark secret. 'Tis thy pride,
And not the shame and grief of thy contrition,
That locks thy secret up!

BERTRAM. I have no secrets
From God, to whom for judgment I must go;
No hope from man, of whom I have no fear,
And no confession for his ears, whose judgment
Can do me hurt or service now no more.

FRIAR. Beware, my son! This stubbornness! This woman—
Francesca—who hath perish'd in her guilt—
She was to thee no wife? Her full confession—

BERTRAM. Ah! now I know thee! Get thee to Leoni:
I have no secrets for thy keeping, father,
Or thy revealing. Yet a prayer I make thee;
Leave me to God—in quiet.

FRIAR. If I leave thee—
Thy conscience unrelieved—the truth unspoken—

I leave thee to the enemy of man,
Who lurks in waiting for thy soul—

BERTRAM. Away!

FRIAR. The curse—

BERTRAM. Oh! fit for curses only—hence!
Thou hast usurp'd the white wings of the dove,
To do the serpent's office! Who is there?

IV.

FRANCESCA. BERTRAM. FRIAR.

BERTRAM. Ah! now is Heaven most merciful! She comes!
She glides, a form of light, athwart the darkness;
I see her radiant beauties, starr'd by Heaven
With supernatural brightness; and I feel
The lightness of a breath, that's balm for angels,
Uplift me as with wings! Oh! blessed being,
That hallowest where thou com'st—how doth thy presence
Prepare me for the sacrifice! One moment;
I shut mine eyes in doubt! I open them
Once more to rapture! Dost thou see, old man?
Thy lips had spoken curses as from Heaven—
Lo! now, its angel!

FRANCESCA, [*to the Friar.*] Hence, father, to Leoni.

BERTRAM. Leoni! Can she speak of him—Leoni!

FRANCESCA, [*to the Friar.*] He summons thee! He needs thee! Hence with speed!

FRIAR. Then hast thou answer'd wisely. All goes well!
I leave thee.

FRANCESCA, [*to the Friar.*] Hence!

V.

FRANCESCA. BERTRAM.

BERTRAM. Is it Francesca speaks—
And speaks she of Leoni? Thou wert mine,
Francesca—and in robes elect of heaven,
Speak'st thou of him who was thy enemy,
As he is mine? I tremble, with a dread
That tears my very heart-strings! Oh! Francesca,
Pure spirit of the purest of earth's mortals,
Speak, and uplift me, with a voice of mercy,
From this dark sphere to thine.
FRANCESCA. Bertram!
BERTRAM. That name!
Which still was the dear burden of thy lips
When thou wast mine, and mortal—sounds to me
As thou hast ever said it. There's no change,
To eye or ear, in thee. O heart! be hopeful;
Since death makes free the living to their mission,
Nor robs the loved one of those precious beauties
That fashion'd thought and sense, and fiery passion,
To one sweet frame of love!
FRANCESCA. Dost think me dead,
Dear Bertram?
BERTRAM. Dead, my Francesca—dead to earth—
But oh! not dead to me! They show'd thee to me,
Even through these grates, array'd in innocent white,
And robed as for a bridal with the stars,
In pure white blossoming flowers.
FRANCESCA. They mock'd thine eyes,
As they have mock'd my ears. I am not dead . . .
I live as thou hast known me. I am thine,
As still I was before; but, rouse thee briefly,

For we have little space. Reserve thy wonder
Till we go hence in safety. We must fly—
While the dread baron sleeps. Leoni sleeps—
Sleeps soundly! I have left his bed but now!

BERTRAM. Thou! Left *his* bed but now!

FRANCESCA. Marvel not, Bertram,
However marvellous all seemings be
That check us in this dungeon. Thou shalt know
The dark, dread truth hereafter.

BERTRAM. Left his bed!
His bed! The lustful murderer—the foul satyr,
Whose very eye but taints the thing it looks on,
Whose very breath is incense of pollution,
Whose very touch is sin! O God! I hearken
And live! He lives! . . . She lives! Francesca—mine!—
All live! Yet hath she left his bed but now!—
Death! death! O friend! where art thou? I had lost
The sense of fear! I lived but for one hope—
That the short, rapid interval of time
'Twixt this impatient consciousness, and that
Which made my faith assurance absolute,
Of life with thee hereafter—would be o'er,
With but one shock—one moment of thick darkness—
And then all light and rapture!—and I wake,
To feel the scorpion sting of agony,
That tells me of the death that follows death,
In which all hope lies buried—smother'd sure
In loss of that most precious of life's fancies,
Its dream of the pure angel, whit'st of all
Above the cloudy confines of the grave,
Waiting with welcome! Death! Oh, death! Oh, terror!
That I should live for this!—that thou shouldst tell me,
Francesca, with no crimson on thy cheek,
No gushing eyes, no husky, tremulous voice,

That thou com'st freshly from Leoni's bed,
No longer fresh—yet living! [*Falls on his face.*

FRANCESCA. Were thy fears—
Thy dark suspicions true, oh! cruel Bertram,
How vain were tears or tremors, conscious blushes,
Or all the broken agonies of speech,
To show my shame or thine!

BERTRAM. Yet didst thou leave
Leoni's bed but now! Thy own lips said it,
Nor falter'd in the speech.

FRANCESCA. Oh! had I left
My virtues on his bed, there had been need
For faltering and for tears. I left his bed,
But left no living bed, my Bertram! No!
Look on this dagger—let it speak for me!

BERTRAM. It bleeds—it drops with blood. The crimson edges
Gleam brightly dark before me. Oh! Francesca,
I see what thou hast done—yet, do not say it!
I feel the terrible need that stood before thee,
And comprehend the fate that forced upon thee
The dreadful stroke of death. And yet, Francesca,
I would it had been any hand but thine
To do this deed! [*Covering his eyes.*

FRANCESCA. Thy life was on it, Bertram—
And mine—and something more to me than life;
And, in my soul, a voice that cried—"Be cruel,
Or thou art lost to Bertram and to Heaven!"
Thou hat'st—thou fear'st me! Ah! I see it, Bertram!

BERTRAM. Hate thee, Francesca? No! How much I love thee,
No words may speak. Yet there's a deadly horror
That shakes my frame—that seizes on my heart!
Look how thy hand is crimsoned!—up thine arm,
Even to thine elbow, drips the clotting current!

God! what a terrible stroke! *Thou* didst *not* do't—
Thou once so gentle, whom a wounded sparrow
Had brought to feminine sorrows. Thou hast wept
The fate of the cucuyo when I brush'd it,
To loss of wing and glitter, from thy garments;
And not a beggar's babe, with plaint of hunger,
But, with thy bounty, won a boon of tears,
Sweet as the angels weep o'er woes of mortals;
And thou to strike this blow! I'll not believe it;
Some other hand than thine, Francesca!

FRANCESCA. Mine!
Mine only, Bertram. Do not curse or chide me;
Turn not thy face away. 'Twas for thy safety.

BERTRAM. As if Death had one terror in his keeping,
To wound a fear of mine!

FRANCESCA. Yet, have a thought
Of poor Francesca's danger. See her struggles,
At midnight, in the darkness, with her tyrant;
That bold, bad man, with all his power around him!
Hear her wild shrieks, which all refused to hear:
How vain were all her pleadings! How the danger
Threaten'd the whiteness of her innocent bosom,
That knew no claim but thine; and think how madly
The spasms of fear and horror in my soul
Impell'd the deadly weapon to the heart,
Grown viperous with its lusts—its snakes about me,
Ready to sting with deathsome leprosies!
Oh! think of this, my Bertram!

BERTRAM. My Francesca,
Dost think I blame thee! 'Twas a fate that made thee
Thus stern and fearful; yet, to me, thy beauties
Were those of meekness only. In mine eyes,
Thy mould was still of those celestial beings
That find their virtues in their tenderness,

Chasten'd by love to purity. All passions
Grew modest in thy presence. Every feeling
That minister'd to make thy loveliness,
Seem'd to have had its birth in angel meekness,
That spread a hallowing moonlight at its coming,
Making the rugged soft. How could I know thee,
Thus terribly incarnadined with vengeance
For any purpose! Could I dream of thee,
Thus robed in crimson horrors, and believe thee
The pure white thing thou wast, when first I found thee
In groves of green Val d' Arno, singing sweetly,
With eyes of dewy glistening, to pale sisters
That watch'd above in fondness? Oh! thy nature
Hath been o'erwrought to madness! May I fold thee
Once more to this lone bosom, and remember
The thing thou wast, but art not?

FRANCESCA. Let me save thee,
Even though I lose thee, Bertram.

BERTRAM. Lose me, never!
The flight that saves thy Bertram—

FRANCESCA. Saves not me,
Since thus he holds me alter'd—if he alters
In the dear faith he gave me. The worst death
Grows up before me, though we fly together,
In these so foreign glances—in this speech
That tells how much he loses in the change
That outraged what I was, and, in my terrors,
Made me achieve the deed, however needful,
That makes me thus a terror to his love.
Yet must we fly. These keys undo thy fetters—
See how they fall about thee! Rouse thee, Bertram!
Thy hands, thy feet are free. Thy tyrant sleeps,
No more to cross thy fortunes; and Francesca,
If stain'd with blood, is pure for thee, as ever

In happy vale of Arno. Yet I ask not
That thou shouldst deem me so—that thou shouldst love me,
As then, in those sweet hours.

BERTRAM. I've done thee wrong
By this ungrateful chiding. I will take thee,
As all-confiding to this hopeful bosom
As when thy hands were innocently white.
We'll fly together. I am thine, Francesca,
Never to wrong thy hearing with a thought
That love may deem rebuke. Let us away!

FRANCESCA, (*aside.*) Yet is the thought the shadow to the soul,
Though never shown by speech. My doom is written
In the deep horror which his spirit feels,
At what this hand hath done. Oh! in the future,
I see the icy dread—I hear the accent
That speaks the chill'd affection—forced and idle,
As born no more of fondness. I must perish,
In the denial of the love which made me,
At first, a breathing woman. I must perish;
Yet, to the last, in loving him, I cherish
The hope, that when the ice-bolt falls between
Our lives, our hearts shall reunite once more,
And death retrieve the whiteness life hath lost.

BERTRAM. Why lingerest thou, Francesca?

FRANCESCA. But for prayer!—
Heaven's mercy may be yielded to our flight
If not our hearts. Dear Bertram, let me lead thee;
But take the dagger—I will bear the keys!

BERTRAM. Oh! give it me; far better graced in mine,
Than in thy hands, Francesca. Give it me!
O heart! 'tis my infirmity that speaks—
But I could easier strike a host of hearts,
Than see it in thy grasp! And yet, Francesca,

I would not wrong thee by reproach. Thy danger
Made the dread weapon a necessity
Thou couldst not 'scape, and shouldst not. Let my arm
Enfold thee; and should danger threaten now,
Thine eye shall see this arm more red than thine,
In shielding thy white bosom.

FRANCESCA, (*timidly.*) May I hold
Thy hand, my Bertram?

BERTRAM. Heart and hand, Francesca. [*Embracing.*

FRANCESCA. Now could I go to death!

BERTRAM. We go to life,
To love and safety, dear one!

FRANCESCA, (*aside.*) Through a night,
Where all is cloud before me, never-lifting
Till the last cloud descends. Oh! love no longer,
As once we knew it—wings and sunniness,
With music in the pauses of the breeze,
While leaves drop down in odors; but a love
That chills while it embraces—and sweet accents
That never warm to meaning.

BERTRAM. What say'st thou?

FRANCESCA. Of cold and darkness, Bertram.

BERTRAM. Soon, the light
Will gather round us with its cheerful aspects,
That smile among the stars; and Heaven's fresh breathings—
'Scaped from the pestilent atmosphere of death—
Will lift our spirits with a glad surprise.
The bolts unclose! Oh! see you not, Francesca,
How swiftly darts the messenger of light,
As glad to do us service, o'er the threshold,
And waves his glow-worm torch to guide us on;
While the fond zephyr, through the yawning portal,
Wraps us in sweet embrace, and bears us forward
On wings made free like his? Come forth, Francesca!

FRANCESCA, (*faltering.*) Whither?

BERTRAM. To life—from death!—Dost see?

FRANCESCA. The blessed stars!

BERTRAM. Now fly we with the urgent feet of fear;
This valley must not hold us. To our hills:
There we may breathe in safety. But thou shrink'st!

FRANCESCA. The light! They see—the stars! These bloody proofs—

BERTRAM, (*averting his eyes.*) And I—alas!

FRANCESCA. Lead where thou wilt, my Bertram.

BERTRAM. Among the hills! I know where runs a brooklet,
Shall cleanse thee of these stains—Jesu! how black!

FRANCESCA. How black! how black! (*aside.*) Alas! the stream may cleanse—
The arm be white once more as when he took it
To wrap about his breast!—but oh! my heart,
The dread impression fasten'd on his soul,
Leaves only night to mine! I follow, Bertram!

BERTRAM, (*aside.*) How terrible! How had she heart for it!
So fearful, even in her innocent ways,
So tender still, and merciful!

FRANCESCA. Thou speak'st?

BERTRAM. Of the great debt I owe thee—of the struggle
That nerved thee to this blow! And yet, Francesca,
Would we had died before—together died—
Even at the moment when our lips first met
In love's first sweet delirium!

FRANCESCA. Thou art right!
Would we had died, O Bertram! in that hour,
And had not lived for this!—Would *I* had died!

THE DEATH OF CLEOPATRA.

AUGUSTUS CÆSAR. DOLABELLA.

AUGUSTUS. Dead! say'st thou? Cleopatra?
DOLABELLA. She sleeps fast—
Will answer nothing more—hath no more lusts
For passion to persuade—nor art to breed
Any more combats. I have seen her laid—
As for a bridal—in a pomp of charms,
That mock'd the flashing jewels in her crown
With beauty never theirs. Her bridegroom one
Who conquers more than Cæsar—a grim lord
Now in the full'st possession of his prize,
Who riots on her sweets; seals with cold kiss
The precious caskets of her eyes, that late
Held—baiting fond desire with hope of spoil—
Most glorious gems of life; and, on her cheek,
Soft still with downy ripeness—not so pale,
As sudden gush of fancy in the heart
Might bring to virgin consciousness—he lays
His icy lip, that fails to cause her shrink
From the unknown soliciting. Her sleep
Dreams nothing of the embrace, the very last
Her eager and luxurious form may know,
Of that dread ravisher.
AUGUSTUS. If it be true,
She still hath baffled me. My conquest sure—

My triumph incomplete! I had borne her else,
The proudest trophy of a myriad spoil,
In royal state to Rome. Give me to know
The manner of her death.

DOLABELLA. By her own hands!—
That, conscious still, commended to her breast
The fatal kiss of Nile's envenom'd asp;
That subtle adder, which, from slime and heat,
Receives a gift of poison, whose least touch
Is a sure stoppage of the living tides.

AUGUSTUS. Her death commends her more than all her life!
'Twas like a queen—fit finish to a state,
That, in its worst excess, passionate and wild,
Had still a pomp of majesty, too proud
For mortal subjugation! She had lusts
Most profligate of harm—but with a soul
That, under laws of more restraint, had raised
Her passions into powers, which might have borne
Best fruits for the possessor. They have wrought
Much evil to her nature; but her heart
Cherish'd within a yearning sense of love
That did not always fail; and, where she set
The eye of her affections, her fast faith
Kept the close bond of obligation sure.
This still should serve, when censure grows most free,
To sanctify her fault. In common things
Majestic, as in matters of more state,
She had, besides, the feminine arts to make
Her very lusts seem noble; and, with charms
That mock'd all mortal rivalry, she knew
To dress the profligate graces in her gift—
Generous to very wantonness, and free
Of bounty, where Desert might nothing claim—
That Virtue's self might doubt of her own shape,

So lovely grew her counterfeit. O'er all,
Her splendor, and her soul's magnificence,
The pomp that crown'd her state—luxurious shows—
Where Beauty, grown subservient to a sway
That made Art her first vassal—these, so twinn'd
With her voluptuous weakness—did become
Her well, and took from her the hideous hues
That else had made men loathe!
                                        I would have seen
This princess ere she died! How looks she now?

DOLABELLA. As one who lives, but sleeps; no change to move
The doubts of him who sees, yet nothing knows,
Of that sly, subtle enemy, which still
Keeps harbor round her heart. Charmian, her maid,
Had, ere I enter'd, lidded up the eyes,
That had no longer office; and she lay,
With each sweet feature harmonizing still,
As truly with the nature as at first,
When Beauty's wide-world wonder she went forth
Spelling both art and worship! Never did sleep
More slumberous, more infant-like, give forth
Its delicate breathings. You might see the hair
Wave, in stray ringlets, as the downy breath
Lapsed through the parted lips; and dream the leaf,
Torn from the rose and laid upon her mouth,
Was wafted by that zephyr of the soul
That still kept watch within—waiting on life
In ever anxious ministry. Lips and brow—
The one most sweetly parted as for song—
The other smooth and bright, even as the pearls
That, woven in fruit-like clusters, hung above,
Starring the raven curtains of her hair—
Declared such calm of happiness as never
Her passionate life had known. No show of pain—

No writhéd muscle—no distorted cheek—
Deform'd the beautiful picture of repose,
Or spoke the unequal struggle, when fond life
Strives with its dread antipathy. Her limbs
Lay pliant, with composure, on the couch,
Whose draperies loosely fell about her form,
With gentle flow, and natural fold on fold,
Proof of no difficult conflict. There had been,
Perchance, one pang of terror, when she gave
Free access to her terrible enemy;
Or, in the moment when the venomous chill
Went sudden to her heart; for, from her neck,
The silken robes had parted. The white breast
Lay half revealed, save where the affluent hair
Stream'd over it in thick dishevell'd folds,
That ask'd no further care. Oh! to behold,
With eye still piercing to the sweet recess,
Where rose each gentle slope, that seem'd to swell
Beneath mine eye, as conscious of my gaze,
And throbbing with emotion soft as strange,
Of love akin to fear! Thus swelling still,
Like little billows on some happy sea,
They sudden seem'd to freeze, as if the life
Grew cold when all was loveliest. One blue vein
Skirted the white curl of each heaving wave,
A tint from some sweet sunbow, such as life
Flings ever on the cold domain of death;
And, at their equal heights, two ruby crests—
Two yet unopen'd buds from the same flower—
Borne upward by the billows rising yet,
Grew into petrified gems!—with each an eye
Eloquent pleading to the passionate heart,
For all of love it knows! Alas! the mock!
That Death should mask himself with loveliness,

And Beauty have no voice, in such an hour,
To warn its eager worshipper. I saw—
And straight forgot, in joy of what I saw,
What still I knew—that Death was in my sight,—
And what was seeming beautiful, was but
The twilight—the brief interval betwixt
The glorious day and darkness. I had kiss'd
The wooing bliss before me; but, even then,
Crawl'd forth the venomous reptile from the folds
Where still it harbor'd—crawl'd across that shrine
Of Beauty's best perfections, which, meseem'd,
To shrink and shudder 'neath its loathly march,
Instinct, with all the horrors at my heart.

AUGUSTUS. Thus Guilt and Shame deform the Beautiful!

SAUL AT ENDOR.

A SCRIPTURE LEGEND.

THE sun was dark in Israel! O'er the land
Spread, like a cloud, Philistia's hosts;—and Saul
Grew hopeless as he felt the light of heaven,
God's countenance, withdrawn. His pride of heart,
And insolent presumption, had o'erborne
The favor of his Sovereign. He had stood,
Resting on strength of will, and mortal powers,
And reckless of the warnings, night and day,
Vouchsafed, through holiest prophets, from on high;
Till sacred wrath o'erflow'd, and, from his hope,
Drew all its smiles and succor. O'er his soul
The cloud was dark, like that above the land;
Nor knew he whither, seeking light, to turn,
In the bewildering mazes of his fear.
Vainly he pray'd to Heaven. The usual signs
Denied him answer. In his dreams, no voice
Declared indulgence for the profligate heart,
So long a trespasser. Nor Urim spoke,
Nor prophet, to his pleadings: all were dumb.
And still the tempest grew before his eyes—
The twofold tempest of his mortal fear,
The outcast, he, of Heaven, in wrath denied—
And that which threaten'd, with as dark a doom,

His hapless people—o'er whose cities sped
The fierce invaders. They possess'd the land,
To Shunem, and in multitudes o'erawed
The brave in Israel. Trembling, as he saw
Their darkening hosts, he gather'd his array,
And pitch'd his tents in Gilboa. But the fear—
The feeling, like an instinct—which possess'd
His people, that the favor of their God
Their king no more might challenge—that he stood
The surely-doomed of Heaven—o'er all their hearts
Spread terror like a spell; and, with their king,
They look'd away from their dread enemy,
As seeking succor from the East and West,
Where succor there was none. In terror, then,
The monarch—of his fears, as of their own,
Now fully conscious—in himself no more
Assured, as in his days of innocence,
And hopeless of all answer from the God
His stubborn will had outraged—turn'd his eyes,
Seeking forbidden agencies—the powers
Of darkness—for that knowledge of the truth,
The powers of light withheld.
"Seek me out one,"
He said unto his servants, "some woman that hath
A spirit familiar, whose intelligence
May answer to my quest."
They led him forth,
By night, in base disguise, until he came
To Endor, where a woman secretly
Pursued her dark, abominable trade,
Defying heaven, and mocking human law,
Which still denounced, with deadly penalty,
The practice loathed of God. With trembling feet,
He cross'd the threshold of evil, and beheld

The loathly one he sought. No stately rites
Embellish'd her sad service. Lowly place
She kept, for the reception of a king,
And the responses of her dubious gods.
But knew she not the monarch—a sure proof
How vain was the pretension of her craft
To supernatural knowledge.
"Show to me,"
He said, "by the familiar at thy beck,
Him I shall name to thee!"
A prudent fear
Possess'd her:—
"Wouldst thou spread for me a snare?
By what should I divine, and with what plea,
When, as thou knowest, that Israel's king hath slain
Such as divined by spirits? Wizard and witch
Hath he cut off, in vengeance, from the land;
And seek'st thou for my life?"
"As the Lord liveth,
I seek thee with no snare! Pursue thy art—
Bring me up him whom I shall name to thee,
And profit shall be thine, not punishment."
"Whom wouldst thou?"
"Samuel, prophet of the Lord!"
With lowly heart, the monarch bow'd himself
Before strange altars; hooded his proud head
Submissive, and in anxious waiting, knelt,
While the weird woman, with her mystic rites,
Evoked the awful dead. Her subtle spells,
Sustain'd by potent but still evil powers,
Meant to evoke a semblance, and delude,
By magical presentments and blear shades,
Sufficient for the heart of humble fear,
Grew to a greater power, beneath the will

Of the Most High! He, with a terrible truth,
Responded to the summons that was meant
For the inferior deities. Instead
Of the gross mockery of the sainted shade,
Samuel himself arose; but with such state
Of mightiest angels issuing from the void,
That the weird woman bow'd herself, in dread
Of the true God, whose living rites she mock'd.
Then sank her heart with terror, as she knew
Such answer to such summons well declared
The monarch in her guest. To less than he,
Or in less straits, would Heaven accord a voice
Of such acknowledgment? She cried aloud:—
"Thou hast betray'd me; thou art Saul himself!
Thou whose keen sword hath swept, with glutless rage,
The wizard tribes from Israel!"

"Have no fear,"
The monarch reassured her. "Thou art safe
From sword of Israel's ruler. In his need
He seeks thee now, whom once he will'd to slay,
Having no refuge in a holier shrine,
And a more certain oracle. What seest,
That shakes thee with such terror?"

"Gods, that rise—
True gods, ascending from the depths of earth!—
And now an aged man, from head to foot
Clad in a mantle."

"It is Samuel!"
And, as he spoke, headlong, and cowering low,
The king crouch'd humbly at the spectre's feet:—
The mantle fell—the prophet stood reveal'd!
Dread was the moment's pause that follow'd then:
The woman abash'd, and stricken with awe the king,
In the oppressive shadow of the dead.

Not long the silence—when the prophet spake:—
"Why hast thou vex'd the quiet of my sleep;
Thou, whose deaf ear unto my living word
Gave little tendance? Wherefore dost thou now,
Too lately, from the silence of the grave
Entreat my counsel?"
The familiar sounds
Of that remember'd teacher, sought too late,
Fell with rebuking, but in gentle tones,
On the king's senses. In his grief, he cried:—
"'Tis in my woe, in sore distress of heart,
That Saul now seeks for Samuel. Holiest man,
Too coldly heard when counsel had been worth,
I look to thee for succor. O'er the land
Spread our Philistine enemies. They rage,
In confidence of heavenly help withdrawn
From Israel, by the madness of her king;
And Israel, with a terror, of this fear
Born wholly, weeps and trembles in his tents.
Thou gone, and God against me, 'tis in vain
I seek the voice of Heaven from midnight dreams,
And prophets known for good. They fail me all;
And, in the bitterness of my blank despair,
I seek the wizard arts that rob the grave
To teach the living wisdom. Unto thee,
That first upon this head pour'd sacred oil,
I make appeal. O Samuel! man beloved,
And ever dear to Heaven, in this dread strait,
Show me the way of safety for my people,
Though Saul may plead in vain. On thee I call
For counsel in this peril."
"Why to me,
Since God hath grown thine enemy? To Him!
Yet vainly wouldst thou plead against thy fate:

The evil is upon thee, long foreshown:
Thou hadst thy day of warning. From these lips
Went forth the proper oracles of God,
That told thee thou wert wanting: that thy realm
Should pass from out thy keeping, and thy crown
Descend to him thou still hast sought with hate—
The noble son of Jesse. He hath still
Obey'd the precepts of the living God,
And not as thou, outraging, with a will,
The fix'd decrees of Heaven. Thou didst contemn
His bidding, when thou dared spare Amalek,
On whom He swore to execute all wrath!
For this, the trouble of this day is thine,
And yet another day. To-morrow's sun
Shall set upon thy fortunes. Israel's hosts
Shall fail before the Philistines, and, ere night,
Thou with thy sons, O Saul! shalt be with me."

The voice had ceased! The awful form was gone;
But the dread prophecy was ringing still
In the appall'd one's ears. Then fell the king
Prostrate, as one who, sudden shorn of strength,
Sinks helpless on his shadow, in a heap!

SAUL'S LAST BATTLE.

THE heroic soul still struggles against fate,
And, arm'd with self-devotion, finds resolve
For struggle in despair. Prepared for death,
And hopeless for himself, the soul of Saul,
Though counsell'd from the grave of sore defeat,
Still nursed the dream that God would succor yet
The fortunes of his people. They had sinn'd,
But he, their sovereign, led the way to sin,
And shaped their disobedience. On *his* head
Heaven's vengeance only; and for this he pray'd
With an heroic virtue, at the last,
That honor'd his decline. Weary with grief,
The bitter penalty of a stubborn pride—
No longer cheer'd with promises from Heaven,
The voice of sacred prophets, or the signs
Vouchsafed in dreams; or by the mystic rites
Of Thummim and Urim;—with a sense of peace,
He yielded satisfied to the doom that hung
Suspended o'er his head. Another day,
And he should sleep without the harassing dread
That whisper'd the desertion of his God,
The enemy ever, with a fearful dart,
Above his couch of sleep and weariness,
And a new rival ready for his throne!
Better than this so dread anxiety,
The conflict without hope;—and, though despair

Sat heavy at his heart, it took resolve
From the impending circumstance of ill,
And by his natural courage, moved to pride
At the grim presence of his enemy,
Saul girded him for battle. Israel's tents
He pitch'd beside the fountain of Jezreel;
While the Philistines gather'd their great hosts
To Aphek, and defied him with a shout
That spoke their hearts secure of victory.
But naught did this abate his firm resolve,
Which look'd to battle, though it bring defeat,
As the heroic finish to a term,
That lacks but noble ending—not with hope
Of safety or of triumph. His brave youth
Consider'd, and the songs of ancient days
Remember'd, which had shown his thousands slain,
Demanded the last struggles which should fold
The monarch's robes about the hero's form,
And mantle greatly his great overthrow.
Unmoved he heard the shoutings of the foe,
And mock'd them with his own.
"Let us but raise,"
He said to his brave son, Melchishua,
"The courage of our people to the strife,
And though we perish, we may save the throne
To our successor. We shall fall, I know,
Thou with thy brothers, both; and we shall sleep
This night with Kish, our sire, and the great dead
That have prepared the ever-open way
To all the living. Let this fear us not,
While we invoke, with words of ancient might,
And songs, as of a prophet, the spell'd hearts
Of these, our people, waxing faint to hear
Philistia's insolent clamors. Get thee hence,

And pass among the timorous with proud speech,
As of heroic promise. Jonathan
Already seeks them, and Abinadab,
With voice of fire and martial eloquence:
I too, will follow, teaching with a tongue
That soon shall lack all pleasing—of a will
That not the less resolves on valorous deed,
Because it looks, beneath the frown of Heaven,
Upon the dread, inevitable doom!
Go forth and follow in your brothers' steps,
So that our people, warm'd with proper fire,
May seek the battle with that noble rage
Alone that brings success. If we must fall,
It may be Heaven shall suffer us to fall
Like Gaza's blinded captive, sworn on death—
Our mighty foes crush'd with us—in our fate
Proving Philistia's too!"

The battle join'd;
And Israel quail'd before his enemies!
The monarch saw with anguish, and his soul
Put on the wildest courage of despair,
And braved the thickest dangers of the field,
Still in the face of his worst destinies!
The youth of Saul came back to him—the heart
Of fearless valor and vindictive wrath
That led him, desperate through the opposing hosts,
When first upon his head the sacred oil
Was pour'd by Samuel—and the Amorites,
At Jabesh-Gilead, fell before his ire,
That, from the morning watch till noon-day sun,
Still smote their withering hosts. Again he wrought
As in that day of prime; but not as then,
With God's assuring sanction on his deeds.

His valor raged in vain. In vain he threw
Aside the golden helmet—his white beard
And thin, gray locks, still gleaming through the fight,
Unseemly, with that terrible strength of wrath,
Which mark'd the wingéd passage of his darts.
Again he slew his thousands, and his deeds,
More fortunate then, were never in his prime
More glorious than when now, in his old age,
He smote in vain—and from his lofty brow
Felt the green laurels gone.
        "Where?"—as he sped,
Still smiting with a weapon drunk with blood—
"Where's Jonathan, my son?—I see him not!"
And on he pass'd. One answer'd him that knew—
"To him the battle has no farther voice,
Nor enemy's weapon terror!"
        But one groan
Broke from the monarch's bosom, as he cried—
"Now see I that the day will soon have end;—
God's will be done in mercy!" On he went,
Crossing his dripping spear with other foes,
And trampling o'er his slain.
        "I see no more
The shining azure of Melchishua's shield:—
Who marks him in the fight?"
        They answer'd him—
"He who, with still a foeman at his throat,
May stop to single from the up-piled dead
The son of Israel's sovereign!"
        "How it works,
That fate which I have vainly sought to cross—
That vengeance I have anger'd! Yet, awhile,
Deeds may be done for Israel. If the foe
Must triumph, they shall sing their choral songs

In bitterness, and with a grief that lives
When triumph is forgotten. Thrice the shaft
Hath stricken me"—and he pluck'd an arrow forth,
That, in that moment, quivering in his side,
Stay'd the heroic speech—"but I am proof
'Gainst hate of human foes. They can but slay,
And I am self-deliver'd to the shaft
This day, as one decreed to sacrifice!—
Who calls me from the host?"
"Oh! sire, your son,
Abinadab, is smitten, even to death,
And cries on thee for succor!"
"Let him cry,
But fight the while—the succor is at hand,
Certain to come ere sunset."
Thus he sped,
Himself prevailing in the matchless might
Of his one arm, where'er his weapon flew.
Yet still his people quail'd. His sons were slain;
But he, though smarting with repeated wounds,
Still hew'd a fearful passage through the foe;
Then turning, with his weapon as a share,
Plough'd the dense field again. His arm, at last,
Fail'd him—the great drops gather'd on his brow,
Mix'd dust, and blood, and water. All in vain
His desperate deeds of valor. On all sides
His people fled discomfited. The war
Went wholly against him, and the hope was gone
That dream'd how Israel's banner yet should rise
Triumphant, though above the sovereign slain!
The progress of the battle had led up
The heights of Gilboa. Here, as Saul beheld
His scatter'd hosts in flight, and, close behind,
The foe pursuing with inveterate rage,

Of murder edged by madness, he stood up
And rested on his spear.
"Why should I fly?"
To those who counsell'd safety. "I have lived
Too long already, having outlived my sons,
My fortunes, and God's favor. Get ye hence,
For Israel's future, and another sway
More blest by Heaven and man. For me, no more
The pomp of royalty, the pride of spears,
The joy that's born of battle, and the songs
That hail the conqueror on his homeward march
Through the great cities. I behold the sun
For the last time, and with no vain regret
That he shall rouse me from my tent no more,
Rejoicing in a day of deeds begun!
Hither to me, thou last of many friends,
And faithfullest of followers. Take thy sword
And thrust me through!—for the Philistines come;
And they must never, with their barbarous rage,
Degrade this conscious form!"
To him who bore
His armor in the battle, thus he spake,
The wounded king of Israel, as below
He saw his enemies gather. Wounded sore,
By their superior archers, well he knew
That neither in flight, nor in the further struggle,
Lay hope of safety. But the man replied—
"Now God forbid that hand of mine be laid,
With violence on the heaven-anointed head!"

"All fail me at my need," reproachfully
Exclaim'd the monarch. Then, as came the foe—
"I will not see their triumph!" cried the king;
And turning his own steel against his breast,

Headlong he threw himself upon the shaft,
And perish'd ere they came! Thus, with like deed,
Died he who bore his armor;—silent both,
As the exulting heathen, up the heights,
Rush'd to the bloody spectacle with shouts,
That ceased when they beheld, beneath their feet,
The mightiest prince in Israel. They were dumb,
As stunn'd by their own triumph—which were naught,
But that the God of Israel was in wrath!

Mournfully sweet the dirge on Gilboa's heights,
Sung by the monarch minstrel, on whose brow
The crown of Saul descended, as he saw
The wreck of that dread battle, and bewept
The royal victims. Never elegy
More touching or more beautiful. How wild
The lyrical sweetness from the Arabian caught,
Which pictured Israel's proud nobility
Perishing in pride and valor, on the heights
Their sacrifice makes sacred!
"How," he sang,
"How are the mighty fallen! Israel's beauty
Slain on high places. Tell it not in Gath,
Lest they, the daughters of Philistia, joy
And triumph o'er God's people—triumph o'er him
Who taught them shame and bitter overthrow!
For thee, Gilboa, let there be no dew
Upon thy summits. Be the rains denied
That crown thy summer fields with offerings;
For on thy heights accursèd the big shield
Of Saul was cast away; by vilest foes
His banner overthrown, and he o'ercome,
As though his mighty head had never been
With heavenly oil anointed. To its sheath

His sword return'd not thirsty. Never, in vain,
He smote the enemies' legions, even at the last,
When God denied the victory to his arm!

"And thou, my brother Jonathan—oh! thou,
Fleet as the roe of the mountain; from whose bow
Never flew fruitless arrow at thy prey,
But in the fat of the mighty, and the blood
Of the warm enemy, made vengeance sure;—
I mourn for thee, my brother, sore distress'd;
For, very pleasant, since I knew thee first,
Hast thou been unto me—thy love to me
Wonderful precious, and surpassing still
The love of woman. Thou, with thy sire,
Hast won the fame of warriors. Thou wast slain,
Like him, on highest places, in the thick
Of fiercest battle—undismay'd, though fate
Refused thee, and thy battle-cry went forth
With the sure knowledge of death against thy hope.

"Lovely and pleasant ever in their lives
Were Saul and Jonathan. Nor in death at last
Are they divided. Kindred in their worth,
Stronger than lions in the battle's rage,
Swifter than eagles in pursuing flight;
Their sweet and sure communion to the close,
Makes them heroic for our histories
So long as fame shall last. Weep for your king,
Daughters of Israel. He it was who first
Ye rescued from the bondage of the foe,
And clad your forms in scarlet; who, with gold,
Deck'd your apparel richly, and first brought
Your hearts to knowledge of still more delights.
How are the mighty fallen!—weapons of war,
How perish'd, and what glorious state o'erthrown?"

THE REBELLION OF ABSALOM.

We pay the mournful penalties of guilt
Long after we forget its pleasant sweets,
And sow, in youth, the bitter seeds of pain,
That age shall reap in sorrow. Thus the king,
Heaven's favorite, when his head was gray with years,
For the impetuous passions of his youth
That led him, though repenting still, to sin,
Found in his best beloved, his Absalom—
The dearest to his heart of many sons—
A resolute rebel; seeking with bared arms
And deadliest weapon, after Israel's crown,
Pluck'd from his sire's gray head. From him he stole,
By subtle arts and guilty agencies,
The affections of his people; till, grown strong,
He shook away the webs of policy,
And standing fearless forth, proclaim'd himself
The rightful king in Israel. Through the land
The trumpet voices of sedition rang—
"Absalom reigns in Hebron!" He had snared
His father's nearest counsellors, and had stolen
His way to hearts, forgetful of their faith,
Solemnly sworn to David; while his power
Shook to its centre the great realm which Heaven
Had built up under Saul, and made secure
In hands more worthy and more fortunate.
An hour sufficed—so suddenly it fell—
To spread sedition's tempest o'er the land,

And drive the monarch, unprepared, in flight,
Forth from his royal city. O'er the brook,
Kedron, he sped by night. Through secret paths
He sought strange places. Day by day he went,
While bitter tears, slow coursing down his cheeks,
Declared how bitter was the pang that found
A traitor in a favorite—rebel foe
In the dear pledge of a most faithful love,
The child of his best manhood. Thus he went,
With cover'd head, and feet made bare, in grief,
Up the steep sides of Olivet; while they
Who follow'd, with a rare fidelity,
Took a like form of mourning to their hearts,
And echo'd all his woes. Ere many days,
God heard his prayers, and wrought, by human means,
Confusion to the counsels of the son,
Who, in his desperate thirst for evil sway,
Sought equally his father's life and crown.
Meanwhile, the faithful of the tribes drew nigh,
In succor of the sovereign. Soon his hosts,
Number'd and train'd by Joab, the strong man
And savage warrior, were prepared to plant,
On the high hill-top, in the face of foes,
The Zion banner. Unto Mahanaim
Then David came. Here number'd he his troops;
And when he sent them forth to seek the strife,
He said to his great captains:—
"For my sake,
Deal gently with the youth—with Absalom!"
His people listen'd as he spake. They saw
The weight of his great sorrows in his face,
His stooping form, the dust upon his brow,
And the deep mourning tremors in his voice.
Mightiest in numbers was the rebel host,

Which, seeking battle with an eager rage,
Drew nigh unto the army of the king.
Absalom cross'd the Jordan. Here he made
Amasa captain of his force—a chief,
Kinsman to Joab, fearless as himself,
And with as keen an appetite for blood.
The armies met in Gilead. Ephraim's wood
Beheld the dread encounter, while heaven's arm,
Sustaining the mock'd fortunes of the sire,
Fought 'gainst the rebel legions till they fled
With twenty thousand slain. The fell pursuit
Traversed the thicket with devouring sword,
That slew where'er it came. Then Absalom,
Lost in the intricate mazes of the wood,
Was seen by David's people as he sought
A refuge from pursuit. But they had heard
The entreaty of the sire to deal with him,
For his sake, gently; and they dropp'd their spears,
And turn'd their wrathful eyes on meaner foes.

Not so with Joab. He preferr'd to save
The monarch from the sire. He knew the heart
Of Absalom—his restless vanity,
The ready ear he gave to counsellors
That taught him rude rebellion; and he knew,
That, spared to other days, was but to spare
For worse rebellions still. When that he heard
Where Absalom was gather'd, he, alone,
Subduing in his soul the entreating voice
Of the old father, pleading for the son,
Sought out the unhappy fugitive. With arm
That never, or through fear or sympathy,
Had yet been taught to falter—through his heart
He thrust the unerring javelin till he died!

Then sounded Joab, the fierce conqueror,
The trumpet that recall'd the wild pursuit;
For he that would not spare the king's own son.
Yet knew to spare his people. He had shorn
The head of the offending; for the rest,
They had already, in their thousands slain,
Paid the sufficient penalty of crime.

All day, even from the hour when forth the host
Went at his bidding, had the monarch sat
Between the city gates, with mourning brow
And heart, misgiving of the fearful tale
He soon must yield to hear. The watchman stood
In the high tower above, far looking forth,
Intent, for messenger of good or ill.
And soon he came, for when was messenger
That spoke of evil, slow?
"Thy foes, O king!
This day have been deliver'd to thy hand!"
"But of the young man? What of Absalom?"
"May all the foes that rise against the king,
To do him mischief, share the young man's fate!"

Then burst the anguish of the agéd sire,
Forgetting all the king.
"Oh! Absalom,
Would God that I had died for thee, my son!"
Thus wailing, he ascended from the gate
And wept within the tower, until they brought
The mangled, but still beautiful form of him
Best loved, and stretch'd him on a bier of state
Even in the chamber where the monarch lay,
Prone to the dusty floor, no more a king,
Ashes upon his head and in his heart.

Still was the young man beautiful. His corse
Might still delight the eye. No blemish marr'd
The perfect symmetry of the lofty form
And the fine, noble features, save the wound
That still'd his heart forever. They had wash'd
The blood stains from his bosom ere they brought;
Had smooth'd in wonted flow and natural curl
The long fair hair, that was his grace and pride,
As Samson's was his strength. They had removed
His armor, helm, and shield, and bloody spear,
Ere they had placed him 'neath the eyes of him
Whose state these proofs had outraged; had disposed
His limbs in pure white garments; and he lay
Serene as one who sleeps a pleasant sleep,
Untroubled by a dream. As thus he slept,
The sire, no longer hush'd by curious gaze,
Sunk o'er the unconscious body of the son,
And clasp'd it to his breast. Then gush'd his eyes
With tears, and spoke his bursting heart with sobs
That shook his mighty frame.
"Oh! Absalom,
My son!—my son!—that wast so beautiful—
That art so beautiful, though in thy shroud,
With death's hand heavy on thy cold pale brow—
Thou, grievously misnamed thy father's peace,
That still hast been his woe; and now with pangs
But ill remind'st me of those happy hours,
When in thy mother, fair Macaiah's arms,
I felt in Geshur respite from my griefs,
And named thee, at thy birth, from my own peace,
Which thou hast still destroy'd. Oh! Absalom,
Why hast thou brought me to this woe, my son?
Thyself to this sad fate? To thee my heart
Turn'd ever with a preference, most unwise,

Over more faithful children. Still, in thee,
As pledge of precious loves and peaceful hours,
I found a joy that grew upon thy sight,
And my heart swam in rapture but to view
Thy stately shape, the graces of thy walk,
And the soul-beauty kindling in thy face!
Yet wast thou guilty and ungrateful still—
A rebel in thy service—treacherous
Even when most trusted. But alas! for me,
I cannot now reproach thee, Absalom,
Thou hear'st me not—thou canst rebel no more.
Would I had died for thee beneath the shaft,
Or, at the peril of my life, could now
But give thee back thy own. My son!—my son!—
Would God that I could die for thee, my son!

"What had I done to thee that thou shouldst fly
My presence, and take weapons in thy hand
Against these thin white hairs? Seeking this sway,
That, as thou seest, saves not from any grief;
Which, where the affections still abide with power,
Is still as open to the shafts of harm
As any subject breast. What was thy grief?
What wrong was done to thee? What favor'd voice
Spoke in thy father's ear against thy peace,
That thou couldst not o'erplead? I spared thee still,
When, at the cruel feast of Baal-Hazor,
Thou slew'st thy brother Amnon. I forbore,
Though, in thy lust of power, I saw thee take
A state upon thyself, and dignities
Unfitting son and subject: and I yearn'd,
Even in my secret soul, to see thee wear
This empire for thyself. Alas! my son,
Why, in thy youth and beauty, didst thou strive

Against thy father's love ?—'gainst Heaven's decree
Till thou call'dst down its bolts, my Absalom,
Stricken with the cruel death-dart in thy breast,
Making me desolate! Oh! erring Absalom,
Rebellious, seeking thy fond father's life,
And perishing in thy beauty and thy guilt—
Would I had died for thee, my son!—my son!

"Alas! thou hear'st not. Couldst thou hear, my voice
Should fill thine ear with chiding—but in vain!
I feel the echoes of my words come back,
Though breathed upon thy breast, as from a vault
Where all is dark and hollow. Death, I know,
Is on thee—on this brow where youth before
Had set her richest beauties—on thy tongue,
Which ever in music spake, even when its speech
Had birth in youthful passion, which misled
Too frequently the heart, that 'neath my hand,
Sleeps without pulse of feeling or of fear,
Having no passion more.
"Ah! they will come,
And deck thee for a chamber where no eyes
Shall look upon thy beauties—where, to see,
Were to feel fear and loathing. They will bear
Thy form from my embrace, and I shall go
To homes which thou shalt enter nevermore!
Oh! Absalom, my son, this had not been—
This fate of silence unto thee—this fear
Of human strifes and voices unto me—
But for the vain ambition which had birth
Even in thy strength and beauty. We must part:
Even now I hear the voices at the gate,
Of those who come to take thee to thy couch,
Whose cold thou shalt not feel. The chants arise

From drooping handmaids, who shall time thy steps
To vaults no song shall penetrate but mine.
My victory is mourning. All my host
Fly, scatter'd as a host that feels defeat,
Knowing how great thy father's agony,
Which still they dread to see. My people fly
The city which I cover with my shame,
Though to their fond fidelity this day
I owe my life and empire—saved in vain,
At price of thy most precious life, my son!
I must throw by the semblance of this grief,
And wear it in mine heart. I must put on
The aspect of the monarch and the man,
Lest I do wrong to champions, in whose faith
My crown is made secure. Joab will come
And chide me for this weakness, which declares
How happier it had left me to behold
My perishing hosts o'erthrown and stark in death,
Than the one rebel, whose unnatural power
Makes his life dearer to the heart it wrongs,
Than all Heaven's gifts beside. Alas! too true!
I leave thee, Absalom!—I tear away
From thy detaining fingers. They will take
And hide thee from my sight; and I shall sway,
Once more, the sceptre that thou took'st from me—
Sway with calm forehead and untrembling hand—
Though in the watches of the night, as now,
The voice of my great sorrow cries aloud,
My son, for thee—belovéd Absalom—
Would God that I had died for thee, my son!"

FRANCESCA DA RIMINI.

EPISODE FROM DANTE.

The following is a new version of the fifth canto of Dante's "Inferno," which contains the famous episode of Francesca da Rimini, in which she narrates the manner and the misfortunes of her love. She was the daughter of the Lord of Ravenna, and was married to Gianciotto, the eldest son of the tyrant of Rimini. Unhappily, her affections did not go with her duties. She did not love her husband, but bestowed her heart upon Paoli, a younger son of the house of Malatesta; and still more unhappily, forgot her vows in her passion. Her husband surprised and slew the guilty pair, who were buried together in the same grave. These parties are discovered by Dante, as he passes under the guidance of Virgil, whom he denominates "his master," into the "second circle," which first opens the view of the infernal regions and the terrible sufferings of the inmates. Here Minos sits, at the threshold, and determines, at a glance, the particular doom of the guilty spirits. Those who occupy this first circle are such as have fallen victims to their carnal appetites. Here they are tossed incessantly to and fro, in a region of "brown horror," by fierce and capricious winds, the likeness of their own passions, to which they can offer no resistance. Here, as examples of such as occupy this circle, they discern first the famous Queen of Babylon, Semiramis. In this "band" or circle, are Dido, Cleopatra, Helena, Achilles and others, a vast and well-remembered multitude. Two of these guilty victims, in particular, compel the attention of Dante, as they are borne forward, seeming particularly light upon the tempestuous winds. These are Francesca, and Paoli, her lover. He summons them, at the instance of Virgil; and the sympathy which he shows them prevails upon Francesca to relate their story, she speaking for both. Dante is so much affected by the narrative and by the agonies which Paoli all the while expresses, that he swoons away lifelessly. This is all that is necessary to a proper understanding of the episode. It contains several of the most frequently-quoted passages from Dante—passages singularly suggestive and comprehensive—and affords as just an idea of his manner as could be gathered from any portion of his divine poem. The measure employed here is that of the original, *the terza rima;* and the number of the lines is nearly the same, Dante's being 142, and this 140.

From the first circle thus descending down,
  I pass'd into the next of smaller space,
  But deeper torment and superior groan.
There horrible Minos sits, with mocking face,
  Watching the entrance for the criminal,
  Whom, judged, he quick dispatches without grace.
Near him, the ill-born shade confesses all:

Soul-searcher, he discovers, as he eyes,
To what dire mansion it is doom'd to fall,
And with his spiral snake extremities
Coiling around him, shows how far below,
To what degree of doom the spirit hies.
Ever before him stand a crowd, who go,
Each, headlong down to judgment; they are heard,
And hear, and then speed whirling into woe.
"Oh! thou"—to me then Minos yielded word,
As, seeing me, his office he forebore—
"Look where thou go'st, and whom thou hast preferr'd
To be thy guide; and seek no open door,
Won by its wideness." To him, then, my guide:
"Why wouldst thou hinder that he should explore?
Such is his mission, will'd, where power beside
May do what still it wills. No farther ask."
And now mine ears began to open wide
To dolorous complaints. My sorrowful task
Now led me forward where the numerous wail
Assail'd me; and, as cover'd with Night's mask,
I pass'd into a region full of bale,
Mute of all light, and raging like the sea,
Torn by conflicting winds in bellowing gale.
The infernal tempest, from its coil ne'er free,
Still toss'd the distracted spirits in its sweep,
Sore whirl'd and vex'd, incapable to flee;
Dash'd 'gainst their rocks of ruin, curses deep
Blaspheme the power divine; and all is moan,
Bitter lament, and woes that wail, not weep.
Such was the doom; capricious thus; and borne
By fitful blasts through the unlighted air,
Were those who, by tempestuous passions torn,
Yield reason up to lust: so starlings bear,
Abroad in wintry storms, a trooping host,

Hither and thither, powerless, as they veer.
Hope of less pain, or of repose, thus tost,
No comfort brings; but as the cranes depart
With mournful chant, and streaking the lone sky,
So borne by the impetuous blasts, thus dart
These shadowy hosts with mournful scream and cry.
"Master," I then, with great concern of heart,
"What are these people, shrieking piteously,
Whom the keen wind thus lashes?" He replied—
"She that first comes was queen of many lands:
With lust corrupt, she made the laws provide
That vice should show for virtue. Her commands
Shaped the decree to favor the denied—
Semiramis, who, held in golden bands,
Of Ninus, was his mother, and his wife,
And kept her rule where sways the Soldan now.
Who comes with her is she who, in love's strife,
To ashes of Sichœus broke her vow,
And, with self-slaughtering hand, smote her own life.
The next is Cleopatra." Then I saw
Helen, who for so long a time of ill
Prevail'd; and great Achilles came, who fought
With love the last; Paris, Tristan; and still
Thousands beside, of whom "the master" taught,
Naming them as they rose, whom Love's sad will
Had smitten from our life. Then, as full fraught,
He told the story of old cavaliers,
And noble dames thus ruin'd, pity stole
Upon and conquer'd me; and, in my tears,
Bewilder'd, and with melancholy soul,
I spake: "The cloud, O Bard, that now appears,
Hath two that go together, and do roll
Most light before the wind—with them awhile
I willingly would speak." "When they draw nigh"—

Thus did he answer me—"then shalt thou wile
With adjuration of love—for still they fly
Obedient to the passion which did beguile—
And they will come to thee." Soon as mine eye
Beheld them borne toward us on the blast,
I cried with lifted voice: "If none withholds,
Oh! wearied souls, come hither to us and speak."
Then as two doves whom one desire enfolds,
Fly with twin pinion their sweet nest to seek,
So those two spirits whom one will embolds,
From the same circle which doth Dido keep—
Such was the power of my appealing cry—
Came to us, borne through the malignant air.
"Oh! being most gracious, whose benignant eye
Thus seeks us through this sooty atmosphere—
We who stain'd earth with deep and bloody dye—
If we had favor with heaven, our earnest prayer
Were for thy peace, seeing that on our woe
Thou hast had ruth. Of that which thou wouldst say,
Or that which it would please thee best to know,
Speak freely—we will answer as we may,
The blast as now being still.—Beside the Po,
Where seeking kindred waters he must stray,
My native city sits. Love, which in breast
Of tenderness is ever quickly caught
With that fair form, no more by me possess'd,
Won *him;* and still with grief my soul is fraught
By that sweet prize. Love, which in all confess'd,
Leaves none escape from passion, strongly taught
My heart to joy in him, with such delight
As leaves me not even yet. Love to one death
Conducted both; but Cain's deep realm of fright
Waits him whose cruel vengeance quench'd our breath."
Thus spake they. When that I had heard each sprite,

I bowed me, till at last the Poet saith—
"What think'st thou?" And I answer'd him—"Ah, me!
What were the sweet dreams, what the longings dear
That led them to this fate and misery?"
To them I turn'd—"Francesca, look—the tear
Flows for thy grief. Yet farther would I see—
How Love, in season of youth's sweetest care,
First taught thy heart its dubious want to know."
Then she to me replied—"The greatest grief
Is to remember in our hours of woe
How blest we have been. He can tell, thy chief;
But if thou will'st that I the story show
Of love's first shoots in the beginning leaf,
I will, as one who tells but weeps, relate.
One day together as we sat alone,
We read for pastime of knight Lancelot's fate—
How Love compell'd him. Nothing had we known
To wake suspicion of our mutual state;
Yet, as our eyes met, from our cheeks had flown
The color as we read. The moment came
Which conquer'd both. 'Twas where we found that he
Kiss'd on the cheek the sweet smile of his dame:
Even then *he* kiss'd *my* mouth all tremblingly.
The book was Galleotto. Such the name
Of him who wrote. But in that volume we
Read nothing more that day." While thus one sprite
Reveal'd, the other wept; and with such woe,
That, in my sorrow at so sad a sight,
I fainting sunk, as if beneath the blow
Of Death, and in my anguish fell outright,
As the dead body, hopelessly, falls low.

CPSIA information can be obtained at www.ICGtesting.com
Printed in the USA
LVOW131140240613

339879LV00002B/6/P

9 781611 170559